THE COURAGEOUS LIFE OF
WEARY DUNLOP

**Also by Peter FitzSimons
and published by Hachette Australia**

Kokoda
Burke and Wills
Monash's Masterpiece
Mutiny on the Bounty
The Catalpa Rescue
James Cook
Breaker Morant
The Incredible Life of Hubert Wilkins
The Opera House
The Battle of Long Tan
The Last Charge of the Australian Light Horse
The Legend of Albert Jacka

PETER FITZSIMONS

THE COURAGEOUS LIFE OF
WEARY DUNLOP

hachette
AUSTRALIA

Published in Australia and New Zealand in 2025
by Hachette Australia
(an imprint of Hachette Australia Pty Limited)
Gadigal Country, Level 17, 207 Kent Street, Sydney, NSW 2000
www.hachette.com.au

Hachette Australia acknowledges and pays our respects to the past and present Traditional Owners and Custodians of Country throughout Australia, and recognises the continuation of cultural, spiritual and educational practices of Aboriginal and Torres Strait Islander peoples. Our head office is located on the lands of the Gadigal people of the Eora Nation.

A catalogue record for this book is available from the National Library of Australia

The authorised representative in the EEA is Hachette Ireland, 8 Castlecourt Centre, Dublin 15, D15 XPT3, Ireland (email: info@hbgi.ie)

ISBN: 978 0 7336 5028 4 (hardback)

Cover design by Luke Causby/Blue Cork
Cover images courtesy of the Australian War Memorial (AWM P00406.026) and Svitlana/Adobe Stock (background)
Maps by Jane Macaulay
Author photo by Peter Morris/Sydney Heads
Typeset in 11.1/14.5 pt Sabon LT Pro by Bookhouse, Sydney
Printed and bound in Australia by McPherson's Printing Group

*To the POWs of the Thai–Burma Railway
and their families who suffered so much, and
complained so little. We salute you.*

*And to my beloved publisher over much of the last 35 years,
Matthew Kelly, who pushed me for ten years to do this book
and, as ever, was right. Thank you for everything, Matthew.*

To us he takes precedence over Ned Kelly, Phar Lap, Les Darcy, Simpson and even Don Bradman as the great Australian hero of all time.[1]

Keith Flanagan,
POW with Weary Dunlop

I want to be thoroughly used up when I die, for the harder I work the more I live. I rejoice in life for its own sake. Life is no 'brief candle' for me. It is a sort of splendid torch which I have got hold of for the moment, and I want to make it burn as brightly as possible before handing it on to future generations.[2]

Weary Dunlop's favourite quote,
from George Bernard Shaw

CONTENTS

DRAMATIS PERSONAE

Lieutenant Colonel Ernest Edward 'Weary' Dunlop: legendary surgeon of the Australian Imperial Force, serving in the Middle East, and later providing skill, succour and support as Commanding Officer of POWs while in Japanese detention in Java, Singapore and Thailand.

Bombardier Tom Uren: served with the Australian 2/1st Heavy Battery in Timor. After capture by the Japanese, he was assigned to Weary Dunlop's Konyu POW camp in Thailand.

Private Milton (Blue) Butterworth: after first meeting in Greece, Butterworth became Weary's batman in July 1941 at Tobruk. He accompanied Weary through a series of POW camps in Java, Singapore and Thailand.

Colonel Fred 'Black Jack' Galleghan: commanded AIF prisoners at Changi Prison.

Major General Samuel Roy Burston: Director of Medical Services, 1 Corps AIF.

Sergeant Ern Corrie: born in Bendigo in 1909, he worked as a commercial traveller until enlisting in 1940. After just three months medical training he was posted as Corporal Chiropodist to Blackforce in Java and kept a diary of his remarkable experience thereafter.

Colonel Laurens van der Post: South African who had been stationed in the hills of Java leading a guerrilla group instrumental in smuggling out Allied personnel until his capture. Assigned to Weary's Bandoeng camp, van der Post was quickly embraced as a learned and inspiring addition to the camp.

Chief Petty Officer Ray Parkin: Chief Quartermaster on HMAS *Perth*, which was sunk near Java. Captured by the Japanese, he was assigned to Weary's camp at Bandoeng, and later was transferred to POW camps in Thailand with Dunlop Force. Notable for his many sketches of life in the camps.

Major Ewan Corlette: very fine surgeon who became friends with Weary while serving in the Middle East in the 2/2nd Casualty Clearing Station in Palestine. A senior medico in the POW camps, affectionately known by his colleagues as 'The Gangster' for his swarthy visage, thin moustache and the 'rakish angle at which he wore his peaked cap'.[1]

Major Arthur Moon: Sydney surgeon who sailed to Java with Weary, became a Japanese prisoner of war and worked with Weary at the hospitals in Java and Thailand.

Captain Jim Yeates: surgeon and great friend of Weary. Served with the 2/2nd Casualty Clearing Station in the Middle East and Africa.

Aircraftsman 1st Class Bill Griffiths: 21-year-old Englishman who was a patient at the No. 1 Allied General Hospital, Bandoeng, in March 1942.

Brigadier Arthur Blackburn VC: commanded the 2/3rd Machine Gun Battalion in the Middle East. Upon arrival in Java in 1942 was given command of Australian forces, designated as Blackforce.

Lieutenant Eiji Hirota: officer of the Imperial Japanese Army's 9th Railway Regiment, in charge of the construction of 10 kilometres of rail in the Konyu–Hintok area.

Lieutenant Kishio Usuki: Japanese Commander of Konyu 3 Camp. 'No man,' one soldier records of him, 'was more sadistic than the Japanese camp commandant Lieutenant Usuki.'[2]

Corporal Seiichi Okada: Medical Corporal at Hintok Mountain Camp, called 'Doctor Death' for the fact that he daily forced seriously unwell soldiers to undertake exhausting work.

Yi Hak-Nae: Korean guard renowned for his cruelty and nicknamed 'The Lizard'. He was subordinate officer during the months of March and April 1943 at Hintok Mountain Camp.

Boonpong Sirivejjabhandu: Thai trader, fondly known as Boon Pong, who sailed the Kwai Noi River dispensing lifesaving food, medical supplies and money to the POWs.

INTRODUCTION AND ACKNOWLEDGEMENTS

Weary Dunlop?

My publisher, Matthew Kelly, had been at me for years to write a book on him.

Of course I knew who he was, and have vague memories of both of my World War II veteran parents – Lieutenant Peter McCloy FitzSimons and Lieutenant Beatrice Helen Booth OAM – speaking warmly of Weary and his legend, though neither claimed personal contact.

But still I resisted for, frankly, reasons I can't remember now other than I was always in the thrall of other projects I found more alluring. Happily, the more I resisted and desisted from half-starts, the more Matthew persisted and insisted, and I finally began to dig a little more. At last I made the breakthrough to my first understanding of just how staggering the whole story was and what all the fuss was about. (Starting with the fact that the *sixteenth* match of rugby he ever played was for the Wallabies and they beat the All Blacks!). I went from there, quickly getting to the extraordinary saga of his wartime valour.

What a man! What men around him! What an extraordinary trial he lived through, and what amazing things he did to prevent so many more men perishing. Most touching of all were the accounts left by the POW survivors of just how highly they regarded him, the man they referred to as the 'Christ of the Thai–Burma Railway'.

And so it began.

My principal researcher in diving deep and scouring wide was the indefatigable Barb Kelly, who digitally trawled and crawled as mightily and as far as ever, regularly returning to bring to the surface long-lost treasures of previously unrevealed detail. Happily, she became as obsessed with the story as me, and was able to provide the exact material to help bring to life previously obscure and unknown episodes. As with some of my previous books it was wonderful that her son Lachlan was able to lend valuable assistance.

My long-time researcher and beloved cousin, Angus FitzSimons, was as insightful as ever, constantly turning up new angles to pursue, even while finding fresh information on previously covered ground – and being a terrific sounding board.

This book is in his great debt.

My warm thanks also to Dr Peter Williams, the Canberra military historian who has worked with me on 15 books now. As ever, I relied on the depth and width of his military knowledge and lore to inform my writing, and on this occasion his knowledge of the Japanese language and culture was of great help.

Meanwhile, I record my gratitude to Brendan O'Keefe, who trawled the copious archives on Weary Dunlop at the Australian War Memorial and indeed came back with many previously unexamined nuggets. In February 2025, I journeyed to Hellfire Pass to see for myself the principal landscape for this book, and came away stunned. Only then, did I truly get it. While there, I of course visited the Thailand–Burma Railway Centre and found their resources as moving as they were informative. Bravo, all who have had input to it.

As ever, my friend Dr Michael Cooper – who I met when walking the Kokoda Track, seeing as you ask – was more generous than ever in sharing his expertise on matters medical concerning Weary and the Thai–Burma Railway, and doing further research on my queries that he did not already know the answers to. I thank him profoundly, as I do Associate Professor Lachlan Miles of the University of Melbourne, who gave me wonderful help on other esoteric historical medical matters, particularly on the innovative ways Weary and co. manufactured their own drugs. I am also indebted to the National Film and Sound Archive of Australia for allowing me access to some precious footage that helped explain a lot.

As ever, my long-time *Sydney Morning Herald* colleague and friend, Harriet Veitch, took her fine-tooth comb to the whole thing before submission, untangling hopelessly twisted sentences, eliminating many grammatical errors and applying – I kid you not – her staggeringly wide and oft esoteric general knowledge to point out minor errors of fact and reference that would otherwise have escaped me. She gives my work a sheen which does not properly belong to it, has strengthened my stuff for three decades now, and I warmly thank her.

In all my books, I give a draft of the near finished product to the eldest of my six siblings, David, who has the best red pen in the business. When his interest flags, it is a fair bet so too will that of the reader, and I generally slash what doesn't grab him, so long as it is not key to the story. In this book, he was as astute as ever, and I record my gratitude. Another early reader who went through the final manuscript to give great feedback was my friend Steve Conroy, and I am grateful.

All books used are listed in the Bibliography, but in terms of those authors who have done previous work that focuses or touches on the life and times of Weary Dunlop that I am particularly keen to acknowledge, I dips my lid to the late Sue Ebury, otherwise known as Lady Wilton. Her 1995 book, *Weary: The Life Of Sir Edward Dunlop*, was both a wonderful source of information itself, and a great navigational guide whenever I lost my way midst the mass of diaries, letters and other contemporary accounts. She and Weary were extremely close for well over a decade and he told her things he had never mentioned elsewhere, and her book is all the stronger for her chronicling many parts of his experience that otherwise would have departed with him.

Margaret Geddes' book *Remembering Weary* was also terrific, containing many candid, humorous and humanising reminiscences of his associates over the years. *Blind to Misfortune* by World War II veteran Bill Griffiths was invaluable, as was the fascinating trilogy by Ray Parkin, *Out of the Smoke, Into the Smother* and *The Sword and the Blossom*. Tom Uren's book *Straight Left* was yet another war memoir by someone who was there with Weary, and wonderfully helpful to complete my picture of the man, rather than the legend.

My most loved book of all, however, in terms of getting to some of the fine detail of the POWs' experience on the Line was Pattie Wright's wonderful opus *The Men of the Line: Stories of the Thai–Burma Railway Survivors*, a collection of survivors' accounts. I highly commend it to you, as I do her other book, *Ray Parkin's Odyssey*, which was also highly informative for me. It was equally wonderful to be welcomed by Pattie into her home on the Mornington Peninsula, where she was more than generous in offering sage advice – and in many follow-up emails responding to my endless queries by sharing her knowledge and contacts. The fact that she also scanned my work to look for errors, and suggest alternative lines of inquiry, was testament to her desire that I do justice to Weary and the men who served with him, many of whom she had become very close to. Thank you sincerely, Pattie.

Just as I had finished the first draft of this book, I read Richard Flanagan's Booker Prize winning *The Narrow Road to the Deep North*, and found it – if I can put it like this – emotionally informing as to the mindset of the Australians, whose numbers included Flanagan's father, Arch. At a more granular level, Gavan McCormack and Hank Nelson's book, *The Burma–Thailand Railway*, also proved to be a wonderful source of fine detail, insights and occasional quotes.

Similarly, many moons ago when I was writing my book *Kokoda*, the academic who helped me most, who went out of his way to place all his expertise and resources at my service, was the late, afore-mentioned Professor Hank Nelson. For this book, it was wonderful to be able to call on his expertise once more, in this case the long interview he did with Weary back in 1983 for the Australian War Memorial, covering so many of the particular episodes I was writing about and giving me an overall feel for the kind of man Weary was, in his own voice. Similar interviews with Blue Butterworth, Ray Parkin and Tom Uren were also extremely valuable. And for one episode in particular, I relied on a 1983 interview conducted for the AWM by Tim Bowden with Lieutenant Ben Hackney of the 2/29th Battalion, which was an absolute breakthrough in chronicling what happened. Robin Newell, the driving force of two great documentaries on Weary Dunlop and the Thai–Burma Railway – *The Quiet Lions: The Story of Weary Dunlop* and *Spirit of the Railway* – could not have been more useful in helping me source some of the fabulous material they used, and I warmly thank him.

As ever, and as I always recount at the beginning of my historical writing, I have tried to bring the *story* part of this history alive, by putting it in the present tense and constructing it in the manner of a novel, albeit with nearly fourteen hundred footnotes as the pinpoint pillars on which the story rests. In bringing that history alive I have used terms and language that were considered acceptable during the time in which the lives I am sharing were lived.

It was a great pleasure to revisit previous Australian sagas I have worked on, like my books on Kokoda and Tobruk, which gave me handy familiarity of some of the building-blocks of Weary's life and times.

When the book was completed, I was delighted to be able to have Weary's surviving son, John, read it from first to last and have further input – just as Andrew Corlette did, with a view to affirming the accuracy of the account of his own fine father, Major Ewan Corlette. It was also wonderful to talk to Weary's long-time PA, Valda Street, to gain further insights, and to Tom Uren's second wife and widow, Christine Logan. I record my warm gratitude to them all.

For the sake of the storytelling, I have occasionally created a direct quote from reported speech in a journal, diary or letter, and changed pronouns and tenses to put that reported speech in the present tense. When the story required generic language – as in the words used when commanding movements in battle – I have taken the liberty of using that dialogue, to help bring the story to life.

Always, my goal has been to determine what were the words used, based on the primary documentary evidence presented, and what the feel of the situation was.

My thanks also to my highly skilled editor, Deonie Fiford, who, as ever, has honoured my request that she preserve most of the oft esoteric – I'm told – way I write, while only occasionally insisting that something come out because it just doesn't work. And to my diligent in-house editor, Karen Ward, who has worked on many of my books over the years and is now retiring, so this will be our last.

I am also grateful to my friend and publisher, Matthew Kelly of Hachette, with whom I have worked many times over the last three decades, and who was enthusiastic and supportive throughout, always giving great guidance, as did my long-time friend at Hachette, Vanessa Radnidge, the Head of Literary and Head of Non-Fiction.

I have felt privileged to do this book, and hope it helps cast light on one of the darkest and yet most inspirational episodes in Australia's military history.

Peter FitzSimons
Neutral Bay, Sydney
January 2025

CHAPTER ONE

RUGBY DAZE, MEDICO DAYS

I went up to the university feeling that there I could find a new world with people to whom I could relate, and instead I found a lot of overgrown schoolboys.[1]

Weary Dunlop

Rugby football is a game I can't claim absolutely to understand in all its niceties, if you know what I mean. I can follow the broad, general principles, of course. I mean to say, I know that the main scheme is to work the ball down the field somehow and deposit it over the line at the other end and that, in order to squelch this programme, each side is allowed to put in a certain amount of assault and battery and do things to its fellow man which, if done elsewhere, would result in 14 days without the option, coupled with some strong remarks from the Bench.[2]

P. G. Wodehouse, *Very Good, Jeeves* (1930)

11 August 1934, Sydney, tested

He is a mountain of a man – six foot four for nearly fifteen stone, and all crags! And yet he moves with the speed of an emu, is as light on his feet as a dingo, and has the heft of a wounded bull on the fly.

And yes, the man in black running flat out the other way has seen him, and tries to change course.

But it is too late.

At full tilt, Weary Dunlop launches his body horizontally and has the satisfaction of feeling his hard right shoulder hit the man in what he knows is the softest spot of the torso, just under the rib cage – a little below the liver, in front of the kidneys and bang on the gall bladder – resulting in a massive 'OOOOOOF!'

But Weary isn't done yet. For, with his arms still around his victim, he drives his legs forward with little steps for maximum traction on the turf, which sees the All Black lock now going five frantic yards *backwards*, before the man from Benalla drives him down hard into the SCG turf – resulting in another deeply satisfying *oooooof!* as the air goes out of him – all as the crowd roars and the ball comes free.

Unnecessary roughness?

There really is no such thing against an All Black forward and, most importantly, the referee doesn't think so.

But the mighty All Blacks, the most feared rugby team in the world, do. In the ensuing brawl, Weary has his nose badly broken for the second time in two weeks. Still, not to worry. The first time had been while boxing in the Melbourne University Boxing Championships, and, as the incumbent Australian Universities champion, he had done as well then as he does now, unleashing a blistering array of uppercuts, right crosses, left hooks and counterpunches that fell all men in black foolish enough to come in range. He does try to protect his broken nose from too much attention – having set it himself last time, by putting a couple of toothbrushes up both nostrils – but it hampers him little.

It is not quite that Weary is the last man left standing, but after winning the brawl, he is so angry – which is rare for him – that he plays the game of his life, by his own estimation 'like a mad tiger',[3] and the Wallabies go on to win the Test, 25–11. Two weeks later they have the coveted Bledisloe Cup.

And that is the most extraordinary thing.

If they had had to *design* a game purely for the strapping 27-year-old, they would have come up with rugby. He can not only break tackles when he has the ball under his arm, but also break those he is tackling when they have the ball under theirs. He has great hand-eye co-ordination and such massive hands that he rarely drops passes. When he runs, his high-knee action makes him nigh on impossible to bring down, unless several players hit him at once – meaning that in club football the most common cry heard among those facing him on the fly is '*Yours!*'

'All Australia's forwards excelled,' *Truth* newspaper notes of this game. 'Second row men "Bimbo" White and Dunlop revelled in the tight going, and it was in this phase, even against such foemen as Max and McKenzie, that our superiority was most marked.'[4]

The wider press leans in further, specifically to Weary. Where did his extraordinary strength come from, and how did a *Victorian* – prior to him, there had been no Wallaby from that state – make his way so quickly into the national side?

The answers are interesting. He had been born at Wangaratta to James and Alice Dunlop and grown up on 580 acres of mixed farm – sheep, cattle and wheat. There, at *Summerlea* – near Shepparton in the north-east of Victoria, right by Sheepwash Creek and not far from the Black Stump and Lower Woop Woop – he had been engaged in hard physical work from the age of five onwards. The bigger he grew, the more work his father had loaded him up with. By the time he was fifteen he could do the work of two men and his father had no doubt he was destined for a life on the farm. His older brother, Alan, can go off to university, but Ernie can stay here. He was needed to work on the farm, particularly as the Depression had taken hold, and his father had insisted that it was time for all hands to the pump, and the cook to the helm. After all, Ernie was clearly 'cut out for farming pursuits, a life of horses, sheep, dogs and hunting'.[5]

And Ernie felt the same.

'Life as we grew up,' he will reminisce, 'was dogs, horses, back-breaking work, wild riding, hunting, swimming, fishing, shooting, and fighting when necessary. This seemed to be my life and my future . . .'[6]

It was only for the pleading of an impassioned teacher at Benalla High – 'Edward is very smart, and must go on to higher education!'[7] – that his father had reconsidered. Things are helped by the fact that, despite the family being as poor as *three* church mice, Edward had won a £10 scholarship to study at the Melbourne Pharmacy College, while working as an apprentice at a local Benalla pharmacy. After topping that course in every year and gaining First Class Honours, he had gained another scholarship, to study medicine at the University of Melbourne, with accommodation at the prestigious Ormond College. (For a lad who had been home-tutored by his mother for his first years of schooling, until judged old enough at the age of seven to ride a horse to the local school, he had come a long way.)

Which is where it had become interesting . . .

For while Weary was recovering from an injury sustained as a ruckman during an Aussie Rules match representing Ormond against Scotch College, his Queenslander room-mate had *begged* the fourth-year medical student to try rugby by turning out for the Melbourne University Rugby Football Club Fourth Grade team. Weary had been so strong, and scored so many tries, that four weeks later he had been in the Firsts for the National Intervarsity Carnival, and been so outstanding that he had in turn made the combined Australian Universities side.

In only his sixteenth match he had been in the Wallabies, picked as a hard-driving number 8, at the back of the scrum! That successful debut in 1932 had been followed by a representative hiatus in 1933, when he had declined to go on the six-month tour of South Africa with the Wallabies. (Not only would such a tour interfere with his medical studies, but with no pay in this strictly amateur game, he simply could not afford it.) But now here he is again, and playing better than ever!

'Although I have been playing rugby for so short a time, I like it better than my old game,' Dunlop had told the press after his debut, 'and that is saying a great deal. I think rugby is the better game to play, though our Australian game is more interesting from outside the fence.'[8]

The thing that particularly distinguishes rugby, he had said, was that it was more of a 'team game' and he has always prospered best in team environments. But, yes, did he mention the game's physicality?

'The whole team gels into action at one time, and moves like one man in great dashes down the field, striving to defeat the opposing side and put the ball over the line. The "tackling" also appeals to me. To me the tackling is more thrilling than anything in the Australian game. I am speaking as a player.'

(It was a physical capacity he had actually demonstrated off the field as well, most particularly against a 19-year-old student loud in his support of nothing less than *revolution*. Yes, in a university debate, this callow, shallow youth, Sam White, had dared to argue that democratic institutions were a failure, while also putting the case for – get this! – communism. Dunlop was one of those who manhandled him out the door, and White had only narrowly escaped a ducking in the lake for his trouble by the arrival of the police. They had quickly escorted him from the campus, though he could not escape condemnation by his fellow students for besmirching the reputation of the University, and being 'disloyal to the Empire'.[9])

All up, Dunlop had loved the game of rugby nearly as much as the game had loved him, and had made friends in both his own and opposing teams, and become one of the stars of the game. The press had loved the stories about him growing up on the farm. One incredulous reporter asked, 'Is it *really* true you could hold two hundred and ten pound bags of wheat under each arm?'

'That's nothing,' replied Weary. 'Where I come from plenty can do the same. There's one bloke who can hold a third bag from his teeth!'[10]

The only problem is time. For it is not only on the field that Dunlop is fast. Off the field he is a young man in a hurry.

He had earned the nickname 'Weary' in his first days on a residential scholarship in Ormond College. Firstly for the fact that, while he was striding out in the final leg of an intercollegiate relay, a rival supporter had cried out, in an attempt at wit, 'Dunlop tires!'[11] a pun on the famed brand of 'Dunlop Tyres' now giving the wares of the Michelin Man a run for his money, and the whole thing had evolved into Weary . . . which had stuck.

And secondly there is the irony of it. Ernest Edward Dunlop, the second name proffered as 'a tribute to the sovereign at the time',[12] is anything *but* weary, for his energy is simply astonishing – and beyond his rugby, he somehow manages to fit in boxing, Aussie Rules, debating, socialising, drinking, rat-bagging and . . . pranking. One highlight of the last had come from the college asking the famous aviatrix Amy Johnson to be their guest. When she declined, Weary and co. pretended she had accepted, dressed up a dummy as 'Amy' and caused a riot by hiring a car and chauffeur for the dummy Amy to be driven down Swanston Street, hailed by saluting police officers and hundreds of onlookers, who assumed Miss Johnson would change her facial expression occasionally, or at least wave.

And, of course, he is anything but weary when it comes to . . . *work*.

For in the realms of academics, his capacity to study, to understand, to get to the bottom of things is nothing less than astonishing. When it suddenly comes to the attention of the university that their star student has no qualification in Latin – which is a requirement of his degree – Weary must fit crash-course studies to that in, too.

Quo vadis?

It is our Weary, burning the midnight oil, actually into the *wee* hours. *Veni, vidi, vici.*

Here, in the 'charmed circle of Ormond College', as Weary will describe it, 'my ideal was that of the scholar athlete like C. B. Fry, Fairbairn of Jesus, and some of our more luminous Rhodes scholars'.[13] Of more rustic influence is the motto printed on the Furphy water cart that had been used so extensively back at *Summerlea*, when irrigating crops:

GOOD BETTER BEST,
NEVER LET IT REST,
TILL YOUR GOOD IS BETTER,
AND YOUR BETTER BEST.[14]

Going hard is just in his *bones*.

By the end of the year, he has earned his First Class Honours in Botany, Chemistry and Zoology – having topped the year in the latter two. Just before Christmas 1934, he graduates with a Bachelor of Medicine and Bachelor of Surgery and, with all of his splendidly begowned fellows in the Royal Exhibition Building in Carlton Gardens, gravely intones the words of the Hippocratic oath to always attempt to preserve life, to do no harm and to do his best to heal the sick:

'I swear by Apollo the physician, and Aesculapius the surgeon, likewise Hygeia and Panacea, and call all the gods and goddesses to witness, that I will observe and keep this underwritten oath, to the utmost of my power and judgment . . .'

It is done.

Step forward, *Dr* Weary Dunlop MBBS.

•

Who is that exquisitely beautiful young woman? Though having just left school the year before, Helen Ferguson – he is advised of her name – carries herself in such a sophisticated manner that she appears much older and is definitely the sort, as he will put it, that 'you wished you could get to know better'.[15]

And yet she is also the sort that is used to suitors and dismissing them with just a glance from her dazzling dark eyes. She is a stunner, with high cheekbones and a shock of black hair. And she looks just like what she is: elegance, grace, beauty and intelligence all wrapped up in a shelter of wealth, used to being and having the best. Weary falls for her in an instant; but she is a catch that even a Wallaby fullback would struggle to take. Escorting Helen home from a dance to the family's grand home at 605 Toorak Road, *Falkirk*, Weary is hoping for a goodnight kiss, only to see her race through her front gate and bang it after her in case he hasn't yet got the message.

Oh, he got it, alright. But, no matter that she is Weary-wary, he is determined to pursue, woo and wed her. Her beauty is intimidating and so is her family. They are not just rich, they have generations of that best of all things – 'old money' – behind them. They don't have dinner parties, they have banquets. The boys of the family don't just go to school, they go to, if you please, *Geelong Grammar*. (They have a way of intoning the school's name, which says that, although they are not so gauche as to add an exclamation mark, all those from non-attendee families really should. Never, in their entire collective lives, have they heard of Benalla High, let alone known someone who attended it. And that's *not* the fork you use for oysters.) The girls don't just see friends, they go to grand silverware luncheons, lawn tennis parties at Royal South Yarra, and golfing at the Peninsula. The odds of Helen going out with a farm boy who thinks he might make a doctor are low – even if he is topping his year in medicine, and playing some strange game for Australia.

But, look, at least last year's school captain of Morongo Presbyterian Girls College is studying pharmacy, despite this annoying her father, who wants her to do nothing other than enjoy life. The fact that Helen wants to be part of the modern world and independent gives Weary some hope.

She likes him; but that's all for now. She is off to Europe soon and an ocean will separate them; he will see if she will give him the time of day on her return.

•

And so to work.

That strikingly tall man striding about the wards of Melbourne Hospital from January 1935 as a junior medical officer is, of course, Dr Dunlop.

Not that there isn't still time for high jinks, as there had been at Ormond College.

As it happens, Weary is a live-in resident at the hospital with two other junior doctors – Ben Rank and John Bolton – and happens to be nearby when a crisis occurs. For it is Rank who has the bad luck to be the sole resident on site at eight o'clock one evening when an insistent 'reporter from the *Melbourne Herald*' calls.

I'd like to know about the leprosy case you have . . .

[Pause.]

But we don't have ANY cases of leprosy, as far as I know?

Well, that's NOT what we've heard at the Herald! *We've been told not only does the patient have leprosy, the symptoms are advanced and the case is being hushed up to prevent panic!*

Not unreasonably Dr Rank starts to feel exactly that. And not being exactly up to speed on all the symptoms of leprosy – what with this being Melbourne in 1935 and not Judea in 33 AD – rushes to find a textbook to answer the reporter's detailed questions. As soon as he hangs up, Rank races through the wards looking for the leper. Each nurse tells him the same thing: there is *no* leprosy here. Relieved, Rank calls the *Melbourne Herald*. He has glad tidings.

'No leprosy patients exist in Melbourne Hospital.'

'My God!' says the reporter on the other end of the line. 'What! WHAT! What case of leprosy?'[16]

But I just spoke to another reporter who knew all about it?

Well, the *Herald* doesn't know who that was and within minutes a reporter from their journal is in the hospital being shown around by Dr Rank, who is telling him there are no lepers here. While he is doing this, the phone rings. It is . . . *another* reporter from the *Melbourne Herald*. Yes?

Ah, I'd like an update on the leprosy case please . . .

The penny drops. On the phone is the other resident, Dr John Bolton, playing another reporter, but not very well.

The first 'reporter' was Weary Dunlop, who was bored and had decided to have some fun on this slow evening. It is less funny the next day when the *Herald* publishes its story headlined 'THE LOST LEPER'. And one of the real reporters from the *Herald* had gone for a drink at Mrs Orr's pub late last night, where every drunk journalist in town goes to relax of an evening, and told them about this leprosy case, and now every bloody paper in town is calling every hospital and the Victorian State Health Officer has to reassure the public and the press.

Dr Rank, Dr Bolton and Dr Dunlop are all yelled at next morning by the Chief Medical Officer of Melbourne Hospital, who tells them never to contact the press about anything ever again and never even dream of saying the word 'leprosy' in Melbourne.

Well, if you can't take a joke . . .

GET OUT!

•

Typically of Weary, as busy as he is with his work as a doctor, he makes time for other activities, joining the Australian Army Medical Corps in July 1935.

Now, as one who had been in the cadets at Benalla High – which had included a little training on the Lee-Enfield rifle and Lewis gun – Weary already has a feel for military matters, and his qualifications as a fully fledged doctor see him immediately commissioned with the consider-able rank of Captain, attached to Coburg-Brunswick Battalion . . .

All the while, his career at Melbourne Hospital continues to prosper, as, after his careful observation of senior surgeons, he is invited to assist – making initial cuts, removing diseased organs and suturing the incisions – before conducting such surgeries as removing appendixes himself. (Even at this late point, there are many nascent surgeons who become squeamish and decide surgery is not for them, after all.) By the following year he has become the Senior Surgical Resident at Melbourne Hospital, blitzing the regular exams that go with his growing qualifications, which see him, as he will describe it, 'pretty well at the top of every medical year'.[17]

•

In January 1937 Dunlop joins the Children's Hospital, the most confronting area of medicine possible because your patients are help-less children, with terrified and often stroppy parents as protectors. Things do not go well from the first.

And what seems to be your problem, little fellow? he asks a trau-matised child on his first day there.

The short answer would appear to be, *YOU, doctor.*

At the very least the fact that the young tearaway toddler grabs his stethoscope and yanks it hard, while also – with remarkable force – kicking him in the shins and shouting with remarkable diction 'Bastard! Bastard! Bastard!'[18] is some indication that this is not going to be an easy round.

Playing for Victoria against the Springboks – whose forwards are so big they are rated 'ten to a ton'[19] – is a tougher assignment, even if his medical work prevents him again getting to Test level. (Part of the issue is that as he is no longer a student, he is not eligible to play for the Melbourne University Rugby Football Club, and must make do with captaining the University's Old Boys team – which proves to be less a rugby team with a drinking problem than a drinking team with a rugby problem.)

The good news is, in September 1937, he graduates as a Master of Surgery – and now that Helen Ferguson has come back from her overseas tour of London, Paris and Vienna the two are going strong as a couple. However, as one who reads newspapers avidly every day, Dunlop knows better than most that there are troubles looming, some of which might see the world descend into war once more. A lot of the troubles are coming from Germany, where their new Chancellor, Herr Adolf Hitler, has seized command in brutal fashion by outlawing all rival parties, executing political rivals, persecuting Jewish people, and expanding the nation's armed forces, the Wehrmacht, to 600,000 – six times the limit imposed by the Treaty of Versailles. Other ominous signs are that he has taken Germany out of the League of Nations before reoccupying the demilitarised zone in the Rhineland.

Even more worrying, from the Australian point of view, is Japan, where extreme militarists have also taken over the government and are insisting that 'Nippon', as they term themselves, is set on expanding its national borders and that those who do not embrace that concept are guilty of 'treason'.

As if this is not alarming enough, it is the brutality they bring to that Nipponese intention which most shocks. For it is just around the time that Weary fully qualifies as a surgeon that the appalling news breaks . . .

The Imperial Japanese Army had attacked Nanking in China and had no sooner surrounded the surrendering Chinese soldiers than the prisoners had been put up against the wall and cut down by machine-gun fire. They were the lucky ones. Others were used for bloody bayonet practice before being thrown into the Yangtze River.

Still, the Japanese were not done. For *weeks* afterwards the victorious soldiers had looted the city, destroying more than a third of its buildings, while murdering many of the city residents and raping – almost as a military policy – women. Many civilians weren't simply shot, but were disembowelled and decapitated by soldiers who seemed insane with bloodlust.

The whole episode became known as the 'Rape of Nanking' and, given the delight the Japanese had in demonstrating their brutality, its notoriety spread far and wide. (Later, the International Military Tribunal for the Far East – the war crimes assessor – will officially estimate that the Japanese soldiers had been responsible for over 200,000 murders and at least 20,000 cases of rape.)

1 January 1938, Melbourne, bliss was it in this dawn to be alive, but to be young was very heaven

On this New Year's Day, Weary and Helen have partied through the night at a University of Melbourne ball, and now, in the first rays of the sun, the massive Wallaby walks her home, ambling by the shores of St Kilda Beach, hand in paw, and making their way to her family's gracious mansion at Toorak.

'These were charmed hours,' he will later reminisce with her, 'and I can remember clearly everything you said and did and the little questions and expressions which fascinated me so. It was a sparkling morning, you trailing a purple evening cloak, and we walked happily hand in hand. You were part of the glory and freshness of the morning and the loveliness of the first light on the sea and you must have been conscious of me rather obviously adoring you.'[20]

A breakfast of peaches is served.

'And once in quite unfathomable impulse you leaned against my shoulder and brushed a very soft cheek against mine, whilst I sat very, very, still fearing to break the charm. Helen dear I love you so!'

And yet, despite being immersed in a blooming romance, Weary now decides to take up an extraordinary offer. For having had the audacity in his last year of studying to be a mere doctor to have sat an exam for the primary fellowship of the Royal College of Surgeons of England – a highly prestigious graduate scholarship – the news comes through.

He is accepted; England and the Royal College beckons – an incredible opportunity for one so young, with only three years of experience in hospital. And yes, it would mean leaving behind Helen, but the offer is nigh on irrefusable. To qualify as a surgeon in England at that august institution – in Weary's eyes the 'mecca' of training surgeons worldwide – is the highest qualification of all and will help secure not only his future, but *our* future, Helen.

•

To get there, Weary will have to work his passage on the SS *Ormonde* – due to leave Melbourne in April 1938, bound for London – not shovelling coal but being one of the ship's medicos.

True, it is a dreadful wrench to leave behind his family and friends, and particularly heart-wrenching to take his leave of Helen – they swear their undying love on their last evening together, and she tearfully accompanies him to the dock, so they can have a few more precious hours – but there is equally no getting away from the sheer excitement of departing for distant, glorious horizons.

In short order, with his kit dropped and his cabin arranged, even before they steam through the heads of Port Phillip Bay, Weary is being shown the ropes by Dr Kenwin Harris, the main surgeon on the *Ormonde*, who expands first and foremost on Weary's duties, which go well beyond wielding a stethoscope. Being an assistant surgeon on a ship to England is not exactly a full-time medical job; it is rather more a social one. Tall, good-looking surgeons with nobody to operate on – this means you – are expected to spend their days chatting to ladies and dancing with them. This is nice work if you can get it, and Dr Dunlop is happy to do his bit. One particular passenger is pointed out to him by Dr Harris: a slightly awkward young woman who risks being a bit of a wallflower on this trip if there is no intervention. Is there anything Weary can do? The gallant Dunlop asks the surprised woman out for dinner and dancing. On the third night, Dr Harris finally informs him he is dancing with the wrong woman. No wonder she was surprised.

On D Deck there are a flock of showgirls returning from a theatrical engagement in Perth and they are very good at coming up with imaginary ailments for Weary to cure at length. At Ceylon, Dr Harris gets married and, despite this new impediment, the *Ormonde*'s two medical officers now lose themselves in 'a moving mass of ship's madness love affairs'.[21]

This is *living*!

Early August 1938, English Channel, green and pleasant views
There it is!

After an exhausting eight weeks aboard the *Ormonde* – all that dancing, singing, drinking and cavorting can tire a man, pass another glass of champagne, and let's play a tune – the joy for Dr Weary Dunlop at first catching a glimpse of green off the port bow on this misty morning is profound.

England!

By the very late afternoon, after coming into berth at Tilbury Docks, some 20 miles down the Thames from London, he is in London itself, and getting off the train at Charing Cross station before taking an Austin taxi – all shiny red metal, glass and plush leather seats – to that home away from home for post-graduate students from all over the British Empire: London House in Bloomsbury. After throwing his bags down, he sets off with typical energy to absorb 'London proper', in 'the amazing twilight and warmth'.

'In this glorious sunshine, and under a soft blue sky,' he recounts to his parents, 'I first saw St Paul's Cathedral, the Strand, Fleet Street, Oxford Street, and many familiar London sights . . . the Marble Arch, Hyde Park and Kensington Gardens to Notting Hill Gate.'[22]

Oh, the sheer thrill of it all!

His study and work will be not long in beginning as he must soon immerse himself in the training course at St Bartholomew's, an old, exceedingly worn-down teaching hospital dating from the 1100s – no, really – which is positioned, oddly, between the gracious splendour of St Paul's Cathedral and the madness of Smithfield market. To get there, every morning Weary sets off in the company of two new-found Australian companions doing the same course, Frank Mills and Jim Yeates, the latter a perpetually sunny chap from Queensland – a rugby player himself, educated at Toowoomba Grammar – who Dunlop has particularly taken to. Chattering happily, after leaving London House, 'the Aussie triumvirate' as they soon become known, daily make their way through the hustle-bustle of Gray's Inn Road, the hurly-burly of Hatton Garden and the hoi-polloi of the markets, to finally enter the cloistered confines of this ancient hospital.

Together they learn state-of-the-art surgery techniques through the day before hitting the books each night.

The final exams are . . . terrifying.

Going into them, Weary is convinced he will fail, a pessimistic view which is substantiated when two professors accompany him on hospital rounds and ask him to diagnose a particular patient who has just been brought in, having collapsed with abdominal pains. Given the man is writhing in agony and has a deathly pallor, Weary has no hesitation in diagnosing him as suffering an 'acute duodenal, ruptured ulcer, an emergency'.[23]

When the professors roar with jarring laughter and call the rest of this part of the exam off – for their can be no salvaging such a diagnosis – he knows he is in trouble.

    'Weary Dunlop. FAILED.'

But, as it happens, just two hours later when the patient in question continues to descend, he is opened up for exploratory surgery and the problem proves to be, well, seeing as you mention it . . . 'acute duodenal, ruptured ulcer'. The patient is saved by emergency surgery, as is Weary's medical career!

(True, it is not so rosy for Jim Yeates, who has failed despite his perpetual optimism, and Weary and Frank have a job at hand to restore his spirits – noting he simply must sit the exams again, and all will be right with the world – but, that aside, Weary's own joy knows no bounds.)

Meanwhile, Weary continues to prosper, immeasurably helped by the leisure of his betters . . .

> The surgical consultants here are all famous men around London, but I've seen very little of them as they have been away on holidays. As a result I've done most of the surgical work and have scored as many as six major operations on some days.[24]

All up, it is a glorious time in Weary's life, as, beyond discovering London, he also manages to go on a brief excursion to Paris in the spring.

'Paris is the loveliest city imaginable,' he writes home to his parents, 'with glorious boulevards and gardens, and the great buildings, unlike London, are given proper space, perspective and a suitable environment.'[25]

The most pleasant thing of all in this trip far surpasses even the Champs-Élysées.

While spending some time in the home of a French family closely related to the French President, Albert Lebrun, he has the beginnings of an affair with the daughter, and no-one else in her family seems to mind at all.

'I really think the French are the most tolerant and civilised people on the earth in many respects.'

And it is not as if she is the only beautiful woman he is meeting.

'Did I mention meeting the Duchess of Gloucester? A most charming person, very youthful and pretty, and, of course, exquisitely turned out.'[26]

Most importantly, back at the British Postgraduate Hospital at Hammersmith, Weary is reunited with Jim Yeates, and at the end of long days working together they are able to carouse into the night, talking of just how thrilling it is to be here, to have the opportunity to learn so many things, to be discovering London and Europe together, while surrounded by such eminent medicos, not to mention so many beautiful women, including the ever fetching nurses.

But there is always time to write to Helen, now approaching her final exams back at Melbourne University for her Bachelor of Science degree.

> *Darling my delight,*
> *Just terribly proud of you to find that as anticipated you are doing big*
> *things in the examinations . . . I shouldn't worry Helen dear about*
> *the domesticity friends who frown on 'Careers' for women. You seem*
> *to manage domesticity delightfully with the left hand whilst being a*
> *university success with the right. All very admirable. As for the question*
> *of examinations being a 'masculine' pursuit – well darling you must*
> *know that I think you are the most thrilling feminine person I have met.*
> *Might kiss you about 1.000.000 times.*[27]

And more.

> *I need you very abominably, and so often wish for unattainable things*
> *like holding you ever so closely with my head rather buried in a soft*
> *neck and hair so that at the time one might explore new places to kiss or*
> *whisper in your ear.*
> *I'll have such dreadful arrears to make up for when I see you, that*
> *you will be eaten in the first week.*[28]

•

And yet, these are troubling times.

Despite British Prime Minister Neville Chamberlain's assurance that there would be peace in our time, Hitler is not taking his time to prove that statement false. There is no appeasing the Führer's rush to roam over lands and people that resist him and anyone who reads the paper or glances at the glum faces wandering towards Whitehall knows that Europe is hurtling towards war. In the expectation that London itself might soon be bombed by the Luftwaffe, all of three million women, children and elderly residents have been evacuated to whatever shelter they can find in the rest of the United Kingdom. Weary Dunlop, like most medicos in the grand old city, has been drafted into an emergency medical service team, in his case based at St Mary's Hospital, Paddington.

As busy as he is in surgery and general emergency medical care, more often than not on the weekends Dunlop is doing more than his fair share to send even more patients to hospital! For, as it happens, not only does St Mary's have a very strong rugby team, but Weary is inevitably soon the strongest part of it.

It is not often that you get a barging behemoth of an international playing among the motley medicos – read *never* – and the simply stunned British Army teams of Aldershot and Portsmouth find they have actual competition when they compete. These are service teams, full of actual men and killers, and they are being scattered asunder by this massive piece of fleet-footed meat from St Mary's.

Yes, St Mary's! They are supposed to stitch you up at half-time, not trounce you with tries without even trying. The dashing Dunlop makes friends easily on the field and gains admirers off it; both from local ladies and from the delighted senior staff at St Mary's, who love the fact that they have something to celebrate of a weekend; at least outside of a surgery. Weary is invited to play for the Barbarians against the Combined Services; he is asked to play for British Commonwealth, he is requested everywhere – including black-tie dinners and balls – and is always ready to play, on and off the field. A gentleman scholar, who can tackle as well as he can quote Shakespeare and tell amusing stories from the Antipodes, is a man in demand and his social circles briefly include even the likes of Lord and Lady Mountbatten. (Though the former, a famous captain in the Royal Navy, doesn't quite call the king his uncle, it is close.)

It is through his social interactions with those in the services sides that he becomes ever more certain that war is really on the way, and he must be in a position to react when it arrives.

'The more people I saw in uniform, the more morbid I was getting about this that I just had to get into the army.'[29]

Alas, the Dean of St Mary's, Sir Charles Wilson – soon to be Lord Moran but more popularly known as 'Corkscrew Charlie' for his skill in negotiations with the British Medical Association and the Ministry of Health – simply won't hear of it.

'You shouldn't go into the services at this time,' he insists time after time, 'and will be doing a better job for the country at St Mary's operating on the sick and injured of London!'

The Australian doesn't believe it is medical matters that concern Corkscrew Charlie at all, however.

'The old wretch,' Weary deduces, 'what he wants is to keep me on the rugby union team.'[30]

He is relentless!

> I tried the Army, Navy and Air Force in England and every time Sir Charles blocked my entry into the services and said that I was essential to the Emergency Medical Service.[31]

12 July 1939, Melbourne, two-faced Bob each way

'History,' Prime Minister Robert Menzies says firmly, at this meeting in Anzac House, 'will label Hitler as one of the really great men of the century.'

There are cries from the back of the room!

Hitler?

Hitler! The very man who had plotted *Kristallnacht* and launched an *Anschluss* that threatened to hurl the world into war? Yes, that Hitler. The ridiculous-looking chap with the Chaplin moustache, who has already declared war on the Jews in his own nation.

This is the European leader that the Australian Prime Minister so vaunts. The outcry grows. Right at the back, a fetchingly good-looking young woman jumps up and waves a placard, while she continues to shout, soon joined by a fellow who hurls his own insults. The calls of both, however, are soon drowned out by others in the crowd who also call out in protest at what the PM has just said.

Undeterred, Menzies goes on.

'Whatever outside nations thought of Hitler's aggressive methods,' the *Mirror* will record of the thrust of his remarks, 'the Fuehrer had certainly dragged his people from the depths of the despair which followed the Great War and gave them another place among the great powers.'

And this is Menzies' point.

'As far as the German people are concerned,' he says, 'Hitler has proved himself a great man and a tireless worker. He dragged his nation from bankruptcy and revolution, and I think he has too much intelligence lightly to cast them back into another war.'[32]

He continues.

'Let us judge Hitler soberly and fair . . .'

But the shouting starts again. It is the same good-looking young woman with the placard.

To Mr Menzies' right one of the organisers whispers, 'Would you like her thrown out?'

Yes, Mr Menzies would. It will be best if she and the other inter-jectors are removed. It takes a few minutes for the police to do the business, but it is done and he proceeds, expanding on the theme that what some saw as the outrages done by Germany can be forgiven when you focus on what Hitler has done to lift the German people.

(Presumably, the Jews apart.)

Menzies closes with a little wit that makes the papers the next day: 'I would like to thank all those present . . . [*pause*] . . . and those no longer present.'[33] [*Laughter.*] Mr Menzies is referring to the protesters removed from the meeting, not the Jews removed from their homes.

'MR MENZIES' DEPARTED FRIENDS' reads the headline in the next day's *Mirror*, Hitler not newsworthy enough to get top billing in Australia yet.

•

Good news, for Weary.

The Wallabies have just landed in England, disembarking at Plymouth from the P&O liner *Mooltan*, to embark on the first leg of their ten-month, five-Test rugby union tour. Right now, on this Sunday morning of 3 September 1939, they are settling into the Grand Hotel on the esplanade of the picturesque British seaside town of Torquay, England's Riviera, and as soon as Weary finishes this shift, he intends to take the train down to see them, and catch up with so many of his old mates . . . but now what?

The word suddenly goes around that the British Prime Minister, Neville Chamberlain, is about to make some kind of national address and they should turn their radios on.

'I am speaking to you from the Cabinet Room at 10 Downing Street,' Chamberlain begins in his clipped, but rather unsteady, tones.

> This morning the British Ambassador in Berlin handed the German Government a final note stating that unless we heard from them by 11.00 a.m. that they were prepared at once to withdraw their troops from Poland, a state of war would exist between us. I have to tell you that no such undertaking has been received, and that consequently this country is at war with Germany . . .

At the very moment that Weary crinkles his brow to better grasp the gravity of the British Prime Minister's words, the declaration of war is, 'eerily punctuated by the first mournful air raid warning . . .'[34]

Weary and his fellow surgeons exchange glances. It cannot be long before bombs will start dropping and their resources at Emergency Medical Services will be stretched to breaking point. But, do go on, Prime Minister.

'At such a moment as this the assurances of support that we have received from the Empire are a source of profound encouragement to us . . .

'Now may God bless you all. May He defend the right. It is the evil things that we shall be fighting against – brute force, bad faith, injustice, oppression and persecution – and against them I am certain that the right will prevail.'[35]

•

It is a very odd thing to be a 21-year-old Pommy bricklayer lying under the bed of an English girl in a grand Killara home of the northern suburbs of Sydney, with your head next to a vat of shit . . . but that's just the way things are at this very moment for 'Blue' Butterworth.

As a new 'Jimmy Grant', immigrant, he'd taken some work on a Turramurra poultry farm helping the one-armed owner, and, on this Sunday night, had gone to quietly visit Edwina and Amy, two girls he'd met on the ship the year before. And yes, it is a risky business, 'cos they now live in the grand home of the bloke who is the 'trump' of the Sydney Stock Exchange – with a name like 'Darganheart' or something, Blue can never get it straight – and are forbidden to have men visiting.

So, when there had been sudden movement in the hallway, of course he had ducked under Edwina's bed – Mrs Darganheart had heard voices, and is investigating – and of course Edwina had quickly turned on the radio as an explanation for how voices were coming from her room. It was just unfortunate that she had used the 'gazunder', just before he had arrived, though at least Blue is able to use her contribution to put out his fag with a sick sizzle.

But, what now?

ABC Radio interrupts normal programming to make an important announcement. It is the Australian Prime Minister, and he is sounding very grave. Christ, that gazunder stinks.

Go on, Prime Minister . . .

'Fellow Australians,' Prime Minister Menzies is saying, 'it is my melancholy duty to inform you officially that in consequence of a persistence by Germany, and her invasion of Poland, Great Britain has declared war upon her and that as a result Australia is also at war.'[36]

Britain is at war, therefore Australia, her loyal dominion, is at war.

Christ Almighty!

'Oh,' Blue thinks. 'Gotta go and join up. Another job.'[37]

•

They really are a weird mob, these Australians.

Milton Butterworth had known that from meeting his first 'Aussies' on the way out to Australia.

The first one he'd met had said to him, 'You're Blue.'

'Why?' Milton had asked.

'Because you're red.'[38]

For some *weird* reason, they called people with a shock of red hair 'Blue' and he'd been 'Blue' Butterworth ever since, but that had been only the beginning of the odd way they went about things.

The Australians are so steeped in irony, with laconic as their resting speed, that simply getting through the day coherently requires mental acrobatics for a newcomer like him.

But this *is* serious.

As soon as war is declared, the following morning, Blue Butterworth has quit his job at the poultry farm and has turned up at Victoria Barracks in Sydney, eager to join up. If England is at war, and Australia is at war, then *he* is in no doubt that he is at war.

In short order he has signed up to the Second Australian Imperial Force, 2/1st Battalion, listing his occupation as bricklayer, only to find they have a job for him out at the Liverpool Army Camp: build some new latrines.

What are latrines?

Shithouses.

'Listen, sport,' he says to the snooty corporal, 'I'm not the battalion poop carter. I'm the battalion bricklayer.'

'I'll have you know,' the corporal snarls, 'you'll do as you're told.'[39]

Well, we'll see about that.

Spying a tall sergeant over the corporal's shoulder, Blue Butterworth goes up to him and snaps off a salute, only to be rebuked.

'Soldier, you don't salute a warrant officer,' says he.

'Look, you're so tall I couldn't see if you'd had anything on your shoulder or not.'

'What's your problem?'

'Well, do you know of any jobs, sir, that I could do?'

'Yeah, I want a batman.'

'I'll take it.'[40]

Later on, he can work out what a batman does. But he will *not* be spending this war building shithouses or carting poop.

CHAPTER TWO

DOGS OF WAR

*Once upon a midnight dreary, while I pondered, weak and
weary,
Over many a quaint and curious volume of forgotten lore –
While I nodded, nearly napping, suddenly there came a tapping,
As of some one gently rapping, rapping at my chamber door.
"Tis some visitor,' I muttered, 'tapping at my chamber door –
Only this and nothing more.'*

Edgar Allan Poe, 'The Raven'

September 1939, London, war in our time
Now that war has come, Weary dashes off a quick note to his love;
at least, his true love, Helen.

*The ball kicked off today by Mr Chamberlain to the relief of all.
Our mind just boggles as to the consequences . . . There is a curious
detachment on the personal affairs as though we were a particle seen from
another planet. We must make ourselves believe that some day when all
this beastliness is over that some of the beauty will remain.*

*London of course is taking on the appearance of a fortified city.
Evacuation has gone on smoothly, and the organisation of it all
has to be seen to be believed. Endless sand bags everywhere, the sky
studded with balloons and the population being trained to live like rats
underground as much as possible.*

*Preparations have been made for sensible civilian loss but somehow
we surgeons all feel that it won't be surprising if we are on the Continent
before very long. Defence has a habit of getting on top somehow . . .*

*One small note of personal regret does intrude persistently. I should
give so very much to have seen you again before all this. I am so hungry
for the sight of your darling face, and the sound of your voice, and so*

many lovely things. . . . Now that the continued separation I have so feared is definitely to be I feel my faith in us is stronger than ever before. It is happiness in itself to be so in love with you.

Your ever devoted Edward.[1]

Meantime, the most important thing he wants his parents to know, in the wake of this massive historical event?

'If you are worrying about me – don't!' he writes in his educated if slightly rustic hand. 'I shall almost certainly be depressingly safe.'[2]

London is remarkably resilient, despite what it faces, and is girding its loins for what is to come, as are Weary and his colleagues. Both he and his now best friend Jim Yeates are certain they must join up. The question is with who, and how quickly can it be done?

For while Dunlop wants to serve with his own Australian army, rather than the British one, the problem is that 'enlistment in the 2nd AIF requires that I first return to Australia . . .'[3]

However, a man like Weary – a doctor, surgeon and Wallaby – scoffs at any such notion of doing things by the book, like everyone else. For him, going back to Australia to join up is obviously 'a tortuous way to get to a war in Europe',[4] and as one who not only knows people, but knows people who know people, he is confident he can find a way around such administrative red tape.

Sure enough, back in Australia, it is his old chief at the Children's Hospital, Major General Rupert Downes, the Director General of the Australian Army Medical Corps (AAMC), who steps up. For, after an exchange of cables, which 'broke all the laws of God and man that no Australians were being enlisted in England',[5] Weary Dunlop is signed up as Captain Edward Dunlop of the AAMC – the same rank he had attained in the militia. He is assigned to be the Deputy Assistant Director of Medical Services at the Australian Overseas Base in Jerusalem, Palestine, which is where the bulk of the Australian soldiers now flooding recruitment centres across Australia are being sent, to train in the Middle East before being sent on to join the British Expeditionary Force bound for France. All up, there should soon be 17,000 Australian soldiers of the 6th Division AIF in these parts, dispersed in six tented camps running north along the coastal road from Gaza, and their medical care must be organised.

And what will the DADMS *do*, exactly? That is not particularly defined, but as near as Weary can work out, he will be the staff doctor to senior officers of the 6th Division.

It's a start!

Alas, he and Jim Yeates will not be able to join together, as Jim's contacts are not quite the equal of Weary's and it will take him more time, so for the moment, Weary is on his own. But not even Weary can make the quartermasters at home move faster.

For, as an Australian officer so far from home – let alone one of his highly irregular size – getting the regulation uniform will take *months*. So, in the interim, he adapts and dons himself in the trappings of his previous militia service, which, beyond braid, gold buttons, a staff armband, plus a rakish cap and a cane, includes 'some form of boots and leggings and corduroy britches and the spectacular tunic that might have come from the South African war'.[6]

Most wonderfully of all, it also boasts the famous slouch hat of the Diggers, complete with emu feathers – a leftover from the hat worn by the Light Horse in the Boer War.

'I'm telling you that when I ultimately put this on in London, one of the better uniforms, I really caused a sensation.'[7]

No, really!

For no sooner is he out on Fleet Street than one passer-by stops and stares. And now another. And another. And still more of them. And they start clapping, before . . . rushing forward to shake his hand and clap him on the back. Weary Dunlop is the first 'Digger' – heirs to those famed fighters of the Great War – on the streets of London in this, the British hour of need, and London is *determined* to make it known to this worthy soul just how very welcome he is.

Bravo! *Bravo!* BRAVO!

> It so embarrassed me, that I fled down Shaftsbury Avenue to Morris Angel's Shop to be equipped as an officer and gentleman! I emerged indistinguishable from British officers save for a keen inspection of the bright buttons worn by Australians in World War I.[8]

Whatever he is wearing, the main thing is that he will soon be on his way to war!

Weary is *beyond* thrilled.

Apart from everything else, this turn of events offers an alternative route to becoming what he wants to be, a highly qualified surgeon doing interesting work. Without Herr Hitler, he would be facing as long as ten years with his 'nose to the grindstone' entering a 'professional rabbit warren', in the mere hope that 'you will . . . make the bracket of successful surgeons after very long arduous training'.

But this is different.

> Suddenly [we were] presented with a marvellous alternative of a great war with a certain amount of excitement and unusual things to do – a very attractive thing to enterprising young men.[9]

And beyond even the possibilities of rapid professional advancement, there is, too, this sense of tremendous adventure. Weary had prospered on the rugby field for his physical prowess, yes, but also because of his unusually cavalier approach to facing great danger. So, too, with this war.

He cannot wait to be in the thick of the action, one way or another.

Early 1940, Jerusalem, and did those feet in ancient times

It is the best of times, it is the worst of times . . .

For Weary, it has all happened so very fast – no time for even taking a fitness test, or getting a paybook to make sure he will have enough money to live on in the short term – all while taking *so long*.

Having left London on New Year's Day 1940, 'Captain Dunlop', if you please, had first boarded a British India liner, the SS *Mantola* – the only man of the armed forces on board – bound for the Suez, and thence Jerusalem. And yet, after first struggling to get through a frozen Thames, the ship is blocked by a magnetic mine at the river's mouth, and it is a whole week before it can get to the Channel! Dodging German U-boats from there, they practically go across the entire Atlantic in convoy before making their way back to Gibraltar.

Dunlop has diagnosed himself with the worst hangover ever known to modern man. His head throbs, his heart pounds, his mouth feels like someone has left the Dead Sea Scrolls in there overnight. It had come at a brief stopover in Malta, where he and two other Australian officers, 'wild devils', had gone on a massive bender. And the worst thing, the 'medicine' he had proposed for them all, was a concoction he'd suggested – a 'Prairie Oyster': mustard, pepper, Worcestershire sauce, egg yolk and . . . desperation.

If it had been a case of the cure being worse than the ailment, he'd at least have the consolation of *some* good having come from it. But, as it is, the concoction just makes him want to throw up, added to all the other ailments.

'It baffles me often,' he writes to Helen ruefully, 'why I . . . have something of a flair for attracting hell-bent company.'[10]

Finally however, by 21 January 1940, they have successfully made it to the Suez Canal – all shimmering sands, cavalier camels and devastating heat around a thin strip of water – and they are able to definitively disembark at Port Said, whereupon Weary's intent is to head straight to Cairo on the morrow, intending to 'do the town over' for a couple of days before reporting in.

Alas, he has no sooner had a shower in his Port Said hotel room than there comes *a tapping, a tapping at his chamber door.*

Dunlop opens it to find an extremely officious and immaculately turned-out Sergeant Major standing there – every bit as bristling and spiky as his moustache – advising that he is from something called 'Movement Control' and Captain Dunlop should be ready to move out to catch the train to Jerusalem on the morrow.

No ifs, no buts. These are orders.

Inwardly, Weary groans: 'And that's the end of my trip to Cairo.'[11]

And so it is that after a slow journey through a land of dust, sand, sandy dust, dusty sand and camels he finally approaches his destination. Keenly aware that in one day he has traversed the lands that it had taken Moses 40 years to cover, and even King Richard a couple on his own Crusade, he steps down onto the platform at Lydda outside of Tel Aviv, to be greeted by his new Commanding Officer at the AIF's Overseas Base, Assistant Director of Medical Services, Colonel Clive Disher.

This way, Captain Dunlop. Our truck to Jerusalem awaits.

And here now is the city itself straight out of the Bible, still peopled by its characters.

Merchants with glittering goods, beggars with peeling palms, palms with peeling fronds, barefoot boys on donkeys, and all things produced either by God or mammon are on sale. If a couple of the disciples were to appear and try to flog you a testament or two, you would not be surprised. Jerusalem doesn't just seem ancient, it *is* ancient. Look, for just a couple of Palestinian pounds, you can buy splinters guaranteed to come from the cross of Christ.

'In the old City of Jerusalem,' Dunlop writes home, 'one finds a maze of winding, tortuous streets, steps and dark alleys, with no motor traffic or indeed any concession to modernity except electric lighting in shops and bazaars. There are, of course, four quarters – Moslem, Christian, Jewish and Armenian. Jerusalem is the third most sacred city to Moslems, and so it is the sacred place of three religions related to Jehovah, Christ and the fact that here Mohomet's spirit was said to ascend to Heaven.'

You really have to see it, to believe it.

> Jerusalem is perched up on the gaunt highlands, with the Mount of Olives, 2680 feet up approximately and from there you can look down on that immense rent in the Earth's surface, the Great Rift, which actually constitutes the Jordan Valley . . .
> The road to Jericho goes through Bethany, where lived Mary, Martha and Lazarus, and is to this day otherwise utterly lonely except for one inn.[12]

There is room at this inn, at least for one Australian who cannot get over the fact that the ancient stories told from Sunday School and pulpit alike are now alive before his eyes, with no mod cons introduced to spoil the illusion of waking up 2000 years ago.

> Amid the harshness of the locality the Mount of Olives seems very peaceful and gracious.[13]

There are times when you need to remind yourself there is a war on.

Early February 1940, Palestine, Mary not contrary

True, as a breed, potential mothers-in-law tend to have standards so high most men would have to stand on their tippy-toes, on a fruit box, to even get close. And Mary Ferguson is no exception.

But Weary is not most men, and as a six-foot-four surgeon, international sportsman and proud officer in the AIF, he stands sure. It is not only clear that she wants him to marry Helen, but Mary openly says so in a missive he has just received, hoping that he and Helen might 'enjoy some happiness' in the coming year.

So now, after making his way to an old Russian church atop the Mount of Olives, he sits 'neath the shade of some cypress trees and in his hasty if heartfelt hand, pens a proposal . . .

•

Good news, sort of, and the best of it comes on Weary's 33rd birthday, 12 July 1940.

Weary's superior in Jerusalem, Colonel Clive Disher, has been promoted, and will be moving to Gaza as the Assistant Director Medical Services for the 6th Division, which means the towering Australian medico is now – at least until Disher's replacement arrives – 'Medical Pooh-bah Jerusalem'.[14]

Which is fine.

But just as had been the case in London, Weary Dunlop has little interest in being promoted when the result risks being the exact opposite to what he actually wants to do. 'I was anxious to avoid being a Half Colonel, because majors are the chaps who do most of the surgery in the army.'[15] He wants to be of *use* to the men directly – and on the front lines – not just a paper warrior.

A quiet word, please, Deputy Director of Medical Services to 1st Australian Corps, Colonel Roy Burston (or 'Ginger' as Weary called him on civvy street, back in Melbourne)?

Weary wishes to volunteer for 'the most active service available'.[16] Burston promises to look into it, but appears far from convinced that it is a good idea.

There will at least be plenty to keep Weary busy, including liaising with the doctors of all the units of fresh Australian arrivals, which are even now on their way up the Suez Canal in ships about to disgorge Diggers at such ports as Suez, Port Said and El Kantara. It will be his role to find out who is ill, what can be done for them, and to which hospitals they should be sent in the interim while he works out exactly where Australia's own two general hospitals should be established.

And here is the first ship filled with Australians now, just coming into the main wharf at El Kantara.

But, what's this?

Striding up the gangplank in his admittedly rather dandy uniform, swinging his cane, Weary suddenly hears cat-cries from above – 'Mind the step, chum!' is the kindest of comments now called, most revolving around what a poncy Beau Brummell he is – as a sprinkle of pennies descends all around.

Well! Well, he *never*.

Reaching the deck, Weary throws a salute at the Commanding Officer, and says, offering a gimlet eye to his would-be persecutors, 'Can't you bastards recognise a chap from Melbourne?'[17]

They fall back. Christ, he is *big*.

•

Now in Gaza – where the Australian Overseas Base has been moved since the arrival of the troops – life is nothing if not hot under the Middle Eastern sun. Even in the evening the sweat pours off Dunlop so furiously that he aches to open the window for some night air, and sometimes gives in, only for the room to be engulfed by whole swarms of insects. All he can do on such occasions is maintain that discretion is the better part of valour and retreat to his camp bunk positioned just above the tiled floor, draw the mosquito net, and keep slapping until all the insects inside the net are at least dead, before resuming writing.

Sorry, my dearest darling Helen, where were we . . . ?

Ah, yes. Their wedding, upon his return! For to his great delight, Helen has not only said yes but her father has given his blessing, and their happiness had even been considered newsworthy enough that it makes the papers in Melbourne on 6 June 1940.

Engagement of Wide Interest

The engagement is announced between Captain Ernest Edward Dunlop, A.A.M.C., Palestine, formerly of St. Mary's Hospital, London, second son of Mr. and Mrs. J. H. Dunlop, of Benalla, and Helen Leigh Raeburn Ferguson, only daughter of Mr. and Mrs. Mephan Ferguson, of Toorak.

Captain E. E. ('Weary') Dunlop, in addition to having a fine medical career, is an international Rugby player. At present with A.I.F. in Palestine, where he is assistant director of medical services, he was a member of A.I.F. Rugby team.[18]

True, it is not quite the conventional thing to be trying one's amorous chances on the very evening that one announces one is off the amorous market forever, but – very quietly – Weary scoffs at such conventions. They are for other men, and good luck to them. He can make his own rules.

This is looking like a long war, and though he might be in the desert, a man is not a camel when it comes to *amour*, and as ever one for more and more *amour*, he is up for it.

So, when a very attractive woman happens to walk through the door of the watering hole where the newly engaged Dunlop is drinking – alone, mark you – he does not just give her the once-over; he sends a young companion to call her over if she would like to have a good time.

That fellow soon returns with a stunned look on his face: 'She says she's the Duchess of Roxburgh!'[19]

So, is that a yes or a no? A likely story. They resume carousing but Weary's eyes keep returning to the glory of that solitary beauty. What might have been! On the way out, Weary stops at the cloakroom and is given his hat. The head waiter passes and Weary stops him and points out his target. Who is that gorgeous creature? 'She *says* she is the Duchess of Roxburgh?'

'She is,'[20] replies the waiter.

Ah. Well, if you're going to strike out on the night you are betrothed, that's the way to do it. Weary and his scofflaws are out into the night looking for women with less title and more give.

•

What is that?

Perched high on the escarpment above Sollum on the Egyptian–Libyan border, the Australian war correspondent John Hetherington and a mate are gazing down onto the endlessly brown plains of Egypt stuck in dull repose by the enormous blue bay of the Mediterranean. But as seagulls dive, glide and screech their displeasure at the intruders, they see something . . .

Yes, there. Right on the very hundredth of the hundred horizons in the sand that stretches before them, a small brown stain of something appears, and is, ever so gradually, getting bigger. What could it be . . . ? They stand up, and now lean forward, in the instinctive manner of humans towards curious things seen at a great distance . . .

A nearby Tommy soldier, who knows who and what is coming, tells them in a broad West Country voice thick with excitement:

'T' Aussies are movin' up! They'll give bloomin' Itie some 'urry-up, them laads will an' all!'

Sure enough . . .

Hetherington will describe it:

> The great cloud of dust rolled on to meet us and presently we saw the vanguard of the trucks. Then behind them, huddling through the dun fog churned and lifted by their own wheels, we saw more trucks stretching away mile on mile. I looked at the men who sat behind the driving-wheels of trucks and the men who perched under the canopies behind, cuddling their rifles. Their faces coated with dust, looked like the faces of film actors made up to go before the camera . . .[21]

But this is for real. This is the Australian 6th Division, moving forward, answering the battle siren that has just sounded for them . . .

'They really went through country like a hot knife through butter,'[22] Weary will recall, of the Australian advances, until they arrive at the gate of the most important Italian stronghold of all, Tobruk.

Frustratingly, it is a gate closed to Weary now through sudden illness. The newly promoted Brigadier Burston takes one look at Dunlop's yellow face and knows he can't go anywhere, let alone the Western Desert. Weary is so badly jaundiced that he could play the final role in the childhood ditty about traffic lights, 'Stop says the red one, go says the green, ready says the yellow one, blinking in between . . .'

Despite protests, Burston orders Dunlop into his own staff car and takes him straight to the hospital that his patient had helped set up! The reluctant Weary is now detained against his will in the 2/1st Australian General Hospital at Gaza Ridge.

'I'm in hospital with infective jaundice,' Weary soon writes, 'thin, yellow, dyspeptic, nauseated and depressed.'[23]

January 1941, Tobruk, Go on, you bastards!

Private Blue Butterworth has come a long way in the last fifteen months since war had broken out. Not only is he not building shithouses or carting poo, but – as batman to Regimental Sergeant Major Wally Delves, the 2/1st's Intelligence Officer – he has seen genuine action.

Now a proud member of the mighty 6th Division, he and the 2/1st Battalion had finished their training at Liverpool Army Camp before, like the rest of the AIF, being shipped to the Middle East, where they had trained in the shade of the Pyramids, just like the

Diggers of the Great War, before launching themselves against the Italian stronghold of Bardia with great success.

Next on the list is the jewel in the Italian crown in these parts, the harbour of Tobruk, lying 50 miles to the west of Bardia and the only port for miles of North African coast – a crucial supply post for the war machine of the Axis powers, as well as berthing three destroyers, two squadrons of submarines, and . . .

And pipe down over there, or I'll have your guts for garters! *No* whispering!

There are 25,000 Italian soldiers defending the heavy barbed wire perimeter around Tobruk, sprinkled with pillboxes, and it has fallen to us of the 2/1st Battalion to sneak forward in the darkness and get close enough to blow the wire. Once the guns of the Royal Navy just off the harbour entrance open up and plaster the Italian defences on their side of the perimeter, it will be for us to blow the wire and pour through, hopefully followed by the rest of the 6th Division.

So it is that in the darkest part of the night, when the sun is well gone and the moon still not yet risen – in this, the wee hours of 21 January 1941, Bluey and his fellow soldiers move into position, just back from the designated spot on the wire.

Clearly, the Italian defenders are still not aware we are here – though the same might not be said for some of their camp dogs in the far distance, which are barking.

As the dim moon rises, the desert is bathed in a curious light that is just strong enough to see in, without quite being able to throw shadows.

As Captain Delves' batman, Bluey now goes with him to see that all is in order for the attack. Their hearts in their mouths, they move to the rendezvous point, a small and flickering kerosene light with a solid back, meaning the Australian attackers can see it, but the defenders cannot.

There! Up ahead, they can see the expected dim shapes of Delves' fellow officers and, sure enough, it proves to be the Commanding Officer of the 2/1st, Colonel Ken Eather, with the Battalion adjutant, Captain Don Jackson. All is in order. This light will guide their own soldiers when the curtain goes up very shortly.

'Right,' Colonel Eather whispers, 'now all the watches have been synchronised.'[24]

The plan is for the 2/1st to lead the ground attack at exactly 6.25 am.

But, right now, it is exactly 5.40 am and with that utterance, a sudden boom is heard in the distance. The guns of the Royal Navy are opening up, for the boom is followed by the sound of whistling and now many explosions as the shells land, as 'the arty' focuses saturation fire on a rectangle measuring 2500 yards wide by 800 yards deep on the southern perimeter of the Tobruk defences. Saturation is exactly what it is, a soaking in shells as the shriek of falling metal is met by the roar of rising debris. That such damage is done ashore by those at sea seems somehow wrong. Surely there is some Newtonian law which means flinging such fire can't be done while staying so deadly still; but Blue and each man watching sees the same illusion come true before their eyes. It is dreadful, and it is wonderful to see when you are the next warriors due to approach.

Again, *precisely* as planned, at 6.05 am the barrage of artillery fire ceases and the next part of the plan is smoothly swung into action. For now, the 'Bangalore Torpedoes' – essentially, twelve-foot lengths of three-inch water pipes packed with high explosives – are brought forward and placed just above the ground amid the rolls of concertinaed barbed wire. At Bardia those little Bangalore beauties had blown gaps 25 foot wide in the wire and the hope was they could do the same here, once they are detonated from a distance, courtesy of a wire that had been carefully attached to their detonator.

And sure enough . . . and sure enough . . .

Heads down, boys, 'cos we're about to blow her. With great explosions through narrow passages, the wire is blown to smithereens, and the way is clear.

There is a sudden stunned moment as the assembled Australian troops of the 2/1st Battalion see the gap, and now at 6.25 am the clear voice of a lieutenant rings out.

'Go on, you bastards!'[25]

And with a mighty roar, so they do. Up there, Cazaly, and into 'em! Charging through the blown corridor, the Australian soldiers swarm.

Some of the stunned Italians have sufficiently recovered from the barrage to quickly return ferocious fire, but the first of these defenders don't last long. So numerous are the Australians, and so fast are they in charging forward and firing as they go – with the ground so flat that they could see the flashes of the guns of the defenders ahead, just as they could see the flashes of their own guns behind – that the first of the Italian posts fall almost immediately. With that breach in the Italian perimeter now assured, within minutes six 'Matilda' tanks – so-called, affectionately, because they had a protective metal 'skirt' around their tracks – are aiding the troops to knock over the Italian defences, post by post.

Private Blue Butterworth is with Captain Delves following up – with Blue the regulation two steps behind Captain Delves, ready to answer any need he might have. Beside Delves is Colonel Eather, who is using a cane for support.

It is Blue's first time in the midst of fire, and he is thinking of all the bad things he has done in his life and whether God is about to make him pay for them all.

'Oh,' he says to himself, 'this is the time you're gone.'

Suddenly there is indeed the chattering of an Italian machine gun up ahead and the cry goes up, 'Down!'

Blue indeed throws himself down, only for the tip of his bayonet to penetrate the back of Captain Delves' pants, and even getting a short way up the Khyber Pass, mercifully without breaking his skin.

'On your feet,' Delves roars, while checking his backside for damage. 'Who gave that bloody order?'[26]

Who knows, but it didn't seem like a bad one under the circumstances. Massive clouds of dust billow towards them, carrying the unmistakable stench of cordite from the exploding shells.

Some posts fall to the rampaging Australians almost immediately, with the Italian soldiers coming out with their eyeballs rolling and their hands up, frequently holding silky white handkerchiefs that seem to have been kept pristine for just such an occasion. Others resisted solidly. These were usually brought under severe artillery fire, causing huge amounts of billowing dust. Into that heavy dust cloud, the leading Australians charge, bayonets drawn and grenades at the ready. Clean 'em out, clean 'em out, clean 'em out, and go again.

It is a busy morning, and the road back from the Australian front lines to the breach in the perimeter is soon *thick* with Italian prisoners, thousands of them heading towards the comparative safety of an Australian stockade, seemingly happy to be away from these wild men from the south insanely charging at them with death and destruction pouring from their every barrel. Rome Radio had been shrieking for days that the 'Australian barbarians have been turned loose by the British in the desert',[27] and now that these soldiers had seen them close up, few of the Italians want any part of it.

The Australian rampage continues for the next two days, and it is hard to keep up with the swarm of Italian prisoners. There are so many that when a cable query comes from Cairo HQ on 23 January inquiring how many there are, the answer is sent back: '20 acres of officers and 100 acres of other ranks!'

The prisoners were fed the same biscuits and bully beef as the Australian soldiers, but as Blue Butterworth will recount, 'our blokes used to back up to the fence and just grab the cases of bully beef, toss them over the fence and the tins of biscuits over the fence. Consequently the big Italians got the bully beef and biscuits.' Noticing that a lot of the other Italian prisoners were missing out, Blue started tossing biscuits to some of 'the poor little fellas who didn't have the energy'.[28]

Those poor bastards.

•

Weary Dunlop is at last released from hospital in time to head to Alexandria, where the hospital ship *El Amira Fawzia* is bringing wounded soldiers from the action to their west. The work is 'Interesting enough . . . if one were not pining to be in Libya doing surgery.'[29]

Perhaps he might be able to visit Libya by other means?

Yes!

After a heavy drinking session with some RAF pilots, the pilot of a Bristol Blenheim bomber invites Weary to go on a bombing raid on Benghazi, west of Tobruk.

Yesh, shplendid idea!

Which is why he is here now, holding on to a roof-strap for dear life as red and green tracer bullets try to knock them from the skies, and the said pilot – roaring imprecations that on translation would make Hitler blush – hurls the plane to left and right, up and down, round and round. Below, searchlights are seeking them out, buildings are being blown apart by bombs, and Weary knows his life could end at any moment.

When finally he gets back on the ground at Gaza, it is with a resolution as strong as a wedding vow, NEVER to go on such excursions again. (Actually, maybe *stronger* than a wedding vow.)

Hopefully something else will turn up, in the way of action, that might be a little easier.

•

Now that Tobruk has been secured, the new British Prime Minister Winston Churchill changes his focus in this part of the world to the other side of the Mediterranean.

Greece. British Intelligence has no doubt. With the Italians having been beaten back to their own borders by the Greeks themselves, Hitler is about to declare war on Greece and invade with as many as ten divisions! Who can Churchill send to Greece's aid, to fulfil the terms of the British–Greek treaty?

He has an idea, heavily involving Australian and New Zealand troops, and, as the extremely loyal Australian Prime Minister, Robert Menzies, is in London at the time, attending meetings of the War Cabinet – Churchill puts it to Menzies on 20 February 1941.

The British Government wants the Australian 6th and 7th Divisions to leave North Africa, where they are doing so well, and go to Greece, as the foundation stone of 'Lustre Force' under the command of British General Maitland 'Jumbo' Wilson. They will be joined by the 2nd New Zealand Division – to form 'ANZAC Corps', and supported by the British 1st Armoured Brigade with 100 tanks – 58,000 soldiers in all. Greece has already agreed to accept Lustre Force, and a flotilla is being assembled to transport them across the Med. We believe the Germans will likely attack mid-spring, say from April onwards, and we need your men on the ground, quickly.

Very quietly, Menzies is not only underwhelmed by the plan, but by the British Prime Minister in person and much of the government. In the last war, it was Churchill himself who had come up with another plan filled with adventurism in the world – to invade the Dardanelles – and it had been a debacle.

And now Churchill wants the Anzacs to go again, on another shore, to be at the pointy end of the arrow aimed at Hitler's rampaging forces led by Panzers and bearing bigger guns than the world has ever seen? All that, and *Menzies* watches as Winnie gets no resistance to his whims.

'The Cabinet is deplorable,' he writes in his diary, '[consisting of] dumb men, most of whom disagree with Winston but none of whom dare say so. This state of affairs is most dangerous. The Chiefs of Staff are without exception Yes Men, and a politician runs the services. Winston is a dictator, he cannot be overruled, and his colleagues fear him.'[30]

The more he thinks about it, the more appalled he is.

'The problem of a couple of good men to prop up Churchill is acute. He is not interested in finance, economics or agriculture, and ignores the debates on all three. He loves war and spends hours with the maps and charts, working out fresh combinations. He has aggression without knowledge.'[31]

Menzies presses for more information, but is told very little, and drops the pursuit. Menzies' first weekend in England had been spent with the British Prime Minister at his country residence, *Chequers*, where the British bulldog had made it wonderfully clear that in his view, 'Australia is Dominion No. 1'.[32] It would almost be rude to counter him now, whatever his misgivings. Yes, as Menzies notes in his diary, 'This kind of decision, which may mean thousands of lives, is not easy.'[33]

Nevertheless, on 24 February Menzies agrees that the 6th Division can be sent from Africa, under the command of General Thomas Blamey. After all, Menzies reasons, Australia helping Great Britain in this manner against the Germans must make it more likely that Britain will offer support should the Japanese attack Australia. All up, he remains deeply troubled, not least for his own vaunting of Hitler just before the war had started. And before that he had earned the nickname of 'Pig Iron Bob' for his successful insistence as Attorney-General in the conservative government of Joseph Lyons that pig-iron be sent to Japan from Port Kembla, against the protest of the union movement that such iron would more than likely come back in the form of bullets and shells to kill Australian workers.

If he is wrong on Greece – and he has had to make the decision without approval from his Cabinet, due to distance and lack of detail – then his position as PM will likely be untenable, as his party defends a majority of just one.

General Archibald Wavell himself – the Commander-in-Chief of the British Empire forces in North Africa – is strongly against the madness of sending his finest troops from Libya where they are winning, to Greece where they will lose. But he is powerless to stop it.

The Australian troops will be sent, at least with the British promise 'that evacuation, if necessitated, will be successfully undertaken'.[34]

12 March 1941, Suez Canal, dangerous liaison

Weary, is that you?

It is, and this is Deputy Director of Medical Services to 1 Australian Corps, General Roy Burston, calling him on a very crackly line from Cairo HQ. That appointment as surgeon to 2/2nd Australian General Hospital? It's off. We want you to go to Greece instead as Deputy Director of Medical Services on the staff of Lustre Force. Your job will be to work with the liaison staff, acting as the conduit between the British HQ in Athens and the Lustre Force HQ in the forward areas. You are to do your utmost to ensure that the Australian forces get the best medical care possible, and if things go south to have the means of evacuation.

(This is what comes from sitting down 13th to a table. Last week Weary arrived late at a luncheon party at Major Scott's. At that lunch, a polite brawl had broken out between Major General Tomlinson, Colonel Boyd and Colonel Hamilton over who exactly was responsible for 'stealing' medical stores in Libya. Weary had acted as peacemaker and offered to set up an impartial investigation. When Weary is off investigating, he is transferred!)

•

It is not until Weary gets his formal orders to leave for Greece on the SS *Brattdal* that he realises that the days of mild danger are over. That same day, 26 March 1941, he writes out his will, sends a farewell telegram to Helen and packs his bags.

Tomorrow, we sail; 'we' being Weary and his batman Private George Bennett. The next morning, they find themselves aboard and unwelcome. You see, there is no cabin set aside for a Chief Medical Officer, let alone an important liaison officer. Yes, but he is both and he is here. Well, that may be but there is no cabin and round they go again, on deck, fully packed, and apparently staying there! Weary can't believe it. 'No accommodation has been provided for a medical officer. Present position Chief Officer refuses accommodation since no order . . . No one has any authority! This I think I can manage.'[35]

The next day the medical stores turn up on board. Well, this will be interesting. Is he supposed to operate al fresco, or will the future injured get their dressings applied in their own quarters? Not that they will have much luck with that as the 'stores' include only one packet of bandages! And the entire set of medical stores arrives in an old petrol tin, which is not exactly the hygienic condition a doctor prefers. If the petrol tin had actual petrol in it, it might be of some use to the ship.

As it stands, as he stands on deck, Weary finds he has 33 clothing pins as his most impressive supply, along with one bottle of castor oil, and one giant temper tantrum which results in somebody in GHQ actually sending them some proper stores that are clean.

The *Brattdal* is not terribly clean, although it does have six toilets. Yes, look and wonder, six portable on-deck seats with 'shoots' over the side. Well, what did you expect? There is a war on and this is a cargo ship; *you* are the cargo at the moment and the fact that you can complain is a novelty, but it doesn't change your status.

Their skipper is a model of calm or indifference, depending on your perspective. He is Norwegian so it is very hard to tell if anything is capable of upsetting him, as Weary discovers that Friday when the *Brattdal* is at sea and being bombed by Italian planes.

The Captain shrugs.

'We are,' he observes placidly, 'always bombed between Crete and Rhodes.'[36] Well, as long as it is expected. Weary finally gets access to a cabin and the first thing he does is write another letter to Helen. There is nothing like the prospect of death to make a man open his heart. How long is it since they have seen each other?

'It can't be three years. I still sense your presence, the touch of your shoulder and a sweet, low voice, it's only when I face reality squarely that you are gone and I am lonely, so lonely, and pain is my companion.'[37]

Three years. That is an eternity. But on this day in 1941 eternity is arriving for many men. Unbeknownst to Weary, the Battle of Matapan is underway between the Italian Navy and the Royal Navy's Mediterranean Fleet. The *Brattdal* will reach port without further trouble as the Axis forces are otherwise engaged.

CHAPTER THREE

GREEK MARATHON

Cry 'Havoc', and let slip the dogs of war;
That this foul deed shall smell above the earth
With carrion men, groaning for burial.

Shakespeare, Julius Caesar, Act 3, Scene 1

Either the British or Australian Government or both were
prepared callously and cynically to sacrifice a comparatively
small force of Australian fighting men for the sake of a political
gesture – that is to gamble with Australian lives on a wild
chance, wilder than Gallipoli.[1]

Kenneth Slessor, Australian war correspondent

30 March 1941, Athens, Grecian Ern

Arriving in Athens, it does not take long to get his bearings, but who – truly – wants to find them when you can get so wonderfully and mesmerisingly lost in this ancient capital? This is where great and enduring Gods were invented and where democracy was born. And you can still see all the bits of the Parthenon that Lord Elgin didn't get around to stealing.

Dunlop is to be lodged at the King George Hotel in the heart of the golden quarter, just down from the Acropolis, and he will work at the Acropole Hotel, where the British HQ of Lustre Force is situated. His job is to be responsible for the medical care of the Australian soldiers and to find sites for makeshift hospitals, for General Thomas Blamey is determined that the Australian soldiers of the 6th Division – who have themselves arrived in Greece 10 days earlier – will have the benefit of their own General Hospital. (They are *not* to be dependent on the good graces of the British for their hospital care, such grace tends to be distributed on national lines when push comes to shove, and Blamey still remembers the shoves from the Great War.) Once those units are established, in old schools, new ruins or anywhere flat, then Weary is to ensure that they are well supplied with as much medicine and as many staff as he deems necessary to care for the wounded and sick, whether their ailment is from Italian shells or Greek women. All woes, whether arterial or venereal, must be anticipated and catered for. Military medicine ordered and arranged from afar is a bureaucracy so Weary is to be on the ground, making sure these hospitals will be able to operate at maximum capacity instead of just overwhelmed in a trice and turned into a fixed triage.

So, Weary? Better make them *big*. We will need a couple of hospitals capable of holding at least 1200 patients each. If the growing reports are correct, we Australians are going to be caught by an overwhelmingly large German force, and the likely result will be bloody carnage.

And it is not as if Weary does not have his hands full from the beginning.

For the first medical issue he faces is something of an epidemic of VD spreading among the Diggers still based in the Greek capital.

Going to see General Christopoulos, the Greeks' foremost medical General in Athens, the Australian tells him: 'General, despite the marvellous charms of these Greek girls, we are having a certain wastage.'

The General raises his eyebrows.

'What is the cause of this wastage?'

'Gonorrhoea,'[2] says Weary simply.

Now the General rolls his eyes.

'This gonorrhoea is just a cold in the nose.'

(Yes, the Greek is a medical General, but it is possible the physiology of the body, and the position of its various parts, is not his strong suit.)

The General insists. This gonorrhoea is the price of temporary love, nothing to get excited about.

'. . . a little malady from *la petit mort* is worth it.'[3]

If gonorrhoea was considered a serious medical complaint, the Greek army itself would never leave the infirmary.

(Not that Weary himself takes any moral view on Australian soldiers visiting brothels or – just as he used to occasionally do – drinking way too much and raising hell, for that matter. 'Australians don't behave well on leave,' he will later note. 'If you compare them with British . . . units, they don't wear their uniforms well, they're untidy, they're over friendly [in] their relationships with the [local] people and they are apt to get a bit drunk, things like that. But these are sort of non-essentials really.'[4] On *the* essential – fighting – they are very strong indeed.)

Such problems become minor, by comparison, however, once the news breaks that . . .

The Germans are attacking!

Hitler's orders are followed exactly, and the German forces begin pouring into both Greece and Yugoslavia from dawn on 6 April 1941, and are now roaring towards Athens, with their Panzers to the fore and crushing Greek resistance wherever they find it.

As it happens, on this day Weary is at Foula Bay at Volos – some 200 miles north of Athens – looking for a site for a second hospital near Athens, but another sight literally stops him in his tracks. Past Lamia there are so many refugees heading to the south, cattle and carts trundling in retreat, that he must stop. For the Greeks, the Germans are a new enemy – the two countries were not at war until this invasion commenced – but now they are coming and so it's time to go. Weary's own hopes of completing his task are dashed as looking for a hospital site the Australians won't be occupying in a week is to build a castle in the air. (And that castle will just get strafed by a bunch of Fokkers, so don't bother.) More importantly, there is no getting round or down this road. Sheep, cattle, goats, men, women, kits, cats are flooding towards him – each detour just leads to a shorter stop.

So, atop a high point in the Mount Parnassus range, Weary stops. His bed for tonight will be a pile of leaves. As the sun sets, the noise begins, far off, frenzied and ferocious, German bombers hurtling overhead in the dusk, their engines throbbing. God help whoever is on the receiving end of their bombs . . .

9.30 pm, 6 April 1941, HMAS *Perth*, Piraeus Harbour, fatal sure

The Germans are coming.

Late that morning they had seen a single plane come over at high altitude that circled Piraeus in the manner of a reconnaissance plane and on the strength of it – for he did not like the look of it at all – the Captain of HMAS *Perth* had given orders for his vessel to move out to anchor in Salamis Bay, over 12 miles from the rest of the shipping. But that won't necessarily save them.

As the air-raid siren goes off, Chief Petty Officer Ray Parkin and his shipmates rush to their action stations on their 562-foot light cruiser, manning the machine guns and Ack-Ack guns that they hope will allow them to beat off the attack by this swarm of Dorniers and Junkers, protected by a gaggle of Messerschmitts, flying over the harbour for a good look.

And now the sailors see what is happening.

These are not ordinary bombs. They're not dropping down, they're . . . floating?

Yes, floating! They are mines on parachutes, dropped directly above the biggest mass of ships the planes can find.

The sailors watch, fascinated, as the first chute makes a landing, and Ray Parkin's mouth drops open as he sees a great column of pure flame silently climbing higher and higher to at least 300 feet. It is only after they see the top of that flame flick the blue, that the wave of sound hits them, the massive explosion shaking the nerve of each man in this anchorage. The damn thing had fallen 'just where we had lately come from'.[5]

If they had been there, every man-jack of them would be right now either knocking on the Pearly Gates, or noting how Hell was at least a whole lot cooler than where they had just come from.

The horror, oh, the horror!

The guns of *Perth* blaze, even as the beams of the searchlights do much the same, scanning the skies and trying to stay with the bombers to give the gunners a better chance. The bombers, in turn, send down streams of tracer fire straight at the searchlights, trying to extinguish them. Aboard *Perth*, the stench of cordite from the explosives is more acrid than ever, right up until the first of the billowing black smoke drifting towards them engulfs them.

'We could hear the scream and clatter of fighter combat somewhere up there too.'

Look out!

One of the mines is drifting straight down upon them, only to be caught by a puff of wind at the last instant, which sees it hit the nearby shore instead.

'The force of its explosion was powerful enough to be strongly felt across the sea to where we were.'

The nearby *Cyprian Prince* is not so lucky. The 10,000-ton merchantman is hit by a floating mine amidships and is instantly enveloped in a white cloud of explosion and debris. By the time the cloud has cleared – no more than three minutes later – she has gone to the bottom in two pieces.

Christ!

Boats are quickly lowered over the side with crews told to steer towards the cries of voices in the water.

Parkin is among those devastated when the boats return with no more than four survivors from the ship's company.

'There were now fire and explosion all around the harbour. Ships and barges had broken their moorings and were drifting, some on fire. One of the ships that had been hit was the *Clan Fraser*, with 5000 tons of ammunition she had been discharging into rail trucks alongside. She was now well on fire.'[6]

The Luftwaffe continue to concentrate their deadly efforts on the Allied ships in Piraeus Harbour.

Four hours after the *Clan Fraser* is hit, she blows up. The blast is so strong it knocks Parkin from his bench on the deck of *Perth*, even though he is a mile away.

'All the air around the harbour was suddenly filled with screaming red hot metal starting fires everywhere,' he will recount. 'The whole port and almost everything in it became an inferno. At intervals, the rail trucks with ammunition blew up also.'[7]

A shattering seven ships are sent to the bottom, crippling the supply line that the Australian and British forces had been relying on. Other vessels are still afloat, but are burning furiously, sending great billowing black smoke skywards over Athens. Still others – including the *Ajax* and the *Calcutta* – are miraculously able to get clear of the harbour and survive unscathed. Most importantly for Ray Parkin, *Perth* itself is undamaged and able to get away.

•

As the dawn of 7 April comes, Weary Dunlop can see that smoke rising with the sun, from the south, from Athens. Heading towards it, he and his driver move quickly, at once drawing the attention of a Messerschmitt which sends a stream of bullets their way.

Weary is thrilled.

'Bloody marvellous,' he thinks. 'At last I have reached a point in this war, where I am worth having a shot at.'[8]

By 9 April the Germans are indeed at the gates of Thessaloniki, 310 miles north of Athens. Can *anyone* stop them?

The AIF's 6th Division forms the bulk of the force in the enemy's way, bracing themselves to try to withstand the coming storm at a line around Vevi.

Weary, you must go to co-ordinate the medical efforts to save as many as you can.

In the face of overwhelming force, the Australians set up a new defensive position along the Aliakmon River. At this point, for the first time since Gallipoli, the Australian and New Zealand divisions are brought under the one command and fight together as part of a combined Anzac Corps. And yet, while holding the Germans back longer than had been thought possible, Lustre Force itself must fall back.

In Athens, at first, the freshly promoted Major Weary Dunlop is dependent on British corporals shouting down the phone lines to their counterparts on the front lines, '*This is Freddie speaking, is that you, Georgie?*' but even when that connection is made, there is little actual information received, and it is all but impossible for him to give orders.

For Weary, day and night becomes a blur of ducking, driving and having meetings with generals, medicos and nurses. All up, the situation is grim and getting grimmer, most particularly as the front line starts to completely crumble and the flood of wounded coming back to Athens becomes tidal.

Weary does what he can, making constant forays by staff car and even motorcycles to the front, but it is soon clear that the situation is hopeless. What chance were 50,000 men ever going to be against the 500,000 Germans coming at them, supported by air superiority and over a *thousand* tanks?

For its part, the leaders of the Greek Army are already negotiating terms of surrender with the invaders, seeking to lay down their weapons to them rather than to the Italians.

On Friday 18 April, Weary's Commanding Officer in the medical ranks, General Burston, sails for safety and Egypt, travelling on the hospital ship *Dorsetshire*, which is filled to the gunnels, stacked by the funnels, with grievously wounded. Before leaving, Burston instructs Weary to make sure that all the Australian nurses are evacuated for their own safety – whether they want to go or not. And he also volunteers to take a letter from Weary for Helen.

Weary quickly dashes one off: 'Just ever so much love dear heart – I wonder if it is possible to send enough to last the time which may be necessary.'[9]

Thank you, Weary, I will see it gets into the post at Alexandria. Good luck.

And with that, Major Weary Dunlop is on his own, responsible for the hands-on medical welfare of 17,000 Australian soldiers in the face of 500,000 German soldiers.

•

If only it could have been like the Battle of Thermopylae, where 300 Spartans had held off 300,000 Persians in a narrow pass, simply because the superiority of those 300 against the first 300 Persians in the pass was endlessly replicated.

But this is not like that. For one thing, unlike glorious Spartan fighters, these men aim to get out of this battle alive. For another, this time, from 21 April, the Thermopylae Pass is being held by General George Vasey's 3000 Diggers of the 19th Brigade of the 6th Division. And yes, even though that means they have ten times as many men as the Spartans, the modern Germans will be a touch more difficult, especially as machine guns and fighter pilots have been invented. But the Australians fight hard, the spirt of Sparta is with them, and these rocks and narrow paths block the attackers, just as they did thousands of years ago. The Diggers shoot, thrust and parry with care and skill, shooting well and dodging better. But as they are stormed at with shot and shell, bombed from on high by the Luftwaffe, plastered by German artillery, and facing weaponry the likes of which the Spartans could not even have *imagined*, General Blamey takes the decision. The 6th Division must withdraw, all save Vasey's 19th Brigade. It will be a Gallipoli job, a skeleton force to hold back the hordes while the others escape.

Blamey gives the bad word to Vasey, who now gathers his senior officers to bellow some morale at them. Gentlemen, here are your orders:

> Here we bloody well are and here we bloody well stay. And
> if any bloody German gets between your post and the next,
> turn your bloody Bren around and shoot him up the arse.[10]

(Look, it's what Demosthenes might have said if he was an Australian.)

Pass it on to the men, word for bloody word.

RAAAHHHHHH!

Vasey's Brigade Major, Alfred 'Ding' Bell, rings the orders through the ranks: You heard the man, the whole bloody brigade will 'hold its present defensive positions come what may'[11] – keep firing, keep shooting, defend with the confidence of a man who still intends to be here at dusk; and be a bunch of bloody heroes until such time as the rest of Lustre Force has got away and then we can scarper too.

While they fight, 47,000 men make fleet retreat from the ports of Nafplion, Monemvasia and Kalamata in the Peloponnese peninsula south of Athens, across the Corinth Bridge. There is so much movement it is hard to tell whether you are coming or going, but all are going, bit by bit, as the fire increases.

'Then the nightmare drive over the mountains through the blackness of the night with no head lights . . .' Sister Sylvia Duke of the 2/6th Australian General Hospital records the experience, 'the boys clearing the road of obstruction every little while for us to proceed . . . driving at reckless pace around bomb holes on the roads that had sheer drops down to the sea – abandoned trucks on every side – the awful sense of complete desolation everywhere . . . enemy planes overhead, when the convoy stopped we left our trucks and scattered running for cover into barley fields lying face downwards hugging Mother Earth and wishing our tin hats were somewhat bigger to cover more of us.'[12]

This trick was done 25 years ago at Anzac Cove, now thousands of coves become smuggled goods as Vasey's bloody-minded boys blast away. It is a brilliant bluff and it succeeds.

The battle will rage for four days and four nights before Vasey's men lose their Lustre. The Germans are unstoppable, and the Australian 6th Division must fall back to save themselves.

God, with this and Dunkirk, we have heroic retreats down pat.

•

Being invaded?

The Greeks are old hands. From the beginning of history, which they and Herodotus invented, they have been at it. The Persians, the Romans, the Germans, the Germans again; it is a routine and a ritual. Those who want to flee, do; those who don't, stay and wait for the next triumphant lot to come through. For Weary Dunlop it's different. He is not used to being in the sweep of history; he would prefer to get out of the way of it and right now if possible. All around him the pieces and people of Athens are vanishing; and now those in Australian uniform have been ordered to do the same. Quickly. But Major Dunlop is not just jumping in a jeep and heading thataway; he has to arrange passage and transport for the sick and wounded. Getting things done quickly in Greece is not easy at the best of times; at the worst of times, like now, it is bloody near impossible.

Bluster, bluff and bloody-mindedness are needed far more than any red tape. And as Greece goes to hell in a handcart, the Australian's primary concern is to gather as many handcarts as he can, as many drays, ambulances, trucks and train carriages as possible, and evacuate, evacuate, evacuate – ideally around the night of Anzac Day when there would be nigh on no moon.

All wounded must be removed from all forward Casualty Clearing Stations. Yes, we are clearing the clearing stations, but there is no time for irony – just get moving! Mobile hospitals must be marshalled onto ships to be sent to Cairo and El Kantara. Complicating things is that Weary has to assemble a haystack worth of needles to even begin, for the Australian wounded are scattered around hospitals in Athens; they weren't expecting to be invaded and evacuated in their diagnostics, and now Dr Dunlop is making house calls across the Acropolis, past the Parthenon, hither and yon to dig up every Digger from whatever sickbed or ward he rests in and gather them together. How? Ambulances. A 'crazy little fleet of ambulances',[13] the maddest fleet assembled since Helen scarpered to Troy, retrieving each and every wounded man they possibly can and setting him aboard a waiting ship.

Such organisation is exhausting not only for Weary but frays every last nerve of his staff; tiring the tireless, including his exhausted batman, Private Bennett. Weary takes the wheel as they hurtle back from the front line. The car is difficult to control, due to the fact that a bomb that exploded too close has given it a drifting axle, but Weary is doing his best, when . . . when . . . when, *allaaaaay-OOOP* . . . they go straight over a narrow pass and are momentarily in flight!

By an extraordinary stroke of good fortune the car does a complete forward somersault and their fall is broken by landing on a tree.

Certainly, good fortune might involve not landing in a tree in a car in the first place, but such is the way of war. Further good fortune blesses Weary now as his fall is further broken by the remarkably soft thing beneath him, which proves to be the unfortunate Bennett with a broken arm. Yes, it hurts, but they're *alive* and can keep going, once we get a lift. The tree can keep the car. Onwards! (Backwards!)

With things going so badly at the front, there is no shortage of lifts to get them back to Athens.

•

In London, watching on with abject horror, is Prime Minister Robert Menzies. Yes, the most severe of the risks of the Greek campaign had been substantially kept from him going into the venture, but the results are becoming all too clear, as much as Churchill tries to hide them.

Menzies goes through the reports with a leaden heart – 'It is a terrible anxiety',[14] he notes in his diary as the first reports come through of the evacuation to Crete and the high casualty numbers – but also with a rising fury.

As the London *Daily Mail* will put it quite openly. 'As a military adventure it was madness. As a political gesture it was stupid because it was doomed to fail.'[15]

Churchill clearly realised it was doomed as he had not shared that information with his Australian counterparts. And even now he is lying through his teeth!

'War Cabinet,' Menzies notes in his diary on 28 April. 'Winston says, "We will lose only 5000 in Greece." We will in fact lose at least 15,000. W. is a great man, but he is more addicted to wishful thinking every day.'[16]

•

When retreating, any decent officer needs his batman to get away from trouble in a dignified and orderly manner. Or, the batman could be Private Blue Butterworth. Things have been busy since he took this position for a Sergeant and Sergeant Major in the first weeks of the war, and he has been everywhere with the 2/1st Infantry Battalion since, from Cairo to Bardia to Tobruk, but things have never been quite as grim as now.

Major Miller, who is on his way to the port to catch a ship to Palestine, throws him the keys to a 1941 Chevy and says, 'You can drive, Butterworth.'

Now, Blue does not like to say he's never actually driven a car before – but he figures he'll work it out as he goes along. He does, only to be told, 'Butterworth, you've got to go and report to Major Dunlop [at the Acropole Hotel].'[17]

Only a short time later, Butterworth – with his knees still knocking from negotiating the Athens traffic – is knocking on the door on the third floor of the Acropole. Upon the door opening, the Private is greeted by a British Brigadier in full regalia and clearly about to set sail.

After snapping off his best possible salute – which means making it look less like a casual wave and more like swatting a military fly near his temple – and presenting his apologies, sir, Butterworth says, 'I'm here to pick up a Major Dunlop?'

'Oh, Dunlop, old boy,' the Brig calls in his plummy accent, 'your driver's arrived.'

From somewhere in the bowels of the room behind, Butterworth now hears a remarkably quiet but distinctly Australian voice – a rare combination.

'Ask him where is he parked,' the voice says with smooth authority, despite speaking to a far superior officer.

'Right opposite, near the park,' Butterworth informs both officers.

'Good. I'll be down there shortly.'

Fifteen minutes later, Butterworth looks up to see one of the largest men he has ever seen approaching, with a greatcoat that goes nearly all the way down to his boots! It must be Dunlop.

'Shit,' he thinks, 'he'll never get in here.'

And yet?

And yet no sooner does Major Dunlop introduce himself than he settles his massive frame into the passenger seat – straining the springs on the right side so hard they threaten to desert to the left – and they are on their way to the King George Hotel to pick up his luggage. Alas, in the growing madness of Greek traffic as word spreads that the Germans are on the doorstep, a car in front of them on Omonoia Square stops suddenly and – brace! – they run up the back of him and their bumpers are locked. Without a word, Major Dunlop gets out and physically *lifts* Butterworth's car off!

They are on their way once more. Major Dunlop barely blinks.

'Who the hell is this fellow?' Butterworth wonders. 'I think he must be Intelligence.'

And sorry, you were saying, Major Dunlop?

'Now,' Weary says as they are on their way once more and approaching the King George, 'I don't want these people to know that I'm actually leaving.'

Disappearing inside, and pausing only to leave a tip, Major Dunlop is back shortly afterwards with various bits and pieces and they are on their way to the northern front, where the German Army is advancing at a rapid rate.

Late that night, still pushing, Butterworth is indeed feeling sleepy when the giant beside him says, 'You must be tired, Butterworth. I'll take over.'[18]

It is said so quietly, so kindly, that the young man is taken aback. Is this how spies talk in Intelligence? *Something* is different. It is no small thing to drive under these conditions as, despite the darkness, and the late hour, the road is filling with evacuees from the north, most of which are huge British Army trucks, driven by Tommies with haunted eyes, slit in their determination to keep going, to get away from the Germans. But the Major's words are neither a request nor an order – simply a statement of what is happening.

And look, the truth is that, if driving was cricket, Weary Dunlop would not make 12th man in any even half-decent team – his confidence outstripping his ability many times over – but there is nothing for it.

Butterworth does his best to help, trying to guide according to what he can see – 'A bit to the left. A bit to the right. Over to the left. Over to the right . . .'

LOOK OUT!

Over the edge.

They have run into a ditch and no amount of roaring the engine in reverse will get them out.

'Have you got the trenching tool?' Weary asks calmly.

'Yeah . . . *Yes*, sir, there is one in the boot.'

'Give it to me.'

What? The officer, now taking off *his* greatcoat, is going to do the hard yakka of getting them out?

Yes.

Butterworth watches as Major Dunlop sends huge clods of earth skywards, each one landing before the next one is launched. Warming up now, Dunlop also removes his shirt and singlet and is soon shovelling with bare torso.

'He looks like Hercules!' Blue thinks.

The big man hands Blue a small torch.

'Now hold it like *that*. Keep the light down.'[19]

Blue takes a closer look at the torch, a pencil light with a purple globe.

Ah.

'This bloke must be a doctor,'[20] he twigs, as this is exactly the kind of torch used by doctors when gazing down the throats of patients.

In short order they are on their way once more, and in the wee hours have arrived at the 1st Australian Corps HQ. The plan, they learn, is to evacuate the troops on the night of 26 April under the new moon when it is darkest.

Everyone is awake and scrambling, ready to be out by dawn when the Germans are expected to arrive.

Major Dunlop makes the necessary arrangements – the well can make their own way, the sick will follow him – and after filling the boot and the back seat with four-gallon cans filled with petrol, they are soon on their way back to Athens.

Passing the previous spot where they had come off the road and the not-so-weary Weary had dug them out, Blue Butterworth can't help but notice: 'You'd have thought a bulldozer had been in there where he'd been.'[21]

They stop to pick up two Kiwi soldiers trying to get back to Athens and, only a short time afterwards, there is a roar overhead and they see a German Stuka that has just spotted them.

'Stop, Butterworth,' Major Dunlop says as calmly as ever, before running up a railway embankment to get a better look, even as Butterworth and the New Zealanders jump out of the Chevy to take shelter in a ditch.

'Who *is* this fellow?' the Kiwis ask. 'He's bloody mad.'

'I've only just met him,' Blue replies, but he, too, is hellishly impressed. This bloke wields a shovel like Hercules, commands like Churchill, and has no fear of Stukas!

'This bugger, he's different,'[22] Blue thinks.

This view is further confirmed a short time later when the Major decides he wants a shave and gets out his mirror, razor and soap when they find a pool of water to get lathered up. Even though there are still bloody Stukas around! Blue tries to get Weary to do it in a safer spot, but the massive Australian's only concern is for his driver.

'Get yourself undercover,' he says quietly, while whipping away the first of his whiskers.

•

Some evacuations are harder than others, and some are impossible, Dunlop, if you want to go by rail, now. *Why?*

'This is the last train with a Greek crew in Greece,' says the AQ, the branch of the Adjutant General and Quartermaster General. It's out of the question, especially as Weary serves under Brigadier David Large, who the AQ hates.

'Well,' says Weary, 'I shall have to report to General Blamey that the last train has not been given to transport Australian soldiers. General Blamey will inform the Australian Government.'[23]

And then the AQ can tell them that the train was unavailable due to spite . . .

Very well, you may have your train.

In short order, Weary and Blue, and two wounded Diggers they have picked up, are approaching the railway station at Thebes where their train awaits. Only moments after they have pulled up, however, and just as Weary is indeed about to climb aboard what feels like the last Greek train leaving this area, he suddenly hears, even above the *choof-choof* of the engine, that previously distant drone getting louder, followed by cries of alarm from the crew of the Greek train.

Seeing the familiar formation of three waves of nine – with each wave itself made up of three small arrows of three planes each, one plane leading a wingman on either side – they know all too well it is the Luftwaffe. Now, normally the fact that their train has a huge Red Cross symbol draped across the engine should mark it as an ambulance train that is protected from attack by international agreements and base-level decency. But either the Germans are too far away to see it or simply don't care because only 10 seconds after hearing the drone Weary and his charges first hear tiny pops . . . which soon enough become metallic pings, followed by a fast ROAR of the planes overhead.

They are under *attack*!

There is only just time to get themselves and those patients who can move out and under whatever cover presents itself. Weary watches now as the planes dip and turn, to come back for second helpings, as they 'start hammering away again'.[24]

Suddenly, and from out of nowhere, Blue Butterworth jumps up from their bare bit of ground, yells out, and runs for a low crop of rock to get better cover. To Weary it seems like a miracle that Blue makes it, but he also has no choice but to follow – as Blue's yell says he has surely been hit and is likely in need of medical assistance. After completing the same mad dash with bullets spitting up the dirt all around, he comes in for a landing beside Blue to inquire where he'd copped it.

Oh.

Oh, indeed.

'A tracer bullet had scorched his posterior,' Weary will recount, 'burning a hole in his pullover!'[25]

Well, that's lovely. But now Weary sees something more worrying: the Greek train crew is also making a run for it! And it is not for mere cover. They are heading for the horizon at such a pace they are rapidly becoming part of it. Pausing only to grab a rifle, Weary now makes like the 'Man from Snowy River' heading out after 'the colt from Old Regret' that got away, the one that had 'joined the wild bush horses'. Racing across a landscape strewn with the rubble of the Luftwaffe's previous efforts, he realises the urgency of his task.

He *must turn* them!

For if there is nobody to drive the damn train, they will all be stuck here at the damn Germans' mercy. The ex-Wallaby races over the field of battle yelling curses and telling them to COME BACK, YOU BASTARDS! The Greeks elect to keep running. After the Luftwaffe strafes the ground around the train once more – while stopping momentarily so they don't fire on the train itself – they again dip round to the point that the Greeks and Weary find they are running *towards* the Germans!

Ah. Suddenly realising that deserting is a bad idea, the Greeks turn and all run back to the train, joined by a spray of bemused bullets from Luftwaffe pilots who can't figure out what in *Gott*'s name they are watching, or what the Greek *Dummköpfe* are doing.

As the planes' guns produced sputtering spurts of dirt all around, Weary throws himself behind some cover, even as the attack finally recedes. Alas, he now looks up to see the Greek train driver standing over him and posing heroically!

Glancing with pity at the prone Weary at his feet, even while beaming with pride for his own national characteristics, the Greek proclaims with a level of vaingloriousness that surely reaches the heights of the Parthenon itself, 'We Greeks have no fear!'[26]

Weary doesn't know whether to laugh or cry so he goes with the former. The Greeks do have panache, he will give them that. Come on now, stop posing, start running and let's get back on our Red Cross train and get going! Whether it is Greek posing or the Red Cross markings seen at last, they are able to escape and the crew live to pose another day.

Now that the evacuation of the first lot of wounded Australians is complete, Weary and Blue devote themselves to checking the boundary fences to see what others might be gathered up.

Making their way now to a place in the Athens northern suburbs called Kifissia, where the 2/5th Australian General Hospital is to be found, Blue takes a short kip while . . .

While Weary is urgently called to the phone.

It proves to be his senior officer, Lieutenant Colonel Odbert, who does not mince words.

'Dunlop, get the hell out of there, you've only got five minutes to get to Daphni!'[27]

The German land forces really are close, very close. And it is important that another Australian medical facility at Daphni – 15 miles away, on choked roads – be confirmed as satisfactorily evacuated, with no major equipment or papers left behind for the invaders.

'Good lord,' Weary replies, 'that's miles on the other side of Athens. I can't do that, Odbert.'[28]

The line goes dead.

Weary remains stunned.

The Germans can't be moving *that* fast.

Alas, nobody has told them that.

•

Blue's back under Edwina's bed at Killara, and Mrs Darganheart has caught him, and is shaking him . . . shaking him . . . shaking him . . .

Ah, no. He is being roughly woken by an officious orderly telling him, 'Private Butterworth. Report back to your car.'

This time, as Blue approaches the Chevy, he can see it is weighed down on the right side as Major Dunlop is in the passenger's seat, with the engine running, ready for a quick getaway. 'Now don't panic, but I've just been told that the Germans are on the way. No panic.'[29]

Blue doesn't panic, per se, but does take the shortcut across the hospital lawns, instead of bothering with the circuitous drive. And if he and Weary aren't panicking, they are pretty much the only ones who aren't.

Everywhere they look as they make their way through Athens to get to the Acropole Hotel on their way to Daphni – for Weary has left sensitive papers in there, including details of 'niche evacuation sites' which must be destroyed – cars and trucks are racing; a marathon of panic is taking place before their eyes.

Seeing that the falling sun is shining right into his driver's eyes, Weary removes his own officer's cap and, without a word, puts it on Blue's head, pulling the peak down so he doesn't have to squint.

Blue can now see even more clearly the panic around him as soldiers of different half-dressed uniforms are scarpering, ordinary Greeks are weeping, worried shopkeepers are scurrying with their goods, plumes of smoke are billowing not from shellfire but simple lit-match fires, piles of paper on footpaths are being burnt to keep them out of the hands of the invading army, cars on footpaths are being piled high with belongings, and people are driving off, tottering at speed like mobile geometry experiments. All eyes keep gazing to the north, where clouds of billowing black smoke caused by the swarms of German planes are coming closer. Seemingly all of Athens is leaving.

There proves to be just two exceptions . . . LOOK OUT!

The first exception is the stationary donkey cart that Blue tries to avoid, only to skid sideways into it. (And in moments like this, it can be good not to speak Greek. What the aggrieved cart driver is yelling at them is not clear, but it does not sound good.)

And the second exception, once they finally screech to a halt outside the Acropole Hotel, is this flower of Scotland, complete with kilt, standing at rigid attention before the front entrance, as all around him, the last of the officers and other soldiers of the British HQ are streaming away.

Weary takes pity and stops long enough to yell at him: 'What the hell are you doing here?'

'I don't know, sir,' says the Scot. 'Orders seem to be that I stay here and hand over to the Hun.'

And he simply *must* follow orders.

'You damn fool! I *order* you to get into the car!' says Weary.

'No, sir, I must stay here!'

Bloody hell. A short argument takes place, the only type possible with a stoic Scotsman when you've only got TEN MINUTES before the silence and stoicism of eternity begins. He won't move. But the Germans . . .

But nothing. Orders are orders.

'You poor sod,' Weary says with a sigh. If not shot dead, which is the most likely thing, this dutiful Private is going to follow orders right into a prison camp for the rest of this war. 'Is there anything I can do for you?'

'Will you take a letter to my missus?'[30]

Yes, Weary will, and he and Blue get to the Daphni medical facility – north-east of central Athens – before the Germans do. Outside in the garden, supervised by an officer, two Privates are burning whole *piles* of large drachma notes, originally intended for the payroll of the 6th Division – to deny them to the oncoming Germans. (Crowds of devastated locals have gathered round and are pleading: 'Why? *Why* they burn? Why not give Daphni, make people rich?'[31] Because, dear friends, the Germans would only take it off you when they arrive, and they are the ones we are worried about.)

Mercifully, beyond that, the place is all but deserted, meaning the evacuations of the wounded have been successful, and there proves to be just a few Australians remaining: two staff officers of Weary's acquaintance, John Rogers and Ken Rules, in the Officers' Mess sharing a whisky, perhaps several.

Would Weary like one?

Yes . . . alright.

(*They do know there is a war on, yes? And that the Germans are just miles away, if that?*)

Halfway through his whisky, however, Weary does feel obliged to ask.

'How are things going?'

'Oh, not bad,' Captain Rogers replies mildly. 'We've all got to be through Corinth tonight but things are going alright.'[32]

Hopefully. But really, might it be time to hurry? Weary already knows that the Corinth Bridge – the key span between the Greek mainland and the Peloponnese peninsula – is going to be blown tonight to slow down the Germans pursuing the forces of the British Empire to the three ports on the other side, but he also knows that the Germans have been bombing the road there and parts of that road are likely to be impassable.

Bottoms up, gentlemen, and good luck!

Weary and Blue must cross the Corinth Bridge and get to the port called Nafplion! Of course, that will take all night. And given that Weary has not had a wink of sleep for the past two nights, this is going to be a damn interesting drive.

•

The problem comes, of course, from the fact that they are not the only ones fleeing the Greek capital and trying to get to the ports, and they soon come to an impossible traffic snarl of army trucks. Britain's promise, 'that evacuation, if necessitated, will be successfully undertaken',[33] is now being shown for the absolute sham that it is.

Making matters supremely difficult, though, is not just too much traffic on too small a road, it is that the Germans have given the road a lot of bombing attention, leaving massive holes, and the retreating Greek cavalry have also shot a lot of their horses. This means all the truck drivers are engaged in driving a slalom of holes and horses – with only mixed success.

Fortunately, one of the officers trying to sort things recognises the giant figure in the passenger seat of Blue's Chevy.

'Is that you, Dunlop?' he asks.

'Yeah.'

'Right, the Brigadier's up front, waiting for you.'

Very well then.

'Right,' Weary says to Blue, 'just go round the convoy.'

Alas, in the darkness it is difficult, if not impossible, to see the perils in front and in short order they have first hit a shell-crater, before veering off the road and . . . are now teetering on a forty-five-degree angle over a seaside cliff! Both men are shaken up, but still alive!

'Oh shit,' says Weary quietly. 'You alright, Butterworth?'

'I'm okay, sir.'

'Try and get out.'

Butterworth puts the car in reverse and roars the engine, only for the wheels to skid and the car to teeter even more appallingly every time he eases off. Weary carefully gets out to help pull it back, even as – with his eyes adjusting to the dark – Blue peers over the edge and sees two other cars shattered on the rocks below.

'No, sir,' Blue calls to the Major, who now has his shoulder to the car, trying to *push* it back. 'If this slips, you'll go. No.'[34]

Even more carefully now, Blue himself climbs out and uses just one foot in the car to push the accelerator while keeping the other foot on solid ground. But it still won't move.

And now out of the darkness comes another English voice, that of a notably officious officer.

'You'll have to abandon your vehicle and get in the vehicle at the back of the convoy.'

Oh, really?

'I don't know who you are or what you are,' Weary Dunlop replies pleasantly. 'Will you please fuck off.'[35]

Which he does.

(Butterworth is *seriously* impressed, thinking, 'He's my boy. He's good.'[36])

Momentarily, all is quiet bar the crashing of the waves on the rocks and cars below. But hang on, what's that?

What?

That.

Yes, off in the distance, in a nearby village by the coast, they can hear singing. With the Greek capitulation, many local soldiers have returned whence they came, scarcely believing they are still alive after the horror they've known – but once Blue alerts them to the Chevy's predicament, they prove more than happy to help pull the car back out of the shell-hole. Blue empties the glovebox of Woodbine and Player's cigarettes – gifts to Greeks, happy ones at that – and in a very short time Dunlop and Butterworth and the Chevy are on their way once more, this time with *Weary* driving.

Some 30 minutes later, crossing a bridge, Weary says to his passenger, 'Do you know where you are now?'

'Wouldn't have a clue,' comes the response.

'We have just crossed the Corinth Canal.'[37]

Unseen in the darkness behind them, the Germans have captured the bridge and, being orderly and methodical fellows, now begin to remove all the charges on the bridge preparatory to taking them away. How? Well, watch them now, painstakingly gathering up *all* the charges to put them in a BIG pile in the middle of the bridge.

A thought occurs.

Yes, for the Australians, it might be a shot in the dark to try to detonate that pile with rifle fire, but why not? A Digger takes careful aim in the moonlight and gently squeezes the trigger, the way his father had taught him to, knocking over kangaroos at 150 yards on a dark night and . . .

The explosion lights up the night sky, the reflection from the stunned clouds just above revealing the Corinth Bridge falling into the canal and taking a lot of German soldiers, trucks, and one too-intrepid German journalist with it.

By this time, 'Weary' is eponymity incarnate writ large. 'So tired,' as he will write to his family, 'that I found myself nodding over the wheel almost oblivious to the consequences.'

In short order Weary and Blue have arrived just outside the port of Nafplion and manage to secrete their vehicle beneath the cover of an olive grove, while they work out what to do next.

'With the dawn,' Weary will write home, 'there was much ditch hopping while merry German aviators strafed the roads, but eventually I found a party on the beach with whom to take pot luck. An amazingly beautiful day was spent for the most part lying up in a little flowering orange grove, surrounded by cypress trees and mountain slopes ablaze with flowers of all sorts, notably giant poppies, yellow marguerites, little white daisies, and so many other unknown ones.'[38]

•

After two days hiding out in the orange grove, it is nearly time to leave, with one notable problem. That is, a German air raid is taking place, bombing every floating thing they see in the harbour, one of which is the very ship Weary and Blue are meant to leave on.

And where is Weary right now?

That is what Blue Butterworth wants to know. Wherever it is, he is without his tin helmet, which Blue has just noticed in the back of the concealed car. Retrieving it, he goes looking for his boss and, sure enough, there he is, sitting calmly on the sea-wall, earnestly taking notes – as if the Stukas roaring overhead are of no more interest than noisy birds. Less than 500 yards away, a troopship is on fire, simply *blazing* away, not that the Major seems remotely concerned.

'Here you are, sir,' Blue says, proffering him the helmet, 'you'll need this.'

'Go to buggery,' Weary replies mildly. 'And get out of here before you get hurt.'

Blue doesn't have to be told twice.

Strange bugger, is Major Dunlop – supremely uncaring about his own welfare, but very concerned about everyone else's.

•

And *stroke*, and *stroke*, and *stroke*. The time has come.

Soft oars on the water in the moonlit night, Weary Dunlop and Butterworth are making their way to a British anti-aircraft cruiser *Calcutta*, their faces illuminated by burning ships in the bay, courtesy of the Luftwaffe's bombing work only hours before. They pass so close to one burning hulk that the heat radiated from its reflected agony could just about peel skin.

Nevertheless, before long the *Calcutta* appears dead ahead, and in short order, they are in the shadow of its bulk, with its officers appearing over the side and pointing to the scramble nets that descend to the water.

'Officers, NCOs to the right,' they call. 'Other ranks to the left.'[39]

You Australians are on a British ship now, and must strictly observe the formalities of class division, even if it doesn't come naturally to you. Weary Dunlop does not like it on principle, but this is not the time to argue the toss. For Blue Butterworth, returning to the system he had been born to does not come easily, but at least he is soon installed below in the mess with a heavy curtain drawn across the portholes to prevent any light escaping, and blessed with a steaming-hot cup of cocoa to warm his bones, before being offered a big plate of bangers and mash. There are *some* British traditions he still likes.

Nearby, the crews of other ships are working equally furiously to get every soldier they can on board. Among them is *Perth*, which has raced there from a raiding fleet that had been bombarding the Germans at Tripoli.

'We arrived off the beaches at 11 pm,' a *Perth* sailor will recount, 'and began embarking troops including walking wounded, departing at 3 am to be well clear by daylight. We had embarked more than eleven hundred . . . packed through the ship like sardines.'[40]

Other ships are doing the same, with no fewer than 10,000 troops being loaded within just a couple of hours.

For Weary and Blue's part, within minutes of their boarding the *Calcutta* it has weighed anchor and they are fully on their retreat to Crete with the rest of this twelve-ships-strong convoy, bearing more than 50,000 soldiers – and indeed the Greek Government, which had abandoned Athens for the island in the Mediterranean, some 200 miles south of the capital.

'I drank a pot of beer and went to sleep in a chair, still clutching the pot,' Weary will note to his family, 'not to move until our anti-aircraft guns thundered into action at 7 am.'[41]

For yes, of course the Luftwaffe now finds the ships once more, and a furious battle begins as those on the ships fire for all they are worth at the Stukas and Fokkers.

Shortly after the battle begins, Blue, just back from the bridge of the *Calcutta*, watches gobsmacked. For there is Major Weary Dunlop, bare torso, glistening with sweat, helping to shovel Ack-Ack shells for the Royal Marines.

Who *is* this bloke?

For some reason, the sailors of the *Calcutta* remain confident, continually shouting, 'They'll never get this bloody tub! They'll never get this bloody tub!'[42] and on this occasion, at least, they are proved correct. For, finally, after having sunk two ships in the convoy, the Germans depart, and by nightfall the *Calcutta* has miraculously made it into Suda Bay on the north-west coast of Crete, where they are greeted by the sight of what remains of the famed British cruiser HMS *York*, with just the top part of its superstructure still above water and still burning.

The British sailors on the *Calcutta*, so joyous earlier in the day in their conviction that the Luftwaffe would never get their tub, are struck dumb at the sight of the destroyed cruiser, and immediately wonder out loud just how many aboard might have been saved before she went down. Is this to be their own fate, sooner or later?

An extraordinary few days ensue for both Weary and Blue as, offloaded with all the others, they essentially must live off the land, trying to meet up with whatever organised forces there are, while getting ready to meet the Germans, who will soon be storming ashore on the northern part of the Cretan coast. And yes, there are a good number of Australians there, most of them completely leaderless – and not at all unhappy about it. After a disastrous campaign in Greece, getting their bloody heads shot off, they are now *free*, and *alive*, in a place with easily available food and water, not to mention women.

And this big bastard, this Major Dunlop, wants them to do what? Answer to him, so we can get organised as a fighting force?

Not bloody likel—

Stand to attention when I am talking to you, Private!

And so, they do.

'Weary had reason to pull 'em into gear a bit,' Blue Butterworth will recount, 'which wasn't bad for a medico.'[43]

They are not a bunch of refugees, they are Australian *soldiers*, with a responsibility to be organised and ready to take on whatever the Germans throw at them – which will be considerable. Now Weary has formed them into something of a unit, and has even managed to secure some weaponry and ammunition from other units getting similarly organised.

'Within a day or two,' Weary will recount, 'we were fast developing into my guerrilla band.'[44]

(Still, he makes time to check on the evacuated Australian nurses, many of whom are now working in a British tent hospital that has been set up, dealing with the daily and bloody flood of new victims as the Luftwaffe continues to drop its explosive eggs. These women prove to be brave Athenas, eschewing any idea that they should look after their own safety first and retreat to the Cretan hinterland.)

Weary himself is as crook as Rookwood from exhaustion, from the aftermath of a bout of hepatitis, from sleeping in cars and ditches – his body is covered in boils and carbuncles, with a temperature soaring to 104 degrees Fahrenheit – and he still has a throbbing ear both from an infection and being next to the endless blasting of the big guns on the *Calcutta*. But he, too, feels the joy of being alive against all odds and even having the novelty of organising a band of combatants.

There is, however, a problem, and that problem is standing in front of him now, having journeyed into the woods to find him. His name is Lieutenant Colonel Jack Barrett, and he had been Weary's superior officer back in Athens, overseeing the Australian Liaison. And he has a question for him.

What the HELL do you think you are doing, appointing yourself a guerrilla leader! Out you go, chum.

You are a medico, Major Dunlop, and that is where we need your skills. There is a ship leaving for the Suez this evening, and you will be on it . . . *tonight*, with me.

The following evening, sure enough, by a wharf at Suda Bay he can see the British destroyer *Hotspur* has pulled in, and makes his way along the wharf, Blue Butterworth inevitably by his side.

And where do you think *he* is going?

Colonel Barrett, loaded down with red braid for the occasion, speaks firmly.

'Dunlop, he can't go with you.'

Weary pauses, but puts it firmly in turn.

'I *want* him to go with me.'

'Dunlop, he can't go with you and that's an *order*.'[45]

There is a pause, and finally a nod of acceptance.

Blue Butterworth looks at Major Dunlop with some emotion. It is extraordinary. They have only been together for little more than a fortnight, and yet somehow have become much more than officer and driver. They might even have become that most precious of all Australian things . . . *mates*. In the English way of things this would be unthinkable, but the Australians are different. And Blue is already convinced that the best way for him to get through this war is going to be to stick to Weary like glue. But right now they have no choice. They must part.

Quietly, Dunlop slips the young man a thousand drachma note – before summoning one of the Australian officers he has come to know on Crete, Lieutenant Bob McLeod.

'I want you,' he says, 'to look after Butterworth until such times as when we get back to the mainland. I'll catch up with him again.'[46]

And with that, pausing only for a quick handshake, he is gone.

Butterworth feels 'bloody awful',[47] and no mistake, but somehow feels sure that they will find each other again.

And so does Weary Dunlop – what he most loves about this young bloke is his eternal buoyancy, whatever the situation – though the first thing he must do is get through this shocking night on this cripplingly overloaded destroyer. (The problem is too few ships for far too many men. No fewer than 3000 Australians have been left behind in Crete, to soon be prisoners of the Germans. The British 'evacuation plans' have been a cross between an upturned bowl of moussaka and a shit sandwich.) The only place to sleep is on the back deck, above the vibrating engine room. At least, by late the following afternoon – after having their entry into Alexandria blocked by German mines – they are able to continue and dock at Port Said, where Weary is profoundly shocked.

After getting through hell on earth, and escaping it by sea, he has returned to a world, as he will describe it, that is, 'the most polite place you've ever seen with everybody dressed for dinner. [It was all] black ties and several old Army and Navy people and Canal officials and "You must have a rubber of bridge, old boy", and so on.'

Precisely *no-one* asks him about his experiences in the far-off worlds of Greece and Crete, let alone how it is he has a fever, a middle ear infection and carbuncles, and is almost falling over through sickness and exhaustion.

With his last bit of remaining strength he is able to get himself to the 2/2nd Australian General Hospital at nearby El Kantara that he had helped set up.

•

In London, Winston Churchill is doing his best to rise above the whole debacle, blaming others, spinning grand speeches as to how what went wrong was not his fault at all, but on one thing he is particularly insistent:

> I see the German is trying to make bad blood between us and Australia by making out that we have used them to do what we would not have asked of the British Army. I shall leave it to Australia to deal with that taunt.[48]

Only a short time later, Australia begins doing exactly that . . .

•

Order! Order!
The Honourable Member will continue.
Thank you, Mr Speaker. In the Australian Federal Parliament in Canberra, the Labor Member for Batman, Frank Brennan, is more than happy to continue, as he is disgusted, Mr Speaker, *disgusted*,

with the way Prime Minister Menzies has completely botched the entire Greek campaign – by sending Australian forces into harm's way, by making the decision without even the imprimatur of his own government on it, let alone the Australian Parliament, and the whole thing was a decision made by the government of *another country* – you heard him, Mr Speaker. And we all know the devastating result! It meant that 17,000 sons of the Southern Cross had been sent into harm's way and we've suffered nearly 600 dead, just over a thousand wounded and more than 5000 now taken as prisoners of war – all for the sake of being part of an historic defeat at the hands of the Germans!

(Very quietly, General Thomas Blamey, the Australian commander in Greece, agrees with him, having already told the war correspondent Kenneth Slessor, off the record: 'The politicians, with encouraging words, continue fine arguments, but I am thinking of the men I sent on the mountains of Greece. What is a gesture to the politicians is death to us.'[49])

How could this happen, Mr Speaker?

'The fact that we took up arms in Greece arose from the pledge given by Great Britain to Greece to come to her assistance if she should decide, by force of arms, to resist the German aggression.'

And the problem was . . . the Prime Minister himself!

'Mr. Menzies never demonstrated a real Australian outlook. Australia was the *only* Empire country which had sent troops into the war without first consulting her Parliament. Mr. Menzies had left Australia's decision to the Imperial Government generally. [Australia] played the butler with complete subservience to the United Kingdom Government so far as she could make out.'[50]

Order! ORDER!

CHAPTER FOUR

TOBRUK

This great tract . . . stretched with apparent indefiniteness over the face of the continent. Level plains of smooth sand – a little rosier than buff, a little paler than salmon, are interrupted only by occasional peaks of rock: black, stark and shapeless. Rainless storms dance tirelessly over the hot crisp surface of the ground. The fine sand, driven by the wind, gathers into deep drifts among the dark rocks of the hills, exactly as snow hangs about an alpine summit; only it is fiery snow such as might fall in hell. The earth burns with the quenchless thirst of ages and in the steel-blue sky scarcely a cloud obstructs the unrelenting triumph of the sun . . .[1]

Winston Churchill, *The River War*

Mid-May 1941, Gezira, in the rear with the gear

After defeat in Greece, Weary starts thinking about where he might be part of a force that might at least hold its own.

Tobruk?

Yes, Tobruk, where – since ousting the Italians in January – the Australians have been under siege by both the enraged forces of Mussolini and Hitler's Afrika Korps, but holding on against all odds. When Weary discovers there is a vacant spot for the position of senior surgeon with the 2/2nd Casualty Clearing Station of the 7th Division – due to the fact their last senior surgeon has had to be evacuated – he puts in a request with General Roy Burston to be transferred.

'Surely you don't want to go there?'[2] says Burston.

After all, that's where the bloody fighting is? Yes, that is the point. Jack of administration, Weary wants to 'get back on the tools again',[3] be a *surgeon* once more and put his great skills to actual use saving grievously wounded soldiers. If Tobruk is where they are most to be found right now, then that is where he wants to be. Burston is dismayed, as he has high hopes for Weary reforming and reorganising the medical field units, and in fact has offered him the rank of Lieutenant Colonel if he will stay out of fire and organise care for those who have been fired at, yes?

No.

Roy promises he will get Weary appointed to the 2/2nd Australian General Hospital as a surgeon.

And yet, for the moment, the physician still has to heal himself. Weary is an official invalid, ordered to rest and recover on the Anglo-American steamer, the *Victoria*, moored by the Gezira Club, situated on the island in the Nile in central Cairo. It is doubly annoying, as he has already ordered other men to recover on the bloody *Victoria* and now the men get to see Weary having a taste of his own medicine.

One man briefly aboard is Emmett McGillicuddy, who had boxed against Weary in Melbourne days. Emmett is up for a court martial, violent behaviour and insubordination apparently, but Weary had prescribed medical rest instead of a trial. Unfortunately, once aboard the *Victoria*, McGillicuddy gets into an argument with the ship's captain and throws him overboard! So, Dr Dunlop, more rest recommended? No, unfortunately court martial it is, and please try to hold it where the judges are nowhere near a large body of water.

The Hotel Cecil has seen Winston Churchill and Somerset Maugham walk through its doors; today it sees Weary Dunlop totter into its bar, gazing at . . . it looks like the sea? The Mediterranean! That's the one, and perhaps more than one too many are had on this Saturday 31st May, but it's alright, they are all doctors. The booze flows down their gullets as they sway out of the Cecil and towards any restaurant that won't kick them out. When Weary sobers up he finds himself back in the Greek hospital in Alexandria, with the most unglamorous injury possible: boils. And carbuncles on his bum.

Colonel William Hailes, Senior Medical Officer, takes a grave view of Weary's bottom. He has clearly been talking to General Burston because he has what he feels might be very useful, sobering news.

'Weary, they get boils in Tobruk.'

Yes, well, he already has boils.

'Look, sir,' replies Weary, 'you wouldn't dream of putting me on the sick list? You wouldn't tell the old man I'm too sick to go to Tobruk?'

Hailes sighs as though the weight of the world rests on these boils. 'I don't know, I don't know . . .'

Weary does know: a rat is at work and sure enough his place on the boat out to Tobruk today is gone.

But there is more than one way to get there. After another week or so in the hospital, Weary spies an auld acquaintance not forgot, the Brigadier 'Roley' Pulver. Pulver, he knows, has been newly promoted and a few quick inquiries establish that he is due out in charge of a convoy to Tobruk tomorrow. How fortunate, for – after returning to his room, to get dressed in his best uniform so he at least *looks* the part – Weary has a quiet word in his ear.

Listen, Roley . . .

'I'm in a terrible hole. I had a convoy listing to get to Tobruk, and frankly, I got pissed the other night and I missed my draft. Could you take me up there as staff officer?'[4]

Of course, but be discreet. That is exactly what Weary was thinking. At 5 am the next day he exits his hospital bed permanently, leaving a thoughtful note on his pillow for Dr Hailes.

'Sorry, gone to Tobruk.'[5]

Even though he's as crook as Tallarook, by hook or by crook, he is determined to get to Tobruk.

•

And yet, while it is one thing to be posted to Tobruk, it is quite another to actually get there. The only way for the Allied troops to enter the harbour is to charge in on darkened ships in the middle of the night, surging at full throttle along what is known as 'Bomb Alley', the last 30 miles into the port.

On this night, Weary's destroyer, the HMS *Waterhen*, whose turn it is to run the German gauntlet, starts loading men and supplies in Alexandria at midnight, and now slips the surly bonds of the harbour just before dawn, and is soon doing 20 knots in the open sea. The aim is to be well away from the shore and prying eyes by sun-up. Into the Mediterranean proper, they turn west, towards Tobruk, staying just beyond the vision of the shore, secure until such time as they clear the current Allied front lines at Mersa Matruh and . . .

And what's that feeling?

Could it be . . . sea-sickness? Indeed, it is. Weary had been just down in the engine room, being shown around by an old rugby mate who is an officer on the ship, when the feeling comes over him. A mad dash to get up on deck in time just does the trick before he loses his breakfast over the side while his amused friend with the cauliflower ears, Petty Officer Tony Edwards, holds his hand and tries to console him, saying: 'It would be just the same with us . . . but we're busy.'[6]

Passing Mersa Matruh to port, from this point on they are on their own in enemy territory, with that aloneness only occasionally leavened when one of their own fighter escorts drones overhead. When those escorts leave, the Captain calls to the engine room for full speed ahead, cranking up the old tub to as high as 27 knots, as they head in on the terribly dangerous last 200 miles into Tobruk. 'Bomb Alley' is particularly hair-raising as the Luftwaffe patrols heavily in those parts, snarling back and forth, looking for the phosphorescent wake made as the tubs churn forward, and swooping down accordingly when they find it.

For Weary Dunlop, as for all the first-timers, it is a weird thing to make your way into a harbour where, in the menacing moonlight, you could see poking from the waters the many masts and funnels of the ships that have passed this way before you, now standing silent sentinel to their watery graves beneath. It is almost like an aquatic version of an elephant graveyard; a place where the big ships had come to groan and die. Eerie, Weary.

Beyond the harbour and the few desultory buildings that ring it, there appears to be little but shimmering desert pounded by blazing sun and endless sandstorms and – as he will soon learn – it is in that desert that the Allies have formed the 'Red Line' a defensive ring of anti-tank ditches, barbed wire and mines extending 28 miles to keep the Italians and Germans out. It is their constant efforts to break through the Red Line into Allied territory that is causing so many casualties for the 2/2nd Casualty Clearing Station, for which Weary is now to be the Senior Surgeon and second-in-command behind the Commanding Officer, Lieutenant Colonel Wilfred Park, from Brisbane.

And so to work.

Their 'surgery and hospital', such as it is constituted, is housed in a deep shelter, which is accessed by a tunnel that goes under the major building by the harbour, Admiralty House – on the simple grounds that even a direct hit on the building above, and it has had many from the endless raids of German Stukas, should leave those far below untouched.

Weary's job is to minister to the thousands of Diggers now holding the Germans and Italians at bay. (His other job, *noblesse oblige*, is to grow a moustache suitable to his station; a thin trim specimen soon appears below his august hooter, never to leave it again.)

As it happens, today is a day when there are many casualties and so, within hours of arrival, Weary Dunlop finds himself doing once more what he has long wanted to be doing again – operating. Soldier after soldier is scrubbed down and prepared for his scalpel. This one with a chest lacerated by lead that must be plucked out; this one missing a hand, requiring the stump to be cauterised; and still another one with shrapnel from a shell that must be removed from his abdomen. Many of the others Dunlop is working on prove to be *gravely* wounded and there is plenty of further surgical work to be done before they can be evacuated in the ships that come and go every night. By the light of a lantern, it is very dim work, but he is saving lives.

His enduring frustration remains, nevertheless, that he and his team are too far from the action. While the CCS has been divided up into two sections – for light and heavy wounds – his section is the light one, while the heavy one is five miles away on the front lines.

Still, it is not just those who are wounded who need his care. There are also many men suffering from dysentery, dehydration and sunstroke – those afflictions that often come with living in the desert, with such heat, and with such a poor diet and so little water, there is only so much that the human body can stand before it starts to fall apart. Many soldiers complain of a complete lack of appetite, while others are beset by vomiting and diarrhoea. On average, the front-line troops have lost a stone in weight, with some men having lost as much as *two* stone, in just over three months. Among the Diggers, the running joke is that some blokes have lost so much weight that they have to take three steps before their trousers start to move!

Every chance Weary can, when there is a break in the traffic of patients, he emerges from the CCS hospital via the tunnel to stride along the docks and even go for a swim in the harbour, seemingly completely unconcerned by the frequent shellfire landing all around, let alone the diving Stukas.

Concerned for him, some of the Diggers beg him to at least do what they do – to wear a helmet when in the harbour – and some even manage to get him to dive into slit trenches when the bombs are thicker than flies on a cow pat, but mostly he impresses for his complete insouciance.

Still, wonderfully, it is not *every* bomb that hits that explodes. Part of the legend of Tobruk is about a bomb that landed so close to an Ack-Ack gun, it could have blown all the Diggers to kingdom come, but instead all they suffered was their gun suddenly jolting upwards and throwing them backwards. When the bomb disposal squad had arrived and carefully opened the bomb up, it was to find a note on which the words were scrawled from some worker in one of the Nazi-controlled factories in Occupied Europe:

> *Keep it up, Tommy.*
> *This is the best we can do for you now.*[7]

•

Well, he'll be buggered.

After weeks of trying to track down Weary Dunlop, to follow up on the promise made in Crete, Private Blue Butterworth could have put Marco Polo to shame. After finally getting away from Crete on a Greek ship bound for Syria, he has been everywhere since, from Nazareth, to Haifa, to El Kantara, to Alexandria. He's used boats and barques, camels and cars, trains and trailers, and lately on Shanks's pony, getting still more frustrated with every misadventure – as he *always* just misses his target.

At last, however, Blue just knows he is closing in.

Now, arriving at Amiriya 2/2nd Casualty Clearing Station he is quick to ask the Adjutant, 'Excuse me, sir. Where is Major Dunlop?'

'Don't you know?'

'No, where is he?'

'He's in Tobruk.'

'Oh shit. Don't tell me I got to go back there again!'[8]

As a matter of fact, you do. But happily, as Major Dunlop has been asking after you, just as you have been asking after him. It shouldn't take *too* long to get the paperwork done so you can join him.

•

In Tobruk itself Weary Dunlop is dumbstruck by the sheer resilience of his fellow Australians. No matter what is thrown at them, they are holding on! Yes, the whole campaign through the Western Desert had been completely derailed by the 6th Division being pulled out to go to Greece, and their destruction there has meant that such momentum won't be regained any time soon. And yes, it has left those in Tobruk completely besieged by German and Italian forces all around the perimeter. But here is the thing.

The defenders really are digging in, digging down and holding on, to the complete dismay of the Germans!

Weary Dunlop has been in Tobruk no longer than a day before he hears the story of the Diggers' chosen sobriquet. For after the Australian and British soldiers had seen off the Afrika Korps's first big attack last Easter, they had come to the attention of the infamous British traitor and propagandist Lord Haw-Haw, who had broadcast from Berlin his view that Tobruk was now being held by 'the sons of sheep herders', and these 'self-supporting prisoners of war'[9] who were now surrounded by the mighty German and Italian armies, were caught like 'rats in a trap . . .'

'These rats of Tobruk . . .' he had sneered. 'Living like rats, they'll die like rats.'

The Diggers had reeled. Looked at each other. Laughed.

The 'rats of Tobruk'!

They loved it. It was perfect. In fact, make that the 'Rats of Tobruk' with a capital 'R'!

How have these ramshackle Diggers on the Red Line managed to hold off the elite divisions of the best-trained, best-equipped, most brilliantly led army the world had ever seen, for months on end?

The great ABC correspondent Chester Wilmot, who has witnessed much of it up close, does his best to explain it to those at home.

'The spirit which has made Australia,' he intones, in words that will become famous, 'is the spirit which has held Tobruk. The inspiring and binding force in Australian life isn't tradition or nationalism or social revolution. It's quite a simple thing. Henry Lawson called it MATESHIP . . . the spirit which makes men stick together. In Australia by sticking together, men have defied drought, bushfire and flood. In Tobruk they've scorned hardship, danger and death, because no Digger would ever let his cobbers down. In Tobruk for the first time in this war the Germans were thrust back by a spirit that even tanks and dive-bombers could not conquer.'[10]

•

And here it comes!

Out of the gloom, in that part of the night caught between being *very* late, and *very* early, HMAS *Vendetta* is just appearing in the moonlight out in Bomb Alley and cruising in towards the docks.

Speed is everything. Hurry.

That which is to be unloaded must be done quickly. Fresh wounded are to be brought immediately on board.

Fresh reinforcements are to file down the gangplank and immediately mustered away from the docks, to let the dog see the rabbit and allow more on.

From the distance comes the regular boom of 'Bardia Bill', the Italians' famous gun, peppering the perimeter with something admittedly a lot stronger than pepper – the pell-mell hell of shells.

Among those being mustered now just away from the wharves is a figure looking around in wonder in the moonlight. Not because he has never seen Tobruk before, but because he has, and this time it is so different. Last time Blue Butterworth was here, the Allies had just taken it from the Italians and there was little damage done to the buildings around the harbour area, or to the docks. Now, he sees destruction all around: enormous craters, caved-in roofs, rubble and ruins of recent vintage, to go with the destruction in the harbour. It really is a bloody *miracle* that anything is still standing and . . .

Fall in!

The new arrivals are led away to a holding camp, where they can spend the rest of the night before their paperwork can be sorted by the light of day, and it is not before the afternoon that Blue is finally able to make his way back to where he had started the night before, down by the docks, to present himself at the 2/2nd CCS shelter in Admiralty House, where he expects to find the Major.

The questions begin.

'Where did you meet this bastard? He's mad.'

Stories pour out of Major Dunlop's propensity to swim in the harbour during raids, to show no concern for shells landing when he was out and about, to be completely fearless when –

'Listen, mate,' Butterworth interrupts, 'that's why I'm here. I could have bailed out when they told me he was back here, but the episodes I encountered with him . . . *That's* why I'm here. Anyway, where is he?'

'He's in the hospital operating. Up in the main hospital.'[11]

'What time will he be back?'

'Ah, on dusk.'[12]

Which, by now, is not far away.

In fact, no more than an hour later Blue Butterworth is just outside Admiralty House when he sees a familiar, huge silhouette loping through the twilight towards him along the wharf, as light on his feet as ever, despite his mass.

Weary!

I mean Major Dunlop!

Blue Butterworth, British-born, but feeling more Australian all the time, walks up to him, stands to attention, and snaps off a salute.

Reporting for duty, Suh!

'How the bloody hell did you get here?'[13] asks Weary, before a huge grin breaks out on his face and the salute is returned. Despite the offhand jocularity of his greeting, he is clearly touched that Butterworth has made such an effort to find him, keeping his word and proud promise. This one is a keeper, and they have much catching up to do.

But wait . . .

That whistling, getting louder . . .

It's not, is it?

It is. Bardia Bill has just unleashed, and when it comes to reading the whistling, Blue knows enough by now to know that this shell is going to be close. He is just about to throw himself to the ground when he can't help but notice that the good Major Dunlop has not broken stride. So, what can he do? He keeps walking too.

A realisation comes to him that will never leave Butterworth thereafter.

'No, if I'm alongside of you, mate, I'm right.'[14]

The shell misses. Not by much, but it misses.

Blue quickly becomes part of the rhythm of life – while working to also preserve it – touring the perimeters in the morning to gather in the wounded and stabilise them, then getting them back to the hospital where Weary would work on them and, if there was no hope for recovery at Tobruk, sending them back to Alexandria.

How? Under the cover of night, midnight in fact, Weary, Bluey and other more orderly orderlies carefully get these supine soldiers on stretchers and take them out on barges to await whichever one of the 'Scrap Iron Flotilla' – as Lord Haw-Haw had referred to it – is coming. Sometimes the wounded are loaded from the off-side – winched up – to keep them clear of all the slings and swinging derricks.

And while Blue and Weary load men, munitions are unloaded from the other side onto other barges. Yes, there is an ironic symmetry at play: the wounded go up; the weapons to cause wounds come down in exchange.

Say, hurry! The tiniest glimmer of light to the east signals the danger of the dawn and pushes the ship's company into a frenzy as they hurl everything overboard in their eagerness to get away, and strap in tight those wounded or ill soldiers who are coming back with them. Weary and Blue sweat and strain to have all work done before the sun can even think about peeking above the horizon.

Now the cargo hold is at last empty of munitions, the galley and cabins are full of the new chums, and the skipper on the bridge is champing at the bit.

The ship starts gliding away from the jetty, throbbing forward, straining for the open sea.

All hands being on deck, and all else being equal, they want to be up to 50 miles away from Tobruk by the time the sun is fully up, and have only a few nervous hours to get through before an Allied fighter patrol from Mersa Matruh escorts them back to safer waters.

•

There are many challenges that must be faced in Tobruk.

One of Weary's fellow surgeons is Polish, and whenever German wounded are brought into their makeshift theatre, he immediately downs tools with the grumpiness and commitment of a striking coal-miner against bastard bosses. He will not be using his scalpel, nor skills, to save Germans. This is, of course, a breach of the Hippocratic oath that all doctors take to heal the sick, not to judge or deny them treatment on their own whim, and the Colonel in charge of the operations sends for the Polish surgeon, to put him straight.

'Captain . . . you must deal with the wounded as they are brought in irrespective of race.'

'Is that an order, Colonel?' the Captain asks, in his thick Polish accent.

'Yes, Captain, it is.'

'Very good, Colonel. I will obey you but you must understand that with regard to the Germans, my mortality rate will be 100 per cent . . .'[15]

In that case . . . as you were.

When Weary's own Commanding Officer of the 2/2nd CCS, Lieutenant Colonel Wilfred Park, falls ill in early July and is sent to hospital, it is Weary himself who must take command – something he takes no joy in at all.

Commanding the unit means that all the administrative load – which sees his scalpel replaced with a pen with increasing frequency – falls on him. At least one upside is that he is able to make Blue Butterworth officially, from this moment forth, his batman – and signs the paper-work accordingly.

Not that Blue does more than the bare minimum of 'batmanning' for all that. For 'the boss', as Blue comes to call him, continues to have zero interest in shined boots and pressed uniforms, and still less in having someone prepare his meals. What he mostly wants is an extra set of hands and if Blue does not quite become a nurse, he could certainly argue the toss with a few who are on how to bandage a wound, how to transport a patient and even how to insert a cannula.

•

Winston Churchill is not happy, but so what?

After six months of successfully manning the principal defences of Tobruk against the constant attacks of the Germans and Italians, the view of the Australian Government and High Command is that their troops are exhausted and the only way to preserve them as a serious fighting force is for them to be relieved. General Blamey will note that getting an Australian unit of soldiers back from the British is 'like prising open the jaws of a crocodile'.[16]

At British General Headquarters in Cairo, it is all he can do to explain to the British General, Sir Claude Auchinleck, and his senior officers, that while they might not like the Australian withdrawal – Churchill is rabidly against it – that might be just too bad.

'Gentlemen,' he tells them, 'I think you don't understand the position. If I were a French or an American commander making this demand, what would you say about it?'

'But you're *not*,' replies Auchinleck, clearly mystified by just what Blamey is getting at, and as Blamey is not French or American, there is nothing left to discuss.

'That is where you are wrong,' Blamey returns evenly to Auchinleck. 'Australia is an independent nation. She came into the war under certain definite agreements. Now, gentlemen, in the name of my government, I demand the relief of these troops.'

'Well,' Auchinleck says finally, 'if that's the way you put it, we have no alternative . . .'[17]

•

On 21 July 1941, the word comes through for Weary's unit, the 2/2nd CCS:

```
Evacuation of the unit to Australian Base Area Palestine
. . . to enable refitting, reinforcing and rest . . .[18]
```

Pack up, Blue, we are moving out.

Further orders establish that every man can take just one valise or kitbag with them, as well as essential medical equipment.

10.30 pm, 24 July 1941, Tobruk, hanging on for a hero

Quickly now, *quietly*. On this night, Major Weary Dunlop and Private Butterworth are among five officers and 82 other ranks who make their way, 'under cover of darkness with strict road discipline to No. 6 Jetty'.[19]

And there it is, HMS *Hero*, waiting for them. By way of farewell, Bardia Bill burps and a few desultory shells are sent their way, but even then – with all the loading and unloading that must be done – it is nigh on three hours before they are finally underway and the shadows of Tobruk fall back in the dim night.

At least, once they have cleared the harbour proper, it does not take long to be at full speed – and what a speed it is!

Hold on to your hats, but the British destroyer HMS *Hero* does an extraordinary 42 knots, and is more like a speedboat than a destroyer, surging ahead with such speed it creates a wind and a glowing phosphorescent wake behind them. Inevitably, there is a fellow on board, an English officer who Weary had played rugby with before the war, and the two stay on deck talking of old times, and the games they had played; back when such things had seemed like life and death. Now their memories are just the things to get your mind *off* life and death! As they steam up Bomb Alley in complete darkness, all lights extinguished, and proceeding at full throttle, the whole ship shaking under the strain, they talk of great tries they had seen scored, greater tries they had stopped, tackles executed and matches won, the fun of the fray and those shimmering moments that shine still in their talk, until finally Weary goes below to get some kip.

So fast is the *Hero* that they are back in Alexandria by the following afternoon, and back in Palestine only two days later – after four changes of trains and a transfer to truck – and they are soon settling into a dusty camp by the name of Kilo 89, just outside of Gaza. (It will take another three months for the bulk of the Australian troops to be withdrawn and five months till the last battalion, the mighty 2/13th, is out.)

The question is, should Major Dunlop's temporary command of the 2/2nd CCS be made permanent, or should he return to being a surgeon only?

•

As ever with Weary, it doesn't take long for him to resume the rhythms of – pass the port if you will – civilised life, once he is back in a big enough city to provide it.

The Metropole Hotel is a brilliant example of Egypt as a sparkling outpost of Empire – five storeys of opulence, with a thousand stories within. On the outside it looks like a Matisse painting of a perfect pink hotel, transplanted from Paris via some dusty dock; on the inside, every room looks like an excellent place to be murdered in an Agatha Christie novel. It is old world and new, with vivacious velvet, cane furniture and high fans twirling, and it is bedecked with statues and sculptures, with red chairs so opulent they intimidate the sitter, and finery and dinery all around this great ground floor that Weary is currently gazing at. The plum of this palace is the dining room, and it is here on this evening that Weary settles, dressed to the nines, and ready to shovel some grub daintily.

He is accompanied by two other dapper soldiers. The gentlemen are seated by the maître d' with his snoot at full cock. Australians.

Shudder. Their accents and behaviour are known. The Aussie gentlemen are nature's aristocrats and don't care if the maître d' is looking down his nose more than Pinocchio on a bad day, they would like to order prawns. Three dishes please.

Well, gentlemen, we are very busy tonight and that order will take some time.

No problem, Weary and co. will reseat themselves at the bar, and you, *garcon* with the fez, just give us a shout when the crustaceans are in danger of nearing the table.

Thirty minutes and as many gulps of beers later, a thought occurs. Something about a dish they ordered? How long can it take to scrub up some shellfish? They hail passing waiters, but none can give them an update on the order; worse, none remember *any* order about prawns. Well, get the bloody head waiter, and he'd better be here before I finish this beer. He is, but he has no record of an order of prawns either, neither does the maître d', who rushed over to shush these swaying Australians. Alright, let's go to the kitchen and see if any of the chefs remember it?

Sadly, that is not possible, gentlemen, as it is now past 10 pm and no further food orders will be taken.

But this is not further prawns, this is past prawns, and these three singular persons would like some past prawns pronto.

Well, there is nothing that can be done.

Really? Weary senses a crustacean conspiracy and demands to speak to the manager – all part of a typical Australian evening of fine dining, but now things take a turn. Because the maître d' is a big chap, almost as big as Weary, and instead of taking Weary to the manager he decides to take Weary to the floor using a half-nelson. A short scuffle ensues, with a full bar watching in delight, before Weary rises carrying the maître d' aloft by the scruff of his elegant neck.

I would like very, very much to speak to the manager. And to get some prawns.

To aid this process, Weary now grabs the maître d' by the seat of his pants as well and holds him up in the air like a trophy as he makes his way to the sacred kitchen that cannot be disturbed after 10 pm. His companions follow him, fighting waiters and wrestling tables and chairs that threaten to impede their progress. The manager, who has heard the row, which means he was within a two-mile radius of the Metropole Hotel, now appears to render judgement. It is a credit to him that he backs his staff and his kitchen and tells the Australians to go to hell. Well, at least they got an answer. Some English bloke once wrote that discretion is the better part of valour, and given the fact that they can now hear police whistles tootling at increasing volume, Weary decides to drop the matter, and the maître d', and the Australians flee into the night, proud if prawnless.

Perhaps somewhere that serves pies, in future?

•

Look, General Burston has been enormously impressed with all the reports he has had from Tobruk on how well Weary Dunlop has managed his unit; however . . .

However, he takes the view that Weary is 'too junior in army standing to be given the command permanently'.[20]

Excellent!

To Burston's bemusement, Weary of course could not be more pleased at his lack of promotion, and even more pleased to hear that the man who will command the 2/2nd CCS is Lieutenant Colonel Norman Eadie – who he knows to be a good egg, committed and co-operative. And the arrival of two splendid new surgeons in Majors Arthur Moon and Ewan Corlette makes things even more collegiate and jolly – and all the more so because, as a First XV fullback at Cranbrook School, Corlette had followed the Wallabies very closely, and knows precisely Weary's grandeur in that (and on that) field.

Beyond everything else, the fact that Weary does not have to take on an administrative burden frees him up with the time he needs to develop a plan that has long been gnawing at him.

If the mountain will not come to Muhammad, then Muhammad must go to the mountain.

And if they cannot get enough critically wounded soldiers to surgery before they die in this fast-moving war – quite unlike the static trench-warfare model of the Great War the Generals had planned for – then Weary wishes to establish a 'first operating unit',[21] a mobile surgical unit. Yes, he wants one that can be set up just behind the front lines in any battle and immediately get to work stabilising men and saving their lives. The central idea is for the units to have their own transport, dedicated staff, equipment and power supply from light generators. They would, thus, be able to move forward and back under their own steam, and once on site, quickly put up two tents for surgery – the first for triage, the second for operating.

It is not simply a matter of time saved in getting to the operation, it would spare the soldiers from having to be transported on long and bumpy ambulance rides, which frequently exacerbated their distress to the point that it killed them. The urgency of coming up with a new solution is that with more and more Diggers being pulled out of Tobruk – there have been 6000 evacuated by the end of September – it seems likely that a new campaign in the desert will be launched before Christmas. More likely still is that the British will launch a campaign, and so eager is Weary Dunlop to test out his ideas that he urges his superiors to put his unit to the test as a part of the British battle plan.

It takes some agitation on his part to convince his superiors of the virtues of his idea.

His theme, as he warms to it with the Director General of the AAMC, Major General Rupert Downes, over lunch, in the presence of other senior officers, is that as they are currently constituted, 'Units are not suited to the type of warfare we are having. New things are needed.'[22]

'There's nothing wrong with the units, Dunlop,' Downes replies sharply, 'it's the way you use them.'[23]

But Dunlop persists, and keeps pushing his 'pet project to design a mobile field hospital which would cope with about 50 casualties, [at a time] expanding to 100, [that] could operate in advanced areas'.[24]

Finally – after endless negotiations with the likes of Generals Auchinleck, Blamey, Tomlinson and Burston – he is given leave to explore it and work up a formal proposal. With typical Weary energy and thoroughness, constantly consulting with colleagues and heading out on field excursions where different formats are tried, an entirely new kind of mobile medical facility begins to form under his fingertips.

Five trucks. Two large tents, and five smaller ones holding 50 beds for pre-op and post-op patients. One operating theatre, with two operating tables lying parallel, with two yards in between so surgeons can easily move around both and, if necessary, go easily from one to the other. One triage area. Heavy reliance on the new injectable anaesthetic Pentothal, which will be kept in the second drawer of the third cupboard, above the gauze and below the bandages.

The resuscitation and X-ray ward to be positioned just next to the triage tent. The instrument table to be positioned at the head of the operating table, with the scalpels to the right, and the forceps to the left.

Surgical instruments will be boiled by the second Corporal, the moment we start setting up, and from the moment the truck stops we can be ready to operate – *check stopwatch* – just a little over 20 minutes later. But we can get that down with practice.

'Best fun I've had since playing trains as a small boy,' he writes to Helen of the process, 'just like having your own circus.'[25]

Yes, it will be a flying circus of medicos ready to go with the winds of war, not just shunted to the side of the fray. So often the transportation of injured troops dictates their treatment and odds of survival; now the mobile units can beat these bugbears at last.

By 20 October, Weary's notions and arguments are canonised in paper form entitled, 'Suggested Establishment and Equipment Tables for Mobile Surgical Units forming Sections of a company of an Australian Casualty Clearing Station.'[26]

All up, his report covers 30 tightly typed pages,[27] and is nothing less than a blueprint – not just for one mobile Casualty Clearing Station, but for many, across the board.

Official approval arrives just 10 days later: For Major Dunlop. Authority to raise experimental unit granted.[28]

RAH!

Wherever the next battle takes place – likely somewhere in North Africa – Weary will be able to bring his mobile operating unit forward to just behind the front lines, and set about saving lives. With the Afrika Korps still rampant, proof of the concept shouldn't take long.

Most wonderfully, as he forms up his surgical team, he is able to arrange for the transfer of his best friend, now Captain Jim Yeates, to leave his 2/5th Field Ambulance and join him here with the 2/2nd CCS.

Not that it is easy for all that, as Weary writes to his beloved, noting that in terms of properly reorganising the Army Medical Corps, 'the type of man needed is a cross between Houdini, Lord Kitchener and Jesus Christ of this unhappy land. However, in this unhappy person you see one likely in the immediate future to become C.O. of the first Australian mobile surgical unit . . . surgery on wheels.'

It's exciting and frustrating both in one.

'From the inordinately good tempered person you remember I am fast degenerating into an irritable, pugnacious, ruthless even ferocious old gentleman . . .'[29]

At least he has his faithful offsider to keep him sane.

'Butterworth is a pleasant smooth-faced boyish rascal who loses my things in an engaging way. He is golden red of hair and English in origin and at least is good at repartee always catching me out at that hour when the wits are at the lowest ebb. e.g. this morning, "Bad luck about the old queen, sir."

'"What, is Queen Mary dead, Butterworth?"

'"No, Queen Victoria, sir!"'[30]

•

By mid-November 1941, they are finally ready and the No. 1 Australian Mobile Surgical Unit, as the five trucks packed with medical staff and their equipment are called, is moving across the desert.

For the first time in this war a serious mechanised force is mobilised to neither kill nor supply the killers. This one has come to cure, to heal, to save.

As Weary will delightedly recount to Helen back in Melbourne, his newly established unit 'moved off in convoy with everything and everybody on the vehicles and in 1½ hours laid out a small field hospital with our own electric lighting and technical gadgets working – had lunch provided by our own field kitchen, struck camp in under the hour and off again. Altogether this is the most complete job I've had entrusted to me in the army and the success or otherwise . . . is of considerable importance in our organisation.'[31]

It works, it really works!

Returning to camp, Dunlop confidently waits for the orders to go into action, wherever the Allies are to be thrown into action next, only to read something completely staggering in the *Palestine Post*.

The Allies have launched a massive attack in the Western Desert involving 120,000 soldiers, code-named 'Operation Crusader', led by the newly formed Eighth Army, and under overall command of General Claude Auchinleck, with the aim of relieving the still besieged Tobruk and sweeping Rommel and his Afrika Korps out of North Africa.

And yet Weary has been told nothing about it?

Angrily, frantically, he sends a cable to Cairo.

`Ready to move, one hour's notice.`[32]

As it happens, they could have been ready to move on a year's notice, and it would have made no difference.

Despite their readiness, despite the promises, General Auchinleck has left them off the Order of Battle, deciding to attack without them, and they are left, as Weary puts it, 'stranded in the Sinai'.[33]

'And so there we sat on our bottoms while the battles raged in the desert and the British took a bit of a knock on the nose.'[34]

The outrage of it!

'Our flag has fallen out of the map,'[35] Weary writes to Helen.

'He was very disappointed,' Blue Butterworth will recall. 'We had it right down to a fine art, that we could get in there in X number of minutes, have a bloke on the table and operated on.'[36]

But there is nothing for it.

'I was so disgusted that I decided to shake the dust of the . . . off my feet and transferred back to my unit [the 2/2nd CCS].'[37]

Nevertheless, once back, he is asked once again if he would like to be promoted to Colonel to command the 2/2nd CCS. He declines, as ever, far preferring to remain a Major conducting actual surgery.

They will not be joining Operation Crusader, no matter how bitter they are.

In desperation Weary keeps refining his mobile unit operation, in the hope that a call-up will follow to another battle, perhaps in Syria, where Helen's brother, Captain John Boyd Ferguson, is about to go into action with the 2/33rd Battalion.

The sense that the Allies are losing this war is unspoken, but felt. All they can do is fight on, hoping, like Mr Micawber, that 'something will turn up . . .'

CHAPTER FIVE

FROM THE LAND OF THE RISING SONS

The Digger asks no beg-pardons. He has adapted himself from the heavy-equipment desert war with the Germans to this individual war in the jungle and he has had to learn the hard and bloody way. He has outfought the Jap with the same spirit as he held the Hun at Tobruk, and smashed him at Alamein. The Jap can commit his hari-kiri for the Emperor and the Imperial Nipponese Empire, but the Digger has fought, and always will fight for his cobbers: for Bluey and Snowy, for Lofty and Stumpy.[1]

Damien Parer, 'A Cameraman looks at a Digger'

7 December 1941, Pearl Harbor, bombs bursting in air

It feels like just another quiet Sunday morning in Hawaii. While some US sailors and assorted military personnel are nursing hangovers, many of the residents are just getting ready to head off to church, when they hear something.

Listen there. Can you hear it, too? It's coming from the north-west and is like an insistent mass . . . *droningggggg.*

What the *hell* is that?

O Heavenly Father above, it is not, surely, the Japane—?

Yes. In numbers. In the heavens above.

Bombers. Torpedo planes. Escorting fighters. Coming in successive waves. There are no fewer than 200 in all, and they have taken off an hour earlier from a secretly assembled pod of six aircraft carriers some 250 miles to the north of Hawaii. Just as the Japanese intelligence had determined, most of America's Pacific Fleet have returned to Pearl Harbor for weekend leave and are moored tightly together, with little in the way of active air defences protecting them. And there they are!

It is just before 8 am when these Japanese squadrons arrive directly above the American airfields and harbour and – following the direct orders of Prime Minister Hideki Tojo – unleash hundreds of tons of bombs. The resultant devastation sees five battleships sent to the bottom, badly damages a dozen more ships, kills 2400 military personnel and civilians, and wounds over 1000 more.

When Winston Churchill hears the news from an aide at *Chequers* of what has happened at Pearl Harbor, he is . . . thrilled. Now, America *must* join them!

'We had won the war,' he will record his feelings. 'England would live; Britain would live; the Commonwealth of Nations and the Empire would live.'

Yes, there will likely be 'terrible forfeits in the East', but that is so immaterial to the main news that he goes to bed 'saturated and satiated with emotion', to sleep the 'sleep of the saved and the thankful'.[2]

For his part, in that East, the new Australian Prime Minister, John Curtin, reacts swiftly to the terrible tidings. Woken in his Melbourne hotel room, he responds with a simple: 'Well, it has come . . .'[3] before gathering whatever Australian resources he can for the country to defend itself.

Both leaders follow closely the reaction of the USA and are not disappointed when an enraged President Roosevelt quickly declares 7 December, 'a date which will live in infamy', in the process of declaring war on Japan. A mighty giant, now enraged, stirs itself after two years of formal neutrality.

The response of the Japanese is . . . nothing if not lyrical, in the first instance. For the Japanese Emperor, the direct descendant of the Sun Goddess, merely releases to the ethereal ether: 'We by the grace of Heaven, Emperor of Japan, seated on the throne of a line unbroken for ages eternal, enjoin upon ye, Our loyal and brave subjects: We hereby declare war on the United States of America and the British Empire. The men and officers of Our Army and Navy shall do their utmost in prosecuting the war . . .'[4]

•

In Jerusalem at the time for meetings at Hadassah Hospital, Major Weary Dunlop happens to be with other surgeons when the news of Pearl Harbor comes through and all are soon hovering around the radio to devour the BBC reports. The pride of the American Pacific

Fleet now lies on the bottom of Pearl Harbor. The implications are obvious, at least to Weary, and he has no hesitation in opining to his fellow surgeons of the Southern Cross that their time in North Africa might be coming to an end, as they must be called back to face the new threat. A big night of drinking ensues for all . . . for the sake of auld lang syne. Who knows what the future holds?

•

This is war at Australia's door.

Without waiting for Britain's lead, Prime Minister Curtin declares war on Japan. In the wake of the Pearl Harbor attack, both Germany and Italy observe the terms of their Tripartite Treaty with Japan, declaring war on the United States, with the Americans returning serve.

Just half an hour *before* the bombing of Pearl Harbor, another Japanese force had landed in northern Malaya and is now fighting its way down the Malay Peninsula towards Britain's enormous naval base at Singapore, a site which Australians had long considered their principal source of security in the region.

With woefully inadequate support from British forces, the forward elements of Australia's 8th Division await the Japanese onslaught as the invaders move inexorably towards Singapore. Four days after Pearl Harbor, Japanese bombers unleash their fiery fury to send two British capital ships, the HMS *Repulse* and *Prince of Wales*, to the bottom. There are hundreds of casualties, who are soon flooding into Singapore's Alexandra Hospital, suffering burns, bullet wounds and shocking shrapnel gashes.

With savage speed, Japanese forces are soon also laying siege to Hong Kong, Wake Island, the Dutch East Indies, Burma, British Borneo and Thailand.

The Australian War Cabinet quickly gives the nod to arm and train another 100,000 Australian men and to send more troops to Darwin and Timor.

Among those heading to Timor is Bombardier Tom Uren, a strapping young front-rower for the Manly Sea Eagles who, nevertheless, had had to cajole his mother into signing his AIF papers, as he was under 21.

Within *hours* of the news coming through about Pearl Harbor, he and his mates in Darwin are bustled onto HMAS *Westralia*, and are now pounding through the tropical night, o'er the westerly swell towards Timor. If the Japs can hit Pearl Harbor, who knows what else is at risk? Timor? The Dutch East Indies? Darwin itself, and even a full-blown invasion of Australia? At least everyone can be sure that the British bastion of Singapore will never fall, but the horizons are suddenly dark.

Most importantly, Curtin and the Australian Cabinet urgently debate bringing the troops of the 2nd Australian Imperial Force in the Middle East home at all speed. With the way the war is turning, Australia is now threatened by Japanese invasion, and whatever Churchill's government might think about it, the more Australian soldiers heading for home shores the better.

And in the meantime, Singapore, where the AIF's 8th Division has been based, must be saved. But it needs reinforcements!

'I am particularly concerned in regard to the air strength, as a repetition of the Greek and Crete campaigns,' Curtin notes archly in a cable to Churchill, 'would evoke a violent public reaction and such a happening should be placed outside the bounds of possibility.'[5]

Churchill is appalled, *appalled*, at Curtin's presumption. Blaming the British Prime Minister for what happened in the Greek and Crete affairs? Outrageous.

As to the 'Singapore fortress',[6] as he refers to it in a cable to Curtin, there is no need to worry. It is amply defended, and will not fall. Nevertheless, he follows up with another cable assuring him that it would still be reinforced 'with all speed'.[7]

•

There is just time before Christmas to write to Helen.

Hélène Beloved,
All sorts of things to thank you for this week. The first of them
something which you will have quite forgotten, notably a lovely picture
which a long, long time ago was despatched to me per Boyd. That sound
fellow had a delightful frame added and no doubt after possessing it so
long must feel I am a robber.

It is nearly as lovely as you, and such a consolation for the loss of
your [other picture] from which blow I've never quite recovered.

Butterworth asked if it were a picture of Princess Elizabeth, and
I reported very gravely that it wasn't, but it was of a princess just the

same. So this sweet, grave, adorable, beloved person lives in my hut and makes it just a tiny little bit more like home.[8]

Late January 1942, Port Tewfik, Suez, anchors away but guns to stay

The official movement order comes in late January. The personnel of the 2/2nd Casualty Clearing Station are – with nearly all the other Australian troops – to leave North Africa.

And, the troops want to know, they are to go *where*, exactly?

Exactly.

Blue and Weary Dunlop – together with another 85 members of the 2/2nd CCS and another 3000 or so Australians from various units – simply have orders to get on a fast ship by the name of RMS *Orcades*. No other details or even clues are provided, though other sections of the 2/2nd CCS are placed on other ships in the convoy.

'Most of us believed that we were headed for Australia,'[9] one soldier of the 2/3rd Machine Gun Battalion will allow, but no-one can be certain.

Other members of the 6th and 7th Divisions will be part of a large convoy leaving in coming days and protected by a flotilla of warships, but the *Orcades* is so fast it is to go on ahead.

Those leaving are simply obliged to march four miles from the nearest station and straight up the gangplank.

And now you can see it there, by the dock at Port Tewfik, Suez: sleek, and with engines already purring. She's a beauty! Not your usual troopship, the *Orcades* is a converted 23,500-ton luxury liner, with enclosed decks, a well-stocked library and even an open-air swimming pool!

Around the port, all is flurry and worry.

This is not the usual way of preparing a ship for departure – the calm, orderly, methodical manner of putting each thing in its place until it's ship-shape.

No, this is like the mad scramble that comes when a stationmaster on a railway platform shouts, 'All aboard!' and blows his whistle two minutes into what was meant to be a ten-minute stop. There is no time to load properly, the ship is leaving. We need speed, speed, speed!

Still, most amazingly, the *Orcades* still has – please hurry this way, gentlemen, as we show you to your quarters – the original officers and crew of the Orient Line, which owns her.

While there is an entire convoy of ships also assembling that is soon to head out across the Indian Ocean, taking the survivors of the 6th Division and the 7th Division back to Australia, the *Orcades* will not be a part of it. As one of the fastest ships in the British Navy, it has been singled out to go first, go fast, and get the 3000 Diggers on board to their destination as quickly as possible.

None of which is known to Weary as he and his men continue to pile on board with soldiers from such units as the 2/3rd Machine Gun Battalion, the 2/2nd Pioneer Battalion and the 2/1st Anti-Aircraft Regiment – many of whom are distressed to find themselves pulling away from the dock when they know for a certainty that their Vickers machine guns, .303 rifles and Ack-Ack guns haven't yet arrived.

Too late now. As is the army way, and particularly the way of the AIF, they will just have to make the best of it.

Now, as per the orders, Lieutenant Colonel Norman Eadie becomes the Senior Medical Officer on board, and Weary's 2/2nd CCS will staff the ship's hospital.

In that case, Blue Butterworth is quick to claim the cabin next to the ship's surgery for Major Dunlop, while Weary himself is pleased to soon meet the ship's presiding surgeon, Prince Gardiner, and more particularly the ship's nurse, a fetching Irishwoman in her early thirties, Sister Kitty Murphy.

All good!

But where they are going remains unknown, with rumours ranging from India to Istanbul to . . .

No, it's Bombay . . . no, Burma. *I heard* Singapore, Java or . . . don't even jinx it by thinking it . . . Australia. Well, we are leaving in less than an hour, on the dot of 10 am on this first day of February. And our baggage is *where*?

Still to come. Your belongings, your weaponry and your ammunition are on other trucks, and will be put on other ships. Later.

The 2/3rd Machine Gun Battalion's Lieutenant Colonel Ted Lyneham – a bull-headed kind of man, ever prone to bristling bluntness – will record the feelings of the men while avoiding the language actually used: 'All ranks felt rather annoyed at the situation as the Q.M. had not arrived and all were without change of clothes, razors, towels, cooking equipment, office records.'[10]

Everything that might be of use, in other words. Still, mustn't grumble! You don't need any official clobber to do PT on board;

and all are now forced to, which does at least give them something new to grumble about.

Colonel Lyneham's own Commanding Officer at the 2/3rd Machine Gun Battalion is none other than the legendary Great War figure of Lieutenant Colonel Arthur Blackburn VC. He is a spare, grey, bronzed figure who regularly strides the decks, chatting to the soldiers in a friendly, if still formal way. With the air about him of a deeply experienced warrior, he is nevertheless always interested – if sometimes bemused – to find out how the young warriors are getting on.

'And what do you think we have in store?' the 50-year-old asks some young gunners on the foredeck on this day.

'Leave at home first, sir.'

'Mark my words, you lads,' he replies cheerily, 'you'll be lucky.'[11]

Lieutenant Colonel Blackburn is firmly of the view that they are on their way to fight the Japanese.

If so, more's the pity they are not at full strength.

'[We were],' Blackburn will note, 'less about 200 officers and men, all our vehicles, all our machine guns and practically all of our fighting equipment.'[12]

Rather than being all dressed up with nowhere to go, they are going somewhere, nigh *naked*.

•

A few days later, a pamphlet on jungle warfare is distributed. (So they are probably not headed for London.) Among those bemused to be perusing it is Sergeant Ern Corrie, a Bendigo boy who used to flog soft drinks and tomato sauce as a commercial traveller before the war – only to enlist, get three months medical training and, bang, become a corporal and a chiropodist! Well, he has risen in rank and stature to be an everyman orderly who can now do a good impression of a medico if required. Back at home he has a two-year-old boy cared for by his darling wife, Doris. But now he is here, reading over a small guide on how to fight World War II in adverse conditions.

He gives Weary a nod and is pleased to get one back, Ern to Ern. Corrie is not a doctor but the doctors like him and trust him implicitly; a trust he returns in kind every time.

On the late afternoon of 9 February 1942, after proceeding across what is obviously the Indian Ocean, they anchor in Colombo Harbour and are told to be ready to disembark. Then they are told to just remain where they are. Curiouser and curiouser.

The main thing, for Weary, is that they are heading in at least the broad direction of Australia, and Helen!

What will it be like to be with her again?

He has no doubt he is a different man to the one who had left her, and she, too, will no doubt have changed. Her letters display, even proudly, a newly assertive tone of one who has had to make do without him, and is a long way from the young student with whom he had first fallen in love.

It is enough to make a man – even one who has withstood bombs, bullets and bastardry, without blinking – nervous. And as a matter of fact, it quickly emerges that they might well be home even sooner than in a few weeks, because the ship that the 2/2nd Australian CCS is assigned to, the *Orcades*, is – praise the Lord and pass the caviar – as a former ocean liner, very fast indeed.

Early 1942, Malay peninsula, honoured in the breach

In the two months since the attack on Pearl Harbor, the Japanese have stormed through all of Indochina and the Malay Peninsula, while pressing the shores of the Dutch East Indies, including Timor – and are even on the point of taking Britain's famed citadel of the Far East, Singapore itself! Against all odds, and more particularly all British military planning, the Japanese Imperial Army is approaching the island from the direction of the Malayan jungle just a few hundred yards across the narrow causeway to the north.

By 10 February 1942 things are so grim that Churchill sends a stirring cable to his Commanding Officer of British forces in South East Asia, General Archibald Wavell.

In the kind of language that gave the word 'Churchillian' its punch, Churchill essays to give mettle to his men from afar, asserting that Wavell and his most senior officers should abandon any 'thought of saving the troops or sparing the population. The battle must be fought to the bitter end at all costs . . . Commanders and senior officers should die with their troops. The honour of the British Empire and of the British Army is at stake.'[13]

•

Doing his morning constitutional around the deck with Blue Butterworth, Weary Dunlop suddenly finds the ship astir.

For what's that?

There is excitement all around as soldiers and sailors alike spy a dash of black smoke on the horizon. Friend, or foe? Inevitably the men look to the bridge and note that the skipper and his officers are calm so the smoke must be coming from a friendly ship.

Sure enough – but as a clear sign that they are moving into dangerous waters – by dusk the *Dorsetshire*, one of the cruisers that had helped to sink the *Bismarck*, is bristling on their starboard flank, on the lookout for any German raiders or U-boats. By the following morning a fast British destroyer has joined them, quickly followed by two Dutch cruisers.

'It makes one feel much more secure against possible raiders,' one soldier notes, 'to see [the *Dorsetshire*] racing around us like a greyhound dog. We have been thoroughly trained and warned what we are to do in case of an air raid or an attack from the sea.'[14]

And while the units on board the *Orcades* still have very few of their own guns, such ones as they do boast have been combined with the ship's modest armoury and set up on deck, so that if an enemy plane comes overhead it risks being met with fire from the 'Bren, Bofor and anti-tank guns lashed to the rails and of course our rifles'.[15]

One way or another, they feel ready for whatever the Germans can throw at 'em.

•

And so it has come to this.

John Curtin has continued to urge Winston Churchill to send more troops, ships and air-support to bolster the defences of Singapore, but so far the British Prime Minister has continued to send little beyond more magnificent Churchillian prose. Worse, it is the Australians of the 8th Division who have been placed right at the prow of the British defences, with insufficient support.

And now, after four days of bitter fighting in this last burst of January 1942 – where some 4000 Diggers of two AIF Battalions of the 8th Division, backed by a smattering of a scattering of a battering of Australian gunners and the remnants of the 45th Indian Brigade, have managed to at least severely slow the advance of 10,000 crack Japanese Imperial Guards on Singapore – these Australians at the forefront of the fighting retreat have arrived at Parit Sulong on the west coast of the Malay Peninsula.

Alas, with their lives in the balance, and carrying some 145 of their severely wounded number in 50 vehicles – lots of whom are 'delirious, some mad from pain, torment and thirst'[16] – they find their way has been blocked by Japanese forces who have leapfrogged them and are now holding a bridge on the outskirts of this small village. Worse, the Japanese are refusing to even allow their ambulances of severely wounded through. After attempts to take the bridge by force fail, the Commanding Officer of this battling brigade, Lieutenant Colonel Charles Anderson – who has personally led many bayonet charges against the swarming Japanese in the last bursts of battle – orders the remaining fit men to disperse into the jungle and get away the best they can. The 110 wounded Australians and 35 Indians who complete 'the maimed and bloodstained'[17] group, who are no chance of getting away, will be left here to surrender to the Japanese, in the hope that the usual rules of war apply and they will receive the medical care they so desperately need.

Alas, no sooner have the Japanese approached than they open fire, including with cannon. One shell sends two pieces of shrapnel straight into the back and right knee of Lieutenant Ben Hackney of the 2/29th Battalion.

And so it begins.

For no sooner have the Japanese – enraged by their own losses at the hands of this force in recent days – taken charge of the wounded in the mid-afternoon of this oppressively hot day than many of the Indians are beheaded, while they ruthlessly beat and kick the open wounds of the Australians, as well as unleashing many blows of rifle butts at their head. Survivors are beaten and forced towards two small buildings by the bridge, a 'coolies' accommodation' block and a shed. After being stripped naked – strangely bar their socks and boots – their clothing is searched and a pile made of all their wallets, watches, rings, pens, paybooks and personal effects. Now, at the point of bayonets, they are forced into the shed, with so little room that they must step on each other, with the most grievously wounded inevitably suffering most as they fall midst the forest of trampling boots as ever more naked men are forced in.

Some soldiers are incapable of following Japanese orders, and as Hackney will chronicle, 'the Jap would immediately begin yelling and making more signs, and the soldier still not moving would be bashed about with the rifle, kicked and on some occasions eventually either run through many times with the bayonet, or with the rifle close to his head, shot. This was the fate of a good many wounded men.'[18]

The horror continues for a long time.

'Some of the prisoners were killed, and many knocked unconscious, when struck with terrific blows on the head with rifle butts. While the prisoners were in the nude many suffered unpleasant treatment to the more private parts of their bodies pulled, bounced with rifles and swords, hairs plucked out or pulled, punched and sometimes kicked and hit with rifles – while many of the Japs made crude sexual signs.'[19]

As for himself, still outside and bleeding so heavily from his wound he can only just stay upright, Lieutenant Hackney is relieved when the screaming Japanese accept that no more can go into the shed, meaning he can breathe – and bear witness to what happens next.

For now, in the wake of a convoy of motorbikes, cars and some tanks, a large vehicle pulls up, out of which a 'shortish stocky fellow',[20] who is clearly a high commander, alights. Despite Hackney's shock at what he is witnessing and suffering, he is able to remark that very few orders seem to have been given. To his eyes it looks like 'a very, very well-rehearsed procedure. The Japanese did not have to keep on giving instructions. Everybody seemed to know just what to do and when to do it.'[21]

But that changes now as he closely watches this officer, 'dressed in shiny boots and spurs, with a sword hanging low with a great amount of braid around the butt'.[22]

After swaggering about for twenty minutes inspecting the prisoners, the newly arrived high officer barks orders in Japanese. He will later be identified as Lieutenant General Takuma Nishimura, and one of his soldiers will later assert that his words are, 'Instruct the officer in charge of the Prisoners Of War to execute all the Prisoners Of War by firing squad.'[23]

With this the officer and his convoy depart, 'with a great amount of yelling and saluting and bowing by all the Japanese'.[24]

Hackney at least takes satisfaction that after the Commander goes, so too follows the mass of the Japanese attacking force. 'Lorry after lorry, tank after tank, gun after gun. It seemed as if the stream was never ending, and all these forces had been massed and attacking two depleted AIF battalions and some Indian Army engineer troops; and yet our fellows had held them up for five days during that battle which raged along the road.'[25]

Still, for the remaining Diggers, it is clear that whatever the departing commander has just said is not good, as in short order 'machine guns were brought from where they had been resting between tours of duty and placed in front of the building'.[26]

Perhaps not? For now the first of the prisoners allowed out are suddenly given cigarettes and bowls of precious water, all while a Japanese film crew that has just arrived roll tape.

But no sooner has that crew been hustled away than the cigarettes and water are slapped away, and the prisoners are joined by the rest of those inside. Their wrists are tied together behind their backs with rope, including a loop around their necks, before being joined to the next man, and so on. When the rope runs out the Japanese use wire. And now the prisoners are moved into position, towards the southern end of the coolie building, where the machine guns have been set up. When Lieutenant Hackney collapses, some soldiers step forward and put a couple of bayonet thrusts through him to make sure he is good and dead, and the line moves on without him.

In a few minutes the machine guns chatter, before Japanese soldiers use petrol siphoned from the abandoned Allied vehicles to douse the bodies and ignite them, though some men are still alive. Hackney, downwind, can smell the burning flesh – reminding him of life back on the family farm near Bathurst when, on occasion, they had to dispose of dead cows and sheep without going to the trouble of burying them.

Villagers will later insist that, for the amusement of the Japanese soldiers, some of the few surviving Australians still roped and wired together are forced to stand on the edge of the bridge, before one Digger on the end is shot. As he falls into the water, it takes the next man, and the next man still, and so on, until all must fall in and drown. And now Japanese trucks are driven back and forth over the grisly remains of what had been the 2/19th and 2/29th Battalions and the 45th Indian Brigade.

Some 100 yards away, Lieutenant Ben Hackney comes to. Every breath is an agony and comes with bloody bubbles forming on his chest, where the bayonet thrusts which missed his heart have clearly penetrated his lungs. As darkness falls, he is able to crawl under the coolie accommodation building where, by laboriously rubbing the rope on his wrists against the angle of the brick foundations, he is able to sever it, and free his hands. After crawling away into the jungle, he is joined an hour later in the moonlight by two others, both smelling of petrol.

14 February 1942, Alexandra Hospital, Singapore, red double-crossed

Get down! For the medicos and nurses, not to mention the sick and wounded, in Alexandra Hospital on the western edge of Singapore – still filled with those citizens, soldiers, sailors and airmen wounded by the Japanese attacks over the last two months – it is terrifying. For the last 24 hours they have been hearing the sounds of battle getting inexorably closer as the Japanese draw near this British Military Hospital.

Australia's 8th Division had been placed in the direct path of the Japanese, and have fought like tigers, but it is obvious now that it can only be a matter of time before the invaders arrive. The hospital has itself been so overwhelmed with British, and more particularly, Australian wounded that despite being built to a capacity of 550 patients it is now completely overflowing.

There are so many corpses to dispose of that for the moment they are just wrapped in blankets and stacked up.

But now, after a morning of heavy shelling actually hitting the hospital, the 18th Division of the Imperial Japanese Army has arrived, and the staff can see the first of the soldiers marching down the street. With great bravery, a British medico – an officer of the 32nd Company of the Royal Army Medical Corps – puts a Red Cross armband on and, pointing to the internationally recognised symbol of medical neutrality in armed conflict, walks towards the Japanese.

The first Japanese soldier doesn't care. He lifts his rifle and – in another internationally recognised symbol, this one of wanton brutality, fires at him, miraculously missing. The officer runs back to the hospital, but nothing can prevent what happens next.

For now, the Japanese enter the hospital and simply go from ward to ward, using bayonets and bullets to dispatch doctors, nurses and patients alike. Patients are killed lying in their beds – every bed a death bed, nowhere safe – and the huge red crosses on the wall to mark the hospital as an internationally recognised neutral place of medical care are frequently splattered with angry blood. One patient is killed while undergoing an operation intended to save his life, the bayonet trumping the scalpel.

One officer, Captain Tom Smiley, also points at his Red Cross brassards when the Japanese enter the hospital, not realising yet that this is a red rag to a bully.

A bayonet is pushed to his chest, but he reaches out to move it aside. His reward is life, because although the blade cuts his hand it is diverted by a fraction and hits his silver cigarette case. Sometimes smoking is good for your health. The blow still knocks him to the floor, where he stays, realising that playing possum is the only chance he will have to escape or fight. An unwitting Private Alf Sutton passes and Smiley comes to life for a moment, dragging Sutton to the floor.

Play dead or you will be.

In the first hour the Japanese kill 50 people. In the afternoon they round up 200 medicos and orderlies and force them to march to a distant building. Those who are too ill or wounded to walk are summarily killed. Survivors are crammed into three rooms so small that some die during the night. Others are executed the next day. Some of the nurses are killed. Only five of the medicos and orderlies will survive the final wave of atrocities.

More than 300 are killed in total.

Mid-February 1942, aboard the *Orcades* in the Indian Ocean, better out than in

Of all the surgical procedures, removing a ruptured appendix remains among the most simple and yet usually the one with the most dramatic results.

Nurse, scalpel.

Nurse, forceps

Nurse, swab.

Nurse, needle.

A groaning, dying man can be laid out on the table as poison from the appendix courses through his system. And yet with a simple incision by the scalpel in the lower abdomen and liberal use of the forceps to whip the appendix out, followed by careful, simple suturing to prevent bleeding, the same patient can be, as they say, 'resting comfortably' within minutes of the operation concluding.

At least, usually, such operations are simple.

Not so, on this occasion.

For the patient before Weary, Private Eric Beverly, has been rushed to the ship's infirmary at the height of a raging Indian Ocean storm in the middle of the night, and is in thrashing agony. To perform an operation under such conditions is not easy, as by a closely held hurricane lamp Dunlop must sway exactly against the sway of the ship on the torturous ocean, ruck as it bucks, rise as it falls but . . . it works. No sooner have two strokes of his scalpel cut deep enough than yellow pus pours out and – forceps, please – the offending appending is removed, and within minutes Beverly is, indeed, resting comfortably.

Sister Murphy looks at the strapping surgeon with admiring eyes that warm still more with every stolen glance.

(Her adoration of the Australian is obvious to all, including the ship's surgeon, Prince Gardiner, who regularly teases her about it. She doesn't care, and seems to like nothing better than doing all she can to pamper the Australian. *Can I get you some more tea, Major Dunlop? Some of these scones? Why yes, I did make them myself!*)

The *Orcades* keeps scything through the Indian Ocean, as speculation continues about their destination.

Blue Butterworth is one of many who gets his compass out, and asks the question that all are at least thinking.

'Are we still going back to Australia?'[27]

Alas, alas . . .

'As more days passed,' one gunner will recount, 'we seemed to be heading too far east, even for Fremantle or Perth.'[28]

And now, a few days after their escorts had arrived, they first steam past some small emerald isles and now find themselves with land on both sides, which clearly means they are in a strait. Which one?

The wise heads tell them they are in the Sunda Strait, which separates the islands of Sumatra and Java.

But now what?

They turn to the west, staying off the southern coast of Sumatra, seemingly heading towards an enormous dark mountain ahead, so tall its summit is lost in the clouds. Right by it, they enter a long sound and steam on for a full two hours before the shores on each side start to narrow. Rounding a bend, they enter a 'bay the shape of a fan, as fantastic in colour as a fan made of feathers from a peacock. The mountains that rose sometimes sheer from the sea were like a patchwork quilt in every shade of green. Sampans, with brilliant sails, were paddled by men wearing huge hats of coloured straw.'[29]

They have arrived at Sumatra's Oosthaven, as in East Harbour.

It is indeed a colourful scene. But there is something else, too.

For an ominous silence hangs over this port. There is trouble abroad. And the mountains towering over them all have a distinct brooding aspect.

The men are still clothed in their winter battle dress, suitable for the desert nights of the Middle East but wretched for equatorial climes, and they try to work out what is going on.

Before long, the ship's grapevine gives them the answer. The *Orcades* has been ordered to land at Oosthaven to reinforce the hotch-potch of Dutch colonial, British, American and Australian forces trying to defend those shores from the Japanese, who are expected to be landing shortly. Specifically, they must defend a crucial airfield at a spot called Palembang. They are on an important mission.

On the one hand it makes sense, for aboard the *Orcades*, apart from the 2/2nd CCS, they have at least their fair share of fighting units, including the 2/3rd Machine Gun Battalion, the 2/2nd Pioneer Battalion, the 2/105 General Transport Company and the 2/1st Anti-Aircraft Regiment – some 3000 Australian soldiers in all. But they are all still near weaponless.

What to do?

•

As the *Orcades* is anchored off Oosthaven on this late afternoon of 15 February 1942 – and about to send its troops ashore – a key decision has been made. General Arthur E. Percival, the buck-toothed Commanding Officer of the Allied forces defending Singapore, walks purposefully out from the Allied lines towards the most forward elements of the Japanese attacking forces – as the sun goes down on Singapore, and on the British Empire in these parts.

For one of his aides carries a Union Jack, while another carries a white flag, generating what will be a famous picture of Caucasians bowing to Asians. *Britons never will be slaves*, but they are about to be prisoners en masse, alas. It is over.

The 'impregnable bastion' of Singapore – or '*Syonan-to*', Light of the South, as it is promptly renamed by the victors – has fallen to the murderous Imperial Japanese Army, despite the attackers being outnumbered two to one and almost out of ammunition.

Almost 1800 Australians of the 8th Division have been killed, while the remaining 15,000 are captured. (Many of them are just glad to be alive, having seen the heaviest of the fighting. Though Australians had been only 14 per cent of overall combat strength defending Singapore, they had suffered 78 per cent of the casualties.) All up, 30,000 Japanese soldiers have routed 100,000 armed defenders of Singapore, at a loss of only 3500 of their own.

Oh, the *humiliation*.

In the words of Winston Churchill, the fall of Singapore is the 'worst disaster and largest capitulation in British history'.[30]

•

With the ebbing of the light at Oosthaven comes the rising of action.

'The order has come,' one soldier dashes off a note to the folks at home, 'we are to go off on a tug and it's now pitch dark and raining, not very pleasant, but the boys are all in good humour. Well cheerio till I get another chance of writing, if at all.'[31]

Before embarking on the steamer, they all must gather around Blackie VC. Weary listens closely to Colonel Blackburn as this veteran warrior spells out the situation.

We are going ashore, travelling the four miles aboard the small Dutch steamer that is approaching. Prepare to embark upon it in battle order. You will be issued with enough iron rations to last for several days.

'Gentlemen, you realise that this is a suicide mission and [I] leave it to you to decide what you say to your troops, but I suggest you spend 10 minutes or so to settle down and absorb the situation before you call your orders group and talk to your men.'[32]

The machine-gunners are without machine guns, the Ack-Ack regiment is without Bofors, and for the normal soldiers ... even basic rifles and bayonets are in short supply.

To help make up for the lack of weaponry, Colonel Blackburn has been able to 'obtain 500 more [rifles] from the armoury of the *Orcades* through the kindness of the ship's captain, Capt. Fox'.[33]

True, all the rifles have 'V. R.' stamped on them, meaning they date from the age of Victoria Regina, Queen Victoria, whose rule had ended over four decades earlier, but it is something.

And on the reckoning that there is no problem so great for an Australian that it can't be tackled by the liberal application of some fencing wire, gumption and plenty of elbow grease they . . . adapt.

The orders are given:

If you do have a rifle, disembark with it. If you don't, disembark anyway with some of the ship's mortars, and these pick-handles so you'll have something to swing with.

'And when someone is killed, take their rifle.'[34]

Sounds like a plan!

'Some of the boys have been issued with Tommy guns,' one soldier records in his diary, 'and believe it or not, not one round of ammunition for them, I don't know what they are expected to do with them.'[35]

Perhaps to be used as clubs?

The situation for those with rifles is at least a little better and between them, they have – dot three, carry one, subtract two – ten rounds of ammunition each, and a will to fight despite the odds.

'The boys,' Weary will later note, 'were eager to drive the "Nips" off, even at the point of the bayonet.'[36]

At least those men with actual bayonets are, for even they are in short supply.

Just as the hour falls when the tops of the mountains become indistinguishable from the suddenly black skies behind, they head down the gangplanks on to the small steamer that has come alongside and get ready to cast off.

'We were crammed onto the ship,' Corrie records, 'all 2500 troops, so close we could not take our haversacks off.'[37] Space is so tight they even have to put men in the engine rooms, standing just clear of the engines. Perhaps they should be renamed the Sardine Battalion.

But what a send-off they are given, as Weary Dunlop and all those who remain aboard the *Orcades* line the rails to cheer them on.

•

Just as they head to shore, the skies open up, leaving the three battalions of Australians far from home in the midst of 'a pitch-black night and in absolutely soaking rain that made us all look like drowned rats'.[38]

Dirty balls of thunder roll over them as they get closer.

Approaching the dimly lit wharves at Oosthaven – and noting how 'the town and harbor were in complete darkness [as were] all the ships and transports lying out in the harbour'[39] – they can see something more than passing strange, just as the rain eases.

Can it be?

Yes, it is.

On the wharf, they can make out the dim figures of men who are – as unlikely as it sounds, but yes I am sure of it – cutting sandwiches. So, the British *are* here. Someone has told them of the Australians' forthcoming arrival, and so in the absence of being able to give them guns and ammunition, they – B Squadron, of the King's Own Hussars – are instead intending to provide them with corned beef and bread.

And now, out of the darkness as the Australians pull in alongside the wharf, a thickly accented voice rings out.

'Who is in charge?'

The skipper of their steamer yells out his name, which sounds Dutch enough to pass the first test. Now for the second one.

'Shine a torch on your pips!'[40] the voice yells. Again, it is done, and the glint of said pips appears to provide enough confirmation that the skipper and all the men on board can now be told the news.

'The Japanese have made a three-point landing, about a hundred paratroopers. They've taken the aerodrome. Another hundred have taken the oil refinery.'[41]

And yet more Japanese have made landings up the Musi River near Palembang.

Christ Almighty.

In short order, Lieutenant Colonel Blackburn and his senior officers have descended the gangplank to assess the situation and determine the veracity of what they have been told. It does not take long.

A 'pukka' English Major like they just don't make them anymore confirms the news, and adds to it.

'The railway has been blown up. You had better go back to [the *Orcades*] if you don't want to get trapped.'[42]

And there's worse news still.

Singapore has fallen!

British commanders there surrendered this morning. Tens of thousands of soldiers, including 15,000 Australian soldiers, are now POWs.

When Blackburn arrives back, he calls the men onto the foredeck of the steamer so he may address them, beginning by telling them the news of Singapore.

A chill goes through the Australian troops. The very idea that Singapore – SINGAPORE! – should have fallen so easily is shocking.

Blackburn also confirms news of the Japanese landing on Sumatra.

'We are,' he says gravely to his senior officers, 'in a spot. The enemy is nearer than had been supposed. With our shortage of ammunition, it would be sheer murder to offer fight. I call on every man here for patience and the utmost discipline. As black as this night is, we are going to head back to try and find the *Orcades*, somewhere out in the bay, right now. Every man should know just how bad our "spot" will be, if it cannot be found.'[43]

And make no mistake.

'You are in shark infested waters, the harbour is mined. So, we will return in *complete silence* so the pilot can get his bearings by the sound the *Orcades*' engines are making while idle.'[44]

Got it?

Got it.

Let him repeat it anyway.

'For God's sake, men, keep quiet!'[45]

They will. They have no wish to be blown up and be eaten by sharks. They leave at 1.15 am, in darkness and in silence, but they have a nice surprise in store: 'Our lovely English crew had baskets of sandwiches and buckets of coffee for us.'[46]

Chew quietly, boys, and sip don't slurp. So, silent and enjoying a very late tea, they are taken out in the bay as, following direct orders, all eyes stay peeled for the *Orcades*, with the principal problem being that, because of strict blackout conditions in this graveyard shift of the wee-est of wee hours, it is supremely difficult to tell where their ship actually *is*. Yes, very dark shapes emerge, but in a bay filled with islands, in this tense situation, most of them bear an uncanny resemblance to the liner and the men suffer disappointments by the dozen. Doubling their trepidation is the real risk that they will come to ground on a sandbank, making them, as one of them will recall, 'a lovely target for the Nip bombers when daylight came'.[47]

Just as they are starting to despair – are they really to be marooned here? – a storm hits, which mercifully comes complete with flashes of lightning.

And there it is! A mile off their for'ard starboard quarter they can clearly see the mast and funnels of the *Orcades*, and it does not take long from there. Before dawn they have all embarked once more, and are safely out of the bay before the sun comes up, and on their way once more, apparently now bound for Java.

Sumatra is to be abandoned to the Japanese.

•

They awake and find themselves looking at the most important city of the Dutch East Indies, Batavia, which is sobering in itself.

'The harbour was filled with ships,' one man will recount, 'transports crammed with troops, Dutch battleships, British and Australian cruisers, and smaller vessels. But in spite of the apparent activity, this port – the busiest port – of Java seemed comatose. It seemed as if every human being, every slab of concrete, every blade of grass, was doomed, and knew it.'[48]

Many of the ships have fled from Singapore, or had been on their way there only to be diverted – Mayday! Mayday! Mayday! – once the news of its fall had broken.

What now?

They must wait, until their fate is decided, their orders issued. For the entire day the men are placed on standby to disembark, and are on deck with their gear packed . . . but nothing happens and darkness finally falls. They are part of a fleet ready to flee. The following day, the same, except at least this time there are rumours flying around that they may stay on the ship after all, and return to Aussie! It momentarily lifts everyone's spirits but again the day ebbs, the darkness rises and they are exactly where they were.

•

Finally, the orders come.

The 2/3rd Machine Gun Battalion, 2/2nd Pioneer Battalion, 2/6th Field Company Engineers, 2/105 General Transport Company and the 2/2nd CCS are to disembark with whatever equipment and medical resources they have. As hopeless as the situation appears to be, they must get off the ship and try to help the Dutch to stop the Japanese – or at least extract a greater cost from the Nippon subjugation.

'It was a gesture of course to the Dutch,' Weary notes. 'Resistance was crumbling, there was no hope.'[49]

Captain Jock Clarke agrees.

'Most of us fairly cheerful,' records the former dentist, 'but all realise what a criminal show the whole business is. No illusions about our fate. What a way to finish the war. So near and yet so bloody far. [The others are] off to Australia and we are to be marooned here.'[50]

Only the specialised 2/1st Anti-Aircraft Regiment – who are needed back in Australia – are to stay on board.

As they prepare to go, the *Empire Star* passes, clearly fleeing Singapore, upon which they can see some grey-uniformed Australian Army sisters.

'They waved, but there were no "Coo-ees".'[51]

So it is that on the night of 18/19 February, indeed around midnight, the *Orcades* pulls into the docks of Batavia, berthing beside 'a modern concrete pier, groaning under the weight of guns, aeroplane engines, tanks, ammunition'.[52]

Officers and gentlemen all, soldiers and batmen, for those of you disembarking – and that is all of you, bar the 2/1st – the time has come.

As Weary hoists his copious kit, packed with all his medical para-phernalia and reference books, Sister Kitty Murphy is inconsolable and hovers close. Before the merry Major departs from her warm embrace, she gives him a silver flask filled to the brim with whisky to remember her by, not that there should be *too* many worries on that account.

It is all done in heavy silence. Neither those remaining on the safety of the ship, nor those leaving it, are under any illusions about just what danger those who are landing face, and the fact that there is every chance that men are now saying goodbye to each other and will never see each other again.

But everyone is trying to downplay it. There are a few handshakes, and more than a handful of friends quietly saying to each other, 'Cheerio, Dig.'[53]

Once they are all down on the wharf, one of the Diggers who has been landed tries to lift everyone by calling up to a friend on the deck of the *Orcades*, 'See you in Aussie, mate!'[54]

CHAPTER SIX

DUTCH TREAT

*When Weary was around everyone with our mob felt that we
were safe. If Weary wasn't around for a while and he came back,
they'd say, 'Ooh Weary's back, we're right. Weary's back!'*[1]

Blue Butterworth

*The Japanese regard anyone who wages war against Japan as
a criminal, and as such treats him according to the Japanese
criminal code. It is not a nice code; it has no decent civilised
concept.*[2]

Brigadier Arthur Blackburn

19 February 1942, Batavia, ill winds

'We have just berthed in the harbour,' Private Thomas Fagan of the
105 General Transport Company chronicles, 'and have seen a lot of
boats going out, on their way to Australia. On the wharf are some
Australian soldiers who have escaped from Singapore and Dutch
soldiers all in their nice green uniforms, they look very neat. The
natives are a very clean lot.'[3]

For Weary, it is on the pier that, for the first time, he learns something of the detail of what has befallen Malaya.

'Two bearded Diggers who had escaped from Singapore,' one soldier
will recount, 'told us that the Eighth Division had "copped it".'[4]

The shock of swift defeat, the panic and peril that swept over the
city, the truth of that fiasco is given now by these unshaven men; all
illusions of order dispelled by their earthy, bitter tales. They copped
it, and they are the last cops left, a limb of empire left to be cut off
at Japan's will.

The fact that the outlook is grim is evidenced by the extreme
anxiety on the face of General Wavell, who has come down to the
docks to either greet them or assert his rights to corral the *Orcades*
to get him and his staff out before the Japanese arrive; no-one is sure.

With him is the Commanding Officer of 1 Australia Corps, General Sir John Lavarack, with his senior officers – most of whom have been here since January, commanding the sparse Australian forces currently arrayed against the Japanese, and awaiting the Diggers arriving from North Africa.

Just one look at this graveyard group on the dock, their anxious countenance, their huddled conversations, gives a fair clue on how fares the war in these parts.

One reason that General Lavarack has a face like thunder is because he is so infuriated that these fresh Australians are landing at all. He has fought bitterly against it. The Japanese are rampaging across Asia, have already landed in Sumatra and various parts of Java, and will soon be here in Batavia. It makes no sense to sacrifice Australian troops to a battle that cannot be won at the behest of the British. His men, he will later insist, were 'sacrificed to the cause of Dutch friendship'.[5] And he is right, Wavell himself insisting that the Australians be landed – some will say sacrificed – 'to avoid compromising British relations with the Dutch, and lowering British prestige'.[6]

No, really.

Prime Minister Curtin intends to stop the rot, sending a cable to his High Commissioner in London, Earle Page, informing him that, 'The destination to which [the rest of the Australian troops] should now proceed is obviously Australia which is in imminent danger of attack.'[7]

•

The Australian forces are soon deployed to do what they can.

The primary deployment is that of the 2/3rd Machine Gun Battalion, which is assigned to defend the key airfield at Kemayoran – a few miles south of the port. The men are soon in position all around it, having even secured 50 Bren and Tommy guns from the locals. True, as a unit they had never trained with Bren guns, but at least they are able to take some quick instruction, and in short order their mother's brother Robert is indeed their uncle.

And Weary's 2/2nd CCS?

Here are your orders.

You and your team are to take the train leaving shortly for the inland town of Bandoeng three hours from here – where the Dutch military has its HQ – and there you will establish the No. 1 Allied General Hospital, and receive British, Australian and Dutch wounded. There is apparently an empty ladies' college, the Christelijk Lyceum, well behind the lines, in which you can set up beds, wards and surgeries.

On this morning of 19 February 1942, smaller boats, including the high-hulled native *prau*, pull up alongside the *Orcades* and are promptly loaded with boxes of medicine and medical equipment before being, just like the men of the 2/2nd CCS, promptly loaded into lorries heading to the station. The air is thick with the pervasive scent of the glowing clove cigarettes, *kretek*, that seemingly every male of the local population has dangling from his mouth. Sadly, that mere scent can make little headway against the heavy stench coming from sweating soldiers in heavy battle dress, and that other distinctive odour that comes through the ages – fear.

As they proceed towards the train station, Weary observes the scene closely from the back of his leading lorry and is quick to note that the streets are filled with the baffled, the beaten and the bewildered. Hollow-eyed Dutch are now facing the reality that all is lost. Against a mighty Japanese war machine that has already destroyed all before it, few hold any hope that the Japanese can be stopped.

The Dutch troops they meet look like what they are – middle-aged, plump reservists. They aren't quite Dad's Army, but they are a Dutch Uncle's Army, commanded for the most part by barking brutes, unmatched by any bite in the soldiers themselves.

'We had only just a skeleton force or of what you might call real Dutch defensive people in Java . . .' Weary notes. 'By and large the Dutch Army of the Indies was civilian people wearing uniform who knew very little about war and the army and had no great enthusiasm for battle, which is probably understandable.'

Their people have ruled the locals here for the better part of 300 years, without serious challenge, and now that challenge has come, they are not remotely ready for it. Yes, there are forces raised from the native people, including the Ambonese. 'But nothing like a force to defend Java against the sort of numbers the Japanese sent.'[8]

For Weary, though this is his first time in Batavia, it all feels eerily familiar – a city about to fall to an invading enemy, just like Athens.

The local Javanese are a little more sanguine. If the Dutch who have been here for generations are about to be chased out, it is not an altogether terrible thing – and maybe even a wonderful thing. For it won't be the Javanese the Japanese are hunting, but the white man.

In short order, Weary is front and centre with the 2/2nd CCS's Commanding Officer, Colonel Norman Eadie, and the rest of the men as they are – *all aboard!* – shuffled onto a steam train, and are soon puffing their way away from the teeming streets of Batavia, and up towards the highlands of central Java. Soon enough they are surrounded by impossibly green and fertile paddy fields of rice, and mountains thickly covered with jungle . . . before, after a few hours, the landscape flattens out, wide rivers ribbon all around, the air becomes cooler and they are in the plateau uplands, in the area around the centuries-old colonial town of Bandoeng.

Upon arrival at the station, trucks take them just a couple of miles down the road to the former college for daughters of the Dutch settlers, Christelijk Lyceum, soon to be a general hospital with 1200 beds.

Waiting for them, right by the entrance of the school and under some trees where they are taking shelter from the blasting sun, are three senior officers, led by General Roy Burston – a long-time friend – who takes Weary aside and has a quiet word. He is getting out of Java with the rest of the high military command. This means that those who remain will suddenly be in an outpost rather than a bulwark, and it is almost certain that they will soon be overrun. Look, that is just the way that war goes . . .

A singularly busy 24 hours of trying to settle in ensues and the following evening, after a day spent visiting a hospital in the nearby town of Lembang – trying to grab medicine, bandages, beds and everything they can – what he most needs is a long rest . . . but this is war.

Weary wakes to find Burston and the others are all packing up, their cars being backed up to the compound, their boots opened, as a convoy of workers take suitcases and boxes. They must get away and back to the *Orcades* before it departs this very afternoon.

But a word before he goes, Weary. Other things are changing.

Now, as per the details of a cable just received, with the evacuation of all the most senior Australian officers of 1 Australia Corps, it means Lieutenant Colonel Arthur Blackburn VC is to go up to the rank of Brigadier, and will become the temporary Commanding Officer of all the Australian forces in Java, which is henceforth to be known as 'Blackforce' – about 3000 Australian soldiers strong. Lieutenant Colonel Eadie will become Senior Medical Officer to the AIF, reporting directly to Blackburn, and . . . the new commander of the 2/2nd CCS and No. 1 Allied General Hospital will be you, Weary, promoted to the rank of Temporary Lieutenant Colonel, whether you like it or not.

The first decision Weary makes with his newfound authority is to prioritise the safety of the 17 British and 15 Australian nurses who have been assembled here at Bandoeng to work in the hospital. Things are just too dangerous for them to remain. Against their bitter protest, Weary and Eadie gather the nurses in, arrange for their luggage to be put in carts, and personally escort them to the train station. They are to head back to Batavia immediately, to sail that very night on the *Orcades* with the senior officers of 1 Australia Corps staff and the last of General Wavell's South East Asia Command. It's coming into the dock at 4 pm, and is due to cast off just before midnight, with two escorting destroyers to get them clear of the Sunda Strait.

General Burston has one more thing to say to Weary before he departs in the early afternoon.

'Weary . . .' he says sorrowfully, 'I'm afraid I don't know what happens to you people but would you like me to take a letter back to Helen?'[9]

Yes. Yes, Weary would.

And it is as they say: if history doesn't repeat, it rhymes. Once again, his superior officer is heading off to relative safety with the other officers, while he is left behind to face the invaders – and their only concession to circumstances is to bear a note from him to Helen.

Still, it is something.

In short order he dashes off a quick note to Helen – using a pencil on some loose paper, still with the letterhead of AIF HQ Middle East on it – sending his love, and that impossible instruction: don't worry. He will be alright. He will find a way through this, get home, and they will get married. *Promise.*

(Oh, and given that you're heading that way, Colonel, please also take this note from me to young Kitty Murphy – you know, the fabulously fetching nurse on the *Orcades*?)

He gives both letters to Burston, and within minutes, the General and the other senior officers are gone in a swirl of dust.

Lieutenant Colonel Weary Dunlop must get to grips to establish a large working hospital. It is a mixture of Brits, Aussies and even the occasional Yank, which makes it appear as cosmopolitan as Constantinople in these parts; where uniformity has arrived long before their uniforms.

'Equipment was gathered from most diverse sources,' Weary records, 'such as the debris lying about the docks after timely diversion from Singapore, scattered minor Medical Centres, salvage from Sumatra, purchases from shops and very generous donations from our Dutch allies.'[10]

A rough kind of surgery is set up, with a triage room right beside it.

And how to replace the departed nurses?

Mercifully, Weary is able to recruit a pleasing 80 Dutch women from among the local population, the wives and daughters of merchants and farmers. They are placed under the command of a truly formidable Dutchwoman and already professional nurse, the fetching Matron 'Mickey' Borgmann-Brouwer (de Jonge), who happens to be the daughter of the second-last Governor-General of the Netherlands East Indies . . .

She is in her mid-thirties, keen and dependable, and Weary likes the shapely cut of this handsome woman's jib from the first, interested to know she has a troubled marriage, and she clearly returns his warmth in kind.

'Matron,' he tells her, after allocating the basic resources needed, 'please make this into a hospital.'[11]

For doctors, they have those of the 2/2nd CCS still intact, and Weary is particularly grateful to have superb surgeons like Majors Arthur Moon and Ewan Corlette by his side.

Arty Moon is a gynaecologist and obstetrician from North Sydney and while those two specialities are not in hot demand come wartime in this man's army, his surgical skills most certainly are, and he performs without dropping a stitch, so to speak. After enlisting in 1940, he had first shone in the 2/4 Field Ambulance, before operating in military operations all over the Middle East.

Major Ewan Corlette, affectionately known by his colleagues as 'The Gangster' for his swarthy visage and thin moustache that makes him look like a henchman of either Al Capone or Jimmy Cagney, is a witty, laconic young doctor who has a simple, old-fashioned form of patriotism that his humour keeps well hidden. The reason this man with the sparkling blue eyes joined this war is simple: 'Because my King called me.'[12]

He answered that call and will give his all; even if considerably less is required. (His first injury treated in this war practically defied belief: he was confronted with a young man who had been shot, not unheard of these days, but when the injury was explained it became ridiculous: the lad had had his mouth open when he got shot through it by a sniper's bullet that 'missed all his teeth, missed his spinal column and missed vital arteries as it exited through the back of his neck. A few stitches and he was as good as new.'[13])

Only a short time after the beds are assembled and cleaned sheets placed upon them with – what else but? – 'hospital tucks', the first contingent of wounded arrive, many of them suffering from bullet and bayonet wounds from the first serious clashes that have taken place, east of Batavia, as the British, Dutch and Australians try to stop the Japanese march on the Dutch capital.

In vain. Every bit of news that Weary and his staff can garner is that the invaders look to be unstoppable.

The thing that the Australians find most disconcerting is how attentive the Dutch soldiers are to any sort of air-raid signal. *Not* to rush to weapons, more to dive under tables and wait for the sound to stop!

Captain Jock Clarke – Weary's dentist mate – finds himself in a cafe when one of these air-raid sirens goes off and, after everyone vanishes, he serves himself and sits down to have a beer. Jock can't hear any planes, or bombs. (The long whistle and the BOOM are usually the signs.) These people are shell-shocked before the shells have even arrived. When the next air raid sounds, Jock wanders out on the deserted streets to have a look; if he squints he can just see some planes not coming in their direction. It is a change from Tobruk, where, if you bothered with sirens, you would never have had any sleep at all.

A similar scene occurs when Weary attends a meeting with local authorities, trying to scrounge some medical supplies from the Dutch, when another air-raid signal begins to roar. All the Dutch officers and soldiers immediately leap under the tables, Weary . . . goes to the window to have a look. There are no planes. Apart from the siren there is no noise at all. Weary tactfully jangles some coins in his pockets, in a manner he hopes will be seen as casual, stares out the window some more and clears his throat meaningfully. Eventually, the Dutchmen get up, sit down and their meeting resumes. This is not exactly stirring stuff, and the medico begins to wonder who on earth will be defending them when the Japanese actually turn up in person.

•

The key interest of Winston Churchill in the wake of the Singapore disaster is to prevent the Japanese continuing their western thrust towards India. The best way to stop them, clearly, would be to have the soldiers of Australia's 7th Division – those in the convoy behind the *Orcades* – to divert from going home to defend Australia and instead make a landing in Burma to try to defend India.

And while that might not suit Australia, Churchill is insistent about where his priorities lie.

The needs of Britain still come before the colonies, no matter how loyal 'Dominion No. 1'[14] might have been. In an effort to till the political ground for what he is about to ask the Australian Prime Minister John Curtin to do, Churchill cables Curtin:

```
I suppose you realise that your leading division,
the head of which is sailing south of Colombo to
[Netherlands East Indies] at this moment in our scanty
British and American shipping, is the only force that
can reach Rangoon in time to prevent its loss . . .[15]
```

Indeed. The stage is set.

In an effort to further convince Curtin, Churchill even engages the support of President Franklin Delano Roosevelt, who sends cables to the Australian leader agreeing with the British Prime Minister's line of reasoning.

Curtin is equally insistent that the Australian troops be brought home immediately to Australia to defend Australian soil. And he is staggered by Churchill's presumption. Australian troops have performed above and beyond all expectations against the Germans and Italians, while serving European interests. But because of Churchill's previous insistence on mad schemes Australia's 6th Division had been shattered in Greece and Crete; the first of the 7th Division had already been landed in the catastrophic chaos of Java which is clearly about to fall; the 8th Division had been captured in Singapore and are now mostly in the old prison located at Changi; and they had only just got the 9th Division out of Tobruk and Syria against Churchill's wishes that they stay. And *now*, Churchill wants to throw Australians into yet one more campaign, this time to defend India, not Australia – even though most of the soldiers are not on the same ships as their weaponry and despite the fact Japan threatens Australia's north? Madness, absolute *madness*.

Curtin puts the unbelievable situation succinctly in a cable to General Thomas Blamey in Cairo:

```
With Singapore, the bastion of Empire defence gone,
and with [the Dutch East Indies], the outer screen to
Australia indefensible, they propose to leave Australia
bare. 16
```

Nevertheless, Australia's representative to the United Kingdom, High Commissioner Earle Page – convinced by Churchill that England's needs must come first – implores Curtin to change his mind. Robert Menzies, from his position on the Advisory War Council, equally urges Curtin to cede to British desires and place the 7th Division in Burma's capital of Rangoon – which is even now falling to the Japanese!

Curtin's response is one for the ages: 'There are numerous geographical centres where an AIF or any other Division would be useful,' but from the viewpoint of Australia, 'there is none east of Suez of greater importance than Australia [itself].'[17]

And yet, Churchill – so dismissive of Australia's concerns that he privately characterises Australians as being 'jumpy about invasion' because they come from 'bad stock'[18] – orders that instead of returning to Australia, the troopships are to continue on their course to Burma. Yes, Winnie has railroaded them and it is a full 24 hours before he informs Curtin of what he has done!

The British PM further adds that he 'could not contemplate'[19] that the Australian PM would refuse his request for this diversion. Curtin, shocked that it has come to this, goes for a walk around Canberra's Mount Ainslie. A long one. It is so long that his principal adviser on defence issues, Frederick Shedden, organises for messages to be put up on screens in the city's movie theatre, asking that Prime Minister Curtin return to his office or at least contact it. When Curtin does return, just after midnight, he sends a cable to Churchill, affirming

Australia's right as a sovereign nation to determine where its own troops would be sent.

'We feel a primary obligation to save Australia . . . as a base for the development of the war against Japan.'[20]

Churchill replies that the ships would have to stop at Ceylon anyway for refuelling, which would give the Australian Government three or four days to consider its position. Curtin replies immediately, informing Churchill in no uncertain terms that there would be no change of heart.

Churchill accedes to Curtin's insistence. With the exception of two brigades of the 6th Division that Curtin allows to stay in Ceylon as a temporary garrison, nearly all of the rest of the convoys are headed home, home to Australia.

February 1942, Timor, Tommy guns

If only he had listened to his fine mother.

Mrs Uren had always been against young Tommy joining up, and had only relented after he had begged her, and finally overcome her fears that he would be killed. He had started by being a gunner with the Royal Australian Artillery before – after some difficulty – transferring in the middle of '41 to the AIF, which he felt would get him closer to the real front-line action.

'I wanted to be a returned soldier,' he would recount. 'I'm quite a sensitive person and . . . I couldn't take the criticism that Darcy had taken.'[21]

(In the Great War, the great Australian boxer Les Darcy had been vilified all the way to the grave for declining to join up.)

And he'd seen action alright. After he and his cohort from the 2/1st Heavy Battery had been shipped to Timor to defend it, the Japanese had started bombing their positions from Australia Day onwards.

•

The sun is shining nearly as hotly as the wind is blowing, and the savvy seagulls of Darwin Harbour have already sought shade in the mangrove trees that ring the water.

For the Australian sailors on deck of the minesweeper HMAS *Gunbar*, the best they can do is to put their backs on the lee side of the ship's bridge and talk languidly in the tropical torpor, when one glances up to see a tiny flock of . . . something . . . approaching from far away, all of them in remarkably neat formation. At first he thinks they must be a flock of birds flying high, but looking closer he realises: they're planes, and remarkably well-flown ones at that.

They must be bloody good pilots to keep it that tight.

And what now? As more of the gazing sailors watch closely, they observe the planes releasing tiny silver objects, like a whole bunch of sixpences, before . . . all hell breaks loose. Before their very eyes, it seems like half of Darwin starts exploding. The sound of bursting bombs rolls over the water, angry plumes of flame and smoke shoot skywards and the crash of buildings being felled fills their ears.

It's Pearl Harbor! It's bloody Pearl Harbor, all over again!

Well, nearly.

In fact, these are Japanese bombers with escort Zeros – 188 planes in all – from the same aircraft carrier fleet that had destroyed Pearl Harbor, and they have much the same plan as then. Recognising that Darwin is a base for naval and air operations against Japanese forces, and also an important conduit for transporting *matériel* to Allied troops across South-east Asia trying to thwart them – it is important that it be destroyed as quickly and savagely as possible.

By the time the first wave of these demons of death have shrieked back whence they came, eight Allied ships lie at the bottom of Darwin Harbour, the RAAF airfield is destroyed along with 23 of its planes, buildings around the port are in ruins, 243 Australians are dead and a lot more than that are wounded.

Australians in the Territory panic, as it seems clear that the bombing is merely a prelude to an invasion of their substantially undefended shores – with most of Australia's fighting men still in the Middle East, or on the high seas coming back, or now POWs in Singapore which had fallen just four days ago!

Such is the certainty that an invasion is occurring that many people – before fleeing on the ever more clogged roads heading south – burn their houses and sheds to deny the Japanese any succour.

Very little of this wild panic and certainty of invasion shows up in the public pronouncement of Prime Minister John Curtin, who calmly says: 'In this first battle on Australian soil it will be a source of pride to the public to know that the armed forces and the civilians comported themselves with the gallantry that is traditional in the people of our stock.'[22]

It is a statement to allay wider panic in the country's main population centres, and the only way Curtin is able to get away with it is because wartime censorship still restricts more truly alarming news getting out from remote Darwin. But his government becomes still more worried as day by day the bombing on Darwin continues.

23 February 1942, Timor, eye is on the sparrow

There they are!

Bombardier Tom Uren and the rest of Sparrow Force – the Australian soldiers dispatched to Timor from Darwin just after the bombing of Pearl Harbor – have been expecting exactly this for several days, but the sight is still a shock. Now appearing over the rise on these northern shores of Timor – actually coming at the Australians from behind – are so many Japanese soldiers, literally hundreds of them, that it is clear the Australians have two choices.

An emissary has even come forward with a message to that effect: 'Surrender or be annihilated.'[23]

Given the Australians have already lost 150 killed and wounded by Japanese bombs, and are themselves running out of both ammunition and rations, the leading officers of Sparrow Force are quick to make the decision.

They not only throw down their weapons and put their hands up, they command the soldiers to do the same.

It does not come easily to Tom Uren and his mates from 2/1st Heavy Battery, but they follow the order. They are soon manacled to each other, beaten up, and marched to Koepang Bay. From now, they are POWs.

One thing that strikes them is the seeming uniformity of the Japanese; they look as though they have been pressed out of a factory. Tom Uren keeps thinking how odd it is to be captured by foes who are so much shorter than you. It doesn't seem right somehow, but it is real and they are conquered.

But even after they surrender, the Japanese still attack! Yes, a bloody Japanese aircraft bombs them and their captors before their status is made clear: they are prisoners, for the duration. (Whether that is the duration of the war or the duration of their lives is the next question.)

With the bombs having taken out many of the Japanese trucks – one of which, happily, had been filled with Japanese soldiers – they must march 25 exhausting miles back to Koepang Bay, where their first task is to build the rudiments of their own POW camp.

There is only one upside.

'The Japanese front-line troops treated us well as they respected us for the way we fought . . .'[24]

The Japanese respect for Tom Uren goes up when, hearing that he is a boxing champion, they insist he fight their regimental ju-jitsu champion. As POWs and captors momentarily forget their situation to cheer on their own man, the six foot two giant effortlessly parries the ju-jitsu blows. All the Australians know – because they have seen him in action – that Tom could give the Jap a beating like a red-headed stepson, but this is not the occasion for such a beating. Instead – and as gently as he can – Uren simply drops the fellow, with a left cross to the jaw, and catches him before he can go down too hard.

'That kind of built my reputation with the Japs as well.'[25]

•

For those 681 Australians aboard HMAS *Perth* – now journeyed here from active duty in the Greek campaign – the news is alarming.

Two Japanese invasion convoys have been spotted approaching the eastern and western ends of Java. The Allied convoy of shipping that *Perth* is a part of – including the Dutch light cruisers *De Ruyter* and *Java*, the heavy cruisers USS *Houston* and HMS *Exeter*, and nine destroyers – is ordered to engage, to stop them.

And there they are!

Almost immediately, *Exeter* is hit! From the first it is obvious that the Japanese firepower is simply overwhelming, and ship after ship is hit. For the moment, *Perth* moves to put up a smokescreen between the Japanese armada and *Exeter*, to help it limp away, which inevitably brings still more shells *Perth*'s way. Some are devastating but at least none do mortal damage, and *Perth* is able to hang on till dark, when it breaks off and heads to Batavia. It is a fortunate escape given that, in its wake, the armada leave three British destroyers and two Dutch cruisers on the bottom, with 2300 sailors lost. Both sides retreat to assess the damage, with the Allied ships heading to Tanjung Priok, the main port of Batavia, arriving at two o'clock the following afternoon to refuel, only for that process to be paused as a Japanese air raid occurs in the middle of it! Of the original Allied fleet, it is only *Perth* and *Houston* that are in shape to go out again now, with the Dutch ship HNLMS *Evertsen* following two hours later.

They are well underway again by dark, and on *Perth* the skipper's voice comes over the loudspeaker once out of port to say, 'We are heading for the Sunda Strait, and don't expect to meet any enemy force.'

Able Seaman Frank McGovern's first thought is, 'Oh you beaut, we're right.'[26]

That is the exact sentiment of Captain Hec Waller himself. The Dutch have assured him that the strait is clear, and they should know.

Five minutes to midnight, 28 February 1942, Sunda Strait, full fathom five

Not long after they have entered the Sunda Strait, Captain Hec Waller has woken from a brief kip and arrived on the bridge to find his navigator, John Harper, looking intently through a rangefinder, when . . . he gives a start.

Can it be?

There seems to be a dark blob off to starboard where there should be only moonlight. Suddenly, an alarmed cry from one of the look-outs above.

'Ship, sir, bearing green oh five!'

All eyes on the bridge turn to see, indeed, a dark and rather menacing blur off the starboard bow, perhaps five nautical miles away.

'Very good. Make a challenge.'[27]

In short order, the challenge – via the flashing lights of an Aldis projector on the foredeck – goes out. There is no response, bar two letters, 'UB', which means nothing in any language.

'Challenge again,' says Waller.

No reply at all. Instead, the approaching blob turns broadside and looks a lot like a . . .

'Jap destroyer!'

'Action stations. Sound the alarm!'

Aboard the Australian cruiser, sirens are wailing and every man is scurrying through narrow gangways and up and down ladders to get to their action stations.

Chief Petty Officer Ray Parkin races to his post at the lower steering position. *Perth*'s engines are roaring at full steam and the whole ship is vibrating under the strain as it surges forth at 32 knots, but the sound of shells exploding overwhelms all. Just off to their stern, five cables behind, Parkin can see the USS *Houston* – a heavy cruiser – coming under the same attack, with her own guns blazing, which at least gives them some hope of surviving this.

Alas, the Japanese warship they have spotted is just one of many and both *Perth* and *Houston* are soon engulfed in a battle royale. Just minutes after contact, they have flashes of big guns coming from their port and starboard, from perhaps as many as a dozen ships. Christ, they have had the incredible bad luck to bump into a bloody Japanese strike force. And the ships are now striking them instead of the west coast of Java!

Right on midnight, *Perth*'s Captain Hec Waller, with little ammunition left, decides the best hope is to force a passage through the Sunda Strait, and orders all engines on full speed ahead.

'The whole ship,' Ray Parkin will recall, 'was alive with orders streaming out and information streaming in, like the blood pounding through the heart of a human body. The glare of searchlights; the flash, blast and roar of her own guns, tracer ammunition stitching light across the sky; phosphorescent wakes entangling; ships on fire; star-shell festooned in short strings in the sky – all these confused the evidence of one's own eyes. Brilliance and blackness struggled for supremacy.'[28]

The worst thing, though?

At one point, when star-shells throw an ethereal light over the whole area they can see just what they are up against. *Dozens* of Japanese ships! One sailor will later comment that he 'did not know that there were so many destroyers in the world'.[29]

And those destroyers are now so close, wolves closing in on an already wounded prey, that they can actually see the Japanese flag – 'the fried egg'[30] as the Australian sailors refer to it – fluttering from the bows of some of their attackers. They are *so* close that *Perth*'s six-inch guns are set at just two degrees elevation, as the opposing forces fire at each other at point-blank range, and some Japanese sailors are even seen to be firing pistols and rifles at them! It is 'just like a bar room brawl',[31] but *Perth* and *Houston* remain so badly outnumbered that their only hope remains to force a passage through and get into open water.

Rrrrramming speed.

Perth is like a raging racehorse, whipped into frantic motion, straining with every sinew, fomenting in foam, and now racing at her maximum speed of 32.5 knots, when suddenly, the entire 7000-ton ship *lifts* out of the water, like it has gone over a major aquatic log, before settling down once more, albeit with 20 knots knocked off their speed. A blast of heat and light rolls over the ship.

Was that . . . ?

A *torpedo*!

'I was on the upper deck,' Frank McGovern will recount, 'and I was thrown off my feet and a few of the others were too.'[32]

They have been struck for'ard on the starboard side, just below the waterline.

With his ear to the voice-pipe, Parkin can clearly hear the crackly if not yet cracked voice of Captain Waller say, 'That's torn it.'[33]

Within two minutes, however, Captain Waller's voice again comes through, this time on the ship's speakers: 'Prepare to abandon ship.'

No sooner does he say it than a second torpedo hits, also on the for'ard starboard side – and that's *really* torn it, with ever more water now pouring through the shattered hull – just as shells start to land all over the ship.

'Abandon ship!'

And now a third hit, well aft on the starboard side, and finally a fourth torpedo on the starboard.

The Captain barks his orders:

'Lower steering position! Chief Quartermaster! Leave both engines half speed ahead – I don't want the Old Girl to take anyone with her.'

It is important that after the men jump, the ship is well clear before she goes down, and doesn't suck survivors with her.

'Do you require anyone to stand by the telegraph, sir?' Chief Petty Officer Parkin asks.

Mercifully, however, the skipper has no such desire. Rather, with 'all the warmth a father would use to tell a silly child to do something for its own good', his next words are ones that Parkin would always remember: 'Get the buggery out of it!'[34]

Chief Petty Officer Parkin – dressed only in shorts, sand-shoes and a belt from which hangs his service knife and a small marlinspike – is scrambling.

'The captain has given the order,' he yells. 'Every man for himself, get out!'[35]

'Righto,' he yells, 'chuck everything over the side and follow it!'[36]

The rafts are thrown and Parkin pauses only long enough, using the illumination of the Japanese searchlights, to look for a clear bit of water that is not cluttered with wreckage, or other survivors, and leaps. The impact of the water knocks the breath out of him, strips his sandshoes off, and breaks his belt but, somehow, miraculously, he is still alive.

After some time, Ray Parkin and a few others scramble onto one of the three dozen small balsa rafts the ship had had on deck, and consider their next move, even as Japanese destroyers bear down upon them, awash in a farrago of flotsam, wreckage, oil and dying men – the Japanese searchlights now seeking them out. Yet more shells land all around. On other rafts, and in the water, men are screaming and dying.

Still chugging forth, just as Captain Waller had planned, *Perth* is now 500 yards onwards and continues to be pounded by torpedoes – now seven in all – and shells. They know it cannot last and . . . sure enough.

A great cry goes up – 'She's gone'[37] – and so she is, tragically taking with her Captain Hec Waller and two thirds of her crew. The *Houston* meets the same fate shortly afterwards, as does the Dutch ship *Evertsen* which has arrived just in time to be destroyed, much closer to the shore.

In short order, a Japanese destroyer arriving in the waters where *Perth* has sunk towers over the Australian survivors on the little rafts, and whatever else they have found that floats like boats. They look up to see white-suited Japanese officers gazing down upon them, with one of them even calling out with remarkably well-articulated English: 'We bloody good boys now, eh, Aussie?'[38]

For the moment, the Japanese make no effort to bring them on board, preferring to look for their own survivors first.

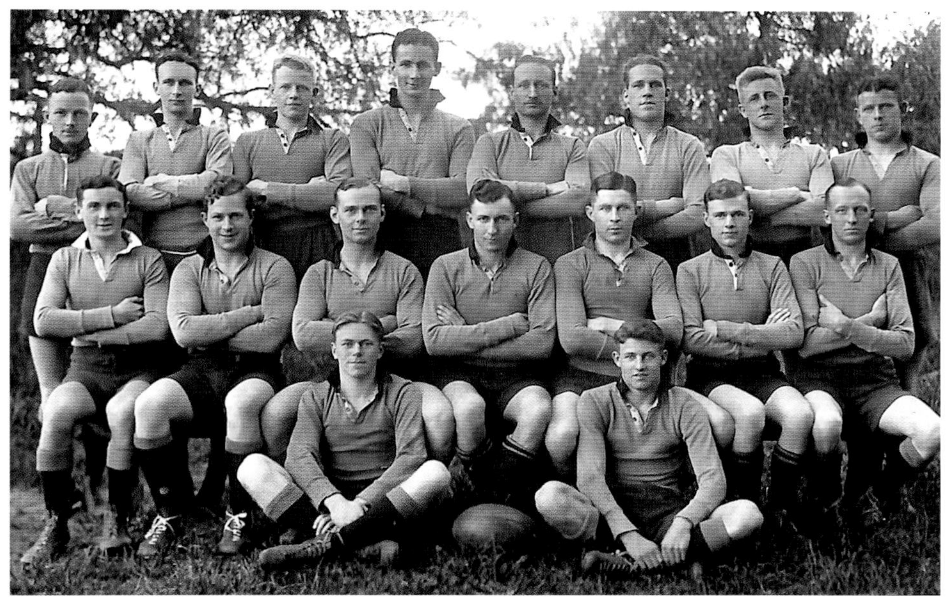

Melbourne University Rugby Football Club, Inter-Varsity Champions, 1931. Weary is fourth from left, top row — towering above his team-mates. He would go on to become a Wallaby, playing memorable Test matches for Australia in 1932 and 1934.

Australian troops disembark from the *Orcades*. Many, including Weary and the 2/2nd CCS, disembarked at Batavia and travelled to the inland town of Bandoeng to establish the No. 1 Allied General Hospital, before being made prisoners of war by the Japanese. (AWM 011779/29)

Major Arthur Moon, 1940.
(SLV)

Laurens van der Post.

Major Ewan Corlette.
(Courtesy Andrew Corlette)

Members of 2/1st Heavy Battery, which formed part of Sparrow Force, tasked with the defence of Timor. Bombardier Tom Uren is fourth from left, holding a tin mug and a newspaper. With the fall of Timor, they became prisoners of war and worked on the Thai–Burma Railway construction. (AWM P10957.002)

Changi Prison. (AWM 117645)

AIF POW theatre, Changi, pen and ink drawing by Murray Griffin, a captured official war artist. The building had been a workshop and was used by an Australian POW Concert Party until it was required for accommodation. (AWM ART26496)

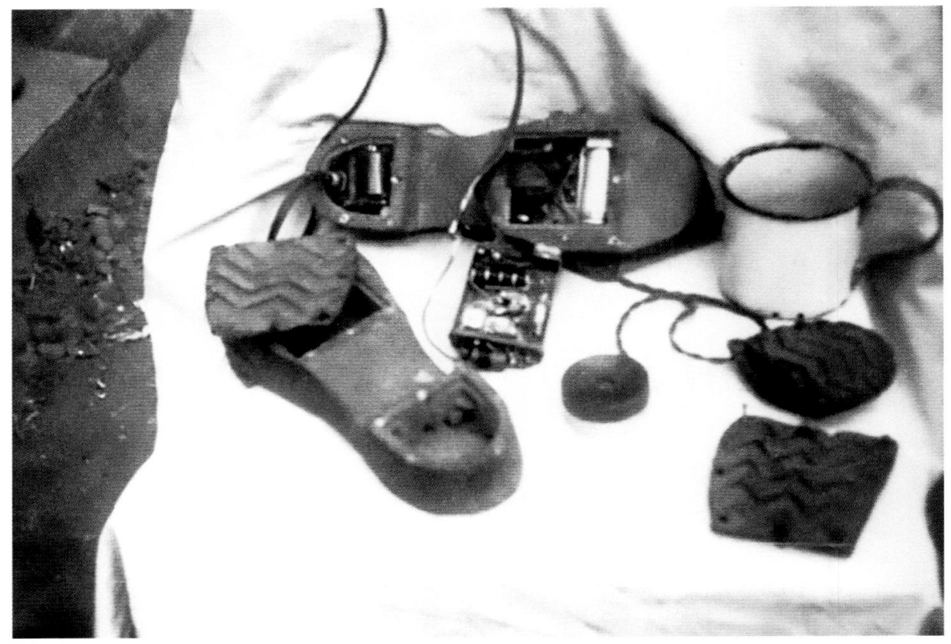

A small wireless set built into the heel and sole of a pair of sandals by POWs in Changi. Hidden radios were the only way to get news of the war's progress. At huge risk, Weary hid several radios over his time as a POW. (AWM 043597)

Interior of a prisoner hut, Changi Prison. (AWM 019189)

Watering point near the Thai border. Men briefly are allowed out of the stifling and crowded box cars being used to transport them to the Railway work camps. This photo was taken at great risk by POW George Aspinall.

Chief Petty Officer Ray Parkin, RAN.
(Parkin Family)

'Rice in the rain, rain in the rice'. Drawn at Hintok by Ray Parkin. (Parkin Family)

Ray Parkin's watercolour, 'Mountain at Sunset, Konyu River POW Camp, January 1943'. (Parkin Family/SLV MS13601)

Ray Parkin's watercolour of butterflies. Parkin was a devotee of their beauty and painted them as often as he could. (Parkin Family/SLV MS13601)

Cholera hospital, Hintok. Watercolour by POW Jack Chalker. Chalker secretly made drawings of the various camps and conditions endured by the prisoners. (AWM ART90845)

Cholera tent, Hintok. Watercolour by POW Jack Chalker. (AWM ART90844)

'Two malarias and a cholera'. Drawn at Hintok camp by Ray Parkin. (Parkin Family)

'Ghosts!' Men sitting on a log outside Weary's clinic, Hintok. Original drawing by Ray Parkin, which he later reproduced as a drypoint etching. (Parkin Family)

CHAPTER SEVEN

POW POW-WOW

He was a man. As a doctor, it made him a great doctor because everybody that came in front of Weary, a no-hoper, anybody, was a person. And he was an equal of Weary in Weary's mind. He was a person to be helped, to be served. That made him a great doctor. But it did more than that. It made him a great human being . . . His self-effacement made him . . . the men sensed this, they knew it. And they would back him to the hilt.[1]

Chief Petty Officer Ray Parkin, 1987

1 March 1942, Bandoeng, black and forth

The situation is more than desperate, and the 3000 Australians of Blackforce are fighting for their lives. With the Japanese now on the outskirts of Batavia, the Australian orders are to hold them off for as long as possible, which is no easy task as Blackforce is facing an entire Japanese division, 20,000 strong with air and artillery support. (After the sinking of *Perth* and *Houston*, together with other smaller ships, the Imperial Japanese Navy is now unchallenged in these seas and has been able to land its entire invasion force without trouble.)

And yet still the Australians under Brigadier Arthur Blackburn VC do not budge. With every flanking move by the Japanese, the Australians shift in turn and fight. Blackburn has never been prouder to be an Australian, particularly as his men are fighting like alley-cats in a sack, despite having no more than rifles, a few light machine guns, three small mortars and just 600 hand grenades between them. All they can do is make each one count, just as they make every shot count.

'In the frantic endeavour to get round us and encircle us,' Blackburn will proudly recount, 'the Japanese had extended nearly four miles south of our original position. But my men had moved south parallel with them, and were *still* holding them. They were doing more than holding them. They were actively attacking them, instead of waiting to be attacked.'[2]

•

As the days pass, the tide of the battered, bloodied and wounded washing up on the shores of Bandoeng only thickens.

Today, however, one of the new patients looks strangely familiar to Weary, though he cannot be sure, as much of his jaw has been blown away, while the rest of his face has numerous wounds.

The only way to be certain is to lift his shirt . . . and there it is. Just down on his lower abdomen is the fresh scar where Weary himself had removed Private Eric Beverly's appendix two weeks earlier. Then, that simple operation had immediately saved him and put him on the path to recovery. Now, it is going to be touch and go whether he can even be kept alive for the next few hours. The only thing going for him medically right now is that at least his appendix won't burst . . .

Bluey, pass the clips, the syringes and the scalpel. We begin anew.

It really is touch and go, but . . . Eric Beverly lives.

8 March 1942, Bandoeng, licked and ticked

Outgunned, outnumbered and nearly out of ammo, Brigadier Arthur Blackburn VC and his brave men of Blackforce are still able to prevent the Japanese outflanking them, and are able to keep the road and rail link between Batavia and Bandoeng open for a crucial 72 hours, allowing the Dutch forces to get away.

And yet still the order had come from the Dutch Commander-in-Chief – after his own forces had successfully retired from Batavia – for Blackforce to itself withdraw, which appals Blackburn.

'My men were still as full of fight and as confident as when they first met the enemy. The spirit shown was not enthusiastic bravado. A number of them wanted to know why we were withdrawing when we had licked the Japanese, licked them badly.'[3]

Perhaps, if the Dutch themselves had been able to hold on and help the Australians, they could have become a successful guerrilla army, living in the mountains and coming down to strike the Japanese wherever they found them. But they cannot, and all that Blackforce can do is to act as a rear-guard to the Dutch and British forces that withdraw to Bandoeng through them.

•

As the flood of wounded coming to Bandoeng from the coast intensifies, Weary Dunlop and his fellow surgeons hear more and more stories from the shattered and battered survivors of Japanese atrocities, of swarms of the soldiers from Nippon overwhelming all before them and leaving behind almost nothing but corpses.

And, in fact, more appalling news comes from even further afield.

'The tide of disaster flowing from Singapore,' Weary will record, 'brought sensational news of rape and mass killing including the Alexandra Hospital massacre of staff and patients. We were too busy to feel much fear. The daily flow of casualties due to air action swelled heavily on 4 and 5 March 1942.'[4]

On 6 March 1942, Weary gets word from the Assistant Director of Medical Services, Lieutenant Colonel 'Pete' Maisey: 'The Dutch are about to capitulate and British Forces will retire past Bandoeng toward the south coast. The hospital must continue functioning and will most certainly be captured.'[5]

Weary does not hesitate.

'I shall remain with the hospital,' he informs Colonel Maisey. 'I hope that some staff and fitter patients shall have the opportunity to move . . .'[6]

And good luck to them. But what choice does he have?

None. He simply will not leave the seriously wounded, for he has little doubt that, if the sick are abandoned, the invaders will show no mercy. But perhaps if he and some others stay behind, looking after those who cannot look after themselves, the Japanese will have the humanity to allow their continued care. It is the only chance the wounded have.

Others can choose a different fate, and may still escape.

After contact with a remnant of the army is established and arrangements made, Weary is able to make a handsome offer to his staff and patients: 'I will guide those eligible and willing to escape to a night rendezvous with the column twenty miles south of Bandoeng and then return.'

A hurried consultation takes place without him. The verdict?

'We would prefer to remain with you, sir.'

All of you?

So it seems, but still he must be sure.

'If you want to go,' he repeats to a mass of them that inevitably includes Blue Butterworth, '*go.*'

There will be no hard feelings, no repercussions. Weary will stay here with a skeleton staff, and that will be that.

Their answer remains the same: 'We prefer to stay with you.'[7]

And Blue, for one, will ever after be proud of that fact.

'Not a man,' he will tell anyone who will listen. 'Everybody . . . wanted to stay with Weary. Nobody left . . .'[8]

Weary informs the incredulous Dutch. His people, his doctors, his nurses, his officers, his men and his patients – some 620 of the latter – are all staying.

'I'd love to be going on, trying to escape, but there we are.'

Of the patients and staff, *all* want to STAY?

Yes.

'Bit of an embarrassment, really,'[9] Weary will note.

But also more than a bit bloody moving. They will all stand together, even when no troops are there to defend them. The thought of Alexandra is in Weary's mind; this may be a very short display of bravery, but there we are.

'Consequently,' he will recount, 'I made the lone journey to the rendezvous through jumpy road patrols.'[10]

After delivering the news, he makes his way back to the hospital, where he and his senior medicos and officers set about destroying all sensitive documents that the Japanese might find useful about just who their patients are, and where they might have been deployed.

Positions everyone. They are close. And remember: upon being questioned, you are only obliged to give them your name, rank and number.

For the next three days, the British flag flying above the No. 1 Allied General Hospital at Bandoeng is the sole such symbol flying in the Dutch East Indies.

And in the end – for they all know the end must come – it is like the detritus that blows before a coming cyclone.

First come the refugees, the fleeing Dutch settlers who have lost their homes, their livelihoods, their entire worlds – everything in fact except their lives, which they are determined to save now, as they rush through. And now come the retreating Dutch troops, shattered men, who have seen the horror up close and can barely believe they are alive when so many have been killed. They have the eyes of men who have seen shocking things they never conceived could exist. Some of those passing through pause for treatment. Most of them just keep hurrying on, flittering phantoms of a fading empire.

The Japanese have sent forward word that all Allied flags are to be lowered as a sign of surrender as they approach.

To hell with that, Weary orders the British flag to be flown high. All of them. The Japanese can lower it when they arrive. And now he walks out into the street to watch his captors enter. The Japanese troops are marching through the empty street towards them, the silent crowds watching as though it is a ghoulish parade. It really is 'a most orderly occupation of Bandoeng', at least until a Dutch woman in a small car starts 'driving madly through the Japanese army'. The soldiers are too stunned to shoot; they can't see what she is playing at, and the car cleaves the troops and drives right up to Weary! The female driver gets out and says: 'Oh, Colonel, come quickly, they are looting my house!'

By 'they' you mean the invading Japanese Army?

'Well, Madam,' answers Weary, 'what did you expect?'

'WHAT!' bellows the woman. 'You will not come to assist a Dutch lady?'

Actually, madam, I have some patients to look after and the troops you just drove through are about to arrest me.

Oh, there's always an excuse, isn't there?

The woman looks as though she is about to spit in Weary's face, she cannot believe that such bad manners exist in Java!

'So, I shall get a Dutch officer?' she says sarcastically. Well, Weary knows many Dutch officers, but they all left just a few hours ago. 'There are two of your Red Cross nurses in my house! They shall be raped!'

Well, you might have led with that, instead of the looting. Alright, Weary will go with her. Before he does, he will just quickly get some weapons. Weary has two .38 pistols in a safe, at the ready for an emergency. This qualifies. He frees his guns and realises he has nowhere to keep them. He can't hold them in his hands, he'll get shot. So, feeling slightly ridiculous, and a little like that star in the cowboy movies, Gary Cooper, he sticks one in each pocket of his bush jacket. Weary is not going to win a quick-draw shootout, but it's something.

His annoyed Dutch constituent is still waiting.

'Very well, Madam,' says Weary. 'If you wish, I will come. I don't think much good will come of it.'

Neither does Staff Sergeant Alan Gibson, who rushes forward:

'Let me come with you, sir!'

The three of them get in the car and . . . drive once more through the Japanese troops. Weary holds up his Red Cross insignia as though it is a magic totem, and it seems to be exactly that, because the heavily armed soldiers part and let them through. There is a lot to be said for bluff, nerve and stupidity in getting you through a crisis. They arrive at the Dutch woman's house and, sure enough, it is full of Japanese soldiers. They seem very tired, but every weary eye is gazing at Weary now as he gets out of the car. In that instant he realises that if they touch his jacket they will feel a gun, two guns actually, and one bullet will be going into him. Weary waves his arms and yells at them, displaying his Red Cross brassards.

There are nurses here! Dutch nurses! *You heard me.* They are under my command! I may be about to be your prisoner, but these women are under my orders and I want them at the hospital, *at once*!

Well, two fewer nurses means there is room for two more tired soldiers in the house, and the Dutch nurses are bundled out and into the car. It is the last moment of pure freedom that Weary Dunlop will know for many, many moons. From now on he will have to ask the Japanese for permission to move. He and Staff Sergeant Gibson slowly drive back through empty streets to what used to be their workplace, and is now their prison.

For yes, the realisation has truly struck.

They are now POWs, under the command of their Japanese captors, 'in the bag',[11] in the Diggers' vernacular.

Bluey, for one, is shocked that it has come to this.

'Fancy being collared,' he will record, barely able to believe that the little Japanese soldiers are taking over.[12]

I mean, we've been knocked over by *them*?

Look, yes, their discipline is extraordinary, and they are clearly superb soldiers, trained to within an inch of their life, and then two inches. Even though it quickly becomes obvious that, as military machines go, theirs is well-oiled and formidable – witness their morning PT training, where they collectively go through their moves in such synchronicity you gasp. But they *are Japanese*, for Christ's sake.

There is one form of open rebellion left – bunting. Although many local houses now feature a craven collection of hastily created Rising Sun flags, waving in their windows and flapping from flagpoles, when you enter the hospital, you can still see the Union Jack, the Southern Cross and the Red Cross flying. They will be torn down soon, but they are there to salute when any Digger walks to their prison at present.

And speaking of salutes, their captors quickly make one thing clear – on pain of beating for those who do not instantly obey. Every time an Allied prisoner sees a Japanese officer or soldier, you must immediately stand and salute them. Yes, even an Allied colonel must get to his feet to salute a Japanese private. It is humiliating but makes the point: even the most elite of the prisoners are no more than dirt beneath the feet of the Emperor's forces.

You have so disgraced yourselves in surrendering it is simply not right you even attempt to look us in the eye, so look down as you salute!

•

Mercifully, for the moment, the newly arrived Japanese leave those in the hospital alone – and there are many, as no fewer than 1300 patients have been treated since Weary's arrival, most of them still here – as they await orders. The only substantial effect is that all supplies of medicine have stopped, even as the numbers of wounded coming their way become a bloody *flood*. Not only are all the wards soon full but so too are the corridors and verandas soon covered with supine figures, to the point that one has to pick one's way carefully through them, as through a minefield, to avoid stepping on grievously wounded men.

For that problem there will be no cure bar an armistice, but in terms of getting more medicine and bandages, Weary is at least able to help solve that problem by finagling his way to see the newly arrived Japanese General Masao Maruyama, who is in command in this area, to arrange a pass for himself and a Dutch Liaison Officer to move around Bandoeng in relative freedom – which they use to secure more medical supplies from Bandoeng and surrounds.

True, the passes provided are only for three days, but using the skills of one of the Australian soldiers, who used to be in the printing game, they are able to extend it by a week!

•

As it is, the Dutch order for its own and all Allied forces to surrender comes through at 10 am on 8 March.

Sorry, what? We Australians have come to the Dutch East Indies to save you Dutch, and now *you* are surrendering after barely more than a fortnight's fight and 'ordering' us to do the same? After risking our lives to save you, we are meant to just lay down our arms, with no further support from you, and be taken prisoner for the rest of the war?

Treachery!

Brigadier Blackburn ignores the order.

And even when the British order – via Air Vice Marshal Paul Maltby, the highest-ranking Briton in Java – arrives at 2.30 pm on the same day, ordering the same, Blackburn ignores that, too.

We are Australian and do not choose to surrender.

'Being unwilling to join in any surrender until compelled to do so, and being completely confident that we could go on defeating the Japanese at least for some time to come, I ordered a further withdrawal into the mountains south of Garoet [50 miles south-east of Bandoeng].'[13]

We sons of the Southern Cross will fight on.

'I occupied a position on the roads leading to the mountains to the south coast, intending to continue my resistance in this area,' Blackburn will recount. 'In Garoet, there was a reasonable quantity of food and ammunition and my supply officers commandeered a large supply of these as to enable my forces to be self-contained.'[14]

For now, they will push on down one of the roads to the south coast in the hope that one of his previous messages to Australia to send ships to evacuate them at that point had got through.

•

Others, however, have little choice but to obey the order to surrender.

Among them is Aircraftsman 1st Class Bill Griffiths, who, when the news comes through, is on assignment with a couple of fellow Englishmen trying to pick up a group of stranded RAF men up in the mountains and deliver them to safety, back with the main body of British forces. They arrive to find the RAF men exactly where reported, albeit with the white flags of surrender already flying above the schoolhouse in the village where they have taken shelter.

Griffiths feels useless, but there is absolutely 'nothing to do but sit tight and await developments'. Alas, those very developments prove to come dressed in Japanese uniform and carrying rifles, a whole squad of soldiers, 'looking extremely arrogant and proud of themselves',[15] as they surround the school and stop any who attempt to leave. It is a bitter thing to be complicitly conquered, and the sting of it is felt by every surrendered soul. In short order they are bundled into the back of a truck and are on their way to a newly formed POW camp:

> I can remember looking out at the countryside, green and beautiful and apparently quite normal, with the natives strolling about leading their everyday lives, cars on the road, kids coming home from school. Nothing had happened, up to that point, to prepare us for what was to come. The truck left the villages and the paddy fields behind and started to grind its way up into the mountains. After a quarter of an hour or so we stopped, and the Jap guards ordered us out of the lorries.[16]

•

Brigadier Blackburn and Blackforce proceed on the track winding back to the south coast of Java, hoping for their rescue by Australia's answer to Dunkirk, only to find nearing arrival that all the radios capable of transmitting to Australia had been systematically destroyed and no ships have been sent for them. The jungle presses, hunger rises, the rain never stops falling and their supplies run low.

What now? Blackburn estimates that they have enough food and ammunition to last for 30 days if they fight on. But in this area there is bugger-all shelter and the rain simply does not stop falling. Medical supplies they have ordered have not come, and his medical officer, Eadie, advises gravely that these conditions are so ripe for malaria and pneumonia that the diseases might well fell half of the 3000 men they have with them.

'I cannot accept responsibility for the health of the troops,' Eadie tells him, 'if we take to the mountains as proposed.'

Very well, then.

'I reluctantly decided that in the best interests of my troops and their lives I must capitulate. Despite the fact that my troops all desired to continue resistance, until compelled by force of arms or shortage of food and munitions to surrender, I [decided] that I would join in the surrender.'[17]

But if you are going to give up, you have to do it properly. To the victors go the spoils, so let's get cracking and spoil the spoils before they get here. Wreck as much gear and equipment as you can.

Put your ammo on open ground, and the rain in these tropics will soon render it useless, with any luck. If you have a rifle in good working order, fix that by pouring some acid from a truck battery down it, which will also wreck the truck – a win for all. To be on the safe side, why not wedge your rifle behind the bumper bar of a truck while you're at it and bend it as much as you can.

Be creative in your destruction. There is a strange, end-of-school feeling to this open sabotage; it is a topsy-turvy feeling to be ordered to engage in behaviour which would have had you in the stockade or a padded cell if you'd done it last week.

Now, the next piece of mischief will take some nerve. We are going to hop in some tanks, armoured cars, trucks and the Bren carriers and drive them over a cliff. It is a bizarre spectacle and oddly satisfying to watch the men leap from slow-moving machines that chug on towards this army Armageddon.

And it doesn't stop there:

> All our precious presents we bought at Colombo, stores, tobacco, typewriters; and many of our trucks were pushed down the steep hillsides to render them useless to the Japanese Army. Chaos reigned . . . Many of the lads were drunk on whiskey obtained from the natives who appeared from nowhere to make a quick buck . . .[18]

Now, Blackburn tells the men, when the Japanese do arrive, simply go on parade without arms. You only get one chance to make a first impression and a good parade will: 'show the enemy that we are better trained and disciplined than they are'. (Now this is a few steps beyond clutching at straws, it is grabbing at haystacks, but what the hell, it's worth a try.) This will be the last order they get from Blackburn of his own volition; soon all their orders will come from men born in another land. No, not England: Japan.

But it does not take long. In short order they can see the Japanese approaching, rifles and machine guns at the ready, clearly prepared to shoot if there's the tiniest sign of further resistance.

Accompanied by other senior officers – Colonel Searle, Air Vice Marshal Maltby and General Sitwell – Brigadier Blackburn goes forward under a white flag and they are eventually steered to the Japanese Commander-in-Chief General Maruyama, who orders them *all* to sign a document of unconditional surrender.

Blackburn agrees, on one condition – the negotiations taking place courtesy of an interpreter – that they signed, 'Subject to our rights as prisoners of war [under the] Geneva Convention of 1929.'[19]

It is done.

General Maruyama's officers insist that Blackburn and his own senior officers return to their troops and keep them under control, until such times as the Japanese are ready to take them in as POWs. They must immediately hand over all weaponry, ammunition and vehicles.

Blackburn does exactly that, and for the next fortnight has his men make camp in tea plantations situated just south of Garoet.

In the whole episode Brigadier Blackburn has just one satisfaction. As the Commanding Officer he is heavily interrogated by Japanese Intelligence officers and senior officers of the invading force, and both refuse to believe that he had commanded just 3000 Australians. Both he and his senior officers are threatened with severe punishments if they don't tell the truth about the true numbers.

'That is a lie,' a Japanese colonel says to Brigadier Blackburn with no little force. 'Nothing less than a division could possibly have held us up the way we were held up. I must know where you have hidden the rest of your division.'[20]

Brigadier Blackburn has never been prouder.

'The same colonel,' he will recount, 'admitted to me that they had had more than 500 dead in the fighting against Blackforce and a corresponding number of other casualties.'[21]

16 March 1942, South Java, back of the net

On the Javanese coast, the lorries newly purloined by the triumphant Japanese Army come to a halt, and the British POWs are pushed out by their guards, at the point of bayonets. One of the POWs, Aircraftsman 1st Class Bill Griffiths, is immediately trepidatious.

By the side of the road he can see some camouflage netting covering, something, but is not sure just what it is.

Whatever it is must be important, for twenty guards thrust rifles and bayonets in their specific direction as yelled orders are fired at high velocity.

動け！動け！動け！

Their meaning is obvious: 'Clear away the netting or get a bayonet in your guts.'[22]

The reasons for Griffiths's fear – one of some 200 POWs ordered to do it – are equally obvious.

Whatever is under that netting must be deadly, or the Japanese guards would have done it themselves. But, what can he do?

He takes hold of the netting and – holding his breath as the guards suddenly step well back – pulls on it with a big heave.

BOOOOOOOOOOOM!

[*The stage suddenly goes black.*]

There is an explosion so violent he is thrown backwards. He moves his hands to his face, but he cannot feel it.

'God!' he says, 'my face has been blown off!'[23]

But . . . this is . . . strange.

He has said this, and heard this, so how can his face be missing? Is it maybe his hands that are missing? Certainly, there is excruciating pain in his arms, and in his right leg. And he can feel the shards of metal in his face. Trying to stand up, he immediately crashes to the road. He is fully conscious and behind him can hear another truck pull up, and now deeply concerned English voices, all around him, as he is bodily lifted and put back either on the lorry or the newly arrived truck, he can't tell. One of the voices in this passing convoy of British POWs – who have successfully begged their Japanese captors to stop to pick him up – is asking about a hospital. Bill remembers seeing one not far back in the village of Garoet.

'Carry on to the bottom of the hill,' he manages to gurgle out, 'turn right, and you'll see it on your left.'[24]

He is indeed taken there, but now experiences a new sensation – cold and pain. It is as if he is being lowered into a vat of icy water, but instead of going numb he feels only shattering agony in what he now realises is his shattered arms. 'Please put me out,' he manages to get out, praying for the pain to end. 'For God's sake, put me out!'

'All right, my boy,' a calm English voice answers, 'we will.'

Hours later, as he comes to, he can hear another voice.

'We're going to move you to another hospital, quite near. You'll be all right.'[25] Bill Griffiths does not care.

Such words mean nothing. The only thing he wants to do now is die.

26 March 1942, Bandoeng, none so blind

Good God.

Just when things are starting to quieten down, and Weary has time to read and sleep, this happens. Four RAF chaps have arrived, with a total of just three working eyes between them.

'One poor chap had both eyes blown out and both arms blown off.'[26]

His name?

It is an Englishman by the name of Bill Griffiths.

Apparently, he had been ordered by the Japanese to clear booby-trapped ordnances, only for them to blow up in – and through – his face.

It is the sort of thing that happens when you are breaking the terms of the Geneva Convention and all principles of human decency. Now, both arms are no more than bloody stumps, his right leg more a collection of shrapnel than bone, both eyes are severely damaged and his pallor is so grey it is obvious that he has very nearly 'bled out'. Weary's first act of putting his stethoscope to Griffiths's chest is not so much to check on the strength of the heartbeat, as to determine if he has one at all. The answer is . . . *concentrating now* . . . just.

And with one look at his fellow Englishman, Blue Butterworth knows that the poor bastard is not long for this world. With so many men needing his attention, Weary has little time to spare for one who is going to be shuffling off this mortal coil in short order anyway, and goes on with his rounds.

In his absence, Major Arthur Moon comes to two quick conclusions. This fellow Griffiths might actually live after all, as his pulse has strengthened. But if he is correct in that assumption, there is no recourse but him doing so without his eyes.

'Ewan,' he calls to Major Corlette, 'looks like we'll have to take them out.'

For such an extreme course of action, Private Butterworth feels that Weary should be informed, and races off, finding him in the former school's foyer.

'Chief, they're gonna take Bill's eyes out.'

Weary Dunlop does not hesitate, and rushes to the schoolroom that has been set up as an operating theatre.

'Arthur,' he says with some urgency, 'are you certain?'

Yes, Major Moon is certain.

'Look for yourself. They are *destroyed* by shrapnel.'

Weary does look for himself, at the 'bomb-shattered body of [this] young man', and can see exactly that:

> His eyes were shattered in the wreck of his face, his hands blown away, one leg with a severe compound fracture, he was peppered everywhere with imbedded fragments, and was exsanguinated and shocked.[27]

The danger of leaving his eyes in is that the wounds would become infected and the infection spread from there, killing him – if the loss of blood, or his arms, or leg, don't get him first.

Indeed, as Weary will recount, 'his torn bloodstained clothing removed, it seemed less than kindness to try to prolong his life'.[28]

But they must.

And so, with a sigh, Weary agrees, insisting only that he will do the operation himself.

Weary, with the assistance of the Gangster, operates, and, with careful use of forceps, scalpel and scissors, manages to extract the shattered remains of the Englishman's eyeballs, leaving only two empty sockets. And now the two surgeons clean up the stumps of Bill's arms, before suturing the terrible wounds on his leg, the best they can.

Quietly, Major Corlette says to Blue afterwards, 'You know what? It's so silly. This poor fellow, if he should survive this, has no future.'

All this pain, for that? So Blue now replies to Corlette with a dangerous suggestion, half unspoken but instantly understood.

'Major,' he says carefully. 'Why can't you . . . ?'

Corlette is silent.

'All we've got to do is chop the oxygen off.'

Corlette looks at Butterworth ruminatively. It would save everyone, including Griffiths, a lot of trouble. But there is a higher duty, a Hippocratic oath.

'No, not allowed,' he replies. They are doctors, not gods.

Butterworth knows the fine arguments that doctors make. But he is just an enlisted man.

'Well, if you look that way, sir,' he says. '*I can*.'[29]

Major Corlette admittedly pauses, but the answer remains the same. The Hippocratic oath is sacred and has no loopholes.

For the moment, at least, Bill Griffiths will live. Whether he thereafter has a life to live is another question.

And he *wants* to die.

'Being totally blind and having lost both hands,' he will later recount, 'it was indeed beyond my comprehension to go on living a life that was fully, swiftly ebbing away.'[30]

•

It has been two weeks since the Japanese had arrived, and still the hospital has been allowed to operate with minimal intervention.

But now what?

Suddenly the hospital is besieged by 'extremely truculent and offensive'[31] Japanese staff officers who scream all kinds of unreasonable demands at 'DUNROP!'[32] These demands include the removal and obliteration of all Red Cross insignia on the walls and on signs outside. Weary had ordered the signs to be put up as a statement under the Geneva Convention that this hospital was a neutral place of healing beyond the diktats of war outside, but the Japanese do not accept that. Their statement is more direct: we *are* at war and you will do exactly as we say. The fact that Japanese guards are now posted at all entrances to the hospital is further confirmation of this.

('It is,' Brigadier Blackburn will maintain, 'an interesting indication of the Japanese character and untrustworthiness that, although the Commander-in-Chief of Java added these words to our actual surrender document, never at any time subsequently would the Japanese admit that we had any rights as POWs under the Geneva Convention or otherwise.'[33])

Weary protests bitterly, as does the Swiss man who is the local representative of the Red Cross, but the Japanese don't care: Colonel Dunlop will do as they say, or face the consequences.

•

There is something about the groan coming from the bed in the corner that tells Matron Mickey that the most gravely wounded patient they have is coming to after a long period of being in a near coma.

Sure enough, though Bill Griffiths can't open his eyes, because he doesn't have any, for the first time he is moving the stumps of his arms around in the manner of a man trying to work out why he not only can't see anything, but can't feel anything.

Settle, Billy, settle.

But he will not.

He is so convinced that this must be a nightmare that he can wake up from, he rolls himself from side to side with such vigour that he falls out of bed, but instead of waking from the agony, he only finds that the agony is even *more* excruciating.

There is some relief with the shot of morphine Matron gives him, which she repeats every evening, but after a few days, when he fully understands just how dire is his plight, how grim his future even if he gets out of here, he is firm.

'I can't accept being like this,' he says. 'I can't. Give me an injection, something, anything, and let me drift peacefully away. It's no good. I can't spend the rest of my life a complete wreck.'

Mickey nods to herself.

'I would do it,' she replies quietly, 'but I have to have Colonel Dunlop's permission. I can't do it without.'[34]

As good as her word, that evening, deeply distressed and overwhelmed with compassion, she takes Weary aside.

'Colonel,' she begins, 'Bill wants to die. If you do not have the guts to kill him, I will!'[35]

Weary says no.

'Even the flickering candle of life seemed precious in a world collapsing about us in which many or all of us might die.'[36]

And so he sternly forbids Matron Mickey from taking any such action. As a personal *priority*, he is going to preserve this man's life whatever the cost.[37]

That evening, Weary makes a special visit to see the young man lying now in perpetual darkness.

He speaks soothingly, and with infinite care.

'Things won't be too bad later on,' he says. 'You will get stronger and should come to accept your situation.'

'What about my sight?'

Will it come back?

The Australian is non-committal – and won't tell him the truth, that he has no eyes. The important thing now is to heal your body. Later, we can work on your sight.

Bill Griffiths is not pleased with his doctor or his diagnosis.

He pleads with another patient, 'Here am I, twenty-one years of age, with no sight, no hands, and for all I know only one leg. What use am I? How can I cope with this lot? I've asked Mickey to give me something to put me out of my misery, but she won't. Will you ask Colonel Dunlop for me?'

He will not.

Weary continues to visit him, despite the fact that he now has 1350 other patients.

'The Japanese,' he says to the 21-year-old, 'will soon be defeated, and when you get home you will get the best medical treatment, and your excellent constitution will see you through. The pain in your arms will gradually ease and you will get stronger.'[38]

Bill Griffiths doesn't want to get stronger, he wants to die. But Weary Dunlop wants him to live, which means his fate is sealed. Little by little, Griffiths's spirits start to lift. Of course, he still can't see, but he knows that soon after the hospital begins to stir at dawn, Dunlop's soothing voice will come: 'Well, Bill, how are you this morning?'

Not great, Colonel, but maybe a *little* better?

'You'll be alright, it will take time.'[39]

In the midst of his darkness, both visual and mental, such a sentiment is precious.

'His calm, confident words,' Griffiths will recount, 'gave me my only flicker of hope.'[40]

For there is no doubt about it.

'There was a certain magic when he was around, somehow. Just the thought of him being around. He seemed to be completely unflappable . . . He was a very cultured, highly educated chap, skilful surgeon, [but] he was one of the lads as well.'[41]

And whatever, else, as Weary sometimes reminds him, the fact that Bill Griffiths has a wife and daughter waiting for him in England is everything. He *must* live for them.

•

Hospitals are used to brief visits from the sick but not so much from the dead. But today is an exception as Weary is surprised and delighted to see – despite persistent rumours as to his death – Brigadier Arthur Blackburn, in the flesh!

In fact, though Blackburn is under Japanese authority, he is not even yet imprisoned and, being a trusted prisoner, has come to inspect the hospital to ensure that all is in order. Extending Blackburn all the courtesies due his rank, Weary shows him around and they discuss just what must be done to improve things further. What puzzles them both is how to get things done as prisoners.

Through endless negotiations, Dunlop succeeds in having the Japanese officer in control of them, Lieutenant Sumiya, agree to the establishment of an international advisory committee – the senior officers from the Australian, New Zealand, American and Dutch prisoners – who can represent all the prisoners and make requests and concessions in turn.

17 April 1942, Bandoeng, do no harm
Weary, quick.

A Japanese officer, flanked by several grim, armed soldiers, is approaching off the starboard quarter and is clearly intent on storming aboard to set a completely new course. That is the way he looks, anyway.

Ah, yes, it is Captain Nakazawa, the Medical Staff Officer.

Nakazawa barks out the order to Weary, without preamble:

'You are to disband your hospital in ten minutes. Everyone must get up and march.'

All those who can't march are to go to prison – and everything is to happen, at once!

'This is impossible!' answers Weary. 'You can't dissolve a hospital in ten minutes. Look, let me show you some of these people.'

And Weary leads the Japanese officer to the worst patient he has. Have a look, Captain Nakazawa.

'This is a blind boy named Griffiths. We had to amputate his hands, his eyes were blown out by a bomb and his leg is broken.'[42]

Now how is this fellow going to march out of here in eight minutes and counting? He isn't. And next to him is another blind young soldier whose face is shattered, and next to him is a paraplegic and next to him is a fellow who has been shot through the chest, and in front of Weary is an annoyed Japanese officer who doesn't give a damn.

Bayonet o tsukeru!

If Weary doesn't understand the exact words, he certainly understands the cruel thrust of his intent, as the soldiers all grimly *fix bayonets* to the end of their rifles. One of them, perhaps a little more civilised than the others, puts a bullet in the chamber of his rifle.

Captain Nakazawa has ordered them to kill Weary's most feeble patients, and those soldiers are now approaching the beds of these very men, yelling wildly and clearly intending to execute . . . their orders.

'You can't do this!' Colonel Dunlop yells at Nakazawa. 'You'll have to kill me first.'[43]

He means it, and now tells the guard in a much calmer voice, pointing to his own stomach.

'If you are going to do that, you must go through me first.'[44]

The Japanese soldier yells threateningly and appears about to shoot him or stab him, it is not certain. But it clearly won't be a problem.

Weary Dunlop does not back down and glares at Nakazawa.

The two begin to argue, loudly, furiously, desperately.

'Sir,' the outraged Australian says, 'I have in my possession a signed letter from General Maruyama, the Commander of the Japanese Army, that you will honour your place as signatories of the Hague Convention! As we have surrendered on Java, graciously, you will also observe the terms of the Geneva Convention.'

'I refuse to see this letter,' Nakazawa replies. 'The General didn't sign it!'

Well, if you looked at it, you could see that he did.

But Captain Nakazawa goes on.

'I won't . . .' he says, and these words are the first time that Weary thinks they will live. A few weeks earlier, the Japanese officers at Alexandra hadn't even remotely negotiated or argued the toss with their captives and had just come to murder. The fact that Nakazawa is arguing is a good indication that Weary is going to be a prisoner, not a corpse. So he might as well be a demanding prisoner.

'Well, if you will tell me who was responsible for this order, Captain, I will hold him accountable,' Weary counters. 'But if you cannot do that, Captain Nakazawa, I will hold you responsible and, in due course, one of the governments concerned will have you hanged!'[45]

'Good,' Nakazawa says, seemingly untroubled. 'Now you will lead the march to gaol.'[46]

But first . . .

Nakazawa now shifts his glare to another patient, a paraplegic who would appear to be the next one at risk of being summarily executed. This man does not have the advantage of Bill Griffiths in not being able to see the terror approaching. He knows only too well that, in all likelihood, the guard's bayonet is a one-way ticket to meet his maker. But Weary takes three steps to his right and stands in front of this man, too. The tension is palpable, all the patients in the ward knowing that the only thing that stands between them and death is Colonel Weary Dunlop.

Finally, Captain Nakazawa moves off with his soldiers, pausing only to contemptuously strike the legs of one of the paraplegics, saying, 'Man walk.'[47]

Whoever cannot walk, or be shifted, will be executed on the morrow when the time for movement comes – for yes, instead of the original 10 minutes to pack up, the Japanese officer finally agrees they may have until the following morning at dawn. Sharp.

There follows a night that no-one will ever forget: 'We spent the whole night pulling down all the orthopaedic traction and clapping people in plaster and making railings for very sick people to be shifted.'[48]

Medical instruments, stores and drugs that the Japanese refuse to allow must be stealthily smuggled out now, to be rapidly regathered later.

By dawn all is done. Blue Butterworth and Weary have even fashioned a long bamboo pole from which they have suspended bags filled with medicines, medical equipment, books, bandages and bloody heavy boots. It is a great idea, so long as Bluey will be strong enough to lift one end. (There are no worries about Weary at the other end. He remains not only the leader, but the physically strongest man of all the POWs.)

And one . . . and two . . . and *lift*!

Yes, Blue's knees are knocking a little, but it can be done. A couple of the passing Dutch VADs – nurses for the Voluntary Aid Detachment – amused by the long and the short of it, pause to take a photo. Alas, it is at this very moment that a Japanese soldier runs up to start kicking and hitting both of the women, while screaming. Both run away, crying, leaving Weary and his eternal offsider completely stunned at the viciousness of the unprovoked attack.

'You bastards . . .' Blue thinks. 'You're a horrible, horrible people.'[49]

A people, too, with no penchant for patience.

For, already – beyond such basic Japanese words as '*benjo*' for 'latrine', '*ashita*' for 'tomorrow' and '*takusan*' for 'very' or 'lots' – they are starting to learn, the Japanese are coining some new pigeon English commands to bark at them.

'*Speedo! Speedo!*'

'*Hurree Uppoo! Hurree Uppoo!*'

'*Pickee!*'

'*Changey! Changey!*'[50]

('A particularly obnoxious trick is to set a task for a body of men for the day,' Weary notes in his diary. 'Then when they finish, "Changey, Changey" plans and do a lot more work.'[51] It will be very late in the day indeed, before the merciful order comes, 'Back, *campo*.')

And the prisoners continue to learn a handful more Japanese words, as most of their orders seem to boil down to, 'Get going, you miserable *bakaeroo*, idiots!'

They will, presently.

But before they go, a few things.

Weary requests a cart to allow them to more easily transport some of the heavier cooking gear and medical equipment.

Ah, that is easy, Dunrop: No.

'Can we at least have one of our three remaining ambulance cars to accompany the party to pick up those falling by the way?'[52]

Easier still: No, again.

Very well then. Weary is at least determined that somebody should know what has happened to them so far; and what might happen next. The answer is his diary. Somebody must have a copy, and that someone should be Matron Mickey. The problem is that she is already beyond his reach in a building across the street. Sentries block both his exit and, if he gets across the street alive, his entry. But there is one way past: pure bluff. An American pilot, Flight Officer Cicurel, once gave Weary some advice which has stuck in his head ever since. It is this: if ever you are captured – recite.

What?

No, it works!

'Have something to recite with great emotion.'[53] Cicurel uses 'The Gettysburg Address' himself, but any old guff you know by heart will do. 'Then brush aside any resistance and walk through.'[54]

Why? Well, when you speak with certainty, without pausing, you are a man of confidence, especially to people who don't speak your language. It will buy you some time, some space, and maybe your freedom if you can distract your captors for a moment.

Any old guff? Weary picks Shakespeare's Sonnet 64, the lines of which he learnt at school. Diary in pocket, he approaches the first sentry:

> *When I have seen by times fell hand defaced*
> *The rich proud cost of outworn buried age!*
> *When sometime lofty towers I see down-raised!*[55]

Weary gesticulates wildly and the guard looks at him puzzled.

What the 地獄?!?!

> *And brass eternal slave to mortal rage;*
> *When I have seen the hungry ocean gain!*[56]

Ah. Weary pushes the guard's bayonet aside and 'my back felt exposed and uneasy'.[57]

But then the guard yells out to . . . somebody else, and by his tone Weary knows that he has passed! Weary crosses the street looking furious and speechifying, or sonneteering (whatever it is, it is working):

> *Advantage on the kingdom of the shore,*
> *And the firm soil win of the wat'ry main!*[58]

The entry sentry nods, and Weary enters with a bow. Down the hall, Mickey Borgmann-Brouwer can hear a baritone lunatic shouting Shakespeare:

> *Ruin hath taught me thus to ruminate,*
> *That Time will come and take my love away!*[59]

It is Weary Dunlop. Who would have thought he would be the first to go off his head? Weary enters her room and speaks prose at last.

'We are leaving for prison in a few hours.'[60] He hands her his diary; this must be kept. She nods. Ah what the hell, Weary takes her in his arms and kisses her. But now he must go.

'Oh, what a pity . . .'[61] says Mickey.

> *This thought is as a death, which cannot choose!*
> *But weep to have that which it fears to lose!*[62]

Farewell, Mickey.

At 10.15 am, the men move off under heavily armed guard, as they nominally 'march', but more accurately hobble, bobble and wobble their way forward, trying to stay fast enough that the Japanese guards won't hit them, but slow enough not to collapse from exhaustion – all while helping those who cannot help themselves, the many sick and wounded patients, to keep moving.

The four-mile march for these 700 of the damned, in this intense heat, is not led by Weary, it is followed by him, as he labours under his load. Having ordered all the officers to carry their own baggage, he is doing the same – it is just that his baggage is so much heavier than everyone else's.

He is not the only one struggling.

'Three hundred of those discharged were quite sick,' Weary will recount, 'and only about fifty were fit for a march with all gear. If, however, they fell by the wayside, boots and bayonets were applied and this was a strong deterrent to weakness.'[63]

'I was staggering under a hellish load of about two hundred pounds of stuff which I thought was essential.'[64] Still, he oversees the help given to those who cannot go on. It has become Weary's personal mission to do everything possible to see blind Bill Griffiths survive. From the first he has been committed to the notion that it is the job of the strongest to help those who are weakest.

Mid-April 1942, Toorak, love from afar

A letter! A letter from Weary.

Helen Ferguson can barely believe it, but here it is, passed on from the Australian Army, via General Roy Burston, who had got it from her fiancé himself in some place in Java. The main thing is, after all the terrible news that keeps coming over ABC Radio, her love is alive and well!

Helen Darling,
In Java and in haste!
There has been no opportunity to write a line for a few weeks, as you will understand.
As usual I am using a courier a departing general! He is now waiting.
This is a lovely country with superb mountains and a gorgeous tropical colour everywhere, I should love you to see it sometime – with me.
You will understand darling that things are tough here and that I have little hope of seeing you for some time, if ever.
So I am writing to say that I shall love you always and that you have made me more happy than I can ever express by this feeble medium.
Thank the Lord that old ruffian Boyd did not get here.
I must just send you all that love and longing to see you again and just myriads of kisses.
God Bless you darling and your family and here's hoping the bitter tide will turn soon.
Jolly my family up a bit won't you . . .

Love always my fawn.
Edward.[65]

18 April 1942, Bandoeng, Dutch oven

By midday, mercifully, they have arrived at their destination, an exceedingly old prison which comes complete with ancient stone walls, rusting iron bars and a stench that would kill a brown dog. It is called *Landsopvoedingsgesticht*, a name so long and difficult it would earn a nod from a Welshman, and had been set up by the Dutch as a prison purely for the worst behaved of Javanese 'bad boys'. The fact that 500 of them are still there, side by side with 1300 Dutchmen – some of whom had first put the Javanese bad boys in there in the first place – means that there are now 2500 men in a place designed for 500.

How long does it take to get everyone in, and with at least one flat spot to call their own?

'It felt,' Weary will recount, 'like an eternity.'[66]

But eternity is just starting. Phoney prison is over.

It is 18 April 1942, and hell has begun.

The first thing is to try to get some rest. But *how*, exactly?

As the new arrivals are assigned to just three large cells and one smaller cell, they simply can't all fit in, inevitably leaving a hundred of them standing out in the rain waiting their turn to get shelter. Even those in shelter don't have it easy when it comes to trying to get to sleep. The biggest problem, oddly enough, is . . . well, excuse me! The smooth tiles on the floor lead to many a rough greeting as one man slides into another as they roll in their sleep. Your face meets feet, your crotch is crushed, it is like being part of a human beanbag. Yes, it is manageable for moments, just, when they settle, but as you fall asleep so does your sense of space and propriety: 'Eternally all night you kept slipping and rolling onto the next chap.'[67]

Unable to sleep, Dunlop decides to begin anew his diary of daily events in a small black notebook he has, following the one he had given to Mickey in Java.

But . . . careful!

The Japanese have been explicit on this. No diaries are to be kept on pain of severe punishment, and even execution. (They don't detail why, but the answer is obvious. There will be *no* documented proof of whatever atrocities they might commit.) In it, he draws a small plan of their prison, and notes of their cramped quarters, 'every square foot of veranda was covered with bodies, there were still 150 approximately obliged to take turns out on the sodden earth in the rain'.[68]

As the reality that they are now POWs sinks in, just one thing gives solace.

'Of course we knew it would be for only a few months,' one of the Diggers, Private Donald 'Scorp' Stuart, will recall, 'three or maybe four.'[69]

As bad as it is, what is three months in a lifetime? Just the blink of an eye. Surely, it should take no longer than that for the Allies to get on top of things and liberate them.

•

At a nearby hospital where he has been moved, Bill Griffiths is as lonely as he has ever been in his life. After endless negotiation, the Japanese have allowed that he will be cared for in another hospital at Tjimahi – which sees him shoved on a stretcher and put onto the back of a lorry, separating him for the first time from the two people who had most cared for him to this point, Matron Mickey and Colonel Weary Dunlop.

'I was unloaded and dumped in a corner on my own,' he will later recount, 'no one took any notice of me, but I could hear people dashing about and the Japs yelling and screaming. I was bursting for a pee; but although I shouted, there was no one who knew how to help.'

And soon enough, the true shock hits like a hammer:

> I suddenly realized with horror that tonight there would be no Mickey to give me my 'fix', and no 'fix'. It was a shattering blow, and I got no sleep at all that night. Life had become even more unbearable – but what choice had I but to bear it as best I could? For me, then, it was one long night of pain, of unending darkness like the grave. Only, unfortunately, I was still alive.[70]

•

For Colonel Weary Dunlop, the question now is what he can to do to help his charges survive the prison privations to which they are now subjected. The first thing is to negotiate with their captors to get more space, more security provisions against the regular prisoners, more food than the two small bowls of rice a day they are being ludicrously asked to subsist on, and more access to medicine for the many sick men. In the normal way of things it would be the most senior officer among them who would take the lead. But as the key matters at hand are driven by medical imperatives, it is Weary Dunlop himself to the fore and it is quickly agreed by both the Japanese and the Australian officers that Dunlop will be the senior Allied officer who will be the conduit between the Japanese and their POWs.

Very well then. Weary begins by giving the Japanese a formal list of the things that his men require, under the auspices of the Geneva Convention.

None of the demands is met – and the Japanese maintain that General Maruyama had no authority to add any such things as Japan was not bound by the Geneva Convention[71] – and food is cut off from the prisoners for a day for even having the temerity to ask.

But, again, there is at least something in the fact that the Japanese are choosing to justify why they needn't follow the Geneva Convention, rather than just putting a bullet in their prisoners' heads.

They're even giving their prisoners a bit more food. For the most part it is rice with a little vegetable soup, occasionally with a small slice of bread, and even more occasionally little bits of meat are to be found in the soup. Mercifully, the prisoners still have some of their own supplies with them, and are able to hand out two tinned sausages a man a week and a weekly issue of dried potatoes.

To alleviate the situation of space, Weary is quick to negotiate with the senior Dutch officer on site, Lieutenant Colonel Overste van Lingham, who has been here for a fortnight, and arranges through him and the Japanese commandant for 100 of the Dutch men to take their sleeping gear with them and spend the night on the verandas of some nearby administrative buildings, outside the prison gates.

Furthermore . . .

'I arranged a parade each day with daily routine orders appointing fatigues and orderly duties.'[72]

It is not just the Australian prisoners who observe his actions closely, and draw strength from them. For so too do the prisoners of other nations, including the Ambonese soldiers of the Dutch Army, who give him a name in their own Malay language, '*Singa Yang Diam*'.[73]

Yes, that's him, Singa Yang Diam, 'the quiet lion'.

•

The barked Japanese commands bite through the air, through the long day's journey into night, and from the early morning onwards – and they never stop!

'*Tenko!*', the Australians now know, is time to muster, to have a roll call, accomplished by each man calling out his number in Japanese, as it is marked off by the presiding Japanese or Korean guard.

'*Roku-jū-nana!*' Sixty-seven!

'*Roku-jū-hachi!*' Sixty-eight!

. . .

. . .

'*Roku-jū-kyū?*' Sixty-nine?

'*Roku-jū-kyū wa doko desu-ka?*' Where is sixty-nine?

Turns out that 69 is *byoki*, sick.

He might very well be on the *benjo*, latrine.

Maybe they are *takusan byoki*, as in 'very sick'.

Look, if you are *takusan byoki* yourself right now, and have to go quickly to the toilet, you tell the guard, '*Speedo benjo*.'

Oh, and '*Kura!*', *jump* to attention, when I even *look* at you! If I say, '*Hayaku!*', I mean hurry, hurry!

'*Makan!*'[74] It is time for a quick meal.

On and on it goes: barked commands, regularly sprinkled with bursts of violence to make the point that no resistance will be tolerated.

At least, occasionally, they are allowed *yasume*, rest, but for the most part any request for a smoko is met by '*Yasume* no!'

As hard as it is for the Australians to be in this prison so far from home, it seems harder still for several Dutch settlers who had taken up arms against the Japanese, only to be captured. For them, it is an agony to have their homes and families only a few short miles away, and one night three of them managed to get out and over the walls, only, alas, to be caught once more.

To Weary's horror, the Japanese call for a full parade and the three Dutchmen are marched out, put up against the wall and *bayoneted* as they all watch – their bodies slumping, bloody, to the ground.

The Dutch Medical Officer faints just to see it, to the complete contempt of the Japanese officer who presides over the execution – and it is the latter who now strides forward, withdraws his pistol and shoots the only man still groaning, through the head, to put him out of his misery.

It is disgusting, inhuman, and against everything the Geneva Convention stands for – all of which points the outraged Doctor Dunrop makes shortly afterwards to the Japanese officer. But the bemused Oriental gentleman doesn't care.

You are our prisoners. You will do what we say. Or you will be killed for your trouble.

Bayoneting to death remains the Japanese's preferred form of execution. Nevertheless, as Weary notes, 'Occasionally, people are honoured by beheading.'[75]

•

The Japanese adjutant of the camp, Lieutenant Sumiya, is inspecting his prisoners. He expects deference: bowed heads and salutes. He gets a soccer ball. Flying just past his head. The ball doesn't hit him, but

Sumiya is sure it was *meant* to. It is dishonour. The inspection ends immediately, and is followed by Sumiya reappearing with an armed guard, with fixed bayonets, ready to puncture any soccer ball and anybody. As for Sumiya, he now has a sword by his side. A Samurai sword. The prisoners are ordered to line up and it is clear to Weary that Lieutenant Sumiya is so angry that he can barely keep still.

'All hell is going to break loose,' Weary thinks.[76] It is like watching the twitch of a cobra, knowing that it is about to strike. When giving a public speech it is important to start with a bang to get the attention of the audience and Sumiya delivers:

'You are scum. You are parasites. You are dying.'

Worse than that, they are *ungrateful*, parasitical, dying scum. They have not even said thank you for the provisions they have been given. He knows these men are scum because they have surrendered, an utterly shameful act – and yet they lack even the decency to *be* ashamed, which is infuriating. It is as if they have murdered their best friend, their honour, but still insist on looking you in the eye as if they have a right to even *exist*! And he will not have it.

'You have bitten the hand that has fed you! You are snakes!'

So, no more soccer?

Sumiya's rage rolls on and on before he finally exhausts himself. He finishes in front of Dunrop, staring, glaring.

'You may dismiss your men.'

Weary, unperturbed, simply says, 'Dismissed', and the men begin to move off. Weary salutes Sumiya and Sumiya punches him in the mouth. Weary reels as the men look on in shock. That was an uppercut right to the teeth! It rocks Weary back, he totters, but he does not fall. Instinctively, Weary's hands come up to fight and with a flash Sumiya's sword is drawn. Of course! That's what he wants. A fight to the death; Weary's death. The sword gleams now and darts at Weary, who moves his boxer's body sideways as though dodging a glove instead of death. The blade misses his body, the flat of it hitting him in the larynx and Weary gasps. He can't breathe, he can't speak but now in an instant he sees his men gathering, ready to charge the Japanese; ready to die for certain.

No, *this* is what Sumiya wants, not just one man, but all of them. It will start with Weary and end with a mass grave. Well, Weary is not going to give Sumiya the start he craves. He drops his boxing hands and bows, low, elaborately and formally. He bows so low it is over the top, an ironic gesture the British and Australians understand and the Japanese do not. At last, Weary's head rises from supplication to speak.

'You've got the sword,' Weary says, pointing at it. Oh yes, Sumiya does, and he knows Weary's men are itching to attack. Will they watch their commander murdered? Let us see. The blade flashes again. They are going to be treated to 'an exhibition of Samurai swordsmanship'. Sumiya cuts the air all around Weary's head, the blade breezes past his ears, slices around his hair, faster and more furious with each thrust. Inches away, away from death. Weary stands and waits for the show to stop. The men watch, every hand clenched into a fist, every man ready to die after the first drop of blood they see.

If it's to come, better it come quickly.

A final jab and . . . the blade is returned to its scabbard. Sumiya has punched him, insulted him, toyed with him, threatened him; but Weary has the honour. 'This is the beginning,' he thinks. This is how to do it: to rise above, to elevate by bowing; literally don't lose your head. This is discipline of the hardest kind – the heroism of humility – and his men have just seen Lieutenant Colonel Dunlop defeat the enemy. *It has begun.*

'When despair and death reached for us,' Private Donald Stuart observes, '[Weary] stood fast, his only thought our well-being. Faced with [officers and] guards who had the power of life and death, ignoble tyrants who hated us, he was a lighthouse of sanity in a universe of madness and suffering.'[77]

28 April 1942, Bandoeng, saluting the Emperor

Such a palaver.

Among Australians, salutes between officers tend to be nothing if not casual. Yes, yes, yes, we both know it is the military form to do this, and we more or less must, but don't come the raw prawn with me. We will give each other real respect according to our abilities, not our mere rank.

The Japanese have no such protocols.

Saluting between Japanese officers is elaborate and precise. And when it comes to Australian officers saluting Japanese officers who are also their captors, a good thirty seconds must be set aside. Every Monday, Colonel Weary Dunlop, together with 12 Dutch Colonels who are also in the prison, must go through the elaborate ritual:

a salute with your cap on. Removal of cap. Another salute. A deep bow. Another salute, to each of the Japanese officers there.

On this day, after Weary has gone through the whole wretched pantomime he – as respectfully as he can – raises the issue he has come to raise.

Food. The lack thereof. The fact that his men are slowly starving.

'You Japanese you do not feed us! You're abusing all the rules of . . . war.'[78]

And it is not just that. It is that if we are not fed more, you are going to have ever more deaths on your hands.

And so it goes.

'Nobody feels much like exercise. There is a tendency to slight giddiness and stars flash at times when one rises to the vertical.'[79]

But Weary must rise now, giddy or not, because he has to report to the Police HQ. There is exciting news.

'A special parade will take place tomorrow,' a Japanese captain tells him, with some gravity. 'It is in honour of the Emperor's birthday. All troops are to assemble at 1015 hours.'

Very well.

'They will then face the north-east and salute'.

One gathers that it is to the north-east that the Emperor is to be found. But in Weary's view, the Emperor will sadly remain unsaluted from his own men.

'I am completely disinclined to ask my troops to salute the Emperor of an enemy people,' says Weary. 'I refuse to give such an order.'[80]

Very well.

The captain will not try to talk Lieutenant Colonel Dunlop out of it. Instead, he takes a rifle and bayonet from the nearest sentry, and pokes it into Weary's abdomen.

'I see your point,' says Weary.

Sadly, the joke is lost in translation.

'I shall discuss the matter with the British troops.'

The Japanese point is returned to the sentry, for now.

Weary talks to the British officers and they tell him *not* to be a hero. Captain Pat Lancaster speaks for all: 'Please don't get killed for such a thing. If you live with madmen you must humour them.'[81] Humour it will be then.

The next day, at 10.15 am, the men assemble on parade, the armed Japanese guards watching and waiting, and Weary takes a careful compass bearing. Not to the north-east but to the north-west, towards London and the King.

'Gentlemen, you are about to receive a very extraordinary order, to salute an Emperor. On the command: "To your front, Salute." You will be saluting an Emperor. I refer, of course, to the King Emperor!'[82]

The guards watch approvingly, the men try to look serious. Most fail.

'If you don't know who that is, you bloody well should! To your front! Salute!'

The men salute King George, the Japanese see them saluting Emperor Hirohito. All are happy. 'This gesture was well received by beaming guards, and the quiet grins of our soldiers.'[83]

Honour is satisfied.

'All damn nonsense anyway.'[84]

If they are going to die, let it be a good death with meaning, not a birthday tantrum.

CHAPTER EIGHT

A CAPTIVE AUDIENCE

Although almost wanting at times to call him by his nickname, the men and medical orderlies right through those POW days always called him 'Sir' or 'Colonel' . . . This was a measure of the respect he earned, and received, from the men under his command.[1]

Sergeant Ern Corrie

31 May 1942, Tjimahi, radio waves

Before rainstorms, there is a flurry of wind and a swirling of leaves as the front approaches.

Before mass POW moves, there are earnest Japanese messengers going back and forth on motorbikes, a sudden surfeit of trucks, an animation in the aspect of the Japanese officers and . . . one other thing.

Weary and his cohort truly know a move is imminent when the 'Kempis' visit. The Kempeitai are the violent brutes that pass for military police in the Imperial Japanese Army. (How bad are the Kempis? Well, even the rank-and-file Japanese soldiers are openly terrified of them. They are like the Gestapo, but without the charm.) Kempis administer military law while being a law unto themselves, and now they conduct a search for contraband, which is always a sign that something is about to change.

It is in the middle of such a tense situation in late May that Weary looks up in his nearly bare cell to find Warrant Officer Rod Allanson bearing a large parcel wrapped in camouflage sheeting.

'Compliments of Lieutenant Naarhuis [of the Dutch Army],' he says, 'and would you please hide this!'

It is a radio. Yes, the very item which guarantees that the bearer, if discovered, will be taken out and shot.

'Rod, I don't suppose you could find the perisher to give it back?'[2]

Allanson smiles. That is not an option.

The essential thing is to hide it now, and Weary moves quickly.

Securing the radio under his shirt, in much the same place as his stomach used to be – for he has never been skinnier in his adult life – Weary strolls outside, with his hands clasped at his belly in the manner of the contemplative man. And now, 'all in a leisurely, careless style but with my heart decidedly racing',[3] he drags the tip of his right boot back and forth behind him in a sloping bit of soft ground behind, all while he remains standing and gazes about. There are guards, but mercifully none are particularly looking his way as he scratches a hole in the opposite way a dog does. Finally, it is done, and he quickly buries his bone, but still his anxiety remains.

'It rained during the day and that night, and I had to smear mud over the exposed parcel which stuck out like a whale's rib.'[4]

Before the move the next day, Weary carefully retrieves the radio and proceeds to carry it under his left arm, hidden among all his other baggage of medical equipment, medicaments, textbooks and his tiny personal kit.

He gives a crashing salute to the guard on the way out, and keeps walking. The guard allows him to move on.

'All you need is a bit of cheek,'[5] thinks Weary.

And now, another move, this time a very welcome one.

While stone walls do not a prison make, their absence certainly makes one feel a whole lot less imprisoned, and on the final day of May the Australian POWs are marched four and a half hours to a newly set up open-air camp, at Tjimahi, near a racecourse. The heat simmers them with each step, every man coated in sweat and drenched in full sun. Their kingdom for a horse, their empires for an ice cube, but the final halt lets them take a breath and a look.

'Quarters a bit crowded but good,' the newly promoted Major Jock Clarke notes approvingly. 'Bed boards. Huts with concrete floors – matting walls and tiled roofs. Very large – plenty of open ground. A canteen – coffee shop – food very much better.'[6]

Some new arrivals who had joined them before the latest move are also worthy of great note.

The most interesting of them is a South African who introduces himself as Colonel Laurens van der Post. An elegant man, despite his filthy uniform, he has the appearance of a minor aristocrat, or perhaps even the forgotten younger brother of King George, his cavalier comb-over revealing his vanity while maintaining his good looks. Highly intelligent, and let's not be falsely modest about it, for he isn't, he has great proficiency in languages – starting with many African native dialects, but including Dutch, Malay, Russian and remarkably polished Japanese – and had been commissioned by the British Intelligence Corps to come to the Dutch East Indies and organise the Dutch settlers into the kind of local resistance movement that had been so successful in Europe. Straight after the Dutch surrender, Colonel van der Post had embarked on 'Special Mission 43', a new top-secret program to assemble surviving Allied soldiers and organise them onto ships to get them away to the safety of Colombo, but the plan had gone awry. For it was only a short time after meeting up with Blackforce that they had capitulated, although they had stayed at large for nearly three months, he tells them, before they had finally been caught in the Japanese net.

About to be shot as a spy, he had only been saved by saying 'in a loud and clear voice as of a stranger with special and singular authority over the occasion', the only words that might save him: *'Makotoni osore – irimasu-ga shibaraku omachi Kudasai-ka?* Would you please excuse me and be so good as to condescend and wait an honourable moment?'[7]

To his infinite relief, the Japanese had done exactly that, declining to shoot a Westerner who had showed their nation such respect as to learn their language and know much of their culture. Inevitably, Weary immediately puts Laurens' skills to use negotiating better conditions with the Japanese – and he will soon be superb in dealing with the local Dutch, and Javanese underground, not to mention the Chinese traders.

'He was the most fascinating man . . .'[8] Weary will note of the South African. 'A Secret Operations character . . . Churchill man. He never wanted to stick his neck out, but [was a] magnificent guru and advisor.'[9]

With Laurens is Wing Commander W. T. H. 'Nick' Nichols, a senior officer with the Royal Air Force. Nichols had recently been captured by the Japanese while trying to lead a small band of troops to the Javanese south coast, in similar manner to Brigadier Blackburn. He's quiet and self-effacing, but Weary finds him 'nervy and a bit jumpy',[10] while Major Jock Clarke is less diplomatic: 'Nichols turning out a complete shit,' he notes in his diary. 'Treating the [officers] very badly. His teeth chatter every time a Jap comes near him.'[11]

Yet another significant officer in the latest batch of arrivals is Major Bill Wearne, a 30-year-old Duntroon graduate from Queensland's 2/9th Battalion.

Weary's reservations about Wing Commander Nichols notwithstanding, the medico is glad to see such senior officers arriving.

'I was a little bit embarrassed at this stage,' Weary will recount, 'to still be the commandant.'[12]

For the moment the matter is left, as, in any case, all must be allowed some time to settle in . . .

•

In June 1942, Ern Corrie is a prisoner at Garoet camp. The Japanese guards there are already beyond brutal. Take this Warrant Officer, who is glaring at them all; he has a special Nippon ability which he now informs them of: 'I can tell if you are thinking bad thoughts.'[13]

Oh really?

Yes, he will prove it to them.

They stand rigidly at attention and the WO walks along and pauses to stare into their eyes. WHAM! That man was having bad thoughts! And so he got bashed. Point proven! Well, they are all having bad thoughts now, but try to look neutral as this psychic – or, more accurately, psychopathic – guard walks the ranks and WHAM!

More bad thoughts. Yes, a lot more as it turns out.

But on 20 June, they have good thoughts at last: of wives, sweethearts and children in Australia. For the men now imprisoned in Garoet are told that they will be allowed to write home.

They do so, but their letters are wrong. A special directive is placed on the noticeboard in all POW camps to teach the Aussies how to write properly:

FOR AUSTRALIANS ONLY

Yes?

Full name, Army Number, Rank and Unit must be on the letter

Right. And the following points must be made in the letter:

1. How they fought.
2. Where they fought.
3. Promised help did not come from England or America.
4. The Dutch and English fought badly.
5. Only Australians fought well. (*Accurate. Funny they should say that, but they will be damned if they will be ordered to write it!*)
6. Japanese showed themselves as formidable opponents.
7. Radio news was and is misleading.
8. Japanese forces were and are stronger than the radio says.
9. Treatment of Japanese POWs is very good (*at least if they have good thoughts . . .*)
10. It is true that Australia is strong, but Japan is stronger.
11. After some time, Australia will be beaten, as promised help is too late.
12. After a short time, Japan will attack with terrific force, which it will not be possible to repel or defeat.[14]

After that, you can squeeze in some stuff about the weather (start with, it's hot, damned *hot*) and ask about your nieces and nephews, I love you, darling etc, whatever guff you like. You have a free hand. Now, all letters must be handed in to Warrant Officer Clarkfield at the hospital orderly rooms, between 0945 and 1000, next Wednesday.

Strangely enough, *none* of the Australians write letters.

Mid-June 1942, Bandoeng, camp to prison

And what now?

On the move again. Now they must march all day in the belting sun to a massive new camp, this one again near Bandoeng. A straggling convoy that goes for over a mile, of men and handcarts – with a heavily armed Japanese guard – the workers in the paddy fields they pass barely look up. Conquerors come, conquerors go, work goes on.

'Little Jap corporal at the head of our column,' Major Jock Clarke records in his diary. 'Amazed when we heard him humming "*La Traviata*" to himself. Whistled with him for a while and he opened up a bit. Could speak some English – a Christian – he sang a few hymns for us. Turned out a very decent little chap.'[15]

Despite their collective brutality, there really are *some* decent ones.

Finally, nearing the end of the day, shattered with exhaustion, the men walk back through the eerily deserted and shuttered Bandoeng, and are soon arriving in their new camp, 'Java-Z', which can accommodate 9000 POWs without burping. It is neither prison nor concentration camp, but more in the way of a hamlet of barracks carved out of the jungle; its perimeter formed by wet brush and fierce foliage, which threatens to invade them daily.

Officers, and even Sergeants, have their own cottages, and the barracks are spacious, *without* leaking roofs.

'Exceeds our wildest dreams,' Major Jock Clarke notes in his diary. 'Australian and English troops in separate areas but not segregated. Officers in a street of beautiful little furnished cottages – 6 rooms – 6 officers. Each with two bathrooms – 2 Kitchens – 2 W.C.s – marvellous . . . Our street out of bounds to the troops but we have access to them.'[16]

As the Commanding Officer, Weary is provided with a cottage of his own, as is his adjutant, Major John Morris.

'We are wondering what this terrific change in our treatment lately means. There must be something behind it.'[17]

(Perhaps the war is going badly for the Japanese, and on the reckoning that there might be a day of exactly that coming up – a reckoning – it might be better to err on the side of decency?)

Though as they settle in to their new camp there is an enormous amount of cleaning to be done, within days everything is up and running fairly smoothly . . . when their numbers suddenly expand.

The new arrivals are survivors from the cruisers *Perth* and *Houston*, sunk three months before in the Sunda Strait, most of them in a shocking state of weakness through a combination of sickness, malnutrition and ill-treatment. The tattered rags over their battered bodies make them look like a ragtag bag of ghost gypsies who have wandered into the camp by some cosmic mistake.

Good Lord, what a time they have had, particularly those from *Perth*.

After being sunk in the Sunda Strait in the early hours of 1 March 1942, most of them had either been picked up by the Japanese immediately, or captured shortly thereafter. In the time since, they have been imprisoned at a camp near Tjilatjap, the spot where they had landed on the south Javanese coast.

One of them, particularly, stands out to Weary Dunlop – Chief Petty Officer Ray Parkin – and Weary is fascinated by the story of this career naval man from Collingwood.

Refusing to accept that their prospects were as sunk as their ship, Parkin and another officer, Horry Abbott, had no sooner drifted to Sangiang Island in the Strait than they had purloined a two-masted schooner. With 21 others on board, and Parkin installed as skipper, they sailed away. Recalling *Perth*'s last intended destination, they immediately set sail for Tjilatjap, a port in southern Java. Perhaps, if their luck held out, they could even make it to Australia . . . They would work it out.

Sailing down the coast of west Java, and reaching Princes Island, they realise that the number aboard cannot be sustained for the rest of the journey. Some men, therefore, decide to take their chances on land. Parkin and nine others continue in the schooner, and make it to Tjilatjap, where they are promptly taken prisoner and marched to a local POW camp, eventually being transferred to the larger Bicycle Camp in Batavia.

And now . . . here we are, with many of the other survivors of *Perth*.

One thing both van der Post and Weary Dunlop note about this fellow Ray Parkin from the first is that, as Weary puts it, he is 'quite a genius . . . credible artist, highly articulate, he could write'.[18]

Once the new arrivals are themselves settled and their new camp has a rhythm to it, Weary Dunlop again raises the issue of who should be Commanding Officer.

But here's the extraordinary thing.

None of the senior combatant officers who have arrived – Nichols, van der Post and Wearne – are inclined to take over. Even after a short time with this conclave of POWs, it is obvious to the new arrivals the amount of respect the men have for Dunlop and that he is their natural leader. To take over as Commanding Officer would make them feel like interlopers.

It is too hot to argue with gusto, but Weary Dunlop tries to talk them into it, charming and disarming with cool logic. After a few days Nichols seems to agree, but Laurens van der Post is equally insistent: Weary must remain as Commanding Officer.

'It will be a war for sanity of mind and body,' van der Post insists to Weary, 'and who could be more fitted to conduct such a war than a doctor and a healer?'[19]

Still Weary persists, noting in his diary: 'van der Post is a natural leader and diplomat, very persuasive with both D and Ns. I wish he could take over the job.'[20]

But this curious cove won't budge, and so Weary must stay in the role while Colonel Laurens van der Post devotes himself to making contacts with the local population, both native and Dutch settlers alike. By wording up the work parties that are daily making sojourns out into the country, he is able to smuggle in food supplies, access the best approximation he can of the medicine that Weary needs, and gain more information on how the Japanese are faring, how the natives are being treated and how disposed they might be to offer more help to the POWs, for a price or a promise of fortune to come once this war is done. Once an Intelligence man, always an Intelligence man: all of this information is written down in code, and all of it secreted; for the present and the future.

Van der Post and Weary also work together on instituting a program to keep up the men's physical health by keeping their minds actively engaged – no easy task in an open prison camp.

Why not institute a wider education program than the one Weary had established in the prison at Tjimahi, whereby those who are expert in one field can give lectures to those who wish to learn about it, and do the whole thing on a mass scale?

'We devised the scheme that we would have a university in captivity,' Weary would recount, '[so that] instead of people suffering a complete suspension of purpose, we would build this magnificent educational activity into life.'[21]

Though Weary is too busy on medical matters to lecture, van der Post gives erudite lessons on Afrikaans and basic Japanese, and Ray Parkin on both art and the art of drawing. In his naval career, Parkin had delighted in sketching ships he'd seen in port around the world. And he is soon drawing superbly detailed sketches of their surroundings now, fellow POWs, and even some of their guards.

Gunner Penry Rees gives daily lessons in the French language.

RAF Squadron Leader Alex Jardine teaches navigation, and one of his pilots gives lectures on English law. French, book-keeping, *The Odyssey*, a POW degree in Ancient History – all are on offer. At the other end of the scale, Captain Pat Lancaster of the King's

Hussars teaches men basic literacy. Now, how to get paper for such lessons? They use the one thing the notably hygiene-conscious Japanese are happy to provide in bulk – toilet paper. Because it is so valuable for this purpose – and because it blocks up their crude toilets – Weary gives the order that such paper is *not* to be used after mere ablutions.

(Such is the shortage of good paper that some blokes are using pages from the Good Book as tobacco paper so that they can continue to smoke. Weary officially frowns upon it, but, oh, forgive me Father, the flesh can be weak, no matter how strong the spirit. 'Unhappily,' he will later acknowledge, 'at one stage I think I smoked through the New Testament . . . But I read it as I smoked it.'[22] Ashes to ashes, durrie to dust.)

Once these men were required to carry a gun. Now Weary requires them to carry a book. One each at all times. You have heard of a circulation library? This is a marching one. The men surprise him with their choices and taste; no pulp fiction for them: 'A number of them had good literature, anthologies and books of poetry.'[23]

Shakespeare and Bernard Shaw make a good showing, but this might be because they don't have any Biggles on hand . . .

As the heat beats, Sergeant Ern Corrie sits among the new bugs today, about to get a greeting and a talk of welcome from Colonel van der Post and Weary Dunlop – both of them giving a brief bio for the benefit of the men. Van der Post tells them extraordinary tales from his exotic past, covering among other things just how important a family he was from in South Africa and how he is descended from a long line of fighters and, though his father and grandfather had fought the British for the better part of the last 100 years, he is glad to now be fighting by their side for such a noble cause as this.

Weary tells them that he would have joined the British Army, except that his senior at St Mary's Hospital, Sir Charles Wilson, valued his services as a surgeon a little and his services as a rugby player a lot:

> So, I joined the 2nd AIF via cables, with no medical examin-
> ation of my fitness, which was fine; and no pay, which was
> not. I've been to Jerusalem, Gaza, Cairo and Greece, where
> I saw some action but mostly suffered carbuncles, boils and
> middle ear infections![24]

After that I went to Tobruk as a surgeon and now I'm stuck here with you lot. Do we know each other now? Pleased to meet you.

But now, here is something else.

Thanks to the Red Cross, their British Camp Commandant informs them, they have a chance to send a *real* letter home, at least after a fashion.

'I can't guarantee all letters, but some will be picked out and broadcast to Australia.'[25]

How? It will be done on the ham radio run by the Red Cross – with the reluctant agreement of the Japanese, who will have an English-speaking guard supervising – on the strict proviso that its access is controlled by them, so that it cannot be used for anything other than precisely this: transmitting information on the prisoners' welfare. So if your letter is picked and broadcast, someone at home may be listening, and they may pass word on to your family. It is the faintest of multiplied hopes, but they write anyway.

Ern has no way of knowing if his letter will get through, but it feels good just to send. At the very least, somebody at the Red Cross will be learning what he is getting up to . . .

Weary and his senior officers will not content themselves merely with the Red Cross ham radio, as all solid news from the outside world is so prized inside the camp and all hunger to hear the BBC World Service. Of course, if you are found with a radio of your own you can be shot, but it's swings and roundabouts, isn't it, even if one of the swings in question might be from the end of a rope? Weary and Laurens have decided to risk it, and they 'put word out to our Chinese suppliers that we needed a radio'.[26]

Part of the hefty price they are prepared to pay is a form of insurance, because some of the Chinese suppliers have a gentlemen's agreement with some of the prison guards. A corrupt gentlemen's deal anyway: for a commission the guards will look the other way on surplus goods coming into camp. Not radios, but fruit and vegetables. And so, the Chinese will hide the radio under the fruit and veggies, which won't be inspected, and the BBC World will be at their service. Illicit payment is made and this morning Weary and Laurens watch the produce arrival with fascination.

Sure enough, beneath the bananas, beans and sweet potatoes, a radio is hidden. Barely hidden, it is a whopper, with gleaming metal edges they hasten to cover with cloth as their forbidden fruit is stashed away for later listening. Tonight, they will hear how the war is really going! Ears drawn close, the volume so low it could be mistaken for the buzz of an unusually literate mosquito, they listen and hear that the war is . . . really not going well. It is 'cheerless listening',[27] the BBC does not churn out propaganda, it details their losses and defeats in clipped detachment, but at least they know.

The next day something else unusual arrives in camp with their fruit and veg. It is another radio. Well, it is unusual to have two of them. The second radio is stashed away, a contingency in case something happens to the first. The day after that, something usual arrives with their fruit and veg, another bloody radio. (It's like buses: you wait all war and then three come at once.) The third radio is hidden, but at this rate the radios will have to have their own hut built for them. The next day 'to our horror',[28] Laurens and Weary get another radio! This is not only ridiculous, it is bloody dangerous. The guards keep changing; not all are on the take and it is a miracle that four days of delivery have gone by without a single search. Surely there can't be more radios arriving? Oh, but Weary is sure, these things are like the Sorcerer's Apprentice magic, they will keep coming and coming. By now they are sweating bullets, and not just from the sun as usual.

They can't be lucky five times in a row, and the next morning a very anxious Weary is pacing up and down the camp perimeter, waiting for the fruit and veg to turn up. Laurens joins him and they wait at the gate, smiling reassuringly at the guard glaring at them. And now the hand wagons are coming, trundling towards the gates and looking suspiciously bountiful this morning. The wagons are through and . . . and now a Japanese private rushes out.

'Halt!'[29] The private looks at the handcarts, looks at Weary and Laurens and then looks for his superior. 'I am summoning the Corporal of the Guard to search these supplies.'[30] There is very little suspense about what the Corporal might find, Dunlop and van der Post can peg it from here: 'Our Chinese providers had grown so careless that we could see, through the ragged screen of fruit and vegetables, shining streaks of the deep red-brown sides of another mahogany radio cabinet.'[31]

(Don't these Chinese know they already have a radio? They practically have a platoon of them. It would be funny if it weren't literally deadly serious.) Laurens does not have to say anything, they are both thinking the same thing: 'If the Japanese found, as they could not fail to, the radio among our supplies, it would mean not only the end of a vital source of food, but judging by what had happened in other camps, the execution of the people concerned in the smuggling of the radios.'[32]

They are one minute away from disaster now as they watch the guard scurrying towards the office where his corporal is resting. But if he's scurrying that way, that means he isn't looking this way, and Weary walks casually up to the cart and whisks out the radio.

'He did it as lightly and easily as if he were merely extracting a rugby football from another ruck.'[33] Ruck me! Weary thinks he is going to get away with this! There is hiding in plain sight and then there is walking into a prison camp with a LARGE RADIO tucked under your arm. He doesn't avoid the guard or the guardroom, he walks past both of them, whistling on his way to the prison hospital.

It is an outrageous bluff, barely even that, and it is called by an awakened and annoyed corporal.

Hey!

'Nani o hakonde imasu ka?'

'What is it you carry under your arm?'[34] Laurens translates, and Weary looks at the corporal quizzically for a moment before giving the obvious answer, 'Medical supplies.'[35]

Laurens, refraining from blushing out of sheer fear, translates it for the corporal as Weary waits.

Medical supplies?

'This is the doctor in charge of the sick people in the hospital,'[36] Laurens adds, a tautology produced by terror, but the guard does not even pause before waving them on. Medical supplies, of course. Who would be stupid enough to just walk past guards carrying a radio under his arm?

The only problem now is where to put the fifth radio. Perhaps they can start selling to Chinese suppliers? They seem to need at least one a day.

After his pulse returns to normal, Laurens grins in delight at the memory. The nerve! The pluck of this man! The gall! If every Colonel was like Dunlop, the war would be going a hell of a lot better.

•

With the camp moving into a rhythm, van der Post and Nichols find the time to begin a camp newspaper called *Mark Time* – printed on the strangely large Japanese-issue toilet paper, measuring eight by nine inches – giving news from the war and outside world gleaned from a few secret radios, news from the camp, poems and short stories and a few inspirational editorials. Van der Post himself – whose magnetic personality and ability with languages sees him gain ever greater influence – writes a popular column under the *nom de plume* of 'The Walrus'.

For those less inclined to things literary and academic, Weary also institutes a sports program whereby the men regularly compete against each other in everything from boxing to cricket to hockey to soccer and athletics. It is a heated contest, even when conducted at dusk, but games make the humidity bearable; the distraction of action making the effort seem effortless.

One day while Ray Parkin is sitting down quietly drawing in the crowded prison yard, van der Post spies him from afar, 'a bearded young man with a battered coolie's straw-hat on his head, sitting as far apart as possible from the crowd and impervious to the clamour. He was engaged in painting.'

And not just any painting. Coming from behind, the South African stands quietly over his shoulder, and watches in stunned amazement as a whole section of prison begins to appear on the canvas:

> In the centre of the picture like a symbol of triumph over defeat and confinement, a flaming Spathodia (or, as the Malays have it more feelingly, a Slippers-of-God Tree) soared above the high barbed wire fence.[37]

The two are soon chatting animatedly about Parkin's extraordinary adventures aboard the ill-fated *Perth*, how it had been sunk, his evacuation and then attempted escape to Australia aboard a rigged-up lifeboat, his encounter with a typhoon, and subsequent capture on the shores of Java.

'That's a great maritime war story,' says van der Post. 'That should become a book.'

'It is a book,' says Ray.

'How can it be a book? We've only been here a week.'

'I've written it all down.'

'I mean it should be bound.'

'It is bound.'

'What do you mean it's bound?'

'I met a bloke who was a bookbinder and he bound it.'[38]

It's true. In the downtime since capture, Ray had written the whole story in pencil on small sheets of shiny toilet paper, and found a place to secrete it in a hollow he had carved in the heel of his boot. Van der Post tells him he published books before the war and once the war is over he'd be delighted to introduce Parkin to his publisher. The spring in Parkin's step thereafter is not for the lump of the secreted book alone, but for its promise. Even more wonderfully, the South African soon uses his contacts on the outside to secure for Parkin an extraordinary array of colours from the black market, specifically Dutch watercolour paints from Bandoeng traders, all of such exquisite brightness, Ray can barely believe his luck.

The key to cheerful survival in this camp is perspective, and today all receive it from someone who can't see at all. An old friend has turned up with the latest motley: 'About seventy arrived from Tjimahi . . .' Weary records on 7 August. 'Bill Griffiths, the sightless, armless boy, now moves about cheerfully.'[39]

The most touching thing of all is how the Australians go out of their way to look after him. For beyond the hard unity forged by Japanese brutality, there is a softer unity in the humanity displayed by Dunlop's mob in their desire to look after the weakest among them.

'My fellow prisoners and POW doctors did all they could to keep me occupied,' Griffiths will recount. 'One doctor set me up with a pestle and mortar crushing herbs and leaves in an effort to make medicines. Another had me taking secret messages to the other parts of camp. I always did my exercises and tried to keep fit. My fellow prisoners helped me to survive.'[40]

In the most severe contrast are the Japanese guards who 'carried on with their brutality',[41] and would clearly prefer that he just die.

11 August 1942, Bandoeng, smoking them out

聴. *Kiku.* Listen.

聞こえますか. *Kikoemasu ka?* Hear it?

There, through the usual sounds of the sleeping camp that lightly fill the night – a few snores, a couple of groans and quiet curses, mixed with the eternal sounds of the jungle, the buzz of the birdcalls, the distant screech of hunter and quarry, the ripple of the river – something else is discernible.

There! That tiny, tinny sound.

What is it? Music?

Something, anyway. Something unnatural.

Two Japanese guards move towards it, padding across the compound.

In his hut, Weary is taking a big chance by listening on his ham radio even though Blue has taken ill and cannot stand guard on this night. But it is so late, and all but certain the guards themselves have surely gone to bed. And he is keen to catch up on what is happening on the Kokoda Track. The Japanese have made a landing on the north coast of Papua and at last call were advancing rapidly overland to Port Moresby, only to be met by a small group of valiant Australians. (Weary is particularly interested in this campaign as he knows that his old unit the 2/2nd CCS is involved, as is his great mate, Major Jim Yeates.)

And so he has no sooner flicked the forbidden wireless on than the BBC is crackling through the air of the Pacific with the patriotic marching song 'Heart of Oak':

> *Come, cheer up, me lads, 'tis to glory we steer,*
> *To add something more to this wonderful year;*
> *To honour we call you, as freemen not slaves,*
> *For who are as free as the sons of the waves?*

It's not exactly the 'Boogie Woogie Bugle Boy from Company B' but it will have to do, and it is doing a bit too loud as a soft signal turns up into a brief roar:

> *Heart of Oak are our ships, jolly Tars are our men,*
> *We always are ready: Steady, boys . . .*

Realising it is uncomfortably loud, Weary leaps unsteadily in the direction of the set but at the very moment he does so he hears feet stamping towards the door. *Damn!* The set goes off, the plug is snatched from the overhead light socket and Weary grabs the war wireless and shoves it soundlessly into a box cupboard, stuffs a shirt over it and leaps back to where he was sitting; adopting a pose of meditation. Christ, even Buddha would be sweating to make it through this one.

In the last split second before the guards fling open the door, the lotus-positioned Weary glances up and sees that the light socket above him is still swinging! Too late, they are here so be here now and pretend all is normal.

Two sentries enter, and their bayonets are fixed; one stays fixed on Weary, waiting for an opportunity to run him through. The other guard starts searching the hut. Weary, feigning surprise and puzzlement, has one clear thought in his mind:

'If they uncover the set, I must kill them. But what will I do with the bodies?'[42]

The search continues and so does the thought. Desperate to distract, Weary reaches for a very effective weapon: a packet of cigarettes.

'Care for a cigarette?'

One guard does, the other continues to search. Finding the radio is just a matter of time, and then at least one man in this hut will die. Suddenly, the guard without a cigarette stops his search and orders Weary outside, marching him to the door as the other man continues the quest for contraband behind them both. Outside the hut, Weary is asked about the men in huts nearby and he struggles to make his answers as helpful and evasive as possible. He can hear the other guard clanging and banging, shuffling and searching as the guard outside watches his eyes. Then, terrifyingly, a silence begins.

The guard orders Weary inside once and they enter to see . . . the other guard smoking a fag while he sits on Weary's bunk. The box cupboard is unopened, the warm radio lies unnoticed within and the guards bid him goodnight. If it were not for that ciggy, a Dutch brand that the men don't even like, death would have come tonight.

The radio will remain silent for the rest of the night, the thump of Weary's heart is enough music to be getting on with. The other huts are all searched thoroughly, but the guards never do work out where that strange song was coming from.

> *We always are ready: Steady, boys, Steady!*
> *We'll fight and we'll conquer again and again*

Mid-August 1942, Bandoeng, kangaroo caught

Trouble. Real trouble.

Private Franklin is one of those rare Australian POWs who is less one-in-all-in and more in-it-for-himself. And now, it is not just that this 'thorough dyed-in-the-wool young scoundrel'[43] has been found to have been embezzling money from his fellow POWs via his promises to 'change money' with the locals, and short-changing the results, it is that he is making a very specific threat that if Weary and his senior officers go ahead and 'hand him over to the Japanese' – something they have no intention of doing – he will inform them that Lauren van der Post is a spy and Colonel Dunlop has a ham radio.

In response, Weary is in favour of 'a very short sharp Field General Court Martial and would even consider the responsibility of summary action by Lt Col Lyneham'.

In layman's terms? Put him on trial and then execute him. Yes, extreme, but what the scoundrel is threatening would have devastating consequences for them all. In the end it is the responsibility of Lieutenant Colonel Lyneham, and that officer decides upon 'proceeding with the court martial as though it were a Test cricket match'.[44]

Instead of the short, sharp, field court martial that Weary wants, with a quick verdict of 'guilty', the whole thing goes for days, but at least Franklin is court-martialled and sentenced to be confined to his cell for the foreseeable future. (On such matters, the Japanese are content to let the Allies discipline their own men.)

The problem is that it is soon discovered that, courtesy of a cleverly concealed latch on his back wire window, Franklin is indeed roaming freely at will. Now his punishment must be increased, and Private Franklin repeats his threat.

'I will tell the Japanese of your wireless, and have you killed if you do not do a deal.'[45]

'Tell them and be damned!' Weary replies with some force. 'I will tell a few reliable men that you are a traitor and to kill you immediately anything happens to me.'[46]

There is a pause.

Franklin heads off to solitary, as silent as the grave.

'Franklin's sentence,' Weary records in his diary, 'announced as six months.'[47]

•

Ever and always since the dawn of time it has been a problem.

When men born to roam are suddenly confined, they can be like too many tiger cubs in a small cave, and turn on each other.

No, in this case it is not that there are many fights per se, but certainly tensions rise, arguments are louder and the tropical torpor is regularly punctuated by sparks of anger that risk turning into fiery confrontations. Words become heated more easily in this humidity; some of these men are at breaking point almost as soon as the day breaks. For the truth is that, despite getting thinner and thinner by the week, these blokes are *so* young they still have energy – particularly if there might be a stink on.

To channel such energy into something more useful, to give the men a focus beyond just getting through every day, Weary has an idea, and, after seeking an audience with the Japanese camp commandant, soon presents it. Why not allow us to have a sports tournament so that our energy has somewhere productive to go? It will allow the men to blow off steam, literally and figuratively, and give those watching some entertainment to pass the long days.

The commandant, a rather short and portly Oriental gentlemen, likes the idea, but comes up with whatever the Japanese version of a 'cherry on top' might be.

'It would be a great honour,' he tells Weary, 'to allow me to demonstrate the superiority of the Japanese race by competing in the tournament.'[48]

Weary rises to the occasion, by balancing a further cherry on his original cherry. 'Would it not be a greater honour,' he suggests to his captor, 'to compete against me as the ranking Australian officer?'[49]

The Commandant looks Weary up and down. Yes, his prisoner is well over six feet tall, mostly muscle and gristle, but . . .

But Major Dunlop is not Japanese, and that is where blood will tell.

The sports tournament takes place, and is a great success. The contests between Weary Dunlop and the Commandant are . . . a fair success . . . after a fashion.

Surprisingly, Weary suffers a series of narrow defeats, going down in everything from the sprints to the 880 yards, to the shotput and javelin. It is only in the high jump that he manages to salvage honour.

Such is the comprehensive nature of his victory that the Commandant takes that minor defeat with good grace, and does not stop beaming for weeks.

And, the Commandant retired from the field, Weary has a remarkable return to form.

'I won three events,' he records on 29 August. 'Hop Skip and Jump, 12m 23; shot put approximately 12 metres; discus approximately 29m. Unfortunate exhibitionism in Hop Step and Jump loudly applauded! (I lost my pants).'[50]

•

There is no way around it, and the evidence grows with every day. The biggest threat that Weary Dunlop must now confront is malnutrition – the men are wasting away before his very eyes. Yes, once burly blokes who had been raised on a diet of meat and three veg, often with three large square meals a day, simply cannot cope with two or three tiny rectangle meals of rice in their dixies, just rice, as their staple diet. Their bodies cry out for meat, for potatoes, for carrots, for beans, for *volume*!

One way to improve the collective diet is to pay for more supplies from the local traders. As Weary will explain, 'I did good business with some of these traders in Java to support the sick prisoners. Just on my signature that George Rex would ultimately pay them they were willing to advance money.'[51]

King George is good for it, he's a sterling chap.

But that line of credit can only go so far, before they need to hand over real money, and for the moment, they have precious little, despite the convention that all POWs doing actual work beyond mere maintenance 'shall be entitled to a rate of pay, to be fixed by agreements between the belligerents'.[52] (Unfortunately for the Australians, while the Japanese have signed the Geneva Convention they have not ratified it, so despite the Hague Convention, despite the Geneva Convention, and with a great deal of spite, all such notions are studiously ignored. And in terms of actual cash, most are like POW Geoff Dewey, 'None of us had any [money]. I hadn't been paid since Gibraltar.'[53]) For the moment, the Japanese remain sticklers for their lack of principles and refuse Weary's impassioned demands.

So, while it is wonderful that they are, yes, able to buy a certain amount of fruit, milk, meat, eggs, bread and butter from a nearby town, such supplies as they can get do not go far.

Typically, Weary is the first to notice the symptoms of malnutrition showing up in his daily mass of patients. Many of them complain of burning feet, the classic sign of nerve damage coming from lack of vitamin B in their diet of mostly rice. Even more obvious than that, a lot of them are already so skinny they have to walk around to get wet in the rain, and others are also suffering beri-beri, pellagra, optical neuritis, and, most particularly, ulcers.

The bottom line is that, despite scrounging all the money they can, and extending their credit to its maximum, they simply have too few resources to feed the thousand Australians for whom Weary is responsible.

There is only one way around it, and that is, with Japanese permission, to grow their own food. On the grounds that he has done farming in both South Africa and England, Laurens van der Post is put in charge, and at Weary's behest, the South African and his men put particular effort into growing *katjang idjoe*, which is the local variation of bean sprout, as it contains copious amounts of the vitamins C and B1, which is what they are most lacking. Ducks are also put into coops, and they are soon able to serve every man one duck egg each week.

But the real solution?

Van der Post is convinced it is . . . pigs. After the Japanese provide half-a-dozen prime sows, they must build sties from the only planks available: which come from the bed-boards. Laurens engages the help of the guard the men call 'Donald Duck' who agrees to gather whatever resources he can so long as Laurens will continue to talk to him about Greta Garbo, Marlene Dietrich and . . . Shakespeare.

Forsooth, what manner of man then is this?

An odd one, but certainly a pleasant change from the usual brutality. At first the plan goes well, but . . . too well. For, although the Japanese quickly provide another 250 low quality pigs, they neglect to provide the feed to keep them going, and the pigs inevitably start to starve just like the POWs.

'The only reason why the pigs do not prosper is because your spirit is bad,' van der Post is told by the Japanese guards, 'and unless things improve, you will be held responsible and severely punished for your wilfulness.'[54]

Fishponds and rabbits are also tried, with mixed success. The problem with the rabbits is the men become so attached to them as pets that they outright refuse to kill them for their dinner.

Rather more successful are the vegetable gardens, which Laurens soon has fully planted, tilled, watered and cared for by eighty full-time assistants, where they grow everything from beans to various varieties of root vegetables. The soil is so rich, after all, that you could plant a toothpick and grow a pine tree, and while there is still not enough food for every man to have his fill, it helps a great deal. Their Japanese captors are content to leave them alone, insisting only that Laurens grows eggplants as they personally want to eat a vegetable that brings good luck, and also believe – and Laurens, to Weary's amazement, confirms – the eggplants will even grow by the light of the full moon.

With the food situation improving, there is even enough energy to work on another project, and at Weary's direction some of the men have soon built a rough stage, complete with an orchestra pit. As some of the POWs had been actors, producers and artists before the war, stage productions are soon underway. For scripts of plays, the Japanese give them access to some of the English literature library they have confiscated from one of the Dutch schools and several wonderful shows are put on.

'These conditions are almost unbelievable luxury compared to our treatment so far,' Jock Clarke records. 'Most of the Japs are strangely pleasant too. We are extremely suspicious about this change . . .'[55]

And yet, as the weeks go by, the men continue to lose weight and that pinched look in the face of those growing emaciated is becoming the norm, rather than the exception. To keep track, Weary has all of them examined with notations recording their overall 'state of health. (O = good; A = below usual; X = illness).'[56]

By 18 September the news is starting to get grim as ever more malnutrition is showing up.

> Normal health (O) 69%, Below Par (A) 27%, Definite Illness (+) 4%. (Bad illness.) . . . Criteria for A were mainly loss of weight, recent illness, feeling and appearance of patient. Malaria: many having relapses and very little plasmoquine available.[57]

Weary becomes sick with worry. The diagnosis is obvious as their chiselled facial features and bony ribs come into shockingly stark relief: they are slowly starving.

September 1942, Bandoeng, dummy war

'We now have new guards,' Weary notes in his diary on 8 September, 'Koreans who have not, I understand, had any real active service.

They are rather brutal and most of those slapped down do not quite know why.'[58]

Things had been bad enough with the Japanese guards, with face slapping one of their preferred means of communication. But these Koreans – mostly big men, with dull eyes – seem to delight in hitting all and sundry with closed fists and don't even bother pretending they have a reason to do so.

Korea has been part of the Japanese Empire since 1910, and now the Japanese have conscripted a staggering 250,000 of the young men of these subjugated people into service as guards in their latest war.

One thing these guards clearly don't like is any congregation of men for any reason whatsoever, and they simply wade in with fists flying to break it up. This includes the lectures, to which some of the newly arrived Korean guards take a *particular* dislike, and arrive with clubs swinging to put an end to the whole thing. Quite what it is about such lectures that infuriates them is never clear, only that their rage seems real, as they unleash in what Weary describes as 'a tide of fury'.[59]

Even when that tide ebbs, it is not over.

'When they got tired of hitting us, they made people line up and hit themselves.'[60]

At one point, a fortnight after the brutal Koreans have arrived, a softly spoken English chap named Denman – a prominent surveyor before the war – is lecturing on an engineering subject when *something* he says or does enrages one of the Korean guards so badly that he charges into the lecture, yelling and throwing punches at every POW in reach, before throwing the Englishman to the ground and unleashing heavy kicks to his ribs.

In moments, a Wallaby is between them. In times of peace, in a place like a boxing ring, or a pub, Dunlop would be beating the hell out of the Korean. Today, he is acting as a tackle dummy, throwing his massive frame into the picture to soak up each belligerent blow; until the absurdity of this situation dawns in the mind of the guard and the notion of shame stops him, however briefly. Weary pushes the guard away now; and for a mute moment the men wait for their commander to be king-hit. The moment passes, the guard moves on.

But Weary will not leave it there, '[ignoring] the two soldiers' bayonets which followed my back closely as I walked away in contempt, taking with me the battered Denman'.[61]

After putting the still bleeding officer in the care of the Gangster, Weary stalks off to see the Japanese Commanding Officer, to register his outrage and disgust at this appalling brutality. It is not only against the Geneva Convention but all sense of human decency!

The Colonel is . . . bemused.

'Colonel, I am very sorry,' he begins. 'I have new soldiers, they think you are savages.'[62]

And they really do. Walking back to his own hut, Weary can't help but notice the Koreans furiously putting up rolls of barbed wire around their barracks, clearly convinced that the Australian savages might attack them at any moment, and quite likely *eat* them.

Things do not improve, as Weary notes that the guards play 'hell like the little tin horn inferior sons of bitches they are'.[63]

And such violence begets more violence among the guards themselves, and certainly in their interactions with the POWs.

Still, it is the Japanese who remain the prisoners' most persistent persecutors. Weary struggles to get to the bottom of just why it is that they are so vicious, so extraordinarily inhumane, almost always without the tiniest hint of anything resembling common decency. Little by little, it becomes clearer:

> The Japanese despised anybody who became a prisoner. In their own culture, it was a matter of honour to arrange for somebody to decapitate you rather than submit to become a prisoner, or to commit Hari-Kari. Therefore, those of us who did not do this, in the eyes of the Japanese, were the lowest form of animal life.[64]

Against that?

Well, against that, many of the Australian soldiers have an innate view that the Japanese are nowhere near their equals as men.

'My generation had been brought up under the influence of the White Australia policy,' one Digger will note, 'and considered ourselves superior.'[65]

Yes, it is a clash of men, of nations, and of cultures – but right now only one of them has the guns.

October 1942, Bandoeng, making the world go round

Good news.

'At a formal ceremony,' Weary will recount, 'we were received as prisoners of war officially and that from that point on we would receive pay for work.'[66]

From now on they have, at least nominally, some rights, even if there are many caveats.

One is that while the Australian officers will ostensibly receive the same pay as Japanese officers, it will only be paid 'in the local currency, less a deduction to be put in the Yokohama specie bank', soon enough nicknamed the 'Yokohama suspicious bank' by the Allied officers. And if you are sick and can't work, you get no pay, because to the Japanese sickness is shameful.

The coming pay will amount to 220 yen per month for Weary, less a further 60 yen that are to be 'deducted for food, quarters, electric light, gas, water'. There is also a 'dependents sum' for their families at home in Australia, which is to be paid when Japan captures Australia, 'and defeats UK to establish new order'.[67] Right. Well, fingers crossed then.

Right now, though, the officers will be getting some real money, actual guilders. Each officer of field rank is to receive fourteen guilders a month, while each NCO and soldier will get four guilders a month. The mood of the camp lifts . . .

•

It is Laurens van der Post who first puts the idea to Weary Dunlop.

Why not live like communists?

Sorry, what?

'Like *real* communists,' the South African says, with everyone being genuinely equal.

Goodness! The last time someone had proposed communism to Weary as a solution to what ailed the world, it had been Sam White back at Melbourne University, and Weary had personally manhandled him out of the room where he had so disgraced himself.

But in response to the inevitable Weary query, the answer comes back. Van der Post wants the officers to live on an equal footing with the men.

'All officers to put everything into the pool and live purely on the men's diet.'[68]

To Weary it sounds less a political idea, and instead 'rather like the New Testament. It has me in, but I fear it is impractical.'[69]

On the other hand?

Well, such a collective fund really would be more than useful to buy additional food and medicine for the men from local traders, and from that realisation on – coupled with the fact that illness from malnutrition and lack of medicine continues to get worse all around – Weary needs no more convincing.

This money, he is soon telling his fellow senior officers, should go into one collective pool (which sounds a lot better than a 'communist' pool, a word he quickly bans van der Post from using again).

One for all, all for one – and one in, all in.

And yet, Weary soon learns how mean-spirited some officers are, as there is a strong backlash coming from certain quarters at the very *idea* that they not keep every guilder they have coming to them . . .

The next day, the officers are split and the camp is in two camps. Camp One, backed by Weary and headed by Wing Commander 'Nick' Nichols, wants to take all pay from officers, except two guilders weekly, and pool the rest to buy goods for all the men. If they win the war, well, His Majesty's Government will reimburse them. Probably. But if each of the 36 officers keeps just two guilders per month this method will enable them to raise – dot three, carry one, subtract two – a more than useful 452 guilders a month. And if the men do the same, keeping just two, they can raise a grand total of 1200 guilders a month for the general welfare.

Camp Two, headed by Lieutenant Colonel Ted Lyneham of the 2/3rd Machine Gun Battalion – who still looks to Weary like a one-man scrum, solid and fierce – wants every officer to keep every bit of their own pay for themselves.

Why? Well, how should one put it delicately? Who cares, let's just say it: 'Certain troops are not worth being given officers' money.'[70]

And why is that? Because certain troops have not been grateful when they were given money in the past. And certain other troops are just bloody awful. Weary cannot believe it: 'This is magnificent – it seems that an officer's duty is something which is only carried out if the troops are worth attention.'[71]

Worthy troops will be given money, on a case-by-case basis, or as Weary puts it: 'buying gratitude'. Not if he has anything to do with it.

In short order the officers are in conference and in loud disagreement. Nichols wants the officers to sign an agreement on pooling their pay. (Weary had been wrong in his initial assessment of this English officer, adding an addendum to his original notation that he was 'nervy, and a bit jumpy'.)

'I subsequently found that Nichols' diffident style cloaked a dedicated, brave and virtuous officer.'[72]

Other officers are less virtuous and are very dedicated to hanging on to their brass.

'I will never sign such a thing!' says Lyneham. 'I'm being requested to sign a *ridiculous* document to do with unauthorised seizing of officers' money!'[73]

Oh, for God's sake, you are not being robbed in the high street. We are in a POW camp, trying to stay alive! Yesterday, the trumpeter collapsed on the parade ground before he'd blown the bloody trumpet! What other indications would you like? These men are starving, we can feed them, or feed them better, now. *No.* Meeting adjourned. But more meetings take place, privately, on 'Officers' Street', organised by Lyneham's adjutant, Major Beaney, and a furious Weary is told that Lyneham has gone over his head and told Group Captain Gilbert Nicholetts – a newly arrived high-ranking officer, who he hopes may lend authority on the matter – that there is no need for the officers to hand over any money to their lessers.

The next day's conference is senior officers only, all Colonels, and Weary goes at Lyneham like a stray All Black forward on the edge of a ruck.

'I was in a fighting mood,' Weary will recount, 'and just gave [Lyneham] everything straight on the chin.'[74]

And so, Weary, you have the floor.

'I am disgusted in you, Lyneham,' he begins. 'You went to the Group Captain without discussing the situation with me; which is a breach of military procedure but also of normal decent behaviour between human beings.'[75]

The Group Captain is broadly with Weary: 'It is not often that five Colonels meet to discuss such a matter.'[76]

But he will make no such edict to that effect. He has no authority to order the officers to hand over money. If it is done, it will be done voluntarily.

Late September 1942, Bandoeng, magic bullet

It's hot; hotter than usual, which is saying something. So why is Ern Corrie smiling? Because he is, if not happy, at least happier than he was. The food situation is slowly improving.

'Every man was given a bread roll per day as well as his bowl of rice,'[77] something often augmented by local Dutch settlers giving those out on work details whatever food they can spare.

Alas, the Korean guards do not take kindly to the Dutch being kindly, as Ern and co. discover when walking back to camp on this day, carrying the dairy ration. For now, they see a poor Dutch lady, who has been so daring as to walk out of her house with two hands of bananas for the passing prisoners, being chased by a Korean guard. The woman screams as she runs back to her own property, but that is no protection, the Korean raises a whip and brings it down hard on her legs. Not once, but several times as the screams grow louder and the Australians burn with anger at the shame of it: 'It was terrible to watch and not be able to do anything about it.'[78]

That such things can happen . . .

Some of the food they get in camp is watery rice, which is excellent at giving them the trots. One evening, Ern wakes up and staggers out, half asleep, towards the toilets at the double only to hear a cry from a Japanese guard.

'KURA!' he roars, using his pidgin for Corrie. 'Why you no salute?'

Ern is wide awake now.

'I didn't see you,' he says.

'You Australian?'

'Yes,' says Ern.

The guard smiles and points at his watch chain. On it there is an unusual decoration, a silver bullet. Now the guard points to his leg, where the bullet once was.

'Australian,'[79] says the guard.

Ah. And Ern is smacked in the face by the guard's open hand, the start of a beating for the bullet.

He tells the story to his fellow prisoners after he returns from the loo and they grin. That guard has a name. It is 'Silver Bullet'. He asks every lone prisoner where they are from. If they are from the USA, his bullet *came* from the USA; if they are from Britain, why that bullet *came* from Britain. That bullet comes from everywhere but it always ends up handing out a beating!

CHAPTER NINE

DEATH IN THE JUNGLE

Weary had already become a bit of a legend. Everyone was so glad to be with him, they looked up to him. Although the officer quarters were separate – it was an old army camp and therefore it was arranged in that way – he used to come and mix with the blokes and of course we'd see him on the sports field. Although he was a doctor he was so much of a leader that he was actually put in charge.[1]

Chief Petty Officer Ray Parkin

October 1942, Bandoeng, having a ball

Weary opens his diary with the most important entry: 'Helen's Birthday. God bless her wherever she is.'[2]

He is in a sick camp, with some very sick men: 'over a third of them now look quite ill, thin, pale and drawn'.

Their unshod feet are burning and so are their testicles. Yes, 'Bandoeng Balls'[3] is a new medical condition. It might not be getting into the *Lancet* soon, but it is in Weary's diary every day. The first symptoms? Well, it is a raw and weeping scrotum, accompanied by ulcers at both corners of the mouth. The cure is relatively simple, if mostly unattainable. For yeast is a help. (That is, yeast on your scrotum – as yeast in your mouth is a luxury beyond imagining in this camp.)

Not surprisingly, Weary is now *desperate* to scrounge whatever extra money he can – from officers' donations, contributions from the underground and on-side Chinese traders who continue to accept IOUs redeemable after the war – to supplement the food they are getting. Calories in are far below calories expended. These men will get thinner and thinner until they are *so* skinny they need no longer shuffle off this mortal coil – it just slips off. Weary's greatest frustration is that so many of the conditions the men are suffering

184

have such a simple solution, for the real medicine is nothing other than . . . *food*.

'We hadn't had enough time for these deficiency diseases to become really lethal,' Weary will recall of this time. 'They were a terrible nuisance, a misery with your own mouth [ulcers] and raw scrotum and burning feet. And you might even start to go blind. But it was *still* reversible, if you got a bit of yeast or a source of vitamins, you could reverse things, and we hadn't lost all *that* much weight.'[4]

So long as they get food, and soon, things are salvageable.

On 13 October, at least, the money comes in – which is a good start. Two full months' worth of pay for all officers, delivered overnight. There is no prizes for guessing what the morning conference will be about today: money. The 'Regimental Fund' is where all the standard money goes, the 'imprest' is the term used for other money, whether it is given by 'sympathetic' Chinese traders as a secret loan to be repaid after the war, or donated by British and Australian officers, or any underground donations, including from Dutch citizens. So, how big will the imprest fund be now? That is something that will be discussed by *all* senior officers at a special meeting today. Yes, every one of you. In the one meeting, so we can *all* hear what you have to say. Weary has had enough of the little 'indignation meetings of Aust. Officers'[5] which he keeps hearing whispers of every evening. It is time to settle this once and for all, before the men find out what the hell is going on and give their officers hell for the rest of the war. Are they going to be live communists or dead . . . free marketeers?

We shall see.

But, no time to tarry. He must get on with the endless paperwork that goes with being the commander as, despite the fact that they are POWs, all men must be accounted for and records kept of their health, disposition and discipline. With around 1000 men currently in camp, it is *endless*, but must be done – or at least all signed.

•

And so it has come to this. In this stinking heat, a trial for decency will be held in the camp's 'Radio City' – the spot where they stage their plays and concerts – as the glaring officers assemble well away from the men to thrash the money situation out. It is like a council meeting held in the jungle; all have mini-speeches and points of order at the ready.

It is Weary Dunlop who has called the meeting to resolve the crucial matter before them, and he sits as Chair, with Arthur Moon at his right-hand side, ready with the pertinent medical facts.

Weary begins:

> I am asking you all for absolute observance of confidence as I wish to give frank information about financial matters involving dangerous observations, such as:
>
> One. The serious decline in the troops' health.
>
> Two. The iniquitous nature of the diet. Everything possible is being done with Nips but we must help ourselves.
>
> Three. Origin of the Regimental Fund and its battles.
>
> The total cash available for expenditure at present is 4024 guilders. The anticipated minimum expenditure from now on to be 1200 guilders monthly; this must be greatly increased.[6]

Over to you, Major Moon.

Major Moon outlines just how grim the situation is, how many men risk dying unless their diet can be improved, and just what ravages malnutrition is taking on them. He concedes that 1200 guilders a month alone won't solve all the problems, but it will certainly help.

Very well, gentlemen, you have the nub of it.

'Now,' Weary goes on, 'you have heard the minimum required. But let us do better than this and put in *all* September's pay.'

A hand is raised.

Yes, Lieutenant Colonel Lyneham, my fellow Australian?

For once, Colonel Lyneham concedes that 'some help should be given'. Alas, he devotes the rest of his speech to highlighting just how poor his officers are, and how sick they are. He not only does not want to contribute any more, he and his supporters want to be paid *back* the minimal amount of money they have already had to hand over.

Wing Commander Nichols in return is every bit as curt as he is to the point:

> What are we giving men? Little more than two handfuls of *katjang idjoe* and two eggs a week, which will only keep men

alive. Our duty is to put money in and we can't rely on outside money. Let us ensure that the monthly sum reaches 1600 guilders. Donate September's pay and all above 2 guilders a week . . . It is our *duty* to give at least the sum suggested.[7]

Very well then, Weary now opens the floor to those who wish to speak, expecting Laurens van der Post to come in over the top, in full support. Strangely, however, the South African remains mute. A captivating man one on one, spinning tales of great grandeur, he unaccountably recedes in group situations.

It leaves the floor once more to Lyneham, who fills the vacuum by leaping to his feet and decrying the injustice of levying Australian officers of their hard-earned money, particularly the younger ones. Was not their own health impaired? Where better for their own money to go than in paying for their own food? And besides all that, he insists there is 'sufficient money [in regiment funds] to look after the troops for 10 months'.[8]

He is supported in turn by his adjutant, Major Jim Beaney, who questions the accuracy of the figures given, and maintains that the fund as it stands is quite adequate for six months without officers' aid.

Weary Dunlop keeps his peace and holds his fire, but finally, he cannot hold it in anymore.

Choking with disgust, he speaks now.

'It is,' he grates out, 'a difficult job to run this camp with all the grave responsibilities it entails. I am prepared to make way at any time for any senior officer who could make a better job of it. If, however, I am to continue to discharge these responsibilities, I will not flinch from the task. I thank you therefore for expressing your views, but I shall now write to each of you personally requesting your donations at the level we have recommended.'

Weary is not going to let them hide behind a collective decision; each man, individually, will have to record whether he will give over money to support the men or not. And the record will be kept. *NOW*, do you want to renege on your duty? He cannot fathom that they dare to call themselves Australians:

I left this melancholy affair in almost the lowest frame of mind imaginable and disgusted at the light in which Australian officers had been shown. Imagine, after a clear statement of the miserable health of the troops and low finances, to hear a discussion by officers as to whether they would give the help required. Where is the principle 'my horse, my men, myself'? The leadership in this matter disgusting, and I feel I handled the meeting badly.[9]

Which is as may be.

But after he writes to each officer, nearly every man-jack of them contributes the money he has asked, and his authority as their leader has never been higher. For, it works.

'An astonishing transformation took place in our camp,' Laurens van der Post states. 'All traces of confusion, bitterness and in-cohesion vanished. We rounded up all the public money we could find in the possession of senior officers in the camp, established contact with Chinese merchants outside prison and bought food on the advice of the Australian medical team to supplement inadequate and unbalanced prison ration.'[10]

The common soldiers certainly appreciate it and are not surprised to hear that Colonel Dunlop is behind it. He is dinkum different from other officers, and has no airs about him of being superior, let alone *a* superior.

•

Every day, the same.

The postman blows his whistle and Doris Corrie – 'Dorrie Corrie' to her friends – wipes her hands on her apron and goes out, hoping against hope for a letter from Ern, a sign that he is alive, that he can speak to her by letter the same sweet way he has since they married in 1935. It is a dream she carries that will not be put down by what happens each morning.

For every day, it is the same. Stone, cold motherless *nothing*. It is like he has disappeared into the void. Last thing she knew he had been serving with the Blackforce, then the terrible day had come when she had heard over the radio that Singapore had fallen and, since then the news of Australian defeats and retreats in Java compounded her fears. The only comforting thing is their toddler son, Robert, but as the days, weeks and now months have passed with no word, even Robert can't lift her, and she has all but given up ho—

A whistle.

Again, she wipes her hands on her apron, and trudges out, expecting the usual array of bills that she will struggle to pay on her Servicemen's Dependants Allowance. But what's this?

It is a letter with a postmark from, let's see, Kalgoorlie in Western Australia. But she doesn't know anybody from there? With great interest, she opens the envelope to find a missive in neat copperplate writing from a woman she has never met, and who does not even know how to spell her name as she has never seen it written, only heard it:

> *Dear Mrs Coray,*
>
> *I was listening to the Batavia Broadcasting Station tonight and heard a letter read – written from your husband to you. I am sorry I could not write quickly enough to repeat every word and some I could not quite catch but if no one else has sent it on to you I know you would like what little I can repeat for you. It commenced:*
>
> *Dearest,*
>
> *I often wonder how you are keeping these days. I do trust you are well dear and not worrying about me. The food is a little different to what we have been used to – I am very well (he said something here about where he once had curves they had now given way to healthy muscle).*
>
> *We have a very good camp – concerts – some very good artists – a choir. I am one of the choir.*
>
> *Now Dearest I must close – love to yourself – and Robert.*
> *Your Ever Loving Husband & Daddy,*
> *Earnest'*
>
> *I am,*
> *Sincerely Yours,*
> *Miss E. Roth.*[11]

Doris's heart sings.

God bless you, Miss E. Roth!

•

Extraordinarily, there is even some direct response back to the POWs from Australia.

Back in Melbourne, Thelma Parkin had no sooner heard of her husband Ray's message via the Red Cross than she has left her two small children in a neighbour's care and gone to the post office to send a telegram, *just on spec, addressed as follows*, to 'Petty Officer Ray Parkin, Prisoner of War, Java'.[12]

And on this day, just days later, it somehow gets through, and is even handed to Parkin himself by a Japanese guard.

```
DARLING, TERRIBLY GLAD TO KNOW YOU ARE SAFE. ALL WELL
HERE. SEND OUR LOVE. DO NOT WORRY. KEEP HOPING. LOVE.
THELMA. 13
```

Parkin's feet won't touch the ground for days.

•

Great news! And after it comes over the ham radio, Weary joyfully records it in his diary in his typically illegible doctor's hand.

3 November 1942 – Australians have taken Kokoda (New Guinea) and pushed further on.[14]

He knew it! In a straight-up fight, he was always sure the Australians could take on the Imperial Japanese Army and win. It's an enormous feather in the cap for the Diggers. Beyond everything else, it is one in the eye for – no names, no pack drill, but it rhymes with 'Finston Burchill' – all those who wanted to throw the mighty 7th Division into an insane excursion into an already fallen Burma, instead of coming back to fight in what John Curtin is calling the Battle for Australia.

For Weary, the growing success of the Kokoda campaign means Australia is less likely to be invaded, *and* Helen is safe. All he has to do is to survive long enough to get back to her. Onward, Christian soldiers.

Now as summer starts to rise, the days begin to melt into each other, in a blending blur of light and heat that has no respite, bar the brief bursts of intense rain in the late afternoons.

More troubling still is that another move is soon afoot – a chunk of it on foot – which will take them from Bandoeng to Makasura Camp, positioned by the main road out of Batavia leading south.

It is with some regret that Weary must take his leave of Nichols and Laurens van der Post. Sadly, he doesn't get to say goodbye to Lieutenant Colonel Ted Lyneham, who will be coming with them to wherever it is they are going. There had been yet another issue with him in recent weeks, with money that he had been administering in trust from the Japanese to distribute to the officers having gone missing.

For those remaining in camp, it is Nichols who will now take over Weary's formal command. The two take their leave of each other with firm handshakes and enormous respect, despite their rocky beginning.

Far more distressing for many of the men, as it happens, is that those men who have pet rabbits are firmly told by the Japanese that – at least for the moment – the animals will not be allowed to go with them. But, never fear. Their captors firmly promise that the rabbits will be sent afterwards, and they even have a method of determining which rabbit belongs to which prisoner. To the men's amazement they are issued with some indelible pencils and each rabbit owner writes on the inside of his squirming rabbit's ears their name, rank and serial numbers.

(Their rabbits, in fact, will never be seen again once the prisoners have left, but simply issuing them the pencils and making the promise has calmed them. The attachment of the prisoners to their pets is nothing short of *extraordinary*.)

Fall in!

'Kura!'

As is the Japanese way, every POW must stand rigidly to attention in front of all their worldly possessions, so they can be searched for contraband.

That done, the next order comes, just as the first lustre of dawn makes dim headway through the thick mist.

Move out!

Leaving behind the 500-odd English soldiers, Weary Dunlop and his 1000 Australian soldiers – with their packs on their backs – begin their march to Bandoeng Station at 5 am on the morning of 6 November. There, a train awaits, to take them down from these Javan highlands, back to Batavia.

'The high towered lights cut illuminated fans in the cold mist,' Ray Parkin records, 'enshrouding the railway yards. Crowded in the boxcars, we rattled and shrieked over ravines and around red-soiled, rain-soaked mountains . . .'[15]

Clickety-clack, don't look back, the men gaze out upon an outside world many had near forgotten, of small villages, gaily attired women and ever smoking Javanese men, all going about their daily chores to start the day, balancing jars of water on their head, heading to yonder rice paddies, gathering eggs and rounding up small children.

Oh, to be free once more themselves!

Gradually the ranges give way to coastal plains and finally a large station where they come to a halt.

'Tumbled us out of the train in a hell of a rush,' Major Jock Clarke chronicles. 'Up the road at a hell of a pace . . . The march – seven miles flat out – absolute agony – men falling over & left by the roadside with a guard to be picked up later. At the end of my tether when we arrived at the camp. I have not been too strong since that bloody fever I had. God what a comedown this camp is after Bandoeng.'[16]

Makasura proves to be a swampy bit of acreage that was once a coconut plantation, with a curious collection of bamboo huts, many of which have those same coconut trees growing through the ceilings, which occasionally sees – *look out!* – the coconuts themselves crashing through to pay a visit. While there is a little brickwork in the centre to give the huts stability in storms, the roofs and the walls are thatched fronds of the attap palm tree, and the interiors are little more than bamboo beds lined up tightly side by side, the whole camp surrounded by no more than a relatively benign barbed wire fence.

Despite the heat and humidity, the most wonderful thing about Makasura is the sheer space – enough for Weary to not only organise an athletics carnival, but also to personally win a 440-yard race around an admittedly rough – and clearly badly measured – track, against Wing Commander Ron Ramsay Rae in a time of . . . 50 seconds. (This is pushing perilously close to being a world record for this 'distance', but Weary chooses to accept his glory at face value.) He knows he is not the swift athlete he once was back in his heyday at Ormond College, but such a good race is at least a sign that, despite the ulcers he has recently developed on his legs, his health is holding and the vitamin course he has put them all on is actually working. Others report the same, and the numbers on the sick list are slowly diminishing, in no small part due to the essential decency – a rare surprise – of the Japanese officer who has been placed in charge of them.

But for now . . .

'*Kura!*' Stand to attention!

'Nip commander (Lt Tanaka) had a parade of all troops marked unfit to march,' Weary notes in his diary. 'He inspected them all sympathetically and marked his movement rolls without comment. He is a very intelligent fellow who speaks a little English and has always behaved well to prisoners here.'[17]

Such basic humanity makes an enormous difference to the POWs.

'This camp has done us good in many ways,' Major Jock Clarke chronicles. 'We have become quite resigned to the idea of being shipped to Nippon. It has shaken us out of the lethargy we had fallen into at Bandoeng – we are taking more exercise. I am feeling 100% better myself . . . We can buy a greater variety of goods at the canteen and plenty of fresh fruit. The nights are hot and one goes to sleep sweating profusely and half stifled under a mosquito net. The mosquitos are not bad but some are malarious. I certainly could not afford to get Malaria until I have built up a bit.'[18]

19 December 1942, Makasura, caged bird sings

Stone walls do not a prison make, and neither does a thick jungle, if you can let your mind go free. The best way not to lose your mind is to lose it in a book, and as part of a revolving POW 'lending library', Weary finds himself captivated by a Chinese work by Lin Yutang, *My Country and My People*. Its lessons are simple but deep and Weary takes them in whole, as he notes in his diary:

> It is a striking error to assume that the comforts and ameni-ties of Western society necessarily bring happiness. On the contrary, possibly most of the happiness of this world is that of simple people living close to the soil. Even my present squalid conditions with their terrible limitations do not make me really unhappy. Happiness is something rather individual and internal.[19]

What makes him happy, internally, individually? Helen. The thought of her, the love they share, it is something that transcends. Lin Yutang makes Weary philosophise further about the society he is fighting for; he has no doubt the 'Western world is sick' somewhere in its unhappy soul. And it really might be that the Eastern world has something of the cure. (Not the Japanese part – the *rest* of it . . .) There is every chance that he could die any day. Every soldier knows this, every prisoner of war knows it better. But what of it?

'Supposing our Java adventure ends in death; somewhere, somehow in the southern soil under these eastern seas, there is something in the thought that perhaps my love was a thing which soared wondrously above other things in life.'

But his love is not 'was'; it *is*, and Helen has been his love for five years now. She is absent; but she was absent when he was in England too, and yet she is with him. Now, why is it, when the war was not happening, they were apart? Could they be too much in love with the dream of each other to let reality ruin it? Weary ponders it now: 'Some deep subconscious instinct not to risk something very precious in the ordinary commerce of reality?'[20]

Oh, what he wouldn't give for five minutes commerce with her now. What a fool he was not to be with her when he could. You don't need a philosopher to explain this to any young man, it is the old 'have your cake and eat it, too'. Now he just has rice.

•

The *joy*.

Weary's racing pen records it in his diary, just before Christmas.

'Momentous day: received per radio by means of the Batavia station and the ABC the following message from Helen: "Delighted to get your message. Splendid efforts commanding your hospital. Am happy, well and not worrying. Keep cheerful. Our future holds so much. Love [Helen]." '[21]

He is even able to reply:

```
I AM NOW IN A JAPANESE PRISONER OF WAR CAMP IN JAVA. MY
HEALTH IS EXCELLENT I AM CONSTANTLY THINKING OF YOU.
IT WILL BE WONDERFUL WHEN WE MEET AGAIN. OVERJOYED TO
RECEIVE YOUR ADORABLE MESSAGE AT CHRISTMAS TIME. VERY
WELL AND CHEERFUL. FOND LOVE TO YOU AS ALWAYS DARLING.
    EDWARD. 22
```

Christmas Day 1942, Makasura, tidings of discomfort and joy

It is not merry this morning, it is melancholy and quiet; a solemnity that is as unnerving as it is unfamiliar steals over the men. Usually, good cheer and bad jokes start the morning; why, it is as compulsory as roll call or being bitten by a mosquito. But this is a holy day; you didn't feel it so much at home, but now, so far from home . . .

The night before at least had been merry, with a Christmas Eve cabaret called 'Xmas Krackers' being a riotous affair. What it lacked in wit it made up in filth and slapstick, which had not pleased everyone.

'Community singing taken over by some RAF people,' Major Jock Clarke had noted in his diary, 'lots of dirty songs interspersed with quite good music. One very filthy monologue – very bad taste. Tommies produce much more "studied" filth than the Australians.'[23]

Happily, the tone had soon lifted, and even featured the world premiere of a new song, written by Weary's adjutant, Major John Morris.

Cunningly marketed to an upcoming occasion, it's called 'Happy New Year' and its chorus is so catchy that all are singing it before the song is done:

> *Happy New Year to you – good cheer to everyone*
> *Put on your brightest smile and let's have lots of fun*
> *Leave all your cares behind, for bright days are in view*
> *LIFT UP YOUR VOICE IN SONG – there's a happy new*
> *year for you!*[24]

Well, there might be, but this morning it's just bleak. They have never felt so alone, together. Each man is picturing the family he is not with today. At 9.30 in the morning, 1400 men assemble, not for roll call but for hymns. They form a square and the best voices are gathered in the east to be the choir.

'Hark! The Herald Angels Sing', 'God Rest Ye Merry Gentlemen', 'I Saw Three Ships', and, the one that is so well sung it hits them in the chests: 'Silent Night'. They are all used to that contradictory Christmas of Australia, winter carols sung in high summer, but here, in Java, in prison, the sweet words are so rich in irony that it is almost too hard to bear their beauty.

> *Silent Night, Holy Night*
> *All is calm, all is bright*
> *Round yon Virgin Mother and Child*
> *Holy infant so tender and mild*
> *Sleep in heavenly peace . . .*

They think of their own wives and infants; the parents who will be thinking of them now; and it is a struggle to retain their composure while the choir finishes.

Anyone for a beer? Not a whole beer, but half a mug at least? And a smoke! God bless the local Dutch women, who have known exactly what each man would want for Xmas. Sadness turns into high spirits with every sip supped, high jinks and japes soon follow and Weary roars with laughter as he sees the dignified face of no less than a Wing Commander being hit by a well-thrown banana. The high-ranking officer, a pompous git, spots the man who threw it and leaps like a tipsy gazelle at the New Zealander, only to miss his man and plant his face spectacularly in the dirt, which makes every man cry with delight. Now that is great slapstick!

It is all so riotous and joyous, it even sees some of the Japanese guards watching quietly from the shadows – not quite sure what is going on, but not wanting it to stop. (They are *takusan* strange these Australians. Despite having disgraced themselves and their families by surrendering and not fighting until their own glorious death they don't . . . look very ashamed at all.)

There is even a respectful visit from the enemy: a Major Anami, who Weary describes as 'a bearded, elderly fine-featured N'. The Major appears to recite a learnt phonetic phrase: 'I send you happy Xmas.'[25]

He also allows the POWs a piano, which they may play all night if they wish – and they do. Every type of song is sung, from, fittingly 'The Singing Soldier' to . . . 'a few in much lighter vein'.

(They all start with men who have boarded a good ship named *Venus*. It is not exactly traditional Christmas fare, and rather more in the way of traditional army songs for drunk men.) Weary has promised the men will all be on parade tomorrow, and it already is tomorrow; it is 4.30 in the morning and it is time for bed otherwise how can they get up?

Before he sleeps, Weary writes one message in his diary: *Happy Xmas to you Helen dear*.[26] And to all a good night.

On Boxing Day, the men are allowed to play sport. Weary begins his day with basketball and ends it with a relay race. The conditions are not ideal; the track is terrible and features the unusual hazards of barbed wire and open drains. The Senior Officers team consists of Fred Camroux, Hec Greiner, Bill Wearne and Weary Dunlop. They make the finals to complete one 440 each. Sadly, the finals are won by the bloody RAF, but there is one satisfaction in the fact that the fastest individual lap is run by one Lieutenant Colonel Weary Dunlop, 'which surprises me in view of the fact that I never run or train'.[27]

One odd thing is noticed today, white officers are seen, being saluted in the distance by the Japanese.

Nazis.

Why are they here? Something must be up.

And something is down.

The screens – the thin bamboo walls that surround them, more to obscure vision than anything else – are being taken down around the camp. That can only mean one thing: the camp itself is being taken apart. The wire will be next. But where are they going? One Japanese guard guesses their thoughts and whispers the answer as he walks past, 'You go Nippon.'[28]

What? Taken to Japan? Does that mean they are winning the war or losing it? Why would the Japanese bother to move them into their homeland? Some paper propaganda is handed around now in camp. Apparently, according to the Japs, they have, 'staggering success Solomons, New Guinea and much talk of Pearl Harbor and Philippines'.[29]

Well, if the Japanese are doing so well, why are they moving their prisoners backwards? The next day comes the surest confirmation of rumour and speculation: Weary is asked to give the names of any men unfit to march. They are moving on. Oh, and the Japanese would also like to see stool samples from every man who claims to be suffering from diarrhoea. Of course. It might be runny but Weary has an almost endless supply if they are interested.

They are very interested, and an apologetic Lieutenant Tanaka has more shit news for Weary. At tomorrow's parade at 9.30 am each man is to be on parade with 'a specimen of faeces on a bit of paper, a somewhat dextrous and malodorous feat'.[30] Now word comes, some cards for travel are marked with 'S', some with 'N'. As far as Weary can make out, those letters stand for Singapore and Nippon – and it seems the Australians are bound for 'S'.

That is, if they are well enough to march.

If not, 'N'? Or will they just be left here? Who knows? Weary looks for the bright side: any movement is better than torpor.

'God knows what lies ahead in the way of hardship, short rations, disease and death before the end of the road, but the mind does not speculate much about such things.'[31] Not if the mind wants to remain sane. 'As for me, I am perhaps a *vrai* voyager and hanker for new countries and new experiences that we sum up as "adventure".' The last few years have tested him, but Weary thinks he is stronger for it, as he has 'a nervous system as strong as an ox'. He still feels fear, but he knows what can cure it, the greatest terrors can be 'trampled underfoot by self-discipline and a resolute and steadfast way of living'. You must construct order out of chaos: being a prisoner is a job; do it. You know, if you look at it the right way (try upside down): 'Life really hasn't been too bad, even under the squalid circumstances of this camp.' Who knows? The next camp might be better.

'Everyone on parade this morning with the jolly old faeces in hand – but worse was to come with rectal swabbing.'[32]

It is, however, a shit New Year's Eve. For four bloody days in a row they have been told to parade with their faeces by their side. They have been probed, swabbed, inspected, examined and now they are doing it again?

'They are faeces crazy and at 9 pm we were again issued with cellophane for another parade (faeces in hand) at 0900 hours tomorrow!'[33]

As it is December the 31st, the Japanese decide that lights out will be at … 8 pm. As per usual. It is a 'miserable travesty of an evening' and if anyone sings that New Year's Eve song, sarcastically or otherwise, they will get a bollocking. Even cheery Weary notes that he feels 'rather murderous towards anyone who talks about Happy New Year'.[34] Roll on 1943, for we've had enough of 1942.

On 2 January, Weary is given the numbers by his captors: 895 men are to move on, including 15 Officers and 12 Warrant Officers. (Scanning the list, Weary is at least pleased to see one thing. Lieutenant Colonel Ted Lyneham will *not* be going with them, wherever it is they are going – and is apparently to be sent to the Japanese-occupied territory of Formosa.)

Stores can be drawn by the men – coats, buckets, boots, mosquito nets, plates and forks – or each man that Weary thinks fit enough to bear the burden. They will march tomorrow night.

Night?

Yes, 'too hot for march by day'[35] says the commandant. Oh, and there will be another faeces inspection before they march. The fact that they are even given boots is some indication that the march will be an arduous one.

Weary inspects the stores and finds that the Japanese idea of a 'large' boot is small by Australian standards. Hopefully, this won't be a long march. There is much to do before setting off, including sewing his diary into his cap, and having 'Angus', as they have code-named the ham radio set, broken up into separate pieces and hidden in his effects and medical paraphernalia to be re-assembled later. (The other four ham radios are broken up and thrown deep into the latrines. It will be a brave Japanese soldier that does a search there!) Yes, there is a risk in carrying such things, but he is the one who must bear most of it – though, at their insistence, majors Jock Clarke, Bill Wearne and Allan Woods will also take pieces with them, rolled up in their socks. If a search is on then ideally they can – God bless their cotton socks – simply throw the socks away.

Finally, all is done.

That night, Weary is attacked as he sleeps, bitten by a large rat 'that got inside my mosquito net and chewed my hair, finally running over my face and becoming tangled in the net'. Weary tries to beat it to death with his torch, but the light keeps going out with each blow and the rat escapes 'he bit my chest twice – damn him and his family'.[36]

This is starting to look like a long war.

•

Fall in!

Yes, it is still just 2.30 am on this fourth day of the New Year, but the Japanese are insistent. *Quick march!* In the sweltering heat, the men move off in what really is meant to be a march, but is closer to shambling rambling, carrying whatever personal belongings they still have, with Makasura Camp soon falling behind and the men even taking up a song as they march along the Java roads.

How I love the kisses of Dolores
Aye-aye-aye Dolores
Not Marie or Emily or Doris
Only my Dolores

From a balcony above me
She whispers 'Love me' and throws a rose
Ah but she is twice as lovely
As the rose she throws[37]

The mood, despite that, is exhausted angst. Just what awaits? The only thing that becomes clear, for now, is first a railway station before dawn where – sir, your carriages await. Actually, they are goods carriages, into which the men are crammed unceremoniously before, a few hours later, they disembark at Batavia itself, and must march once more to the port of Tanjung Priok, where they are told to board a very small rusty hulk by the name of *Usa Maru*. She is no more than 4000 tons and soon christened the *Byoki Maru*, very 'sick ship'.

(Was it really less than a year ago they were here, disembarking from the *Orcades*, full of hope if not optimism that they could stop the Japanese? It feels like at least a decade.)

In the half-light, another party of Australians – some thousand strong – files on first, and now their own order comes in a guttural bark:

Embark!

To get on the actual gangplank, however, they must pass by a Japanese team that showers them with a strong spray of carbolic solution – all over both them and what little kit they have – designed to kill off any pestilence or plague lurking upon them.

In short order they are pushed down into the hull of this crowded cargo ship, and physically *squeezed* into a space measuring no more than 30 yards by 16.

But, good God, we are over 400 men! How could we *possibly* fit onto and into such a small tub? It is a question that occupies Weary and his senior officers over the small breakfast they are served on the dock as they work out who to send on board in the lead of everyone else, on the grounds that whoever is first will inevitably go to the bowels of the ship, with less light, air and space than those who follow. The answer is, it must be the strongest among them who lead, on the grounds that they can best withstand it. Weary himself picks some of the healthiest men and by 9.30 am he is leading them on board:

> There were two small gangways to our hold for 433 men and all were drafted like sheep to these, duly stumbling down to a scene which surely is some figment of the imagination when one ponders over the black hole of Calcutta. A typical hold of a rusty old tramp, a square vent above practically covered

> with heavy planks, rust and cobwebs everywhere. Every square
> inch of space is occupied by a man or his baggage . . . rats and
> cockroaches plenty.[38]

Two days of hell on earth and worse on water awaits – even if the ocean itself proves to be 'as flat as a shit-carter's hat' – and they finally emerge on the wharves of Singapore. Fall in! They are to immediately be trucked to a prison camp by the name of Changi, which some of the Australian soldiers on work detail on the docks tell them is nothing less than the worst place in the Pacific.

Changi is the largest Japanese POW camp in the whole regional theatre – with 50,000 men crammed into a prison designed for just 4000 – a place where men are held until being sent to work camps around Asia, including back in Japan. (Their real worry is about being taken to its older and more solid namesake, Changi Gaol, but it turns out that this is only used for civilians. They are relieved to know that they will be heading to some kind of camp, or at least that is what they are told.)

Piling on to the back of lorries as the darkness falls with its usual rapidity in these tropical climes, they are able to proceed through the quiet and moonlit boulevards of a city under occupation, every street corner held by Japanese sentries on the lookout for any resistance from the locals.

(Weary can't see any, either.)

After crossing myriad bridges from which they can see fishing boats bobbing in canals and junks lying in the mud – the lorries stop a long way before Changi itself. Some long marching follows before, exhausted, the men finally get to what appears to be their designated three-storey stone barracks late in the night, only to be initially put in the wrong one, and have to decamp to another, three blocks down.

Finally, shattered with exhaustion, battered by so many miles under their belt in so many conveyances under such appalling conditions over so many days, they get some kip at 4.30 in the morning – though Weary, for one, finds it so surprisingly cold, he must get his greatcoat as extra cover above, while he has just a single blanket between him and the hard concrete floor.

Paradddddddde . . . attennnnnn-shun!

Paradddddddde . . . riiight . . . turn!

After just two hours sleep – a remarkably solid one, given that their cells are coarse concrete and *not* 'tiles that are very smooth',[39] meaning that for once, they don't slip on to each other in a confined spot – Weary and his men have been woken at 0630 and told they must be on parade at 0700 hours, to be presented to 'a full retinue of the 8th Division'.[40]

And so here they are, weary and bleary, dearie. Gazing at their surroundings, and seeing Changi for the first time in daylight, it is simply unbelievable.

For Weary's mob have been hearing a lot about Changi and how dreadful it is from the moment they have arrived in Singapore. But now that they are roughly assembling in the centre of what appears to be a well cared for parade ground and can look around, it does not seem to be like that to them!

'The magnificent stone barracks of three storeys with red-tiled roofs,' Weary will note, 'occupy a lovely bluff overlooking the sea.'[41]

Those barracks, get this, even have electric lights and running water. And that, of course, is not all. For, once descended on the tightly packed gravel of the road, the men are immediately surrounded by a bunch of Australian officers from the 8th Division, with a distinctly British feel about them, 'neatly dressed . . . carrying canes, blowing out puffy moustaches and talking in an "old chappy" way'.[42]

And even then, the surprises keep coming. For as they head back to their barracks, they pass *brick* latrines that are missing the usual stench that would kill a brown dog, and right beside them are shower blocks! A little further down, beyond the neat lawns, they can even see a building marked 'Mess Hall'.

'Well, I've got to say as far as we're concerned,' Blue Butterworth will later say, 'Changi was a convalescent depot. Changi was easy.'

And then there are the soldiers facing them. For inevitably, the two groups of soldiers – those newly arrived with Weary and the long-time residents of Changi, the 8th Division – look at each other with some amazement.

Weary's men are quite stunned to see just how . . . how . . . how *young*, and neat the 8th Divvie blokes are.

'We see all these polished soldiers,' Blue says, 'just as if it was normal days, normal wartime?'[43]

I mean, just *look* at these coves.

'They were all done up. Sam Browns. *Brylcreamed* hair . . . pork pie hats from the South African Red Cross and good boots.'[44]

Beyond that, they have recognisable uniforms – many of which fit well because the soldiers have the same well-fed weight now as when the uniforms were issued – and polished boots. Their hair is clearly cut with actual scissors by the barbers among them, and no-one seems to have the thousand-yard stare that belongs to veterans who have known terrible battles and seen things too shocking to ever forget.

Weary's mob is not like that at the best of times, let alone after two days in the bottom of a leaky boat. For, over the months in Java, the men from Makasura had been obliged to wear whatever they could get their hands on as their own clothes fell off them, including second-hand Dutch uniforms, saris, rags, and often bare feet.

And that is what many of the 8th Divvie men see: Wild men from Borneo, or thereabouts.

In sum?

> We were veterans and they were all new chumps. Some of those poor buggers . . . only just arrived over there in Selarang in Changi, in Singapore I should say, and the war they're straight into it and over, five minutes. No training. Practically no training at all. Poor devils.[45]

The lack of welcome that Weary feels for himself and his men is palpable, and clearly expressed in the eyes of the 8th Division's Commanding Officer, Colonel Fred 'Black Jack' Galleghan, now standing before them and clearly gazing with contempt at the new mob that has blown into Changi 'like the leaves of the trees'.[46]

With just a look, this towering figure of forged steel from the military establishment, who has been with the Australian Imperial Force since 1916 – priss and polish to some; piss and wind to others; but either way with a ramrod where his spine should be – can see they are anything *but* military.

I mean, just look at them! Many of the newly arrived are even wearing straw hats – through which, their hair springs in all directions, for they have not had the time for haircuts, nor the need, nor the clippers – and they look like nothing so much as a ragtag mob of ruffians. Why, at least a third of them have no boots, and some of them are completely barefoot! (And don't even talk of the stench. After four days in the hold of a Japanese tramp steamer, sweating, covered in lice and bugs – despite the carbolic spray – all of them just a mess of heaving flesh, and gross garments, it means that just one whiff of the new arrivals could kill a kookaburra in mid-flight stone-dead, down-wind at 50 paces.)

And why are they staring, open-mouthed, at his own soldiers?

It's because of what the men of the 8th Division opposite them are doing. They are actually standing there on parade with – *get this*, Jacko! – 'broomsticks for guns'.[47] You just couldn't make this up if you tried. Fuck this for a game of soldiers. But hark . . .

Attennnnnn-shun!

Colonel Galleghan is about to speak. Or maybe *bark*, as it turns out . . .

For yes, as he now makes clear, he is firmly of the view that there is a right way and a wrong way to do things, and the good Colonel is very much of the view that Lieutenant Colonel Dunlop has gone about things the wrong way. In his book – and he is a man who operates by a very thick one – they are first and foremost men of the Australian Imperial Force, and must behave as such, irrespective of their POW status. There is a great chance that British forces are going to break us out of here, and when that day comes, we will be ready to pick up as an army, where we left off.

'You're *soldiers*,' he has frequently told his own men on parade, 'and when I march you out of this camp I'm going to march you out as soldiers. I'm not going to march you out as a mob. You'll still be soldiers on the day it's over.'[48]

This new mob that has arrived under this Lieutenant Colonel Dunlop are clearly no more than a mob, and Galleghan is not happy about it. They will have to be brought into his disciplined way of doing things.

So let us get to grips.

In a meeting with Colonel Dunlop straight after the parade is over, Galleghan's remarks are nothing if not sharp. (One of his underlings will later say of him, 'His personality left no room for half measures. He did not necessarily seek your regard or goodwill.'[49])

Dunlop and his men are going about things all wrong. Once arrived, no matter that it was in the silent watch of the night, sentries should have been posted, and compliments sent to the Commanding Officer of the unit just joined – which, to be precise, is him, Colonel Galleghan.

But had Dunlop and his men done any of these things? You have not. You have simply crawled into the bunks you were shown to grab some sleep, which was extremely unsoldierly. We will only survive this war with our bodies and dignity intact if we always behave like soldiers, and that starts with observing military command structures.

(Weary can't see it. Sentries? What for? Who is going to attack? The Japanese? Rather unlikely, under the circumstances of them already running Changi prison. Present his compliments at 4 o'clock in the morning? He had few compliments to spare at that time, and there was no-one to present them to.)

But Colonel Galleghan doesn't see it like that, *at all.*

'Black Jack,' Weary will recount, 'was really furious that compliments hadn't been paid or the right things done, and the guards and sentries were not posted properly and so on.'[50]

And that is not all. Black Jack does not like the command structure. Why on earth is a mere non-combatant Colonel in charge of a unit of soldiers, when he is not even the highest-ranking officer there?

Such is the substance of what Weary finds to be a pompous and presumptuous letter from Lieutenant Colonel Galleghan on this, the first full day since their arrival:

> Comd. AIF desires following information. Name of senior combatant officer with party.

(As in, who is the SOLDIER in charge, not the doctor. Who is the one who can restore DISCIPLINE?)

> Suggesting changing O.C. party to combatant officer. Is there any reason for not making change?[51]

Weary's reply is quick and clipped. The name of the officer? He is Major William Wallace Wearne. Oh, and about Weary giving up command:

> Your suggestion welcomed. Present arrangement result of Nip policy in Java . . . As senior officer Lt.-Col E.E. Dunlop was instructed to command the party in transit. Before making any change your further advice would be appreciated. Could this matter be discussed with Comd AIF tomorrow 10. Jan 43?[52]

In the meantime?

Weary receives a visit from the senior officer he had been with on the *Orcades* and then seen in Bandoeng when he had come on inspection, Brigadier Blackburn VC. He is far and away the most senior combat officer among them, and happens to be briefly passing through Changi at the same time as Dunlop and his men. Blackburn has, in fact, come to say goodbye to Weary as he is about to depart for a POW camp in Formosa, in accordance with the Japanese policy of removing all senior officers above the rank of Lieutenant Colonel from their men.

What do you make of it, sir?

In response, Brigadier Blackburn is furious.

The *hide* of Galleghan to seek to impose his preference for a combatant officer on what is already working very well. Well, Blackburn won't have it, and – because he is being shipped out the following day – quickly pens Weary a note to pass on to Galleghan, saying, 'I have considered this matter & desire Lt Col Dunlop to retain command for administrative & disciplinary purposes so long as the troops brought over by him remain together as one body.'[53]

At dinner that evening, the heat goes on.

Unaware of the note in Colonel Dunlop's pocket that already settles the matter, Black Jack Galleghan goes on at some length.

'Your position is quite incorrect,' he says in his dismissive tones, as if he is the very one who *wrote* the book on such matters. 'As a non-combatant you have no authority whatever to give commands to or punish combatant soldiers. It is laid down by the book.'[54]

Having read the said book, Weary knows this to be absolute nonsense, but cannot be bothered arguing. He simply agrees with everything, before coldly saying, 'You are the Commander of Australian troops here, so take appropriate action.'[55]

But now it happens.

Within Weary's earshot, one of the British officers refers to the Australians as the 'Java Rabble'.[56]

Oh, really? It requires a response, and Weary is the man for the job. For he is descended from the Dunlops of the Lowlands of Scotland, and his great-grandfather, the Reverend Walter Dunlop, known as 'Our Wattie', had been so famed for his twinkling sermons – all without notes – that a monument still stands to him in St Michael's churchyard in Dumfries, bestowing a blessing upon all his descendants. The largest and most accomplished of those descendants rises now, to give a mocking toast from the new boys in response, pausing a moment for silence and to have the room in the palm of his paw.

Thank you, thank you all, with a particular thanks to our hosts of the 8th Division. But as to the so-called Java Rabble, I cannot help but note . . .

> The prisoners I command have fought in the Battle of Britain, battles across the Atlantic, the Mediterranean, Greece, the Western Desert including Bardia and Tobruk, Crete, Syria and finally Java. And now we, the Java Rabble, salute you, the 8th Division, who have fought so gallantly here in Malaya.[57]

Shots fired!

The rabble leave rubble in their wake.

The rabble also now take to referring to the 8th Division as the 'Malay Harriers' in honour of the amount of ground they had covered in reverse – and in such quick time, too, so bravo, you Harriers – getting away from the Japanese.

Nearing the end of the evening Weary finally produces Blackburn's note, in the manner of one who has just a short time ago received it by messenger.

After reading it, Black Jack is beyond furious. He refuses to accept the authority of Blackburn: '*I* am the commander of the troops in Malaya,' he tightly informs this upstart Major medico. '*I* do not take orders.'

'Well, very good, sir,' Weary comes back brightly. 'You are *my* commanding officer . . . Do anything you like. I am not even interested.'[58]

Well, Galleghan remains interested and, refusing to give up, seeks out Major Wearne, imploring him to assert his authority as a senior combatant officer and replace Lieutenant Colonel Weary Dunlop as Commanding Officer.

Sorry, *what*, Colonel Galleghan?

The *Brigadier* has already decided matters; and that is where this matter will rest!

But . . . but . . . but . . .

I want you, Wearne, to take over command from Dunlop.

'What do you have to say if I refuse, sir?'

'That would be a gross dereliction of duty.'

'In that case, I should give you my reasons against it in writing.'[59]

Is that really necessary?

Yes, if you insist on this, but Major Wearne equally makes clear that, 'no other officers . . . will accept the assignment'.[60]

True, Major Wearne is regarded as a first-rate officer – and one of the youngest in the history of the British Empire to be made a Major – but he also knows better than most how valuable Lieutenant Colonel Dunlop is, how highly regarded he is by all and sundry. And no matter that Weary is not a combat officer, no-one will be superseding his command on Wearne's watch. And, he has no doubt, his fellow officers feel the same. Weary, not Wearne.

In the end, Colonel Galleghan, as Weary will recount, 'was unable to find any officer in my command . . . to accept the change'.[61]

At last recognising that he is beaten, Galleghan grandly tells Weary that he will now give him the 'formal authority to command' the combatant soldiers in 'Dunlop Force', as it is now to become known.

'Thank you, sir,' Weary replies in as bland and friendly manner as he can muster. 'I assure you I bear you no resentment, and it is very nice of you to go to all these pains on my behalf.'[62]

Very well then. Galleghan even asks what can be done to help the 878 members of Dunlop Force. What do you need?

'Clothing and boots,'[63] tops Weary's list, though he also adds a request for such things as 'rice polishings'[64] – the husk off rice, which is even better than the rice itself for Vitamin B, for the 8th Division seem to have plenty of it, and his own men continue to suffer from lack of sufficient or proper food – with one of his recent diary entries having noted, 'Our number now showing malnutrition amongst the 1000 is now 160+.'[65]

Colonel Galleghan promises to look into it.

Of course, Weary's toast at the dinner defending the valour of Dunlop Force spreads round Changi as fast as a bushfire with a southerly buster behind it. Lieutenant Colonel Dunlop decides not to record any of it in his diary. His legend is already being burnished by his fellow prisoners, no need to write this part down for posterity.

Unable to command Dunlop Force, Galleghan does the next best thing and gets rid of them. For they have been at Changi for no longer than two weeks before they get the word. They are to be sent away, on a work detail in parts unknown. Whether it is indeed Black Jack who has organised this with the Japanese is unclear – but there is no doubt he will be glad to see the back of them.

Weary, for the record, is convinced that Black Jack is behind it. 'I'm afraid all this did was to get us perhaps promoted in the order to depart.'[66]

Despite the fraught relations between Dunlop Force and the men of the 8th Division, there is inevitably an exchange of information between them, and for the first time Weary's men realise that they and their mates put ashore at Batavia had simply been sacrificed as a sop to Britain keeping faith with the Dutch – it was not a battle they could ever win!

'A lot of them when we found out,' Blue Butterworth will recall, 'were very upset.'[67]

None more than Weary: 'God help the [Australians] if Churchill had succeeded in throwing them into collapsing Burma in this scrambled state with essential weapons on other ships!'[68]

Moving on. For they really are. Galleghan and his men are to remain in Changi, as the previous rumour that Weary and his men are to be sent away on a work detail is now taking shape with added detail. Unless it's all a furphy, which is possible, they are to go to Siam, now apparently known as Thailand, to build a railway to supply the Japanese forces in Burma laying siege to India – so that Japan won't have to risk their shipping, going around the Malay Peninsula – but who knows? Just about any option that will get them away from Changi and Galleghan seems like a good option.

Weary himself is more than ever convinced of this when Galleghan gravely informs him that the 8th Division has no rice polishings to spare and if Dunlop Force wants any they should buy it from their own funds. Oh, and those boots and that clothing you wanted for you and your thousand men of Dunlop Force?

In a response that gives some clue as to where the 'Black' part of 'Black Jack' comes from, Galleghan is heard to say he will 'give nothing to that Java rabble'.[69] In fact, he finally manages to donate – dot three, carry one, subtract two – six pairs of size 11 boots, together with a couple of dozen caps, 150 pairs of socks and, rather than even a dressing-gown, gives the Australian another dressing-down about just how poor he finds the Java Rabble in everything from marching to saluting.

Weary Dunlop is appalled and astounded in equal measure. The dressing-down is neither here nor there – just blather. But the lack of willingness to help them is extraordinary. In the reverse situation he would not have hesitated to give those who were suffering more than his own, whatever was possible to help alleviate the situation.

His rage is matched by those of his men, with the likes of Ray Parkin noting that, 'the "Singapores" started their captivity with seven pairs of shorts and seven shirts EACH. They have never shifted camp nor been made to hand their gear in.'[70]

Meantime, Weary can't help but note that advanced medical treatment in Changi is nothing if not singular: it comes daily from the rear of a chicken. Yes, as 312 men of Dunlop Force are currently diagnosed with sore mouths, they each get an egg a day. Now, they will have to pay for their own care; an extra egg a day costs them 49 cents a week. Severe cases get two eggs a day. It is effective, and the miracles that some paltry poultry can work in the realm of ulcers is pleasing.

All up, Dunlop Force is getting more organised by the day, and at Weary's command is now structured on three units – O, P and Q Battalions – allowing him an easier way to exert command and hold officers accountable for the men's health and discipline. The unit will be part of a much larger grouping, known as 'D Force'. Mercifully, on the day before departure, many of the blokes in the 8th Division, as Ray Parkin notes, 'despite official decrees, have given us boots and shirts'.[71]

The next morning, before leaving, Dunlop takes the time to write a note to Galleghan:

> Two weeks ago, my men arrived in a pitiful condition in this camp from Java. You have done nothing to alleviate their needs. Tomorrow at 8.30 they leave in the same pitiable condition bootless and in rags. You have done nothing.[72]

Again, these prove to be Weary's opening remarks, for he does not leave it there.

'We certainly left in a pretty poor shape and bootless and so forth,' he will recount, 'and I left some strong protests at their headquarters in Singapore, which didn't endear me. I was chased into the utmost corner of the jungle with letters minuting their displeasure.'[73]

THAI–BURMA RAILWAY

Happiness lies with harmonious relations with one's fellows and service to mankind other than a dirty, unprincipled self-seeking existence.[1]

Weary Dunlop, diary entry, 28 February 1943

Obviously the Ns have a great reserve of manpower here and at Singapore and they are showing every intention of just breaking men on this job, with not the faintest consideration for either life or health. This can only be regarded as a cold-blooded, merciless crime against mankind, obviously premeditated.[2]

Weary Dunlop, diary entry, 19 March 1943

[Weary became] a lighthouse of sanity in a universe of madness and suffering.[3]

Private Donald Stuart, 2/3rd Machine Gun Battalion

20 January 1943, leaving Changi, Changi the guard

In these parts, there is nothing so cheery as *'All aboarrrrd!'* to impart that it is time to get on board the train.

Instead, after being put into trucks at Changi and taken to Singapore's main station, they are pressed at the point of bayonets into 22 cast-iron boxcars designed to carry two tons of rice to a truck – or indeed 30 tightly packed men, as you choose – which will take them on the beginning of a long journey. With that many men plus their luggage in a space measuring just 7 feet by 18 feet, there really is no room to even change your mind, 'crowded as sheep or pigs in a saleyard'.[4]

The last ones on board must make their way into iron hot-boxes where blokes are banging on the sides and frantically crying out, 'We can't breathe! Open Up! Open Up!'[5] – but, bayonet or burst, they must keep filing on. Many of the men have been told by the

Japanese that they are going to a 'better land far away, and we should be sure to take plenty of sporting gear',[6] so this is not remotely the start they have been expecting.

Beneath the blazing sun the atmosphere is stifling. Just as it had been on the ship, the only men who can lie down are those who are seriously ill with the likes of malaria, dysentery and diarrhoea, so for the most part the rest of them must sit, slumped against each other, waiting for this hell-on-earth journey to begin. Men vomit, faint, urinate and excrete without anyone noticing particularly – such is the overall stench, and barely conscious exhaustion.

At last the train starts to *l-lu-lur-lurch* forward, and more or less keeps moving for the next three days – apart from stopping to fill the boiler with more water. There are also occasional stops like when they pull into Kuala Lumpur Railway Station – a superb Victorian structure that now stands as a massive tombstone to what had been the rule of the British Empire in these parts, now under Japanese control. At least the Australians are able to barter things like watches, fountain pens and even rings for fruit and vegetables with some of the local vendors on the platform, though this only makes their gastric troubles more devastating, and it is not just the carriages now moving once more.

Given that no air circulates and there are no facilities for relieving yourself, other than taking turns to lean out of the doors, the situation is beyond appalling.

In these parts, as the sun belts down on their trucks, the sides become too hot to touch, and for the men of Dunlop Force it feels like they are in an oven – their situation made worse for the fact that the rice rations they have been given for the journey have started to rot, and there is not enough of the still edible rice to go around.

Aggravating things even further is that now, more than ever, they are under the control of guards who are habitually even crueller than the Japanese – the Koreans – who continue to serve the Japanese Army by performing the lowest of all low jobs befitting ones of their own exceedingly low rank: guarding and bashing the Australians.

Open parenthesis. As ever, it all goes back to the culture of their captors.

'We learned very quickly the hierarchical structure of the Japanese,' Weary would note, 'in that a colonel would have no hesitation in

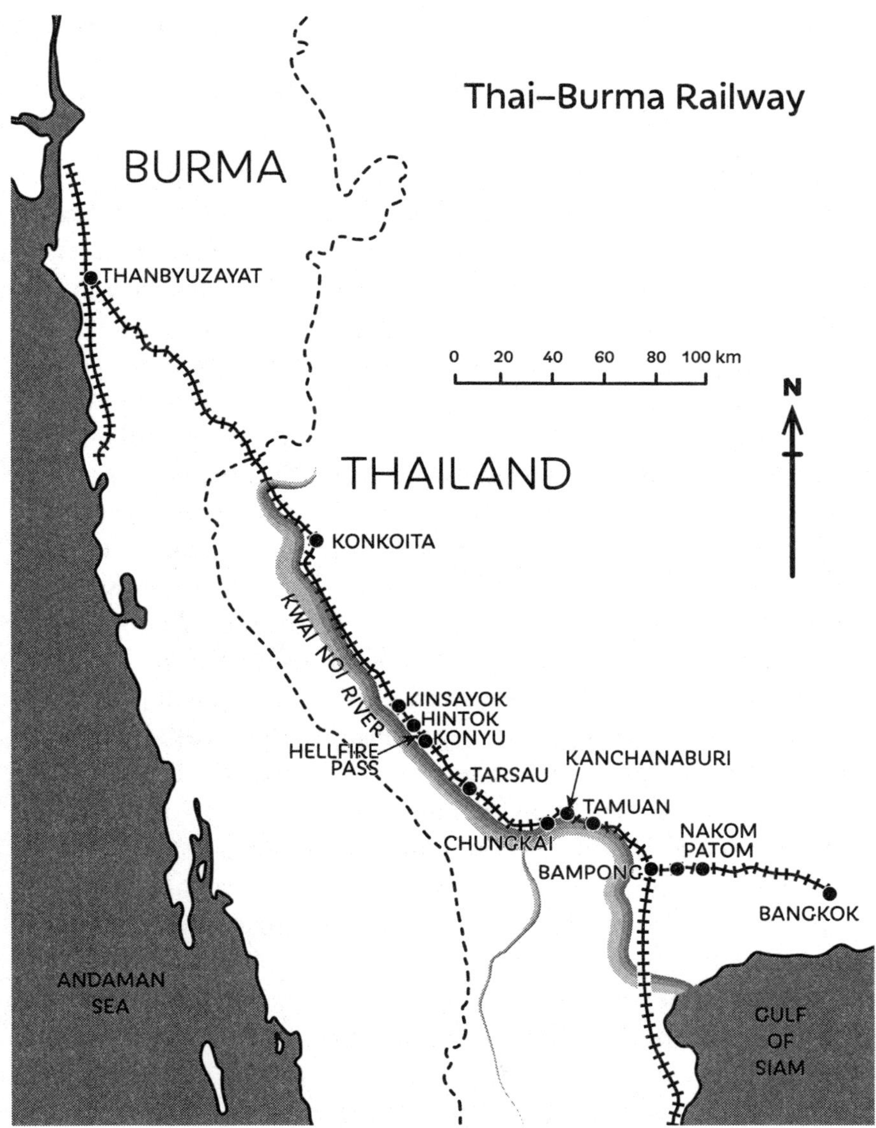

dealing out physical punishment to a major, and then he in turn, to a captain, and so it went on.'[7]

That physical punishment filtered down through the Japanese got more extreme still through the Koreans, and then a deep hole has to be dug to get low enough to indicate where the Australians stand on this sliding scale of brutality.

'The Japanese used to knock hell out of one another and then the poor old Korean,' Butterworth would recall, 'he used to really cop it and as soon as he copped it, then we copped it.'[8] Close parenthesis.

Onwards!

But just where are they going?

No-one knows for sure.

But in the crippling heat and humidity, the landscape becomes ever greener and more lush, with their anxious eyes noting every new tree for something distinctive, something unique beyond the endless array of rubber trees, something that will give away their destination before any guard does. Sure enough, when on the third day the rubber trees give way to rice paddies, and the stations they pass through have อักษรอียิปต์โบราณแปลกๆ strange hieroglyphics on the platform signs, and not an English word to be seen, it seems a fair bet they are in Thailand. In short order the landscape changes again.

'The razor mountain outcrops suddenly rise . . . from the plains which are level like the waters of a flood. The outcrops are sheer on some faces so that in the sunlight with the hard blue shadows upon them they look like cathedrals or old castles.'[9] Even as the track rises and the train strains, the towering ranges and thick jungle that press close are mixed with tight agricultural plots where 'coolies' in sarongs and curiously peaked hats ceaselessly cultivate crops with hard toil in a soil that looks rich and *very* wet. Some of the blokes who are farmers reckon you could make anything grow here. Christ, if the guards stand in it for much longer they will probably get taller.

Finally, mercifully, their train grinds to a halt in a dusty place called Bampong, some 50 miles west of Bangkok.

'Helping some of the sicker men off the train,' one soldier will recount of this journey, 'I noticed a teenage soldier lying at the rear of the carriage. One of the lads jumped back up and tapped his foot. "Come on, son, we're here." Lifeless eyes stared back. I turned my back and walked away. I did not want to see his face and carry that image with me; anything that sapped the will to live had to be avoided.'[10]

A long hot day in the back of dozens of lorries followed before finally they arrive in a guarded compound by the name of Tarsau, enclosed by 'a rickety bamboo two-rail fence'[11] and seeming to consist mainly of huts that Jack built, stinking trench latrines, and truly emaciated British POWs with cadaverous eyes. They mumble of the horrors that await the new arrivals on 'the Line' that they have just left after working on it for months. Yes, a railway line. In the jungle. We have been pulled out, and you are being put in. But that is all these 'nitwits',[12] as Weary calls them, give the Australians – bad news. They even deny the new arrivals any of their stored water with which to wash. That night the filthy, ragged and raging Australians – those bloody Poms! – sleep head to toe on bamboo mats before, the following morning, they are loaded into the lorries once more to begin the last long haul of their journey.

As the lorries roll and the hot sun rises in sync with the smothering humidity, Weary Dunlop takes a moment's pause to admire the sheer beauty of the towering ranges, the green of the jungle, the way the sunlight must *find* its way through the thick canopy to illuminate what is clearly a very poor, badly eroded track as they bounce their way forward over the next 15 miles or so.

The more they climb, the steeper becomes the track, and several times when the lorries get bogged the men have to get out en masse and push.

When the trucks can absolutely go no further, no matter the push, the men must gather themselves, their few belongings and climb off, to form up into rough lines as Japanese and Korean guards shout at them.

Compannnnnnnny! Fall in!

Kura! Stand to attention!

From here, you will have to march the rest of the way, deeper into these jungles, starting . . . now.

And off they go, indeed ever deeper into the thick jungle – the bamboo towers over them, growing as high as 50 feet, all of it tangled with vines – and they keep marching into the mid-afternoon.

With his artist's eyes and literary flair, Ray Parkin notes that 'the vines writhe and twine and grip the living trees and the grip is so tight that in places above and below each coil there is a bulge of strangulation like those of an uncooked sausage between the fingers'.[13]

Weary's shoulders are aching and his legs are buckling but he must stand. The last five days have been hell. Last night he had shocked himself by looking into a mirror: 'Just a pair of haggard eyes looking out of caked dust and sweat.'[14]

For while the saying is right that rank has its privileges, it has a price too: the men are *always* looking to him – and it just never stops.

He cannot fall, he must stand. Today, while one of the orderlies will carry Weary's small suitcase, Butterworth will carry his greatcoat and all Weary has to carry is his pack, two haversacks, his 'medical companion, his instruments, his incredibly heavy valise, and a roll of books'.[15]

And yes, of course there are plenty of other blokes offering to help.

'But Weary,' Ray Parkin notes, 'would tend to carry everything himself. And then when someone snatched it off him and carried it, he'd pick something up off someone else and help them. You could never get ahead of him. He did it so unselfconsciously, as a matter of course. It was just Weary.'[16]

And yet his burden is not just weight alone, but the fact that he is carrying contraband. For he, like many of his officers, also has secreted on his person many of the medical supplies the Japanese had refused to allow them to bring.

'I could feel my legs trembling and my shoulders were like hell.'[17]

Drenched in sweat, they walk down a steep mountain path into a river valley, for an eternity that Weary pretends is only an hour to a roughly cleared patch of jungle known as Konyu camp. Home unsweet home.

'A small native village on the opposite side of the river was almost deserted when we arrived,' one soldier will describe. 'Where we were halted was a small clearing in the jungle on the banks of the river.'[18]

The Thais call it the *Kwai Noi*, but it will soon be known to the POWs as the 'River Kwai'. The Kwai is a shimmering ribbon that winds its way through ravines, gorges and jungle, bursting with life. Impossibly bright red and pink hibiscus flowers compete with birds of infinite variety to catch your eye. There are huge clumps of bamboo and towering teak and kapok trees as far as the eye can see, all draped with vines, and no-one is more animated in their welcome than the myriad monkeys that swing from them, all while engaging in vigorous chatter about their arrival. In strict contrast, as the newly arrived soldiers gaze about in exhausted wonder, are the studiously incurious Thai villagers going by on their gaily coloured 'longtail boats' – like dinghies if they were stretched to be three times as long – trading and fishing as they have for centuries.

'*KURA!*'

The Japanese Commander of this camp, Lieutenant Kishio Usuki – a swaggering brute of a man, with a head like a robber's dog – tells

Weary to parade his men in five sections, so a headcount can be done. (It would be the unlikeliest escape in history, with more weight on you than Phar Lap, escaping into an impenetrable jungle down a mountain, but still . . .) Well, if that is what Lieutenant Usuki wants, then that is what the doctor orders, and a parade it is: 'This was difficult among the semi-cut jungle, but the check was ok.'[19]

Now Lieutenant Usuki will address the troops, in a roundabout way. He speak to translator Susuki, who only speak pidgin English, then Weary turn his word into King English and call out to men. Ready? Here go, Susuki begin:

'He speak for . . . Commander of area, Commander Tanaka. Name camp . . . "Konyu". First, he . . . glad that troops have come such . . . long way to come under his command.'

Well, we would have preferred a shorter way, but understood.

'He will do best to help. Please accept apologies no camp.'

No camp?

Yes, no camp.

'And very little food at present. Must build camp and things then perhaps improve.'

We can only hope.

'Very important to work hard. You must obey all orders.'[20]

Yes, they had guessed that part. Weary is then instructed on who should be saluted – *all person in Japanese uniform* – and told to report at 1500 hours for a detailed briefing, presumably in more detailed pidgin.

And so it proves, as they get to know their captors, and particularly this one, better. On first impression, out on the parade ground, Usuki had the appearance of being little but a gilded youth, pushed much higher than his natural station by the war, a fact he gloried in.

'Darker than the other Japanese soldiers, he strutted around like royalty, his beefy gut protruding from beneath a shabby uniform. He despised us totally. We were scum to him.'[21]

And yet first impressions do not quite do him the injustice he deserves. For on second impression, he's *much* worse. You see, close-up, one on one, he really is, 'a one-pip beardless little youngster (few hairs on chin) with a face like a spoiled boy and much laughter but hard as flint'.[22]

He is vicious, vulgar and drinks like an alcoholic fish.

With him is another Japanese man, 'a long-haired businessman type of Nipponese with a hook nose — egregious, smart, pidgin English and instincts of a snake'.

Both prove to be polite, but completely implacable.

'The most sinister feature of the whole talk,' Weary will record, 'was the insistence that if many men are sick we will draw less food!'[23]

It makes no sense, which is why Weary believes it must be true. The Japanese have their own ways, and it seems that for many of their officers, illness equates to weakness, and weakness must be punished by deprivation – at least until the POWs learn their lesson. It is the Japanese way.

(And in fact, there is indeed method in their mad cruelty, Susuki later explaining his master's reasoning for giving less food to the sick. For when those who are ailing are given less rations, 'the sick then die and are no longer a drag on the others'.[24])

A tour for Weary and his most senior officers is now arranged to visit the British POW camp that is set up just a hundred yards away, where he is wanly greeted by their Commanding Officer, Lieutenant Colonel 'Mackie' More, and his 2IC, Lieutenant Colonel 'Hookey' Hill, together with some other senior officers.

'Their appearance shocked me,' Weary notes, 'all dressed in pyjamas and sarongs, unshaven or bearded, sallow and dull of eye, full of a sort of hopeless depression.'[25]

Petty Officer Ray Parkin feels the same: 'It is a bare, spiritless place. Many are sick. They say that only twelve per cent are fit for work. They have been here three months and claims of their dead range from eighteen to sixty-four. They think we look well fed and very fit.'[26]

Weary's men are equally profoundly shocked, as they now spy some of their British brethren, many 'very badly stricken with beri-beri'. Christ, this looks grim. *This* is the place the Japanese said they could play a lot of sport? The only things that look like sporting paraphernalia here are the poor sick bastards who are, 'carrying their testicles that were the size of footballs in their hands'.[27]

Dunlop Force has work to do, and Weary arrives back in time to greet the latest arrival – one of his officers, advising that his 'Q' Battalion of 375 Australians, under Captain Jack Hands and Captain Tim Godlee, has been assigned to the 'Hintok Mountain Camp'.

(This, they're told in the curious Japanese measuring system, is 'six kilometres' away – about four miles in the old money.)

Good luck to them. Weary gives the orders for his 'O' and 'P' Battalions, totalling 900, to be roused, so they can get to grips.

Those very grips are soon wrapped around the machetes that the Japanese have handed out – carefully counting, to ensure exactly the same number will come back – which are now used to hack into the massive clumps of bamboo. Not only must the clearing be made bigger, but the mature bamboo needs to be harvested and handled – just as the remaining trees must be chopped down and hauled away.

'The glade rings continuously with the swing of axes, crash of timber and thud of picks and shovels and . . .'[28]

And what now?

Major Arthur Moon rushes up. There is a barge approaching on the shimmering river, sent by the Japanese and loaded with the attap thatch the camp inmates will need to build their roofs. But the Thai boatman also apparently has 900 duck eggs, which they can buy if they just have a bit more money to the amount already committed. One of the officers hands over the required sum, and Major Moon rushes off once more to secure the precious eggs.

Back to work!

Tonight, with no huts completed – and only five heavily mildewed tents erected, 'one for the Nipponese guard, one orderly room, two hospital tents and one medical inspection room'[29] – the POWs must sleep in their new camp as it is, with nothing bar mosquito nets for shelter, at least laid out as a reflection of the camp that must be built.

'Each man,' Parkin recounts, 'dropped his pack on the most likely looking bit of dust and called it "home".'[30]

And it starts to take shape from here.

'Nets have been rigged with bamboo fences in company area with a maze of streets and lanes,' Weary notes. '"Weary Lane" etc. Huge fires were lit to give warmth, and as Nips emphasise, to keep the wild animals away. I think they like to have these to give light in patrolling, although the reason advanced was leopards.'[31]

Leopards? Yes. Well, Weary and Major Wearne will risk them because they would like to have an evening bathe in the river. That, and a cup of rice, feels like heaven. The men are spread out in the open air, many rising warily throughout the night, via cold or nerves or both, but Weary sleeps deeply and gloriously. He is wearing his greatcoat; a sweat burden through the past weeks of walking, but now a bedsheet that is worth its weight in gold. In the morning, a new camp must be built. Tonight, we dream. Tomorrow, we build again.

From one of the tents, as he drops to sleep, comes the sound of one of the men serenading the camp with his superb baritone rendition of 'Waltzing Matilda', his lilting voice floating out over this small Australian outpost so very, very far from home. Weary drops to sleep to the familiar verses . . .

> *Once a jolly swagman camped by a billabong*
> *Under the shade of a Coolabah tree*
> *And he sang as he watched and waited till his billy boiled*
> *'Who'll come a-waltzing Matilda with me?'*

Soon enough Weary will be *jumping up, one, two, three*, but for now he is tuckered out . . .

•

Keep going!

Weary is so insistent on good *benjo*s, that he has Major Jock Clarke take official charge of the 'Benjo Squad', who exclusively devote themselves to constructing hygienic latrines, with 20-yard-long pits that are at least two yards deep, complete with timber flyproof seats well away from the supply of fresh water.

'This is terribly hard work,' Weary notes, 'and beautifully done.'[32]

Which is as well, because to Weary the danger of so many voiding their bowels in such conditions are obvious – if ever faecal matter gets mixed with the water supply, they risk cholera breaking out, which could wipe half of them out in mere *days*.

And so to work, as they continue to clear the ground.

'The jungle is ringing with the sound of axes. Bamboo clumps are roaring in flames and there is a tremendous crackle as the 80 to 100 foot bundle collapses.'[33]

The camp continues to thicken with new arrivals.

'Here they come now!' Ray Parkin notes of the Dutch battalion that arrives the day after his own mob. 'We reckon we are old hands – we have been here twenty-four hours. So we are jeering the new-comers. They are staggering as we staggered yesterday, falling over roots and kicking up dust and coughing.'[34]

Yes, this newly arrived battalion is large, 625 strong, but to Parkin's eyes they are weak as piss. Roundly beaten by the Japanese, they are completely demoralised and very nearly leaderless, bar one Captain Johann Smits. For his part, Weary soon determines they have two doctors who confirm what the Australian medico can see with his own eyes. The Dutch are in dreadful shape medically, and in worse shape when it comes to morale. They are, in fact, so downtrodden that the Japanese Commanding Officer, Captain Tanaka, soon determines that the newly arrived Dutch – now designated 'R Battalion' – will simply be absorbed into a newly established and separate Australian–Dutch camp five kilometres upriver, and Weary will command the soldiers and officers of both nations.

What?

Not on your Nelly, he won't.

Successfully seeking an audience, Weary tells Tanaka, 'It is an impossible arrangement to make an Australian commander administer the Dutch in a mixed camp. It would be much better to transfer all Australians to one camp [to keep everyone separate].'[35]

Captain Tanaka listens sagely, but in the end gives an Oriental gentleman's version of a Gallic shrug.

He can do nothing, he tells Weary, as the order has come from on high. Very high.

'He then gave me a clout on the shoulder, as much as to say "Buck up".'[36]

Off the Dutch go, under Japanese guards, Weary promising to visit on the morrow.

The mood is grim, and for more than the obvious reasons that they are POWs beneath a belting tropical sun, marching to places unknown.

'The Japs told us that where we were going, there would be plenty of tobacco; but of course there is none. The lads are smoking leaves . . . Tobacco shortage is causing bad temper and much bickering. Heat, hard work, shortage of tools and too many people trying to get them, add an enervating confusion to the days.'[37]

Equally giving them the shits in these parts is the insistence of the Japanese that they *all* be saluted, bringing your hand right to your hat – other than when actively working, where it is the NCO of the working party who will do the honours for them all.

It is dinkum disgusting, and against every fibre of their being, but at least it is better than the worst of all – *bowing*. If you have no hat to bring your hand to, you must elaborately bow, bringing your head right down to the level of your waist, fer Christ's sake.

And when on parade in the presence of any of the big Japanese commanders – Colonels and above – you have to bow en masse, or be bashed and thrown into solitary.

These are hard, hard days, when such indignities are the least of their woes.

'We were starting to be starved,' Blue Butterworth will recall. 'We had hardly any food.'[38]

Those Japanese bastards! When the Australians had had the upper hand over Italian POWs at Tobruk, the whole lot of them had gone out of their way to break into stores to give their prisoners cans of bully beef and packets of biscuits. But now that they are the POWs, their own captors could not be more callous and uncaring about them.

27 January 1943, Konyu, pickle of a trickle

In these parts the sun doesn't just beat down, it throbs.

Slowly roasting beneath it, Lieutenant Usuki, Weary and Wearne; one captor, two prisoners and no chance of guessing wrong which is which. All three are sweating profusely as they clamber up this jungle hill and occasionally slip down it with choruses of curses. But it is important to keep going, to see up close how the Dutch–Australian camp – Captain Smits' 'R' Battalion, and Captain Jack Hands' Australian 'Q' Battalion – is faring, upstream. But what an effort! With a Japanese escort, they keep toiling along this mountain path so rambling it might be a lost dog. The sun beats down and beats them up, the sweat draining, their bodies straining, but it must be done. Weary must make sure the men are setting up with their health in mind, starting with ensuring they are getting the bulk fresh water that is needed in these parts.

Sure enough, when they arrive, it's a real worry.

'The water supply is not good: a little trickle down the mountain with some shallow, rather stagnant pools near the camp . . . probably malarious.'[39]

Weary does his best to suggest what they should do, including digging a canal from a better water supply nearby.

Weary is firm about who should have command between Captain Hands and his Dutch counterpart, Captain Johann Smits.

'I informed them that Capt. Hands would be regarded as camp commander.'[40]

And yet little he says seems to have any effect on the Dutch Commander, Captain Smits, or on his men. For even while they are visiting, the Dutch lines begin to look, 'like China-town, almost everyone having built a crazy hut of . . . leaves, bamboo etc'.[41]

God help them all:

> The Dutch are an ill-disciplined mob with a tendency to wander all over the place in search of this and that, Smits meantime waving his hands like King Canute and using his voice weakly.[42]

The Dutch might now be forcibly made part of Dunlop Force, but it is no easy fit.

•

Back at the Australian camp, over the next week the Japanese guards continue to keep a close watch with their machine guns always trained on Dunlop Force as, with machetes in hand, the men keep cutting the huge bamboo clumps, with the bamboo poles then dragged back to the camp site. Under the supervision of soldiers who had been carpenters before the war, the basic structures of the huts rise quickly, even while other soldiers are soon put to work building their 'own attap huts out of bamboo, constructing them much as the natives themselves did',[43] all while the engineers of the Imperial Japanese Army's 9th Railway Regiment – their new masters – are settling into their own already well-appointed compound right beside the POWs' own digs.

'We are now building our camp,' Ray Parkin records with his keen eye for detail. 'Clearing is going on all day. Fires burn, smoke curls . . . Axes ring, trees crash and bamboos are torn out of their clumps with the noise of ripping thorns. Men call, "Oh-h-h . . . HO! H-a-a-u-u-L-L!" as they drag and work. They are stripped to hats, boots and shorts. They are red and bronze and moving; dark in the shadows and rich in the sun.'[44]

Happily for Ray Parkin, the hard work coincides with the timing for the weekly wash they are allowed by the Japanese and, after spending the day by the river, making the thatching for the roof, they are allowed to wade in, as glowering guards watch their every move.

'There is no lending of soap,' he chronicles, 'each man jealously guards the little he has. I don't even share mine with Blackie. It is a piece as big as my thumb and dried as hard as bone, which will make it last longer. After the bath we stood naked around a big fire we had lit. We stood in the red, glowing cave it burnt in the grey river mist, like smugglers, shivering and baking by turns.'[45]

They continue to get themselves organised for the long haul, Weary chronicling that 'temporary cooking trenches have been dug for *cwalis* [huge iron rice bowls], with wood fires, and we asked for drums for water containers, chlorine for chlorination, buckets in greatly increased numbers and boots for the men'.[46]

Of the last, there is still next to none, meaning that for Weary's mob trying to make do with the tiny things the Japanese have provided remains like trying to put Thumbelina's ballet shoes on a clod-hopper.

Still, on the upside, a rare *yasume* day is a thing of joy, as Weary records: 'Troops spent an amusing day on the river ranging far and wide, swimming, fishing with improvised gear and diving for giant clams, of which there are plenty. Very few fish caught.'[47]

(And Major Greiner had held such high hopes that his mosquito net might do the trick, only to find even the tiddlers were able to break through it.) Some crabs are captured today, the first time some of these Australian soldiers have caught crabs since they went to a Greek brothel.

Today Weary has a morning walk to a nearby mountain with Lieutenant 'Happy' Houston.

But there is a real problem. In pidgin English, some Japanese guards warn the Australians that panthers and tigers will be awaiting them, if they are thinking of escaping. (It must be the leopard's day off?) They wander through the brush, looking at the 'constant flurry of life',[48] not for its beauty but its protein. Weary spots wild pigeons and fowl, now there is no way the Japanese are going to let them have a rifle, or even a bow and arrow, but if they did, the men could live off this land. One thing that will be permitted is finding fruit and Weary is delighted to see a banana tree but, sod's law being what it is, 'did a recce and no fruit'. When they return to camp they find rations sorted in spectacular fashion, the troops have killed a huge cobra!

'Typical hooded snake about five feet in length, dark green back, mottled whitish belly and very thick.'[49]

The cobra is roasted and Weary's diary records his share in parentheses: ('I was given a small "steak" myself, which was rather stringy but with quite a nice flavour.')[50]

Tastes a bit like chicken.

And yet, now that it is obvious they will be struggling for a proper amount of rations from the Japanese, Weary is quick to affirm among his fellow officers that the previous system of gathering in the better part of their stipends from the Japanese will apply – a system now all but universally accepted by his countrymen of all ranks.

'I received the same pay as a captain in the Japanese Army, 122½ rupees,' one Australian officer on the Thai–Burma Railway, Dr Rowley Richards, will recount, noting the currency of choice in Thailand. 'The Japs took 52½ rupees for board, and then the balance went into the bank account. No matter what rank you were, the officers could only get the maximum that the troops got, and a warrant officer got 20 rupees a month. So the difference between what the Japs took and 20 rupees went into a canteen fund and with that we purchased food for the sick and so forth. That money made all the difference.'[51]

The common soldiers took exactly the same approach.

'You worked every day you could for [a pittance], but you knew the sick boys would get [half] of it.'[52]

That money goes straight into the Regimental Hospital Fund. If they are going to get through this, it will be together, as they did in Java.

•

It is the way of big, athletic men, with a lust for combative sports . . .

Upon meeting for the first time each one does a subconscious calculation. If it came to it . . . would I win a fight against this bloke?

For Weary Dunlop, it is an extremely rare thing to waver in his conviction that he would. At six foot four inches, with a background with the Wallabies and boxing . . . he knows he has the measure of most men if it comes to it. (And a great left hook if it comes to that.)

But on this day of late January, as the remnants of the 2/1st Heavy Battery from Timor arrive at Konyu, he meets Bombardier Tom Uren for the first time, and wonders. Yes, he's got him for height.

But Uren is at least his weight, has fists the size of pineapples, has played rugby league for Manly Warringah in the front row, done a lot of competitive swimming, and been a professional boxer – once even fighting Billy Britt for the Australian heavyweight championship.

And yet, just like Weary himself, despite his physical prowess (or, perhaps because of it), there is a gentleness to Uren, a humanity, that is refreshing in one who could pulverise you good, sunshine, if it came to it.

And pleased to meet you, Tom.

Tom's first impression is one that will only deepen over coming months.

'Weary's leadership wasn't pronounced or boasted about or loud-mouthed in any way. He was a very kind, quietly spoken human being. He led by example.'[53]

It does not take long to sum up their new digs. Just as a farmer measures space by paddocks, Tom Uren, like Weary, has a tendency to measure things by football fields. The Konyu camp, he estimates, is 'about twice the size of a normal rugby football ground'.[54]

But that's all it is. The jungle presses in from all sides.

When he had become a POW back in Timor, the first task assigned to Uren and his mates had been to build their own huts. At Konyu the task is one step back – they must begin by building the accommodation huts of their Japanese masters, together with kitchen, mess hall and *benjos*. Then, and only then, will they be able to start building their own – in the interim they are sleeping on rough mats on the ground, with tarpaulins pulled over them when it rains.

Weary is quick to harness the pre-war skills of many soldiers to help make their environment more amenable to survival, and there is no better example than a large urinal. It has been created by one of Dunlop Force's favourite soldiers, Private Bob Fox – an old carpenter from South Australia in civilian life and former esteemed member of the mighty Australian Light Horse in the Great War. At Weary's request, Fox takes an enormous bamboo pole, some 20 feet long and six inches in diameter, and lays it horizontal. Then Ol' Bob suspends it on two forked sticks with one end higher than the other, but both at mid-thigh level. It means the urine runs down to one end, where, as Ray Parkin chronicles, 'it drains into a vertical pipe set over a hole in the ground. It is known as "Bob Fox's Piccolo", and fifteen men can play it at once. Hordes of black bush flies and gorgeous clouds of kaleidoscopic butterflies frequent it.'[55]

Amidst those flies, stories swirl about what the POWs are here to do in this particularly thick and mountainous section of the Thai jungle. The Poms back at Tarsau had told them they were being sent to build a railway line, but there has surely been some mistake. Not . . . here? Not through an area like this, which is so mountainous, and so covered in impenetrable jungle? Some say it is true. Others say they are going to build a road through the mountains, while still others insist they have it on good authority that they will be building a camp so remote that it will eliminate any hope of escape or rescue. Weary himself has no reason to disbelieve the nitwit Poms at Tarsau. They really are here to help build a Japanese railway through singularly difficult country.

The POWs continue to look around, aghast. A railway, here? In the middle of this fungal jungle of mountainous mess? It defies belief!

But, yes, they are apparently the first Australian contingent to be sent to work on the nascent Line, which extends over 400 kilometres and has work camps of 1500 men or so, every five kilometres along the Line.

Only shortly after arrival, Dr Weary is bemused to be summoned to the *shoko*'s house, the officers' residence, where he is sternly ordered to treat the Quartermaster's . . . sore toe.

Oh, and another Japanese officer has a pain in the belly. Now, what is the fee for a prison MD house call?

'Retainer: one packet of cigarettes.'[56]

Smoke 'em if you got 'em, and Weary's payment is distributed to the Australian officers that night.

3 February 1943, Konyu, of grave importance

At the English camp, Lieutenant Colonel 'Mackie' More has a trip in store for his Australian counterpart today, to an area in this jungle he is quite pleased with. A graveyard. Well, it is grim, but it is necessary and Weary accepts the invitation to come and journey to the fresh site. The way Colonel More speaks, Weary assumes that it will take about a day to get there and back. He is amazed to find that: 'It is about 150 yards.'[57] It is a stroll to the side of the riverbank, not a trek across country. The 'cemetery' itself is similarly underwhelming; a bamboo fence marks out the ground, right next to the 'church', another bamboo boundary; and both church and cemetery share the same cross, the only marker that would help you guess what either is. Instead of headstones, each grave is marked by a cross of – what else but? – bamboo, and a tiny nameplate. Rupert Brooke, this ain't. Still the British officer enthuses, 'on the whole show with the pride of a sexton in a village churchyard'.[58]

For the life of him, Weary cannot fathom the pride with which the Pom speaks.

'There are just twenty-nine graves,' he says, puffing up, 'but with terrific scope for more.'

And now he pauses,

'Are you a Roman Catholic or a Protestant?'

Weary confirms he is a Protestant.

'Would you . . . er . . . would you care to . . . er . . . *share?*'

Bemused, Ray Parkin watches closely as 'six foot four of Weary bent forward in patient, polite attention as, with a disarming smile, he asked, "Is there room?"'[59]

'Of course,' the English officer replies enthusiastically, before pointing to various tracts of land.

'First, I want to fill over *there* . . . and then *there*! . . . then over *there*! . . . I think I could fit you in.'[60]

Hmmm. 'Would you like a *separate* part made, as an extension?'

Actually, they would prefer to remain above ground. But if they are headed six feet under, well . . .

'Not if it will take up too much of the accommodation,' says Weary.

'Oh no!' replies the Brit. 'I want to fill up this part first. But there is plenty of room here.'

Good to know.

The Colonel talks and talks about possible cemetery delineations, as a disbelieving Weary just manages to hold his tongue. Enthusing over a cemetery on the River Kwai is simply a bridge too far for the Australian – and completely beside the point. All of his own energies are devoted to keeping men *out* of the cemetery, not having them properly arranged while in one. Finally, mercifully, the British Colonel falls silent. It is silence that envelops, Weary notes, it broods over this tragic tableau: 'the pathetic newly-turned earth, the stones and bamboo crosses, the soft murmuring of the River [Kwai] and the rustle of bamboos in the tall jungle'.[61]

As if on ghoulish cue, a work party comes out of the jungle, their gaunt, sallow faces and emaciated frames, 'pitifully thin', look to be heading straight for the graveyard. A metaphor enacted. Weary can't help but wonder 'how many more will eventually find peace there'. As for the cemetery, they are not in England, it will not last, and the only question now is, 'How long it will be before the relentless jungle obliterates all trace of their coming and their departure?'[62]

Who will know they were ever here? Who will survive to remember? As for dividing the graveyard, who gives a damn?

In the land of the living, at least the huts are done, now large enough to accommodate 200 men to each one, and they come complete with raised bamboo platforms that will have to do as bunks for the moment.

Grub is still the main game in town, including actual game today as a talented lad named Denny throws a stone straight and true at a wild fowl in the distance and kills the plump feast . . . yes, stone-dead! And Weary is told the men have future kills in mind: 'There are traces of game tracks here including pig, elephant, buffalo and panther.'[63]

Now, how big a stone do you need to kill an elephant? Some goods can't wait, cigarettes for example, and Weary 'borrows' a couple from Staff Sergeant Gibson. Smokes are in short supply these days and their price on the black market has gone up. Not to worry, Gibson sold his Rolex Oyster watch to pay for these beauties. How much? Twelve ticals. In Australian currency that is . . . about a dozen packs.

7 February 1943, Konyu, and also with you

It is a bad sign when God's chosen gets the trots. The camp tries not to take it personally, but the padre is now so unwell that Weary tells him not to perform services, only communion. The soldiers will do the service themselves today, as best they can, as much as they can remember. But, however meagre the service, however weak the Father, there is something special here, as Weary sees plainly: 'There is beauty in this spot, with the quietness of the river and the large stone of the altar with the simple bamboo table and cross built over it.'[64]

He especially loves dawn, saying of the sun peeling away the darkness from the jungle – illuminating the trees, awakening the birds, and setting off the chattering monkeys swinging from tree to tree – that the beauty of it all, 'sometimes positively hurt'.[65]

God is with them, even here. The shimmer of the River Kwai is as far from the stately River Jordan as any pilgrim could imagine, but it will serve for exultation while in exile. The altar and seats are built from bamboo too, a cane congregation that rises up into the bank behind them like a little theatre. How strange it is to sing ancient hymns here, but their voices ring about, bass and tenor attempting 'O Come All Ye Faithful' as 'all around the green life of the jungle and the challenge of a little cross down by the river'.[66]

As Ray Parkin possesses the artist's eye for beauty, wherever it may be found, he is stunned by just how exquisite a scene the river presents. As its gleaming band of silver dances under the green jungle canopy, it is in breath-taking contrast to the viciousness that surrounds it.

'When the weather was cooler,' Parkin will note, 'an early morning mist would hang just above the water. It was very beautiful.'[67]

The colours? Don't get him started.

'The flowers in that area are among the most beautiful I've ever seen,' he will later note. 'We were lucky to be there at that particular time of the year.'[68]

Others just see a jungle.

Parkin sees 'hooded scented lilies, several iris-like orchids which look like the first shoots of Bermuda lilies and cannas . . . the trees are flowering and on their branches and trunks are clumps of yellow orchids, which are like large corsages of yellow jonquils'.[69]

9 February 1943, Konyu, mortality maths

And so it has come.

In response to Weary's demands for fresh medical supplies to deal with the myriad medical challenges he now faces, as Dunlop Force copes with living in the tropics on too little food, with too little shelter and too little rest, the Japanese have provided . . . too little humanity.

Opening the small packages that have been dumped in front of Weary's hut, they find a grand total of 10 bandages, 300 aspirins and the other totals for everything from iodine to tinea lotion are similarly pathetic. There are 4000 men in these camps at the moment, 300 are sick in hospital in the British Camp alone. The next supplies will be here in . . . a month? Two?

Weary muses on the problem today as he and the other officers continue to build the officers' hut. Now this would seem logical, but it is remarkable from the British point of view. Their way is for officers to instruct *others* to do manual labour, they don't do it themselves until an enemy appears.

But an enemy is here – fatigue, hunger and sickness – so Weary decides the Australian officers will set an example and haul this hut together themselves. Weary himself goes hard and the result is surprising: 'most foully blistered my hands which are very soft'.[70]

Well, that will change. What shocks him is just how tired he is: 'I am ashamed at how little energy one has in this climate.' Heat, sweat and too few calories make you weak and tired. You can bluff yourself through an ordinary day with good spirits, but when you have to work, it tells. God help you if you have to work hard. At least the nights are pleasantly cold but Weary will find them very cold now because he gives his beloved greatcoat (temporarily, mind you) to the pleurisy-ridden Bob Haddon. Meanwhile, the reviews for the new bamboo beds are in and they are not raves: 'Bamboo beds are diabolical, owing to their hardness, smoothness and irritating irregularities.'[71]

Unfortunately, irregularities are now a regular way of life. The only upside is the widespread reckoning that the men will likely only have to be here for three months or so.

•

How to make up the difference, between the food that is delivered and that which is truly required?

Starting their own farm as they had at Java-Z is not a realistic option, but another solution soon becomes feasible. Here in Thailand they are not in a prison per se, or even an enclosed camp – allowing much more liberal interaction with the locals.

When one of Weary's senior officers, Captain Reg Newton, makes discreet inquiries about whether any of the local traders speak English – one name keeps popping up.

'Boon Pong', or Boonpong Sirivejjabhandu to those who can master it – a group that includes no Australians – is a trader who, with his wife Boopa and brother-in-law Nai, has a large contract to supply the Japanese. Of all the families plying their trade by selling fruit and vegetables from barges going up and down the River Kwai, Boon Pong's is one of the busiest.

A meeting is arranged with Boon Pong and Newton is soon able to establish that the trader – who proves to be small, neat and bespectacled, always in the crisp white shirt and neat trousers of one who is an educated businessman – is operating a successful business in the old city of Kanchanaburi, some 75 miles north-west of Bangkok. Boon is already providing food supplies to the Japanese, loading up barges and bringing them up that ribboning waterway that brings triumph and despair (market price dependent), the River Kwai, and selling to different POW settlements along the way.

Would he be amenable to providing more, in return for immediate remuneration, and an IOU for more when the war is over? He would. Newton does the deal on the spot, arranging for Boon Pong to bring an extra barge with food along the River Kwai Noi, and drop off to Dunlop Force at an agreed spot.

And so it begins.

In short order, Boon Pong is sending their way barges laden with everything from duck eggs to tobacco to whitebait and such crucial condiments as salt, cooking oil and sugar. Better still, hidden deep within the tobacco are small amounts of the drugs that Weary has requested.

10 February 1943, Konyu, many unhappy returns

The Japs are searching all the quarters today. For weapons? For diaries? Hidden orders? No, *vegetables*. Yes, word has reached them that, as sure as eggs is eggs, contraband pumpkins are to be found. And cabbages. This is hardly high stakes stuff, but the fear is that while they are searching for extra food, the guards will find something extra. Sure enough, three compasses are found, along with several binoculars and some little cameras. *Bugger.*

One piece of food is not discovered: a tin of salmon. It is being kept by Weary as a birthday present for Ewan Corlette, the Gangster, today. (By now, Weary, Arthur Moon and the Gangster are the wartime version of 'the Aussie triumvirate' he'd once been a part of in London, with Jim Yeates and Frank Mills. They are inseparable, and delight in working closely together.) It's not exactly chocolate cake, but it is precious and proper protein and that evening the birthday boy celebrates his 35th in style . . . Konyu style, anyway. Weary for one is glad it's done, he has been eyeing that salmon for a week and 'that damn tin has been gnawing at me for days to go off quietly and eat it by myself'.[72]

They toast Ewan with coffee. *To happier birthdays!* If Ewan did want a birthday cake he could have it, as long as it's made of bamboo. Everything else here is, as Weary notes: 'I have a bamboo water carrier, bamboo wash basin, bamboo bed and will soon have a bamboo house and bamboo furniture.'[73]

Henry Ford used to tell customers that they could have their cars in any colour they liked, as long as it was black. Well, here you can have any bamboo you like, for anything. If you don't like bamboo, well, you'd better hope the war ends soon.

Weary is grateful to have such a man as the Gangster by his side.

'He was,' Weary will note, 'a real man for tough days, stern faced, but full of kindness, disarming humour and a kindness of heart which I never felt that I could equal. I always thought that he exceeded me in true compassion and rapport with the sick.'[74] For the record, Corlette takes the opposite view, regarding Weary as 'a better doctor and someone possessed of greater compassion'.[75]

Either way, Corlette's care of the POWs is spiced with a black humour that the sick soldiers love. One shaking hospital patient, lying on bamboo slats in a dim light as rain pounds on the canvas of their hospital roof, manages to gurgle out his worst fear to Dr Corlette.

'Major, am I going to die?'

'I haven't decided yet,'[76] is Corlette's deadpan reply and now the patient shakes with laughter.

There is droll and then there is Ewan Corlette. He is always there for curious patients who want to know the precise nature of their condition: 'Do you know what's wrong with you?' says the doctor gravely. 'You're totally buggered, not a thing left.'[77]

There is indeed a lot of it going around, you know. And while at the daily sick parade the Japanese have a grading system for the ill that they insist on, 'fit', 'light sick' and 'heavy sick'. Then, this really is a new one from the Gangster, and is him all over:

Worse than heavy sick?

'Totally buggered.'

And yet the men love him for it.

'He wore his cap over one eye and was as tough as they come,' one of the Dunlop Force men will say of him. 'But to a sick Australian his heart was as soft as that of a new mother.'[78]

But to protect his patients from the Japanese? There are none more fierce than the Gangster and Weary admires his suave colleague deeply.

One man that both the Gangster and Weary go the extra mile in protecting is a gentle Englishman by the name of Jack Chalker, who has demonstrated a splendid ability to patiently paint and draw the scenes around him.

'And in return for [being kept away from the Line],' Weary would recount, 'he did all these magnificent sort of drawings for me.'[79]

Alas, when a Korean guard discovers some of those paintings and drawings, Chalker is dragged out of his tent, tied to a post and left there for two days and nights, with beatings at regular intervals. Let him be a lesson to you all – this is what happens to those who would dare try to chronicle, in any manner, what is happening here.

When Chalker is finally cut down, his life hangs in the balance for days, but little by little, it is the Gangster who manages to pull him through.

16 February 1943, Konyu, by George, he's got it!

A good time to talk to a guard is when he is merry, or in the case of the guard they call 'Pushface', after he has been very merry. Weary knows that Pushface went on a bender last night, and he will be in a sympathetic mood this morning. Push comes to shove when Pushface asks how the hut building is going. The huts are not the problem, Weary says, gearing up for a pidgin briefing on what is, starting with Dutch dysentery: 'Yesterday I go mountain camp. Many Hollanders hospital, very sick. Many, many men.'[80]

Pushface nods, he savvy.

'No good I speak,' Weary continues. 'No medicines. No good.'

Another nod.

'Also must boil clothes. No drums or boilers. No good. Very, very urgent. Soon all men sick. Hollander, Australian, Nippon soldier . . .'[81]

Now Pushface is very interested.

'*Sama, sama*, all go sick,' Weary follows up, 'quickly die, finish. No good.'

Pushface agrees and Weary again emphasises the point. 'Must have medicines – very, very urgent. Also wire and boilers. Medicine from Tarsau three days. No good – quickly, quickly. *Mushi, mushi* Tarsau. Otherwise all men die – quickly finish!'[82]

The result of all this? Pushface will have a word to the Japanese medical Corporal. And, come with me, Dunlop. Mystified, Weary follows him, through the English camp, past the cemetery (where Pushface bows!) and on into the jungle, towards the Menan Kwai Noi and there! See, Dunlop? Hot springs!

Weary sees that, yes, 'a large log has been felled to wall off a little rectangular area roughly where the water is more than comfortably hot'.[83]

Pushface examines the waters with enthusiasm and asks Weary to do the same. Now, these are healing waters, all know this. So, how is it healing?

'Dysentery?' he asks Weary.

'No good,'[84] says Dunlop.

'Malaria?' Pushface asks hopefully.

'Good,' says Dunlop, joking, and Pushface nods. And now he points at Weary's leg, the sores on them.

Weary nods.

'OK!' Pushface grins.

And one last disease might be helped but Weary can't understand what it is. Pushface has a go at his own pidgin:

'. . . er – er- er- suck-er, diph-er er, diph- ther – ia?'

Diphtheria?

Yes, that's it!

'No good,'[85] says Dunlop.

Ah well, one out of three isn't bad these days. Weary and Pushface and an English Corporal named Doherty now wander back to camp, and Doherty and Dunlop both exchange a glance as Pushface again bows slow and low to their dead.

In Weary's view, it is a 'meaningless bow'.[86]

18 February 1943, Konyu, an evening at the theatre

Weary has many medical duties to perform today, but first some admin business. Last night, a guard by the name of Takayama wandered around camp looking to buy a watch strap, as a present for the commander, 'No. 1'. He doesn't get the price or the strap he likes so starts slapping Australian soldiers in the face. Well, this morning Weary is set to meet with, *Ichi Ban*, No. 1 – on this day the very lowly ranked Private Ikimoto – and have a word.

'Nippon soldier smack face, many face, no good,' says Weary.

No. 1 is shocked! Absolutely shocked!

'What, hit face?'

'Yes, hit face!'

'When? Where? How many?'

No. 1 is distressed, and asks everything bar 'Which way did they go?' But, most certainly, a search will be made to find the soldier who did this! *(Yes, but it was Takayama.)* None shall rest until this man is found!

'Of course every soldier was produced or discussed except the one in question. After much face saving they assured us they would "examine".'[87] Good luck with your investigation, gents.

Weary retires, only to shortly thereafter be hailed by Dr Corlette, who has come from the hospital tent with news that one of the patients has taken an alarming turn for the worse.

Private Jones, who had previously collapsed with abdominal pains, is now writhing in agony and has a deathly pallor. (This all seems strangely familiar, like *déjà vu*, all over again?) Weary accompanies the Gangster back to the tent and, after further conferring with him, Major Moon and Jock Clarke, they are of the same mind: an operation must be done at once, a perforated duodenal ulcer is suspected – an ulcer in the highest part of the intestines. If they are right and no operation takes place, Jones will die this night.

Of course, if Weary mucks up an operation, performed in the open air with jungle surrounds, on an operating table made out of bamboo set up on four vertical posts dug into the dirt, Jones will still die this night, but at least they will have tried. Now, how to get enough light? You can't. But a circular white tent, twelve feet in diameter, currently being used to treat dysentery patients will provide reflective light. They request lights from the Japanese, and their Medical Corporal is interested, but all he sends is two hurricane lamps and a torch. Oh, they also have some candles. And a small torch. Bloody hell. Roaring bamboo fires are lit outside the operating tent, partly for warmth, mostly for light. In essence, they are putting the band back together, and the 2/2nd Casualty Clearing Station rides again, with a 'mobile surgical unit', well removed from a general hospital, being configured in a way they never imagined it.

Cyril Cahill has a bamboo mask made to administer anaesthesia; Bert Lawrence sprinkles water over the tent floor to lay the dust. (Thank God that Florence Nightingale is not alive to see this.) The officers are all up and boiling instruments for Weary, they have some towels and three sets of gloves at the ready. Blue Butterworth has swabs ready at Weary's command, as ever his swathe of red hair standing out, just over the Boss's right shoulder, and showing up even in this light. *Now this is going to be a show*, the Japanese guards gather to watch. At midnight the patient is examined again and all doctors agree, the operation must go ahead. Poor Jones is washed and shaved and a Japanese guard gets caught up in the excitement.

Surely they should put a blanket over this man? Won't he get cold? No, seriously, give him a blanket!

'He was restrained!'[88] Weary will note, amused that they have to keep a guard prisoner for a few moments until he settles down. We know what we are doing. Major Corlette will be anaesthetist, with Major Moon assisting (as is the actual moon, with backup lighting). Here we go . . .

The part of Jones's abdomen to be cut is first swabbed with pure alcohol, previously distilled through 'the fermentation of rice with a suitable strain of fungus'.[89] For a scalpel, Weary must use a pocket-knife that has been so sharpened it could kill any boy scout that attempted to open it, while the only anaesthetic that can be offered is a small amount of chloroform that the doctors keep for precisely such emergencies.

'This was one of the strangest operations I have ever been at,' Weary will note in his diary, 'the fitful light of weak hurricane lamps and the large fires, a beam of a torch and on one side of the tent a fantastic audience of mixed Nip soldiers, our officers and the CCS laddies who were up. (Of course, one doesn't notice spectators when operating any more than the crowd surrounding the football oval.)'[90]

That said, the former Wallaby and the crowd are relieved when the peritoneum is opened and a puff of gas emerges. We were right! The diagnosis was dead on, now they just have to save Jones's life.

The stomach is opened, with some rice in it revealed, oozing out and . . . and don't worry about the CLUNK behind you, it is just one of the Japanese guards, fainting . . . Weary continues. The ulcer is folded inwards, transverse mattress stitches are done, 'and the rice stopped oozing out'.[91]

One of the men manning the fire outside will never forget the vision he sees of Weary and the operation through the tent flaps.

'[Jock] Clarke kept saying, "More light . . . more fire" and the sweat was rolling off me. It was still dark, but I could see Weary doing bloody awful things like pulling the intestines out, which Clarke wrapped in towels – pulling, pulling until they got the twist out. I left. I couldn't stand the blood.'[92]

Sewing Jones up again is done with a needle made from 'hardened copper wire' and catgut thread made 'from the intestines of animals, peeling off the peritoneum, drying it, boiling it twice in saturated saline and storing it in alcohol'.[93]

The operation takes two hours in all before Weary can sew up Jones's abdomen, at which point hot bottles are produced to lie as close as possible to the patient, who is wrapped in blankets. Against all odds, the patient will live and likely be as good as new.

One of the Japanese officers who has watched the whole thing is simply stunned.

He . . . LIVE?

'He should have a good chance,'[94] Weary says.

'You No. 1 doctor!'[95] the officer cries, reaching up to pat the enormous Australian appreciatively on the back.

It's 5.30 in the morning before Weary can sleep.

And yes, of course he is still there for breakfast. That is just the way he is. It is not that he can get by on just two hours sleep, but when it comes to cat-naps, Weary is a lion, the biggest cat-napper of the lot, and able to keep going for hours after just a ten-minute kip.

•

Having a bit of a chin-wag with his mates from *Perth*, Ray Parkin looks up to see an enormous figure towering over them. It is Colonel Weary Dunlop. And this time, instead of just a chat, he has come over with a specific query.

For you have, Ray, apparently, written an account of the night the Germans declared war on Greece and blew up Piraeus Harbour in Athens. Weary was there, too – or at least close enough to hear the result and see the billowing smoke, before witnessing the destruction up close the following morning – and would love to read it.

The two end up talking over what had happened for the next couple of hours and deepen what is already a strong bond.

'He tells me that all his life he has been a scoffer,' Parkin will recount, 'but he knows the conventions at which he has scoffed are the necessary weft and woof for the many, and he respects that. But I know he is a most kindly and gentle scoffer – except at the unrighteous. He is a man who shoulders his own burdens so that they will not worry others, and then heedlessly piles on his own shoulders the worries of anybody who comes to him. He is a man the Japanese have already tortured several times; but about this he says nothing.'[96]

For his part, Weary is equally impressed with Ray Parkin – he is just his kind of humble, hard-working officer who looks after his own – but right now he must away on a curious endeavour. For yes, their Japanese Commanding Officer has called for him and a fellow officer to come to his personal quarters, for reasons unknown.

It does not take long to find out. For, after stumbling their way along a very dark and hazardous track, they arrive to find the said officer sitting up in his bed with a mouth organ.

The result?

Weary and his fellow officer must sit up until the wee hours, 'listening in forced admiration to the murder of "Auld Lang Syne" and "Home Sweet Home"'.[97]

•

Is it not strange the kind of things that can give a man not just pleasure, but joy, in such conditions?

Before the war, the idea of spending any portion of a day of rest killing bugs would be the most unheard of thing anyone had ever heard of. But not here, not now. Not after how much the men have suffered at the hands of these bugs, these flies, these ticks, these white lice, these *worse than senseless things*!

First the sufferers get a fire going and wait till it's down to glowing embers. And now they take the lattice strips of bamboo off their beds, the ones that are so completely infested with bugs that all their nights are spent only dozing while regularly waking to slap the biting bastards but never winning the battle. And now, with one POW on each end of the lattice, it is lowered down to just above the embers – not low enough to burn, but low so the bugs start jumping out in their *thousands*, and onto the embers below. Oh, how the men cheer.

'And it was really, with joy and delight,' Tom Uren would recount, 'that you could pay back such a cruel vicious person as a bug.'[98]

Shortly thereafter Uren is in a close confab with his three closest mates here, starting with big Bill Belford, the former amateur heavyweight boxing champion of Queensland who – rare for such a big man – had been a Spitfire pilot. One of the others, Kevin Wylie, had also been a pilot, while the final one, Donald Stuart (known as 'Scorp' as he had once been stung by a scorpion), had been a machine-gunner and . . .

And . . . *quiet*!

Yes, the grasp of English of the Japanese and Korean guards who regularly walk by is only scant, so it is unlikely they'd understand even if they overheard but, given the subject matter, the Australians simply can't be too careful.

They want to escape. There are rumours aboard that the Pommies are driving down from their strongholds in India in an effort to 'break the Japanese lines of communication between Mandalay and Rangoon'.[99]

All prisoners need to do, thus, is get away from this hell-hole and make their way through the jungle, travelling say, 10 miles a day, for the next hundred days or so, and they could join the Brits! After all, between the four of them, they have a great number of skills and should be able to live off the land, while dodging snakes, crocodiles, whole swarms of deadly insects, not to mention the damned leopards, and . . . starvation and all that. Yes! Already they have fashioned some catapults and have practised using them to kill wildfowl at a distance of up to 30 yards. Of course, all such plans have to be run by Colonel Dunlop, and though he is 'not unsympathetic'[100] he remains to be convinced, and steers them to his friend, Major Wearne.

What do you think, Billy?

Major Bill Wearne is deadset against it insisting, 'your information is wrong'.[101]

He has looked closely at this very issue, talked to villagers and those familiar with the area of what they would face and is in no doubt their likely fate: a grisly death in the jungle, or at the end of Japanese bayonets. *Do not do it*. And beyond all that, why bother when we should win this war soon, anyway? Privy to the news they get over short-wave radio, now carefully secreted, there have been fine tidings from an island called Guadalcanal, in the Southern Solomons. Allied forces, led by Americans and including a scattering of British and Australian coast-watchers and others, had landed back in August of last year and, after a long campaign, have finally secured it from the defending Japanese. A serious and perhaps even catastrophic blow struck on the forces of the Japanese Empire, it gives the Allies a secure staging post to start to launch against the rest of the Nippon forces in the Pacific.

Either way, for Tom Uren and his mates, that is the end.

'I never talked about escape from then on,' he will recount, 'because I realised that it was futile, the distances and inhospitable terrain were too great.'[102]

CHAPTER ELEVEN

SETTLING IN, DYING DOWN

Article 2. Prisoners of war are in the power of the hostile Government, but not of the individuals or formation which captured them. They shall at all times be humanely treated and protected, particularly against acts of violence, from insults and from public curiosity. Measures of reprisal against them are forbidden.[1]

Geneva Convention

Habitations were made of bamboo and palm leaf held together with jungle fibre, ingenuity was indeed tested. Astonishing uses were made of bamboo, which served for such varied construction as beds, brooms, brushes, baskets. containers, water-piping, tubing [and] splints.[2]

Weary Dunlop, *British Medical Journal*, 1946

21 February 1943, Konyu, as the river runs

On this pressing hot Sunday morning, the visiting Church of England padre from the English camp is presiding over a sad service. Sad, not because of his flock but because of his own state, as a shocked Weary notes: 'His robes and communion kit battered, travel stained . . . a gaunt, bearded, spiritual face.'[3]

This reminds Weary of someone. Jesus Christ . . . it is Jesus! It is the hollowed, barely flesh and bones of a martyr that presides over them now. His robes still have faded splendour, but at their bottom you can see two thin stick legs stubbornly standing incongruously in army boots.

The man is not long for this world, Weary thinks, and as ever with his doctor's instinct, he will sadly be proved right.

As bodies decompose so rapidly in these climes, the padre will be quickly interred beneath the sod, as the somnolent tones of 'The Last Post' – played by the only trumpeter they have, on the only battered trumpet they still possess – ring out over the jungle and the Australians take pause.

The greatest enemy they have at the moment is not the Japanese, but malaria. Using the medical textbooks he always lugs with him, and consulting his fellow medicos, Weary finds out everything he can on this devastating disease: 'Information reveals that malaria is highly endemic in [Thailand] especially in the hills . . . The *Anopheles minimus* mosquito breeds especially in slow-running streams with grassy edges, also in pits, rice fields and seepages.'[4]

Once a POW has the disease, he goes through a completely debilitating series of fevers and chills mixed with such uncontrollable shakes he can't drink a cup of tea without spilling half of it all over himself. Oh, yes, and it can bring headaches, 'like an anvil under the repeated blows of a sledge, the same ring and thump'.[5]

Well, Weary had better get rid of those insects as soon as possible. The anti-malaria squad is formed, and the men in it do all they can with the few tools at their disposal, burning back jungle under the watchful eye of guards, finding water patches and ponds that can either be drained or have some precious kerosene poured upon them, which spreads out and kills the swarming enemy with remarkable speed. But there are other more immediate and present dangers that occupy the men at their camp: 'Another curse of this site is the frequency of very painful scorpion bites.'[6]

On the plus side, many times when men report being bitten and panic that it must have been a scorpion, Weary can reassure them that it is only a snake bite after all – so, bloody well calm down. If you want something to complain about you have come to the right place: 'There are many huge tarantulas and centipedes, not to mention multitudinous ants (many of these in dreadnought class) and every type of fly, sandflies etc.'[7]

In sum, if you wanted to pick the worst possible place to be imprisoned and healthy, you have found it.

It would depress any normal doctor, but Weary is not that and he tries to turn his mind to the higher things in life, or what he can remember of them. Even as another, inevitably dreadful day begins,

Weary looks, genuinely, on the bright side: 'Shortly after parade there is a slight lightening in the sky to the east and then eventually there is usually seen pale rose streamers, apparently an effect of the light mist and cloud. This strongly reminds me always of Homer's description: "The rosy fingers of dawn showed through the mists".'[8]

Or, as the POWs would say: 'It's bloody early.'

23 February 1943, Konyu, house calls

The problem with being a success is that you are suddenly in demand. After his famed night-time abdominal operation, Weary finds he is even more annoyingly popular with the Japanese guards: 'all the Ns now look at me with bated breath as No. 1 doctor and are chasing me for advice'.[9]

Around him, Weary has severely sick Australians and many ill Britishers who also require treatment, but it is their hypochondriacal gaolers who have to be humoured first: 'They are like a lot of frightened children about their health; worry re chest, stomach etc. etc. Much fuss about any scratches.'[10]

They are also more than fussy about their medicines. The guards are now very fond of Vicks VapoRub, but, as one guard informs Weary, 'Eyedrops – Nippon soldier no like.'[11]

It is beyond infuriating.

'Suffering cats!'[12] is Weary's last word on the absurd situation, where prima donna prison guards insist their own light ailments are treated before the oft severe illnesses of the POWs can receive any of his attention.

In camp any source of food is prized, but snakes have become the protein of choice. Snake hunting is not a traditional sport, but the Australians embrace it with gusto. Weary is informed that, just last night, one Australian soldier did not have to hunt at all as he woke up to the terror of a large snake crawling into his bedsheets. With a scream, the panting Private beat the snake to death and then looked up to see his hut mate declare: 'Some people have all the luck.'[13]

Another favourite is catching lizards, with the men becoming proficient at making traps for them. By setting a string with a loop at one end, delicately poised on a small catch around a lizard hole, while the other end is attached to a bent bit of bamboo, all they have to do is wait. As soon as the lizard emerges into the loop the trap is sprung, and their rice that night will be leavened with small but delicious chunks of reptile.

Most wonderfully, of late they can eat such fare while discussing the rumours circulating that the war is now over in Europe. Can it be true or just another dream that runs through the camps as fast as fevered word can take it? There is also word that there are 'protests in Geneva about the treatment of British POWs in [Thailand], quoting the extremely high death rates'. True, there is an extremely high chance this is just prisoner-generated propaganda – these days no-one knows what is a furphy and what is the good oil – but the truth of that death rate among all the POWs here *is* appalling. As one who keeps a daily tally of the sick and dying, Weary knows better than anyone just how rapidly it is growing. An overwhelming 130 are listed as sick today. Two more Dutch have died this morning. A number of the English will likely be joining them this afternoon. One truth is unchanging: 'The state of health in these camps can only be regarded as an everlasting appalling disgrace and a perfectly natural result of the administration and general treatment.'[14]

Weary would write more, but there is a groaning guard with a very slight tummy ache who has asked for his attention.

25 February 1943, Konyu, mind your language

On this morning's list of complaints: the camp. If only there could be one. The officers are still sleeping rough, in the open air. At least the patients get spoilt with three tents serving as a hospital. Weary is asking about anti-malarial protection from a Japanese officer when Sergeant King appears, looking like he has fallen out of the bleeding ugly tree and been hit by every branch on the way down – because he effectively has.

What happened?

Well, sir, there was a disagreement.

Soldier Susuki had not been happy with the way, or the amount, of bamboo that King had been carrying. The two had argued, in their respective languages mostly, and Susuki warned that if King did not do as he was told, he would be struck.

Oh really?

Well, said King, to all in earshot: 'If I'm hit, I'll knock the fucking Nip down.'[15]

Now, as Weary knows, swearing is not a good idea as the Japanese 'do not like this word which is a point in favour of their taste'. And it seems Susuki, *particularly*, doesn't like it.

For, as King recounts, the work party had been on the march once more when, as irony would have it, they had been just passing a cemetery when Susuki had reappeared, holding a large chunk of wood.

'Where is *fucking fucking* soldier?'

Ah, Susuki saw him before any man could lie about King's whereabouts and he viciously swung the club at King's head. It would have killed him if King hadn't shot his arm up quickly enough to take part of the blow. He fell to the ground and Susuki beat him as he was prone, King's arm held up again as a shattered shield.

His arm now? Swollen and broken, says Weary. (Between us, Weary does not think it is broken, but always better to be on the unsafe side if you are trying to get the Japanese not to kill your men.) Weary escorts King to see the commandant and starts to give his 'pidgin patter'.[16]

There are two sides here, Weary tells both of them: 'Sergeant speak Nippon soldier, say "fucking". No good. Nippon order Sergeant speak back. No good, very bad. Nippon soldier hit Sergeant with big stick very hard. No good, very bad. Please see.'[17]

At this point, King looks suitably pathetic and theatrically strains to hold up his arm.

'Perhaps bone break,' say Weary. The commandant, he furious. Soldier Susuki, he summoned, berated, front of Weary. Then Susuki stand attention front of Lieutenant Colonel Dunlop for 15 minutes as gesture of respect and humiliation. Later that day, Weary watches as Susuki approaches King with some cigarettes. 'Please accept apology.'[18]

No. King waves him off. *Fuck off.* The tension simmers. At least it would if the sun was not always so blistering hot, the humidity so endlessly enervating. Out here, the tension stews.

27 February 1943, Konyu, survey says

Despite the daytime humidity, the nights are cold and bitter and so are the men. Who can blame them? As Weary knows: 'one's whole body aches if one wakes up on this damn bamboo'.[19]

And one does, several times a night. More if you have malaria – which brings us today to the 'hospital' they will no doubt be needing. Major Moon, Major Wearne and Weary gather today to inspect the 'hospital buildings', which are barely either of those things in any sensible sense of the words. What they are is 'shockingly jerry built with no roof as yet in the most deplorably low and uneven areas of the ground available'.[20] What the camp needs is two huts, quickly, with at least 'four rows of beds 1 metre wide [times] 2 metres long allotted to each patient'.[21]

There is another matter to be dealt with today: a questionnaire that needs to be filled out for the Japanese Army. It seems a General would like some information on how the enemy officers feel about their camps? Please fill it out with regard to the following: 'impression of camp, impression as to the future progress of the war, impression as to Nipponese Army, impression as to camp sanitation and accommodations'.[22]

These forms will then be read by the General in order to spare senior Japanese officers the bother of visiting the camps themselves.

Thoughts? They have a few.

'It was decided to put our case fairly strongly,'[23] Weary notes. Mainly focused on malaria, dysentery, the maggot-ridden food, the lack of medical supplies, the lack of clothes, the absence of boots, the fact that a lot of the food tastes like boots, no chlorine, no disinfectants and no toilets that work. Apart from that, they're fairly happy.

As ever, they will have to do what they can to improve things themselves and when it is decided that more and deeper latrines are needed, it is Weary himself who is the first to pick up a shovel – displaying exactly the same spirit that Blue Butterworth had first witnessed back in Greece, when their car had to be dug out of a spot of bother. The important thing is getting the job done, and when the boss can, he does it himself.

In the face of seeing 'No. 1 doctor' working in this manner, some of the Japanese officers are confused – in their world it is unthinkable that an officer would so sully himself, as manual work of this kind is only fit for ... Koreans. And as hard as they will push the Australian POWs, for the moment at least, Nippon does not insist that their officers join them on the tools, believing their energies are better spent maintaining discipline, and running the camp.

For their part, British officers think it is work only fit for Privates. And sometimes even the Australian POWs themselves think it is wrong, believing that the Japanese officers must have put Weary to it, as punishment of some sort. But the huge Australian doesn't care, either way.

'Weary just carried on in the old tradition, and he dug the latrines and he wouldn't want any fuss made of that.'[24]

All that counts is that the work is done, and the men made safer.

Meantime, as always, he records the sick and can't help but note a correlation: 'Seventy-one men in hospital today. 15 out of 30 cooks have been down with malaria.'[25]

Half the cooks, and most of the bottle-washers! So there will be more men in hospital soon and far more will be *benjo* happy . . .

These days, the *tenko* musters . . .

'*Roku-jū-nana!*' Sixty-seven!

'*Roku-jū-hachi!*' Sixty-eight!

. . .

. . .

'*Roku-jū-kyū?*' Sixty-nine?

'*Roku-jū-kyū wa doko desu-ka?*'

. . . take much longer for the fact that so many are *byoki*, sick, their once serried ranks now look like those old combs where lots of teeth have fallen out.

28 February 1943, Konyu, like a brief in the night . . .

Every evening, talks are given in the camp. Tonight's topic: death. Oh Christ, can't the Catholics pick a cheerier subject for their talk? Like sex for instance? Or Hell? But Weary will give them a hearing. The first speaker is very insistent they stay vigilant: 'Death always comes like a thief in the night when you are not expecting it and are in a complacent state of mind.'[26]

Well, no worries there; these men *are* expecting it, they aren't complacent, and there is a pretty bloody good chance that death will come during the day out here. Weary makes it through the lecture but the faith does not make it through to him, much as he would like it too: 'In a sense, I am perhaps less a Christian even than I was before the war, but I have been taught very soundly that one must believe in some religion, or sink into the terrible mire of utter selfishness and materialism.'[27]

Religion is good for the men, good for the spirit and if you are an officer who doesn't believe a woman once took an apple from a talking snake and that is where all the trouble started, well, keep it to yourself.

'Man seems to be still far too unintelligent an animal to realise that happiness comes from harmonious relationships with one's fellows and service to mankind.'[28]

And not hearing long talks about death. Try and do Salome and her sexy dancing or Sodom and Gomorrah next time, please. Think about morale!

•

How to survive this hell on earth?

Some refuse to even try, and once they give up it never takes long for most of them to find their way to the cemetery. Others pray, while others gaze forlornly at treasured photos of loved ones somehow still preserved, willing themselves to *live* to see their families again.

Ray Parkin draws. Sometimes he draws his fellow prisoners, sometimes the Japanese guards and officers, sometimes the country around them. What he most loves to draw is ships, both from his memory and the memories of his fellow prisoners. Remembering the details of a particular vessel that he had seen in one port or another, he would start to sketch it, then approach other POWs who had sailed in it, and check: Were the funnels positioned where I have them? Further forward, you say? What about the curve of the bridge? Just like that? A little flatter? Their combined memories are strained to conjure each detail.

It takes him out of himself, his current hell, and helps him to recall happier times and . . . stay sane.

2 March 1943, Konyu, something rotten in the state

It is no easy matter for Weary and Major Wearne to visit the Dutch camp up the way as they have promised, and it is made all the more difficult as they clamber up the mountain by the obvious disdain of the monkeys at their plight. Swinging from vine to vine above them as though they are auditioning to play Tarzan, they never stop chattering in derision at the absurd way these giant apes get about. As it turns out, these small furry fellas are the last spirited creatures these two monkey's uncles will see today, as the Dutch camp at last comes into view.

Greeted by the nominal 'leader' of the Dutch prisoners, Captain Johann Smits – a dour, depressed figure who seems to have lost all but the will to live, and even that hangs in the balance – the only good news is that he is about to resign his command. And it is not just because, as Weary can see, he is 'quite hopeless as a leader',[29] it is that he inspires hopelessness in others.

With 204 men in hospital as of last night, dysentery is nearly as rampant as despair. It starts with the Dutch and extends to other former locals languishing in camp.

'When the Javanese leave Java they lose heart,' Smits says. 'It is no good trying to drive them.'[30]

Right, so giving up is the new strategy? How about constructing something, you know, like we Australians have?

Smits shakes his head.

'We have too many old men; we cannot work like the Australians.'[31]

Well, how about starting with something basic to combat dysentery, we have a new system with latrines that –

'We cannot dig the deep latrines. It is too hard for us.'[32]

Well, how deep have they got so far?

'Two feet.'

And that has taken many days. Weary is darkly amused to hear that even the Japanese guards have started criticising how slow the Dutch are at digging the damn things.

Perhaps they might try –

No, trying is out.

'The work is too hard, we cannot do it,'[33] says Smits flatly, and this is his response to all Australian suggestions, as it becomes ever more clear that this sad officer is unlikely to have descended from 'The Flying Dutchman', whoever he was.

'There is the same hopelessness about anything one speaks about.'[34]

Well, does Smits have any plans for the future? Oh yes, one: escape.

Seriously? Weary is spectacularly unsurprised to hear that Smits has 'damn all in the way of a plan. I did all I could to discourage such foolishness.'[35]

If you are too weak and sick to even produce a pot to piss in, God help you if you think you are strong or resourceful enough to escape.

When they inspect the Dutch 'hospital', Weary himself is sickened. Orderlies are rare, the Dutch are too ill and the Javanese are 'frightened and will not help'.[36] The patients lie abandoned, their sheets soiled, and the stench of the place is so terrible that, coming from the fresh air outside, it is like being hit in your mug with a shit-bat. If you weren't ill before you arrived, you will be before you leave. If you leave. *Why the hell aren't the bedsheets cleaned?*

'There are not enough containers.'[37]

Well, how about just folding the sheets up and giving them a boiling wash?

Not our job.

'The friends of the patients are supposed to wash the clothes but do not come.'[38]

As for the doctors, they impress less than the patients. Weary asks a Dr Brower about one man he spots twisting in delirium. Brower tells him that the man is in a semi-coma, as a result of meningitis. Well, has a lumbar puncture been done? 'No,' replies Dr Brower. 'As I have no adrenalin.'[39]

Weary promises he will do what he can to get some supplied, but is then told there is no problem with supply, Dr Brower just hasn't got around to asking for it!

This place. Weary looks in disgust at the 'dysentery latrine', it is 'a sort of rough garden seat. All men then clean themselves with water, using their hand, and go through the process of sticking their hand down into the one disinfectant container, a single, long and narrow, stick of bamboo. No thought of soap and water even.'[40]

These men are asking for death and they will get it. Even then there will be no dignity as, 'the dead men are hardly below the surface due to the difficulty of old men digging graves!'.[41]

Shocked, Weary returns to the Australian camp to be confronted with more loo problems, this time of a non-life-threatening nature. The Japanese are 'making a great fuss about their *benjo*'.[42]

They would like a *private* toilet built with excellent walls so that no prisoner can watch them answer the call of nature. Really? Even 'despite the fact that they publicly pee all over the place about their hut and foul the scrub about without covering the mess'?[43]

Yes, despite that.

Very well, Weary will add it to the list of priorities: Private Loo With No View. Oh, while you are here, Dunlop, do you remember that questionnaire you filled in about how happy you were with conditions in the camp? You got the answers wrong. Please do it again and say you are happy, particularly with 'attitude of mind as to camp'.[44]

No. 1 has ordered it so. The interesting thing about this for Weary is it shows No. 1, the camp commander, might be worried about the safety of his job.

It is something, anyway, a crack in the otherwise implacable face of total Japanese control.

And there is other news, which seems significant.

'We are warned today that soon we are expected to supply 500 men a day for outside work on road and rail.'[45]

3 March 1943, Konyu, report retort

Ask and you shall bloody receive. No. 1 wants Weary to fill out the questionnaire anew? Well, he will get new responses and a new attitude: 'My attitude is one of gross disquiet and fear for the lives and health of the troops placed in my care.'[46]

Specifics? 'The following matters worry and perplex me. Although I have found that our soldiers do not remain healthy with the full Nippon ration, only a fraction of the promised scale of vegetables and meat has been supplied.'[47]

More? Well, for one thing – no, make that two things – 'after many weeks many of the soldiers have no house and most sleep in the open, although some have almost no clothes'.

Truly, by this time even such uniforms and clothes that had survived from their time at Changi have so rotted off them that most of the men have taken to wearing things they call a 'Jap-happy' or 'cock-cloth' – no more than a small bit of material, often sacrificed mosquito nets, that goes from the bit of string around your waist and under your legs from one side to the other.

Weary goes on:

> Supplies of medical stores and hospital and sanitation arrange-
> ments are not satisfactory. Out of a total of 873 men I consider
> that only 350 are suitable for heavy work outside the camp.
>
> It causes grave alarm that other troops I see in the area should
> look like living skeletons. As I have always been informed that
> the Nippon army has an honourable tradition, I cannot under-
> stand why prisoners of war should have been shifted to such

an unhealthy place, or that conditions should be so inhumane and discreditable to the detaining powers.

E. Dunlop, Lt. Col.
Konyu No. 3 Camp[48]

Weary calls on No. 1 personally to deliver the report. Result? The very next day a Japanese major arrives to inspect this camp personally. His verdict: 'I am satisfied that the food is very good and cooking satisfactory. In fact, everything good.'[49]

No Australian officer is allowed to meet with him.

Report over.

Any more questions?

No.

And no more questionnaires.

5 March 1943, Konyu, holy roller

Of all the people who cause you trouble when you command a camp, the last one you expect to be involved in a barney is the Chaplain! But Weary has learnt to expect the unexpected on a regular basis on his watch, and today is no exception. For right now, he has to run on the double to stop a punch-up between Padre Gerard Bourke and Lieutenant Usuki, who is already red-faced with fury. (Actually, both are red-faced with fury at the moment, and Bourke looks as though every blood vessel in his face is about to burst.)

What the hell has happened? A poor choice of words because it seems Padre Bourke was readying a holy service and Usuki ordered him to stop that nonsense, and Bourke said it wasn't nonsense and he wouldn't stop and now Usuki has his sword out and they are YELLING at each other. The exchange is recorded word for wondering word by the watching Weary:

Usuki: 'Why do you disobey the orders of the Japanese Army?'[50]

Bourke: 'I take my orders from a higher authority!'

Usuki: '*NUNDA! Nunda!* Higher authority? Where?'

The Chaplain points to the sky.

Bourke: 'My orders are from up there!'

The guard is puzzled for a moment, and then decides what to do. He'll kill him.

Usuki: '*BUGERO!*'[51]

His sword gleams in the air and Weary is quick to see that Bourke welcomes his fate. Jesus *Christ*, his face is even 'happy with the prospect of martyrdom'.[52]

Weary jumps between them and taps his head as he talks to Usuki, pronouncing his opening word as the Japanese do, avoiding the 'r', wherever it is found (something they compensate for by restoring it in any word that has an 'l' as in 'Dunrop'):

'*Kistian!*' he yells, by way of explanation. 'Kistian priests very eccentric men!'[53]

Lieutenant Usuki – looking completely ridiculous, as all the Japanese officers do, with their huge thigh-hugging boots and tiny caps – smiles, at least the best he can, with his face like a twisted sandshoe. Of course! *Kistian*. That explains the madness.

'Ah, eccentric man.'[54]

His sword is sheathed, his face is saved, as is Bourke's head. Weary thinks back fondly to Australia, where church services were boring.

Bourke returns to his rounds, which are becoming ever more difficult as it is so hard for many to believe there can be any God at all, when He allows such things as they are seeing and suffering every hour of every day on 'the Line' to exist. You want me to believe He loves me, when He is allowing this ulcer to eat half my leg?

No. Just no.

•

Welcome, welcome, welcome!

Weary has the floor, filling in at the last minute of tonight's concert, after Sergeant Wynne, who had been meant to do it had . . . well . . . fallen into the *benjo*, twice! It was not just that Wynne could have gone to a fancy-dress party as a Werribee duck, covered in shit from top to toe, it was that he had injured his arms.

So, welcome.

Sergeant Wynne is sorry he can't be here, Weary notes, but 'he has got himself into a hole or two'.[55]

The first roar of laughter . . . and they are away!

A more enthusiastic audience would not be possible, as they devour the show, which comes complete with a touch of vaudeville and a side helping of ham. Everyone who can do a turn, gets a turn; the 800 men watching roaring with laughter or showering them with applause.

The whole thing had started with a scrawled note, pinned to the outside wall of the most central hut:

Wanted for Pow-Wow

Concert Party

Actors – acrobats – comedians –

comediennes – crooners

croonettes – musicians – magicians

and

Buxom Beauties for Bosomy Ballet

Note: Chorus ladies are requested to leave their phone numbers with the management. 'Call girls' being in short supply. Apply Pig Net, Hut 3.[56]

Jocular, yes. But amidst all the turbulence of their lives, the home-sickness and generally depressed air, Weary has recognised it from the first for the great idea it is.

To begin, half-a-dozen Diggers start singing their favourite song of all, to the tune and lyrical structure of 'Bless 'Em All', albeit with their preferred word stuck in to the recurrent phrase. Ah, sing it!

Fuck 'em all,
Fuck 'em all,
The long and the short and the tall,
Fuck all the sergeants and W.O.1s,
Fuck all the corp'rals and their bleedin' sons,

'Cos we're sayin' goodbye to 'em all.
As back to their billets they crawl,

You'll get no promotion this side of the ocean, so cheer up,
my lads,
fuck 'em all.
Fuck 'em all!
Fuck 'em all![57]

In the black Thai night, the ribald laughter of the men soon fades as the Australian POWs all join in, their soaring voices rolling through the jungle with force enough to give all of the monkeys, leopards and even elephants pause.

Fuck 'em all!
Fuck 'em all!

As the singing goes on, it is momentarily possible to forget that you are a beaten, starving POW working in a hell-hole in Thailand and instead to think of yourself as a free man, surrounded by your mates and having a good time.

Fuck 'em all!
FUCK 'EM ALL!

True, it's not quite the same hymn-like song they recalled singing around Uncle Bob's old piano on Sunday afternoon after the roast. (Another favourite of the men on the Line is singing to the tune of 'She'll Be Coming Round the Mountain', with some gusto, *'They'll be dropping 1000-pounders when they come / They'll be dropping 1000-pounders when they come / They'll be dropping 1000 pounders on those little yellow fuckers / They'll be dropping 1000 pounders when they come.'*[58])

And so the concert goes on, with Weary bringing each act on and off to robust applause. The jewels in tonight's crown include Private Herbert Smith, known as 'the singing soldier', and Private George Page on his battered old trumpet which used to do 'Reveille', but now brings the house down with a marvellous 'Boogie Woogie Bugle Boy'.

'Great fires lit the scene,' Weary records, 'and the crackling of bamboo with showers of sparks drifting up to mingle with the stars so multitudinous and bright. The surrounding jungle was black and mysterious and forgotten.'[59]

But in truth the night belongs to one of Weary's friends, Major Allan Woods. He can't sing (not that the lack of such a talent stopped the others), he is not good at telling jokes, but he has one party piece: a poem. Yes, it's one they all know, it's Banjo. As his slow bass voice rings out, the men fall silent:

> *There was movement at the station, for the word had passed*
> *around*
> *That the colt from old Regret had got away,*
> *And had joined the wild bush horses – he was worth a thou-*
> *sand pound,*
> *So all the cracks had gathered to the fray . . .*

His listeners know the words, they are like a rosary to Australians, they have heard them spoken in the schoolroom and in the pub, and Major Woods transports the men now back to their homeland, to the outback, to the bush so far away from this jungle, to a past now present as he speaks:

> *When they reached the mountain's summit, even Clancy*
> *took a pull,*
> *It well might make the boldest hold their breath,*
> *The wild hop scrub grew thickly, and the hidden ground*
> *was full*
> *Of wombat holes, and any slip was death.*
> *But the man from Snowy River let the pony have his head,*
> *And he swung his stockwhip round and gave a cheer,*
> *And he raced him down the mountain like a torrent down*
> *its bed,*
> *While the others stood and watched in very fear.*

The spark of the fire is the only sound heard now, save for Major Woods, and even that takes them into the tale they know so well. Speak it, say it, make it live. And the tale of that lone rider, that one man against the odds, braving death and winning, fills every heart. Weary Dunlop has been at many of these shows, but he has never heard anything like this. Woods plays the Banjo's tune and every man is caught in its taut emotion; those words gaining new meaning in this place:

> *And he ran them single-handed till their sides were white*
> *with foam.*
> *He followed like a bloodhound on their track,*

> *Till they halted cowed and beaten, then he turned their*
> *heads for home,*
> *And alone and unassisted brought them back.*

After finishing, there is a moment of silence, before Woods tilts his head in the barest bow and the applause rings out and on.

They are Australians and, for a few precious minutes, they are in their own land beneath the Southern Cross once more, Aunty Martha's put the roast on the table, and Bob's your uncle again . . .

7 March 1943, Konyu, body willing, flesh weak

Sex.

Thoughts of it intrude at the most inopportune times. Like during church for instance. Weary tries to chase the thoughts away, but it is too hard. For his part, poor Padre Webb is doing his best, cobbling together his own substitutes for the usually sacred necessities. (Today, the body of Christ won't be bread, but rice. As for His blood, well, the wine is 'some sort of synthetic produce of the padre's'.[60] Like most religion, which Weary quietly scoffs at, it goes down better if you don't ask questions and don't think about it too much.)

During the service, Weary's body is present but his mind is elsewhere and everywhere: 'Somehow my thoughts were racing all over the world in a crazy kaleidoscopic way. I thought of Helen often, and of many [women], though few were holy, I'm afraid.'[61]

Padre Webb hands Weary a chalice made from – of course – bamboo, and he sips. Other thoughts intrude now and one thought persists: moving. There is a rumour growing that they will be leaving; some of them, somewhere up in the hills, nearer to a railway that is being built . . .

(In the meantime, Weary is not the only one with thoughts of sex. One dark evening, Ray Parkin finds himself isolated and is suddenly confronted by a Japanese guard, rubbing his groin.

'*Bashabish-ca?*'[62] he ask the naval man.

Sorry, what?

'*Bashabish!*' the guard repeats, making the sign for coitus, by putting the forefinger of his right hand back and forth through the small circle formed by the thumb and forefinger of his left hand.

Oh!

NO.

'He seemed to be in a state of roused childlike passion,' Parkin will recall, 'which was strong enough to overcome shyness but not enough to obliterate embarrassment. But he was making a scandalous proposal with odd hope. He went away abashed and disappointed.'[63] Better abashed than a *bashabish*.)

11 March 1943, Konyu, moving to the mountain

News. And it comes at nine o'clock at night.

Weary records it in his diary, '[The English camp] warned me of movement tomorrow to [Hintok] mountain camp . . .'[64]

It is situated some seven kilometres to the north – the camp previously occupied by the joint Dutch and Australian unit that has now been assigned to a camp at Kinsayok, which is 16 kilometres further north again. The POWs of Dunlop Force will cover most of the journey there by lots of 50 men to a lorry, before walking the last few kilometres to what Weary already knows to be a mosquito-infested 'waterless bog'.[65] God help them all.

'This news is as bloody as could be received,' Weary notes, 'in view of the fact that the river here is the life-line and to be away from it in wet weather is too unpleasant to contemplate.'[66]

Instead of supplies being delivered on that shimmering life-line, everything will now have to be heave-hard-hauled higher. With the reluctant blessing of Lieutenant Usuki, Weary pays a rushed visit to the camp they must decamp to, and the short verdict is: 'bloody awful'.[67] The long version is that the Dutch, particularly, have 'fouled the whole area'[68] with a mixture of indifference, incompetence and incontinence. And the biggest worry is indeed the lack of fresh water available. Instead of a glorious river like they have now, there is nowt but a tiny mountain stream, which more *seeps* than *streams*. There is a real question about whether it will be able to sustain so many new arrivals, and a real risk that their move will see the stream further fouled.

Weary retreats to have a visit and a moan with the British camp, where Lieutenant Colonel Mackie More receives them, while Japanese Warrant Officer Tadano, who is proving a reasonable man, offers them a drink of precious Thai whiskey. They have a drink . . . and another drink. Colonel More commiserates, they drink some more and a high-spirited Weary suggests that if the English have to move too, it will be no great loss.

'The only really good thing you will be leaving behind if you shift is the cemetery, and the view from the officers' hut. So why not take the cemetery with [you]?'[69]

Colonel More laughs and then much joking begins about how their bamboo palaces can be broken up and mailed ahead. *Another drink? Why not.* Gallows humour and cheap liquor go well together: 'I felt rather like one at a late afternoon sherry party and in great form.'[70]

Duty continues and, move or not, Weary has promised to go out for a malarial recce with the redoubtable Sergeant Honeyman, and the slightly less redoubtable Jock Clarke. Clarke and Weary look at each other as Honeyman 'set a terrible raking stride up the rough rocky ravine to the north'.[71] The bloody man makes mountain goats look like sloths, but dammit if Weary is going to let him know that *he* is tired. Then again, he has had a boozy lunch for once and the conditions are not exactly encouraging for a stroll, let alone a hike from Hell but twice as hot: 'The sun beat down intolerably and I could feel it concentrated as from a burning glass, so that steams of hot sweat poured down my face and blinded my eyes.'

Honeyman calls to Weary from on high ahead: *Should I slow down?*

Not at all!

(He was in the Wallabies, dammit, and will be buggered if he is the first to cry for mercy. Hopefully, Jock will do the honours.) Onwards and upwards into the heat, and Weary is just wavering on declaring himself a piece of exhausted meat when Jock yells out: *For Christ's sake! Slow down!* A puzzled Honeyman turns and Weary shrugs. *Well, I suppose if it will make Jock happy we might take a breather?*

After they take a panting break, they come across something far more potentially lethal than hidden ponds or brush breeding grounds for mosquitoes and pests: it is a track. A railway track.

And Weary sees now that although it is 'still being cleared, it is an astonishing affair. It seems to run without much regard to the landscape, as though someone had drawn a line on the map!'[72]

They look in amazement at a parallel trail of surveyors' pegs placed there by still barking Japanese engineers; pegs that run down the 'precipitous slope of a hill instead of the ridge'.[73]

Madness. Everywhere you look, you see, 'terrible gaps and boulders and descents'.[74]

It is all to be cleared regardless and the ridge of granite speckled with crystal quartz ignored. This hard and heavy work, the Japanese engineers make clear to Weary, is what his sick men will soon be marched towards and set to. In this land of jungle, mountains, culverts and chasms, the straight line will go through, come what may: with the felled trees and broken rocks from the mountains providing the raw material for the embankments and bridges to get across the culverts and chasms.

It makes Weary sober very quickly to contemplate joining the British soldiers sweating just ahead of them now. The stripped Tommies have been tasked with tree felling and Jock points out the broken axe handles leading up to the mighty tree they are working on now with blunt axes, hemp ropes and mass exhausted exertion. And look at these already 'cut' trees!

'They look as if they've been gnawed down, by someone with inferior false teeth,'[75] says Jock, ever the dentist. The Japanese guards take no notice of the three Australians with the appalled expressions. Weary and Jock have taken their shirts off while sweating up the ravines, and they look just like the other British prisoners slaving away today. Chastened, they slowly retrace their steps. Honeyman's efforts will protect them from malaria, but who on earth can protect prisoners from that railway?

Positioned 100 miles from the start of the railway at Nong Pladuk – itself 40 miles west of Bangkok – about 500 Brits and 2000 Tamils have already been on this Konyu section for three months, building a railway through the pressing jungle, around its mountains, across its gorges, towards its goal: Burma, hundreds of miles away. Dunlop Force has been assigned to finish building a particular section of railway that will be two and a half miles long, extending through country that is very particular in nature. For just as, back home in Australia, God had legendarily made the platypus from every spare part of bills, beaks, claws, hands, tails, pouches, paws and feral furs He had left over, so too is this area a jumble of jungle, gullies, ravines, rivers, valleys, escarpments, mountains and molehills that He emptied from the bottom of his landscaping bag just before He called it a day – let's see, 'Saturday' – before He rested on the seventh day.

Specifically, Weary and his men are part of the force that has been assigned the carving of six cuttings into hills of solid rock, and the building of nine bridges and two major embankments.

As they will later discover, Dunlop Force is just a part of a contingent of 60,000 Allied POWs brought here for this purpose, including 8000 Dutchmen, 30,000 Brits, and even a few American airmen who've been shot down – together with another 200,000 Asian 'coolies', labourers from Japanese-occupied territories, shanghaied here at the sharpened points of bayonets for a pittance of pay. They are being overseen by the 5th and 9th Railway Regiments, some 10,000 men strong, in turn supported by 3000 Koreans.

•

The first two sections of railway the new arrivals must work on are a couple of cuttings to avoid long detours around mountains – one is 460 metres long at a depth of eight metres, while two kilometres to the north is the other, which is 75 metres long and 25 metres deep. They are positioned respectively at the 'Kilo 153' and 'Kilo 155'[76] marks of the 415-kilometre line.

The task of the Australians will be to blast through the sheer rock and remove the thousands of tons of detritus to the spots where they can build embankments. The machinery they have to help them is practically non-existent and most of the work is done by sheer muscle power, plus dynamite.

And make no mistake, they are told, there are POW camps all along 'the Line', but few, if any, are doing work as hard as this, on such a long cutting, so remote from any town. The Australians have been brought in because the British and Dutch, heavily flogged, have badly flagged.

After 12 weeks of this hell, the British and Dutch workforce is withering and starting to lose men to a variety of ailments, from malnutrition to – most particularly – beri-beri, not to mention through accidents such as rock falls in the shocking conditions.

And yes, engineers among them have pointed out that in many ways it would be easier to build a tunnel, but the problem with that would be only a limited number of men could work from both ends. With an open cutting, the whole lot of them can work at the same time.

I see.

Weary et al. have only just made it back to camp, when the orders come through.

'Transition of Troops'[77] will be commencing . . . tomorrow!

There will be '2 lorries daily at 1030 and 1530 hours (same lorry back and forth), with approximately 50 troops per lorry load'.[78] Baggage in the afternoons only, morning troops to carry just a water bottle and 'eating gear'.[79]

The sick are to remain; some may be sent south 20 miles to the staging camp of Tarsau, which now has a rough hospital, with some healthy men remaining to tend them. Weary lodges a protest about the troops not being able to move with their own baggage; the men and their officers have little faith that all will be transported after them, and it is distressing to think that whatever meagre reminders they have of home and their lives before this war must be abandoned.

As for 'organisation', it just seems to be a giant game of leap-frog, 'each camp chases the next one',[80] and they will once more be constructing quarters and attacking unforgiving undergrowth: 'Perhaps we are regarded as jungle shock troops!'

Despite the jokes, the men are shocked tonight. They had something of a home beginning, now they are going again, on into unhappiness and darkness. The guards are unsympathetic and are enjoying the flurry of moving everything onwards at once: 'this is (as always) the N method of combining inefficient behaviour with "hurry", "hurry", "speedo", "speedo".'[81]

Don't want to be late for your next prison!

That night, of course, it rains heavily and the weather matches their mood, and masks more than a few tears.

•

Moving day and 50 men are ready as ordered, waiting for a lorry, when a Japanese guard runs up and tells them of a new, revised plan:

'Now two hundred men *marchy marchy, hurry hurry!*'[82]

'Lunch?' asks Weary.

'Don't need,' replies the guard.

Yes, we do.

Alright then, six of the cooks can go marchy marchy too. Speedo a-go-go, righty-ho, tally-ho. Onwards.

13 March 1943, Konyu, bombs away

Another 200 men are *marchy, marchy, marchy* for the mountain camp today. There will be no lorry for the baggage and all must carry their own bedding rolls. Their new camp has just two huts built, frames for eight more up and no beds in any – a situation that must change today. There are 155 men present, fit and working, Weary informs Susuki. And seven elephants, Susuki adds. What? Oh yes, down at the British camp, the Japanese have enlisted seven elephants which will escort 80 men to do railway construction today.

Is he serious? Deadly serious, in fact. The elephants have not entirely been a success, Susuki informs him. Susuki does not blame the elephants, he blames the British for not knowing how to handle them. Why, one British soldier annoyed one elephant and Susuki relates the consequence: 'Elephant very, very angry. Soldier climb tree.'[83]

(Susuki now helpfully pantomimes climbing up a tree in case Weary is unable to imagine what this might look like.)

'Too late. Trunk seize. Hospital! No good.'[84]

The main business of the day is getting more of a roof over more of the heads that are arriving. The camp is muggy, which means, soon enough and sure enough: 'Rain, rain with a vengeance.'[85]

The enlisted men have shelter, the officers are 'of course still in open and got a thorough drenching'.[86] At least they are setting a good example to the men. A wet example, but a good one. They do their best to sleep on their bamboo beds, covered by their coats and canvases; but at two in the morning, Weary wakes to find the water 'rose above my bed bamboo and our backs were in the water'.[87]

Noah had it easier.

The next evening, they get a rare bit of detailed military intelligence from a Japanese guard: 'Nippon bomb bomb Darwin, bomb bomb Brisbane, bomb bomb Sydney, bomb bomb Newcastle.'[88]

Sobering news. The Australian response? A single voice yells out: 'Bullshit!'[89]

'Yes!' replies the triumphant guard, 'Bullshit bomb!'[90]

But keep building.

Today, among other things, they must build the Japanese HQ for the growing number of Kempis, whose main job remains to make everyone live in dread, by frequently searching the prisoners' huts for ham radios, diaries, contraband – anything for which the POWs can be tortured or executed. A much-grander affair than the other buildings, their HQ, the *Kebetei*, will come complete with cells. (A prison within a prison, is exactly the sort of idea that most pleases the Kempis.)

At Weary's insistence, plumbers and carpenters in the ranks are also put to work building a water system of hollow bamboo for piping to deliver clean water from a nearby mountain creek in an area well removed from the latrines.

Mid-March 1943, Konyu, hard landings

Physician, diagnose thyself. And Dr Weary does.

'I have mild dysentery, a little blood and mucus. Damn.'[91]

That is not going to stop an orderly meeting of the officers, featuring Major Hec Greiner giving Weary a run-through of arrivals and departures of men and structures. The next morning, 'still feeling rather poor with a tongue like a birdcage',[92] Weary walks to the Dutch camp and right 'into a Dutch funeral, the 14th in 28 days'.[93]

All are silent as they stand over the open grave: 'The body was wrapped in a mosquito net and on a rough litter with a small D flag and a large wreath made of jungle flowers and leaves.'[94]

For yes, the Dutch are being pulled out of this camp as they have finished their section of rail, at much the same time it has finished them.

In conversation with Dutch medicos and officers, it is clear to Weary that the brutality of the Japanese has known no bounds in their desire to get the railway done. The Dutch that survive are drained and done; more death is in train and the Australians are about to be mown down by the indifference of their captors.

The dead buried, talk turns to those still alive and what they are being asked to do. This railway is already out of control, and they have barely begun: 'Men yesterday went out at around 0915 hours, had 50 minutes for lunch then worked until 1825 continuously.'[95]

This would strain very fit, very well men. It is going to kill them, and the guards have an eye for any slackers: 'One man was beaten up.'[96]

Oh, and there is a four-mile hard walk, each way, to and from the railway. Last night the men arrived back at camp just after 8 pm. They are achingly active for 11 hours a day at best, a ridiculous situation. Tomorrow the Japanese engineers will give a figure for the men needed that morn; and the result will be the same as today, every man not seriously ill in hospital is on the railway. There will be more jungle wreaths soon.

Weary's surgical skill is needed today when RAAF Sergeant Geoff Dewey has a workplace accident. He is hacking away at a tree and his axe slips and cuts his foot into a bloody mess. Or, more professionally put: 'breaking metacarpals near heads and severing all the tendons on extensor aspect of 4 small toes'.[97] The poor soldier is run to a lorry on a litter, and the lorry is driven to Weary, who demands that they be taken to Konyu, where an anaesthetic can be given to Dewey so he can endure what needs to be done. Permission by the guards is given and they race 'down the rather terrific new road to the camp'.[98]

Dr Dunlop is quick, unorthodox and precise: 'Made a right-angled splint out of a kerosene tin and wire';[99] bandages and plasters are borrowed from the British. Major Moon once more serves as an approximating anaesthetist and, most ingeniously, the 'tendons were sutured with parachute silk'.[100]

Result? Dewey keeps his foot. Soon, he will likely be well enough to be worked to death.

Mid-March 1943, Konyu, unsocial climbers

Alas, alas, they have no sooner finally finished the Japanese facilities and the bare rudiments of their own than the Japanese decide to . . . decamp. Yes, this camp is too far from where the work is to be done, so they must move some eight kilometres still further north.

On this morning packing up everything they own takes 30 seconds, to which they must add a few hours to pack everything they will need for the building work. Laden like mules with tools, they start staggering up the track, through the jungle, to a place called Hintok.

'First,' Ray Parkin will recount, 'we had to get up that Hill on which men on ration parties had collapsed.'[101]

The sun beats down, their lungs burst, the sweat drips from their foreheads, and still they must climb, as whole clouds of butterflies and insects rise before them. It is possible, just possible, that the air is slightly cooler the higher they go, but that still only takes it down from throbbing hot to boiling hot. In the fog of the men's exhaustion, swirling aptly with the billowing green clouds of the endless jungle-covered ranges that balloon all around them, they eventually become aware that the track is 'winding just below the serrated spine of a mountain chain. To the south were other jagged ridges of dark, stained granite resembling the sheer faces of organ pipes . . .'[102]

It is sobering to see other lost souls as they make their way forward, for before long they are passing two other camps filled with POWs who are surely reflections of themselves, albeit as they will be a few weeks on from now. They too have been placed here to work on their own five-mile-long sections of line. These men look so haggard, so weak, as though a fresh breeze could blow them down. Most chillingly, they look back in turn, their eyes filled with pity as they know what the new chums will soon be facing.

Finally, just after two o'clock, Parkin and the rest struggle into the mountain camp – known as Hintok Mountain Camp – a small clearing with bamboo lean-tos and small battered bamboo huts left behind by the Dutch and native workers, who've either just left, or, more likely, just died. To judge by the faeces scattered around the camp, they only departed, one way or another, recently. *Charmed, we're sure.*

The remaining residents – the monkeys and baboons – utter simian screams of protests that the new arrivals still don't get it: these curiously hairless horrors, who can't even climb trees, have no place in these parts.

The camp is situated in an elevated valley at the base of a large foothill that will come to be called 'Elephant Mountain', and hemmed in on three sides by very steep slopes, seven kilometres from the River Kwai Noi.

Collapsing from sheer exhaustion, the men are soon given some fish soup and tea in the hope it will revive them. They are equally given tents, 18 feet by 12, to put up. For the rest of the day they do their best to establish their camp, 20 men to a tent.

How to get themselves out of the mud?

'We cut logs and covered them with a bamboo deck on which we put our belongings. It had rained on the way and been thundery. We were glad to have some shelter . . . '[103]

They sleep meantime on similar bamboo slats, which would have been comfortable if not for the fact that, just like at Konyu, myriad bugs, insects and mighty mites have come to precisely the same conclusion, and swarm in the night, all over the slats and the sweaty bodies. The most terrifying thing is dealing with scorpions so big you can *hear* them as they drop from the roof onto some poor bastard below. Who? You'll know soon enough when an anguished cry rings out, and only hope it's not your own. It is the eternal, infernal nocturnal through the darkest hours, as slaps and curses ring out from every bamboo bunk.

Welcome to Hintok.

With an early start the next morning, when – given no time to establish themselves, and do the work necessary to build latrines, a mess that is not a mess, and a hospital that is more than a notion – they must leave this new camp to get to the actual worksite. For now, another desperate climb begins.

•

And their workplace?

Alas, it is still some three miles away, on a track winding back to make a billy-goat crack, let alone weakened POWs like them. Getting dressed in the dark, they are on parade just after dawn, before breakfast of a small portion of overcooked rice sludge, known by them as 'pap' (rhymes with crap). As ever, it is served by orderlies who, by the light of candles or slush lamps, ladle out seven ounces worth of their daily allotment of 20 ounces into their dixies. And now, after a weak tea to wash it down – and gathering another seven ounces in their dixies to eat at lunch, with two small vegetable rissoles – there is just time to warm themselves in the always surprisingly cold Thai dawn by the embers of the still smouldering night fires, before they are on their way.

'The first few hundred yards of our way,' Ray Parkin will recount, 'was across a short flat valley which looked as if it would be a swamp in the wet. It lay between two escarpments. We climbed an arduous zigzag up the southern one, and up a rock wall for the last sixty feet on a rope.'[104]

And they are still not there. For now, to get to the worksite itself, they have to go up a track so steep that, with just a few more degrees, you'd call it climbing a *cliff*.

Crikey! *This* is the way they get to work?

Indeed it is. The rock surface all around them is a strange mix of granite and limestone, pocked with crystal quartz. After getting to the top, they must now descend a slope covered by bamboo thickets and boulders before there is some relief provided by crossing a large furrow, 'made by elephants hauling out teak logs'[105] to be used in building the bridges.

Not that these massive animals do all that they might.

'It was that time that I lost my affection for elephants,' Uren will note dryly, 'because the elephants had the best trade union in the world. They worked two hours and rested the rest of the day. But we old Aussies had to work *all* day.'[106]

The best thing, oddly enough, is that the enormous piles of dung that the elephants have left behind dry so quickly that they become like poo stepping stones. And now the men start to get the first idea of what they are charged with doing. While some, under the supervision of Japanese engineers, will be engaged in building several large trestle bridges over the River Kwai, others must excavate a cutting through the side of the mountain – blasting out thousands of tons of rock – while still others will have to haul the detritus from that cutting to build a nearby large embankment to cross a gully.

And their starting point is here.

Before the workers can begin to make the cutting into the mountain they must 'clear the rail trace'[107] and remove all the bamboo clumps and trees that grow upon its path. Guided by the theodolite-wielding Japanese engineers, the Australians set to with machetes, axes and plenty of elbow grease, chopping, hacking and hauling.

'We spent a hot forenoon here, surveying and hacking down bamboos and trees in line of sight. It was an almost sixty-degree slope; our feet ached and our haunches tired, playing mountain goats . . .'[108]

There is a small break, and now they are back at it, 'hot, weak and hungry, and feeling a little sorry for ourselves'.[109]

And how could they not be?

Even as they hack and haul to exhaustion, they are endlessly harangued by their Japanese overseers, who never stop with their constant imprecations: *'Speedo! Speedo! Hurree Uppoo! Hurree Uppoo! – Pickee! Changey! Changey! Basketo! Basketoo!'*[110]

At the end of the day, it is . . . night. Exhausted, they at last put down their tools.

'We started for home up the long two-mile hill, through a mass of boulders, and finally dropped, almost vertically, on to our camp.'[111]

17 March 1943, Hintok, flat out like a lizard stinking

Just as often happens in the way of these things, many of the guards and officers have by now been given nicknames to do with their physical features, mannerisms or general behaviour. The deeply hated

Lieutenant Usuki, for example – violent bastard that he is – has now become known as, variously, the 'Konyu Kid'[112] for his juvenile swagger and more specifically the 'Black Prince'[113] for the fact that his dark disposition is only matched by his darker skin tone.

'No man was more sadistic,'[114] one POW will say of him.

One down from Usuki in both rank and estimation is Seiichi Okada, who is a 'medical corporal' despite the fact he has had no medical training whatsoever.

'Short and squat, he took the roll calls and carried out all of the camp commandant's orders.'[115]

And yes, of course, he also, at least nominally, is responsible for the POWs' medical care. But there is a real problem.

'His only prescription was a wooden sword. If you went near him you got a hiding with the wooden sword.'[116]

Not for nothing do the men refer to him as 'Doctor Death'[117] for his insistence that sick men work themselves into their grave.

Meanwhile, 'Billy the Bastard', is a notably brutal guard, a small walnut-hard man with a lean, baboon face. His alternative title is 'Billy the Pig'. Never far away from him is 'Stepin Fetchit' – named for a comedy character actor – who seems to spend his days running around on perpetual errands for senior officers. Nearby is 'Boofhead'.

But already the short favourite to be regarded as the worst of the whole bloody lot?

That is 'the Lizard' a Korean whose unblinking stare makes him look like, well . . . like a lizard. No, he *does*.

Though he has only just arrived, the Lizard, or Kakurai Hiromura as the Japanese call him, is already well on his way to being the most hated man in camp, against some fairly strong competition. He is ruthless, cold, vicious and calculated; his face set in a perpetual sneer, his eyes unblinking and pitiless like his first cousin once removed, the snake.

And the Lizard is just the underling that the bastard Japanese engineer who is in charge of their section of rail, Lieutenant Eiji Hirota, needs to enforce the *orders* he has already passed on to Corporal Seiichi Okada – on pain of death that they be carried out.

Now hear this, Doctor Death announces on this morning.

Each Australian worker will have to work at least 10 hours a day and shift a staggering amount of rock and earth, per man.

Weary considers such a demand 'terrific'[118] for already weakened POWs, but not in a good way. The same applies to the Gangster, who chooses his words carefully and manages to tone down what he *truly* wants to say before at least getting out, 'Fuck off, Okada!'[119]

Mercifully, Doctor Death's grasp of English does not yet extend to understanding the concept of the said 'fucking off', and there are no immediate repercussions.

But Major Wearne still wants to take it further. Once he has been advised of the demands by Corporal Okada, it is Wearne who dares to approach Lieutenant Hirota directly, a man described by Ray Parkin as 'a little pug-faced, fit-looking fellow with a charming, show-the-teeth expression which does not conceal the fact that he is a vicious, spoilt child at heart'.[120]

Alas, though Wearne's case is compelling – this workload will so shatter the men that as a workforce they will be severely debilitated – the young engineering graduate with the perpetual sneer tells him that the ruling stands. And upon his return, Doctor Death goes out of his way to order the Lizard to brutally slap Wearne in the face, continually, for the temerity of visiting the engineer's camp without permission.

'Very stormy affair,'[121] Weary notes, with a brand-new cloud on the horizon: 'No. 2 of this camp "the Lizard", who does all the returns, is a proper little bastard.'[122]

Big Bastards give him competition though, and Lieutenant Colonel Ishi arrives today with Usuki to examine their miserable quarters, which perversely fill him with enthusiasm for more: 'There is talk of putting 2000 troops from Singapore into this little hole in addition to us!'[123]

Absurd. Major Wearne and his recently slapped face gamely raise objections 'on the grounds of inadequate water supply, sanitation etc'.[124]

Usuki considers his case and replies: 'Perhaps only 600 men.'[125]

Well, that is only deeply stupid; so a great improvement.

What horrifies Weary is how unhorrified their captors are by the chaos: 'It has been a fairly smooth move up to date according to Nip standards – nothing at all that some hundreds had a night out in drenching rain, and sick just do not enter into calculations.'[126]

As for the Lizard, he is now 'cheerfully transferring men from battalion to battalion and doing ghastly sums interminably with his

Abacus'.[127] Whatever these sums are they provide no solutions, only problems. The Lizard – left in charge of the whole operation when Hirota is not there, which is mostly – 'bitches all common sense camp arrangements'[128] and now carefully arranges their mornings so there will be no time for the cooks to make breakfast before all must work, 'little sod'.[129]

Their water supply at the Line today will be transported via elephant, which is very picturesque but Weary would rather it were boiled first – for his fear of cholera breaking out remains extreme – something that the Lizard and his abacus refuse to arrange.

When the demands of *speedo, speedo* are getting more insistent, so too are the guards more vicious in that insistence, but Major Corlette is more than capable of rising to meet them. For every morning now, when the Japanese arrive at the hospital with demands for how many patients they wish to be released, Corlette is there to meet them.

'I want forty men from the hospital this morning,' the Japanese officer will bark.

'No!' the Gangster barks back, his blue eyes flashing with rage. 'Ten!'

'Forty!'

'Ten!'

'Forty!'

'TEN.'

The Japanese officer strikes him in the head with his rifle butt.

The Gangster gets up.

'Ten.'

And so it goes.

'In the end,' POW John McNamara would recount, 'the Jap would get about fifteen. The Japanese could never understand the fearlessness of these men. In fact they had an awed respect for them, as they had seen some of the wonderful operations the doctors performed, even on wounded Japs.'[130]

•

Weary and his ranking Japanese commander on this particular day, once more, Private Ikimoto, are working together to select new *benjo* sites. Picking a toilet site would not be considered life or death back in Australia, but here it is, and Weary wants approval for a new site to the south-west where the men can dig deep.

Ikimoto approves Weary's selection and seems in a very happy mood today, which has the Australian's antennae up.

'Soon we will all be friends,'[131] says No. 1, launching into a long speech on this same theme. 'Australia, Nippon, very good *tomodachi*.'[132]

'Okay,' says Weary, bemused. 'You speak Tojo, I speak Churchill.'[133]

It is not simply a joke, because a rumour is flying around that Churchill is dead, a whisper Weary thinks the Japanese have started. No. 1 just nods, and Weary breathes a sigh of relief. It seems Winnie is likely still with us.

'Nippon never surrender,'[134] says Ikimoto.

No, of course not. You will fight them on the beaches . . .

19 March 1943, Hintok, humanity against crimes

The civility of yesterday is destroyed today by a lizard: 'Dreadful news in the evening. Lieutenant Eiji Hirota has been over tearing strips off the Lizard and tomorrow 600 men are required for the railway. All work on *benjos*, anti-malaria and "improve water" schemes must cease';[135] worst of all, 'light sick' and 'heavy sick' men must all work, as must even those men with no boots. To this point the light sick men and the bootless have been engaged in light duties around the camp, helping the cooks, the clerks, the wood and water fetchers of the 'duty section', but now the Japanese want them back on the tools, immediately.

'This,' Weary fulminates in his diary, 'is the next thing to murder.'[136]

What makes it more despicable is the knowledge that the Japanese have great reserves of their own men, here and in Singapore – but they won't use any of them. They would rather just send sick, weak prisoners to their all but certain death, just so long as the work is done.

'This can only be regarded as a cold-blooded, merciless crime against mankind, obviously premeditated.'[137]

The Dutch have lost six men in as many days, and Weary knows the Australians will soon catch that rate. Fuming, he tries to decide whom he will protest to on the morrow. It may make no difference, but it must be done.

Witnessing and suffering such brutality himself, Ray Parkin is another who comes to the same conclusion as Weary:

> I thought now this has got to be recorded. So I started diaries
> in earnest up there on the railway. And while we're in the
> jungle, I was able to keep them concealed fairly well because
> the jungle's a wide place and the bamboos are hollow.[138]

Look, if such diaries are found, you risk death. But if these deaths are not written down, they risk being forgotten. The first risk can be lived with.

20 March 1943, Hintok, all the livelong day

This morning Weary tackles the Lizard as the morning work party is about to head out: 'Twenty of these men are unfit to go out.'

'Okay, okay,' the Lizard says, quite meekly, which surprises and pleases Weary more than a little. Then, as he watches the other 577 men – of whom so many are also crook as dogs and fading fast – head out to the railway, he realises he has been played.

'I felt like a bit of a sucker not to stick out about all the other [sick] men.'[139]

With illness and work both the new normal, men who should be in bed for weeks are wielding hammers and hauling rock till they drop.

Something must be done to improve conditions, and in short order Weary is presiding at a meeting of battalion commanders to thrash out options, starting with providing them with boots: 'Footwear is also a matter for a fight: it is murderous working on rocks as hot as hell and covered with knife like edges with no boots to protect their feet.'[140]

(In truth, not all the boots have been lost to wear and tear. Because the Australian boots are distinctively brown, and the Japanese had recognised Australians as good workers, there had been many occasions when overseers had walked along disparate groups of POWs and picked out those with brown boots for work details. Thereafter, some Australians had preferred to fashion new footwear out of everything from cow hides to old tyres – though regrettably no Dunlop Tyres are to be found in these parts.)

The commanders meet with Lieutenant Hirota and make their case as practically as possible: 'It would be useless for Nippon to send out sick and bootless men to work as they would only crack up and soon be a bad economic proposition.'[141] Money is the best way to get Hirota to agree as 'the humanitarian point of view is quite useless'.[142]

Though he falls far short of agreeing, at least Hirota does not dismiss their point of view entirely and it is with some sense of progress that Weary heads out to see for himself the conditions his men are now enduring. He comes to a siding being cut out of a mountain, slowly and painfully:

> They drill with the crudest of hand drills like a short crowbar with slight annular rings on the side and a hammer. White rock dust flies in all directions so that the men are plastered with rocks and sweat like bakers or plasterers.[143]

Right beside him, as ever, Blue Butterworth is appalled as he realises just how gargantuan the task set for the Australians is.

'They'll *never* build this,' is his primary thought. 'They'll never do this.'[144]

The heat is stifling. It is 130 degrees Fahrenheit in the sun at midday, and these men will work all day. They already look like a bunch of battered brown berries being slowly grilled in an oven.

'If lucky the troops get ten minutes *yasume* an hour – often, however, only one rest in the morning and one in the afternoon.'[145] The work could scarcely be more difficult as 'the ground is very stony and the brick red soil has to be picked and shovelled out from between rocks'.[146]

Whenever one task is finished, another begins, with the hardly inspiring cry of '*Changey, Changey*'.

Disobedience or questioning is not allowed and Weary hears tell of one officer who 'recently was made to stand at attention with a basket of earth held over his head, Atlas-like'.[147]

Atlas meets Sisyphus, it seems, as the task is unchanging and unending, the irony being that these prisoners work to help the 'blasters' but, luckily for the Allied war effort: 'the blasting work is most inefficient as they lay charges stupidly'.[148] They are far too shallow and shoot impressive dirt into the sky, but not nearly as much rock as they could. Now, they are not going to advise the Japanese how to work faster, but they have to take up the shortfall of their explosive shortcomings.

Lieutenant Hirota has been watching Weary all day and now attempts a gesture: 'Would you like to go to the pictures at Kinsayok this evening?'[149]

Well, this is not how he thought the day would end but for 'reasons of propaganda',[150] Dunlop accepts.

Now, while the Lizard is angry at the best of times, on this occasion he is no less than incandescent with rage that Weary should both be invited and have accepted to go. It is against nature for one so low to be treated almost as if he is human.

But a lordly Weary overrules his objections and, waving his hand dismissively, says that *neither* of them, don't you know, can go against the wishes of *Ichi ban*. Lieutenant Hirota is 'No. 1'[151] and of course Weary must accept, and why, here is his transport now, a lorry, upon which he climbs with Japanese heading off on their big night out.

After a long and bumpy ride they pull up, just as it is getting dark, directly in front of a giant outdoor screen, and, well, here is something to, if not write home about, at least record in his diary.

'I found myself in front of some hundreds of N.s sitting on mats or earth. I also enjoyed this luxury, feeling all sorts of crawling pests on the skin (presumably lice).'[152]

As for the films being shown, they are not going to rival *Gone with the Wind*: 'the first a sort of news review, showing Nippon tearing Asia into strips'[153] with the help of every weapon known to man past or present, including a cavalry charge! The main feature is a propaganda film about a Japanese naval officer, 'a Superman who takes part in the [battle] of Pearl Harbor and the sinking of HMS *Prince of Wales* and *Repulse*'.[154]

The US are made to look inept and stupid, and Weary is fascinated to see that, when it comes to the attack on the British ships, the film is poorly shot, grainy and apparently the real thing. The troops cheer and hoot and Weary is very aware he is alone and being watched.

'I was the only European present and placed right in front with thousands of Japanese behind.'[155]

When Pearl Harbor itself is attacked the crowd becomes boisterously exultant.

'*Banzai!*' '*Banzai!*' '*Banzai!*'[156]

Weary jumps to his feet and yells '*Banzai!*' back at the crowd. The puzzled soldiers near him ask, 'You think good? Nippon bomb-bomb, sink American and British ships.'[157]

'Yes,' Weary roars. 'Old ships no good – *takusan* new ships now build – better!'[158]

Bigger, better ships to sink the whole bloody Imperial Japanese Navy!

So ends movie night . . .

CHAPTER TWELVE

ROCK AND A HARD PLACE

What made the difference, [was] that each man was prepared to look after himself, so that he wouldn't become a responsibility on others. He didn't expect others [to look after him], didn't throw up his hands and say, oh, you know, 'Help me'. He did the best he could all the time. And when you saw a bloke doing the best he could, but not doing very well, you gave him a hand, but he didn't expect it.[1]

Ray Parkin

21 March 1943, Hintok, order of the boot

Christ on a bike.

Three thousand more POWs are coming from Singapore to join their camp and workforce. Weary has it from the horse's mouth – or rather Doctor Death Okada's mouth – this morning. Well, Weary says, they will need ether and plaster of Paris to treat the inevitable wounded. Okada is in a charitable mood and will do what he can, even going so far as asking Weary how his medical personnel are faring with their rounds? It is all very civilised, at least temporarily, and Okada extends an invitation to lunch, which Weary accepts, and now 'both of us sitting cross-legged in the N hut with a small table between'.[2]

This is exactly how they are situated when a few English Majors stroll by, and their jaws literally drop. Weary laughs and gives them a wave, which only drops the jaws another notch.

Alas, pleasantries will be followed by unpleasantness, for now an argument with *Ichi ban*, No. 1, is to be had. Weary gets straight to the point, his speech squashed and direct to make his meaning as clear as can be.

'Yesterday's position was horrid. All men – including light sick, working; no boots, no vegetable or meat for five days, no tools for work, no men for canteen or carrying, just rice to eat.'[3]

This summation is greeted with a smile from Doctor Death and he replies in the patronising tone of one who knows an underling will be wasting his time, but may as well learn for himself: 'Okay, you speak to the No. 1 engineer.'[4]

'No good,' answers Weary. 'He is an even harder wretch than you and it would be useless.'[5]

More men will be coming tomorrow, 150 with no boots.

22 March 1943, Hintok, shot in the light

Again, all 'light sick' men are conscripted by Japanese officers to work today. Weary puts his foot down; they are ill and they are staying within camp. If they must work, it will be on sanitation or anti-malaria measures, that is all. A huge row breaks out and Weary and his sick men are marched over to No. 1 to say it again, pausing only to mentally note No. 1's visage, 'his nasty face now set like a ham and lower lip stuck out (the spoilt child touch)'.

What is the objection? They do not understand so Weary states it loud and plain.

'I object strongly to sending sick men to work.'[6]

Simple enough? Oh yes, on the orders of Doctor Death, rifles are now trained on Doctor Dunlop as they wait for him to change his diagnosis. Doctor Death is certain that Doctor Dunlop might like to reconsider?

The men watch fascinated as this uneven duel in the sun plays out. No dice.

'You can shoot me,' says Weary, 'but then my second in command is as tough a man as me, and after him you will have to shoot them all. Then you will have no workmen.'

Weary cannot resist following up, to note that if Doctor Death won't hang his head in shame, he has something else in mind, something he is working on.

'In any case, I have taken steps to one day have *you* hanged, for you are a black-hearted bastard.'[7]

Of course, the said bastard bites back in black-hearted fashion, barking: 'You can stay here as long as you like! You will get no food or water and the sick will do the work.'[8]

Who else but the Lizard is summoned to perform this task, and angrily round up and force out the 46 sick men, as Weary glares at him.

Sergeant Oliver? Would you care to act as interpreter? Weary would like to also be extremely clear while he insults the Lizard.

'After making us administrative officers you do not accept our decisions on the men's health, and therefore you can go to hell and run the camp yourself.'[9]

Did you get all that? Because there is more.

'You're a lot of murderers and . . .' Weary points at a cross stuck in the ground . . . 'that is the fate for all of us! If the sick men are driven to work everyone down shovels!'[10]

The Lizard does not react well as the strike concept is explained to him. In fact, he is thrown into a 'severe rage and he raved at the men as if working himself into a passion to hit me (but I bet he never could if I was looking at him)'.[11]

The Lizard runs out of puff, finishing with a final yell.

'Send the troops off to work in camp.'[12]

That is all Weary wanted – the sick men can work in the camp, but not have to go to the hellish hot horror of the Hintok Cutting. So, after all this *sturm und drang*, they end where they began. Weary himself heads out to the railway to see the usual horrors, including men being injured by spitting drill bits that break off in this impossible rock, but finds himself uplifted.

'The Australian resilience is startling; the men are extremely cheerful and emphatic the Ns will never get them down and they will be square one day.'[13]

But not today.

Today is a day for Weary to aggressively tell the Japanese overseers that some of these men are 'too sick to work', yes indeed, '*Takusan byoki,* very sick!'

For the most part Weary really can get away with taking such a tone as this, as even men this vicious recognise the unspoken truth: without *ichi ban* doctor Dunroppo, they will lose an untold number of workers. They can severely bash and even kill the common POWs with impunity, but might have a case to answer with this one.

Nevertheless, on this occasion, the way Weary has spoken to the glowering Japanese draws such a furious response from one of them that the mortally offended officer shouts for a log. And make it a big one!

'He stood on the log and began whacking Weary across the face with his fist,' one of the POWs will recount. 'It was the only way he could have reached him. Of course, Weary had been a boxer and was rolling with the punches.'[14]

Back in the day, at Melbourne University, Weary had famously held his own, sparring with 'Young Stribling', who only a few years before had been a contender for the Heavyweight Championship of the World. Compared to Strib's hammer blows, the Japanese man is hitting him with a series of ill-aimed powder puffs.

(On another occasion, a Japanese guard displays a little lateral thinking, by having Weary first dig a hole that the Australian can stand in, to bring him down the 10 pegs necessary for the diminutive guard to swing some wildly erratic punches at him.)

To be fair, along the Line, not all Japanese guards are like that.

On another occasion Weary had so infuriated a Japanese sergeant by not showing sufficient respect to him, and arguing too vigorously that his men were too sick to work, that this servant of the Emperor simply charges straight at him with his bayonet thrust forward, only for . . .

Only for, as Weary will describe him, 'a one star private, the lowest grade in the army',[15] to step forward and quietly stand between the thrust bayonet and Dunlop.

(*Call it all even on the card.*)

Not only is the private a decent man, but Weary is his specific charge, and not in the sergeant's group. To Weary's stunned amazement, and relief, the private's courage – and the strict Japanese protocol of not crossing the lines of responsibility – has saved him.

There really are some good Japanese.

Ray Parkin comes to know one of them who not only speaks a little English but also actually sings it:

> He was a pleasant little bloke whose heart was not made for hate. He led us back to camp at the end of the day in single file, singing us most of Bing Crosby's songs. He said he liked Bing's singing very much. He and I finished up singing a duet of 'When Irish Eyes are Smiling' and 'Home Sweet Home'.[16]

It is a welcome relief to have a guard like that. And yet, at another time, when a POW points out a notably kindly guard to one of his mates, saying, 'I think that bloke's not so bad,' the reply is firm.

'I think he's about the pick of them,' his mate drawls, as flat as the Nullarbor. 'But I could still split him from head to arsehole with a blunt razor blade.'[17]

•

Sometimes, when the conditions are just right as you wake in the dawn, you can smell with the familiar jungle perfumes of 'cinnamon, chocolate . . . clematis'[18] that distinct odour made by dew on dry bamboo which takes you back home, to that 'faraway land over the rainbow', as it is a *dead ringer* for the glorious way you remember the Australian bush smells, back in the days when you ne'er had the brains to appreciate it.

And always, as ever, your reverie is shattered by reveille, at least the God-awful Japanese version of it.

By now Dunlop Force has moved into a regular rhythm: dawn, reveille, Japanese roll call, breakfast of rice pap, trek, *work*, work, work, *yasume,* work, work, work, trek, eat, sleep, dawn. Add lots of water from endless rain, rinse and repeat, all of it interspersed with regular beatings.

> The threat of a rifle butt across your head loomed large. For no reason at all, wire whips would lash into our backs and draw blood. Some guards would creep up on you and strike the open tropical ulcers on your legs with a bamboo stick, causing intense agony.[19]

Look, just getting to and from the worksite is not just persistently painful in its physical challenges, but deadly dangerous. When it is raining, making it slippery beyond belief, they must concentrate fiercely just to avoid slipping into the abyss.

As to how they are getting through the heavy work of blasting the actual rock, now that all the preliminary clearing of jungle and soil is done, the process is particular.

The engineers first demonstrate what will become known as the 'hammer and tap' technique.

The idea is to use sledgehammers to pound in a steel drill to make a hole in the rock surface large enough to stick gelignite in, before everyone stands back and – twice a day – it is detonated. And yes, this does mean that at least in the initial stages one poor bastard has to hold the drill still while the man with the hammer pounds it, but there is no choice.

Few are in any doubt who has the worst of it, so exhausting is it swinging the hammer. After every blow, the one holding the drill then lifts it out a quarter-inch to give it a quarter-turn, before it is pounded again. Every few minutes water is sluiced into the hole to flush out the limestone rock that has been turned to powder, a process that is helped by lowering a strong piece of fencing wire with a scoop attached to get the mud out. There is a quick pause to slap the many vicious bugs and insects crawling all over you for your perspiration – leaving a sting as their calling card – and then you do it all again. And again and again.

It is a long and laborious process, with the men on the hammer and drill regularly changing positions because of exhaustion, but finally when the drill is all the way in, the Japanese engineers pack it with dynamite with long fuses attached, and give the men cigarettes. But this ain't your normal 'smoko'. After a few drags, the idea is to light the fuse and then run like the clappers, all the way to billy-o, to get away before she blows.

RUN, I say!

The concussion of the explosion will knock anyone within coo-ee over like sick bandicoots, but mostly they make it, and once the dust has settled, it is for the rest of the swarming workers to come in with baskets and fill them with the debris. Rocks that are still too big must be broken down with sledgehammers, into razor-sharp pieces of granite that can slice flesh like a butcher's knife.

Once the baskets are filled, they are either carried away individually, or poured into *tankas,* 'rice sacks slung between bamboo poles',[20] with a POW on each end. As the *tankas* are lifted, the shoulders of the two POWs sag just as their knees wobble, but now they must stagger some 200 yards before they can empty it at the designated spot, with the aim of making a stable embankment upon which further tracks can be laid. (A wheelbarrow could easily carry what is in the *tanka,* and be manoeuvred by just a man with ease, but they don't have any.)

'It is a long curving affair,' Parkin notes of the embankment, 'secured by a high knoll at one end and reaching out towards a bridge at the other . . . Basket by basket, *tanka* by *tanka* . . . we carry the earth which has to be scratched from between the rocks in the jungle, tramping it out to the slowly forming bank.'[21]

Each full *tanka* emptied is tabulated by a guard, and every POW on this duty must shift at least a cubic metre of rubble a day.

Ancillary work, which Parkin is also involved in, is cutting a road through the jungle, down from a high hill:

> Trying to cut sprung and springy bamboo, and hauling it from a tangled chaos of canes, vines and locking thorn, is exhausting work, and even the Japanese had to give us rest periods. It is during these periods I try to write, while looking at what I am writing about. All the smallest creatures of the bush seem to have been upset, and have become unfriendly. At the moment, sweat-covered, I am a mass of walking crawling, nipping bush bees. They cover my hands as I write.[22]

And of course, there is the job of building the bridges, something that naturally enough falls to the carpenters and timber-workers among them, together with several coves that Weary estimates would be worked to death anywhere else.

'Some of the quite old men went back to the First World War,' Weary will recount, 'so I went to great pains to try to place them in areas in which they were useful . . . and where they have a chance at getting older. Ironically, it is the young, strong men, who are most at risk.'

A case in point for Tom Uren is a 'magnificent-looking fellow'[23] by the name of 'Tiny' O'Neil.[24]

As strong as a bull, no, *two* bulls – and doesn't he know it – Tiny is the biggest bastard in the force with bulging muscles that gleam, and an air about him that you couldn't kill him with an axe. And no-one is quicker than him on the hammer and tap, with him always being three-quarters of any duo.

For with Tiny, it is a point of pride to demonstrate his strength – pounding the drill with endless massive blows – to get through his work and even knock off early. Oh, how Tiny would puff up when approving Japanese guards would walk around and say, 'Sign here. *Ichi ban!* Number one!'[25]

It feels foolhardy to Tom Uren, and not quite the thing anyway.

What are you – a 'white Nip'?[26] (This is the worst designation imaginable for the Australians, and applied to those who it is deemed are *so* co-operative with their captors, it feels like they are on *their* side.)

Uren himself takes the counsel of another bloke, an old cane-cutter by the name of Harry Baker who comes incomplete with two missing fingers.

'He showed me how to use the eight-pound Plumb hammer. And you'd raise it and let the *hammer* do the work.'[27]

Do you get it, young Tom? All you need do once you've lifted it, is guide it down. Don't use up all your strength pounding it down, because there is no need.

'Tom, don't bust yourself,' old Harry keeps telling him, as the glaring Japanese guards hover close. 'Take your time, play it easy. We'll get the darg.'[28]

The darg, Harry?

The darg, Tom. It's an old mining term, for the target, the 'contract' set the miners at the beginning of every day for how much earth and rock must be moved before knock-off time. Their own darg in this case is 80 centimetres, and they are charged with moving mountains – or at least cutting into them – by precisely that much.

'Don't bust your guts, Tom,' he repeats. 'Take your time.'[29]

Tom doesn't bust his guts. He takes his time.

Tiny keeps belting the hammer. You keep going, *Ichi ban*, Tom will sit this one out.

What he *won't* sit out, however, now or ever, is carrying his fair share of everything, and more.

'Tom's creed,' it will be said of him, 'became that the strongest man takes the heaviest end of the log. Tom was the strongest man.'[30]

And of course he carries the tools, back and forth. On a day shortly after they have begun on the cutting, they are heading back to Hintok camp – all of them inevitably covered from top to toe in itchy limestone dust – and Uren can't help but notice that because the Japanese are so pleased with how hard Tiny has been working, they have given him bugger-all to carry, while Tom himself is loaded down.

The former boxer and rugby league player won't have it.

'You big bastard,' he says, 'carry your share, your lot, and carry some of this heavy load!'[31]

Tiny reluctantly does, but as soon as a Japanese sergeant realises what has happened, he moves quickly. Taking a heavy bit of bamboo while standing on a bank above Uren, he swings hard and connects with his head.

Uren goes down.

And yes, of course, once he is up, he could reach out and break his oppressor like a twig – likely about two seconds before the other guards would shoot him dead. He must control himself – and also control his mates who have cried out, and are clearly caught up in outrage.

'It's alright, fellows,' he calls to the others to settle them down. 'I rode my punch.'[32]

I am not hurt, so stay calm. This angry little gnat shouldn't bother me *too* much.

(After all, these men of Nippon don't seem to quite understand the Western fashion of punches, straight out with your weight behind it, and are more inclined to round-house flailing.)

Still, the second time, the guard hits harder and Uren goes down once more, this time, 'like a pack of cards'.[33]

But he gets up, this time to be greeted by another Japanese sergeant coming forward and furiously slapping him in the face.

That is much more like it.

'It was just like a powder puff hitting me.'[34]

Soon enough it is the Japanese sergeant who is worn out, and Uren is simply given *two* eight-pound Plumb hammers to carry, and they walk on.

Just another day on the Line . . .

•

Quickly now, quietly now.

This way, Private Old.

No matter that Ashley Old is a Pom, he has a skill that Major Arthur Moon particularly admires, and wishes to harness. Old is an artist and can draw the wounds, sores and ulcers of Moon's patients with such startling exactitude you can almost smell the weeping pus. Moon has told Old that he wishes to admit him to the hospital as a nominally ill patient so that when the guards aren't looking, he can document the different kinds of body trauma that Moon's patients are suffering from. Perhaps, one day, scientists might use them in their researches on 'the tropical diseases aggravating the wounds'.[35]

And so it is now. Using precious purloined paper, including the waxy Japanese toilet paper, Old takes a seat by the bed of one groaning patient, and while Major Moon holds the lantern close, the Englishman quickly sketches out the suppurating sores that cover the patient's leg, the way the disease spreads and shreds, each grim contour of no relief given relief and shading. Now, using the child's paintbox they have got from a Japanese guard in return for doing hand-painted postcards that he can send home to his children, Old adds the colour, the angry bright reds on the rim of the worst sores, the bulbous yellow pus at their centre, the greenish pallor of the skin all around. (As a matter of fact, he will so often have to draw that yellow pus that predominates that later he will have to use 'wild jungle saffron as a substitute for yellow paint'.[36]) And now on to the next bed, where another patient – only semi-conscious – is held up by orderlies, so Old can capture the strange sores on his abdomen, while also recording the banana leaves that have been placed as makeshift pads over the wounds where the pus has been already drained, to keep the flies off.

And another patient, and another.

And done.

Quickly, quietly, away. Old returns to his hut and places the drawings, the paper and the precious paintbox in the spot beneath the floorboards that he has made to hide them.

Another who Weary taps to do similar work is the young Englishman who the Gangster had nursed back from a terrible bashing, Jack Chalker.

'He was,' Weary will note of Chalker, 'one of these pale slender sensitive sort of fellows who simply wouldn't survive on the hammer and tap sort of stuff.'[37]

Weary not only has him doing drawings and paintings like those of Ashley Old, but also has him try to capture the lives, deaths and experiences of the men in captivity with brilliance and pathos in equal measure. Each sketch is admired quickly and then hidden – often rolled up and pushed into the hollow of various bamboo poles then hidden in the jungle – for he is their equivalent of a camera, documenting what is happening to their bodies, displaying for history how they are forced to live. Alas, even as Chalker's drawings capture the growing deterioration of the bodies of Dunlop Force, his own body all but gives out through malnutrition and it is at Weary's personal insistence to the Japanese overlords that Chalker is evacuated back to Tarsau staging camp.

There for the first time in many moons he will be able to eat something that is more than mere sludge of rice, with a side-serve of lumps of rice.

23–24 March 1943, Hintok, train in vain

How long do the men have left to complete their task? The Japanese insist that Konyu will be reached in eight days.

No, not weeks, *days*. All 'well' men will work; and in this case 'well' means all those who *can* rise from their sickbed even if the instrument of choice to get them to do so is less a thermometer than the prick from a bayonet. And 'work' means heavy, hard and straining labour. Weary now learns that in 'one English camp recently, men worked 62 hours out of 72'.[38]

Today at Kinsayok, the English had 34 men die. For a railway. The Dutch lost 31 there. It cannot get worse; except when it does, every day.

'The hospital patients are repeatedly paraded and kicked out to work, there are no canteen arrangements, the food is bloody and Lt. Tanaka is an awful bit of work.'

Well, to be fair, Tanaka could be as pleasant as Mary Poppins and they'd still be in a hell of a mess. The Dutch have been reduced to digging 'toilets' in their temporary accommodations. Toilets is just being polite, they are: 'holes in the floor for defecation. The last ounce is being got out of the men without any consideration for their health or future.'

Speaking of last ounces, Weary's last scribbled entry in his diary reveals his anger and shock at the latest Japanese diktat: *'The blow now falls. Duty section reduced from 144 to 80.'*

His skeleton staff are already starting to resemble actual skeletons complete with deaths-head grimaces.

The officers hold a council of war and decide what duties must survive. The answer: 'arrangements [are] made to keep cookhouse, anti-malaria, wood and water squads'.[39]

They are on their own; and survival is their war now.

And beyond doing what we can to improve the diet, let us focus on hygiene above all else. Weary is particularly fierce on the importance of having systemically clean ablutions for such a mass of men, and spends the better part of the next morning, using the tiny amounts of kerosene allocated by the Japanese, to set fire to the previous *benjos*, which had become a mass of maggots. The afternoon is consequently spent personally digging new ones 'with the Lizard having exquisite revenge by watching me'.[40]

Too bad.

Weary has a little revenge of his own a few days later when talking to a visiting Japanese officer who, for once, speaks such good English he is aware of some of the nuances.

'English very hard language to learn. For instance, what is difference between "perhaps" and "maybe"?'

'A *very* difficult language,' Weary agrees heartily, before explaining the nuanced difference between the two words with an example.

'*Perhaps* Japan will win the war,' he says. 'But *maybe* not . . .'[41]

Definitely maybe.

25 March 1943, Hintok, frying pan to fire

Sweating, feverish men fill these lorries arriving at a camp near Hintok today. What is strange is that the only men who are not sick are the ones who sweat the most. For they are being taken to die. Yes, 10 lorries come, full of the sick, heading to Tarsau. One lorry carries four men to their execution. They are British prisoners who have had the nerve to try what they have all dreamt of: escape.

'They had run away with a lorry until the petrol gave out. Then the Thais who were guiding them gave them away after the payment of money.'[42]

Tom Uren, for one, feels more than a little green around the gills for what he and his mates might have faced had they tried to go through with their own planned escape.

Weary, meanwhile, gets word that the Japanese will be offering rewards and presents to 'encourage good work'.[43]

Carrot and stick does not begin to describe it.

26 March 1943, Hintok, get a little dirt . . .

There are some slights to the honour of their prisoners that even the Japanese won't tolerate. Weary Dunlop, No. 1 of Prisoners, has been seen working on digging the new *benjo*! The chief officer stooping so low? Well, yes.

'Number one not work *benjo*,' says a guard. 'No good.'[44]

Well, what is the alternative? *Somebody* has to do this crap, to properly dispose of the mass crap – or they will be hit by cholera.

'Therefore today I was given some six men for *benjo* work but no tools!'[45]

Weary asks for the obvious and is amused to be told: 'Use hands.'[46]

So much for dignity. The six start clawing the dirt, while all other men, including Weary, head out to the railway. That is also no good, but the Japanese disagree.

28 March 1943, Hintok, altogether now

No. 1 Dunlop is completely naked today, working on the water-works for the camp with Major Allan Woods. There is a reason for the lack of clothing, 'as one becomes covered in mud hacking roots and shovelling on the creek bed'.[47] Their tools don't help; Japanese axes seem to be designed to have their head slip as soon as a blow is struck soundly, and their shovels have handles that fold like tin when pressured.

Like everything else, the only thing made to last in these parts is disease and death.

31 March 1943, Hintok, breaking pointers

The Japanese sergeant major calls for Weary this morning. He is '"very, very sorry" all men must at present work terribly hard; later we would have rest'.[48]

Really? How long until rest?

Very soon. Until then: 'We must be very careful to look after the men so they don't get sick?'[49]

Yes, of course. Weary will tell the Australian medicos to pull their socks up. The sergeant major wanders off happily, immune to sarcasm.

Tonight, the extraordinary Ron Lum, an Australian who posed as a Chinese cook, tells Weary about his prison stay in Konyu. It is enough to make anyone sick: 'I got five weeks solitary, just in my clothes with no bed or bedding, and a stone floor. I was tied up in chains at night, my hands behind my back. I got one meal at night.'[50]

There was an 'Inquisition' every night, and the questioning was followed by a beating regardless of answers. Soon they didn't even bother with questions and just went straight to the beatings to save time.

For the record, Weary notes the grim details: 'Specific torture methods: room with peculiar waddies and sticks for beating, knotted ropes and on one occasion he was tied with hands up, feet just on floor for half a day. Other trick is to pin one down on floor, head back over a block, and water is poured from a kettle down the nose (idea is to first make the victim drink about 6–7 glasses of water and the feeling of drowning is terrible). God knows how he held out for so long.'[51]

•

At least there are witnesses to the Japanese brutality.

One of them is Boon Pong, who continues to ply the Kwai Noi, sending and bringing supplies to the railway workforce, with Weary regularly sending men down to the river to pick them up, and sometimes accompanying them – just as Boon Pong often accompanies the supplies to Weary's camp.

This access allows the Thai to see for himself, close-up, just how viciously the POWs are treated. And if he had been eager to help before in return for money, he soon makes it clear to Weary that he wishes to do more and is soon passing everything from money, medicine and messages between camps, as well as bribing pharmacists for supplies, holding watches and jewels in safekeeping for prisoners, and passing on rumours and whispers of war, hard news and intelligence gained from careless Japanese and Korean guards. If caught by the Japanese it would have meant his life, but he does not hesitate.

In this cause, he is helped by his wife, Boopa, who has learnt to speak enough Japanese to distract the guards for long enough for her husband to smuggle supplies past them, even while she is able to garner crucial information from them using charm, guile and the irresistible lure of a woman paying attention to whatever you say. In similar fashion, Boon Pong also often brings their pretty 12-year-old daughter, Panee, who charms the guards by singing Japanese songs. Her father has told her they must help because of 'humanity',[52] and that is enough for her. She keeps singing, and charming, even while her father hands over carefully curated supplies – including hollowed-out watermelons and cabbages containing medicines – to either Weary himself, or a *very* select group of officers. For Boon Pong's protection, the medico would like to be able to count the number of those who know on the fingers of one finger, or four at most.

Sometimes, Weary does not have quite enough money to pay the bills for the drugs. With a dismissive wave of his hand, Boon Pong tells him not to worry. They can be paid for out of his own purse. It is extraordinary generosity and courage from a man who, before this war started, knew of Australians as no more than rumours and not good ones at that. Now, he is risking his life for them – if he is caught, he will not be allowed to die until after he is tortured; perhaps beginning with knitting needles forced into both ears to puncture his ear-drums, a Japanese specialty for causing excruciating pain.

In short order, so appalled is Boon Pong by what he sees, that he is doing much more than merely smuggling in food, medicines and money. Journeying to Bangkok itself, he is able to make contact with an active underground resistance group, organised by a mob of mostly British nationals, based in an internment camp there. The camp is situated at Vajiravudh College and is known as 'V'. His go-between is Millie Gairdner, the Thai wife of a captive British architect, who tells the V underground what is needed. They alert the surviving Thai businesses – who have no truck with the Japanese occupiers – of just what kind of supplies and funds are required. Soon Boon Pong's barges wend their way along the River Kwai, distinctly deeper in the water for the secret supplies they bear. Weary particularly requests more supplies of the '*katjang idjoe* bean'[53] – green mung beans in the old money – together with key drugs like chloroquine, emetine and iodoform.

And we mustn't forget what is referred to as 'canary seeds'[54] otherwise known as . . . batteries, many of them actually encased in – what else but? – bamboo. They are to power the ham radio, with a whole system set up by one of the sergeants, who had been a highly regarded AWA technician before going into signalling in the army. The heart of the radio has been put together using a soldering iron made from two melted pennies, some fencing wire, and the tin from a melted sardine can. Part of the solder itself has come from hydrochloric acid harvested from 'the human stomach'[55] – via thin tubes fed through the nose down the throat of soldiers with peptic ulcers and siphoned off – and the whole lot is contained in a coffee tin, with the aerial provided by a very fine wire that goes out the back of Weary's hut and up a tree. The canary seeds are themselves stored in a biscuit tin.

The risk Weary is taking by having a ham radio, let alone listening to it?

Well, against that, on a couple of previous occasions, both the Black Prince and Doctor Death, Usuki and Okada, had managed to carefully hint at upcoming Kempis searches, just before they had taken place. This had been less out of any personal generosity towards Weary than recognising that it would reflect badly on them if such a radio was found.

•

Great eagles have flown over this bit of jungle for millennia and seen nothing but a billowing balloon of green, until now, as an ugly slash of shining silver goes clear across it.

And now look closer, with your eagle eyes. Are they ants?

No, it is 500 men at Hintok Cutting, dressed in rags, with no hats, and boots that have more holes than leather.

With legs, torsos and arms covered in abrasions, they are working midst the dust, detritus and devastation as the sun beats down, meaning – as Ray Parkin notes in his secret diary – 'The reflected heat and glare, almost cooking and blinding us.'[56]

As blast after blast rings out, the men move forward and begin to pick up the rubble as Japanese engineers regularly bark orders and Korean guards hover closely, often stepping in to swish their bamboo canes on the backs of anyone they consider is not working hard enough – or even just displeases them for whatever reason – and occasionally swinging rifle butts to drop them cold midst the blistering heat. Often, one of the workers of Dunlop Force will collapse of his own accord, to be dragged away by his mates to whatever shade is nearest, even while the guards yell at them and again swish their canes. Yes, the guards are happy for the collapsed soldiers to be dragged out of the way of the work, on the same principle they want other completely useless detritus removed. They just don't want to lose other workers because of it. So let them *crawl* away!

Just another day on this infernal railway. And yet it is a strange thing, how the intensity of their experience can change men, and even alter their entire perspective on life itself.

On this day Ray Parkin and three of his mates are battling hollow-eyed exhaustion, scrabbling to keep their grip on a hill with a 60-degree slope into which the cutting is being made, when the need comes to get more cement to build the base for one of the many bridges. Parkin and his mates are sent to the very bottom of the hill, four miles away, to get a barrel of it, as heavy as it is. How to carry it?

'Of course we were bare footed and in g-strings and . . . the only way to carry it was to put two wire slings on it and put two poles through and carry it on our shoulders.'

All of which is hard enough, but when they are halfway back up the mountain, slipping and sliding, falling and floundering, a storm comes that, even by usual Thailand standards, is extraordinary. The wind shrieks, the thunder rolls, the lightning flashes and the rain is so heavily pounding on the jungle canopy that it is like being on the inside of a kettle drum while a fat man pounds a solo on it.

For the four Australians, it is nothing less than complete *bedlam*. This is not just a storm, it is Armageddon and whole trees come crashing down around them. Their only hope is to take shelter beneath the strongest trees they can find, backing into them, and hoping the heavy branches will shield them from the trunks falling all around, as the deluge continues.

And . . . now.

'I happened to look up,' Parkin will recount, 'and there was a bit of a branch above me with a number of leaves on it, big flat leaves and I looked up and underneath one of them was a mosquito, a single mosquito. Probably one of the frailest things in the jungle and here it was riding it out as if nothing was happening outside its orbit.'

Parkin looks closer and is profoundly struck:

> I just looked and the contrast of all the commotion that was going on outside and this frail insect up there that had found a niche and would weather the storm and a thought struck me then, I thought, well, I knew it was a rat race outside and I thought well when I get out there, I am going to find myself a leaf, just like this mosquito and weather it out.

Parkin's whole approach to life has changed.

> It was the beginning of my philosophy, I suppose . . . The thing
> that struck me most was this contrast between civilisation and
> nature and that's when I became a little bit, you know, cynical
> about civilisation and all its wonders.[57]

Right now, it propels him to draw even more. With despair, death
and devastation all around, he takes what chances he can to make
himself as small as possible in his own space and uses what little
time he can get to capture the scenes he sees with his flying pencil.

(Oh. And that barrel of cement they had been labouring to get
to the top of the hill in all the wind and pounding rain? As Parkin
will delight in recounting ever afterwards, turns out the barrel had
some bad leaks, letting the water in, and by the time the Japanese
engineers opened it, it was a block of solid concrete!)

4 April 1943, Hintok, beauty captured in the jungle

It is like Ogden Nash's couplet of what happens when you turn a
bottle of tomato sauce upside down.

> *First a little,*
> *Then a lottle . . .*

While they arrived at Hintok still relatively healthy – at least by
POW standards – it is staggering to Weary just how a handful of
sick cases had become having his hands *full* just a week later, and
he is now simply *overwhelmed*.

The foundation illness is malnutrition, which is now overlaid with
over-work; vitamin deficiencies leading to beri-beri, scurvy, pellagra,
even blindness; add to that dysentery and malaria, which leave the
men weak, with no appetite, and render them shivering, shuddering
wrecks. The body shapes of every man-jack of them are changing,
with Ray Parkin noting the legs of one emaciated POW walking by
were 'not unlike those of a fowl, with the long bony feet right-angled
and splashed past the ankles with the mud and excrement in which
they walk. This is a man.'[58]

Well, at least it is in some manner:

> This grimace of Nature in humanity walks naked in the rain.
> And solitary, or with other similar wretches, crouches like a dog
> without a kennel, helpless on the latrines. Dysentery reduces
> them in body and spirit. In the rain they crawl there and back to

> their soiled blankets, to lie weak and helpless without removing
> the mud of their beastly pilgrimage.[59]

Life on the Line is a nightmare loop of trying to hang on to that life despite endless illness, forced work on fractions of rations, with bashings – where you are at great risk of injuries from falls, falling rocks and flying drill-bit fragments. For Weary, it is trying to keep as many men as possible alive, despite all of the above regularly knocking them over.

And yet today, Weary has a chance to walk in the jungle, alone, to restore his sanity. His pen comes alive to paint a portrait of the beauty that surrounds their daily horrors. Look around and you will see that 'the jungle is assuming a new coat of multitudinous shades of tender green',[60] look up and see 'the atmosphere appears to have been washed so ineffably clean and pure by the rains that the sky is a serene, fathomless blue'.

In the wonder that is before him now, Weary makes sure to see the poetry of the rising and falling of the day:

> The morning and evening sometimes positively hurt with their beauty, especially the lovely quarter hour before dawn when the whole sky is aglow with brilliant crimson bands showing through the clearly etched foliage in a brilliant atmosphere and the softest of pale blue. Vividness and colours everywhere, butterflies of every size and shade, predominantly white and yellow, fly in their schools in long chains who come to rest in little pools of mixed colours, the faint sway of their wings recalling a massive yacht swayed by a slight breeze on a still lake.[61]

Dr Dunlop? This man's sores have been infected by his diarrhoea. *Sigh.* Dusk and dawn, they are times to soar; your head is pulled down from the clouds quickly at any other time of day.

Overall though, even the otherwise healthy men are wilting, withering before Weary's very eyes upon their return every late afternoon and into the evening. Simply put, their bodies are doing work that their minimal diets can't sustain, meaning the fat and then flesh is being stripped from their bones, and being complicated by a malnutrition disease, beri-beri, which manifests itself by weakness and a swelling of the limbs.

To ease the passage to and from the worksite for so many men with so many ailments, a huge tree trunk has footholds carved into it so it can serve as a ladder to reach the lip of the escarpment, over which they must climb in order to descend 80 feet and make their way down the singularly precipitous track that leads to the work area.

The only good part of the day comes when, finally, the work is over and, on their way back to camp, they could stand briefly under the miniature waterfall formed by the creek going over the ledge, and have a shower.

5 April 1943, Hintok, hidden figures

The Lizard is on the attack again today, furious at the men who have dared to get sick during the past day. The hospital is now due for a reptile visit.

'I will inspect today with a view to reducing numbers.'[62]

It is a view with no room for disagreement, but Weary will provide it anyway. 'All men are ordered to stay in bed,'[63] says Weary to those in hospital, an order easily obeyed as that's where they are right now. Meantime, he's off to see the Lizard, who is awaiting a parade.

'It is not possible to parade sick men,'[64] Weary tells him.

Really?

Really.

The Lizard coldly walks to the hospital, quite a feat in this heat, and inspects the men in situ. Weary is impressed with his men's ability to follow his command to the letter as the Lizard glares at each one in turn: 'all in bed lying very still except for a few using the *benjo*'.[65]

The Lizard now launches into an argument with Weary about how his figures of sick men have grown so rapidly, Weary wearily pointing out that this is because of the Japanese, not him.

Go and yell at No. 1 if you like, but there is nothing Weary can do to make the railway or the conditions in this camp disappear. They are now down to getting just 17 ounces of rotten rice a day per man – already down three ounces because of supply problems and general bastardry – and they have to buy anything else from the canteen! They have just spent a fortune buying eggs, onions, dried meat and fat; and in case you haven't noticed, all the Australians are getting thinner! The Lizard retreats for the day, ordering the men to get better before the next morning, if they know what's good for them.

Weary does know, that's why they will stay in bed.

•

Keeping your discipline while the Japanese are being such bastards about things, can sometimes . . . break a man. Weary documents an occasion when a Japanese surveyor, backed by armed guards, has been so incompetently insistent in his demand for speed above all else that for a log-hauling party the log in question falls into the entirely wrong position.

Much shouting ensues, and while the exhausted Australian POWs endeavour to haul the log back by brute strength alone, some of them start expressing their uncomplimentary views about the surveyor, not realising that as the Japanese man had had a stint in America, he understands phrases like 'incompetent arsehole'.

The surveyor barks some orders and one Japanese guard, sarcastically known as 'Happy'[66] for a countenance that only a mother could love – and even then it would be a close-run thing – takes a chunk of bamboo and starts to beat over the head the POW who has most offended him – Jack Ward, a big bloke from Weary's hometown of Benalla. But there is only so much that flesh and blood, time and again, can bear. Finally, Jack is exactly that – jack of it.

'In maddened exasperation,' Weary reports, '[our bloke] tore the bamboo from the Nip.'[67]

In an instant the other guards fall upon the Australian.

'He was,' Ray Parkin will recount, 'beaten with bamboo, fists, and finally, a crowbar. He is lucky to be alive. Happy was beating him about the head and shoulders with the crowbar. Jack was fending off the blows with his arms, as well as he could.'[68]

The denouement looks to be devastating.

For now, Happy draws back the bar and, wielding it like a bayonet, makes a lunge at Jack's groin. It connects, but not fully, the blow designed to hurt but not kill, which – oddly enough – is reflective of the fact that Happy tends not to lose his temper as quickly and completely as his more brutal brethren.

'He is a boxer,' Parkin will recount, 'unusual I think in the Jap, who seem to be a biting, scratching, screeching lot when it comes to a fight. I think this gave him that fraction of control that saved Jack.'[69]

Still, more beatings will follow, when the Japanese sergeant is informed of what has happened.

While outraged at the treatment handed out to one of his men, Weary wants to show a better way: don't react. Accept it. Do what they say. Do not give them the satisfaction of seeing you're upset – or a reason to bash you.

Weary is soon enough given the opportunity to demonstrate his own self-discipline when his expressions of outrage at the Japanese treatment of members of Dunlop Force are deemed to have gone too far. As punishment, Weary is put on parade before the men, and has a thick bamboo pole, with heavy stones placed on each end, placed behind his knees, before he is obliged to kneel on the ground, in a manner that, as Ray Parkin will describe it, 'the pole acted as a fulcrum to force the knee joints apart with the whole weight of his body (this is called the 'knee-spread'). In addition, his bare knees were pressing into sharp gravel.'[70]

It is hellishly painful, but Weary holds in both his rage and discomfort, doing as his tormentors ask. What is more, the men of Dunlop Force – as outraged as they are by the treatment of their leader – take savage delight in the way that Weary grins at every Japanese guard and officer that passes.

'The Nips,' one Australian will recall, 'did not know what to do with him.'[71]

Finally, after *eight hours*, the weary Weary is allowed to stand once more, at least the best he can, cursing himself to Parkin a short time later, for the fact that, 'I staggered like a silly fool when I got up because my legs were numb.'[72]

But his men have seen his display of self-discipline, and understand. Every one of them vows to be like Weary. Self-control. Do not show rage. Give them *nothing*.

Chaplain Gerard Bourke – who has been put to work with all the rest, irrespective of the fact he is a man of the cloth – witnesses it all close-up, and is stunned by Weary's spiritual strength. It is even beyond his physical strength, which is mighty.

7 April 1943, Hintok, speedo credo

'So many men, are not *allowed* to become ill,'[73] says the Lizard this morning. Weary corrects him, so many *should* not be allowed to become ill. *Why?*

'There is of course ample reason for this unfortunate tendency,' Weary points out. 'Starvation rations, miserable, wet quarters, overwork, absence of drugs.'[74]

And it might very well be because the Japanese filter pump now drawing water from the creek does not filter the water at all. The Lizard does not hesitate, insisting that the Australians are to blame: 'Your casks add unfiltered water to the tea!'[75]

So we are poisoning ourselves *deliberately*?

'This is "face saving" tripe,'[76] Weary notes.

Despite Japanese orders, Weary spends his morning digging new *benjos*. Doctors can't be prudish or prissy; this is where so much sickness and disease will spring from if the task is not done properly – so it is done again and again. Sanitation can be their salvation. In the afternoon, Weary makes his way to the railway, which is 'hot as Hades and on the rocks the men's feet nearly fry'.[77]

Everything today is focused on the embankment near the southern end of the works, as the exhausted men continue to carry their *tankas* 200 yards before they can empty them. The cry from the guards and engineers never varies: '*Speedo! Speedo!*'[78]

The men are kept working later and later, 'Hirota having conveniently forgotten his promise about 5 pm knock off.'[79]

Weary spots Hirota in the distance and approaches, but as soon as the Japanese engineer sees him, he edges off warily, 'avoiding me, giving a cautious gleam of teeth'.[80]

Clearly, the only thing that counts is that he has been given responsibility by the Emperor for these 10 kilometres of railway to be constructed, on *schedule* – by July at the latest – and the number of POWs and coolies who die to get it done is completely immaterial to him. (Weary knows that his men have to do half that amount of track, but is determined they won't be suffering anywhere near half the number of casualties.)

The POWs who are drillers have already had their latest darg increased from 1 metre to 1.2 metres. They work as fast as possible to achieve this so they can rest, but Weary sees that the Japanese are not going to reward fast work with leisure, but with added centimetres to their goal. The drillers today finish by mid-afternoon, but they won't be doing the same any time soon. It is a Devil's bargain, but for today they are happy to make it quick, just to escape to shade and breathe some air that is clear. There is another side to this fast work, as one of the leading injuries in camp is now from drill frag-ments; frantic men working so fast – sometimes with the Japanese engineers firing off the gelignite before giving proper warning for everyone to stand clear – that accidents occur on an industrial level that would shut down any normal operation.

If you don't like drilling or digging you can always try your hand at rock clearing, although Weary can see it 'appears rather dangerous, with the possibility of taking a wrong step and falling down the precipitous slope'.[81] And those on the *tankas* are now more exhausted than ever, as their own targets increase commensurately and they are obliged to move one and a half cubic metres a day.

Weary's face drops as he leaves them, wrestling with the unsolvable: how to slow this orderly slaughter. He has given up the thought of stopping it; only the war's end or their own can do that.

In the evening, he must face 'a continuous treadmill in which I used to have to attend the number one works boss of the Japanese and he would say, tomorrow, so many hundred men. And I'd say, impossible, we can't turn out this number. And we would argue until ten o'clock, during which time I could usually beat him down a few men. Then I'd have to wait up and see the last of the workforce, even up till about two o'clock in the morning, you know, some of them would come in practically crawling.'[82]

It is only at that time that he can truly do his calculations, grading the men from *byoki*, sick, to little sick, to fit, to very fit. The defini-tions will inevitably change over time, to the point that 'little sick' will soon become men 'shivering with fierce attacks and malaria, pouring dysentery, tropical ulcers with a great sort of raw ulcers on their legs or their feet, like raw tomatoes, just looking as if they had no skin on them'.[83]

It is like nothing they have ever seen before, as one Australian will put it, 'stinking tropical ulcers that ate a leg to the bone in a matter of days'.[84] (Truly, once the infection gets to the muscle, the evil spreads so rapidly that legs and arms simply fall apart, into a putrescent mess.)

This tropical malaise – one of many conditions and diseases specific to these hot and clammy climes that the Australian doctors are confronted with for the first time, and must quickly try to master – usually starts from small scratches that the men suffer on their twice-daily four-mile trek through pressing jungle on the small mountain track, wearing little more than shorts. It is a frequent occurrence for their flesh to be lightly torn by anything from thorns to jutting branches to stones. Now, in normal times, fully fed and watered, and with enough rest, such scratches would quickly heal. But not here, not now, not with exhausted, starving men whose systems are completely run down – and not even with base-level medical intervention.

'Mild antiseptics were useless,'[85] Weary notes.

Everything just gets worse with remarkable rapidity, 'among famished fever-ridden subjects exposed to blows and trauma. A distressing feature was massive spreading gangrene with acute exacerbations of spread. Frequently the deep fascia was penetrated and there followed gross involvement of bone, joints, muscle, tendon, vessels, and nerves.'[86]

The sores fester, they grow in size, they . . . stink so badly, it makes a healthy man gag just to be near them. To allow them to treat all those suffering most efficiently, Weary gets them in just one hut, as in 'Ulcer Wards'.

How to treat them?

'We tried everything,' Private Donald Stuart will recall. 'We tried hot foments, we tried rock salt pounded up to a powder, heated in a mess tin to cracking point and then poured in. There were no sulphur drugs and no ointments, no bloody nothing.'[87]

Failing that, the infected flesh must be removed.

Sometimes – using the Dutch method – spoons are sharpened around the edges and, while other men hold the patient down, the rotten flesh is gouged out, usually only after stuffing a bit of rolled-up towel in the affected man's mouth to muffle the scream.

A gentler way is to actively introduce maggots to eat the rot, before, sated, they are themselves removed. ('They did a great job,' one sufferer will chronicle, 'but it was hard to sleep with the little wrigglers.'[88]) Yet one more way is to get down to the River Kwai, five kilometres and several hours walk away, and have small fish start nibbling away no sooner than a minute after you put the limb with the ulcer underwater.

Sometimes these methods work, sometimes they don't. In the case of the latter, when the ulcer continues to grow and is sending infection throughout the entire body, the only solution is extreme; in sum – amputation of the affected limb.

To facilitate the cut, they use an ingeniously fashioned implement. It is a frypan, with a hole first cut in the middle a little smaller than the size of the tibia, and a hinge on the end opposite the handle. A cut is made between the handle and the hinge, with another handle placed in parallel to the first handle, on the swinging half. By placing the whole thing around the diseased leg, just above where the tropical ulcer is destroying all, Weary can use the implement like a guillotine, pushing down hard to cut through all the flesh, before wielding a butcher or carpenter's saw to do the honours.

(After one operation when Weary indeed shakes a leg and takes another off with the cookhouse saw, he holds the severed limb up to the Japanese guards who are carefully watching goggle-eyed, thrusts it forward, and says, 'Here, this is all you're gonna get of this bloke.'[89] They take off like the clappers.)

More often than not, when the pain from ulcers overwhelms the patients, there is little resistance to the notion of amputation and it is the men themselves who exhort: 'For Christ's sake, cut my leg off.'[90]

They have little, and can only do their best.

'The biggest [ulcer], I ever saw,' one Australian, Tom Young, will recount, 'was a fellow with his whole hip exposed, a couple of fellows keeping the blow flies away. He died of course.'[91]

Meanwhile, a newly arrived officer in camp, coming from Changi, brings news: 'In Darwin recently N lost 22/27 attacking planes. Supplies by air to China now greater than Burma Road. Churchill in his 25 March speech warned the nation of heavy fighting and sacrifices to come.'[92]

When it comes to Churchill, the POWs are amused to see he has an imitator in Japan, Tojo!

For Tojo's latest speech has a very familiar air to it: 'Tojo: speech re naval losses – cannot and will not lose – fight on rafts if necessary.'[93]

We shall fight them on the beaches, or just off them, on rafts . . .

11 April 1943, Hintok, bad head in the morning

A word, Weary?

Captain Allen of the English camp near the river and the vital barge supply line tells Weary he is being ordered to leave tomorrow, along with many other Englishmen. The problem is Allen only has stores for about 20 of them, and a few eggs will have to do for the rest. Weary decides to confront an officer who cannot escape a lecture, Okada, who has been bedridden with malaria for a couple of days. Okada greets Weary with a gentle wave of one finger, a gesture he thinks shows how gravely ill he is, but looks like a very different one to Australian eyes.

'What?' asks Okada, only up to uttering one word as well it seems. Well, it's about the stores. 'If Captain Allen goes, there will be nobody on the river, no eggs purchased. Men will then go sick and not work.'[94]

Okada considers the dilemma: 'Captain Allen will go. Japanese soldiers will stop a barge and buy stores.'[95]

Weary is not so sure, the traders have learnt to avoid the Japanese: 'Thai traders need very special handling and gratuities',[96] they get neither from their occupiers. Weary tries to delicately make this case but Okada simply groans and pulls a blanket over his head. His interpreter tells Weary what is happening: 'Mr O now has bad head, very bad, please go away and come back.'[97]

That groan speaks volumes apparently. The irony is that on the way back to his own camp Weary is accosted by several Thai traders with carts: 'These apparently had nothing to sell but showed great desire to buy me right out of clothes from head to heel, including my watch. Good watches bring enormous prices in Bangkok.'[98]

The rain is so bad today that the unprecedented happens, work is stopped on the railway at only 2.30 pm. Grinning wet prisoners walk the muddy roads home, delighting in their drenching.

•

The Lizard forces Major Corlette to discharge 12 men from their hospital beds when Weary is away. All these sick men will work, inside the camp or outside, it matters not to the Lizard. Weary is furious but impotent: 'a stand will have to be made, but with what? You can only argue with such people over a gun.'[99]

Sadly, there is none to hand. More and more, Weary thinks of the treatment he would like to give to the Lizard, a quick course of euthanasia administered by a heavy rock.

Such brooding is not good for the soul, but by God it makes the day go better . . .

The next morning, Weary walks swiftly to the Konyu English camp to meet with an amenable Lieutenant Usuki, who not only promises that sick men will not be forced to work, he says mail will be arriving from Australia for them very shortly. Also, he gives Weary a boiled sweet. It's too good to be true for precisely that reason. Goodwill and promises mean nothing when they get back to their own camp and encounter the Lizard once more. His demand? Twenty-five men to be discharged for 'light work'! More than double yesterday's outrage! 'Both battalions already send "light sick" out to the railway course,'[100] protests Weary. 'The engineers frequently send sick men home, saying they are no good to them.'[101]

Really? Well, the Lizard has a solution. 'Tomorrow you will parade the whole hospital, on the parade ground.'[102] The only exceptions are men who cannot walk, who are allowed to sit on the teak logs by the parade ground. What about men with fevers? The Lizard considers their plight. 'Fevers included, since only for five minutes. I will then select the men I want for light work.'[103] No, you won't. Two and a half hours of argument now takes place between Weary and the Lizard; it is, Weary wondrously notes 'exquisitely polite'.[104] The Lizard agrees to cancel the hospital patient parade, and blames the engineers. 'I regret I must argue with such honourable gentlemen, but I am terribly worried by the requirement engineers put upon me.'[105]

Would Weary like a cigarette? Coffee? Both thanks, but he would like the Lizard to agree to stop trying to turn 25 sick men into well men every day. No. 'Finally, we all went to bed in a state of unsettled but polite evasiveness.'[106]

•

Back at Changi, it is time to follow the Java Rabble to Thailand. On this day, Colonel Black Jack Galleghan assembles his men of the newly constituted 'F Force' – 3662 Australians from the 8th Division and 3400 from the British 18th Division – in the parade ground to properly farewell them.

He wishes them well. He is sure they will do themselves proud, and always comport themselves like the *soldiers* they are and will always be. They will be travelling with a good team of medical specialists and three months of medical supplies, so that side of things should be taken care of. As it seems likely that they will be concentrated in fixed camps, they will be pleased to hear that provisions had been made for their entertainment while there.

Good luck, God bless.

In short order, the first of them are on their way, leading off what will be 15 parties heading to Thailand at one-day intervals, in the same steel rice-trucks that had previously transported Dunlop Force.

14 April 1943, Hintok, light and shade

'Rose early expecting trouble'[107] – that could be any day in this camp but today that expectation becomes a certainty very quickly. Weary is determined to bring this issue of military diagnosis with the Lizard to a head. He parades those soldiers who are well, and diagnoses the number of 'light sick' to be 27 in number – though, truly, back in Australia most of these nominally 'light sick' ones would have been hospitalised. Seriously, the normal Australian translation right now for what the Japanese call 'fit', 'light sick' and 'heavy sick' would be 'crook', 'seriously crook' and 'very bloody nearly dead'.

Weary tells them they will not be allowed out of camp today, by his order.

A Japanese soldier, Takata, turns up and yells, '*Speedo, Speedo!*'[108] at these 27 men.

'Take no notice,' says Weary. 'Sit down and look sick.'[109]

The last two things should be as easy as . . . falling off a log, which some of them do anyway.

As ever, the way Weary deals with the Japanese guards is an inspiration to his men.

'His casual matter of fact "cool" and the almost dreary way he treated the guards always gave us great heart,' one of the men, Colin Finkemeyer, will record. 'Weary had the uncanny knack of making the Japs feel inferior and this used to infuriate them.'[110]

Today proves to be a case in point, as the number of men that Weary has told to sit down means that the guard can't send out his designated tally.

'More men work, too many men *byoki*,' the guard says querulously.

'Only these men work,' says Weary in the calmest of voices.

'More men, men not *byoki*,' the guard repeats, pointing to the so-called sick men Weary has told to sit it out.

Weary barely blinks.

'Only these men work,'[111] he replies mildly, pointing to the men standing up.

Infuriated by such insolence, the guard roars '*KURA!*' at Weary, ordering him to stand to attention, before suddenly swinging his right fist at Weary's chin. Bemused, Weary easily calls on his boxing skills of long ago, honed in many a rugby brawl, to sway his head back just in time and grin mischievously, even as he quickly straightens up.

Want to have another go, Sonny Jim?

Japanese Jim does indeed, and swings again, only to miss once more, as Dunlop Force cannot help itself and bursts into derisive laughter. It is with that laughter ringing in his ears that the guard stomps over to the guardhouse and returns with a box which he now stands on.

And swings again! It is a straight to Weary's chin.

This time Weary puts his head to the side and the fist sails past, harmlessly, as laughter breaks out once more.

One more go.

A mighty swing!

It sails past once more, but with such momentum that it takes the guard with it, as he tumbles off the box.

'It all seemed to happen so easily,' Colin Finkemeyer will recount, 'but it was typical of Weary and the heart-warming effect he always had on us. It gave us a great feeling to know that he was always prepared to go in and bat for us.'[112]

And yet, still it is not over. While the guard retreats, the Lizard arrives and is 'obviously upset' but Weary repeats what the officer must know already: 'These are the men about whom I spoke last night. Not fit to go to work.'[113] Weary and the Lizard now have it out publicly, fury and face competing.

The Lizard retreats to consult an engineer. The engineer, he says, has now revealed to him that 'sick men no good'.[114]

Therefore, the Lizard has decided to allow these 27 men to stay in camp.

You shouldn't have, no, really. But, thank you.

And yet everyone who was discharged yesterday from the sick list must chop wood at the Japanese guardhouse. Fine. They march casually off to do just that then report to Weary that: 'they were then sat down and given some food and cigarettes. Incomprehensible people.'[115]

Unfortunately, it is Weary's job to try to understand them. He has one brainwave; he and Ewan Corlette go through the hospital and see who is on the mend. They select 15 men to be diagnosed as 'light sick' tomorrow, and the Lizard is 'very pleased'.[116] A game is being played, and today the Australians and decency are winning.

And yet, it is not as if Weary does not have support, even among the Japanese officers and soldiers. For they notice precisely what one of the Dunlop Force men notices:

> Both [Weary] and Corlette took their share of Jap bashings and humiliations, but they never once refused to treat a sick Nip brought to them. A sick man was just a sick man to them. [117]

15 April 1943, Hintok, worm turns

Troubles arrive in legions.

Right now, for Weary, the biggest problem is the latrines.

For nearby their camp is still a 'big "open" type deep trench horror which is breeding flies'.[118] You add that to patients who are recovering from dysentery and are helping in the kitchen and you have a recipe for disaster. And it doesn't help that 'a foul open trench latrine is only 100 yards away from the kitchen'.[119]

(Good God, but such scenes as are seen at the latrines would curdle your very soul. When one Australian POW has a pain in his tummy, he heads off to do the business over some bamboo slats above a hole, constantly using one foot to brush the swarming maggots off the other foot, before that foot returns the favour. Once done, a bloke already there, says, 'Look behind you.' He does, to see, 'a big black worm, as thick as my finger and about twelve inches long. I had been feeding that thing for goodness knows how long.'[120])

Weary orders that latrine to be closed at once; all rice is to be covered at all times before being served to the men – and they must all wash their hands before every meal, just like their mother taught them.

Do it!

The Japanese are doing their best to kill them already, there is no need to lend them a hand. As it stands, or perhaps as it squats, over half of Weary's men have dysentery of various types.

The worst of amoebic dysentery, oddly enough, is not the endlessly sprayed faecal matter that the half coconut shells being used as 'bed pans' have no hope of containing. After a while the sprayed expulsions become little more than unpleasant mud – and it doesn't actually stink quite the way normal movements do.

It is not even what comes with the stool with particularly bad cases, when the dysentery is so bad that 'men are passing the lining of their innards in pieces the size of a saucer or of a plate and constantly losing blood'.[121]

No, the worst thing is watching men wither before your very eyes, as the life-blood drains out of them. For Weary the greatest frustration is that of all the illnesses, dysentery is one of the easiest to cure, if only you have the right medicine – *emetine hydrochloride* – and they simply don't have any. Urgently, a message is passed to Boon Pong. We need emetine in bulk, and we need it as soon as possible!

But even without it, could they possibly attempt to manufacture drugs like emetine hydrochloride, themselves? It will take a great deal of experimentation, but the answer is . . . yes!

'Sources of hydrochloric acid,' Weary will proudly note, 'included the human stomach.'[122]

By combining that multi-purpose acid – solder, drugs, anything – with the few vials of Japanese ether they could get their hands on, and mixing with sodium carbonate and alcohol, the result is . . . emetine hydrochloride!

The harvested stomach acid is also added to water and given to POWs suffering from hypochlorhydria – a lack of stomach acid caused by malnutrition, which makes patients particularly vulnerable to cholera. Meantime, another surgeon on the Thai–Burma Railway will record that quinine hydrochloride proved effective for 'intravenous use in cerebral malaria'.[123]

Still another medically skilled POW – a Dutch chemist by the name of Van Boxtel – manages to extract cocaine from some tablets a dental officer was carrying with him, before refining it into a solution to produce a spinal anaesthetic.

All of it is extraordinary, and yet nothing changes the central dynamic – the drug they all need is *rest*. But there is simply none to be had. The work must go on, come what may, and for all such fabulous innovations the number of 'fit' men, and even 'light sick' men, available to work continues to fall. While to this point the Japanese have observed the convention that those above the rank of sergeant need not be obliged to do physical labour, that is about to change.

'Officers,' Weary notes in his diary, 'are to be told frankly that it is absolutely necessary that all do manual work, since otherwise not enough fit men.'[124]

Yes, officers doing manual work would bring forth the smelling salts in any British mess, but this whole camp is in a mess and necessity trumps any rank or tradition – and the manual work will still be confined to the camp, rather than the Line. Not for nothing does Weary soon note in his diary, '*Benjo* work and wood and water carrying now almost entirely thrown on the officers, who have become normal labourers.'[125]

In happier news, a Sergeant working for Weary secretly proves to be a mini-Marconi when it comes to creating an even better radio than the one they had – which had gone on the blink – and this one is created out of nearly nothing. His name is concealed in Weary's diary, and this radio itself is labelled 'X', but it is clear how thrilled the medico is when civilisation crackles through the air to them this wonderful evening: 'Sgt C working on my X with an astonishing modicum of apparatus including only [one valve]. Tonight was in contact with BBC. Astonishingly good results – will summarise later.'[126]

London calling, Dunlop Force listening.

The Japanese are struggling across the board, and the singular bit of good news is that the USA 13th Airforce B-24s have successfully struck the Japanese airbase at Kahili on Bougainville, *twice*, on the evening of 11 April.

It feels like the tide is really turning now. Maybe just another three months and the war will be over.

•

What now?

At morning parade further down the Line, a prisoner is dragged before the assembled POWs, a fellow who has clearly been very badly beaten, 'with his swollen and bloody features virtually unrecognisable'.

The Black Prince, Lieutenant Usuki[127] – looking unaccountably well presented, in full dress uniform – addresses them, as ever with the interpreter giving his words to them in pidgin: 'This man very bad. He try to escape. No gooda.'[128]

To the shock of all, the poor bastard is thrown to the ground and made to kneel in front of Usuki.

Head down! With your neck bared!

The man does not plead for his life. He appears to be beyond caring.

And now Usuki strides forward, unsheathing his suddenly gleaming sword. Steadying himself for a moment, he lifts the sword high above the British man's exposed neck, the way an axeman might at the Sydney Royal Easter Show, just before the bell rings to begin the competition. 'There followed a moment of such horror,' Alistair Urquhart will recount, 'that I could scarcely believe it was happening . . . I could not escape the chilling swoosh of the blade as it cut through the air or the sickening thwack as it struck our comrade's neck, followed by the dull thump of his head landing on the ground.'[129]

That suddenly detached head rolls a couple of feet and stops. *This* is what happens to those who try to escape. For lesser sins, like rising up against a guard beating them, and giving the brute the belting he so desperately deserves, men are tied, spread-eagled in the sun, with their wrists and ankles bound by 'wet rattan – the same string-like bark used to lash our bamboo huts together . . . As the rattan dried, the ties would slowly gash into the skin, drawing blood and tearing into sinew and cartilage as they pulled limbs from their sockets. It reduced even the toughest men to agonised screaming. It was a way of torturing all of us.'[130]

•

Abide with me; fast falls the eventide;
The darkness deepens; Lord, with me abide;
When other helpers fail and comforts flee,
Help of the helpless, oh, abide with me . . .

Shhhhh. It is big Tom Uren, on his knees, saying his prayers – just as he does every evening, just as his mother Agnes had taught him to do, and insisted on, ever since he was a little boy. Mostly, Tom thanks the Lord for the beauty he continues to see all around him, in the trees, the flowers and the birds, which he takes as proof that the Lord is still there.

Another man might be mocked for saying his prayers in this manner, but no-one would dare mock Tom. He has hands like dinner-plates and fists like sledgehammers. If he wants to pray like that, good luck to him.

Ray Parkin is such a devotee of beauty, *especially* butterflies and their iridescent colours, that he starts giving names to the different types he finds, including 'Blue Midnight, Moss Queen, High Priest, Jacob's Coat, Little Piccaninny, Sepia Ballerina [and] Crinoline Girl. They helped to take your mind off sore feet, bellyaches, and malaria'.[131]

The other men, seeing his interest, start bringing even more varieties to him. Parkin presses them, paints them, and then pins them to the ceiling of his hut using tiny slivers of – what else – bamboo, and making that ceiling, by his estimation, 'more beautiful than the ceiling of the Sistine Chapel'.[132]

Now while Weary is not particularly religious one way or another, spiritual souls like these two friends of his – and they have become close over the weeks – are not the only ones to impress him. Occasionally, he meets some of the Thai Buddhist monks who pass by. There is something about the compassion in their eyes, their silent warmth – the sense that we are all just passing through, and the current ugliness is as nothing to the overall beauty of the world – that he finds comforting.

17 April 1943, Hintok, all shall have prizes

'*Changey, Changey*'[133] is the order of the day. 'From tomorrow reveille and breakfast will be at 0700, parade at 0730, move off to work 0800.' Why? For all to be finished at 1700 hours supposedly, to work them all the more in reality. Well, you can change the hours but you can't change the condition of the men, which remains appalling: 'The troops are already getting a terrible belting and are looking thin; also septic sores are a grave problem, there being very little to treat them with.'[134]

This does not stop the men with these sores from working, which then increases the severity of the sores and on they go until they fall over.

Thanks to the new schedule, you might collapse half an hour earlier in the day, but it is not much of a gain in productivity. When the men are at work, their bodies propel themselves into irritable ease; but when work and pressure cease, the real pain comes. Weary notes the depressing phenomenon in his diary, furious that the Japanese will be able to profit from just this misery: 'Men move stiffly and miserably in irritable temper and become gradually more comfortable at work, but upon stopping, the throbbing irritation and torment of flies makes rest impossible.'[135]

Weary is sick with worry about the deaths he can see coming.

It used to be that, as the POWs straggled their way to work, the butterflies would flutter by, getting away from the passing parade. Now, they don't bother and line both sides of the track as a kind of deathly honour guard for a funeral cortege. Only Ray Parkin is pleased to see it.

CHAPTER THIRTEEN

HELLFIRE AND DAMNATION

Only the Japanese Army regulations were binding in the Japanese Army. The Japanese did not consider human life of any value when viewed in the light that the railway must be pushed on regardless of the cost. This attitude was openly professed by Japanese camp command, who have frequently stated that 'even if men die they should do so gladly as they are working for the Emperor and the Railway must go on'.[1]

Brigadier Cranston A. McEachern

18 April 1943, Hintok, humility comes before a fall

Every day, it is the same.

With the first lustre of dawn, the tinny tones of a Japanese trumpet warbling some God-awful martial tune of Nippon shatters the remains of the night and sets the monkeys chattering, while the large black baboons that abound in these parts swing away on their vines, to a place where such barbarous and truly *uncivilised* squealing cannot be heard.

(Everyone's a critic.)

As ever, the warbling enters the huts, rounds up the last of the sonorous sounds of exhausted slumber coming from the bamboo bunks, and lightly screeches them to death. It is just the start of another God-forsaken day in this jungle hell-hole, and only minutes later the men of Dunlop Force emerge to struggle about the camp like baby giraffes, trying to get still aching limbs to start working once more. It's bloody early, but Weary knows it is still not early enough.

'Men have to perform what toilet is practicable and have breakfast by 0730. As it takes a long time for 800 men to draw a meal, some have no time to eat breakfast before they are on parade.'[2]

And from parade they will be off to the railway. And they will be there for a *long* time: 'It is anticipated that very soon they will be working . . . late in the evening.'[3]

On this day Weary will be heading off to the railway himself. On the trek to the tracks, Weary is tired, sweating and . . . he slips on the lip of a cliff and falls six feet, his rubber shoes sliding down the muddy earth, before grabbing on to a vine to stop any further fall.

Onwards, as Dunlop Force's main medical man can't fall ill on the way to his daily rounds, and Weary arrives cheerily enough at the railway course.

There stands Lieutenant Hirota, the engineer, and Weary is quick to buttonhole him.

'The men are getting worn out with no rest and poor food,'[4] he says.

So?

Hirota is aware of this, and he displays no more interest than if Weary had told him the sky is blue. So do you have a point to this observation, Dunlop? Yes, there is a truck. Because tomorrow Weary knows many of these same men are going to be asked to carry sugar and supplies for the camp from Konyu, like pack animals.

'Some have already had no rest for one month. Will you lend us your lorry?'[5]

Hirota muses for a moment and then nods. 'I will let you know the time tomorrow.'[6]

It is so odd to have to beg for such obvious graces; these actions will help the Japanese as much as his men, but Weary knows any concession towards sense must be hard won.

'Tomorrow is definitely *yasume* day,'[7] and one with a truck too.

Weary has to treat a soldier who has been, 'struck in the thigh today with a flying stone from blasting – a nasty wound',[8] and an unnecessary one.

At least today some very small boots arrive. And yes, they are 'neither durable or watertight'[9] but the men have the joy of standing on parade this evening for an extra hour while the Japanese distribute the boot booty in the most elaborate, time-consuming and formal manner possible. Every officer, every soldier is 'rushing around and putting a finger in the pie'.[10]

Weary asks permission for the Australians to hand out any future gear themselves; it is granted petulantly by their gaolers.

20 April 1943, Hintok, whistle while you walk

What do you get the man who has everything, or at least all of Germany, all of France, half of Eastern Europe and bits of Africa? The main thing is not to give him anything else, even if Weary does note the occasion in his diary: 'Hitler's birthday!'[11]

There is no day off to celebrate, and in fact the Lizard demands a further 15 discharges today from the hospital. There is a new system in place for those men Weary deems as 'light sick': they are given a special red tab for their uniforms and they will not be shanghaied for rail work that day. The catch? They must walk to the railway to be given their tab! Every day. It is 'a killing walk there and back',[12] and another perverse polity that the Lizard has dreamt up for their displeasure.

Weary has some more serious medical issues to deal with today: 'We are now seeing for the first time some really first class examples of pellagra rash.'[13] Five men are in this class today, their blistered sunburnt skin transforming into a 'brown scaling rash known as a "toadskin"'.[14]

As appalling as the condition is, it is medically fascinating, with its cause obvious, as the rash appears on the skin 'wherever the sun beats on them, all over the trunk on shirtless men working the rail'.[15]

Others with no boots see the skin on their feet turning toady; a harsh natural boot that irritates and stings with each step taken.

Meantime, beri-beri – one of the classic 'deficiency diseases' brought on by malnutrition – continues to cut a swathe through the men, with more and more showing 'marked swelling of the face and legs and shortness of breath, liver enlargement, etc. Owing to the shortage of eggs of late, there is a marked deterioration in the state of those troops receiving treatment for avitaminosis. Some have very bad mouths and scrotums.'[16]

Yes, the local version of 'Bandoeng balls' is now more prevalent, with even worse symptoms as the lower part of their genitals becomes a raw and weeping mess, making it more and more difficult to even walk. But no matter to the Japanese. They *still* insist that the same number of men go out every day to work!

'If they wanted two hundred men they had to have two hundred men,' one POW will recount of this terrible time. 'The guards would deliver two hundred men even if perhaps thirty of them might be on the backs of their mates. In the rain. So when we got there, if the beri-beri was excessive, you might have to lie some of them on their backs with their feet against the side of the embankment to keep the fluid flowing down through their legs into their bodies so their legs wouldn't burst.'[17]

The actual amount of hammering, tapping or carrying you could get out of such men? Please.

'They couldn't work at all. We'd feed them at lunch time when we had a break. They were looked after, hats placed over their faces to keep the rain out, and they were talked and joked to. They understood the position. We would carry them back at night. Usually one would die during the day.'

One treatment that Weary has been relying on is eggs, for it has become apparent that even just one egg a day keeps away the 'avitaminosis' – vitamin deficiency – but the way their supply chain keeps breaking down, it's only a matter of time before the men break down too. For those suffering from the disease – and truly suffer they do – have both their mouths *and* scrotums ridden with raw and weeping sores. Truly alarming to the Japanese is that this disease seems to affect the hardest workers on the railway:

> It is noticeable that the strong workers who throw themselves into work are now coming in looking very broken and will obviously not be fit for weeks, even with hospital rest and treatment.[18]

When the elephants themselves start to break down and die, the workload on the men increases commensurately.

(Despite Lieutenant Susuki's previous complaints about the way the British treat the elephants, the truth is that the Japanese guards are even worse, and their cruelty to the massive beasts has been even *more* merciless than the way they treat the men, beating them with such ruthlessness it had made the elephants scream and the Australians cringe, so the slow demise of these wondrous animals had been shocking, rather than a surprise. But oh, what brotherhood the Australians feel with one of these elephants when, one day, it simply wraps its trunk around the cruel Japanese guard that had been mercilessly hitting it with a stick, picks him up, and uses *him* as a stick to bash against a nearby tree, before leaving him as a bloodied and senseless mess at her feet. Encore! Encore!)

How long are the men going to have to endure such privations?

The common reckoning remains: just another three months.

Sometimes, in the nights, after another day of shattering exhaustion, the POWs are serenaded to sleep by one of the privates blessed with a rich baritone, Len Gooley from Port Pirie – where he lays down his head, Len Gooley – who lies in his tent and sings in a voice that floats over the entire camp, songs like 'Show Me the Way to Go Home', 'We'll Meet Again' and 'Now is the Hour'.

> *Sunset glow fades in the west*
> *Night o'er the valley is creeping*
> *Birds cuddle down in their nest*
> *Soon all the world will be sleeping*
>
> *While you're away*
> *Oh, then, remember me*
> *When you return*
> *You'll find me waiting here . . .*[19]

It would make a man weep, and many quietly do.

Weary will later write of an episode in camp regarding Ivor Jones, who has been working hard on the cemetery.

'Where are you off to, Ivor?'

'I am going down to the cemetery to have a really good cry – would you like to come along?'[20]

These are tough times, getting tougher.

Both the Dutch and the British, the Australians have learnt, had had plans to build exactly the same railway, dating back to the late 1800s, but neither had the will to make the sacrifices necessary to actually build it. But it is becoming clearer that the Japanese are more than prepared to make much darker and faster sacrifices – starting with them.

21 April 1943, Hintok, bombs our way

It is a strange thing to be thrilled to be bombed, but this morning it is true. Just before 4 am, the drone of a plane is heard, perhaps two, and 'some thought they heard bombs or ack ack'.[21]

Can it be possible? Has the war come to them at last? Weary excitedly notes: 'This is the first "sign" we have met with.'[22]

But what is the sign? Weary tries to get an explanation from the HQ Clerk Kanamoto, who obliges in his own odd way: 'Eccentric plane come Chinese, Engine English perhaps, eccentric aeroplane drop bombs between Tarsau and Tonchin. Very, very eccentric.'[23]

Long live eccentricity! What he actually *means* is anyone's guess and, as a matter of fact, the lack of any solid information sees among Weary's men, 'a huge diversity of opinion as to the number of bombs and where'.[24]

Weary has a lot of time to speculate as he and Billy Wearne, with the aid of a pole and a basket, are ferrying supplies from the River Kwai to the camp today. On their first trip uphill they pull off a camp record, carrying two great tins of *guala* weighing in at 130 pounds.

'The trip up the hill is a killer, what with rain and slush underfoot, the intense heat and the nasty way a pole hurts the shoulder. A miserable wet day.'[25]

The day also has a record of a different kind, a paper one. Weary gets a written chit from the Black Prince, Usuki, instructing the Lizard to give extra pay to injured workers and for 20 fit men to be allowed to only transport supplies for the camp tomorrow: 'It is unusual to get a written chit from any Nippon commander or authority and I am sure this is due to a native dislike of irrevocably committing themselves. Much easier to deny subsequently the spoken word. Nip intercommunication seems to suffer a good deal from this dislike of paper.'[26]

Saving paper saves face, each officer can deny what the other said; promises gained, easily revoked. But with a chit comes a bit of security and Weary and Billy won't have to attempt another aching record tomorrow to get the supplies they need.

Their secret wireless also delivers news to the effect that 'Attempt to reinforce Tunisia by troop-carrying planes was intercepted.'[27] No fewer than16 fighters downed. 'Said to be the greatest air victory of the African campaign. The RAF active in the North Sea. Two destroyers sunk.'[28]

It is thrilling to hear of the war progressing, with the Germans clearly taking a belting. The broadcast is interrupted by a late party returning 'with stores in rain and slush carrying eggs and tomatoes'.[29]

Oil, sugar and eggs, all are gratefully unloaded from lorry loads too. As for the few remaining elephants, they are off water duty but they are still helping out: 'The elephants were being used at several points to pull lorries out of the mud today.'[30]

Another beast of burden is not so lucky, for as the men head out to the railway they pass a bullock gone astray; it is thin and straggly and, as they pass it, one guard says, as a joke, '*Makan!*' Meal![31]

Your word is our command: 'one of the lads promptly hit it on the head with an axe before he could intervene. It was then skinned and cut up in the twinkling of an eye.'[32]

The joke is on the Australians though, as the meat is sent up to the Japanese engineers. They cut off the meat for themselves, leaving only the bones: 'the latter were then generously sent to us'.

Stew, anyone? Oh, they will, and the next time they kill a beast they will cut, cook and hide it before any guard sees. How? Who knows. But they can taste that missing meat now, and God help the next bovine that wanders anywhere near . . .

22 April 1943, Hintok, playing it cool

A bounty of stores is waiting at Konyu for the Australians from the blessed Boon Pong, the only trouble now is finding men strong enough to carry them. Weary, Billy Wearne and 20 others head off at 8.30 am. The first trip there and back is fine, the second is damn hard, the third 'was as much as the chaps could stand. Even Billy was just about sunk on the last trip.'[33]

But they have no choice except exhaustion. Boon Pong tells them that today is the last safe hope of 'extra' stores for at least 10 days, and with more Japanese troops moving into their area, there are questions about whether these liberties of purchase will be allowed after that. Necessity may be the mother of invention but today is a mother of exhaustion and a nagging fear that they are clutching at straws with these stores.

Still there is always somebody worse off than yourself, even in a Japanese POW camp, and today Weary sees them. They are Tamil coolies, men and women both, lured to this area with the offer of working for a pittance a day, plus food; little realising how little a dollar will buy them here, and now told that there is no food to be had for them without money. They are marching to Burma in hope of better: 'They are clad in damn all and have no bedding – some merely carry a glass bottle for water, some a small bundle. There were two women in a party of 400.'[34]

Weary is told that the Tamils 'die like flies of pneumonia if exposed to the wet'.[35]

And yet?

Even though these poor bastards are living out their last days trekking 'tween the Valley of the Damned and the Valley of the Shadow of Death, one of them reaches out . . . to offer Weary and Billy cigarettes as they pass. Good God! Even the Tamils are feeling sorry for *them*.

But, thank you. Don't mind if they do.

Puffing away, Weary and Billy watch them go, heading towards eternity very quickly: 'It was a sad sight to see these poor wretches trudging their way up the deep slushy mud of our road guarded by armed Nip troops – a wonderful tribute to the new order in Southeast Asia.'[36] That new order is here to stay, despite the wondering question of another wandering Tamil: 'When are the British coming back to Malaya?'[37]

24 April 1943, Hintok, second service

It will be Easter Sunday tomorrow, and Anzac Day, but there is still an open question on whether or not the men will have to work – so a service for both days will be held tonight. That's if the dangerous padres from the British camp are allowed to enter the Australian camp today: 'The padres were reported to be in trouble at approximately 1915 hours as they had arrived without a pass and were being threatened with being sent straight back.'[38]

How on earth? Well, the local Japanese guards want to make a point to the more casual guards at other camps and so now the ministers are caught in a show of 'face'. Weary shows his own face and, after more supplication, the visiting padres are allowed to enter this, the Australian slice of hell on earth.

Alright, who's for a quick service? The Roman Catholic bags the chapel, the C of E chaps will have to put up with the 'concert area' between tents. In ecumenical fashion, Weary will take a trip to both. All things considered, it's actually a nice night for it, the rain has cleared, the mountains are in mist and Weary cannot refrain from letting his inner poet free: 'Glorious grey-barked trees simply laden with lilac blossoms blazed brilliantly here and there amongst the lovely green. The sky was positively aflame with crimson banners.'[39]

Hundreds of men turn up for the C of E service; the light fading as the padre's candles glow bright into night.

'The theme of the address was suffering, the cross and the empty tomb.'[40] Well, they know of suffering, many think they may know of death soon too, but the minister's words cut deep tonight as he tells them that their Saviour suffered too and that, 'If all suffering ended only in muddled stupidity, the sacrifice of the Cross would not have been made.'[41]

There is a meaning to all this, a purpose; you must believe it and you must endure. Amen. The 'Last Post' is now played, a strange tune to end an Easter service, but by the time the final note rings out it seems fitting.

Right, off to the Catholics now, and Weary sees the Father is no novice when it comes to ceremony, 'the robed and bearded figure fantastically lit by candlelight',[42] and neither is his flock, 'the communicants moving forward out of almost complete darkness from the little surrounding islands of men around the fire'.[43]

Both ministers are more than pleased with their services and declare the evening a great success. We must do it again next year; back in Australia, we hope.

Late April 1943, Hintok, passing parade

As the mornings become hotter and heavier, and the afternoons more stormy, another trickle of trekkers shuffles into sight, but these ones are far more familiar to Dunlop Force.

For it proves to be none other than the shambling vanguard of 'F Force' – the same mob they had derided as 'Malay Harriers' back in Changi after being called the 'Java Rabble' themselves.

But F Force are not spick and span now. Having come to Thailand in much the same railway trucks as Dunlop Force, in much the same conditions – except no food and water for the last 24 hours – these men are already shattered with exhaustion and battered by sickness. And they still have a long trek ahead of them to get to the camps at the furthest reaches of the same Line that Dunlop Force is working on – in their case, right to the Burma end of the Line. With no transport available, they are being force-marched and will cover nearly 200 miles before journey's end. Weary details for his diary the fact that they have suffered extreme brutality. Somebody will know of this, someday, but tonight they are just shambling ships in the night seeking safe harbour, and have collapsed, as those before, 'lying in a sodden heap on the wet ground, sick, miserable and sorry'.[44]

In subsequent days, the tide of Australian POWs only thickens, each lot more ragged than the last. Weary hears staggering stories of their experiences, including how, as they had prepared to leave Changi, the Japanese had told them they'd be going to a much better place – not heaven, but close – a great camp that would come complete with great hospitals. It had been with that in mind they had departed with such things as – no, really – 'three pianos with band instruments'.[45]

Such things had been left behind, not long after arriving in Thailand, with the firm promise by the Japanese they would be sent on. All they are trying to do now is to stay alive.

Inevitably, Weary strikes up a conversation with their Commanding Officer, Lieutenant Colonel Charles 'Gus' Kappe, a very pukka chap of patrician disposition, frequently found in the officer corps, but never among soldiers. He has arrived with no fewer than 600 of the 2/29th Battalion – among whom are the veteran survivors of the Battle at Parit Sulong, including the replacement officer for Lieutenant Ben Hackney who, with 130 others, has not been seen since. Weary is touched by Kappe's enduring faith that everything would sort out, as they are moving in such military formation, with 'a complete brigade . . . ordnance, AASC [Australian Army Service Corps], and everything'.[46]

Weary listens to such ludicrously unfounded optimism for as long as he can bear it, about 30 seconds, before saying gently, 'Well, sir, I hope that you will remain together, because things are pretty rough up here.'[47]

But enough chat. For just a little over two hours after arriving – after Dunlop Force has provided whatever tiny sustenance they can spare – this vanguard contingent of F Force is moving off once more, in the dark, to make camp somewhere up ahead. The flood keeps coming for another four nights, arriving before 9 pm, and moving off again at around 11 pm. Illusions of a wonderful hospital camp ahead are long gone – and one officer reports how when he had fallen out with 37 sick men he had been personally savagely beaten, as had some of the men.

'They are behaving with unreasoning brutality to the sick.'[48]

These men of F Force now realise they are on nothing less than a 'death march', one that is made worse by the fact that, while most of the men are now barefooted, those still with boots have such badly infected blisters from chafing leather they must carry them. Those men who drop out to be cared for by Weary and his medicos until they can try to catch up generally have three complaints at once: malaria, tropical ulcers and pellagra.

God help them all.

•

Way up ahead, in the vanguard of F Force, the nightmare continues in the middle of the night.

A constant cry goes up from Lieutenant Colonel Kappe, 50 paces back from the lead[49] – two soldiers right behind him, struggling to carry Kappe's kit, a large trunk – to his own leading officer, Captain Fred Stahl.

'Stahl, tell that bloody Nip *to slow down.*'

The Japanese guard does no such thing, resulting in another furious cry.

'Stahl, tell that *bloody Nip to slow down.*'

They push on.

'Stahl, tell that bloody Nip to slow down.'

Finally, as dawn breaks, Kappe cries out one more time, *'Stahl, tell that bloody Nip to slow down!'*

Already spent beyond measure, infuriated by frustration, something inside Stahl breaks.

The entire night he has been trying to do as instructed, by a Commanding Officer who is no more than 50 paces away, and has been spared having to try to order a scared and low-ranked Japanese guard to do what he cannot do, which is to slow down. And so now Stahl *hears* himself shouting back to Kappe, what needs to be said, as his own dam of reticence breaks: *'All fucking night you've been telling me to tell this fucking Nip to fucking well slow down. If you think you can do better, fucking well come up here and fucking well do so.'*[50]

A sudden, intense silence falls across all of the leading troops, about a hundred strong. Did they just hear what they thought they had heard? They did. No-one is more appalled than Stahl himself, as he braces for the blast to come, which will surely precede a court martial. But all that can be heard right now is the continuing shuffling of feet of men tottering as they teeter, awaiting the same thing.

The seconds drag by like minutes, until almost as one, they all realise no blast is coming, and the men start talking among themselves again, as before, albeit with a certain muffled if excited jabber about what had just happened.

26 April 1943, Hintok, like thieves in the night

New quarters for new men are springing up now, 10 tents that will have to do until more huts can be made. The tents are not big, but there will still be 20 to a tent. Yes, it will be uncomfortable, but malaria is no picnic either, so stay strong and bear it, that's an order. Weary is told by the Black Prince that 9000 British troops will be passing through soon, stopping for one day and one night only. This camp is turning into a way station, if they charged for admission they could make a fortune. In camp, 20 extra soldiers are to be allowed a break from the railway to operate a temporary mess. Well, take small mercies as you find them.

A smaller number of Dutch now totter into camp. They will be here until 2200 hours, when they will be marching to the next camp, then the next. Weary tells them news of their comrades; they tell him in turn news that he can already guess. They have received 'unnecessarily harsh treatment from the escort. This seemed to be officially inspired these days.'[51]

There is something particularly perverse in the treatment of the Dutch; as though the new occupying power is determined to crush the old one in these lands; a ringing out of the past that is thorough, cruel and calculated.

The way station has troops going through it so fast that Weary barely has time to record who the visitors are; but some of the temporary men leave with a little bit extra: 'The theft of blankets, food and such articles as haversacks, packs, trinkets, etc, has increased alarmingly with these transit parties.'[52]

Now what's the etiquette? Can one guard one's fellow prisoners? Weary is amused when one visiting officer, Colonel Stitt of the 7th Battalion, is told of the pilfering.

'These Manchesters,'[53] he sighs. There is no need to round up the usual suspects, he will visit his Manchester men and get what he can back.

Doctor Death comes to camp today to arrange a departure. The Japanese need an Australian medical officer for the Kanchanaburi

Base Hospital. It can't be Weary, so who will it be? The doctors discuss it briefly amongst themselves and a hard decision is made: it will be Major Moon. 'This is a serious loss as Arthur has done magnificent work with the sick and is one of the most thorough, loyal and capable souls living.'[54]

There is no time for long speeches or emotional farewells, just a handshake, a salute and Arthur is gone. It is only the next day that Weary learns that Major Moon has left with absolutely no money in his pockets. He is due two months back pay that has not arrived and didn't think it good form to bring it up! Weary will send Lieutenant Smedley after him to Konyu, to get supplies and place a small wad of money in the hand of, 'that wretch, Arthur'.[55]

Being noble is very fine, but being broke is dangerous in a new post.

Moon will be missed and not just for the expertise and energy of his medical ministrations. For he has also proven to be an Albert Einstein of innovation, concocting solutions for every medical problem others can't solve, including blood transfusions for the anaemic as Weary would recount.

'Using soldiers trained as technicians . . . transfusions were carried out by simply collecting the blood of a suitable donor into a container while stirring continuously with a spatula or whisk.'

Whisks? Frayed, so. For, yes, after a lot of trial and error to get it right, Moon had demonstrated that by stirring frayed bamboo strands of just the right length and thickness, the tiny clots attach themselves to the strands and can easily be removed:

> Vigorous stirring was carried on for five minutes after clotting commenced on the spatula. The blood was then filtered through sixteen layers of gauze, and administered. Much help in the preparation of drugs and chemicals was given to medical officers by chemists, botanists, and scientists . . . [56]

No wonder it is so painful to see the Moon setting off.

Ah, but such innovations don't stop in his wake, they continue. For once Weary becomes aware of an issue of cross-infection resulting from surgical instruments being insufficiently sterilised, his men come up with the answer, as he will note, using 'small portable sterilizers, made from the mess-tins of dead men and heated by charcoal stoves devised from biscuit tins and mud . . . The steep fall in mortality at this stage was most gratifying.'[57]

Meanwhile, some of the Dunlop Force chemists are also experimenting with making anaesthetic from a combination of sulphuric acid taken from truck batteries, and alcohol distilled from fermented rice.

29 April 1943, Hintok, murder by prescription
Changey, changey.

'It is ordered that officers move to a new site. I discussed this with the Lizard and a few concessions were obtained.'[58]

These include not moving until these masses of troops stop moving through. It is madness at the moment. Weary is treating over 100 individual patients every morning; then he is off to the railway to minister to those who collapse from sickness and exhaustion, before coming back for fresh illnesses: 'Thus I am working all day and fitting in administration at odd moments.'[59]

There is a little bit of rest today, in honour of Hirohito: 'Today being the anniversary of the accession of the Emperor to the throne, it was deemed a half *yasume* and men were back from work early.'

Oh, but one more thing.

'We were also informed that 40 men were to work at night tomorrow.'[60]

It is not going to make them into Imperialists, or Japanese ones anyway. There is larger relief on the horizon for Weary, and that, blessedly, is the chance of being relieved of command.

For a new man is in camp, a senior one. Lieutenant Colonel Cranston McEachern is just 37 years old but he has had that senior rank for seven years standing, which means the burdens of office will fall to him over Weary.

But, and there always seems to be one these days, McEachern 'will not take over command of this camp'[61] until the question of his final placement by the Japanese. If he is to stay here, he will command. But if he is in any kind of transit, even one that is delayed, he thinks that the rule of Weary should not be disrupted.

Disrupted? Oh, to be so lucky, and, as his 'light' night rounds are done, Weary can only dream of a future where he will actually have time to sleep.

•

Constantly sending 'light sick' and 'heavy sick' men out to work, no matter the effect it has on them, really is 'the next thing to murder'.[62]

The next thing for Weary? *Murder*. There is no other way.

Day by day, the Lizard torments him and his men, displaying no humanity at all, not the slightest trace of decency, and on this day something inside of Weary snaps and a red mist rises.

And even though Thou Shalt Not Kill is not only a commandment, but also the heart of the Hippocratic oath . . . maybe there's a loophole? Surely exception can be made when the person in question is a 'proper little bastard' who daily sends sick men to work that is killing them, and desperately deserves death himself? How many Australians will have to die and be beaten before somebody does something to stop him?

Weary has come to the secret conclusion that *he* is that somebody. And yes, it goes against everything he has insisted upon from his men – about the need to always demonstrate self-discipline, and never over-react – but . . . by ending the Lizard's life, he will save Australian lives. It is as simple as that.

Nobody else will be told of the plan; it will be Weary's murder alone.

And look, as murder plots go, it is not going to make Agatha Christie shake her head in wonder at its cleverness. Hearing that the Lizard must soon depart to take a message to Konyu, Weary's plan is to wait out in the jungle, hidden in a site the Lizard must walk past, just a little way away from the entrance to camp, and beat his head in. With a spade or a rock? No, he has something better: a waddy he had carefully fashioned from a rare piece of hardwood, with a big, iron-hard knob on the end of it.

He will bash the Lizard to death and drag the body so far into the jungle that the animals will eat most of it before it can be found. Yes, there is a chance the Japanese will discover the Lizard has been murdered, and the repercussions on them all would be savage – but they can hardly be worse than what the Lizard is doing to them now.

Weary is resolute. Men are suffering beyond all redemption for this bastard's sheer callous cruelty and it must be stopped.

Carefully, quietly, Weary secretes the waddy in his trouser leg and begins to stroll out of the camp as night falls, behind the departing Lizard, who has both a torch and a rifle with him.

If all goes well, Weary intends to launch his attack just around yonder bend in the track, well away from the camp. The sweat pouring out of him right now is not just from the heat.

He's going to beat this bastard to death and . . .

And what now?

A distant voice crackles from the loudspeaker that is occasionally used at the camp.

'*Captain Dunrop report . . . office . . . meet Major Usuki.*

'*Captain Dunrop report . . . office . . . meet Major Usuki.*'[63]

That voice is not going to stop and if he is not at the camp office soon, well . . . murder must wait.

Weary returns, and leaves the Lizard behind, loping ahead, his torch bobbing about like a giant fire-fly in the night.

Oh, how close Weary came.

For now, sanity floods back. It was a *mad* idea all along. Lovely to think about though, and to plan. But how exactly would you get rid of the body? Now, *there* is a medical question they don't ask you at university. And what would have happened, had they found the dead Lizard and worked out that he must have been killed at the exact time Weary had not turned up at the meeting with the Black Prince?

Weary knows: he would not have made sundown of the next day. And how many POWs would have been killed in retaliation? How many more would die for lack of his own medical ministrations?

What had he been *thinking*?

The red mist of rage dissipates, sanity prevails, and Weary vows not to think such things again.

And what exactly is it you want, Lieutenant Usuki?

Weary is not long in finding out.

Speedo! *Speedo!* SPEEDO!

Previously, the word has been used in the immediate sense. Now, Usuki uses it structurally. *Everything* has to speed up! The men will have to start earlier, finish later, penetrate more deeply, and shift even more rubble to the embankments – with no more *yasume* days! And yes, the Japanese will bring in yet more workers, including another 600 POWs, from H Force – a mix of British and Australians – and another thousand coolies, working in the vicinity of Konyu Cutting. But that still won't be enough.

From now on, the Black Prince tells him, 'for every sick man that dies, the percentage who must work will be increased'.[64]

He means it. The pool from which they are drawing the working men might have fallen from 800 to 600, but the Japanese still demand 500 to report for work on the morrow, come what may.

It is as absurd as it is outrageous, something that Weary points out, but it makes no difference.

Doing their calculations, the Japanese engineers have realised they won't meet the target set for them by their Army commanders unless everything is *speedo*-ed up, by everyone, and so Weary's men will have to work harder.

This is *urgent*. Those laying the Line will soon be arriving at this point, allowing the far easier transfer of workers and resources. And if it is not done in time, 'Hellfire Pass', as the longer cutting has become known for the simple reason that it is ever and always a hellish inferno, will be the bottleneck of the whole line, bringing shame on Lieutenant Hirota, who has been put in charge of getting it *done*, come what may. So, look, if they lose more POWs because of it, that is no great loss. As the POWs are, by definition, men who have previously surrendered, what are their lives worth anyway?

The barked commands, thus, now never stop: '*Speedo! Speedo!* SPEEDO!'

The initial target darg the men had been given of penetrating the cutting at just 80 centimetres a day had gone to 1 metre, then to 1.2 and then they had to push through the mountain at 1.4 metres a day! And the blokes on the *tankas* must shift more than a staggering – literally – 2.5 cubic metres a day.

And in fact, along the Line, it is not just blokes. Among the thousands of coolies that have been brought in are women. One Australian POW, Bob Christie of the 2/29th Battalion, will recount working with a Tamil woman who was not only heavily pregnant, but suddenly in labour. Christie's Sergeant, Clive Boan, helps to deliver the baby, whereupon she puts the little one in a piece of cloth wrapped around her back, and returns to work! Filled with compassion, Christie lightens her load by not completely filling her *tanka*, and continues to do so for some time. 'But the Black Prince . . . he saw what was going on, and did he go to town – he ranted and roared. When I resumed working, I had to put more dirt in the basket.'[65]

On the next return trip the woman gives him a betel nut and softly says '*Thank you*.'[66]

No matter how hard any of them work now, even when they reach their darg, they are told they must keep going. *Speedo!*

The only way they can do it is to drill the holes deeper before the dynamite is pushed into them to blow it. And working ever longer hours. Yes, they will have to push the only men left standing harder and longer than ever, while also bringing in whatever fresh POWs they can secure to replace those who fall.

So now, instead of the day finishing at dusk, work goes on and that initial foray into the night now becomes permanent, courtesy of oil lamps and bamboo 'tiger fires' that must be endlessly fed and stoked by glistening dark figures trying to dodge the smoke and sparks, while keeping an eye out for stalking tigers; tigers, burning bright, looking for dinner. Often, they can hear terrifying tiger roars in the near distance. By this flickering light, and that horrifying sound, the ghost-like figures of the exhausted, emaciated men continue the hammer and tap process, just as – *fire in the hole!* – the dynamiting goes on, and the blasted debris is cleared away by the staggering POWs shuffling away into the gloom. Those shuffling too slowly for the liking of the guards are regularly beaten with bamboo sticks.

Into this Stygian mixture of darkness, dust, blasting and wretched wraiths, wanders Weary – as often as he can get away from his other medical rounds. Shouting above the noise of the hammers, the curses, the blasts, he remonstrates with the guards, offers comfort where he can, and attends to recent wounds from falls, slips and general misadventure.

He tends the sick and helps them back to *campo*.

One Line survivor will recount heading back at the end of a 16-hour shift to see Weary ahead, climbing the shatteringly steep steps now cut into the hill, and badly struggling for the fact he has a sick Digger on his back.

'I'll help you, sir!' a voice rings out.

'No, you won't!' Weary barks back over his shoulder. 'Go get one of your bloody own.'[67]

All up, though?

All up, in the age of '*speedo*', at a time when the sustenance the men are given and can secure themselves is not remotely close to sufficient to sustain the work they are doing, there is little that can be done. The Japanese are, literally, working these men to death.

Watching the Black Prince, Usuki, swaggering about like a man delivered on a sunbeam by God among the darkest and lowliest of his peasants, Weary can't help but reflect that it is the tragedy of war that such a lowly man as this should be able to have presumptions of such grandeur.

In the happiest of distractions, courtesy of the Red Cross, a bag of mail arrives from home.

Oh, letters, pray!

True, the messages are not always everything the men hope they would be, and Weary records two extraordinary missives in his diary that the camp is talking about:

'*You will be surprised to hear no doubt, my dear, that I have adopted a dear little two-month-old baby – I know you will love it.*'[68]

No doubt. (But he will also ask the neighbours if they might have noticed his wife putting on a *remarkable* amount of weight, just prior to adopting the bub?) The second is even more fabulous: '*When you come home, you will have to call me mother, as I just couldn't wait and have married your father.*'[69]

Some of them are, true, from remarkably close families, but this is ridiculous.

Back to work.

As May gets a grip, those men deemed to be 'light sick' now find that the special red tab they have been given to mark them out acts like a red rag to their bullying captors: 'The local Nipponese work them like hell all day with very little rest and just completely knock them out, so they even request to be changed to the railway where the overseers at least have some sense.'[70]

When you are requesting to be transferred to the Line, you know some things have gone very wrong. Very furious is Doctor Death Okada today, he wants 30 men discharged for work, Weary says he can only have 15. The argument is familiar to both but it is conducted with such fury today that Weary shakes with rage, and it takes the soothing words of the more diplomatic of his NCOs, Sergeant Brian Harrison-Lucas, to intervene and stop the yelling, as he tells Okada just this: 'No. 1 has personally gone into the question and it is really and truthfully impossible.'[71]

A pause.

'Okay. Fifteen,' replies Okada. All that for just where they started; what is the point of this? Fear. A disgusted Weary records his contempt in his diary for this 'Nippon unpredictability' and 'brutality to the sick'.[72]

It is outrageous, disgusting, appalling behaviour. But as this punk Japanese corporal is his 'immediate medical superior',[73] Weary has no choice but to obey his orders – despite the fact that by now Weary knows Okada has no medical training whatsoever.

And, of course, the workload on the men just keeps getting heavier, as 'drillers must now do 200 centimetres daily instead of 140',[74] or 'rock clearing parties are to be reduced from 35 to 25'[75] while still moving the same amount of rubble!

8 May 1943, Hintok, the Doctor is in

A large, fat old man is eyeing Weary warily.

It is Lieutenant Colonel Ishi of the Japanese Imperial Army and at the request of the always pressing Lieutenant Hirota, he has been brought to inspect the camp. What the old man sees does not please him, particularly all these sick men lying around – most of them 'emaciated dysentery cases massed in tents'[76] – and he lets the nervously hovering Okada know in no uncertain terms. Ishi is the Commandant of Konyu and clearly thinks this title places him in charge of everything, including physics and disease. After wandering the hospital with a gimlet eye that frequently flashes fury, Ishi pauses long enough in berating Doctor Death Okada to finally talk to Weary about what treatment he is giving the patients to get them up and moving.

'No drugs have been made available by your people, not even magnesium sulphate. Therefore, the only possible alternative treatment is by starvation and fluids.'[77]

'How long no food?'[78]

'Usually, two to three days. Sometimes longer, depending on progress.'[79]

Ishi shakes his head in complete disgust.

'Must always give,' he intones, based on no medical training whatsoever, 'no food for one week!'[80]

Brilliant. Why had he not thought of that himself?

Weary is bemused by this 'great contribution to the medical problem!'.[81]

Ishi is full of such advice for every man in authority, particularly including Corporal Okada – though in his case the advice is barked in the manner of an angry dog to a puppy trying not to whimper.

The Corporal is so annoyed that as Ishi's car departs Okada throws a tin of water against the bamboo fence that lines the departure route. There is losing face and then there is losing your bloody block and this is both.

One of the Diggers who has learnt basic Japanese now approaches Weary and tells him some detail of what he had heard Ishi say to Okada, that bit of what-for that would have peeled paint if this camp actually had any. The guts of it is as plain as dogs' balls: the old bastard is pissed off by what he has seen, and they are about to suffer the consequences. Okada sends for Weary and paces up and down furiously before speaking in the same manner.

'You will find seven hundred men for outside work tomorrow,'[82] he orders Weary.

'HOW?' Weary barks back.

('So loudly that both Okada and the interpreter jumped in their chairs.')[83]

They aren't the only ones jumping as Lieutenant Colonel McEachern swiftly arrives to cool tempers. The numbers are negotiated and when it is all over a disgusted Weary is 'forced to discharge 17 men regarded as unfit'.[84]

It is the lesser of 700 evils, but it still stinks to high heaven. The meeting with Doctor Death, ends on a note of farce: 'Six pigs arrived today.'[85]

So?

'Therefore, fifty men better tomorrow!'[86]

Weary will not have it.

Using the walking stick he has lately been forced to use to compensate for a particularly painful ulcer on his leg, the massive medico draws the Christian cross of crucifixion on the ground, and points to the small cemetery they have, which is nevertheless rapidly expanding nearby, and says quietly: 'You murderer Okada. When I go back to Australia I tell them so.'[87]

Translate *that*!

Until that time comes, Weary must work out ways to keep as many men alive as possible, and so must go through his wards, assessing just which of his hundreds of patients might be able to withstand it.

'Could you battle on today, son?' he asks one after another, day after day, to sick man after sick man, but there is no choice. 'I'll give you a spell to-night.'[88]

They would groan, but inevitably say yes. In Weary, they trust.

And there is another trick Weary uses when the Japanese demand he provides 50 men from the hospital on the morrow at dawn, no matter what.

> Often at night he would smuggle 25 worn-out, but not sick, men into hospital as soon as they returned from work, so that next morning when he had to provide 25 men he could send them out and thus save the sick from going to certain death.[89]

Finally, at sick parade the next day, as the Japanese personally survey those who Weary says are too ill to work, the wilting men of Dunlop Force must follow their Messiah medico's strict instructions.

'Whatever the Japs do, sit still on the teak log, don't stand up.'[90]

And so as the men stagger out of the tents to sit on the log they brace themselves. Sure enough, in short order, they have Japanese guards and officers standing over them, roaring '*KURA!*' followed by another flurry of fury, which makes it very difficult not to spring up and stand to attention as they are being told to.

But Weary has forbidden it.

So, now, the denouement.

For Weary himself comes over, and picks up the man being screamed at and, like a baby, carries him over to Okada.

'This man, Nippon?'[91]

Do you really think you're going to get any work out of this fellow anyway, even if you somehow manage to get him *to* the worksite?

'Nine times out of ten,' Ray Parkin would recount, 'he'd let the bloke go. Weary would always take him back and put him on the log. And then he would carry him back to the lines later on just to carry the act through to his full business.'[92]

And all the men know it.

> Always guards demanded more and more of the sick and dying to join the work parties on their sacred railway to Burma, and always Weary Dunlop, quiet voiced, argued and protested and stood up against Japanese might, and we came to know that he was permanent, unchanging, devoted to his duty as senior medical officer and our leader.[93]

Often, he is slapped or punched for his trouble, but always he rolls with the blows, his legs apart and evenly balanced, just like the boxer he used to be – and he *always* resists the temptation to snap his abusers like twigs in two seconds, even though they desperately deserve it.

His legend grows.

Others, alas, cannot contain themselves.

Another POW – who reacted to being hit by a Japanese guard, by giving him the smack in the chops he so desperately deserved, by return serve – is, in the familiar torture, obliged to kneel with a bamboo pole behind his knees, but with two additions. The first is another bamboo pole across his shoulders, across which his arms are bound, in the manner of Christ on the cross.

The second is a sharpened bamboo stake that digs into his flesh just back from his chin. If he weakens, he dies.

Every hour, the padre pleads for his release. But to no avail.

'The man was later strung up by the neck for a slow death, which took 48 hours.'[94]

•

The view that sick men should not eat has spread to the Japanese and Korean guards. On this day Ray Parkin is working with a skinny young bloke by the name of Colin who is so suffering with a severe fever that his work is trailing off. When a Japanese guard grabs him and shakes him, it is all Colin can do to gurgle out, '*Byoki*', he is sick.

'So,' Parkin recounts, 'the Jap led him away to stoke a huge fire like a blast furnace. At 1 pm, *makan* was called. Colin came over to get his rice, but the Jap bashed him back to the fire yelling, "Sick man no-eat! *Bakaeroo!*" [*Idiot!*] So Colin stoked until we went back to camp. I helped him home, and into hospital.'[95]

These days, the distinction between the hospital and the regular tents is ever less. Everyone is sick, suffering – and working.

•

Christ Almighty.

On this day, Tom Uren and two of his mates have been selected to go, under heavily armed guard, up to a Thai settlement near Kinsayok – the camp, 10 miles north of Hintok – and to bring back some 90 head of cattle, which will become part of the food reserve for the POWs. But while this would be a hard enough job for a dozen healthy men on flat country in the dry, for three weakened men in this kind of country, in the wet season, it is very close to impossible. And it is little better for the terrified, exhausted cattle, emitting endless groans as they fall and try to make their way along barely discernible bog-ridden paths.

With a single pause, the animals are viciously beaten by the Australian soldiers to get them moving again. Tom Uren is not a cruel man, except for today as necessity drives him and he shocks himself. That is until he glances down to see a sight that makes him and his desperate drovers seem benevolent. It is the unearthly remains of Tamils and Thais, left to die by the road, maggots crawling out of their skulls, out of their testicles; their grave the open air and their corpses toys for the passing troops.

What is worse, and absolutely disgusting, is the schoolboy-ish glee with which the Japanese soldiers use sticks and poles to push skulls away from corpses and shout with joy as they roll away spilling yet more maggots and sometimes teeth as they bounce down the hill.

Jesus.

Pushing onwards, at one point the men and beasts cross a river and on the other side is a Thai man, clearly near death, just sitting there, with a groundsheet over him. Quietly using his last breaths on earth to smoke a pipe, he is simply sitting there, puffing away, and awaiting death. There is something about his calm that Uren finds profoundly moving.

No sooner have they finally arrived back at Hintok with the 90 head of cattle than Dunlop Force's best butcher, Private Jack Prescott, takes the herd in hand and selects from it the best bullock to slaughter, to make the men some rare and precious stew for that night. Quietly, however – and recognising that the health of the men most depends on the health of their Commanding Officer – he sets aside a prime cut of beef, covers it up, and surreptitiously takes it to Weary.

'Colonel,' he tells him, 'you'll eat well tonight. I've got you fillet steaks.'

Knowing the gesture comes from a good motivation, Weary Dunlop is not angry, but is firm.

'Jack,' he replies, 'you go back and put it in the stew the same as the rest of the men.'[96]

Case closed. In Weary's world, even the idea of officers getting better treatment than the men they command, merely because they are officers, is completely repugnant. They are in this together. They will survive together, or die together.

Prescott returns to the cookhouse and continues preparing the evening meal of stew for the men – with Weary's prime fillet steaks now added to the mix.

All Prescott had had to do was pick them up from where they had been laid out in the sun to dry, knock the maggots off, and throw them all in together.

9–10 May 1943, Hintok, changing of the guard

It is done quickly and quietly, with no argument. From now on, Weary announces to his senior officers, Lieutenant Colonel Cranston McEachern will take over as camp commander.

'McEachern was in no way anxious to take over,' Weary records, 'but I made it clear that I was now too busy with medical work to carry on efficiently with administrative work.'[97]

It frees the medico for the far more important quagmires to deal with at the moment. For instance, tomorrow there is going to be a pantomime. A Japanese General is to visit camp, and Okada would like 40 men to pretend to be well. What? Oh yes, it would be lovely if Weary could declare 40 sick men 'well', they will be marched out of camp, just out of sight, just until the General leaves, and then they can go back to bed.

'I give you my solemn promise they will not be worked,'[98] says Doctor Death. Hmmm.

'We do not trust any Nipponese word in the least, but there is nothing to do but comply.'[99]

Weary tells the 40 men that if they are made to work, in any way, they must collapse at once. (This is unlikely to strain your thespian talents.)

The next day the farce is on again: 'a day of terrific "twit" and window dressing'.[100]

Here comes the head Twit now, Doctor Death, who toddles around nervously like a schoolboy about to be caught cheating on an exam. Real work has been done to set up a new Japanese HQ in the camp, as well as a new guardhouse and new fences.

A bugle blows and there is momentary Japanese excitement as a car is spotted, but it is just Lieutenant Colonel Ishi bringing in a lorry load of fresh vegetables to make it look as though the camp is properly supplied.

Finally, to the sound of more botched bugling, the General Officer Commanding all POWs in Thailand, Major General Sassa of the Imperial Japanese Army, arrives on an inspection of all kitchens, hospitals, waterworks and, finally . . . the POWs themselves, lined up for his benefit. Let's start with a typical POW having lunch. The soldier is eating an egg, which is very lucky as it is among the precious few eggs in camp at the moment. After the men finish their real lunches, it is time to parade and salute Sassa.

Major General, we hardly knew ye and you certainly have no idea about us.

It is hard not to laugh, but the laughter stops later that day when '29 of the sick returned, terribly exhausted after a hell of a day'.[101]

The word of Okada means nothing. Oh, they were worked, they had to roll 500-pound oil drums, three or four men per drum, kilometre after kilometre to a compressor plant. This was done on a narrow mountain track, and they were told that if the drums rolled off the track and down the mountain, they would have to get them up again. Then they were left to walk four kilometres back to camp, despite lorries being present. Weary needs to create new words to express what he feels:

> These were sick men, most of them covered with huge sores and many weakened by fever and various illnesses. This is the most horrible thing I have seen done as yet, apart from their executions.[102]

It is beyond comprehension, feeling, hope and him. 'The most primitive of races would scarcely treat sick and starving dogs in this fashion.'[103]

And for what? For Major General Sassa not to see? What is the point? Face. It is a topsy-turvydom that refuses to be undone.

At least the following day brings good news from the radio: 'North Africa is cleaned up, Bizerta to the Americans, Tunisia to the British.'[104]

Roll on boys, you are needed here; while we are still here.

But the Japanese have news of their own.

From now on, all the men in hospital are to get only *nine* ounces of rice a day, while those who work are to get 11 ounces – about half of their original allotment in Thailand. If their illness does not kill them, slow starvation will. Staggeringly, the Japanese are issuing rations according to the collective weight of the POWs, who they weigh every month, and so they have reduced rations accordingly.

And yes, under such circumstances, the constant birdsong of the jungle can at least be pleasant to listen to, but a frustration for many of the POWs is that so many of those birds would have nests with the very eggs that would keep them alive – if only the POWs had the wherewithal to secure them.

10 May 1943, Hintok, presento tense

Don't you trust me? No, none of them trust anything a Japanese officer says anymore. They could say 'Good morning' and you'd have to look carefully three times to see if the sun was up. This makes any kind of negotiation difficult, especially industrial relations, but there is always someone ready to give it a go and pull the other one. Today, the brute engineer, Lieutenant Eiji Hirota, approaches a group of Aussie drillers and puts a proposition to them: if you can drill 160 centimetres in one day, you will get two days *yasume*. A two-day holiday for one day's drill? They gaze at him sceptically.

'Me no lie,' says Hirota. 'Speak truth. One hundred and sixty centimetres, get two-day *yasume*!'[105]

Deal. Weary is dismayed to learn that the fools have taken such bait: 'Of course, these goats then drilled the extra 20 cm in about the same time.'[106] Aha! So, the Australians *can* drill that fast, if they want to! No, they can't as Weary knows: 'A few fit and experienced drillers can do this, but it will soon become the standard *"presento"* practice.'[107]

Yes, the weak and ill will be expected to perform as well and as fast as the fit and the strong at their fastest, each and every day. And don't say it's impossible, for Hirota has seen it done. For his part, Okada makes it clear that he completely agrees with his superior's assessment. On this evening, 'inflamed with drink',[108] he slams a knife into the table and roars, 'More!'[109]

More what?

Men. Give him more of these malingerers who claim to be sick, when they actually can work.

How many malingerers would he like? Well, tomorrow: 'a party of seventeen men, including three pneumatic drillers, three cooks and one batman'[110] will be needed to serve at a nascent camp 'at the compressor site by the river'.[111]

Very well, they will be there.

12 May 1943, Hintok, cattle call

Malaria, damn it.

Weary confirms his own self-diagnosis today, he has 'definite malaria with a temperature of 103 F, a feeling of malaise and weakness of the back, my spleen feeling full and obviously palpable'.[112]

Not that the men will know it. Weary doses himself with quinine, refuses to go to 'bed' as long as he is needed standing. (In any case, when it comes to his 'bed', he doesn't 'feel enamoured of my bamboo horror anyway'.[113])

Best to get your mind off it with 'the great cow scoop'.[114]

The what? Well, by hook and mostly by crook, the Australians have just finagled themselves some cattle: 'We now have quite a ranch with 52 cattle skeletons and six small pigs delivered by the Nipponese after the general's visit.'[115]

Major Greiner, Captain Piper and Major Woods supervise a stockyard, built of course with bamboo, and the entertainment for today is provided by listening to tips from the guards on how to care for cattle.

Weary's fever might break, but the fever dream of ceaseless requests continues.

'Okada now screaming for the figure to be reduced for sick again. Seven hundred men to go to work.'[116]

The irony that the man in charge of discharging them has malaria is lost on all bar one – Weary himself.

13 May 1943, Hintok, guarding the guards

A postcard.

So difficult to sum up what you want to say in just a few meagre words. Luckily, the Japanese are here to help: 'very stringent orders re filling in: no date, address to be No. 4, POW Camp, Thailand, officers to delete all reference to working or pay, the card to be addressed to someone of the same name as the sender'.[117]

So, 'Dear Same Name, The weather is fine. Wish you were here, non-specifically yours, Sender.' Their families will think they are very cold and brief correspondents, but it's better than nothing.

One thing they would love to write about but can't is the scandal engulfing their guards today. It seems that a group of the guards 'stole a portion of their issue meat from their store and were cooking it in our kitchen late last night when discovered by the [Kempis]'.[118]

The result is half-rations for all guards, and, what is more, the Australians have the rare joy of watching their mostly Korean tormentors enduring: 'an absolute spate of drill tonight under Usuki, with a great deal of standing to attention and running'.[119]

It is saddening to report that they hear 'angry voices raised all day presumably telling them that they are scum!'.[120]

(Copping most of it, happily, is the Lizard himself, judged not up to the task of getting the necessary work out of the POWs, and he will no longer be presiding at the daily work parade. From now, it will be, as Weary notes, Doctor Death himself, Okada, who becomes the 'No. 1 menace around the place, continually insisting on more men being discharged from hospital who are unfit. He is very moody.'[121])

As evening falls, a group of 500 Thai, Chinese and Malay coolies arrive to use the camp's showers. These poor souls are being 'quartered' just outside the camp and Weary and co. are forbidden to speak to them. So they speak to them, and find out that the coolies are rather unhappy because they haven't received any pay yet! They are working on the railway, cutting timber and they have been promised, in the local currency, four baht a day – the equivalent of about 50 pence in Australian currency. Really? The Australians are getting only a quarter of that – enough to buy a coconut.

Frustratingly, Australian and British voices can be heard tonight, the sound drifting into camp, but their owners can't be seen. Prisoners in transit surely, but why can't they meet or greet them? Five hundred foreigners can wander through and bathe, but their own countrymen are kept from them. Is it paranoia from the Japanese, or just another example of their spectacular lack of care?

14 May 1943, Hintok, malaria area

Weary feels so crook he could be Al Capone, but he still has to do the rounds and today they stretch beyond the usual and all the way to Konyu – as he must check on the health of a Major Marsden. A long walk and a quick examination confirms the obvious: Marsden will live, and is in better shape than Weary, who now feels as sick as two dogs. And now he must walk another four miles in the heat to see a Captain Millard and correct a fatal diagnosis or two: 'He has been under the impression that most of his fevers were dengue, an excusable mistake, although of course they are malaria.'[122]

About 25 per cent of Millard's men are presently too sick to work. How many of them the Japanese will make work is a different question.

Meanwhile, back at Hintok camp, there are more troops in transit, but these ones enter in style, to the sound of . . . cats fighting? No, actually it's bagpipes, as the Scots are among them.

Weary has arrived back with a temperature of 103 and is near collapse, but is more worried about somebody else: Blue.

'Butterworth has had a severe malaria, followed by severe and persistent diarrhoea and looks a shadow.'[123]

Yea, verily, though he now looks like the *Mayor* of the Valley of the Shadow of Death, still he is blustering and defiant. Hell, if Weary is up and walking so is he. Otherwise, what is he here for? Of all things, a hospital unit passes through today, bringing supplies from the distant town of Bampong. They have enough anaesthetic to share but: 'No amount of talk of my wretched state induced them to give me anything.'[124]

Cheers.

On the morrow, Weary gets the word.

Boon Pong's barge has arrived, and Boon has passed a message that, buried beneath the potatoes, they will find the precious vials of emetine Weary has requested.

Usually, the way of such things is for Weary to wait for such drugs to be uncovered and delivered to him, but on this occasion, he simply can't wait, damn the risks. Not running outright, but walking fast, he intercepts those carrying the consignment, looks around to make sure he is not being too closely observed, quickly secures the drugs, signs the receipt that Boon Pong – God bless his cotton socks – has requested, and is gone.

•

Cometh the hour, cometh the rain, cometh the wet season. And it hits Dunlop Force in late May.

And yet?

And yet this is not rain like they knew it in the Dandenongs, Deniliquin and Dorrigo. It simply does not consist of so many separate droplets. Rather, as they soon discover, this rain – which on most days starts at around noon and goes for hours – has no drops at all.

Instead it gushes, rather like a tap turned on just above your head. Sometimes as much as 10 inches of rain falls in a single day as part of an average annual rainfall, they find out, of *16 feet*. Yes, that's how these bastards measure rain in these parts, not in inches, but in fucking feet! Buckets of rain from the outside, buckets of sweat from the inside, and such humidity all around that none of it evaporates.

Put together it means that the rags the men now wear are permanently wet, as is everything they have with them, including their '*makan*', meal. When they do make it back to their huts – after work days that are getting ever longer – a veritable river of muck runs through the camp, courtesy of the fact that their ever soggy settlement is indeed hemmed in by hills and mountains that send roaring torrents their way, meaning they are now living in a potentially disease-ridden quagmire.

As to the noise, back in Australia they thought rain on a roof of corrugated iron could make a racket. But here, in this hell-hole, when squall after squall of tropical downpour hits your tent as you try to sleep, it's like being on the inside of a kettle-drum as the Devil himself bashes away with a thousand drumsticks just to give you the shits. It could send a man mad, it could!

•

By now, the track to get to work is so slippery, so treacherous, that bad falls are frequent, and as Tom Uren will note, 'we had no shoes on or anything up there by this time. We strapped rags and all that around our feet, but in the wet season you would slip and your feet would go completely underneath you, and you'd just jar your body down completely.'[125]

Even when you could stay upright, the wetness of the conditions means that much of what is being removed has turned into a sodden mass which sticks fast to the shovel. *Everything* is more exhausting than ever – even eating whatever thinner gruel they are getting. At one point, in a downpour, Ray Parkin has just got back from the Line and has got his own rice for 'dinner' when he looks outside to see one of the biggest blokes on the Line, Tiny O'Neil, who has just got his own rice, but is so exhausted he falls, spilling his precious meal in the mud.

'He cursed and raved like a wharfie,' Parkin will recount, 'and then he broke down. Absolutely broke down.'[126]

It is an appalling scene, but one so emblematic of their common experience right now, Parkin grabs his pencil and quickly begins a sketch, which he entitles, 'Rice in the rain, rain in the rice'.[127]

Despite Tiny fading before his eyes, Tom Uren still considers himself fortunate to be on the hammer and tap crew, where you really can get by if you don't push yourself like Tiny does . . .

'The people who were not so fit were the ones that had to clear the rubble away, and carry it up. And some of those would work 20 hours a day.'[128]

How does a severely over-worked and under-nourished soldier survive in such conditions? Only just, if at all.

And the emotional toll on those trying to care for them, like Weary, is punishing.

'[When] I see men being progressively broken into emaciated, pitiful wrecks, bloated with beri-beri, terribly reduced with pellagra, dysentery and malaria, and covered with disgusting sores,' Weary writes in his diary in the middle of May, 'a searing hate arises in me whenever I see a Nip. Disgusting, deplorable, hateful troop of men – apes. It is a bitter lesson to all of us not to surrender to these beasts while there is still life in one's body. It is squalor and degradation of body and mind. I could never go through it again.'[129]

He prays he has seen the worst of it, and that maybe there are only three months to go.

14 June 1943, Hintok, news of fresh disasters

And so it has come.

In the afternoon, the notably grave Doctor Death Okada passes by to tell them that back at the Konyu camp – now populated by thousands of coolies – there has been a severe outbreak of cholera, and right now 200 men are flooding into the wards, excreting, urinating and hurling from every orifice.

Cholera?

The very word is enough to strike terror into any medico's heart, even those who haven't seen it. For in this game, when the old ones gather to tell their war stories, the very worst are about various outbreaks of cholera they have seen, of how it usually arrives like a crowded steam-train that has gone off the rails, and ploughed straight into a mob of people – about half of whom will die with truly startling rapidity. The Japanese and Korean guards are walking around in masks, terrified of getting any of the faecal spray anywhere near their mouths or noses, and panic reigns supreme. And no, none of the British POWs at the same camp have yet contracted it, but it can only be a matter of time. What worries Weary particularly is the interactions his camp has with Konyu, with some of his own staff there right now. They will have to be particularly vigilant that one of them or some of the coolies coming through don't bring cholera back to Hintok. But, truly? He knows it can only be a matter of time.

In the circumstances, such limited cholera vaccinations as they have are distributed to medical staff. It is against everything he stands for to take one of the vaccinations himself before the most vulnerable, but he knows he must.

While in his whole adult life he has been used to vibrating under the strain as he packs so many things in to every day, now, for the first time, comes some sign that he risks cracking.

Like this day where he had started well before dawn after snatching just a few hours' sleep from the wee hours, and has buried four good men before being called in to help with the latest atrocity from Nippon. This morning, half-a-dozen of those sitting on logs to demonstrate they were unfit for work had been so unmercifully bashed by the Japanese soldiers that one of them, Private Bonzer, had gone into an hysterical fit.

Weary arrives to find the Japanese guards laughing over Bonzer as he continues to shake and dribble, his eyes rolled back.

Something snaps:

> Their laughter so enraged me that I lost nearly all control and advanced on them, calling them every 'cuss' word I ever heard. No doubt the meaning was caught, if not the actual words, and they backed away. I then highhandedly got a stretcher and we carried the lad away.[130]

CHAPTER FOURTEEN

LIFE IN THE AGE OF CHOLERA

Until I saw what Dunlop and Corlette were doing I thought the sort of heroes you read about in storybooks were all my eye. Now I know the blokes they write about are fellows like Dunlop and Corlette. They are the most selfless men who ever lived. They went into the germ-filled cholera compound daily, exposing themselves to deadly infection. They forced our men to keep drinking saline as fast as they could gulp it down. With utter brutality they made the infected men endure the agony.[1]

Private Clarrie Slavin

Dante knew less about infernos than we knew. We could have given him lessons.[2]

Private Donald Stuart

19 June 1943, Hintok, pale riders

It has come. Weary stares at a sick man lying in front of him now. An uneasy group of soldiers are staring at him in turn, wondering just why their evening sick parade has stopped so suddenly.

Private R. H. Harris of S Battalion has just been carried in on an improvised stretcher. His exhausted mates report that while he had worked in the morning, he had showed no interest in lunch, and was so sick afterwards he had been allowed to lie down. In the time since he has been hurling up so much vomit and hurtling so much excrement the poor bastard must be empty.

He certainly looks that way.

After just one glance, Weary feels the cold clutch of fear grip his heart.

Harris is nothing less than *grey*, is clearly totally dehydrated and has next to no pulse.

'Cyanosed, shrunken, "washerwoman's fingers",' Weary records. 'He was speechless, but on questioning indicated severe pains in stomach and cramp in back of legs. Despite his pitiable condition he was quite conscious.'[3]

There is no way around it.

'Diagnosed cholera . . .'[4]

CHOLERA!

Weary barks orders. Get him isolated at once! Stay clear of what he is putting out. Wash your hands.

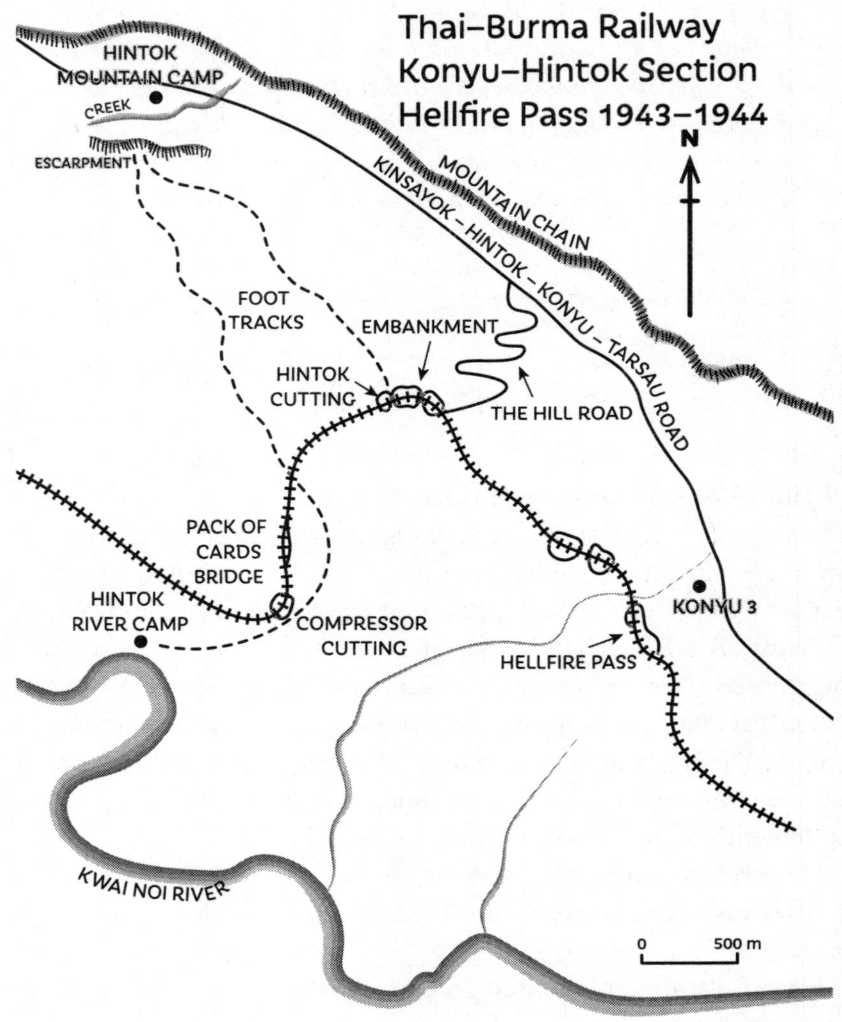

By the time Weary returns to him just 10 minutes later, Harris has already expelled 'a typical rice water stool about one litre and began to sink rapidly'.[5]

With no doubt about the inevitable result and its implications, Weary rushes through the rain to the camp's Japanese HQ – the *kebetei* – where, as ever, 'neath the thick plumes of tobacco smoke, an intense game of mahjong is underway.

Weary only has to say one word, and watch the immediate consternation unfold.

'CHOLERA!'

The mahjong table is not over-turned, but it is close. The Black Prince, Usuki, tries to keep playing the game upon hearing the news, but keeps knocking the pieces over.

He is *shaking*.

'This was the one good thing in the whole affair,' Weary notes. 'I felt like a small boy with a big cracker in the classroom or even an anarchist with a concealed smoking bomb at a WCTU [Woman's Christian Temperance Union] meeting.'[6]

Gathering himself, Lieutenant Usuki calls out, first to himself – 'What to do? What to do?' – and now his underling, right beside him – 'Okada! Okada!'[7]

With rising panic, they ask what Weary needs.

'Disinfectant,' Weary replies. 'Lysol, potassium permanganate, hydronium perchlorate. And drugs to treat cholera. Also, more inoculations of vaccine.'[8]

With a spirit of acquiescence never seen before, let alone this instantly, Doctor Death assures Weary he will send to Tarsau on the morrow for these very things.

What now?

'I would have loved to have yelled "*chorrera*" into the Korean guards' sleeping quarters on my way back,'[9] Weary notes.

Instead, barely sleeping, Weary prepares for what he knows must come.

For just as Private Harris continues his descent, more patients suffering from cholera start to be brought in. When Harris dies before dawn – no more than 10 hours after collapsing – his bedding and personal kit are burnt to ashes before his grisly emaciated form is taken on a bamboo stretcher for burial by his heavily masked mates.

Ray Parkin watches closely as they go: 'six men stumbling and slipping along a path through the bamboo clumps towering like cathedral cloisters above them, dripping green and dark . . . The bearers, muddy soiled individuals themselves, did not curse as normally at a missed footing, but went on silently making a kind of grim awkward progress into the depths of the bamboo cloisters until they were lost from sight – a drab little cortege . . . taking with them a drab, thin little body . . . Half an hour later I heard the notes of the "Last Post" come down the green jungle corridors.'[10]

(They have at least taken the care to bury him *deep*, for fear that, as has sometimes happened, the newly turned earth washes away, and a grisly hand of death is seen emerging, beckoning others to come.)

Weary had not been able to attend, as he is still organising, making sure every officer and all of their men understand what is necessary from here. *No-one*, unless they wish to die, is to drink a single drop of unboiled water, eat from a dixie that has not been sterilised, or even get close to the open wounds on their feet or any of the likely contaminated faeces that now abound all around. In the meantime, Weary gets on with dealing with ever more patients.

All of them have bodies that seem to be expelling the poisoned choleric water in any way they can: excreting, spewing, urinating and sweating, simultaneously and furiously. More deaths come with remarkable rapidity.

Whenever more of them go down with it, while working, the Japanese refuse to either get them back to camp themselves, or to allow their fellow POWs to take them back.

'We'd get a message,' Weary will recall, 'and send out a party over the mountains to get them back.'[11]

Alas, often they are too late and the worst cases are dead before they can get them back.

Before burial, both their anuses and noses are plugged, so that whatever infected fluid they have in them will not immediately leak into the ground water.

Moving quickly, and for once with strong Japanese support, Weary establishes his first cholera ward for the newly sick in a large tent with open sides erected in notably marshy land just below the main camp.

'We called it the arsehole of the camp,' Blue Butterworth will recount. 'It was where all the water came down and made it into a mire of muck and shit.'[12]

It becomes known as 'Cholera Gulch',[13] and with Moon and Corlette by Weary's side – inevitably with Blue Butterworth in support – they all get to work. As the numbers of patients and deaths from this malarial, choleric, dysenteric, beri-beri-ridden, underfed and over-worked slave gang continues to grow, so too does the number of tents pitched in this muddy morass of hell as men cry out in wispy weakness, expel their very souls, and gurgle their last breath.

And yes, of course a thunder-box is installed in the middle of each tent so that the men can excrete, but inevitably few make this catch-as-catch-can can and as the days and nights go by, the muddy floor of each tent beneath their bamboo bunks becomes a 'fouled and stinking'[14] mess.

Weary, now recovered from his malaria, never blinks, and all day and into each night, even as the rain keeps pouring down, ministers to his patients by the ebbing light of the hanging hurricane lamps, with his enormous frame perpetually bent double over each soul – some of them departing – as he goes from one to another.

Truly?

He never seems to sleep, or eat, and it is noticed. A few times, it is noted he has his own tropical ulcers cleaned and treated even while he stays standing, ministering to his patients. He just has no time to do it any other way.

Sadly, despite the many patients that Weary saves, the old carpenter Bob Fox is quickly set a new task to fashion dozens of kapok wood crosses for soldiers' graves – always buried with everything they have touched.

And yet although still more cholera victims keep being rushed in, the Japanese will not relent on requiring workers for the railway. In fact, it is quite the reverse. As the whole workforce is clearly weakening, more weak workers are needed to keep up the output. But the wards keep filling up with more patients, no matter what they do, even as the practice of burying them is abandoned, as the fear increases that the cholera in their bodies will enter the water table. To replace the burials, some of the soldiers, Tasmanian bushmen by trade, establish massive funeral pyres. These piles of old bamboo are set 100 yards away from the camp, to prevent the patients seeing their mates shrouded in rice sacks burning.

(But they are still not far enough away that, at night, when the wind is blowing in the right direction, and God is not in his heaven, one sometimes must try to sleep with the unmistakable smell of your benighted brethren burning. Christ help us all.)

In such extreme times the 'Last Post' is now played just once a week, as it is simply too depressing to have it engulf the camp as often as 10 times *a day*. When the first victims were consigned to ashes, prayers had been said, but the increasing frequency of deaths means it's inevitable that now the most that is often said before the roaring flames is by the two men who are swinging the always remarkably light dead man by either end: 'And one, and two, and . . . on he goes!'

Efficiency is all.

One day when Sergeant Bill Halliday is tending the fires 'neath the canvas that has been jerry-rigged above it to protect it from the rain, his mate Gibbo calls out to stoke the fires up, 'cos another patient has just died. Halliday yells back, plaintively, 'What, only one? There's enough wood for four!'[15]

He will not have to wait long, as the disease continues to rage.

'We could tell within five minutes whether they had cholera,'[16] one of the Diggers, Stan Arneil, notes. 'We would place a bamboo identification disc around their wrists with their regimental number and name on it. Because in four hours it was not possible to recognise a man who had contracted cholera.'[17]

(As to the Japanese, their method of determining whether or not one of their prisoners out in the field has cholera or not is called 'rodding'. Pull down your trousers, or at least move aside the raggedy rags about your loins. Now, bend over, while I do with this bamboo rod what you have been longing to tell us Japanese to do with our Line. If the stool that emerges on the end of the rod is creamy white, you have cholera. If it is brown, probably only dysentery. As you were . . . if a little bow-legged, as if you've spent your life in the saddle, for the next few hours.)

Sergeant Halliday gets more experience than he wants in burning blokes – learning how to first dig a small hollow in which to build the fires so that the body placed on burning logs above it will turn into ashes more quickly from the roaring updraft – and those who join his work quickly have to get used to the shocks, just as he had to at first. The worst is when corpses are thrown on fires already so hellishly hot that it can cause the muscles to instantly contract and bodies are known to suddenly sit up in the flames. When, on one occasion, this is accompanied by the corpse's eyes snapping open, the new pyre tender is not seen for dust!

Still, it is the eyes that close forever that get you.

Ray Parkin will be haunted ever afterwards by coming across a young bloke who is softly sobbing on what is undoubtedly his death-bed, even if that 'bed' is no more than bamboo slats.

'It'll be alright, mate,' Parkin says gently.

'It's not me,' the dying man replies, 'it's Mum.'[18]

Cholera Gulch keeps growing and they have to build more wards to accommodate 100 . . . no . . . 120 . . . no . . . *150* . . . men. The patients are spread out under expanses of canvas, with no sides to stop the rain, and put on bamboo bunks with fewer slats to let them emit more easily – and as Weary records, 'The cases were nursed under leaking rags of tents, in an appalling morass in the jungle.'[19]

Under the feet of the doctors and orderlies as they tend the sick is nowt but a filthy manure of human excretions and expulsions in which they must stand, ankle-deep.

Not for nothing will one of the POWs characterise the whole place at this time as being 'like a cow-yard in winter-time'.[20] Constantly wet, those few blokes who still have boots find them rotting away in days. Tents and remaining clothes also start to fall apart.

With *all* of nature now attacking the Australians, weakening them via sun, rain, disease, insects, animals and their fellow humans – the Japanese and Koreans – it is hard to escape the conclusion that the entire natural world is conspiring to expel the unnatural, starting with a railway being built in these parts in the first place.

Out at Hintok Cutting, the men keep suddenly falling sick.

Tom Uren will never forget it.

'They'd dehydrate and their eyes would go back in their heads. And their temples would sink. They'd go a greyish green colour. They'd age 40 to 50 years in a day. You'd go out to work and . . .'[21]

And by the time you came back, they'd be dead.

'Our friend Freddie is rolling on the ground doubled up with severe stomach cramps,' another Australian will recount, 'his arms and legs twitching and jerking as his muscles seize up. Then his body erupts with vomiting and a violence forced rush of fluid from his bowels, whitish fluid the colour of rice-water.'[22]

When the POW who gets cholera already has beri-beri – meaning his starting point is a bloated body – it is simply extraordinary, as every orifice gushes, all at once. They can go from the Michelin Man to a mere skeleton covered with sagging skin overnight!

The only solution is saline: to replace what is being lost with salty water until the body can flush itself clean. If the patient is not too far gone, it's potable, and Uren would recall with wonder, 'I saw my mate Bill Belford pick up a four-gallon kerosene tin of saline water and drink it . . .'[23]

And yet, day by day it gets worse. At Konyu, they had reached 200 cases of cholera just a few days after the first diagnosis, and it feels like they will soon be well on their way to that here at Hintok, too.

'Hello, not another one,' Blue Butterworth thinks as, day after day, man after man goes down. 'The cholera came, the eyes went back, their voices became like grandma's, they lost weight so quickly, their excreta was like milk and that was it. One minute it didn't look too bad and the next minute, cholera, and gone next day or the day after.'[24]

In desperation to stop the devastation, Weary must again call on the inventiveness that abounds all around in Dunlop Force, and the myriad skills that come from having everything from carpenters to carpet-layers, engineers to engine-drivers, dentists to drivers to divers, and mechanics to musicians in their company. Whatever the need, some or many of them will endeavour to work out the answer, using fencing wire as a stop-gap if necessary. The first challenge is how to force-feed fluids to the afflicted, as many are too far gone to simply drink it. In normal hospital conditions, you'd have an intravenous saline solution, with a needle inserted into a cannula. But here, they will have to adapt.

It is Major Jock Clarke – a dentist – who fashions the first part of a solution, by getting a four-gallon petrol tin filled with water over a fire. Major Billy Wearne manages to convince Doctor Death to allow him to take 'a petrol feed pipe from a Nip lorry'.[25]

And now that copper pipe goes from the sealed tin with boiling water through a large bamboo water jacket – a series of hollow bamboo logs filled with cold water, side-by-side like a radiator, through which the pipe runs – which cools the steam down to condense a thin stream of water into the drum at the other end of the pipe. That water is mixed with salt and put from there into old Japanese wine or beer bottles now closed by corks with hollow bamboo inserted. The tubing that goes to the patients comes from cut up stethoscope tubes.

Now, what can they use for cannulas, to get the water into the men's veins?

Step forward once more, that great old carpenter, Private Bob Fox. Why not try . . . using bamboo? It takes an enormous amount of trial and error, but by taking tiny yet mature shoots, hollowing out the middle and whittling, they are able to get one end to the point, a *finely* sharpened point, that it can be used as a cannula!

Look, there are so many twists and turns in this invention, so many things that could go wrong, you'd reckon it'd be no more reliable than a two-bob watch, but it actually works brilliantly.

In short order there are three stills permanently on the boil, fed by water coming in through bamboo pipes from a nearby spring, and producing some 120 pints a day of saline water for the men and 'these crazy intravenous sets kept 10 or 12 of them going at any one time in appalling conditions'.[26]

Not surprisingly, there is resistance from the first to the painful cannulas.

But, as one Dunlop Force veteran will recall: 'Whenever anyone started to scream with pain they would say, "Don't pull that out. That's your lifeline." If a man couldn't take the pain any longer and pulled out the needle they just grabbed him and bunged it back in again.'[27]

Even then, such saline water as they have is barely enough. In some of the most extreme cases, a single patient could go through as much as 20 pints in just 24 hours.

In another key measure, Weary is quickly insistent that from now on men going out to work will not stand under the miniature waterfall made by the creek tumbling over the ledge. The only water you must come in contact with has to have been boiled, most particularly drinking water. It is with that in mind that another machine is quickly constructed.

'It is an all-bamboo affair,' Ray Parkin will recount, 'a large bamboo at the top with ten spigots in it. The bottles are filled and spigot closed without wasting a drop. A man with a tin of boiled water keeps the large bamboo reservoir topped up as the bottles are filled. There are at least 800 men to fill their bottles after work each night, and the water-boiling party have their work cut out.'[28]

Who builds the bamboo pipes connecting it all together to the creek? Privates Fox and Ward, sometimes supervising other soldiers.

Many further measures are taken.

All raw fruit is banned, as is eating anything uncooked. From now on, all of your dixies and eating implements can only be used after they have been sterilised, and we will set up huge boiling pots for precisely that.

For those caught emptying their bowels away from the latrines, Weary is fierce.

'Look soldier,' he says to one 'if you don't dig a hole to do your shit in, we are in trouble.'[29]

Such is not the way of a British camp that soon springs up on the other side of the creek from them, for, from the first, it is clear that it is not being run for the welfare of *all* the men. The first thing to remark is that the British officers who strut about with their appropriately named 'swagger sticks' have the men laboriously put up all the best tents for . . . the officers. Of the tents that remain, it is the Senior Non-Commissioned Officers – the Warrant Officers, Staff Sergeants and Sergeant Majors – who get the best of them.

'The men got the dregs,' Tom Uren will recount. '[It] was this British tradition.'[30]

The Australians also soon hear that other Pommy traditions are being ruthlessly observed, with officers also getting the best cuts of meat, doing the least amount of work, and are first in line for whatever medical care is required.

Of Henry Lawson's 'Mateship', that spirit which makes men stick together, there is no sign, at least not any between the officers and the soldiers. And with no collective spirit there is no collective discipline – and so they have no such thing as boiled dixies and insistence on clean latrines.

Even when the Pommy soldiers get sick, they are not put in any of the better tents, which could be put aside as a hospital, for the officers fiercely retain them.

'They just had that tendency to look after the few,' one of the men, Tom Young, notes, 'and the rest they didn't worry. Whereas with Weary everything was cooperative. All the money was pooled, everything. No-one got any preferential treatment.'[31]

The inevitable results are tragic to behold.

For in short order, the morning bonfires of the British to burn the dead are twice as big as the Australians', and the ranks of those doing the burning are thinning nearly as fast as the bodies of the soldiers left standing. When the Brits decided on shallow burials as the method of disposal that will take less energy than burning the bodies, sometimes the Australians have to help, after returning from a long day's work.

Day after day, as the Australians make their way to the worksite, they are forced to pass the naked bodies of fallen Brits, lying in the mud. They had collapsed either going to or coming from work, and their bodies stripped of whatever meagre clothes they had, and simply left to rot. Their comrades had no energy to do anything else with their bodies, and the Japanese, no interest.

'Within about six weeks,' Tom Uren will recount, 'only about 50 of those [original 400] men marched out. They'd either died of dysentery or cholera. They got caught in the wet season.'[32]

For Uren, it is a lesson that will stay with him for the rest of his days. 'Only a little stream divided both of us. On one side, the law of the jungle prevailed and on the other side was this collective spirit under Weary.'[33]

And it is that latter spirit – 'a kind of a comradeship, cobberism, whatever you want to call it'[34] – to be cherished, nurtured and grown.

Tom Young agrees, noting, 'Almost everybody was ill, and of course so many people were totally helpless. But the great thing about it, particularly with Australians, was the help that each person helped the other. That was something that sustained me. Everyone helped everybody else.'[35]

•

Yet another tragic contrast with the Australian way is provided by the shanghaied Asian workers, who remain bereft of any leadership.

'Endless streams of wretched coolies from Malaya are plodding their slippery way to the jungle road,' Weary notes in his diary. 'Those who speak English frequently have sad words to say about the recruiting methods the Nipponese used to secure their services. These poor wretches are dying up here in countless thousands.'[36]

Weary is in no doubt what the core problem is, as he will later recount:

> The absolute kernel of survival, is submitting yourself to a discipline. And with good leadership, the survival is enormously enhanced. And the reason why Asiatic coolies perished in scores of 1000s, is that they had no leadership, they had no organisation, it was impossible to achieve and discipline and diverge their circumstances.[37]

And so, their eyes filled with remarkably calm despair, they die . . . in their manner.

One Australian POW will tell of coming across an elderly Tamil coolie standing in the shallows of a creek washing himself, and using silt on his fingertip to clean his teeth. When the Australian tells him that he must stop, as the water is likely infected with cholera and he will die if he catches it, the old man replies with great dignity: 'I know that. But I am doomed to die anyway, and I want to be clean and presentable when that happens.'[38]

The dignified aged one keeps going, and once his teeth are clean, takes out a comb to arrange his thinning grey hair before shaking out his newly cleaned sarong. He will make a neat corpse.

The Australian and his mates press upon him some tobacco, a hard-boiled egg and a couple of limes, which the old man takes reluctantly, on the grounds he can share the gifts with his friends back in camp.

The Digger, stunned by the man's dignity and composure, prays that night to God to help preserve the coolies and all of them.

'God, stay with us. If you know where we are, could we have some indication that you do? Please?'[39]

Alas, alas.

'God didn't answer. I now have no religion. I left it behind.'[40]

And he is not the only one.

In the words of one of his mates, 'No God, who is a loving God, could leave innocent Christians to suffer as we are suffering now.'[41]

He, too, becomes an atheist.

Against that?

Well, against that, the *way* they live could fit into most parables of the Bible, without blinking. In the words of Tom Uren: 'We were following the principle of the strong looking after the weak, the rich looking after the poor, and the young looking after the old . . .'[42]

Yes, they are living a hell on earth . . . while following the principles of heaven.

Ah, sing it, Taffy!

In a night that Uren will never forget, he lies out in the darkness with his mate Taffy Miles, and Taffy softly sings his favourite hymn, his words soaring to the stars above . . .

> *And did those feet in ancient time,*
> *Walk upon England's mountains green:*
> *And was the holy Lamb of God,*
> *On England's pleasant pastures seen!*
>
> *And was Jerusalemmmm builded here,*
> *Among these dark Satanic Mills?*

Uren weeps for the sheer beauty of it.

'It was something out of this world,'[43] he will recall ever afterwards.

•

After a day spent at the hospital, trying to keep men alive who already had no right to be so, Weary Dunlop is completely battered by the deluge of the day. Finally finishing well after dark, he struggles back to camp to find that, although he is too late for the collective evening meal, the ever faithful messman, Lieutenant 'Happy' Houston, has brought him something precious: a plate of dry rice with two – count 'em, TWO – fried duck eggs on top. That amount of protein at once is almost too glorious to contemplate!

Nearly overcome with the emotion of it, 'as strong as if a dear friend had come to deliver them',[44] he decides to take his meal outside to eat it under the trees, to be at one with nature in this act of holy communion with the glory of the world and all that is in her and . . .

And now what?

Across the creek in the British camp he sees two emaciated Tommies doing their best to carry a heavy log while a Japanese guard keeps roaring at them. Wading through the water, they soon pass Weary and, just as they do, happen to collapse right in front of him, their faces in the mud. Rising, wearily, Weary has a few words to the guard and, clearly, has enough grouchy gravitas for the guard to fall away, leaving the starving, beaten Brits in Weary's care.

Which raises a point.

As he speaks to them quietly about their situation, he cannot help realising that, while in his right hand he has a plate of food, glorious food, he is talking to men who will clearly die soon unless they get nutrition. But Happy Houston is all too aware of Colonel Dunlop's disposition on matters like this, and has been keeping an eye on him.

'Now you look here!' Happy shouts at the Tommies in a tone he might use to scare foxes away from the chicken pen. 'We don't get eggs every day, you know! Mostly it's just rice and seaweed soup – same as you. These are the first we have had for a long time. The Colonel would have eaten his by now – only he's working hard in the hospital lines all day. He needs them more than you do. You eat the eggs, Colonel, go on!'[45]

Who knew the Devil could come in such form?

For though he had indeed been about to hand the eggs over, which would be the good and Christian thing to do, it is also true that in terms of the collective health of all POWs, he really does need them more than they do. If Weary dies, or is rendered too weak to work, hundreds will die. He really should eat them.

Rising, Weary goes to his pack and manages to scrape together a few biscuits with some palm sugar on top that the locals call *gula Malacca*, and hands it over to the Tommies. They wolf it down, before returning to their own lines, where their own evening meal awaits.

Weary is desperately disappointed in himself, feeling he has given in to great weakness.

'Then,' he will recount, 'I ate those awful eggs . . . That's the difference between an ordinary fellow and a saint I suppose.'[46]

•

Inevitably, the Japanese demand that the Australians keep up their work production despite the cholera outbreak, which only increases the pressure on those who are sick with anything *else* to go to work, come what may.

At least one part of the problem is the Japanese view that sickness among the POWs is a genuine sign of weakness on their part, a sad example of their complete inability to use willpower to be well again. And Colonel Aketo Nakamura, the senior Japanese commander of the whole Thai–Burma Railway construction, is just the man to put them on notice.

'I am pleased to find in general you are keeping discipline and working diligently,' he writes to them in a frank open letter, '[but] regret to find seriousness in health matter . . . Those who fail to reach objective . . . by lack of health or spirit is considered in Japanese army as most shameful . . . your welfare is guaranteed only by obedience to the order of the Imperial Japanese Army.'[47]

So, get on with it.

Nakamura's acolyte Japanese officers are now empowered to engage in their most brutal instincts.

You, with malaria!

Yes, you, Sergeant Micky Hallam, in your sickbed with enteritis, shaking with severe fever and now shuddering with chills from having malaria, too.

Having collapsed on his way to work, the one-time journalist for the Hobart *Mercury* has dragged himself back to camp and been admitted to one of the regular wards in a severely weakened state. Alas, one of his responsibilities on this day had been to get his work party to Hellfire Pass, all present and accounted for – and they had in fact shown up well short in their *tenko* count. The missing men are discovered still straggling up the trail towards the Line and are accused of shirking not working, or even trying to escape. They, and Hallam, are to be held accountable at day's end.

'キャンプの警備所に報告する！' 'Report to the camp guardhouse.'[48]

In short order Hallam is dragged from the hospital and with the other six ordered to march to the engineer's compound, just a stone's throw from the POW camp, where a big bamboo fire is lit.

All of you must stand to attention until you confess that you were planning on escaping!

When no-one so confesses, the guards line up and take turns to hit each man in the face. When they fall down, they are obliged to stand up so they can be hit again. When they cannot get up, they are kicked. When the hands and feet of the Japanese are too sore to continue in this manner, the guards remove their wooden clogs and hit them with those, before bashing them with 'bamboo sticks, four feet long and 1" in diameter'.[49]

And of course that bastard's bastard, Lieutenant Hirota, the Nippon engineer, doesn't care at all that Hallam is the sickest of the lot. He *orders* Sergeant 'Billy the Pig' and his assistant, 'Mollie the Monk', to give him special attention.

When Hallam insists he is incapable of rising – because he is – he is worked over by the Pig and the Monk and viciously beaten, again and again and again. And now, in front of everybody – bar the only man who might be capable of stopping it, Weary, who is down at Cholera Gulch – Hallam is lifted up by the guards of Nippon and thrown to the ground before they set to, kicking him in the groin, stomach and ribs.

As the brutal bashing goes on, Lieutenant Hirota looks on approvingly.

Work *now*?

Get up, NOW?

It is not that Micky refuses, it is that he is incapable of speaking let alone standing. And it goes on for hours, in front of them all.

Majors Wearne and de Crespigny try to intervene but are driven away with rifles and sticks.

'The orgy went on till nearly midnight,' an official Allied account will run, 'when the victims were carried to their tent more dead than alive.'[50]

Anyone else want to hide from work?

For his part, Hallam, barely conscious, is taken back to the hospital suffering a fever of 103.4 degrees F and dies some days later, with his Cause of Death recorded: 'Contusion to the heart causing cardiac arrest – a result of beating by a Nippon engineer Sgt whilst suffering from malaria on the night of 22nd June 1943.'[51]

Another of those bashed, Private Tuck, loses both his legs through the injuries he receives, and another loses a leg.

'Engineer brutality,' Weary notes in his diary, 'continues without check or abatement.'[52]

Those *bastards*!

As Weary will note, '[Hallam] was slain by these Nipponese sadists more certainly than if they had shot him.'[53]

Only a day later, Hirota strikes again.

When the engineer comes to inspect the work being done by a gang of 'light sick', of which Corporal Cully is in charge, he orders that, 'Instead of gang carrying felled trees up a slope in teams, each man must carry one.'[54]

Corporal Cully cares for his men enough, and is brave enough, to say this is impossible as his men are just not strong enough to do that.

Hirota explodes in rage and seizing a felled sapling – no less than six feet long and four inches thick – brings it down hard on the back of Cully's neck with such force that he is instantly felled. More blows follow.

'His order was then cruelly enforced.'[55]

It is because of such episodes, and uselessly trying to heal men who are now beyond healing, that the hate in Weary's heart near overflows. More than ever, he swears that if he comes out on the winning side of this war, he will do whatever he can to see these bastards are held to account.

In the meantime, with all of Weary's health measures for eliminating exposure to cholera being taken at once, even the number of amputations necessary starts to fall, though for those who do lose a leg, it is again Fox who turns his attention to making the best artificial legs possible. More experimentation reveals that the soft wood kapok tree is ideal for the main trunk, while other wood comes from a variety of such things as clogs, splints and stretchers. For the joints at the knee and ankle, he uses the hinge from the collapsible camp stretchers, while to make the 'bucket' for the stump to fit in, he uses tightly sewn canvas – supported by webbing belts. Before their very eyes, men start to walk again! And no, it is not possible to ever make them see again, but it is *extraordinary* how lifelike an artificial 'eye' made from mahjong pieces can be.

And yet while innovation is marvellous, nothing can beat the basics.

Weary exhorts the men: the only way you can get cholera is orally, so keep masked up. And wash your hands, again and again and again, using the Lysol disinfectant cleanser the Japanese have provided – essentially their only contribution.

'The Japanese showed terror of the disease,' Weary will later note, 'and frequently compelled the patients to be attended in appallingly unsuitable jungle sites with little shelter – in the hope they would die quickly. One notorious case where a cholera sufferer was shot by Japanese order illustrates this attitude.'[56]

Australian measures remain more benign, with Major Corlette repeatedly saying to Blue, 'Listen no smokin' rollin' cigarettes or any old thing because that's the only way you get cholera, through the mouth. And scrub up. Make certain you scrub up,' but in the end Blue gets so sick of scrubbing up with Lysol and not smoking, he says to himself, 'Stuff it. If I'm gonna die I'm gonna die.'[57]

Weary, of course, upbraids Blue for not looking after his own safety, but Blue gives him his own theory: 'I reckon the tobacco saves me from getting cholera.'[58]

Weary is speechless at the stupidity of it, only managing to vigorously shake his head and say 'Oh' in reply, but there is no doubt that Blue is not getting it, and equally no doubt that they would be lost without him – so in the end he lets it go. Smoke away, Blue.

And yet, Weary, too, will make his own mistakes, on one occasion getting so close to the wrong end of a patient at the wrong time that, as Blue will recount, after a sudden internal explosion, Weary's face is covered in the watery excrement. Don't it make his blue eyes brown.

'It was the only time I saw Weary panic,' Blue will recall. 'He crashed about, looking for water. I thought, so you *are* human.'[59]

Against all odds, Weary does not get ill within hours, or even days. Maybe the Japanese are right, for he *wills* himself well. He must stay healthy to be able to help everyone else.

(As it happens, Blue, too, has his fair share of occasions when he is covered from head to toe in the excretions of patients. Yes, the same man who had sworn early in the war that he would not spend the war building shithouses or carrying poop is now living in the former while covered in the latter – but that is simply the way it is.)

Of course, it is not just the cholera patients that take Weary and his fellow doctors' attention.

On this particular day, Major Corlette is sitting in a leaking tent as the monsoonal rain pours down, holding the hand of a young Australian man, just 19 years old, as he dies from a cruel combination of severe dysentery and a haemorrhage. What most aggrieves Corlette is that he knows he could save him if the Japanese had given him even the most basic of medicines, but, no, they have denied him, and with one last death rattle, the lad dies.

'My heart was filled with hatred and I was cursing our captors,' the Gangster will bitterly recount, 'those little yellow bastards who by starvation, brutality and neglect had murdered this boy and many others of his companions.'[60]

It is just another day of disaster in the midst of a litany of the same.

'All the time Dunlop and Corlette had to look after the rest of the sick men in camp,' one Australian will recall, 'but whenever word came down that a boy had been hurt on the line, Dunlop would pack his grip and stride off through the rain and mud to succour him.'[61]

As always, he does so with Blue Butterworth by his side.

Such is the strength of the bond between Blue and 'the boss' that Blue instantly notices if the Colonel disappears from view, even for a short time.

So it is on this particular occasion, when noting his absence, Blue shoots around to the tent Weary is occupying with the Gangster to find . . . the boss is not there, either.

'How you goin', Major?' he asks Corlette.

'Not bad,' Corlette replies, his blue eyes regarding him warily.

With which, Blue blithely pulls back the mosquito net unbidden, saying 'How's the bo—'[62] and stops. For *here* is the boss, Weary, with an earphone in, listening to a makeshift radio with lots of external little batteries, glaring back at him.

'For God's sake, please don't tell anyone,' the Gangster says.

'I won't tell anyone,'[63] Blue assures him.

And he won't.

But at least the news from 'Angus', as the set is still referred to – as opposed to 'Albert', which is the one used in the British camp – is good. The Allies, Weary tells Blue quietly later, have started to fight in the Solomon Islands and under the leadership of General Douglas MacArthur are starting to push the brutes out of the Pacific! If we can just hang on long enough, this war might come to an end and find us still alive . . .

And yet there is also a constant stream of news of newly discovered Japanese atrocities, too, including another massacre, where a couple of dozen Australian Army nurses had been obliged by the Japanese to wade into the waters off Bangka Island, only to be ruthlessly machine-gunned down. There had been talk that one of them might have survived, unconfirmed, but all the rest had been killed.

Hate for the Japanese rises accordingly. As does fear – will that be their own ending, once they are of no further use, and the Line is built?

•

God help them all.

Out on the furthest reaches of the Thai–Burma Railway, the survivors of the forced death march of F Force are only just holding on . . . to life, as after walking four miles just to get to the worksite, they continue to be worked to death hauling heavy teak logs, as long as 14 feet and as thick as eight inches. In the beginning five men would be allocated to each log but, just as is happening with Dunlop Force, their brutal overseers soon insist on doing more with less and they must do the same with just three men – all of whom are becoming progressively weaker. Yes, F Force also has outstanding doctors, and medicos, none finer than the likes of Captain Peter Hendry, Captain Roy Mills and Major Bruce Hunt, who all go well above and beyond the call of duty to keep as many men as possible alive, but they simply do not have the resources, and the situation remains appalling.

When a handful of the desperate POWs decide to make a break for it, and try to get through Burma to India, they are caught and shot.

All this, and of course cholera has hit them, too. And yet without someone like Weary laying down the law on how to proceed, and working tirelessly to keep men alive, all descends into a miasma of misery and mass death.

If not quite leaderless, some sections of F Force are close to it. It will later be claimed by some of the aggrieved members that, while they near starved, Lieutenant Colonel 'Gus' Kappe only got fatter as the months went by.

'He preferred not to have his face slapped by the Japanese,' one account will run, 'and rarely exited his tent. Some officers pooled their extra pay and shared with their men. Kappe took good care of himself with extra food from his officer's allowance. Kappe had even turned over some of his own men to the Japanese for punishment. The men knew it. They detested him.'[64]

A later author will describe Kappe's record as one of 'incompetence, sheer neglect and the total use of abuse of the privileges of command'.[65]

•

In the face of the cholera catastrophe, and the widespread outrage among the men of the Line due to their captors' complete refusal to offer serious resources to help, an idea is floated to Weary and the Gangster.

Perhaps we should deliberately infect the Japanese water supply?

It is an intriguing idea, simple to execute – in both senses of the word – and in some ways seems only fair, given that it would weaken their captors and give those bastards a taste of exactly what the POWs are suffering. Hirota and his horde of mongrels are now pushing the darg out to as much as three metres penetration – no, really – and some of our blokes are now doing 18 hours a day!

But neither Weary nor the Gangster will hear of it.

Weary has not pulled back from killing the Lizard only to wipe out dozens, if not hundreds, of Japanese soldiers. And the Gangster points out some of the more exact wording of the Hippocratic oath they have taken, concerning their fellow man: 'I will take care that they suffer no hurt or damage. Nor shall any man's entreaty prevail upon me to administer poison to anyone; neither will I counsel any man to do so. And I will willingly refrain from doing any injury or wrong.'[66]

Case closed.

As the work goes on, and the toll is taken, Weary notices a certain surprising pattern emerging when it comes to who the angels of death come for.

'By and large, a fellow didn't survive unless he had the right mental attitudes and fellows about 40 were surprisingly better survivors than fellows of 19 or 20.'

For there is no way around it . . . 'A certain amount of maturity of mind and body was useful and the fellow in the first sort of flush of manhood who feels as strong as a buffalo and nothing can knock him over that he doesn't save himself.'

Yes, strange as it is, the strongest becomes the weakest very rapidly, driving themselves into the ground along with their drills; victims of their pace in pursuing 'this dreadful hammer and tap and the fearsome heat of these rock cuttings sort of drilling incredible distances by hand drilling and dynamiting, they really hammer themselves to hell, some of these fellows'.[67]

Even Tiny O'Neil, the strongest bastard in Dunlop Force, is used up. You can only write cheques for so long in terms of expenditure of energy that your stomach can't cash, and after all his fat had been burned up, it is Tiny himself who starts withering, now struggling to even lift the eight-pound Plumb hammer, let alone bring it crashing down like he used to, hard enough to blow the bell off a fairground spruiker's fixed totem.

In his weakened state, it doesn't take long for a deficiency disease to hit, in his case the dreaded beri-beri and one day it begins, tingling in his arms and feet, creating swollen legs and mental confusion.

Everything that can be done is done, including his mates donating their precious weekly eggs to Tiny, but nothing helps.

Alas, as Tom Uren notes, 'he'd just already done more than the human body could stand, and, it's not necessarily a fellow's physical strength [that points to survival], but a combination of mental attitude, mental toughness, together with a physical toughness, which is a little more of a lean, enduring type'.[68]

Tiny fights the best he can, but soon enough has nothing left to fight *with*, and shuffles off this mortal coil as an emaciated bag of bones. Looking at his corpse, Tom Uren cannot help but thank providence, one more time for the road, that he had been taken in hand by ol' Harry Baker and taught to let the hammer do the work. Tom will go on because of it, but Tiny is soon no more than ashes and plumes of smoke heading to the heavens above.

Weary's fury knows no bounds and he personally blames Hirota for such deaths.

'This man,' he will later note, 'caused workmen with horrible inflamed and festering feet, to work barefoot in sharp rocks or haul logs in thorny jungle, and forced men with dysentery to soil themselves while working. He personally struck men with sticks and threw stones at them, and his tours of the works area were accompanied by waves of brutality.'[69]

Bastard, that he is!

For Uren, there is at least sometimes a little respite from the ghastliness of it all, when he can put down the hammer and head off into the teak forests to see troops cut down the huge teak trees and use the surviving elephants to drag them back to where the bridges are being built by both skilled Australian soldiers and hundreds of coolies doing much of the heavy lifting.

Such days at least allow Uren to get a close-up look at the bridges being built, for the most part trestle affairs, solidly constructed with a relatively simple design.

(The main logs are driven in not by anything with horse-power, but *man*-power. It takes about three dozen men hauling hard on ropes to lift a huge steel weight known as a 'monkey' high above the vertical log before letting go so that it drops down in the manner of a hammer – before it is hauled high again. And again, and again, as the day and their very souls wear away.)

As soon as some of the superstructure is added, the most coveted positions are high up, 'out of reach of the guards and their flailing sticks'.[70]

As the bridges take shape they really do look *so* solid you'd reckon they might stand there for centuries to come. But, never fear. As Uren would recount with glee, 'Tassie bushmen would go out and get the white ants out of the bushes and come back and put it into the trestle of the bridges.'[71]

Do your work, you little beasties, and go hard!

And that is not all.

'Men whispered orders to impair the construction of the bridge wherever possible. Some, charged with making up concrete mixtures, deliberately added too much sand or not enough, which would later have disastrous effects . . .' another soldier will recount. 'Out of sight of the guards I furtively sawed half way through wooden bolts, hoping they would snap whenever any serious weight, like a train, was placed upon them.'[72]

In truth?

Sometimes the Australians do their work too well in doing their work badly.

A case in point is a stricken structure they nickname 'Pack of Cards Bridge' for the fact it collapses three times while they are working on it.

•

Though Weary is back at the main POW settlement at Hintok Mountain Camp, many of the workers are now starting to shift to new digs at Hintok River Camp, by a new section of the railway known as Compressor Cutting. Weary remains behind to oversee the mountain camp hospital and to attend to those stricken at Cholera Gulch.

'I have decided to stay on,' Weary chronicles on 18 July, 'despite my leg, as I simply cannot leave this awful mess to [the Gangster] . . .'[73]

Inevitably Weary Dunlop spends most of his time in the cholera camps, trying to save as many patients as he can, though his absence weighs heavily on those in the main camp.

Everywhere, things are shockingly grim.

'In the mud and starvation of those long months,' one veteran of the Line observes, 'we looked back at Bandoeng as the Garden of

Eden, while men died and were buried in shallow graves in hundreds, and in thousands.'[74]

The supply chain gets progressively more strained during the great wet, as the River Kwai becomes too swollen to navigate and even the roads become impassable, and the spectre of starvation sweeps up and down the Line, as some camps are now down to less than four ounces of rice for their daily ration per man. A teacup of rice gruel for breakfast and dinner boils down to four-fifths of Sweet Fuck All – and a fifth of their initial allocation when arriving on the Line.

Men are now so starving that much of their movement is through a mist of such deep exhaustion, overwhelming hunger and debilitating weakness that it is hard to tell which is which.

'Slip on my damp G-string,' Ray Parkin will describe his morning routine, 'seize my pail and dixie and with grim concentrated movements, go slowly through the sea of mud serried chaotically by the feet of moving men coming and going and falling.'[75]

Yes, just over there, a man simply crashes down, taking half of a bunk with him. Now, it is a question of luck. Had he already drawn his breakfast before his collapse? If not, he might still be able to get up and get it. If so, he can lie in the mud, trying to scratch together what he can and get it into him, before facing a day that will now weaken him so much further.

Out in the parade ground, *tenko* is sounding.

'Roku-jū-nana!'

'Roku-jū-hachi!'

Grasping their dixie and hats grimly, late arrivals stumble into place just in time to call their own numbers, trying not to collapse themselves, and just have time to wolf down the three spoonfuls of rice that breakfast consists of, before sorting themselves to get another three-spoonful allocation for lunch.

'As a great queue we advance on the rice basket and have our Dixies filled with rice . . . Then we form up and stand in the rain just as the light of dawn breaks. In ten minutes we are out on our way to work.'[76]

Day after day, just like this, with the only change being that their ranks progressively thin in much the same manner as their bodies.

Soon enough, it is not just their ribs that are showing up as if they were starving greyhounds.

'I'll never forget,' Tom Uren will say of visiting his mate Billy Halliday in hospital, now perilously close to heading to the same fiery pyres he had tended, 'he was so skinny that you could see his backbone through his stomach lying on that bed.'[77]

Others will remember seeing how prominent the anuses of starving men suddenly became – an enduring knob, while all around had wasted away.

The only upside is that there is so little food that even some of their key bodily persecutors are struggling.

While standing above a *benjo*, releasing, one POW hears a Pommy voice from behind.

'Hey, mate, yo' guts are hanging out,' he says.

The Australian looks behind, to see what indeed looks like a part of his intestines, but is in fact 'a tapeworm, a big fellow, about twelve to fifteen inches long. I tugged it away. The poor thing was lifeless, starved to death, no doubt.'[78]

Lieutenant Colonel Ishi's admonition that patients should have the dysentery starved out of them for a week is actually starting to happen in certain parts.

And yet all note that wherever Weary is, things are better, fewer men die and more men are protected from the Japanese.

'Weary was isolated,' Ray Parkin will recall, 'but the news always came back, "how's Weary doing", and all the rest of it. And one day he visited the camp and the buzz went round straightaway, "Weary's back!" "Weary's back!" You couldn't put any deliberate words to it, but it was there all the time. And I think it was a great pride, too, in being with him. We used to be called Dunlop's 1000. And that we were.'[79]

And it is the same up and down the Line, for the various hospitals Weary regularly visits.

'Men dying in jungle camps started to want to live again,' one veteran will recall, 'when the magic whisper reached them that "Weary" Dunlop was coming.'[80]

Mid-July 1943, Hintok, skeleton dance

Oh, Gawd.

It has happened again.

Yet more men are going down with sudden sickness, even while working on Compressor Cutting, this time on Ray Parkin's watch.

First, in the middle of the afternoon, two POWs collapse with what is likely cerebral malaria – shivering and boiling up at the same time – and Parkin is 'able to get them *yasumed*',[81] allowed to rest. Alas, even during lunch another two go down and one of them almost certainly has cholera – for he is so weak he cannot even walk. All afternoon Parkin haggles with the Japanese corporal, Billy the Pig, to have them allowed to head back to camp, but the only response is a lot of shouting and an attempt to hit Parkin with whatever the corporal has to hand at the time, be it shovel, bamboo or hammer. No matter, Parkin sways away, meaning no real damage is done – and by 4 pm the Japanese brute finally relents and says they can go.

'How many men can take them in?'

'None,' is the reply. 'The other sick do it.'

'They can't.'

'*Baka jin!*' Idiot!

Let them crawl.

Parkin does the only thing he can do and keeps trying to sort something out.

'Look,' he says to Billy the Pig, 'the two malarias can take the cholera bloke back.'

Finally Billy agrees, and the cholera bloke is draped between the two malarias, his arms over their shoulders.

'They made a wobble tripod.'[82]

First, some instructions.

'When you get down there,' Parkin tells the malaria blokes, 'there's a big cave just near the bridge, leave him there and send someone back and you can stagger on.'[83]

Off they stagger as Parkin watches closely.

'They were bowed and sweating with pain and concentration, trying not to collapse. The man with cholera was limp between them with his head lifelessly on his chest, hanging like a crucified man.'[84]

Ever the artist, Parkin takes mental notes, noting how the middle man's knees have buckled under him, causing his feet to drag – all while his skinny, fouled buttocks are too bony to hold his pants up, meaning they fall down.

It is all so ghastly, so pathetic, but somehow so heart-warming as 'the others dragged him along with slow, shambling gait, [and] his pants kept falling about his knees. The two men had to stop and pull them up before they could go on.'[85]

But so they do, never leaving him and using their last remaining strength to help him along – which now sees them all fall over. Struggling to their feet they all keep going, and keep going till they get to the cave. Later on, a stretcher party will indeed come out and pick up the man with cholera – even while Ray Parkin, back at the camp, keeps drawing what he has so closely observed.

When reflecting on those times when he regularly 'witnessed the agonies and exertions of those gaunt, chronically starved, diseased, gallant men', Weary is overcome by admiration.

'To this day, I feel uplifted and borne up by their unquenchable spirit and patient endurance of suffering.'[86]

And yet?

And yet, only a short time later, Parkin returns after a brutal day's work 'neath the slogging rain, to find the worst of all possible things has happened. While they have been out, the Japanese have taken their tents for a reason as yet unknown. Where Parkin's tent has been, there is nothing.

A black depression clutches his heart.

All his drawings! All his diaries! All that proof of what they have suffered!

Gone, all gone.

But what now?

Just as he is about to dinkum *weep* from the agony of it all, Parkin sees one of his mates approaching. It is Buck Peters, an interesting bloke. Despite having been 'in every jail from Sydney to Darwin . . . right through the Depression', he is also 'a man in a million this fellow and so honest, it was embarrassing'.[87]

Buck lets his mate Ray know.

'Alright, I got 'em.'

He has risked his life to save both the paintings and the diaries. Ray accompanies his mate to his own tent and affirms it. Buck has them all secreted in his own bag.

'Look,' Buck says simply, 'if we don't get those back, we've wasted our bloody time up here.'

Which is exactly how Parkin himself feels.

'This was a project for me to get this record back, not to complain, but to [chronicle] it.'[88]

These bastards must be held to account, once this Godawful thing is over. *If* it is ever over!

•

Everybody must be counted. The Romans were very strict on this idea back when the Dead Sea was only sick, but they have nothing on the Japanese. Roll call is for all, no exception, no excuses. And this afternoon, Blue, says the guard, 'You one short.'

Yes, but there is no need to worry about an escapee, unless you count the afterlife as a hideout for fugitives. The fellow missing is Dusty, he's busy dying, back over yonder. 'I don't think he'll last an hour,' says Blue.

Well, that is fascinating Blue, and if roll call were an honour system it might be good enough, but as long as Dusty's body is breathing it's a soldier, and all Australian soldiers are to be present for roll call. Blue would ask if the officer was joking, but he is familiar with the Japanese sense of humour, or lack thereof, and knows that he is deadly serious.

Ah, well. Such is death. No, stuff it, let's try reason even if it is never in season with this mob: 'Look, he'll be dead in an hour. Why do we want to bring him over? Leave him in peace there. He's on his own. There's not even anybody with him. You can't get him.'

No, they can't. Blue must. So he goes back, with four men, to find a bamboo stretcher, and they make their way back along the muddy road to find Dusty. Now, there's muddy and there is waist-deep muddy, and you and Sod's Law can guess which one it is today. Oh, did we mention we are all barefoot? Well. They are. But they find Dusty, he is . . . just . . . rasping. Fuck. The men talk amongst themselves. Is it worth carrying him? Is it decent?

'Well, he'll be dead within half an hour.'

Alright, stuff this. Blue walks back to tell the guard, now backed up by witnesses.

'WHERE?' yells the guard as the Dusty-free Blue is spotted. 'WHY didn't you bring him?'

'He's only got half an hour to live,' says Blue.

Really? Well Blue won't even have that if he doesn't get that bloody man here soon. The guard is ranting, he is raving, his fists are flying closer and closer and Blue doesn't care. So what if he gets hit?

'Physical pain is very easy to take. Physical pain won't break you. It's mental pain that beats you.'

But mental pain it is, for he is ordered back. Blue goes again, to find Dusty lying and dying and still breathing. Silently they hoist him on to the bamboo stretcher – which squeaks in protest as soon as he is lifted, as light as he is – determined to bring some dignity to this bloody thing, but failing as they slip and fall in the mud, and Dusty must be gathered and regathered, his bearers slogging through the mud as the bamboo chafes each skeletal shoulder. They get him there, and when they lower the stretcher, Dusty . . . is dead.

Ichi! One! He is counted.

'Everybody is correct.'

The guard is happy, the officer is happy, the roll is accurate. Blue and his men pick up Dusty and take him to the cremation pit.

Dusty, present and correct, is left to his own devices and Blue and the boys stagger back to camp. This war. These people. You would not believe it.

•

Day after day, night after night it goes on.

Many of the Australian POWs risk their own lives by actively helping mates who have gone down with this cursed disease – carrying them, cleaning them up, even just holding their hand as they descend.

'It's difficult for a person in Australia today to understand the depth of the bond,' Sergeant Stan Arneil will recount many years later. 'Difficult to understand death, for example. In Australia one dies in a sterile hospital bed. If the doctors are quick enough they might have the relatives there, but many times the patient is dead before the next of kin get there. In Thailand when a man died, he died in an aura of love and brotherhood which is not available now possibly anywhere in the world. You died with your head in the lap of a mate, with somebody holding your hand, with somebody with a hand on your forehead saying a little prayer, and people actually sorry to see you die. That's a bond which you just cannot obtain now. Many of the people who were there became closer to their friends than to their families.'[89]

The fight offered by some is extraordinary.

One of them, a mate of Ray Parkin's, will stay in his memory for the rest of his days. This mate, Scotty, has been ill with cholera for weeks, but simply *refuses* to die.

'His skull was about the size of a walnut and he never lost his spirit.'[90]

And this is despite the fact that on three occasions he is placed on what has become the dying bed right at the end of the tent, where men who have clearly not got long are laid to shuffle off their mortal coil without disturbing the others.

Each time he is placed there, Scotty rasps out to the orderlies who've put him down: 'Look, no good your boss bringing me out here. I'm coming back.'[91]

And he bloody well does, too, at least this time.

Others?

Well, others just don't have it in them to fight, and Weary must find it in himself, in his own energies, to do everything possible to keep their hearts beating, long after just about everything else has shut down, in the hope they will pull through.

As it happens, 19 July sets a new record for Cholera Gulch as no fewer than 17 *new* cases are admitted, to go with the 30 already under their care.

'[This] night,' Weary will describe the scene, 'the place deserves a circle in Dante's inferno. Extremely low, inferior [Nippon] tents, all leaking. Patients lie on rough bamboo bedding a few inches off the muddy floor and one works bent almost double. The only light . . . is the fitful flicker of crude oil lamps improvised by wicks of fibrous materials suspended in condensed milk tins of oil.'

That constant retching you can hear, in tandem with the stench?

'Patients vomit in gushing fashion into bamboo containers and indeed often all over the place. The orderlies have made little bed pans out of cut-down tins placed in little wooden boxes but of course nothing can deal entirely with the gushing faecal contamination. With these intolerable cramps and abdominal pains and delirium there can be no silence and the air is full of groans, cries for relief and curses in weak, husky voices.'[92]

Men who he had seen walking around just yesterday, before contracting the cholera, now look 'dreadfully emaciated and unrecognisable'.[93]

The hours crawl by, the dead are carried out.

One . . . two . . . three . . . four . . .

And this bloke? Can *he* be kept alive, as crook as he is with cholera? He'd been brought in only hours before apologising to the stretcher-bearers for the trouble he was putting them to.

He is Able Seaman Bob Costin, and he is just 22 years old, a young sailor who had survived the sinking of *Perth*, and everything since, whose only desire is to get back to Australia. For you must understand, Colonel Dunlop, sir. He and his bride in white had been *so* happy on their wedding day, only for him to be rounded up by the navy straight after the ceremony, and obliged to return to *Perth*, *without even consummating the marriage.* And the very last letter concerning his wife, Maud – just before *Perth* had been sunk – had been from her father saying that Maudie had been rushed to hospital for emergency surgery, and it was going to be touch and go whether she'd even live. Right now he does not know if he is a husband or a widower.

And now, *this*? He is pouring his life out from every orifice, getting weaker by the hour!

As the night wears on, Weary does everything he can to help him, even as Costin fades before his eyes. You will get through this, young man, get back to her – for she is surely still alive – and live your life together. But you have to *fight*, have to hold on! But nothing helps as, finally, the young Melburnian has just had enough. And Maudie is probably dead anyway. He might as well join her.

'I was trying to give an intravenous feed,' Weary Dunlop will recount, 'and he just pulled it out and turned his face to the wall of the tent.'[94]

Weary unleashes.

'You're going to die like a yellow rat!' he roars with sudden venom. 'People are fighting to save your life and exposing ourselves to risks of giving up their food in order to help you and you die like a yellow rat.'[95]

It is no easy thing to be 'cursing a dying man',[96] but it must be done.

Alas, though the young man musters just enough energy to turn back to the doctor to hear his speech, it has no overall effect.

When the cannula is put in one more time, the young man pulls it out again, this time saying, 'I want Mum.'

Enough.

'Now just sit back,' Weary says gently, 'and your mum will be able to see you shortly.'[97]

Two hours later, he is dead.

As Able Seaman Bob Costin is carried to the fiery flames of the pyre, his body is so emaciated it barely makes the bamboo stretcher squeak. Just hours after he has gone up in smoke, the three letters that had arrived for him just as he had become sick are opened. They are from Maud, she is alive and well, loves him, is sure he will get through, and can't wait to welcome him home to Melbourne.

Christ.

For his part, Weary can barely register the tragedy of it all, amid so much more dark tragedy going on all around him – together with just the odd crack of light.

For somewhere in the distance, Scotty can be heard rasp-roaring, at least as best he can: 'Look, no good you bastards bringing me out here! I'm coming back!'[98]

And, at least for now, Scotty is as good as his word.

To everyone's astonishment, Scotty survives long enough to be evacuated to Tarsau – even if on departure he is no more than six stone wringing wet, which is mostly, as he is also getting fevers from malaria. Ray Parkin is careful to take a good look at him, knowing he'll surely never see him again, but wanting to savour the fight he has in him to *live*!

Let Scotty be an inspiration to us all.

•

For the Japanese, there is no way around it.

If the POWs keep dying, those who remain will have to work still harder. They will start earlier, finish later, and as yet more POWs arriving from Changi are thrown in, the Japanese will even keep work on the railway going around the clock.

'It looked like a scene out of Dante's Inferno,' one of the Australian POWs, Private Hugh Clarke, will describe the result. 'The Japs decided we would work twenty-four hours a day, two shifts, one was the day shift and one was the night shift. Lighting became a problem but they're a pretty resourceful people, and there's plenty of bamboo, so they formed a light party. Its job was to keep the fires burning all night.'

But could even Dante have imagined such a scene?

> If you stood on the top of the cutting you would see the burning
> fires at intervals of about twenty feet; you'd see the shadows
> of the Japanese with their Foreign Legion caps moving round
> with their sticks belting men. We still had our slouch hats so
> you could distinguish the prisoners by being naked under the
> slouch hats, moving rocks around, hammering and clearing.
> There was shouting and bellowing. And this went on all night.[99]

Never, with all the fires, torches of kerosene-soaked rags in metallic bowls atop poles and writhing bodies, has Hellfire Pass looked so truly hellish as this. Come this way, Mr Dante.

The worst of it?

Well, the worst of it comes when a bloke hard at work on the Line suddenly collapses – usually while vomiting, pissing his pants and, worse, all at the same time.

Because no-one can be spared to take him back to the camp or the hospital, he is just shoved aside until the end of the day, when his mates carry him back on a stretcher – usually tied to it, so he can be manoeuvred up and down cliff-faces – and he gets to Weary and his fellow medicos many hours after first falling sick.

Even as the rain continues to pound down, he is put in the leaking tents with all the rest, and cared for the best he can be.

Weary and his fellow medicos are able to keep, 'the mortality down to about 40%. And most of those were pretty near dead when they came in.'[100]

And of course, beyond the cholera, all the other ailments like tropical ulcers go on, as before – only worse for the fact their bodies are now so worn down.

One of Weary's enduring deep frustrations is the lack of iodoform, which lightly sprinkled on an ulcer where the rotten flesh has been cut away can reduce the burning sensation and begin the healing within hours. (Honestly, iodoform is like a wonder drug, one POW noting, 'you could have a hole inches deep, and sprinkle the powder on, and the next morning the flesh would come up level.'[101])

Though it can be purchased from local traders at the outrageous cost of several hundred pounds per pound – meaning they can only afford very little – Weary's experimentation establishes that it is 'often effective even with such economy as 1 in 20 dilution',[102] with things like flour, but still they need much more.

Other methods they try include mixing up a mash of local plants that the natives tell them they use as poultices to keep wounds clean, and which the doctors know can sometimes 'draw' the infection out, to let the wound stay healthy and granulate up from the bottom.

Everything must be tried!

(All this, and yet the Japanese themselves are singularly well supplied with their own medicine; one Australian doctor reporting after his visit to a jungle hospital for the troops of Nippon, that he 'found it lavishly supplied with drugs and medicines of every kind'.[103])

It is Boon Pong who continues to make up some of the difference between the drugs the Japanese give them, and those that are needed – continuing to risk his life by sneaking in everything he can to help them – including more 'canary seeds' to power their ham radios.

Boon Pong's brave visage brings to mind some Shakespeare for Weary: '*In thy face, I see, the map of honour, truth and loyalty.*'[104] But it is the tireless work of Weary that will make both the difference and the most lasting impression on the survivors of Dunlop Force.

'He was the shining, he was the beam,'[105] Blue Butterworth will say. He was the boss.

Some of them are so staggered by his bravery, his unending work, his commitment to saving them that he becomes known to them by such terms as 'The King of the River' and 'the Christ of Siam'.[106]

Also held in enormously high regard is the Gangster, who is a constant presence in the wards and, despite his reputation for being fearsome, can also on occasion be wonderfully gentle.

'Clean it up, son,' Corlette is often heard to say to soldiers so sick they have only eaten half their allotted rice ration. 'Your passport back to home and mother is on the bottom of your dixie. Go on, eat it up.'[107]

Another exhortation frequently heard is, 'Rice, or rice sack?'[108] as in: do you want to eat your rice, or finish wrapped up in the rice sacks we usually use as death shrouds?

•

The British? They do things differently.

In one case that comes to Weary's attention, when a single British soldier in one camp goes down with cholera, the Japanese decided to shoot him through the tent.

'To spare the lad being shot at repeatedly through the tent, the British Adjutant of his battalion, Lt Primrose, shot him personally. This did not spare the camp much subsequent cholera.'[109]

•

And yet *still* the pressure from Doctor Death, Okada, does not diminish as he continues to pressure Weary to release more of his 'heavy sick' for work.

'Why more sick every day?' Okada demands.

'Am I almighty God to answer this question?' Weary replies. 'Did I make this fever – this unhealthy jungle? Am I responsible that the Nipponese made these men prisoners and then worked them so hard and gave them too little food? Look at them with their skin stretched over their bones! The Nipponese are responsible. Why do you not ask, "Why do men die?" Look at that cemetery – does it surprise you that men get sick before going there?'[110]

Yes, it does actually. The Japanese make Christian Scientists look like a bunch of negative Nellies when it comes to thinking yourself well.

3 August 1943, Hintok, live and let die

It is a red-letter day.

Today, for the first time in six weeks, it happens, and Weary records the welcome news in his diary.

'No deaths. It is still terribly wet and I fear more cholera cases will crop up.'[111]

No doubt. Until such times, Weary and his medical staff cling on like cats to a curtain – just. On 8 August, the Gangster is observed by Weary 'doing sick parade in bare feet, having dermatitis and looking rather fagged and a wild look in his eye'.[112]

•

Occasionally, just occasionally, there is some respite from the hell.

On this day Tom Uren has arrived at the top of the valley where the blacksmiths have set up their forge – cut-down 44-gallon drums – where, with roaring fires, they temper the drills by getting them red-hot before plunging them again and again into water.

As one of the few men strong enough to carry one drill – let alone two, as he often does to give himself more rest-time – it is a task the former Manly footballer often does. But on this day, he pauses for just a few minutes to alleviate the shocking pain in his feet, which he now puts in the warm water of the drums, and is able to momentarily reflect on the sheer beauty of the scene.

Through the massive gorges, around the mountains, the winding river makes its way, bordered on both sides by the most magnificent teak forests. Grown by God over millennia, their splendour and permanence proves His presence.

'You know,' Tom says to himself, 'that's beautiful. A man should come back when he's free.'[113]

When will that be?

A lot of blokes reckon three months.

But today Uren is sent once more on a short excursion to get cattle for their Japanese overseers, and on this occasion passes the same spot where, months before, he had seen the old Thai man sitting by the track calmly smoking a pipe, covered in a groundsheet.

And he can *barely* believe it!

For here he is again, in exactly the same spot, with the same groundsheet and hat, and the same pipe.

But this time, he is just a skeleton.

'This Asian had just sat there passively for the rest of his days,' Uren realises. 'A European couldn't do that; that's how he wanted to finish up and he'd made up his mind. There's something about the Asian soul that can face things so passively like that.'[114]

Australians are simply not like that, but at least right now they are starting to feel more confident about the war's outcome.

One Digger records the words of one of the few Japanese guards who speaks reasonable English.

'You men will die on this railway,' he confidently tells him.

No chance, cobber, the Digger sets him straight.

'We'll be home eating steak and eggs when you bastards are still eating rice.'[115]

He receives a hiding for his trouble, but, Christ Almighty, it was worth it.

•

In the meantime?

In the meantime, the struggle goes on. On 20 August at Hintok Mountain Camp, Weary must supervise the evacuation of some of the 'heavy sick' patients, and he watches closely as the men head for home, starting with an exhausting climb.

'I witnessed the job of moving these up the cliff in the rain and the mud,' he will note in his diary, 'a very sad sight. Charlton, Abbott and Tully were tied onto the stretchers and bullocked up the ladder rung by rung, the rear bearers supporting the stretcher poles on their shoulders.'

All of it is done without complaint, and just in the manner of doing what has to be done. This is no longer the strong supporting the weak. It is now the very weak supporting the weaker still. But it is done:

> Other men managed to get up with assistance, some having to have men behind them to lift their feet up each rung in a combined pull from above and a push from behind to hoist them up that distance. Beri-beri knees are particularly bad on steps; thus the strong men leave in the shadow of that cursed mountain. Many of the bearers are in bare feet, typical ragged tattered figures, emaciated and hag-ridden with sores.[116]

Just another day. And just another night to come.

Weary is humbled, just watching it.

CHAPTER FIFTEEN

THE END OF THE LINE

The men would do anything for [Weary] and are proud to be with him. I am sure it is his presence which holds this body of men from moral decay in bitter circumstances which they can only meet with emotion rather than reason . . . He is a big man – some six feet four inches of him – and a most skilful surgeon; a simple, profoundly altruistic man, with a gentle, disarming smile. This selflessness, this smile, command more from the men than an army of officers each waving a Manual of Military Law.[1]

Ray Parkin

Mid-September 1943, Hellfire Pass, hellfire passes

Finally, the great day has come.

At Hellfire Pass and surrounds, the last blast has rung out, the last *tanka* carried away and put on the embankment, and the last weakened bolt placed on the last trestle bridge before . . . praise the Lord and pass that rotten and infested piece of wood . . . the Tassie bushmen let the last white ants into the bridge's crevasses. Do your fine work, you little beasties, and never stop!

True, other sections along the Line are still not complete, and it will still be some weeks before a train can go through from Thailand to Burma, but there will no longer be a bottleneck at Hellfire. From down in the valley far below, they can even hear the approaching whistle of the engine that is bringing up the rails on flat-cars, for the line-layers who are getting ever closer. Within days they will be here at Hellfire Pass, passing through the cutting the Australians have made, moving upon their embankments and over their bridges.

'Not one of us ever had a feeling of pride in what we had achieved,' Private Ernie Badham notes in his account, 'only sheer relief that it was over.'[2]

What now?

They must pack up their troubles in their old kitbag and do miles, boys, miles, that's the style, to march further up the river to another section that is nearing completion. First, some 20 of the sick men from Dunlop Force's P Battalion are placed on barges and sent some 10 miles up the river to Kinsayok, while the rest will follow on foot in the next few days.

'How glad we were to see the end of Hintok!' Badham records in his diary. 'Our "Rabble" now was down to under 1000 men and not one of us much more than a scarecrow. It was just as well we had no possessions, for we could not have carried them.'[3]

For now, the beat goes on, as Weary and Butterworth pack up their effects, including 'Angus' – with all his parts, as ever, spread across the masses of medical paraphernalia they are also moving. (Over time, one of the successful methods of smuggling has been to place contraband in the empty parts of the trousers of double amputees being carried on stretchers and put a boot on the other end, but Weary forbids it in the case of radio parts, as the men would risk death if caught.)

Raid!

Led by the wretched Lieutenant Usuki barking orders, it is the Kempis once more, the thug military police, suddenly bursting into every hut, over-turning beds, emptying kitbags, bending each suspicious bit of bamboo and eyeing every possession as though it is possessed. They are looking for diaries, drawings, radios, knives, bullets, plans, contraband of any brand and – standing to attention on the parade ground – all the men can do is watch.

Weary Dunlop does so, with rising tension. If they find anything, the best case will be a vicious beating and a long spell of solitary confinement. The most likely result will be execution.

Happily, the Black Prince, Usuki, had hinted at just such a raid the day before, allowing Weary to hide 'Angus' the ham radio in the cholera ward, beneath piles of faecal-covered rags. None of the Kempis would touch those rags, even at the point of a bayonet. Was Usuki being kind? No, he could not risk Weary being thrown into a cell or executed as without his medical expertise and energy the Dunlop Force workforce would be devastated.

Finally, the raid and search is over.

They have found nothing.

Usuki continues to shout, but his eyes meet Weary's.

Don't mention it.

Pausing only to torch Cholera Gulch – throwing a little kerosene on the tents, lighting it, and having the satisfaction of seeing the whole disease-ridden mess collapse in on itself – they are on their way.

Early October 1943, Kinsayok, naked and afraid

It is a hard thing to give a pep talk through an interpreter, but at 5 pm today Okada is in the mood to do just that for the medical officers currently detained by him. The interpreter is called 'Pop', and Pop's pep lets them know that Okada is in a curiously jolly mood today. He asks to see their sick and then their kitchens, and both are deemed satisfactory. Weary is the last officer to leave the kitchen to saunter back to his quarters, and as he does so he walks past the Japanese 'bathhouse'. Lost in his thoughts, Weary does not even register that there are two naked Japanese officers soaping themselves in the distance, buckets of water serving as their tub for tonight. But they notice him.

'*KURA!*' one calls out and Weary turns to the noise. Yes? He walks over to the naked officer who asks him: 'Why no *kura*?'

No salute? Very well, Weary salutes the naked bathers and stands at attention while they continue to bathe, glaring at him. It is times like these when Pop would be handy, and he arrives just in time with Okada. What is the matter? Why is Dunlop watching these naked men? The situation is explained and Okada bursts out laughing:

'Colonel Dunroppo must remember salute Nippon soldier.'[4] Dunroppo is dismissed and the matter is closed. But no, that laughter burns, face has been lost, and a couple of hours later hostilities will resume.

Weary is entering his hut when he is hailed by the yell of a Japanese soldier standing outside the administrative office, a full 50 metres away. Weary turns to the sound and his heart sinks as he sees that is one of the naked officers, now clothed and clearly waiting to make serious trouble. Why did Dunlop not salute him just now?

But you were 50 metres away?

'The officers never salute the office when entering this barrack as it is well away. I did not notice the *kura*,' says Weary.[5] So you say. Stand to attention and salute. Weary salutes and the guard steps forward and swings his rifle butt at Weary's face.

'I countered by raising my left forearm and deflecting the blow smartly.'

The guard staggers and nearly falls over, whether through gravity or shock is not clear. What is clear is that Weary is for it.

A few tense minutes tick by and then he is summoned to the guardroom. Weary's stomach twists as he makes the short journey, reckoning his only hope is that another more senior officer might be in the guardroom to see reason or at least see that things don't get out of hand. As soon as he steps into the room, Weary sees that things will get out of hand because in the hands of the guard now is 'a heavy length of bamboo about 3 ft long and 4 in. across'.

Ah.

Stand to attention.

Weary stands to. The guard swings the bamboo at Weary's face with all the force that he can muster. Weary fends off the first two blows with his left forearm, the next three go lower, striking his left leg and Weary knows with medical precision just what harm is being done to him, as one smack is 'hitting over the peroneal nerve with a horrid numbing effect of the leg suddenly going to sleep and inflicting two lacerations'.

Weary has had enough of this. He grabs the guard's bamboo stick and throws it away with contempt. Furious, the guard grabs another piece of wood and charges at Weary again, only to find that the Wallaby grabs that weapon too and hurls it aside. The guard kicks Weary twice, aiming for the groin, but Weary's weaving means the guard only makes contact with the Colonel's thigh. Right, back to wooden weapons. A small forest must have been destroyed to make up all the 'murderous lumps of wood' that Weary sees lined up now, all destined for his bonce or body. Well, the Rubicon is crossed now, who cares? Weary puts his fists up and prepares to knock this bastard out: 'I was resolved to give him a K.O. and pay the penalty.' But just as the king hit is coming, the small clerk who is in charge of the office, Private Hannamura, rushes in and yells for both parties to stand to attention. What on earth is going on here?

Silence, which speaks all.

'I demand to see the Camp Commander,' says Weary.

Hannamura ponders the request for a moment and then nods. Dismissed.

A battered and furious Weary presents himself to a British ally first, Lieutenant Colonel Francis Hugonin of the Saigon Battalion, and the two Colonels now go to see Okada. Pop is not present but they don't need a translator. Weary strips to show Okada his fresh bruises and cuts, his hands, his left forearm, his legs. Weary tells Okada everything that has happened and Okada grows more silent and pensive as his report goes on. Weary demands once more to see Okada's senior and the commandant of the Kinsayok camp, Commander Hatori Chui. Very well. Now the three officers march to see another.

Yes? Okada introduces Weary and seemingly tells Hatori of the entire incident, complete with pointed reference to Weary's injuries. Weary then gives his own account in English, detailing each absurd escalation and ending with the words: 'I wish to make a strong protest.' Hatori ponders this for a long time and now responds with his verdict: 'You must avoid such incidents with Nipponese soldiers!'

Yes, there we are in consensus. A half promise of half investigation is made, with Hatori pointing out that Weary does not even know the name of his assailant. To find an unknown man is very difficult, you know. Weary knows.

'I suggest Officer Hannamura could help you there.'

That is a point. Hatori is courteous and the two POWs leave his office with polite promises made. We will see. And we will look for that guard and find out his name.

As it turns out, a minor miracle occurs and Hatori keeps his word. Weary never does find out the man's name but one week later a gossiping guard tells him that a soldier has been transferred to Tarsau. Reason: 'He was attempting to hit "Col. Dunroppo".'

'My God, I like that!' Weary comments. The guard's attempts are all over Weary's body in purple right now. But one rotten apple is gone. Only a few orchards left now. Hannamura lets Weary know something else:

'It is now apparent that I had been spirited out to escape being done to death by this character.'[6]

•

Are the Pyramids a wonder of the world or a monument to human suffering? Both.

They are magnificent, but with each block of stone laid at the cost of myriad lives and an eternity of suffering, the wonder for the achievement must come with sorrow for the sheer human cost of it all.

So too, but even more so, for the completion of the Line, as on this day the team of rail-layers coming from Burma on one side, and Thailand on the other, approach each other at Konkoita – at Kilo 263, more than 100 kilometres north of Hellfire Pass, not far from Three Pagodas pass.

As the Japanese engineers hover nervously, making last-minute adjustments, there is a whistle in the distance that portends the arrival of the first train due to go from the Thai capital of Bangkok all the way to the farmlands of Burma. Up front, the Australians can see the 'Nip brass . . . sitting up on the train . . . with their swords and big boots, so that everyone could see them.'[7]

And what now?

As the snorting, belching, shrieking locomotive – the finest and most trusty, if still rusty, steam engine of the Malaysian rolling stock, C 5631 – arrives, there is panic. For, a lot of the Thai villagers, with their eyes darting about like blowflies in a bottle, simply run. Never in their lives have they seen such a noisy, snorting, powerful thing before, and they are terrified. It is against nature.

'But what was even funnier,' one son of the Southern Cross will recount, 'was that the Nip generals all had these little black holes burnt into their uniforms from the ashes thrown out from the train's funnel.'[8]

Those generals alight with due ceremony for the ceremony that is due to take place, and . . . wait!

For the occasion, a desultory Japanese band has been assembled. A film crew that has just arrived from Tokyo in ill-fitting if new uniforms is rolling tape, when a serious problem is spotted. The Australian POWs doing all the work look . . . like slaves? Starving, dressed in rags – it is a terrible look for the Japanese Empire.

Katto! Cut!

If we can't add flesh on their bones, we can at least cover their emaciated forms. The scattering of Australian and Dutch POWs are now issued with Japanese shorts, shirts and black sandshoes and they begin again.

Katto!

For the final dog-spike to be driven in – a golden one for the occasion, as the cameras roll – we need the ranking Japanese general to do the honours.

Action!

The fat officer, who was surely a Sumo wrestler before the war, portentously lifts the hammer high above his head, before bringing it down with massive force . . . alas missing the spike completely and hitting the rail with such a massive clang that seemingly every bird within 500 metres takes to the air in shrieks of protest.

Again!

This time he . . . nails it, and the job is complete.

On this day, 16 October 1943, the Japanese have achieved what the British and Dutch had not dared do anything more than contemplate, before rejecting, and they are thrilled – even though over 100,000 lives have been lost, and others ruined, in the process.

The ceremony is quickly completed with the raising of the Japanese flag, before a sergeant with a large bag walks along and claims back all the shirts, shoes and sandshoes from the POWs, leaving them near-naked once more. But it is neither them, nor generals, who are attracting attention.

For now alighting from the carriages are dozens of Korean *jugun ianfu* – 'military comfort women', teenagers and a little older – who are the latest arrivals from some 80,000 that have so far been rounded up in their native Korea and forced to go to disparate parts of the growing Japanese Empire to service the sexual needs of His Imperial Majesty's forces. Yes, in recent times, the more brutal of the Japanese authorities had realised that what had occurred during the likes of the 'Rape of Nanking' had, in terms of relieving sexual frustrations, lacked efficiency, and so had since instituted something that is nothing less than systemic rape.

In this case, the brothel train stops at each station for 48 hours while the officers and soldiers, in that order, line up. As ever, the queue is so constantly replenished that, in the course of the day and night, many women accommodate as many as 40 men before their shift ends. The next day, common soldiers start at dawn and go until around 4 pm, whereupon for the next three hours the NCOs take their turn. Commissioned officers keep going, into the night. Though most of the women are sick, there are no sick days, and to keep track of how many men they accommodate, a ticket system is used with soldiers, NCOs and senior officers being issued with white, blue and red tickets respectively. After each act of intercourse is completed, the women collect the tickets and present the collection at the end of the shift, so the authorities may quantify the level of 'comfort' she has provided.

Inevitably, Australian interaction with these tragic women is very limited, though one soldier will report a feared Japanese officer known as 'The Tiger' asking one of the Australian officers, Captain 'Roaring Reggie' Newton, if he would like some of the women to be sent over to the Australians' camp.

'No,' replies Roaring Reggie, quietly for once, 'I'd prefer a few more bags of rice . . .'[9]

The completion of the railway is not something any of the Australians can celebrate, beyond their own survival to this point – for they, more than anyone, are aware of the cost in lives to get it done. Courtesy of the slave labour that has been used – their own – a project that had been estimated by civil engineers to take five years has been bashed and thrashed through by the military engineers in just 16 months. It has cost the lives of about 100,000 men, together with many women and children among the Asian forced labourers, particularly the Tamils. Of the dead men, some 3000 are Australians – around one life for every sleeper laid along the overall 400 kilometres of track.

(Though workers on the Thai–Burma Railway were just four per cent of all Australians who saw active service in the Second World War, they tallied just under a third of all deaths.)

•

Where to from here?

With the completion of the Line, most of the survivors of Dunlop Force must leave Kinsayok and head back to Tarsau 'on Shanks's pony', to await their next assignment.

Carefully, Weary secretes his contraband, including his radio – all its parts again put among medical equipment – the best he can. His diaries are hidden in the folds of big medical textbooks, as are some of the outrageous 'Routine Orders' from their captors, all breaching the Geneva Convention. His precious prismatic compass, which he keeps for the day that the worst comes to the worst and they simply must try to escape, he straps behind his scrotum – before setting off, initially a little bow-legged, to Tarsau.

Mercifully, he is able to get through the initial search upon camp entry without discovery. Blue quickly has the contraband placed in secure spots where, if it is discovered, cannot be traced back to Weary, or anyone for that matter.

No sooner has Dunlop settled in at Tarsau than he tells the Camp Intelligence Officer, Lieutenant Colonel Frederick Ian Noel McOstrich – no, really – that he has the set with him.

'Well,' McOstrich says, instantly turning white, 'we need that like a hole in the head!'

'Why worry,' Weary replies with a lightness he does not feel, 'about a hole in a detached head!'[10]

At least it does not take long to get a feel for the place.

'Tarsau,' in Weary's view, is 'actually a filthy hole – unsanitary – open trench latrines and filth all over the place. A good place to escape from really.'[11]

Not that it would be easy for all that, as the camp 'now has a formidable system of parades: a great deal of time is consumed in numbering and checking all the troops (all ordering and numbering is in Japanese) . . .'

Roku-jū-nana! Sixty-seven!
Roku-jū-hachi! Sixty-eight!

. . .

'Discussed my function in the area with Col Harvey. I am to take over the hospital and convalescent depot from tomorrow . . . The lads flatter me by showing extraordinary pleasure that I am now going to stay here.'[12]

One thing is for sure, he will be busy.

With the Thai–Burma Railway now finished, the pressure to send sick men out to work themselves to death is over, and the Japanese can actually send them to hospital. Three hospitals have been established at the southern end of the Line – at Tarsau, Kanchanaburi and Chungkai – and they are all now overflowing with POWs who have been evacuated there from their own abandoned railway camps.

•

Still the sick and wounded just keep coming and coming down the river on barges so heavily laden they are only just above water. The

River Kwai looks more like the Styx, for the damned floating upon it seem nearer the underworld than this world. Some of the men have tropical ulcers, many of them have only just survived cholera and malaria. To a man, none would bet the other would last the next day.

As the barges nudge into the bank, many willing hands are waiting to get the men – eerie in their deathly silence, stinking and sinking even as they float – into the hospital.

'There were about sixty people to a barge, half of them already dead,' one POW will recount. 'They'd been in these barges for nearly two weeks. And they were absolutely silent. None of them could speak. They looked almost inhuman – they were hardly human. It's difficult to describe. They were covered in flies, and their own faeces, and filth. And we took them out, and this really produced a lot of tears.'[13]

And yet, there is one other thing that makes an even tougher impact.

'The stench was worse than that of dead men,' one Australian will recount. 'It was impossible for me not to be ill or to go near them. The men on the barge had to be carried up a precipitous river bank.'[14]

One of those helping is a powerful RAAF man who, after carrying nine men, collapses. He can take no more.

And that other big bloke, who just keeps going and going?

It is Weary, who doesn't even wrinkle his nose. Once upon a time, back on the farm, he could carry a bumper bag of wheat under each arm. That strength is gone, but so is the weight of the men he now carries, and he just keeps going until he has carried a couple of dozen sick patients up the bank, and the barges on this particular morning are empty.

'All this time our greatest worry was that something would happen to Dunlop or Corlette,' one POW will recount, 'that they would catch some deadly disease that would take them from us. Maybe there was a greater force which kept them going.'[15]

One of the patients is so badly gone that Weary decides to operate on him immediately, only for his heart to conk out.

'Colonel Dunlop made an incision over this man's heart, and massaged it back to life.'[16]

That man vows to name his first son after Weary.

•

From the first, it is obvious that things are going to be different here, as the entire camp is *crawling* with Kempis, and even the interpreters appear to be acting as spies for them. It is difficult for the Australians to be away from the penetrating gaze of their captors.

And in these parts, the local Japanese officers prefer to proffer *no* hints of raids to come.

For, now, devastating news comes that the Japanese have indeed discovered wireless sets in a search at the camp of Kanchanaburi, some 48 miles to the south-east. Closer, at Tarsau, an Australian officer, Lieutenant Colonel McKellar, has been beaten, arrested and thrown into solitary.

Worse still, back at Hintok, Lieutenant Colonel Cranston McEachern had suddenly been marched away, presumably because of discovered contraband.

With every day it feels like the noose is tightening.

Weary knows he is 'at risk' of a search discovering his radio, possibly after being named by some of his fellow POWs under torture. At a meeting with his fellow senior officers, it is agreed that things are grave, the talk 'enlivened by some grim accounts of kempis tortures'.[17]

They decide, between them all, that if any of them is hauled in for questioning, the only way forward is to resolutely deny all knowledge of a wireless set, no matter what pressure you are put under. To admit it would be to sign your own death warrant. (And yes, they could throw it all down the latrines, but then that would deny them contact from the outside world, the one thing that lifts their spirits. That is *unthinkable*.)

But just a couple of days later, it happens.

Weary is collared in a civil fashion at first; his 'arrest' is so polite that he will put it in his diary later in inverted commas, and he is at first unsure if he is being detained at all. All doubt is erased soon enough, however, as he is hurled into a cell, knocked over and knocked out, over and out, likely with a rifle butt to the back of his head. As he comes to sometime later, his first action is to carefully put his hands all over his throbbing head to see if his skull might have been cracked – to find that mercifully, no, it had just been a clean KO. As he continues to assess his situation, he rues the fact that, within a concealed pocket he had sewn on the inside of his shirt, he has some coded notes he had taken just the day before of news that had come over the radio. Under the circumstances, what had he been THINKING? Quickly, before they come for him for the inevitable questioning, he chews up the paper and swallows it.

He is just in time, before Japanese guards indeed appear to drag him away.

'Curiously,' he will recount, 'my prolonged interrogation was not accompanied by a search of my gear in the lines. I hoped that it would be dispersed by friends.'[18]

Either way, he is questioned again and again about his strange knowledge of the course of the war. Where does that information come from if not a radio? Why is it that other men have identified him as the source of all the news, if it's not true?

The Japanese know the answer to this; they just want him to admit it so they can get on with killing him. There is no point to being tortured needlessly – for your death will come either way and it is just the condition of your corpse that will differ.

Had Weary been a cricketer at this point, his score at stumps would be no runs taken, no chances given. Everything is played with a dead bat. He answers as little as possible, and gives away nothing, speaking in wide generalities that betray no-one.

But after several hours, his interrogating officer – who Weary thinks of as 'Stone Face', as they have not been introduced and he has nothing else to work with – suddenly changes tack. Leaping to his feet, he pulls down a screen filled with some kind of illustration and Japanese hieroglyphics.

And now, as he points to a central figure in the middle of the drawing, he roars in triumph: '*You* are this person – we know all about you and your set – you will be executed, but first you will talk!'[19]

It is with precisely this in mind that Weary is now clapped in manacles, with all his limbs immovable, while two hefty Japanese soldiers begin to beat him with large lumps of firewood, every time he answers no to a question that Stone Face wants a yes to.

Do you have a radio?

No. (*Whack!*)

Have you ever had a radio?

No. (*Whack!*)

Do you know who else has had a radio?

No. (*Whack!*)

Through the fog of pain, Weary cannot help but think of British officers in an adjacent camp who had been beaten to death in this exact manner. But he cannot break. No matter how much they beat him, he maintains his innocence. Truthfully, however, for all his strength, if he had a cyanide pill right now he would swallow it without hesitation. What is the point in going on? They will never let him go, and his existence now is nothing but agony.

Finally, even Stone Face tires of it and tells him simply: 'You must die.'

Some good news at last.

Weary braces as he is pushed, hit and flogged towards a tree; there his manacles are taken off . . . and put round the tree. His wrists are bound not just behind his back but behind the tree trunk as he stands torn and taut: 'my bare belly exposed to four bayonets wielded by an execution squad of four'. The four grunt, yell and scream; Weary knows that their words mean nothing now, it is primal, they are 'working themselves up to "the moment"'.

And now the strangely long-haired interpreter tells him: 'You are to have the grace of thirty seconds before you die.'

Ichi . . . ni . . . san . . . yon . . .[20]

Weary, while staring straight at Stone Face, feels strangely other-worldly.

'This can't be me,' he says to himself. 'I don't feel frightened enough. It's just unreal!'

If he is about to meet his maker, he is in so much pain, it is not *all* bad. The weirdest thing of all? His mind wanders back to a time at school in Benalla when, after an escapade, he had 'anticipated expulsion and disgrace'. For a reason he cannot quite understand, but it occurs to him now, he had felt more upset about that than whatever distress he feels now.

'Will anyone even know how I died?' thinks Weary. Perhaps that is a blessing.

Is the insistent, jarring voice of the interpreter to be the last words he will hear in this world? Could it really be that in a world filled with Beethoven, Brahms, birdsong and bubbling brooks, the last sounds he will ever hear is this staccato barking?

Juuhachi . . . juukyuu . . . juuku . . . nijuu . . .

'Now ten seconds to go. Have you last message for relatives? I shall try to convey.'

Building the railway 'bund' (embankment) in the jungle at Konyu. Watercolour by Jack Chalker. (AWM ART91846)

Hellfire Pass. (AWM 157859)

A train crossing the Hintok curved trestle bridge, one of six constructed by POWs between Hellfire Pass and Hintok Station, approximately 3 kilometres apart. (AWM 120511)

Jack Chalker's watercolour of camp utensils used in the hospital at Tarsau on the Thai–Burma Railway. Many of the improvised utensils are constructed from bamboo and other salvaged materials. (AWM ART90847)

Colonel Edward 'Weary' Dunlop and Captain Jacob Markowitz working on a thigh amputation, Chungkai. Oil on cardboard, Jack Chalker, 1946. Markowitz and Weary did not actually operate together at Chungkai but Chalker depicted them doing so as a tribute to both men. (AWM ART91848)

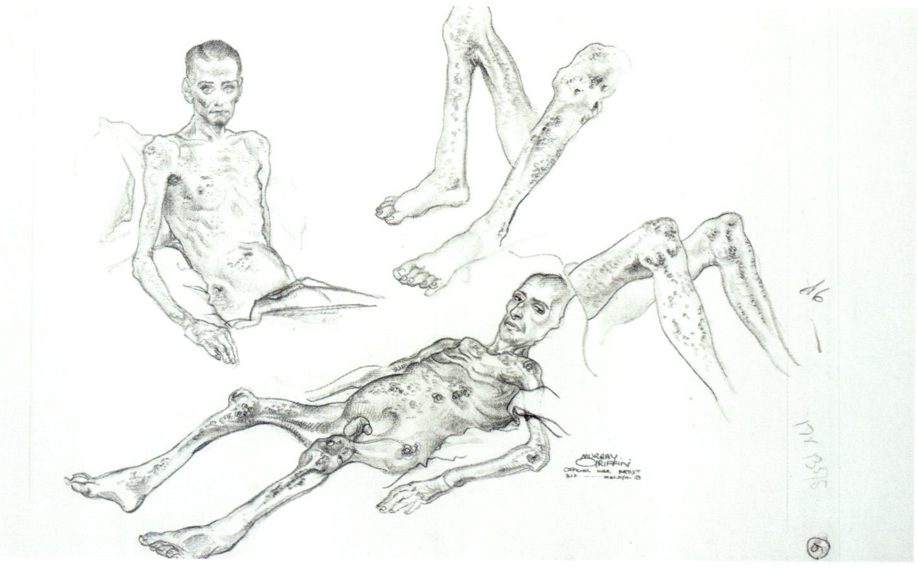

Back from Thailand. Figure studies of recently returned men from the Thai–Burma Railway showing their physical condition, drawn by Murray Griffin in Changi. (AWM ART25103)

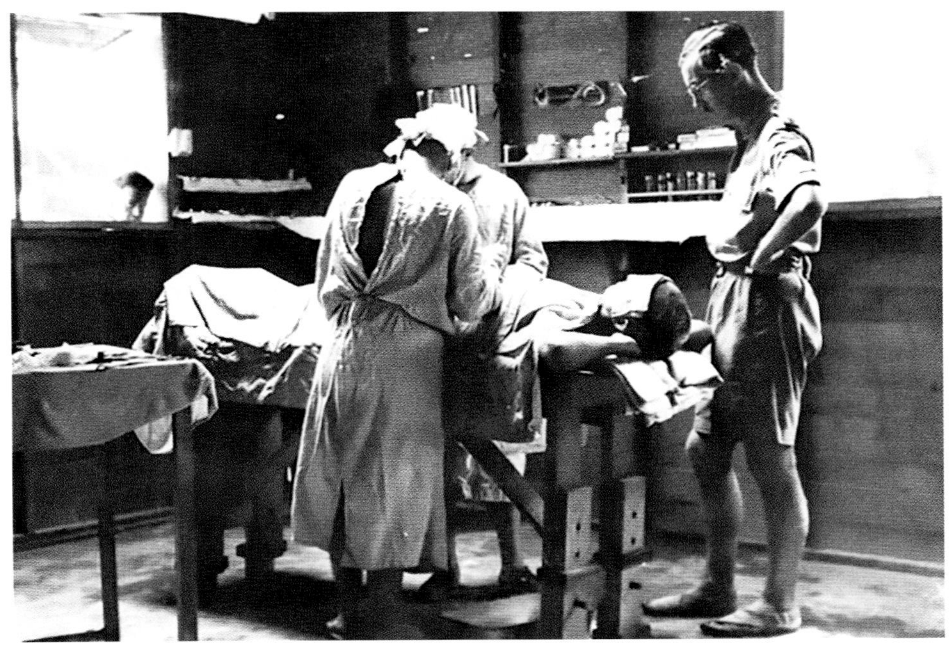

A surgical operation in progress in the operating theatre at the POW hospital, Nakom Patom, 1944. (AWM 157874)

A hospital ward in Singapore showing members of the 8th Division released from the Changi POW camp, 1945. (AWM 019199)

Bangkok, Thailand, 15 September 1945. Weary conferring with Lieutenant Colonel Albert Coates. They are examining the medical record as documented by Jack Chalker and others. (AWM 117361)

September, 1945. Members of the Allied War Graves Commission with Boonpong Sirivejjabhandu, the Thai merchant who regularly risked his life to provide secret assistance to Australian POWs. (AWM P02310.017)

Helen Ferguson. Weary felt he 'needed to get civilised again' before marrying Helen, but in the end they were married on 8 November 1945, just three weeks after his arrival back in Australia.

Weary and former POW guard, Yi Hak-Nae, 20 August 1991. (Fairfax Photos/SMH/Peter Morris)

Weary at the Commonwealth War Cemetery in Kanchanaburi, Thailand, on Anzac Day, 25 April 1991. (Fairfax Photos/SMH/Robert Pearce)

Weary looks him right in the eye and says: 'Last message, conveyed by thugs like you? No, thanks!'

Now the bayonets are taken out of their scabbards, and the four soldiers hover, their rifles drawn back for the fatal thrust.

Weary steels himself, knowing the end has come.

'Stop!' Stone Face suddenly cries out. 'He will suffer a lot more than this before he dies – untie him!'

Clearly disappointed that Stone Face has ruined their fun, the guards down bayonets and in an instant the manacles are removed – before Weary is given yet one more beating, albeit without questioning. And now he is dragged back to a cell so small it is more like a dog-cage and he can only sit there cross-legged 'facing a wall to await execution and presumably meantime to improve my attitude'.[21]

Under the circumstances that is going to be something of a stretch, as one of the sentries who is there to guard him strikes him with the butt of his rifle if ever his body slumps.

What to do?

Weary starts to recite lines from one of his favourite poems, 'Ode to a Nightingale', by John Keats:

> *Now more than ever seems it rich to die,*
> *To cease upon the midnight with no pain,*
> *While thou art pouring forth thy soul abroad*
> *In such an ecstasy!*

As he mumbles the poem, his eye is caught by a lizard in his cell, an actual one, and he watches it with some envy. So free, so calm. Weary concentrates on the tiny reptile, for one very good reason.

'It seemed too painful to think of home, my beloved Helen, or past life.'[22]

Just when he is starting to prepare himself for a long night, it happens again.

Once more he is dragged out and put up against the same tree – to be once more prepared for death with four Japanese soldiers drawing their bayonets back, as the count goes on.

'But again, surprisingly to me, the last second reprieve.'[23]

While not being killed is admittedly a big step forward, he is still dragged back in manacles to a small cage. This time he is thrown in with a man who appears to be of mixed Thai and Chinese ethnicity. And yet that is not what truly takes Weary's attention. Rather, he looks with some envy how easily and loosely the other man's manacles fit around his slim wrists, while Weary's own cut into his flesh and make his hands swell. Making things none the easier is his companion's opening gambit at conversation.

Putting his hand in the shape of a pistol, he points it at Weary and says, 'You – bang!'

Yes, quite, and nice to meet you, too.

In short order when a bowl of rice is pushed in, again Weary must envy the dexterity the fellow has with his hands, 'whilst I made such heavy going attempts to eat'.

As it happens, his appetite is not the strongest anyway as he knows he is in no less than a torture complex, as witness the screams of agony he can hear all around, and he knows all too well what he is likely about to face. It will probably be the Japanese specialty, where his hands are handcuffed behind his back, and he is obliged to stand on a high chair, while one end of a rope is tied around the handcuffs, and the other thrown over a high beam and secured.

Once the chair is kicked away, he will be left, 'dangling with a double dislocation of the shoulders'. And it is at this point the 'real torture then begins, eyes, testicles, etc'.

It can only be a matter of time.

'I frankly wondered whether I had the fibre to take it.'

For in his weakened state, just how long could he hold on?

And what then?

The possible scenarios keep tumbling forth.

'"Yes," you say, "I have the [ham-radio] set — you can have it."'

But would the torture stop then?

It would not.

'[For] then the Judas pit opens: "Who gave you the set?" "Who supplied the batteries?" "With whom did you communicate?"'

Over and over, he keeps going through his fates, while the screams go on through the night. When his Thai–Chinese companion is taken out and 'tidily shot', Weary strangely feels a bit better for it. Perhaps he might get the same, a nice bullet to the head?

Yes.

He is, truly, 'almost hoping for a quick clean end. Shooting seemed promotion.'

And now, finally, late on the second day of his incarceration, he is for the third time dragged out of his cage. To his surprise, and momentary disappointment, he is not put up against the wall before a firing squad.

The torture chamber, then?

Oddly, no.

Instead, he is again brought before Colonel Stone Face, but this time given a chair to sit on. Stone Face wants Dunrop to understand a few things before they get to grips.

'Colonel,' he begins, 'you must understand that though you have not talked, that others have and we know that you are guilty.'

'If they have talked, they are liars,' Weary snarls in reply. 'Why don't you give me a fair trial to throw the lies in their faces!'[24]

Stone Face stares at him as impassively as ever. Finally, after some 30 seconds of silence he asks in the manner of one who really wants to know: 'Is it that you really have not done these things or that you will not talk?'

With something between a snort and a sneer, Weary replies. 'Have I not spent all this time telling you that I know nothing?'

But now Stone Face asks the question that Weary had never seen coming, one that truly shocks him.

'Colonel, if I were to release you this time, would you have hard feelings against the Japanese, hard feelings against me? We kempis do but do our duty.'

'From all I have heard of you kempis,' Weary replies carefully, 'I feel that I have been well treated.'[25]

Which, in a way is true. He has *not* been shot in the head.

But what is going on? Weary does not quite know. Whereas only 30 minutes ago he was sure his end had come, and was looking forward to it, he now seems to have established some 'curious affinity' with this previous brute of a man, as the Japanese officer displays humanity Weary had previously thought was simply not there.

Stone Face suddenly barks some orders. The manacles are removed and Weary is even given beer and cigarettes.

And now it hits Weary.

'Suddenly I realised that prisoners' eyes would be on me being treated to the fatted calf, obviously as a reward for telling all, and this dimmed the surge of joy at my release.'[26]

But, release it is, even if, from now on, with ubiquitous, menacing regularity, the Kempis look him over and cheerily pronounce: 'Colonel, how is your health? We kempis know that you are dangerous spy!'[27]

And yet still Weary will not leave well enough alone, and rejoice in his last-minute salvation.

When Major Bill Wearne and several other officers are savagely interrogated before being thrown into solitary to await their likely execution, Weary secures an audience with Stone Face to make it absolutely clear.

'If Wearne and the others are executed,' he tells him, 'there will be hell to pay.'[28]

Yes. If Japan loses this war, such an atrocity will not be forgotten and you, personally, will be pursued. You have my word. You can't kill all of us, and those that survive will remember every name of those who did not – and who gave the orders to murder them. You.

Wearne and the others are released a short time later.

•

How proudly F Force had left, just nine months earlier.

And now, how shattered are the survivors who on this dark day just before Christmas return to Changi.

'In the trucks sat slowly moving skeletons emaciated almost beyond belief, many with dreadful sores and peeling skin, some unable to move, and others so light [even] a Changi prisoner had no difficulty in lifting them.'[29]

They are ghosts of who they were, their mournful memories haunting all who gaze at them now.

Sergeant Stan Arneil is one of the skeletons shuffling back onto the parade ground, with his few surviving mates. The men already in Changi watch them aghast, in much the same manner as they had once watched aghast as the Java Rabble had arrived. Stan can see their horror, but still stands as straight as he can like the soldier he once was, the soldiers they once were, and *still* are, at least in their minds. 'Those who couldn't stand up straight were on sticks. And those who couldn't stop shaking with malaria were held by friends . . . Our emaciated, cadaverous bodies were covered in rags, we were all barefooted with bandages covering our ulcers and we were almost all rotten with malaria and beri-beri.'[30]

The Sergeant Major bids them stand at ease and he struts to Colonel A. A. Johnson, who walks to Colonel Fred 'Black Jack' Galleghan: 'All present and correct, sir.'

No, not all are present. Just a few.

'Where are the rest?' asks Black Jack.

'They're all here, sir,' the Sergeant Major answers. And so they are.

Stan watches Black Jack Galleghan, the legend, the iron man, break down and cry. It is incredible, but it is true. And still the tottering, emaciated men stand still, waiting to be dismissed.

'We wanted to show them we were soldiers.'[31]

You are dismissed, men. We are glad to have you back.

And they are glad to be back – and all the more so for the fact that the long-time Changi men now raid the stores they had been building up for Christmas lunch and press them upon these wretched survivors of F Force.

'Their joy was our reward,' the History of the 2/29th Battalion, 8th Australian Division AIF will record. 'It was the best Christmas dinner any of us had ever had.'[32]

For who can doubt it?

'Changi was like Heaven compared to what they had endured.'[33]

•

As late Christmas presents go, it could not be better. For just before 1944 rises on the eastern horizon, still in Tarsau Camp, Weary receives, 'by grace of that magnificent man, Boon Pong',[34] the very thing he has been most praying for: 'A valuable supply of drugs and [money].'[35]

The way this Thai trader continues to risk torture and death for them is inspirational, and with the hospital camps – that are now established and overflowing on the southern end of the railway – continuing to fill with the ragged remnants of survivors, all suffering from many ailments at once, Boon Pong's efforts have never been more appreciated than now.

God bless his cotton socks, *and* the Thai resistance movement, V, which continues to support them in this manner. The medicine and money have come just in time for their next move, this time to the 'light sick hospital of Chungkai', where, Weary is informed by his Japanese masters, he is to be the Commanding Officer of the hospital, responsible for the health of all the POW patients.

Which would be fine, except he knows that all the most impor-tant medical cases are being evacuated to the biggest hospital camp in Thailand, Nakom Patom, so that is of course where he would prefer to be. Nevertheless, in mid-January, Weary, together with 200 others, is moved once more, this time in very hot open carriages on the newly constructed railway to the just established POW hospital at Chungkai, where they arrive in the late afternoon to a great and pleasing surprise.

'I was simply astonished,' Weary will recount, 'to see so many well-remembered men standing by the road about the place and without a leg. There were over 100 amputations about, wishing to see me.'[36]

And one other is there . . .

Dr Arthur Moon!

The two have not seen each other since April the previous year at the Hintok Mountain Camp, and can now compare notes as to who has lived, who has died, what happened to the double amputee we worked on back in Hintok, and where that cross-eyed fellow who had lost an arm is now. Sadly, 30 of the men that Weary has sent Moon's way are no more, but, overall, the survival rate has been a testament to the likeable doctor's skills of surgery and care.

Among other things that Moon tells Weary is that, before leaving his previous camp at Tamarkan, he had buried all of his medical documents and diaries documenting Japanese atrocities in a tin in the jungle, which he hopes to retrieve after the war. The documents are significant and list all the names, addresses and military numbers of all the patients he has treated, what they were suffering from, and – too often – the date of their deaths. If the Allies win the war, the records will be invaluable in bringing the worst of their captors to justice.

Still one more POW that it is a particular joy to be able to meet up with again is Jack Chalker, the wonderful artist who had been evacuated many months before, but has against all odds survived. Deputising him as physiotherapist, Weary puts him to work in the 'rehabilitation unit using massage and physiotherapy to rebuild muscles destroyed by tropical ulcers'.[37]

And on the quiet?

He is also able to use Chalker's artistic skills once more 'to keep a visual record of the conditions, illnesses, surgical treatments, and the brutality of the camps. It was a death sentence if caught by the guards, but it was worth it.'[38]

For his part, Chalker – well-known among his fellow POWs for constantly humming Vera Lynn's classics 'We'll Meet Again' and 'The White Cliffs of Dover', something that tends to lift everyone, starting with Jack himself – is thrilled to be back with the men who had saved his life in those early terrible months on the Thai–Burma Railway, and to be doing such interesting work for Weary.

'[Weary] had a little sort of a stool rather than table,' he will recount, 'made of rough bits of wood with a false top to it and in that he kept some of my drawings and I kept the rest in my pack and in the ground.'[39]

Such subterfuge is not always possible.

For at much the same time that Weary is meeting up with Chalker, Petty Officer Ray Parkin – himself separated from Weary since October 1943 – is preparing to move from the camp at Tarsau to the one at Tamuan, with the problem this time being they are given no time to prepare. Move! Move! Move!

Stand out the front of your hut, with all your belongings before you, for a search.

When?

Now!

Speedo! Speedo! Speedo!

Ray Parkin rushes out with all the rest, panic-stricken. Normally, he would have had time to secrete his diaries, drawings and paintings in the middle of hollow bits of bamboo. But now, *in extremis*, he only has time to do one thing.

'All my drawings and diaries, which were flat,' he will recount, 'I'd put underneath the canvas, and then put the rest of my poor belongings on top and make a big show of those.'[40]

For, make no mistake.

'It was all spread with a candid innocence which proclaimed that it could not conceal anything.'[41]

Gazing down upon such sad effects – scraps of linen, a dirty blanket and tatty trinkets, at least laid out 'with some semblance of naval good order' – the guard pauses briefly.

Parkin stands to attention in a more attention-like way than any would think possible.

He knows you can never be too serious for the Japanese, who think that over-the-top is a minimum standard for soldierly deportment. His face is the exemplar of 'wooden seriousness', his 'body strained to an exaggerated "attention"',[42] his chest is puffed up, his arms 'stretched like bow-strings at my side'.[43]

And all for very good reason.

This whole display of exaggerated obeisance he knows, 'appeals to Japanese soldiers'.[44]

The officer inspecting gives him an approving glance.

'For good measure, I threw him a stiff salute.'[45]

You are the man in charge, and I am but your pawn, honoured to be shoved around by you, should you so choose. I offer obeisance to enjoy, not a challenge to be crushed and destroyed.

The fact that the officer now feels obliged to return the salute, checks what would have been his normal progress, 'the crawling predatory picnic he had just been having with the other kits'.[46]

Instead, he glances down and seems surprised at how neatly Parkin's possessions are arranged, almost artistically. It would be a shame to disturb them.

Still, the guard takes a step forward and Parkin crumbles in fear. He is about to be exposed, and the best he can hope for is a savage beating to within an inch of his life – and then three-quarters of an inch.

But now the guard stops, with his feet right on the edge of the canvas.

'*Yuroshi!*' he says, by way of friendly greeting. 'Number One – gooda! *Yasume.*'[47]

And he moves on.

•

For his part, by now Weary is confident that the war will be won, something that he can't resist reminding his captors of.

'You'll die for this after the war,' he tells one Japanese officer at Tarsau who has particularly displeased him for his ill-treatment of POWs. 'I'll see you hang for this.'[48]

And in the end it is like that favourite camp singalong:

'They'll be flying in formation when they come/ They'll be dropping thousand pounders when they come.'[49]

And how funny they should sing that.

For one day in July 1944, they are out and about in Tamarkan, when they hear a drone overhead, and see 27 Liberators – the B-24 bombers of the Allied Air Force – coming in over the low hills in flying formation of three successive waves of nine.

'They ain't coming for tea,'[50] one Australian POW dryly tells another. And indeed they ain't. Billowing plumes of smoke to their south a short time later say they were coming to bomb the Line. And there will be plenty more where they came from.

•

Boon Pong continues to provide Weary with medicine and food, but this, *this* black gold has come from another source – one of the Bangkok embassies – through the mighty Red Cross – and all the Australians who see it are beside themselves with joy.

Vegemite!

At Weary's instigation and insistence, all patients have been assigned one of A, B, C, D, E or F diets depending on what ails them – and as F is for those suffering severe vitamin deficiencies, they are the ones who get Australia's favourite spread, just a spoonful a day. And all you other hungry bastards keep your paws off it!

The results are simply stunning. One of the orderlies, Flying Officer Tom Young, will recall ministering Vegemite to two patients who 'were the most horrible sight I think I've ever seen in terms of human beings'.[51]

Their bloated legs, their swollen hands and grotesque faces are horrors that even the most blasé doctor blanches at.

Assigned other duties, a fortnight later Young runs into the doctor who had the care of those two particular patients, expecting they might well have died by now, so crook, so 'butcher's hook', did they look.

'How are those blokes?'[52] he asks.

Without a word the doctor takes him by the arm and leads him to the ward for patients about to be released. And there they are, with colour in their cheeks and *life* in their eyes, looking fine.

'Completely like you and I,' Young will recount many years later, still with wonder, 'just in that fortnight with Vegemite.'[53]

•

Weary has only just arrived at another camp, Tamuan, when he spies, with his little eye . . . something beginning with 'R'.

Ray Parkin!

Weary has not seen Ray since he'd sent him to hospital at Kinsayok eight months prior, and it is a wonderful reunion as they quickly catch up on each other's news. Among other things, Weary is thrilled to hear that Scotty, Parkin's old mate who had refused to die from cholera, is still alive!

'Here was Scotty,' Parkin recounts of his meeting with him at one of the camps, 'just a remnant of a man, [but] that same old spirit. They brought him in some lime juice, a little quarter of a cup. He wouldn't drink it. Well, he says, "It's not very nice drinking when you fellers haven't got one."'[54] And that is Scotty all over. You could not kill that bastard with a crowbar! And such a gentleman about it.

Alas, only a short time later, it is clear that a bigger move for Parkin himself is in the offing as the Japanese accelerate plans to take POWs who have recovered enough from building railways and send them to Japan to provide the slave labour necessary to work in munitions factories and mines. Among the first to go in these 'Japan parties' as they are called, will be Dunlop Force's O and P Battalions, which include two men that Weary has the highest regard for: Ray Parkin and Tom Uren.

On the night before departure, Parkin comes to Weary's hut to firstly give him good news, and to lay before him a problem.

The news is that, once again, dear Thelma has somehow got through to him, and he has just received three letters from her via the Red Cross, complete with news of his children: 'Jill and John talk about you often . . . he wants you to know he has a car . . . they keep me busy and they keep me loving you too – the darlings. For a while, farewell darling.'[55]

And they have heard that he is still alive, as Thelma confirms in the last letter.

'At last we know you are safe.'[56]

Oh, the joy!

But now, the problem.

For two years now, Ray has been painting and compiling his diary, a minute record of their experiences – and proof of Japanese atrocities. It has been hell on earth to keep smuggling everything from camp to camp, to survive raid after raid. The fact that he has got this far is in itself a miracle.

But now if he is judged as fit enough to be part of a Japan party, could he really risk it all by taking it with him?

Sanity has to prevail, on the realisation that 'I couldn't possibly conceal them any longer'.[57]

Weary steps up to the mark, and instantly offers to take charge of all diaries and drawings.

Parkin is overwhelmed with gratitude. It is not that Weary is the Bank of England, but if anyone is capable of keeping all his material safe, it is him. As it happens, the two talk late into the night.

One of the most sensitive things they talk about is Weary's fiancée, Helen. Not to put too fine a point on it, Weary unloads his fears of whether or not Helen will wait for him until the war is over, and even if she does, whether he will be up to making her happy, and being happy himself. Ray – as the older, married man – offers judicious counsel. As to whether or not Weary's varied infidelities since he'd last seen Helen seven years before might discount him from settling down, that, too, is discussed.

'I knew that he'd been a man of the world, he made no secret of that,' Parkin notes, and also records his own reply: 'Look, it'll be alright.'

Ray warms to the theme of how close a married couple can become and what a joyous state it is, particularly when, like him and Thelma, that marriage is blessed with children. As parents, contemplating their son and daughter, they have truly become *one*.

'Thelma and I,' the naval officer says, 'we get to a situation where I'm her and she's me. And we can't separate us. We really get that feeling, the inter-penetration of personalities, until they're bonded.'[58]

Weary brightens up to hear it, for that is exactly what he wants, but still he can't help but wonder if he could live up to it.

'Of course you can, Weary,' Ray assures him. 'It is only a matter of practice.'

As soon as Ray has gone, Weary rouses Blue Butterworth, and they get to work. After turning the table upside down, they place all of Ray's material on the underside of the top and nail a false bottom on it, before turning it upright once more.

In the morning, it is time.

O and P Battalions are to depart.

Weary puts them on parade to address them before the trucks come. The mood is happy. True, they don't know what they are heading towards, but they know what they are leaving behind.

And yet Weary wants them to go assured of one thing. He has never been prouder to be an Australian than in the time he has spent with them.

What we have gone through, together, can never be understood by anyone else. The friends and brothers we have lost, together, will never be forgotten. We have survived; and it is our duty now to live.

Weary's words are soft, but his voice carries and strikes through every unguarded heart.

In short order, he is done, and wishes them well. Until we meet again.

Auld lang syne.

And suddenly it happens.

'Hip-hip!'

'HOORAY!'

'I retired very discomforted by three very loud and embarrassing cheers which I feared the Nipponese might regard as a demonstration.'[59]

Whatever his pride in them and gratitude for their efforts, it is as nothing compared to how they feel about him. As this new chapter in their lives opens, let the record show one thing.

'Every survivor of Dunlop Force,' one will say, 'owes his life to the "Christ of Thailand".'[60]

And so they march away.

CHAPTER SIXTEEN

THE HOUR BEFORE THE DAWN

The weariness, the fever, and the fret
Here, where men sit and hear each other groan . . .
Where youth grows pale, and spectre-thin, and dies;
Where but to think is to be full of sorrow
And leaden-eyed despairs

John Keats, 'Ode to a Nightingale'

Mid-June 1944, Nakom Patom, a last lap of luxury
Good news. At last Weary gets word that he is to be moved to the newly constructed hospital camp, the Nakom Patom Sanatorium, just 35 miles from Bangkok, in what had formerly been – just four months before – open rice fields.

'The function of the camp,' the Chief Medical Officer, Lieutenant Colonel Bertie Coates, will recount, 'was to provide an asylum for 10,000 chronically sick and permanently disabled European prisoners of war from the Burma–Siam railway.'[1]

It consists of 60 enormous huts made of bamboo, each one containing 200 men. There are no beds per se, not even bamboo ones, just wooden platforms without bedding. In the middle of the camp is one solidly constructed building, which has most things that are not accommodation, from an administrative office section to a dispensary and pathology lab to . . . an operating theatre. The last has – *swoon* – an actual concrete floor and comes complete with fine gauze on the windows to keep the flies out. Nearby cookhouses also have concrete floors and water troughs, while, as Coates notes, the 'latrines between the huts were covered concrete pits.

'Such luxury, we found rather overwhelming.'[2]

Typically, Weary Dunlop's effect is immediate, which starts with harnessing all the skills of those under his command, and, as Coates notes, 'Under Dunlop, recovered patients were soon making apparatus such as splints, rowing machines, stationary bicycles, artificial limbs, stretchers, belts and containers.'[3]

From what, exactly?

Pretty much everything that the POWs can contribute, including, as a previous camp notice has encouraged, 'tins and containers of all sorts, solder, flux, nails, wire, screws, sponge rubber, scraps of clothing, hose-tops and old socks, string, webbing, scraps of leather, rubber tubing, glass bottles of all sorts, glass tubing (transfusion purposes), canvas, elastic, rubber bands or strips, braces, wax, mahjong pieces, and tools of all sorts. Nothing is too old, nothing is too small.'[4]

Wonderfully helpful in such activities is the old builder, Private Bob Fox, who, now transferred to Nakom Patom, has established an artificial limb workshop, and with nine helpers – including an engineer, carpenters, a metal worker, saddlers and boot-makers – has made legs for 189 amputees, using everything from scrap wood to 'leather cured from hide, thread from unravelled packs, iron from retained portions of officers' stretchers, and oddments of sponge-rubber, elastic braces, etc.'[5]

And so it goes on.

'I don't know how they were able to think clearly enough to cope with it,' Jack Chalker notes. 'Because, I mean, they did have to improvise and change methods. And almost everything they did was a kind of one-off each time . . . I think the sort of magic part was the way if you put a lot of people together with different skills, they can move half a mountain.'[6]

That much, at least, had already been proved back at Hellfire Pass.

In the meantime, Coates puts Weary in charge of surgery, physiotherapy and continuing to raise money for the sick.

(A formidable man, is Colonel Coates. At one point, when he contracts scrub typhus, he barely blinks and simply has himself carried around the hospital on a stretcher and conducts his examinations from a rigidly slanted position, all while still puffing on his pipe. *Onwards*.)

For Weary, a long period of stability in the one hospital environment has begun. He is bemused and impressed by the laconic nature of the Australians when it comes to overcoming the struggles they have had with their health.

'What sort of sickness have you had?'
'Oh, not much, doc, not much at all.'
'Did you have malaria?'
'Oh yeah, had malaria.'
'Did you have beri-beri?'
'Oh yeah, I had beri-beri.'
'Did you have dysentery?'
'Oh yeah, I had dysentery.'
'Did you have pellagra?'
'Oh yes, I had pellagra.'[7]

You know, just the usual devastating diseases. Sometimes consecutively, and sometimes concurrently. But nothing really to write home about.

Onwards.

•

On 10 July 1944, Weary is summoned to the guardhouse and accused of 'reporting in late the previous night'.

Well, let the punishment fit the crime: 'In consequence of this, I was repeatedly struck on the face by a Korean guard and then compelled to kneel on the sand in the sun for a prolonged period.'[8]

Yes, as brutal as ever. But Weary is beginning to get more understanding of the Japanese perspective.

'Japan in this war,' an interpreter tries to explain to him, 'is like a desperate vagabond fighting a rich man with a top hat. You have to understand that in such a contest the rules of the game are not clean and gentlemanly.'[9]

August 1944, Nakom Patom, circumcision decision

Blue Butterworth never even sees it coming.

For it is just after the wet season is receding in the latter part of the year, when out of the blue, to Blue, Weary says:

'Blue, looks like you and I'll be parting.'

'Why?' replies Butterworth, stunned.

The short answer is, orders.

'Can't you cook the books?'

No, the boss can't.

'Well, I'm afraid they're sending people out to Ubon [in north-eastern Thailand] and different places.'

'Oh, what a pity. What about an operation on [the] day of movement?'

'What have you got?'

'Well, I got my tonsils. Do without those. I got my appendix. Do without that. I got me foreskin. Do without it.'

Take your pick, Colonel. Pick one of them, and remove it. But don't remove me from you.

In reply, the good Colonel gives his faithful mate a playful tap on the head with his bamboo reflex hammer, as if he would knock him out. It is his way of saying, it's agreed then.

'Right, the foreskin.'[10]

Greater and weirder love hath no man than this, than he will voluntarily lose a part of his penis to stay with the very man who will do the cutting. Weary does not designate the date of the operation, just . . . sometime soon.

•

Every Australian boy dreams of being made Captain of the Australian cricket team. Today for Weary Dunlop that dream comes true. A Test match is to be played at Nakom Patom to ring in New Year's Day 1945; England versus the old enemy, while guards of their mutual enemy watch on amused and confused. England's skipper is the English cricket journalist with the most famed by-line of his generation: E. W. Swanton.

Swanton had pre-war England hanging on his accounts of Tests far flung and at home. Well, they are never more far flung than today, with a bat that is no more than a sawn board (a foot shorter than regulation but two inches broader). And their ball is green and looks suspiciously like a very old tennis ball because that is what it is.

Their ground is about 60 by 30 yards, the batsman's crease is just a few feet ahead of cheering spectators, which somewhat limits any runs behind the wicket, as do the tall trees looking less than fine at fine leg, where squatting spectators hector any batsman who isn't belting the tennis ball. Scoring runs is simple, and not entirely dissimilar to the way it used to be in the backyard at Grandma's.

It's one if you get it into that ditch there, two over this hut here, six over the laundry line and 12 runs if you can cop a sentry on the bonce. Anything past deep mid-off is six and out, minus six runs.

Balls are precious, and the 'bored and sulky Korean sentry'[11] is not going to give them back.

The spectators are dressed very casually today, most sporting a 'Jap-Happy',[12] a tasteful loincloth, and a pair of clogs for the fancy. Real toffs have actual shorts and are allowed to stand in the Members Section. The Australian yobs can sit on the mound at long-on, which of course they christen The Hill, after the famous one at the SCG.

E. W. Swanton is already drafting his Wisden account in his head: 'The sun beats down, as tropical suns do, on the flat beaten earth which is the wicket. At the bowler's end is a single bamboo stump, at the other five . . .'

Wait, what? Five? Yes, that's right, it's a POW innovation to speed the game up and make it easier to bowl the British out. Plus, it will help them to get an LBW with batsmen whose legs are unfairly thin due to Japanese rations. Resume, Swanton: 'There is the hum of anticipation that you get on the first morning at Old Trafford or Trent Bridge, though there are no score cards, and no three penn'orth of comfort to be bought from our old friend Cushions.' GET ON WITH IT! They do. Opening for England today is Flight Lieutenant John Cocks of Ashtead and Lieutenant Norman Smith of Halifax. As one would expect, they bat like English openers, which is another way of saying bloody boring.

Weary brings on the spinners, he tells the quicks to bounce, he tells the spectators to heckle these jackals, but they insist on playing properly, playing 'beautifully down the line of the ball, forcing the length ball past cover, squeezing the leg one square off their toes'.

They also have an uncanny knack of hitting the ball into the swill bucket, which should be bloody illegal, but it is too late now. The barracking grows louder as the runs mount up. 'DO SOMETHING, DUNLOP, YOU USELESS BASTARD!' (And that is coming from his own wicketkeeper.) Weary takes the ball and unveils devilish spin bowling, complete with the rare wet Bosie, but those damn Englishmen keep their heads and their wickets. If it weren't for the dysentery, it would be impossible to get these buggers to leave the wicket.

Swanton is delighted; the Australians in the crowd have to delight themselves. 'As the runs mount up the barracking gains in volume, and in wit at the expense of the fielders.'[13]

TAKE A CHANCE, POM! LIKE CHURCHILL DID AT GALLIPOLI! Traditional favourites are rolled out: 'SEND HIM DOWN A GRAND PIANO, SEE IF HE CAN PLAY THAT!'

He can, they all bloody can, and the smirking Swanton finally magnanimously declares to put the Australians out of their misery: 'the score is acknowledged to be a Thailand record'.[14]

Right! What's sauce for the goose is a flat pitch too for the gander, and the Australians are ready to show these English their best Bradman impersonations with the bat when a sensation erupts. The Poms are cheating! How?

'Fizzer Pearson, of Sedbergh and Lincolnshire, the English fast bowler, is wearing BOOTS!'[15]

Disgusting. Every other player, bowler and batsman alike has played with bare and hot feet, with 'the occasional flint being accepted as part of the game'.[16] It is typical of the English to keep such a secret weapon as footwear all to themselves. How on earth did these buggers get those buggers? A pair of cricket boots in Thailand is like a set of parasols in the Arctic; they are ludicrously unnecessary.

'WHERE DID HE GET THOSE BOOTS?' the roar comes. Followed by a louder roar 'BOUGHT FROM FUCKING CAMP FUNDS'.

Swanton issues an official denial but he is damn grateful that: 'there is no Press box full of slick columnists and Test captains, no microphones for the players to run to – in fact, no papers and no broadcasting.' So, this will not be a Boot Bodyline controversy, it's quite legal, let us all move on, play up and play the game and GET THE AUSSIES.

The field clears of riotous spectators and play begins with the wicked English chanting in delight as Pearson runs in. The result? Well, it's already written, but Swanton dolls up a gleeful draft right now: 'Pearson bowls with shattering speed and ferocity, and as each fresh lamb arrives for the slaughter the stumps seem more vast, the bat even punier.'[17]

But there is one hope left for the side, one huge roar from The Hill as the skipper, Lieutenant Colonel E. E. Dunlop, walks to the crease. (Or creases, this dust is now very well marked.) Pearson roars in, the Aussie crowd ROOOOOOOOARRRRS back, Weary's bat flashes down but too late as his stumps go flying and the English rush the ground to celebrate their victory. It has been a drubbing, but it is the only time the Australians can remember having enjoyed losing. Hands are shaken and spirits are restored. They have played cricket, that strange game of Empire that only the British and their subjects can possibly understand; and they have had a few hours of joy in this damned place. The POW Test Rules will have *many* new clauses added when it comes to fair footwear, but for now all are delighted, save the sentries, who are still not sure this 'game' is over.

•

On this day, Blue Butterworth is doing what he has been doing for a short time every day this month, which is to take one of the most severely ill of the soldiers in the amoebic dysentery ward, Private 'Squizzy' Taylor, 40 leaves of flat fronds to wipe his bottom with. For no fewer than 40 times a day Squizzy would do a penny-size motion of faeces, blood and mucus into the small half of his dixie tin which served as his bed pan, and the leaves would at least help him keep a bit clean. Then, normally, Blue would stay to tell him a bit of a yarn, before taking his leave, saying, 'See you tomorrow, Squiz,' while quietly thinking, 'You won't be here tomorrow.'

The bloke is down to five stone!

On this day, after leaving Squizzy, there is a small surprise. The Regimental Sergeant Major, a Scot, finds him and says with some irritation: 'Butterworth, where you been? The "big fella" as you call 'im, wants you to go to him straight away.'

'Why?'

'Something about an operation.'

Operation . . . ?

Oh, *that* operation!

'But the bloody movement, I'm told, has been cancelled.'

'I don't care. Up and see him.'

A few minutes later, there he is.

'You want to see me, sir?'

'Yeah. Get up to the compound. The operation.'

'It's been cancelled.'

'Just in case.'

After all, if the Japanese can change their mind once, they can change it again.

Better to be safe and sore than sorry, even if he will be missing a foreskin.

Blue feels a bit grim about it, but at least two mates promise to come up with him.

It is a Sunday. *Yasume* day. Rest day. The orderly waiting in the 'operating theatre' – a large tent with muddy floor – is a Welsh mate of Blue's, Taffy Jones, and he is not happy at having been so summarily summoned.

'What is this?' Taffy asks on Blue's arrival. 'Indeed to goodness, man, what are you doing?'

'An operation, Taff. You got to prepare me for an operation for circumcision.'

'*Yasume* day!'

'I don't give a stuff, mate. Go crook on the big fella when he walks in.'

Very well then.

Blue disrobes. And lies back on the table, as Taffy shaves his pubic hair. Blue nervously eyes the honed-down table knife that will serve as the razor with which he is about to be . . . cut.

And here is Weary now. Both Taffy and Blue eye him warily and, for different reasons, decide not to say a word as the enormous medico starts earnestly scrubbing his hands, before now coming over.

'Now, I've only got this much novocaine,' he says to Blue. 'I can only give you a little bit because if you've got too much of this it'd go black.'[18]

Whatever you say, big fella.

Nervously, and all too acutely aware that – did he mention? – the end of his penis is about to be cut off, Blue lies back and thinks of England, or at least of King and country. *It is a far, far better thing he does, than he has ever done . . .*

After injecting the novocaine with a bamboo 'needle', Weary makes a couple of preliminary nicks, asking, 'Can you feel that?'

'No, sir.'

What about this?

Using forceps to pull the foreskin taut, Weary makes an actual cut, at which point Blue yells, 'Holy Hell!' His whole body jack-knifes up, and hits Weary on the shoulders, which knocks Weary back momentarily, until the medico returns serve with an even bigger shove of his own – which could well have solved the problem for them all by knocking Blue unconscious, but still.

'You silly bastard,' Weary says, very quietly. 'You told me you couldn't feel that.'

'I didn't but I –'

There is a thud behind them. One of Blue's two mates who had arrived just in time to watch the operation has fainted.

And now, just one more snip, and a tug.

'Righto,' says Weary, 'do you want to take it home with you?'[19]

•

There is a terrible sensation that doctors know only too well, when a terrible hunch is confirmed and the diagnosis is devastating disaster ahead – starting with your patients and ending with your career . . . ending. For while it is bad enough when you have to tell a patient the bad news, it is much worse when the disaster is of your own making because the 'cure' you have administered is catastrophic.

Tonight, Weary is feeling all of that and more when, after doing his final round of the night, 'with a sense of horror the last thing I saw was two patients suffering from paraplegia'.[20]

And yet these two had not been admitted with any such complaint, and earlier in the day had been fine. What the hell is going on?

The paperwork reveals little commonality. One had come in to have a tropical ulcer scraped out, the other for a hernia operation. They had been treated by different men, with entirely different procedures, and yet: 'both had developed bladder paralysis. Looking at their shrunken pallid faces and despairing eyes, my words of comfort had a hollow ring.'[21]

It is only later, while vainly trying to sleep, that the realisation hits like thunder: 'The spinal anaesthetics of the hospital had changed from my old individually made novocaine preparation for each case, to Percaine.'[22]

Yes, the small speciality dose had been replaced with 'bulk 60 dose-bottles with a rubber cap so that 1cc could be drawn off with a needle each time'.[23] Now, this bulk dose had to be carefully maintained as there was a risk of mould growing in bulk, held solution so 'this led to the introduction of small amounts of phenol, and later trypaflavine, under the careful supervision of Captain Markowitz'.[24] *But how careful?* Markowitz has 'claimed no problem with 1000 personal cases in Chungkai'.[25] But now two men have the same rare and peculiar condition; and the one thing they had in common was an anaesthetic . . .

Hold Christ. These are just the first two Weary has detected, the first two dots joined!

'In alarm I began going over in my mind all the patients I had operated on with bulk spinal.'[26] In panic, Weary wonders if he can risk a beating by secretly examining the patients tonight? No, even if he wasn't caught it would make all the patients panic in turn. But he turns and sweats as he tries to sleep tonight and has 'a hideous nightmare in which I saw all my patients beckoning me in piteous misery'.[27]

That might not be just a vision, it might soon be a grim reality. Before dawn has the chance to even open half an eye, Weary is up and feverishly examining all the men who have been operated on in the last few days. First up is Gunner Jones. Four days ago Weary had performed surgery on him to treat chronic osteomyelitis of the leg. Jones has no feeling in his buttocks and thighs, and his leg muscles are now weak.

'Horror!'[28] is Weary's one-word summation. Twenty-eight patients are checked, one third of them have similar symptoms, 'suggestive of meningeal irritation and minor disturbances of sensation'.[29] Minor for now, but not for long. 'It seemed likely that there was a time lag in the development of a catastrophe.'[30]

Weary cannot eat, he shuns breakfast to shake Lieutenant Colonel Coates out of slumber and tell him what has happened. Coates sits up in bed, lights his pipe very slowly and puffs it before delivering his verdict.

'Weary, do you remember the Bundaberg tragedy?'[31]

'Yes,' says Weary. 'Just a bit. Case of a lot of children vaccinated with staphylococcal infected vaccine. Fatal results.'

Coates nods and puffs again. Weary can feel the sweat growing on his brow now as Coates gently delivers his next terrible sentence; like a barrister leading a doomed man to a judgement that both of them know already.

'And, Weary, do you remember the affair in Berlin in which sulphuric acid was dropped in eighty babies' eyes?'

'Yes,' says Weary. 'Dreadful affair.'

Coates nods again, puffs and looks Weary square in the eye. 'Well, that's what we are up against; what are we going to do?'

Weary feels as though he is going to faint and he is already sitting down. 'We are, alas, going to have to have a Court of Inquiry. And they are never very pleasant.'

No, they ain't. And now both men set to treat the men they may have just wounded; hoping against hope that what they fear will not come to pass.

The strange thing? The damnedest thing? Those first two men never recover; the rest of the men do. The Court of Inquiry will determine that a chemical irritation due to additives is to blame; this mass batching is discontinued, and blessings are counted.

It was that close, just a whisker and a breath of luck. If not for that, the name 'Weary Dunlop' would mean disaster: the fellow responsible for the great anaesthetic paralysis poisoning of July '45.

•

As the worst of the heat goes out of these dog days of summer, tension rises among the POWs, and more word spreads about what is coming over the ham radio. On every front, the Japanese are being beaten back as the forces of General Douglas MacArthur advance through the Pacific, and Allied attacks get ever closer to being able to attack Japan itself. There seems little doubt that the war will be over soon – perhaps three months – but the real question is what the POWs' captors will do in the face of this reality.

Will the prisoners, perhaps, be used as human shields against Allied attacks on the Japanese forces in Thailand? Or maybe, once such an invasion begins, the POWs will simply be slaughtered as Parthian shots, fired from machine guns? None of them can help but notice more and more of just such machine guns being set up along the perimeter walls of the camp, even as a lot of deep ditches are being dug for no obvious reason. Are they, perhaps, right now, looking into the eternal abyss of their own open graves?

(Possibly. Unbeknownst to the POWs, on 1 August 1945 the Japanese Emperor had issued an order that if guards found them-selves overwhelmed by Allied forces, they were to line the prisoners up and 'kill them all'.

'In any case,' His Majesty the Emperor instructs, 'it is the aim not to allow the escape of a single one, to annihilate them all, and not to leave any traces.'[32])

The Japanese are equally tense, but glum to boot.

One day Corporal Ivan McKay is out on work detail when one of the rare Japanese guards who is *not* a bad bastard, *and* speaks a bit of English, 'Joe', seeks him out, looking worried.

'What's wrong, Joe?' McKay asks.

'When war finish, you Australians going to . . . ?' the nervous man says, drawing his thumb across his throat to make the international signal for 'slit our throats'.

'No,' McKay replies. 'When war finish, you go Nippon, we go Australia.'[33]

Japanese Joe beams like the rising sun.

But the only thing that seems certain is that things are coming to a climax.

6 August 1945, destroyer of worlds

At an altitude of some 28,000 feet, the three American planes keep pushing to the north-west, even as the coast of Japan shows up far ahead as long smudges of something darker amidst the endless blue. The commander of the mission, Paul Tibbets, is thrilled that his own plane, the *Enola Gay*, has been named for the mother who had encouraged him to ignore his father's wishes that he become a doctor and instead pursue his own dream of a flying career with the American Armed Forces. So, instead of devoting himself to saving people's lives, things had worked out differently, something never more apparent than on this particular mission . . . as the city of Hiroshima appears ahead, gleaming in the bright morning sun.

In short order, just after 8 am local time, the Americans soon spy far below them the curious T-shaped bridge which they know to be the downtown cross-hairs of their target. Upon Tibbets' command, the bombardier, Major Thomas Ferebee, flicks the switch to open the doors of the bomb-bay in preparation for release. Tibbets reminds all of the crew to put on their heavy, dark Polaroid goggles to shield their eyes from what is coming. Though it defies belief, Robert Oppenheimer, the primary creator of this bomb, has warned them that when it detonates, it will deliver a blast the rough equivalent of 20,000 tons of TNT, with a light intensity that will be like seeing 10 suns at once.

Lining it up, lining it up . . . lining it up and . . . *now*.

'Little Boy' hurtles down onto the oblivious city, with most of its residents on their way to work or school. Just 43 seconds from the moment of release, as Tibbets would describe it later, 'I look up there and the whole sky is lit up in the prettiest blues and pinks I've ever seen in my life. It was just great.'[34]

The other thing he notices is the tingling in his teeth, as his fillings interact with the bomb's radioactive pulses. When the shockwave hits them from the mushroom cloud billowing up behind to an altitude of 45,000 feet, the *Enola Gay* briefly lurches, but steadies and then continues on its way.

At this moment, a Japanese fighter pilot, Minoru Honda, who is flying over Hiroshima, finds his plane is blown violently off course, and drops as if off a cliff.

'I recovered control and looked around me, at the city, but it was completely gone and looked all white. Then, in front of me, I saw a huge mushroom-shaped cloud coming up fast. It was so big, white and shiny, but its inside was red and black.'[35]

Shaken, Honda flies on to Omura and reports to his superiors what he has seen.

'But no-one believed me. They didn't even look interested.'[36]

Soon, however, the contours of the catastrophe will become clear. At the moment of detonation, some 140,000 citizens of Hiroshima had been instantly killed.

•

Ray Parkin, now working in a coalmine in Japan, is suddenly aware that something has happened when all the Japanese miners start talking about something big, something to do with a big plane and an even bigger bomb. Much of it comes through sign language so it is not absolutely clear, but you can see by the miners' countenances that it is serious for Japan's future. Perhaps so serious that there isn't much of a future at all.

For the moment they must simply get on with their work. But just three days later, Parkin happens to be walking on the southern shore of Honshu on this beautiful day, and looking in the direction of the city of Nagasaki on the island of Kyushu over the waters of the inland sea, when, just after 11 am it happens.

'I heard a rumble and I thought, oh, that's ack-ack.'[37]

But . . . no.

To his shocked astonishment, he can suddenly see the instant creation of an amazing cloud formation, something like a mushroom, or an anvil.

'What's happening?' Parkin wonders. There is only one thing he is sure of: 'Well, that's the best meteorological observation I've ever made, I'll remember that. I'll tell them about thunderheads.'[38]

Not far away, where he has been most recently under the gun as a slave labourer in works owned by the Nippon Steel Company, Tom Uren hears and soon sees much the same thing, though is most stunned by 'the whole crimson colour of the sky, so pronounced, you could never ever realise what a crimson colour it was'.[39]

Not long afterwards some Japanese officers with the most basic grasp of English give him the news, 'Big bomb, war over.'[40]

The Japanese pilot who had been over Hiroshima, Minoru Honda, is still at Omura when he also hears an enormous boom from the direction of Nagasaki and within hours has been ordered to go to the local train station to help transfer some of the wounded of Nagasaki, who are being sent to Omura Navy Hospital as all hospitals around Nagasaki are full.

'The trains were already there,' he will recount, 'and the train officer told us the wounded were inside the carriages. I opened the door and I saw the most terrible things in this world. It was as if the carriage was full of red, burnt bits of meat, chucked into the carriage. I couldn't look at them without tears in my eyes . . .'[41]

•

Something is going on, Weary.

One of the Australians who has actually learnt to speak Korean has been talking to suddenly grim-faced guards, and they have whispered that something very serious has happened in the outside world. It is not certain what it is yet, but it might be that Russia has now formally declared war on Japan, too.

Or another rumour has it that some kind of dreadful 'super bomb'[42] has hit two cities, killing 100,000 in each one.

Weary is not sure what to believe.

Is this some kind of ruse by the Kempis, to see how they react? Maybe.

It just seems so extraordinary, he doubts it is even possible.

Against that, as he notes in his diary the next day, 'Hope is rising in my head.'[43]

They must take measures.

For yes, there is an instability in the air, a sense that anything might happen, that *something* is going to happen. It is decided to lift security, to post pickets on gates and make patrols around the camp. Weary Dunlop is appointed on the spot as Provost Marshal, akin to being put in charge of the Military Police.

'We are working on the basis of doing our best to enforce discipline upon the camp at a time when exuberance, or failure to maintain coordination and order, could be fatal. This we term a "camp security scheme".'[44]

15–16 August 1945, Nakom Patom, peace breaks out

The Koreans again. They are beside themselves with what seems an odd combination of grief and joy. Some are in tears. Some are scared. Some are relieved.

They say the war is *over*! The wild rumours that have been circulating for the last 48 hours are in a way confirmed, but still the Japanese themselves aren't saying anything. Everything is in a state of flux. If the war really is over, what happens then? Will the Japanese release the POWs, or gun them down? Should the Australians attack them now? Escape, with the Koreans? Kill the Koreans first, and escape anyway?

'We are ready for "action stations" at noon to clamp on "camp security",' Weary records in his diary, 'but we await the critical moment. There are now mild and persistent rumours that the war is over.'[45]

If only they had a ham radio working they could check, but in recent times the Kempis have been swarming so thickly such radios have been buried until things are safer.

That night, Weary is not the only one who cannot sleep.

The next day, all remains tense, but still different.

For some reason the Japanese themselves are all but entirely invisible. Have they . . . gone?

What *is* here is a sound unheard for years, one they never thought would thrill them. It is the sound of a muster trumpet, calling them to fall in. The bark of Sergeant Major, the blaring of brass, how sweet the sound! No more *tenko* roll call, just FALL IN, YOU HORRIBLE LITTLE MEN. Yes, fall in! Run in!

'Fall in A, fall in B, fall in every company.'[46]

Ah. And here comes a Japanese officer now.

In the early afternoon of 16 August, as Weary watches closely, a black car arrives and out of it gets a very grave-looking Japanese major. He disappears into a building where presumably other Japanese officers are awaiting him. Just after six o'clock, a Korean clerk emerges and tells Weary: get your men on parade.

The commanding officer of the camp, Lieutenant Colonel Shoichi Yanagita – known as 'the Little Colonel' for the fact that, even when standing on the box his underlings always have with them when he makes a speech, he struggles to be more than five foot tall – has an announcement to make shortly.

Sure enough, just as the light of the late afternoon is waning, a visibly distressed Yanagita, accompanied by an interpreter, appears and in short, staccato sentences, gets out the news – pausing only for his interpreter, who himself becomes more distressed as he hears his own words.

'Big bomb. War over. We friends now.'[47]

Good . . . God! Did he just say what we thought he said?

I think so!

'An armistice is now being held between all nations,' Yanagita goes on. 'All fronts are at peace and we have received instructions to the effect that we are to cease to regard you as prisoners of war. Therefore, we cannot guard you.'

A ripple of emotions moves through the men. The war is over? They are free to go?

The Colonel goes on . . .

'Therefore, the maintenance of discipline is your own responsibility. Your repatriation will not be long. I advise you to keep your health and cultivate the papaya trees. We presume you are capable of guarding yourselves and would like to have your suggestions made known.'[48]

It is all true. They are free to go! Or, at the very least, the Colonel, his soldiers and the rest of the guards, Koreans included, will themselves be going – though God knows where.

Weary is beside himself with joy, and can barely believe it.

The war is . . . over.

The Allies have won.

And he is still alive.

He will be seeing Helen soon.

And *marrying* her.

But now, to finish, the most extraordinary thing. For after Yanagita salutes, *he* bows to *them*, before retiring.

Things start to move with nigh incomprehensible . . . *speedo.*

On Weary's orders, the Assistant Provost Marshal places pickets around the camp to ensure that whatever celebrations might take place remain under control.

'I stressed the delicate and "jumpy" state of affairs, and that, for the present, no-one was to be allowed out of camp without special authority. Precious lives could be lost all too tragically at this stage.'[49]

And yet, let the celebrations begin anyway!

For now, every eye watches as hidden flags are unfurled and raised. The Union Jack, the Australian and Dutch flags are all hoisted, helped aloft by the yells, cheers and tears of the men beneath. The emotion is too much, and they cannot get enough of it. The flags flutter and the men saluting them once more are free!

'Those flags seemed to fly proudly in a cleaner, fresher air, charged with deep, overwhelming emotion, a boundless joy still trailing robes of sadness.'[50]

On Coates's orders, a special dinner is arranged to be held this evening, where the men will be able to eat at least three times their normal rations, and whatever else they can fit in. But first, let us liberate a number of Indian POWs who had been brought into the camp in the early months of 1945 and imprisoned in a particularly isolated hut on the edge of the camp, surrounded by a high fence. Despite their complete isolation, in the last couple of months Coates has managed to establish and maintain contact with them – and even smuggled in some drugs and dressings with their food rations.

Quickly calling for a British sergeant major, Coates orders him to 'break down that abominable fence and let them out'.[51]

In short order, it is done, and within minutes the small Indian contingent of 35 or so small, sick, men come out blinking into the light. They are cheered to the echo by the rest of the POWs, which they acknowledge graciously, but right now have a firm purpose. Told that they have been released on the orders of Colonel Coates, they now march in splendid formation straight towards the man pointed out as him.

PLAT-ooooooooN, HALT.

Standing in rags before him, on the sergeant's call, they offer an exemplary salute of thanks.

'I felt honoured indeed,' Coates will recount, 'to take the salute of those poor fellows in their rags.'[52]

The former prisoners are assembled, and the incredible news is broadcast to them by a single voice in their own tongue. Lieutenant Colonel Coates shouts it in English, and Lieutenant Colonel Willem Larsen declaims in Dutch, their joy unconfined; just as they all soon will be. It's done and we've won!

Inevitably, dinner that night is a raucous affair, with the exception of their friends, the newly liberated Indians, who are struggling to take it all in and can do little more than eat, drink and sit there smiling as other POWs clap them on the back.

'Until "Lights Out" at midnight,' Coates chronicles, 'singing and cheering rang out repeatedly throughout the camp. The "All Clear", the "Last Post" and the "Reveille" were sounded. Our hearts responded to our own army calls after three years of the "Toy Trumpet" of the Imperial Japanese Army.'[53]

Happily, discipline is maintained, and at Weary's call of 'Lights out' at midnight, the whole camp of Nakom Patom settles down almost immediately.

On Weary's part, the implications of what has happened keep washing over him as, back in his barracks and still in a daze, he records his feelings in his diary.

'Oh incredible day . . . ! An armistice is now being held between all nations. All fronts are at peace . . .'[54]

The next morning at 11 o'clock in a nod to the hour when the famous Armistice of the Great War took place, a service of thanksgiving is held, with all the British, Australian and Dutch padres uniting to conduct it, so let us pray.

And sing!

Now 4000 voices ring out, with no longer need to be soft about it.

> *And did those feet in ancient time,*
> *Walk upon England's mountains green?*
> *And was the holy Lamb of God,*
> *On England's pleasant pastures seen!*
> *And did the Countenance Divine*
> *Shine forth upon our clouded hills?*
> *And was Jerusalemmmmm builded here,*
> *Among these dark Satanic Mills?*

When Weary takes the makeshift bamboo lectern to remind the newly liberated POWs, 'of the camaraderie which had developed during their debasing captivity, and which would live and flourish in the years to come',[55] men weep openly.

His sentiments on this occasion could not be more clear.

'There will be an enduring bonus for us all in the deep affection and comradeship which has evolved, not only between us Australians, but with men of several nations who have shared this long dark night of captivity.

'There will be strenuous and exciting days working to get the last of these maimed and damaged men on their way home.'[56]

At the service's conclusion, the men crowd around to thank the officers for their salvation, and Dunlop and Coates, particularly, are back-slapped and even hugged by men who had come through their care and lived to see this day.

And yet, even when the thanksgiving service is over, the singing goes on as the camp adjutant takes the stage to sing 'Tea for Two' in his rich baritone, followed by 'If You Were the Only Girl in the World', which sees a concert being launched as impromptu as it is joyous . . . and deeply moving.

The war is over, and they are alive!

But missing mates . . .

'So many had suffered and died,' Weary chronicles. 'Some even now would never see home; but the momentous day had come.'

He takes a moment to take it all in:

> Looking at the gaunt, rapt, and mostly tear-stained faces about me, I recalled my light hearted entry into the war from St Mary's, London, and the happier days of the Middle East War. Wellington's apt comment crossed my mind that there was only one worse thing than winning a battle (or I suppose a war), and that was to lose it.[57]

On the spot, he makes a decision about the men that have been in his care, which will guide his future path.

'I have resolved to make their care and welfare a life-long mission.'[58]

But right now, let us get to work!

With all camps now open, the Allied doctors like Coates and Weary have access to the adjoining Japanese camp, which is filled with 'a large number of Japanese sick and wounded from the Burma front'.[59] (The other Japanese officers and soldiers, like the Korean guards, have been 'elusive' since news of the 'big bomb' has come through.)[60]

Coates and Dunlop, with their medical confreres, are quick to offer their medical services to the Japanese commanding officer. And yet the strangest thing happens. Upon their offer, this stout man begins to weep.

'I thank you for the gesture,' he says. 'But I have no authority to accept it. Therefore, I must decline it.'[61]

Very well then. Overruled. You are our prisoner, and will accept our help because we say so!

That makes more sense and the Japanese officer agrees. Despite the poor condition of many of the inmates of the Japanese hospital, Weary and the Gangster are appalled to see just how well-stocked their medical supply storerooms are, 'with withheld Red Cross parcels and medical supplies',[62] overflowing with the very medicines that the POW doctors have been crying out for.

(At this time, in Ray Parkin's POW camp in Japan, they equally open the stores to find Red Cross parcels from . . . the Great War!)

Before getting to bed that night, Weary manages to find out which camp his favourite blind Englishman, Bill Griffiths, is in, so he can get a message to him – a kindness that the Englishman will never forget.

'When the war ended,' Griffiths will recount, 'the very first day, a message came to me that Weary had survived. He . . . wanted to know how I was, how I felt at that moment, and he passed the message on that he would see me as soon as he could. I thought, "Isn't that marvellous?" A man like that, a surgeon, and humble little me, sending this message that he wanted to see me as soon as possible.'[63]

Right now, however, Griffiths must keep his head down. The end of the war has found him at a camp in Java, where chaos reigns. The Japanese are retreating, and in the subsequent vacuum of power, the local Javanese are fighting with the remaining Dutch as to who shall rule. With staggering rapidity, the Far East has become the Wild West.

'We could not leave the camp,' Griffiths will recount. 'Anyone white was assumed to be Dutch and was shot.'[64]

While they wait for some kind of stability to return, there is endless speculation on how long it will take the authorities to get organised enough so that the men will actually be able to arrive home. The best reckoning is . . . about three months.

•

On this day, 28 August 1945, it is a surreal experience for 28-year-old Lieutenant Colonel 'Duggie' Clague of the British Army Aid Group to be sweeping through the outer suburbs of Bangkok, bound for the Japanese HQ, to find all the Japanese soldiers on the streets *saluting* as he passes!

And yet it is all part of his audacious plan, codenamed 'Swansong'. With Japan's formal surrender imminent, Clague has worked with the secret 'E Group' he has established to have six teams of men, including an officer and a radio operator, parachuted into the vicinity of the major POW camps to attempt to make contact and assist them to prepare for their liberation, in tandem with whatever underground cells can be contacted. For Clague, a former POW himself, who had escaped from the Sham Shui Po POW camp in Hong Kong early in the war, it is personal. The idea is to liberate as many POWs as quickly as possible, while capturing the Japanese and preventing any massacres.

True, there had been rather a major glitch when the Allied Supreme Commander in the Pacific, General Douglas MacArthur had ordered there were to be 'no Allied landings in Japanese-occupied territories until after the official surrender ceremony in Tokyo Bay on September 2', which would condemn the POWs to a further fortnight's imprisonment, and heighten the danger of massacres, but a way around it had been found.[65]

Clague had prevailed upon British Admiral Lord Louis Mountbatten, the Supreme Allied Commander in South-east Asia, to give a covert go-ahead anyway, and it had been done. The E Group teams had been parachuted and are even now making their way to the camps, seeking to make contacts. But not Clague himself. A previous back injury had meant parachuting was out of the question and so, after being flown from his base in China to a remote airstrip in northern Thailand, he had been picked up in a car provided by Pridi Phanomyong, a lawyer who had been made Regent of Thailand in 1941.

The car is flying Pridi's flag and that is why all the Japanese guards are saluting Clague as he passes, making his way to the Japanese HQ in Bangkok, where he intends to roll up and brazenly demand their surrender. No, we don't have you surrounded, but you will be soon, and our teams are already liberating the POW camps. Your best chance of getting home to Japan, and soon, is to surrender, *now*.

•

Things are moving fast.

On 24 August, no sooner has Weary received news that he has been appointed as the Medical Staff Officer for the British and Australian forces in Thailand than he is told he must report to Bangkok.

But how?

He and Blue are contemplating exactly that when – *hulloa!* – a Japanese admiral with a captain aide-de-camp by his side arrive in the camp, in the back seat of a black staff car, driven by a sailor. That'll do. And things have changed around here. Just three weeks ago, grabbing a Japanese driver by the collar and hauling him out of his seat would see a man shot, at best; tortured and shot at worst. But now, with everything up in the air bar the fact that Japan has in fact lost this war, the driver is released from Weary's grasp more content that he is still intact than outraged he has lost his wheel, and as for the admiral and his aide-de-camp, they are so resigned to the new way of things that all they can do is 'bow profoundly'[66] as Weary and Blue drive off.

Alas, the chaos of the day soon intrudes on Weary's and Blue's exultant good humour, as they find with the bridge down their only way across the Mae Nam Tha Chin River is on a vehicle ferry. Weary is just negotiating how much to pay the ferryman when he suddenly must jump for his life as a Japanese lorry barges through them to take its own pride of place. Seeing a beaming Japanese officer with a warrant officer in the cab of the lorry, something in Weary snaps. An hour ago at the camp, he had been relatively gentle with the driver he had collared. But there is only so much flesh and blood can bear.

'I suddenly got a rush of blood to the head, to think that these blooming rascals who had been kicking us around all these years . . . assumed the right to drive onto the ferry when we were talking to the Thai ferryman.'[67]

Jumping onto the ferry, Weary runs to the cab of the lorry, pulls open the door and takes the officer by the scruff of his neck *and* his tunic, ready to throw him over the side, when he hears a chorus of clicks behind him.

Oh. There are 40 Japanese soldiers with their rifles trained upon him.

Very well. As you were, then.

'I decided to accept his apology and cigarettes.'[68]

Onwards!

Once arrived in Bangkok, the two Australians head out to find their new digs, a college that was once an internee camp for civilians. They find the building and also find that it has been bombed, which they were all for a few days ago, but now it is bloody inconvenient. It's also got no electricity. But let's get to grips, with Weary giving Blue a casual order to open the batting: 'Right, get some lights, get some tucker.'

Righto. Blue sets forth with purpose and runs into a startled Thai woman and her husband. They have seen Blue's jungle green uniform and initially assumed he was part of the occupying forces. No, he is a liberator! Delighted, they invite him into their abode to pop open a beloved bottle of wine they had been saving to celebrate the end of this war. Well, Blue does not mind doing his bit for civilian relations and after a few glasses of goodwill, a second bottle is found. After all, it is the end of World War II, one bottle just won't do it. And it *is* his birthday!

Sometime later, Blue staggers back to a darkened college, its only lighting supplied by the cigarette of Weary Dunlop.

'Where the hell have you been?' barks Weary.

'I'm elephant's trunk,'[69] says Blue.

Drunk? Yes, Weary had diagnosed that from the diagonal walking and the salute that nearly took Blue's eye out. Do tell how that happened? Blue tells the tale and Weary is amused despite himself. 'I got waylaid, sir.' Yes, Weary is sure that will be next . . . Go to bed, Blue. We'll forage together when the sun's up.

•

And yet, while it is one thing to be liberated, it is quite another to actually get home to Australia, or Britain or Holland for that matter. The senior Allied officer in all of Thailand at the time is none other than Weary's old friend, Lieutenant Colonel Cranston McEachern, and to him falls the responsibility of repatriating over 30,000 troops on whatever ships are available. The first part is to get the bulk of the men – and in Weary's bailiwick, the sick men – down to the port of Bangkok, where they can wait until their ship has come in or their plane is set to take off. Those who are still gravely ill are cared for in the Bangkok hospitals, as the Thais themselves are more than grateful to the Allies for having rid their land of the invading Japanese.

And yet, by a curious twist of fate, the first patient that Colonel Coates himself must treat in Bangkok's Chulalongkorn Hospital is, if you can believe it . . . Weary Dunlop!

He had been attempting to open a prized bottle of Foster's beer by prying its lid off with a large knife – only for the knife to slip! He cuts himself so badly that the tendons are exposed, and – once Weary is rushed to the hospital in an ambulance – it is indeed Coates who must take suture in hand to sew up the deep wound.

•

As visitors from the outside world go, this is an important one.

On 16 September the Commander-in-Chief of Allied Land Forces in South-east Asia, General William Slim, arrives in Bangkok, with the task of co-ordinating the evacuation of Allied soldiers.

His first task is to visit the Chulalongkorn Hospital. Slim is accompanied by an officer Weary had met a few days before, Lieutenant Colonel 'Duggie' Clague, and it is Weary himself who is given the honour of greeting them.

As Weary offers a salute, General Slim is quick to note the deep wound on his right hand.

'What's this?' he asks.

'Atrocities, sir,' Weary replies, deadpan.

Turning to the officer beside him, General Slim says, 'Clague, have you got the man? Have you got the man that did this? Have you locked him up? We'll hang the bastard!'

Colonel Clague, who knows the story, smiles grimly and says, 'And what would you say, sir, if I told you that the bastard did it opening a bottle of beer!'[70]

As it happens, Weary Dunlop and General William Slim will soon be brought together once more, as the General initiates the process to round up as many Japanese as possible and work out who must be tried for war crimes.

Clague's Operation Swansong has worked well and many senior Japanese officers have been captured and interrogated by officers, who have also talked to POWs and assembled a list of names of possible war criminals. Now that those suspects have been brought back to Bangkok, it requires former POWs like Weary to assist in identifying those who have committed atrocities. So it is that on this day in October, Weary is ordered to attend an identification parade to see if he recognises any of the assembled Japanese officers newly taken prisoner, and whether he knows them to be responsible for war crimes.

And there he is.

Why, it is none other than Stone Face, the very man who had completely terrorised him two years before. True, he no longer has a tunic or even a belt to hold up his trousers, and is using one hand to do the same. And his face is strangely grey and drawn. But as their eyes lock, Weary knows it's him, just as Stone Face must fear the worst is about to happen.

And yet . . .

'Interesting specimen that,' he says, 'but I have not seen him before.'[71]

It represents a change of attitude from Weary, which has come upon him quite suddenly.

'I couldn't have hated anything more than I did the Japanese,' he will note. 'A curtain of hate. When you see so many people die in such misery, the hate is intensive.'[72]

But now the war is over, he can also see close-up their own misery, particularly in the form of the battered, shattered and ragged remnants of the Japanese Army coming out of Burma, many of them dragging themselves down the same Thai–Burma Railway that so many POWs had died to build.

'They were in terrible condition, looked very much like our own fellows.'[73]

The vision of one Japanese soldier will never leave Weary. It is some mother's son, 'who'd hopped God knows how many hundreds of dreadful miles with one leg chopped off through the middle of the thigh, the bone sticking out and sort of stinking gangrenous flesh and still sort of hopping with these ghastly shrunken sort of eyes'.[74]

What's he doing? Just trying to get home, like everyone else who had fought in this damn war, likely with a mother and father waiting for him in Japan, praying their boy will make it, that they will hear news of his blessed return. And yet, on this occasion, no sooner has the train pulled in to the crowded platform and he tries to hop up to get on it, than he falls, and an entire herd of people tramps over the top of him.

As in days of yore, the old rugby forward puts his head down and batters his own way through, to get to him. But it is too late.

'I . . . found myself with a dead man.'

Those parents in Japan will never see him again.

'The hate drained out.'[75]

Other former enemies are not treated with such humanity, and there will be many cases of rough justice.

One newly released Australian POW will tell of his experience of making his way with a mate into the nightlife of Bangkok for the first time, when his mate spies a Korean and says, 'That bastard is one of the guards.'

In fact, one of the brutal ones.

'So,' the Australian will recount, 'he and a bloke from the *Perth* just grabbed him and threw him over the balcony, about 12 feet up. He didn't bounce.'[76]

•

While among many officers there is a rush to get straight back to Australia, Weary is not of their number. His strong view is that, with so many soldiers and so few ships, priority must be given to the sick, to married men with children, to married men and finally to single men, in that order. Their repatriation is so paramount, his own must be postponed.

(Besides, things are not altogether dull in Bangkok. Blue Butterworth will later tell the story of being in a cottage on the outskirts of Bangkok, when he sees a dispatch rider coming down the drive, bearing a missive.[77] It is from no less than Lady Mountbatten, visiting Thailand with her husband, Lord Mountbatten. The missive presents her compliments, and requests Weary comes to meet her at the Royal Palace, as she has heard of his fine work. Blue yells the news for the boss, who is right now having a shower, and in short order, in the best clothes he can muster, Weary is on his way, hoping to renew an acquaintance he had had with her before the war, in London.

True, there is a problem when the guards at the palace refuse to accept the missive as proof of his credentials, but . . . no problem. Again using the trick told him by the American pilot, in what feels like decades ago, to recite poetry or the like with great passion, whenever your way is blocked by non-English-speaking men with guns, before you simply 'brush aside any resistance and walk through',[78] Weary once more launches into Shakespeare's finest, reciting with great emotion: *'When I have seen by Time's fell hand defaced/ The rich proud cost of outworn buried age!/ When sometime lofty towers I see down-razed!'*[79] and finally makes his way to Lady Mountbatten herself!

As fragrant as he remembers, she makes him one of several offers he does not refuse. 'Will you work with me for a few days during my programme in Thailand, and . . . advise me on various matters?'[80]

Why yes, yes he will!

Blue does not see the boss for several days and Weary's own sister-in-law will later be indiscreet enough to opine: 'I always think there was a bit of an affair or something when he met Lady Mountbatten in Thailand straight after the war. They must have been madly attracted to each other because they were both those sort of people.'[81] Another Weary friend will bat off such questions about a romance with Lady Mountbatten with a laugh, noting of the medico Romeo, 'He was a handsome man and an interesting man and there wasn't a love affair with Lord Louis, as you know . . .'[82])

Finally, however, there are no more Australians to put on the planes or ships bar himself and Blue, and on 14 October 1945, it happens.

'We were the last plane to leave,' Blue Butterworth will recount, 'and we shot down to Changi, and we were in 2 Half Moon Street, and Weary's there relaxed, starkers. A motorbike pulled up, it was Lord Louis Mountbatten's front rider. Lord Louis wanted to see Weary.'[83]

(Blue is not surprised.)

At least there is time, before heading home in a few weeks, to dash off a note to Helen, affirming his love.

> *My Darling Gorgeous Person,*
> *Today the first real letter from you in years, with some never to be forgotten snapshots.*
>
> *After this terrible dragging age I just can't say what this means to me. You are the sort of dear, loyal, lovable person who would throw away years waiting for a lost fiancé – that I have never doubted, but oh darling one does want to hear from you that the old enchanted world of you and I still exists and that you can still be in love – with a ghost.*

> *But darling how could you be so clever as not to look any older at all?*
> *And I think even more lovely if that were possible, so that it makes my*
> *heart stop to look at you.*

But she must prepare herself for what *he* will look like when they meet, something that has been ever more on his mind.

> *For of course I'm older even though I am not admitting it . . . It's a*
> *little difficult to explain but I've taken this war seriously like a life on*
> *its own, and just poured everything into it as though five years were one's*
> *mortal span — and everything else in life to follow at the moment seems*
> *like a bonus or something left over.*[84]

At last, the great day comes and their plane takes off for first Singapore – where he is able to send a telegram to his beloved Helen:

ARRIVED SINGAPORE DARLING VERY WELL JOB FINISHED
LEAVING BY AIR TOMORROW LONGING TO SEE YOU LOVE
PRECIOUS EDWARD[85]

before heading to Borneo, then Morotai, and finally the moment he has most been waiting for. As their plane comes in low, he looks out the window, and there it is. AUSTRALIA! So many times, he had been convinced that he would never see it again. But now, here it is. He is alive, the war is over, and he really is coming home. Minutes later they land on the remote airstrip at Egglesfield, right on the point of Cape York.

RAH!

Much later that same day, they arrived at Archerfield in Brisbane to spend the night, and it is here that both Blue and, more particularly, Weary are stunned to see a major feature story in the *Australian Women's Weekly*, naming Weary as the 'King of the River',[86] and more!

The story is filled with quotes from POWs who have not only survived the Thai–Burma Railway, but credit Weary for that fact.

Good God! Or son thereof, now Weary reads that he is publicly hailed as the 'Christ of Thailand'. Christ knows Weary does not hold himself up to be this. Goodness.[87]

That's you, Weary. 'The Christ of Thailand'!

Goodness.

After taking off on the morning of the next day, their plane arrives at Sydney Airport in Mascot just before lunchtime, where Blue prepares to take his leave.

'Right, sir,' says Blue.

'Where the bloody hell do you think you're going?' asks Weary.

Home. And away.

'This is where I enlisted,' Blue says simply. 'I got Wally Delves' wife and sister-in-law gonna meet me.'

Well, they can wait longer.

'You're coming to Melbourne with me,' Weary says. It's a request masquerading as a command. And it is the first order in four years that Blue will not obey.

'No, I'm not.'

He holds out his hand.

He means it. He's getting off.

Weary shakes it.

'Keep in touch.'[88]

Oh yes, Blue will, but it will never be the same and they both know it.

Their war ends now. Once they part, the Colonel will go back to being Dr Dunlop and Blue back to a building site. They have gone through thick, thin and thinner still, right down to bony ribs and worse – and yet what's a missing foreskin between friends? – but now . . . it's over.

Without a look back, Blue departs. If he had turned, he would have seen something more than passing strange. For Lieutenant Colonel Dunlop does not get back on the plane. At least for the moment, he is staying in Sydney too, though Helen is waiting for his return in Melbourne.

While it had been one thing to stare down Japanese guards bearing bayonets, who are sworn to kill him, it is quite another to see again a woman to whom he is betrothed, after *eight years* of absence. The man who could do anything when the war was on, cannot do this. He retrieves his kitbag and walks into the terminal, looking for a phone.

What he most needs, he decides, is time – and a good friend to talk things over with. He has no better friend than Jim Yeates, now Lieutenant Colonel Jim Yeates, if you please, who he has not seen since Tobruk but who he knows is now in Sydney. Wonderfully, Jim arrives at the airport within the hour and they spend the afternoon on Bondi Beach, catching up and talking things through. Jim's own war has been eventful, and never more fraught than during the climax of the Kokoda Track campaign. He had been the most forward surgeon during the Battle of Buna in early '43, and thereafter had been twice mentioned in dispatches.

But the fact that Jim has never been a POW means he is struggling to understand just what is ailing Weary now. What is he doing here instead of Melbourne? Why did you get off the plane? As the waves pound in, and the sands shimmer, Weary tells his old mate that, right now, Australia is the last country he wants to be in. He needs to take a long, long trip around the world to come back home.

'I am not fit to come home,' he explains to his old friend, as the bathers blithely glide past. 'I need to get civilised again.'[89]

The truth is, as Weary knows, 'I have lost my nerve.'

Seriously? The man who could place his belly between bayonets and a blind man the Japanese were intending to kill, now afraid that he is not up to resuming his old life, and seeing the love of his life once more, because he just doesn't feel civilised enough, yet?

Seriously.

'Am I the same person as I was when I left here eight years ago. Will it work out . . .?'[90]

Yeates hears him out, and steers him back to getting his nerve. It will be alright, Weary. You are the same man, and a great man at that. Whatever issues there might be in adjusting from POW life, Helen, who has waited for you for *eight years*, will be able to cope. Jim, after all, had himself been obliged to adjust to again seeing his own fiancée – Pam Bushell of the Bushell Tea family of Sydney's Darling Point – but is now looking forward to marrying her.

As the shadows finally lengthen across the beach, Jim gets Weary back to the car, and they are soon out on Campbell Parade once more, heading back to Sydney Airport. Jim comes in with him and, pulling rank to have a passenger thrown off the flight to make room for Lieutenant Colonel Dunlop, safely sees him on a plane bound for Essendon Airport.

•

Helen has been worried before Weary's return about whether their engagement is still on. After all, it has been so long since they have even *seen* each other. Ironically, she had received a letter from Weary just after pouring out her worries to a friend. The letter said, 'You are the sort of dear loyal, lovable person who would throw away years waiting for a lost fiancé . . . one does want to hear . . . that you can still be in love – with a ghost.'[91]

What did that mean? She still doesn't know.

But after his afternoon arrival had been cancelled with no explanation, she is now back at the airport at midnight – courtesy of an Army staff car sent for her by Weary's old friend, Brigadier Roy Burston – waiting for Weary to disembark.

As Weary comes out, his eyes scan the sea of women waiting to see their men returned and there, standing at the back of them, with a half-smile on her lips, is Helen. He walks straight for her and she cannot believe the moment is here.

'I fainted into his arms to find him exactly the same, not at all grey, wonderfully well and amazingly English.'[92]

It is, she will record, 'the most momentous day of my life'.[93]

And one that goes well into the night.

'We came home in the staff car – had a family reunion here – drinks, then coffee etc. till 3.30 a.m. Got to bed at 4.15 a.m. no sleep at all. No plans yet but he is off to Benalla tomorrow . . .'[94]

Of course he is. Like a rugby player who has leaped high to take a long pass and finds himself in space, Weary has hit the ground running and is not just a man on a mission, but a man on *many* missions all at once. And if Helen is not his absolute top priority on his first full day at home, she is at least somewhere well up *near* the top.

(Not that he wants any fuss. Aware that the dignitaries of Benalla are waiting for him on the station, with the town band, all ready for his homecoming, he gets off the station before Benalla, Violet Town, and quietly walks home. It has been a bloody long war, you know? He wants a cup of tea, and a good lie-down.)

In Sydney just a few days later, Blue Butterworth receives a letter from Weary.

'Helen and I,' he writes, 'are getting married on the 8th of November. You're our guest.'[95]

At the Presbyterian Church of Toorak, Helen is given away by her father. Weary's best man is Jim Yeates.

Helen's wedding gown? It is made of pale green silk that, at Weary's behest, Blue had purchased in Bangkok, just before they had set off for home. The reception, held at Helen's parents' house at 605 Toorak Road in South Yarra, is wildly celebratory, not just for the happy couple but their boozy guests, with Blue Butterworth recording that, 'I was treated like King Billy.'[96]

This includes receiving an offer of work from one Brigadier Stevens, a mate of Weary's who has an important position on Melbourne City Council.

'By the way,' he says, 'I'm told you're a bricklayer. You've got a job.'

'No, sir, I'm going back to Sydney. I've got all my friends there that I met before the war, I want to stay there.'

Deep thanks, but in Blue's words, 'I just wanted to paddle my own canoe.'[97]

And so to the speeches, the dancing, the drinking, the revelry and . . .

And what now?

Late in the evening, there are heated words and clenched fists between the groom and a Scottish piper of the old school, a Mr MacLennon from the Scottish Highlands, who drunkenly dispenses the view that as a breed the Dunlop clan are 'thieves and reevers' – *and*, worst of all, *Lowlanders*. Unfortunately, the man with whom he has shared this view has the last name of Dunlop, the first name of Weary, and a disposition that seems suddenly volcanic, oddly enough, now that the war is over.

Jim Yeates intervenes, Mr MacLennon is shown the door, and the wedding goes on into the raucous night . . . . . . and all the way to the dawn, when the still rowdy Weary and the completely exhausted Helen get back to their room at the Windsor Hotel – with company. It is a bunch of ex-POWs from the Thai–Burma Railways, wedding guests all – if not all of them with wedding invitations, as a number of them had just turned up, and not been refused – wanting to continue the party, you understand, Helen?

Not really, no.

But the bonds Weary feels with these men, and they with him, are so strong she will have to try to navigate her way around them for the rest of their lives together.

For now, at least, after the POWs are finally out and the newly married have a long sleep, they are able to get away late in the day to a house in the Dandenongs, with the only problem being that the set of keys provided open very few of the locked rooms throughout the house.

There is only one thing for it, as Weary will report to Ray Parkin.

'I made love to her all over the garden.'[98]

It has been a long war.

Let the peace begin.

EPILOGUE

How do you memorialise Everest? See, Weary's a man like Everest. It's not until you get away from him that you realise how big he is. His humility, his willingness to serve people, ungrasping. All the paramount virtues are there, but they're never worn on the sleeve. They're just there and I think the only way to remember Weary is thoughtfully, not gushing phrases or anything like that . . . You just think about the man and just ponder over what he's done.[1]

Ray Parkin, 1987

While Weary did his best to settle down and leave the war completely behind him – as he and Helen begin their married life in Melbourne – the war could never quite leave *him* behind.

The first flat that he and Helen rent in South Yarra comes furnished, complete with a fat Buddha on the mantle shelf. Out it goes, with Weary telling the surprised landlady, 'I have had a tummy full of Buddhas.'[2]

In 1946, the Australian Government conducted 23 war-crimes trials, with 62 defendants – many of whom like Yi Hak-Nae,[3] the Lizard, were known to Weary. He was happy to send his diaries, and an affidavit dated 27 June 1946, detailing his own charges against those on the Thai–Burma Railway he considered war criminals.

> I, Ernest Edward Dunlop, of 66 Walsh Street, South Yarra, in the State of Victoria, make oath and say . . .
>
> Between Jan and Aug 1943 in the Konyu-Hintok area, Lt Usuki was directly responsible for causing the deaths of many POWs under his care, by callous neglect to provide food, adequate shelter, hygiene arrangements or medicines and repeatedly stated that the sick should not receive as much food as the fit.

Cpl Okada (Doctor Death) was responsible for the medical arrangements of thousands of men, though he appeared to have no medical training. For many months, and particularly in June–July 43, he daily overruled experienced medical officers, forcing them to send sick men to work under the most exhausting conditions and brutality and directly causing many deaths.

Lt-Col Ishii (The Laughing Colonel) as commander of all Group 4 POW was responsible for the deaths of hundreds of men by his neglect to ensure provision of sufficient food, clothing, shelter and medicines, to the working camps during 1943.

During the period I was at Hintok, Lt Hirota was in charge of the engineer section. This officer is directly responsible for the death of scores of Australians who worked under him in inhuman conditions on railway construction in the Hintok area. In 1943 he daily forced extremely sick men to work and treated all workmen with sickening brutality, and sadistic punishment.[4]

There is one man alone that Weary conspicuously does not denounce.

Yi Hak-Nae. Prosecutors request that Weary come to Singapore himself to testify against the man he had known as the Lizard – who Weary had not even mentioned. Weary, *still* haunted and feeling guilty for the fact that he had once formed the intent to kill the Lizard, declines to make any move that would see Yi imprisoned or even hanged now.

One of Weary's contemporaries who became involved in the war-crimes trials was **Dr Arthur Moon**. Before returning home after the war, he had returned to Tamarkan and, with the help of Boon Pong, recovered all the medical documents he had buried, detailing the Japanese atrocities. They were all turned over to the Australian authorities and were used as evidence by the prosecution.

Weary and Moon were pleased to hear in 1947 that both Hirota and the Lizard had been found guilty of ill-treatment of prisoners and sentenced to death by hanging. While happy for the verdict and sentence on the Lizard – and it will later emerge the Korean had completely denied all charges, and lied unconscionably saying his 'duties were [only] to patrol the camp to see that the prisoners of war would not desert and other duties were to sweep the quarters of the Japanese troops and the officers', and that at no time did he ever 'put the sick prisoners of war out for work parade'[5] – it was at least not on Weary's conscience that he had helped to hang a man who, at another time, he had very nearly murdered.

Weary was also eager to do justice to the men he owed so much to, and no-one more than **Boon Pong**, whose post-war years were difficult. Just weeks after hostilities ceased, Boon Pong was outside his shop in Kanchanaburi with his wife and father when shots rang out and he slumped to the ground with holes in his neck, chest, arms and back – the victim of some people's mistaken belief that he had been a collaborator with the hated Japanese.

A nearby British officer raced to him, and got there in time for Boon Pong to look up at him and say: 'Thai police kill me.'[6]

Amazingly, after emergency British medical intervention, Boon Pong survived. Not long afterwards, a British officer, Colonel Philip Toosey, heard that the bus company Boon Pong had started, with money redeemed from the Australian Government for Weary's IOU chits to buy abandoned Japanese trucks, was in financial difficulty. Moving quickly, Toosey organised a whip-around among former POWs and an extraordinary £38,000 was raised. The company became extremely successful and in 1948 Boon Pong received the MBE to go with the George Cross that the British Government had already awarded him for his heroism.

In Australia that same year, a collection of Western Australian POWs who had survived the Thai–Burma Railway launched the Weary Dunlop Boon Pong Exchange Fellowship, pooling their money to regularly finance Thai surgeons to come to Australia to widen their studies.

In those immediate years after the war, Weary's attitude to the Japanese en masse was severe, telling the press in 1946, 'There was no semblance of honour in their make-up. Their attitude towards life and womenfolk was disgusting, and their standard of morality was appalling. The Jap soldier was little more than an animal . . . The men higher up were even more extreme in their cruelty, and very corrupt.'[7]

A firmly entrenched member of the Establishment himself, in 1947 Weary was awarded an Order of the British Empire, which is not the only empire he supports. He also spoke out on the right of the Dutch to re-establish their colonies in the Dutch East Indies, including at Java and Sumatra.

'[Dr Dunlop,]' one report ran, 'said that the Dutch were nice people, possessed courage, human kindness and were not war-like. They had brought a lot of good to the Indies, and in these days when empires were being readjusted, the right should be conceded to them to go back and settle the same as they have the right in India and other places.'[8]

All up, his post-war life was not remotely as it was before the war. Back then, looking back – *decades* ago, it felt like – he had been not much more than a callow youth. And now, he was famous. Word of what he had done – the courage he had displayed, the men he had saved, his selflessness – continued to spread well beyond the surviving soldiers and their families. Such fame inevitably helped make Weary busier still, as many patients sought the prestige of being treated by him, and they were added to the long list of POWs who naturally sought him out anyway.

Often, it was Weary who would seek them out, as when he and Helen were visiting England a few years after the war.

Bill Griffiths had returned home to find the family trucking business sold, his wife gone, and his daughter in the care of her sister. Not long after remarrying, there is a knock on the door. His second wife, Alice – with an apron on, as she is cooking fish and chips – answers to see a tall and distinguished-looking man there.

'I want to see Bill Griffiths,' the stranger says pleasantly, if forthrightly.

'I'm sorry,' Alice replies, thinking he is some kind of salesman, 'but we don't need anything. We're all right, thank you.'

'But I've come to see . . . '

'Who?'

'Bill Griffiths. I am Edward Dunlop.'

The Edward Dunlop? Weary Dunlop, who my husband has not stopped talking about?

Yes.

Oh dear, oh dear.

'Is your wife with you? Bring her in.'

And in short order, Weary and Helen are in Bill and Alice Griffiths's humble abode, both wives realising they are present at quite the moment as the two men simply sit quietly, contemplating the other.

'They were so quiet,' Alice will recall. 'I thought, Good gracious, talk or something, make some kind of conversation. But it was very emotional. There was plenty there, but they weren't speaking. And Bill looked so well, you see, when Sir Edward had only seen him at his worst.'

'It was absolutely so unreal an event,' Bill Griffiths will recall. 'After all the experiences as prisoners of war, here we were in Lancashire and Weary sat there talking to me. Marvellous. Absolutely. It's difficult to put it into words just now, how it was.'[9]

Beyond doing surgery at places like the Royal Melbourne Hospital and the Royal Victorian Eye and Ear Hospital – where he must scramble to catch up on new, modern techniques that have been developed in his absence – Weary held specialised clinics for returned soldiers and on principle he never charged them a penny. (Nor, for that matter, did the Gangster, Dr Ewan Corlette, on his regular visits to see POWs at the Concord Repatriation Hospital in Sydney.)

In similar fashion, many organisations, particularly those devoted to the welfare of returned soldiers in general and returned POWs specifically, wanted him as their public face and advocate.

As an unofficial adviser to the federal governments of Ben Chifley and Robert Menzies, he began pushing the idea that medical and dental care should be free for POWs – just as he argued for more generous war pensions. With so many POWs still struggling, dying at '*four times* the rate of other veterans',[10] even after the war was over, his continued contention was that it was both a matter of urgency for them, and a moral obligation of the government, to grant special care to them. After all, as he would later note, while the overall percentage of deaths among those Australians who saw active service in World War II was just 3 per cent, when it came to POWs under Japanese control, 8000 of 22,000 overall had died, meaning for them the percentage of death was a staggering 36 per cent.

One breakthrough came in 1952 when Prime Minister Robert Menzies established the Prisoners of War Trust Fund with £250,000 to be used to help those former POWs 'suffering distress or hardship as a result of disabilities arising from the conditions of their captivity'.[11]

Weary and Helen have been blessed with two young sons who delight them both – John and Alexander – and have taken over Helen's old family home at 605 Toorak Road. And yet for Weary, family life is something that has to be squeezed in around so many other pressing commitments and duties he finds so hard to refuse.

•

Another who prospered back in Australia was **Ray Parkin**. Upon his return to his boyhood home in the Melbourne suburb of Ivanhoe, he finds his wife is throwing a party to welcome him. It is open house, joyful, tearful and bewildering. Finally, Ray gets a second to rest and sit down alone in a chair, only to find the local butcher immediately plonk down in the chair next to him. He asks Ray no questions, which is a relief. Instead, he tells Ray about his own life on the home front in Ivanhoe from 1939 to 1945.

'Oh, you've no idea what it was like during the war. Even tea was rationed!'[12]

'Oh, yeah?' says Ray.

Yes. And sugar, *and* butter. Try to make a decent cake more than once a fortnight and you'll find it a bit of a bother. And don't get him started on the price of lamb chops, let alone the price of tea in China.

'God, I'm glad I wasn't here!' Ray remarks. It makes him laugh, but he prefers it to what he usually gets: 'All they wanted to hear were the horror stories, how terrible the Japs were and what was the effect.'[13]

That is what he is still working out. He is glad to be home, but re-entering the world he once knew and settling down will take time. For the moment, Parkin heads back to work as a tally clerk on the wharves of Melbourne – while also continuing his splendid art work. With the drawings that Weary handed back to him at the end of the war, Parkin felt he had the makings of a book. And how funny he should say that.

For not long afterwards, while home in Melbourne, Parkin receives a letter from none other than a man who definitely *is* afraid of Virginia Woolf – her husband, Leonard, a famous British publisher. He had been told of Parkin's work by his friend Laurens van der Post, and wondered if the Australian would like to have a book of his drawing and painting published by Woolf's own Hogarth Press in Britain?

Parkin does exactly that, first publishing a small pictorial volume which he dedicated to Dunlop, before later publishing via the Hogarth Press his own three-volume memoirs of his war-time experiences in novel form, *Out of the Smoke* (1960), *Into the Smother* (1963) and *The Sword and the Blossom* (1968).

In the second of those books, Parkin's dedication reads: 'For WEARY (Who knows so much more of this than I).'[14]

One fellow former POW with whom Ray Parkin keeps in touch is none other than his mate who had refused to die from cholera no matter how many times they put him on the death table.

'**Scotty**,' he would later happily report, 'got back and is now the father of a fine family.'[15]

(I weep.)

•

Despite the fact that in civilian life Weary drove himself as hard as ever, he and Helen also maintained an active social life, more often than not with former POWs and veterans, and their wives.

One he always loves to see in Sydney, or when on overseas sojourns to do with POW matters, is **Blue Butterworth**, who had married not long after returning to Australia, and found employment with the Hornsby Shire Council, in charge of a bricklaying and maintenance gang.

'Wherever we went overseas,' Blue recounted, 'it wouldn't matter what company he was with, or being with ambassadors and consulates and what have you, [Weary would say], "Meet my man Friday," and so it opened up a lot of avenues for me: a Yorkshire lad who come out without a zac. Through Weary I've met people I would never ever have met, if I hadn't have been in the army with Weary.'[16]

By pure happenstance, when the author Pattie Wright met Blue much later in life through research for her book *The Men of the Line: Stories of the Thai–Burma Railway Survivors*, she realised that he was both the bricklayer who had given her brother Johnny his first job, and the man playing Santa in the back of a ute, throwing out presents to the kids running behind at Hornsby's dusty old oval at Lodge Street, in the late 1950s.

•

Alas, Weary's closest friend of all would soon be a notable absentee from his life.

For despite the efficacy of **Jim Yeates'** advice to Weary on Bondi Beach about the virtues of being betrothed, the truth was, Jim's own marriage . . . struggled. (And it was not with Pam Bushell, the woman to whom he had originally been engaged. In 1946, she had married another, and so he had married Diana Dickins in 1949.)

In a story that gripped Sydney, at 5 am on 15 September 1960, Diana, holding a torch, discovered Jim dead in the garage of his Vaucluse home – with his car still outside, the door open, the engine running and the headlights on.

At first, it appears to be death by bludgeoning alone, so badly battered is the Macquarie Street specialist's head and face. But further investigation, led by the famous Detective Ray Kelly, reveals an extraordinary thing. A small puncture on Yeates' chest is established to have been administered by a hypodermic needle, and his heart had stopped through an overdose of adrenalin. Clearly, the murderer is a doctor, and an elite one at that – very familiar with *precisely* the spot medical experts use to inject the heart.

Suspicion soon falls upon one of Sydney's most famous medicos, another Macquarie Street specialist, Dr Eric Hedberg, who was one of Yeates' closest friends – and like him, a war veteran. (Weary had also come to know this blue-blood nephew of the former Australian Prime Minister Sir Earle Page well, in the early part of the war, during their joint posting to Jerusalem.)

To Weary's shocked amazement – as he devours every newspaper account he can find, and calls friends in Sydney to keep up to date – Hedberg becomes the chief suspect as stories begin to circulate that the surgeon had been having an affair with Diana. Coincidentally, Hedberg's own wife, Joyce – not long after reporting she feared she was being poisoned – had died five months earlier from causes unknown and been cremated less than 48 hours later.

So it is not surprising the Coroner's inquest into Yeates' death is held amidst breathless tabloid reporting. One fact that draws a great deal of attention is that, less than an hour after her husband was murdered, Diana Yeates asked a family member if she should talk to her solicitor or the police first . . .

It is also established that Dr Hedberg had purchased a large amount of adrenalin just days before the murder. Dr Hedberg nevertheless steadfastly maintains that, despite not having reported it to the police at the time, this adrenalin had been 'stolen' from his car and he insists it must have been by someone trying to set him up.

Mrs Mary Hedge, of Glenview Crescent, Hunters Hill, gives evidence about her friend of 20 years.

'Mrs. Hedberg came to see me,' she tells the Coroner, 'and told me her husband was having an affair with Mrs Yeates, the wife of a friend of theirs. She was distressed and came to see me for advice. I asked her what had given her the idea. She said her husband had been going out rather unnecessarily at night, taking the station wagon rather than his own car.'[17]

In fact, she asked him directly, and he came right out and did not deny it, but admitted it.

'He said he was very much in love with Mrs Yeates and did not want to give her up.'

Objection! Hearsay.

Mr C. S. Rodgers, the Coroner, allows it, as this is a court of inquiry not a trial.

The late Mrs Hedberg's sister, Mrs Patricia Wilson of Barraba, tells Rodgers that her late sister had indeed alleged Dr Hedberg was trying to poison her. Her suspicions had been raised after Dr Hedberg gave her an unexpected drink.

'She said he did not usually offer her a glass of sherry. My sister said she immediately collapsed and later became violently ill. She thought she was going to die. After this she had a heart attack. I tried to persuade her to come and live with us. But, she said she felt so ill at the time she thought she had better stay and see if she could try and sort things out for the children's sake.'[18]

For her part, Mrs Yeates' housekeeper, Mrs Mary Mason, tells the court Mrs Yeates had not slept in the same room as her husband for four months before his death and that when she had reported for work on the morning of Dr Yeates' death, Mrs Yeates told her that her husband had died from accidental electrocution after he had 'put up his hand to put on the light and touched something and he's dead'.[19]

She thought Mrs Yeates was 'rather calm'.[20]

Despite the heavy suspicion, the inquest returns an open verdict, ruling that Dr Yeates had been 'feloniously slain by a person or persons unknown at his Vaucluse home on September 15',[21] and Dr Hedberg is free to go. The Coroner announces that, while he completely rejects the idea that it was an accidental death, the important thing is that there is still not 'one scintilla'[22] of evidence to connect either Dr Hedberg or Mrs Yeates to the strange murder of Dr Yeates.

Four years later, Dr Hedberg and Diana Yeates marry. Weary and Helen Dunlop are not in attendance. Nor is **Dr Ewan Corlette**, the Gangster, who by now is another Macquarie Street specialist, and had known both men well. Corlette's son, Andrew – by the Gangster's second wife, after his first wife had died during childbirth – will long remember Weary as an occasional visitor to their home at Woollahra, the two men drinking whisky and talking late into the night.

'I remember looking at them talking quietly and privately. I never saw them being jovial together.'[23]

There is much to discuss, much of it sad, and none sadder than the fate of Jim Yeates. As to what had happened on the Line, the Gangster takes the view, as he will tell his son, 'You can forgive them but you can never forget.'[24]

•

A reflection of what Dunlop's life was like in his middle age came in a letter to a friend, 20 years after hostilities had ceased:

> I have been around the world four or five times since the war and have crisscrossed the East – I do not travel light but have the worries and concern that go with a large consultant surgical practice, and numerous ties, not to mention a town house of nearly twenty rooms and large garden, my professional suite in the city, a cattle farm in the country, numerous staff and a gaggle of things which keep me poor. Thus we become so preoccupied all the time with things that we simply must do, that there is no time for the things we want to do.[25]

While Weary's medical career flourished in terms of public renown, and he remained highly regarded for his surgical skills, the same was not always said, surprisingly enough, about his approach to fitting in with surgical teams.

'Weary's legendary contempt for time,' one of his close colleagues, Bob Marshall, will note, 'did not endear him to his professional colleagues, especially his fellow surgeons. He was apt to schedule massive operations at a moment's notice with a sublime disregard for his own or anyone else's convenience; consequently another surgeon due to operate in the session after Weary's might easily find himself cooling his heels for hours on end while he waited in vain for the theatre to become vacant.'[26]

Immense tension was the inevitable result.

'You might be the Christ of Changi,' a fellow surgeon once yelled at him, frustrated beyond all measure, 'but you are not the bloody Christ of this hospital!'[27]

The essence of the problem was clear.

Weary's attributes were . . . more appropriate to the 'hero-surgeons' of the 19th century when the surgeon really was a one-man band. He was reluctant to delegate responsibility and believed, above all, in his own powers.[28]

One top surgeon recounted assisting Weary, then in his sixties, with an operation; when another doctor pointed out that the operation would take half as long if Weary allowed another surgeon to assist. 'Well, if there was anyone at my level, I would,'[29] replied Weary.

His self-regard was not universally shared, and it is fair to say that by the early 1970s – though he had done a great deal of work in the field of cancer treatment and pioneering research, particularly with oesophageal cancer – Weary's most significant contribution in matters medical was before a microphone or in front of a TV camera, rather than with scalpel in hand.

Another insight into the kind of man he was, in later years, came from one of his friends, the author Patsy Adam-Smith who, in Margaret Geddes' book of reminiscences about Weary, recounted how she was driving with Clive James through the streets of Melbourne in the 1980s, when by chance she saw a familiar if slightly slumped figure walking along.

'Oi!'[30] she cried out the window.

At that cry of recognition she is amused to see Weary instantly come to attention. He doesn't want to be an 'old man', and after determining that somebody has recognised him, he instantly becomes 'Weary Dunlop' for them.

Adam-Smith also noted that many of her contemporary women friends did not particularly like having Weary around as their husbands ignored them in his presence. One said, 'I'm not married to him – my husband's married to Weary.'[31]

Yes, their husbands would not even be there if not for Weary, but when he is near, the women's current life disappears and their husbands are back in the war talking with the man who could understand – the leader and saviour of those long-ago events seared in their brains.

Weary's long-time secretary, Valda Street, would recount how, many times, she would look up to see former POWs suddenly show up in his waiting room in Parliament Place and just sit. Can I help you? Not really. I just want to see Weary. No hurry. They would bring him jars of relish or jam, or skinned rabbits. And they would stay there, often for most of the day. They just wanted to be near him. And he understood it.

Weary did indeed remain deep friends with many of his fellow former POWs, and one thing they often discussed was their evolving attitude towards the Japanese – from hate, to understanding that it wasn't actually the Japanese they abhorred but fascism and militarism. In the medico's view, the entire Japanese nation had fallen victim to those forces, just as he had.

'Weary,' one former POW recounted, '[felt] that we were all in the same boat, the Japs and ourselves, none of us wanted to be there. Weary saw this wider view, that it was just what you might call circumstance with a capital C, that you were in amongst and you each had to make the best of it. And there were good ones and there were bad ones on both sides.'[32]

In the late 1970s, one of Weary's nurses, Eileen McCarthy, is stunned to see that a new patient had been none other than the Japanese consul.

'I'm surprised you treated him!'[33] she says.

'Well, Eileen, you know, you must forgive people.'

Weary will even go so far as to say, 'I personally felt that the Japanese had an excuse for getting involved in the last war. I think the Americans put them down as a tinpot economy and really screwed them down as a minor power. There was a lot of provocation.'[34]

For all that, Weary remains haunted by the episode in the war when he had been right on the point of killing the Lizard. What had he been *thinking*? He tells no-one of his angst, bar one of the few who could understand, Padre Gerard Bourke, who he had long ago saved from being decapitated by an enraged Japanese guard.

'I was narrowly saved (by chance) from the full realisation of murder's futility,'[35] Weary writes to the padre, full of anguish. But nothing can change the fact that he had fully intended to kill the Lizard, even if he had not gone through with it. Padre Bourke writes back that what Weary had been contemplating was not murder at all, but 'tyrannicide . . . in the state of war'.[36]

This is a far different thing, and the morality of it, or otherwise, turned only on whether the reprisals taken by the Japanese for such an act – if indeed they found the body and realised he had been killed by a POW – would have been greater than the 'existing evils' of what was already being done to the Australians by the Lizard.

As Weary's conviction at the time had been that the consequences of the cure could have been no worse than the cause of their ills, there is no moral case to answer here, Weary. Stand down. As you were. At *ease*.

None of this prevented Weary, as Chair of the Ex-POW and Relatives' Association – one of the many war- and medical-related official positions he held over the decades – from pushing the Japanese Government to pay reparations to the returned POWs and their families, including most particularly the families of those who did not come home 'in compensation for suffering, disability, and loss of life resulting from inhuman treatment'.[37]

As a powerful voice speaking out on behalf of the returned POWs, Weary was joined by none other than **Tom Uren**. After a post-war venture to become a professional heavyweight boxer in London had failed – with one sportswriter noting that he'd 'never seen a fighter get up off the canvas as many times as Tom did in his first fight'[38] – the giant had moved quickly upon his return to Australia to establish a different life for himself. First things first, Uren married Patricia Palmer, whose image he had first seen when her POW brother, Billy Palmer, had shown him the cherished photograph of his sister he carried with him. After initially working at the Port Kembla steel-works, Uren then became a trainee executive at Woolworths before, in 1951, joining the Labor Party, which opened an entirely new career path.

For on the afternoon of 26 February 1959, the towering figure rising to speak in the Australian Federal Parliament for his maiden speech as the newly elected member for Reid is one and the same.

After some preliminary remarks of his pride to be elected, Uren warmed into an account of the most formative period of his political life.

'I should like to relate,' he says in tones as broadly Australian as the Nullarbor, 'an experience that I had during the war. I was a prisoner of war at a place called Hintok Road Camp, on the Burma–Siam railway. Our commanding officer was Lieutenant Colonel

"Weary" Dunlop. He was a remarkable man in many ways. He was not only a great doctor but also a great soldier. We were known as the "Dunlop Force". As Honourable Members probably know, the Japanese paid our officers and medical orderlies an allowance. The non-commissioned officers and men who worked on the railway were also paid a small wage. This was a sham kept up by the Japanese to save face under the Geneva Convention.

'In our camp the officers and medical orderlies paid the greater proportion of their allowance into a central fund. The men who worked did likewise. We were living by the principle of the fit looking after the sick, the young looking after the old, the rich looking after the poor. A few months after we had arrived at Hintok Road Camp, a part of "H" force arrived. They were about 400 strong. As a temporary arrangement they had tents. The officers selected the best, the non-commissioned officers the next best, and the men got the dregs. Soon after they arrived the wet season set in, bringing with it cholera and dysentery. Six weeks later only 50 men marched out of that camp, and of that number only about 25 survived. Only a creek separated our two camps, but on one side the law of the jungle prevailed and on the other the principles of socialism.'[39]

And Uren's time on the Thai–Burma Railway, experiencing up close Weary's inspirationally humane leadership, indeed provided the parliamentarian with his North Star for the rest of his political life.

'The strong should look after the weak,' Uren would say, 'and the young should look after the old. And if a person gets sick it's a national responsibility, it isn't any individual position. We should be a more collective body. I've always asked people, "Why is it only at the time of crisis, we need each other? Why can't we need each other and love each other in normal times?"'[40]

Inevitably, Uren is quick to emerge as a voice of enormous influence in pushing the cause of former POWs and he and Weary were often able to catch up with each other.

'Weary,' the famous parliamentarian once noted proudly, 'would always say, "Tom Uren's one of my boys," and I was. He was 35 and I was 21 when we met.'[41]

Uren never pulled any punches about his own one-time hate for the Japanese.

'Their brutality was so bad,' he once said, 'I would have exterminated them from the planet. That was their sadistic brutality.'[42]

But, like Weary and Parkin, Uren's views evolved and he became one of the leading voices in the Federal Parliament urging that commerce with Asia be expanded, insisting: 'Trade and goodwill are our front line of defence.'[43]

When Uren became a minister in the Whitlam Government, his and Weary's advocacy for POWs over the last quarter-century finally began to bear real fruit and in 1974 a Gold Card was issued to all former POWs and veterans over 70, which gave them free medical, hospital, dental and optical service.

In the next term of parliament, Uren even rises to the position of Deputy Leader of the ALP. All the while, Uren is up for a scrap for the values he believes in, and never more so than when he heads to King George Square in Brisbane to protest for the preservation of civil liberties against the conservative regime of the new Queensland leader, Premier Joh Bjelke-Petersen – who had outlawed such marches.

After 700 police with truncheons wade in, Uren, with 280 other protesters, is hauled off to the notorious Boggo Road Gaol. But things do not go according to the plan laid out by Bjelke-Petersen's bovver boys.

'I was one of many officers on duty on the day they brought Tom Uren into the Reception Division for processing,' one of the guards, Stephen M. Gage, later recounted, talking of how they had all been strictly ordered to treat this famous politician as just another scummy protester. However . . .

'As the vehicle pulled up and Tom was ordered to stand in front of the reception window, I and many other officers saluted this man for what he stood for. The senior prison officers present could not stop the junior officers from saluting and speaking respectfully to Tom Uren, but the surprise was yet to come.'

Ah, but it will get better still. For, in short order, the most senior officer of the lot arrives, the Chief Superintendent of Boggo Road Gaol, Mr Clyde Lang – who is no less than a former POW on the Thai–Burma Railway and 'a comrade-in-arms with Tom Uren'.[44]

No-one will be treating the big fella badly on his watch. So you blokes mind the shop, while Tommy Uren and I head out to paint Brisbane red with drinks and dinner, while we catch up on old times, and toast our 'friendship from so many years ago'.[45]

RAH!

Inevitably, Weary's own time in public life remained far more firmly within the confines of conservatism, in keeping for one who had by now been honoured *twice* in recognition of his service to medicine, the second time in 1969, making him a Knight Bachelor which formally bestowed the title Sir Edward Dunlop on him. (It is yet one more honour to add to a name now well on its way to its final formation of looking more like an eye-chart than the appellation he had been christened with, and his formal name has come about as far from the simple 'Weary' as it is possible to get: 'Sir Edward Dunlop, A.C., C.M.G., O.B.E., K.S.J., M.S., F.R.C.S., F.R.A.C.S, L.L.D. Melb (Hons), D.Sc. Punjab (Hons.), Hon. Fellow of the Colleges of Surgeons of Thailand and Sri Lanka.'

In 1976 he was accorded the great honour of becoming the Australian of the Year, to the particular delight of his fellow former POWs.

'Thousands of men, middle-aged now, in Australia and across the world,' one of them will note, 'when they read that Weary Dunlop had been named Australian of the Year, would have said: "Yes, I knew him in Thailand. He's the 'Australian of many years'. We'd never have got back home if it hadn't been for [him]."'[46]

In 1979, the television program *This is Your Life*[47] was filmed in honour of Sir Weary Dunlop, and it brought together the likes of Bill Griffiths, Mickey de Jonge, Ray Parkin, Bill Wearne and Ewan Corlette. (A sad absence was **Arthur Moon**, who had died in 1973.)

Most moving is Bill Griffiths, who has flown from Britain. The years since the war have been good to him, as with his second wife, Alice, by his side he had thrown himself into lecturing and advocacy on disability, and in 1977 was recognised with an MBE for his prodigious effort. For this show he had arrived in Australia with Alice, who stays with him throughout the broadcast.

Before entering on stage his voice comes through loud and clear: 'I lost my eyes. I lost my hands, but Sir Edward, I found you . . .'[48]

When the host, Roger Climpson, asks Griffiths what he would like to say to Weary, who stands in front of him now, the Englishman speaks in a strong, clear voice: 'He is a man of very obvious, immense surgical skills; a man of incredible courage, brilliant leadership, and a wonderful example of how one can endure in the most difficult and desperate situation. I survived. So do many thousands of others give thanks to Sir Edward, and I certainly have enjoyed thirty years of wonderful, happy life, enriched immensely by the friendship of you, Sir Edward. Thank you so much.'[49]

For her part the Dutch matron Mickey de Jonge had had a tough time of it. Not long after the Australians had left Bandoeng, she had become active with the Dutch Resistance – providing medical care to Allied soldiers and Javanese fighters – only to have been arrested in June 1942, imprisoned and tortured by the Japanese. After the war she returned to the Netherlands, divorced and reverted to her maiden name of de Jonge – but could not be more delighted than to be here for this occasion, to honour the man she had admired so much during the war, who had stood up to the Japanese aggressors.

In the years that followed the broadcast, as Weary became more famous than he'd ever been, and progressed well into his seventies, his strength of character and willingness to take on aggressors remained.

A fellow surgeon, John Heyward, recounted an episode of being in a car with Weary when he was driving – badly, disobeying road rules and taking absurd risks – only for the old man to seriously anger the young man driving behind, as they all pull up at a traffic light.

Alas, the young fellow is so angry that he gets out of his car, approaches, and because Weary's window is open, is able to unleash a punch that breaks the medico's nose.

Unfortunately for him, the young man has picked the wrong old soldier to assault. For in a split instant Weary has not only opened his door but put his shoulder against it, hard, which knocks the man back – before springing out of the car and unleashing two very hard punches right in the man's chest that would have felled an All Black forward, let alone a young punk motorist.

He then gets back in his car and drives off.

Heyward is aghast, but Weary has rarely been more gleeful, despite the blood pouring from his nose.

'I gave him a shirt-full of broken ribs,' he chortles to his fellow surgeon.

Oh, the joy of it.

'I am sure that is exactly what he did do,' Heyward told Geddes. 'He never picked a fight, but if you picked one with him, beware. You'd come off second-best – twenty-second best. In that case, he knew he had been naughty but he was secretly pleased with himself nevertheless.'[50]

Such episodes were not one-off. When interviewed by this writer early in 2025, his surviving son, John, merrily recalled an episode when he and his brother, Alexander, were in the car with their father while still young lads. Weary had been just about to park in one of the few remaining spaces in a supermarket carpark, when a young man in a convertible, with a woman by his side, stole the spot.

'This,' John said to his brother quietly, 'is not going to end well.'

Weary remonstrated. In response, the young man was rude to him. Before his sons' very eyes, Weary got out, went over, and after lifting the young man a little out of his seat with his left hand, unleashed a punch with his right hand which rocked the man back into his seat. The medico then leaned over, took the handbrake off, and rolled the car back and out of the way, before taking his rightful spot. Problem solved.

When I asked his son if his father ever got into trouble for such things, he said, 'He was "Weary Dunlop". Things sorted themselves out, without legal trouble.'[51]

As to the raising of those sons, it mostly fell to Helen. While Weary's marriage to her was a relatively happy one – tempered by both his roving eye and his extreme level of occupation with so many things beyond the family home – his view seemed to be that the raising of the two sons fell all but exclusively in her bailiwick.

'Dad cared about us,' John said. 'But we boys were a little further down the list than POWs and his many other causes. So long as were basically okay, he was okay with that.'[52]

At least when John appeared on *This is Your Life*, he was touchingly affectionate about his father: 'First of all, I'm sorry, because my brother Alexander is unable to be with you tonight. He's tied up with his own medical duties, and so from the both of us, I'd just like to say, really, we couldn't have had a better father, and we're immensely proud of you.'[53]

Alas, that lynchpin of the family, Helen, would ail well before her husband.

When, in the early 1980s, she began to develop Alzheimer's, Weary recorded that it was 'heartbreaking to see her weep in frustration at her inability to dress herself, turn on a shower or tap'.[54]

When she needed to go into a home, one of the many problems that Weary faced was the ready cash to finance such a move. Money had never been one of his preoccupations and beyond the Toorak mansion he and Helen had raised their sons in, and lived in since, there was little else to go around.

It was for this reason, in 1986, Weary finally published *The War Diaries of Weary Dunlop*, a lightly edited version of his many diary entries during the war, illustrated by the drawings and paintings of such fellow POWs as Parkin, Chalker and others.

(Chalker, particularly, had gone on to a solid artistic career in England after the war, his son reporting: 'My father's notoriety gave him one wonderful experience which he cherished his entire life. In the camps when things were bad, he remembers humming Vera Lynn's "We'll Meet Again" and "The White Cliffs of Dover". In the 1980s Vera Lynn came to one of his exhibitions and one of the crowning moments of his life was to kiss the cheek of this icon and heroine to the troops.')[55]

In his preface, Weary paid homage to others, and one in particular:

> It is also with deep emotion that I pay tribute to the bonds that I formed with men of numerous nations in captivity, many of whom died in alien lands, and to men of the 'underground', like Boon Pong, who risked their lives to help our lot. Most uplifting of all is the timeless, enduring, special brotherhood shared with all survivors of prison camps whose devotion and pride smacks of the St Crispin's Day of Henry V. There can be no gift so rich as the gratitude and love of such men and women. To them I attribute any good there may be in this book and commend their unquenchable spirit to their children, to their children's children and to those yet unborn. In thy face I see the map of honour, truth and loyalty.[56]

Boon Pong had died four years earlier, aged 76 years.

The Foreword of Weary's diaries was written by **Laurens van der Post**. His extraordinary and controversial career included becoming a celebrity guru, famed writer and producer, celebrated African explorer, the godfather of Prince William and a close friend of Carl Jung. In 1956 he produced the incredible documentary series *The Lost World of the Kalahari*, a fascinating study of the 'Bushmen' that propelled both them and van der Post to instant world fame. His first fictional work, *The Face Beside the Fire*, was a thinly veiled portrait of himself as artist and philosopher. His semi-mystical ideas proved attractive to many, including Prince Charles, who accompanied him on a safari to Kenya in the young man's formative years. Van der Post travelled to Russia, which resulted in another best-selling book; he lived next door to Margaret Thatcher in Chelsea, and became the thinking person's guru. He was a brilliant conversationalist and writer, but – as it turned out – absolutely terrible when it came to telling the truth. Despite a life of careful evasion, a series of jaw-dropping frauds began to catch up with him. One of these was that while he had presented himself in Java to Weary as a 'Lieutenant Colonel' he was in fact no such thing. Rather, he was simply a Captain with a hell of a nerve and a poker face that held for the entire war – and ever afterwards.

Fortunately for the South African, none of his lies in the field – and in many other fields as it happened – emerged until after his death in 1996. His anointed biographer got a major shock when researching his subject, discovering that he was 'a fraud, a fantasist, a liar, a serial adulterer and a paternalist. He falsified his Army record and inflated his own importance at every possible opportunity.'[57]

And this, right up until his death.

'He was such an astonishing liar,' the woman who cared for him in his later years said, 'it seemed as automatic and necessary to him as breathing, from some flim-flam to do with socks to the engorged fabrication of his deeds. Consequently, I found it impossible to see him as anything but his own invention.'[58]

Weary's book sold so well that Helen was indeed put into a fine nursing home, where she lived out the rest of her days slowly fading and finally neither recognising him nor their sons – until she died on 21 April 1988.

By now Weary's own complex life was itself ebbing and yet, even in these twilight years, the time he had spent on the Thai–Burma Railway loomed large as the basis of his fame, and the time that defined him, just as it had defined so many of the POWs who had suffered and survived it.

While the common experience of all those POWs in **Hellfire Pass** and adjacent cuttings had formed bonds that could never be broken, let alone erased, in truth the surrounding area of those cuttings that Dunlop Force had worked on was so comprehensively reclaimed by the jungle over the decades that for a long time it was lost – helped along by the fact that the railway was demolished shortly after the war. (There was no need to demolish the bridges. Few of them were left standing in any case, as the Allied bombing and, more particularly, the white ants introduced by the Tasmanian bushies had done their work so well that a military report from 1945 had noted: 'Some of the bridges on this railway are too weak to carry locomotives ... wagons having to be moved over them singly by hand. Many of these bridges are liable to be washed out during the monsoon season. Under present conditions, therefore, its capacity is negligible.'[59] It was more than just one bridge on the River Kwai that had fallen!)

In the mid-1980s, however, 30 Diggers from 3rd Battalion, Royal Australian Regiment, were assigned the interesting task of finding Hellfire Pass, clearing away the jungle and getting the whole area into shape for a ceremony to be held there on Anzac Day 1987.

Under the supervision of an historian, they had indeed found it, and – using hand tools from an era long gone to restore a section of rail – became the first Australians to work in Hellfire Pass since the war.

In late April, Uren accompanies Weary with a delegation of ex-POWs back to Hellfire Pass. It is a deeply moving affair for both men, as all the memories, the horror, the heat, the humidity, the deaths, disease and disasters come flooding back.

The two unveil a plaque on a memorial, honouring the dead. Uren, for one, finds the experience literally overwhelming.

'I went into the cutting,' he will recount, 'and I lost muscular control over the whole of my body for a couple of minutes.'[60]

There to calm and support him – as, after a pause, they continue to walk into the cutting – is a young official in Uren's office, Anthony Albanese. He is like a son to Uren, just as this 24-year-old fellow from Marrickville with big political ambitions of his own will later say, 'I grew up without a dad, but not without a father. Tom Uren was my father figure. He was a big man in stature. A big man in ideas. And a man with a big heart.'[61] This was Albanese's first trip overseas, learning at the feet of the master in the spot that defined the old politician's early years, and he would credit Uren with laying the foundation stone of his own political ideas: 'His beliefs inspired me ... Those values still drive me today.'[62] Uren returned his affection in kind, saying of him, in the last political interview he gave, 'I love the boy.'[63]

After visiting the cemetery and laying wreaths, Uren even managed to call on Albanese's youthful vigour to the point that, together, they were able to climb back to the spot he'd gloried in all those years ago, where he had sworn he would come back when he was free, to drink in its beauty as a liberated soul. Alas, alas, as he gazes out once more on the ancient teak forests of Thailand, it is to stand witness to environmental devastation.

'There wasn't one teak forest left,' Uren would recount. 'They'd all been raped and all they had was bamboo.'[64]

Gone with the teak forests are most of the birds, monkeys, tigers and elephants that used to abound all around.

Not long after Tom Uren had retired from parliament, both he and Weary, among others, received an extraordinary letter.

It was from a famed historian, Professor Hank Nelson of the Australian National University, seeking to arrange a seminar for survivors of the Thai–Burma Railway together with Australian and Japanese historians.

Why?

They were attempting, as his co-organiser, Gavan McCormack, then Professor of Japanese History at ANU, later recounted, 'to bring together as many survivors as possible, i.e. including formerly hostile parties, to reflect on the episode across the gulf of half a century'.[65]

Among those attending was . . . **Yi Hak-Nae** from Korea, the man the Japanese called Kakurai Hiromura.

Who?

No.

It couldn't be, surely?

It is.

The Lizard! Yes, the very man Dunlop had personally contemplated murdering nearly 50 years earlier will be coming to Australia for the event. After his sentence of death by hanging had been commuted to 20 years imprisonment, he had served his time for his war crimes in Japan, and, feeling he did not have long to live, has particularly said he wished to see Dr Dunlop.

Uren decided to go.

And you, Weary?

After long consideration, Weary agrees, and, despite being quite ill at the time the seminar is due to take place, journeys north to Canberra.

And here, in the conference room before him, is the Lizard – stooped with age, yes, and more thick-set, but still strong enough to have come all the way from Tokyo, where he has been working as a cab driver. But Weary is not strong. In fact, he is now so weak and with his leg in a splint while swathed in bandages, he cannot even rise from the chair he is in when the Korean arrives.

The Lizard steps forward and without a word helps him up, immediately making Weary 'embarrassed . . . by his assistance to help me stand'.[66]

But he is also stunned by the kindness. This is indeed an older version of the Lizard he had known, but in so many ways it is not the same man.

They must talk before the conference formally begins, and it is Professor McCormack who accompanies the two men, with Tom Uren – who remains a little standoffish – to sit outside in the morning sunshine on the steps of the H. C. Coombs Building.

With McCormack acting as interpreter, the two one-time enemies talk to each other for the first time in nigh on 50 years, and actually *converse* for the first time ever.

By now Weary is already aware of much of the former guard's story, but the Korean adds details. One thing Weary and Tom Uren are shocked to hear is that the Lizard was only born in 1925, and had just gone 18 when they were dealing with him!

Nor, at the time, had they ever known of the horror of the Korean's own experience, born at a time when Japan had already occupied the entire country for the previous 15 years and viewed Korea's population as vassals to be moved around at will, in the service of the Japanese Empire. All of his early life had been filled with intensive education to regard the Emperor as a god, and themselves as his subjects, with no other role in life but to serve his whim.

Now, he earnestly seeks their understanding for why he and his fellow Korean guards had been so brutal. For we, too, had been victims of a system, tossed around like flotsam on a tidal sea of violence and completely incapable of influencing the course of events. We had been raised in it, come to maturity in it, trained in it, subjected to it. It was the only thing we knew. It was only in my full maturity, long after the war was over, that I realised there was another way.

It is obvious just how deeply saddened the Korean is, by the pain he has caused, and just how regretful he is. Weary leans forward and listens closely, while Uren leans back with one eyebrow raised, as Yi remains insistent that whatever he had done had been less because of his own failings and more because they had been forced into their behaviour by the Japanese.

Weary and Tom Uren must understand!

He was just eighteen. He had absolutely no training in how to handle prisoners. They must put them through a course where they tried to beat the military spirit into them – literally beating them several times a day – bashing them into believing that the Imperial Japanese Army was a glorious thing that they were lucky to serve in. They made them understand that, on pain of death, the first prerequisite for that service was absolute obedience, and strict observation of the code of military conduct. And after just two months of that kind of training they were sent to guard them.

And yet, when the war was over, and the Allies were rounding up suspected war criminals, their captors had made absolutely *no* distinction between those of Korean ethnicity and those who were Japanese.

As it happened, Yi had been one of 62 Koreans put on trial for his life by an Australian court in Singapore, in his case charged with ill-treatment of prisoners, and in just two days of trial – with only 40 minutes of his own testimony, and understanding little of what was happening – his primary memory was the trial's conclusion, when he had distinctly heard the judge say, while looking at him, 'Death by hanging.'

Though Yi's sentence had been commuted to 20 years imprisonment, 23 others – including Lieutenant Eiji Hirota – were in due course hanged. After five years in Changi, Yi had been transferred to Sugamo prison in Tokyo, and finally returned in 1956 to a world he did not recognise – and that truly did not recognise him.

'Except my parents and siblings, no one would welcome me,' he recounted sadly. And they no doubt would have, but still Yi felt he could not take the risk of being branded a traitor, and bringing dishonour to his family, and so never set foot in Korea again, even missing his mother's funeral.

He is absolutely clear on why he has come to Australia. He wishes to try to make amends, and even friends, all these years on.

'From my very soul, I truly and sincerely want to apologise to you,' Yi tells the man who, as he will later tell McCormack, has been in his thoughts as the subject of both his deep regret and great admiration for many, many decades.

Weary pauses, looking momentarily stunned that it has come to this.

But now he proffers his hand, and engulfs the hand of Yi Hak-Nae, before shaking it.

Profoundly moved in turn, the Korean stands up, and bows deeply to Weary, and tangentially Uren, as a mark of deep respect.

'The weight of nearly half a century has been lifted from my heart,'[67] the one they once called the Lizard will note.

And yet, for his part, Tom Uren does not offer his hand in reply. The former heavyweight boxer is all for forgiving their former enemies as a people. But he struggles much more when it comes to individuals like Yi Hak-Nae. And he is not alone in his attitude.

From the podium shortly afterwards, the Korean repeats his contrition to all.

'From the bottom of my heart I wanted to apologise profoundly,' he tells them. 'As one of the aggressor side, to Colonel Dunlop and all the former POWs, for the bitterness and pain of the loss of so many of their comrades under such harsh circumstances. Before you all, I apologise from my heart.'

And yes, there is a stirring in the room at this extraordinary event. The Lizard, apologising to them for what he had done, 50 years on from his atrocities!

But beyond Weary, there is still no move from any of the other half-dozen former POWs in attendance to accept the apology.

The room swirls with so many complex emotions, it is nigh on overwhelming.

Weary's grace in accepting Yi Hak-Nae's apology is deeply moving to those who witness it.[68] And yet several of the other POWs will tell Yi that while they were glad he had apologised, and accepted his sincerity, they cannot bring themselves to personally forgive what had been done to their mates all those years ago. The scars from their time on the Thai–Burma Railway still run too deep.

Weary himself is unrepentant for having accepted Yi's apology.

'You don't understand,'[69] he tells his own doctor, who dared mention his act of forgiveness a few weeks later. The fact that Yi had journeyed to Australia, and given such a heart-felt personal apology was proof positive that there is a 'little bit of God in every man'.[70]

•

In 1991, Weary again ventured north for the Dawn Service at Hellfire Pass, and to unveil another part of the Line that had been turned into a place of sacred commemoration.

He just made it, having only arrived in Bangkok at midnight after a lost passport in Australia had delayed him catching an earlier flight, only for the taxi he had caught to take him north to then break down in the wee hours. After hitchhiking and being picked up by thrilled Australian SAS soldiers on their way to the same ceremony, he had arrived just in time for a 5 am tot of rum to settle down, and brace for the trudge to Hellfire Pass itself.

Some things never change!

Just as it had been half a century earlier, in that half-light of dawn, Weary picks his way along the narrow track towards Hellfire, though part of it now goes by an unfamiliar grove of pawpaw trees. More familiar, a little further on, are the thickets and soaring bamboo intertwined with cruel and thorny vines that snake around and through it, picking at his clothing as he goes, breathing ever more heavily. Finally, the way clears and he is back once more at the bottom of the steep decline where lies Hellfire Pass, just in time for the Anzac Day Dawn Service, even as the temperature rises to 35°C, with humidity at an astonishing 90 per cent.

Waiting for him are numerous dignitaries and 50 former POWs, including none other than Ray Parkin, returning to this place of horror for the first time in nearly five decades, bringing his son, John.

When the last tones of the 'Last Post' fall away to craggy silence once more, and the service is over, Weary and Parkin wander through this cutting of death, their hands occasionally running across the face of the rock, as the memories come flooding back.

'You can still see the marks where the poor wretches drilled,' Weary says to Tony Stephens of the *Sydney Morning Herald*. 'They worked day and night. It was very like Dante's Inferno. It measured up to Hellfire.'[71]

For his part, Parkin, ever the artist, says, 'I came back not to revive war memories, but memories of the land.'[72]

And yet those war memories keep intruding.

'I had thirty-one attacks of malaria here,' he said. 'When I look at this place, all I can hear is hammer and tap, hammer and tap.'

Of course, most of it – at least here – is as it was, including a small section of railway that had been re-laid where it once had been, but even since the clean-up by the soldiers of the 3rd Royal Australian Regiment, some years before, trees have started to re-establish themselves on the floor of the cutting and are pushing their way to the strands of sunlight making their way through the jungle canopy. Weary walks among them, away from the rest of the group, sometimes reaching out to touch surfaces as the memories that flood back overwhelm him.

'The Japanese were totally brutal even to animals,' he says to a man near him. 'They had a deadly earnestness, an instilled brutality.'[73]

Asked of his views about plans to build a museum and memorial walkway on this site, Weary affirms his pleasure and hopes that this 'will become a hallowed place, like the war cemeteries at Gallipoli' while also adding sagely, 'the best memorial of all is in the hearts of men and women'.[74]

Moving on, as the heat of the day starts to get a real grip and the temperature starts to climb, a forward young Australian television reporter pokes his microphone too close to the great man, to ask the obvious question – 'Tell me, Sir Edward, what are you thinking about right now?'[75] – and Weary is less than pleased.

'If you must know,' he growls, as the camera rolls, 'right now I'm wondering how I'm going to get back up that fucking hill, in this fucking heat!'[76]

It is a fair query, and he only just manages to make it, after considerable rest.

Back in the day, Weary's favourite quote on how to live a life had come from George Bernard Shaw: 'I want to be thoroughly used up when I die, for the harder I work the more I live. I rejoice in life for its own sake. Life is no "brief candle" for me. It is a sort of splendid torch which I have got hold of for the moment, and I want to make it burn as brightly as possible before handing it on to future generations.'[77]

Weary Dunlop – now 85 years old and feeling every bit that and more – does indeed feel all but thoroughly used up. And while this has been a worthwhile trip, already he knows it will be his last, at least while still alive. Before leaving this sacred place, there is just time to make like the swagman did with the billabong.

For, after finding a stream with a waterfall in a cool and shady place, he quickly strips down to have a dip, 'wallowing in the water like an old walrus. Women and children from the small settlement recognised him and, shyly at first then more boldly, joined him, laughing and splashing water . . .'[78]

Is he sinking, drowning . . . losing consciousness?

Yes, a little of all that, and more. For only a short time later, on 1 July 1993, Weary, having suffered a bout of pneumonia, collapses at the same Toorak home he and Helen had lived in for decades. He is rushed to Melbourne's Alfred Hospital, the doctors doing all they can to save the most famous doctor in the country.

But as Weary knows better than anyone, some battles will always be lost and the final one must be. He dies.

It is 2 July 1993, and he is 85 years old.

The word of his death spreads quickly thereafter, around Australia and indeed around the world, particularly across what Sue Ebury calls the 'Bamboo Radio' – that vibrant network of POWs, veterans, families and advocates stretching from Melbourne through every Australian capital and hundreds of regional towns, across to Singapore, up to Bangkok, across to Hong Kong, New York, London, Blackpool, Edinburgh and The Hague.

Yes, it is true. The 'quiet lion' is gone.

Prime Minister Paul Keating releases a statement, noting of Weary Dunlop that he was 'courageous, determined, humble and, above all, ever generous in helping those who needed help . . . Sir Edward was admired, even beloved, of many. To have gathered as many friends as Sir Edward did in his life is a tribute beyond any that I can offer. I extend, on behalf of a nation grateful for his work and his life, my condolences and sympathy to his family.'[79]

A State Funeral, perhaps?

Well, the subject had arisen earlier that very year when a friend had floated the idea, only for Weary to dismiss it out of hand.

'Nonsense. I wouldn't allow it,' he had retorted.

'Then you will have to put it in writing, because otherwise you will have no choice.'[80]

But, of course, that is precisely what Weary is honoured with by the Victorian Government and when it takes place at St Paul's Cathedral on the morning of Monday, 12 July 1993, the church is packed tightly.

The front pews are filled with POWs, and their numbers include, most movingly, Bill Griffiths. He has flown from London for the occasion, now just a little over 50 years since Weary had saved his life, first by operating on him and then by standing in front of a Japanese bayonet intended for him. Other POWs include Ray Parkin and Tom Uren, with a seat empty between them for Bill Butterworth who will arrive shortly. (Missing are the likes of **Ewan Corlette**, the Gangster, who had died in 1986 after a stroke the year before, and **Mickey de Jonge**, who is in Holland and has herself only months to live.)

Behind them in the second row of pews are such dignitaries as Prime Minister Paul Keating and Opposition Leader John Hewson, together with former prime ministers Malcolm Fraser and Bob Hawke, who accompany the widow of Sir Robert Menzies, Dame Pattie. Other dignitaries include former Governors-General Sir Zelman Cowen and Sir Ninian Stephen, members of the High Court, the Japanese Ambassador and the Chief of the General Staff, Lieutenant General John Grey.

But hush now as the horse-drawn gun-carriage bearing Weary's coffin, draped in the Australian flag, approaches through streets where the people bow their heads in sombre silence and the only sound heard is the muffled bells of St Paul's, the occasional sob, and the creak and squeak of the iron-rimmed wheels on the bitumen. Right behind the casket solemnly walks none other than Blue Butterworth – who had lost his wife just a fortnight earlier – holding Weary's medals, his faithful servant to the last.

The day before, some members of the Buddhist community of Melbourne – whose philosophy that 'never in this world can hatred be stilled by hatred'[81] had impressed the medico – had gathered around the coffin to 'sing him up to heaven'.[82] Among those singing, chanting and burning incense had been Weary's four-year-old granddaughter Isabelle, along with her father John and mother Chantel.[83]

And, as the coffin now enters St Paul's, some will insist they can feel what Ray Parkin had called 'the subtle presence of the big man'.[84]

All rise.

'It is as a hero that we remember Weary Dunlop,' Sir Ninian tells the congregation in his eulogy, noting that through all the challenges that life threw at Dunlop in the realms of sport, war and surgery, he had quietly triumphed himself, while inspiring those around him. 'Bitterness never entered his soul, for he knew its corroding influence and forthrightly rejected it . . . It is lives such as his that teach us that man can aspire to and achieve true nobleness of character.'[85]

Sir Ninian warms to the theme of greatness, opining that of all Australians who ever lived, it is perhaps only Sir Douglas Mawson who could look Sir Edward Dunlop in the eye when it came to the 'lone eminence of sustained heroism and superb achievement'.[86] And while Weary would be surprised to hear himself described as being very nearly saint-like, Sir Ninian insists that 'to many, his dedication to all that was good and his own sheer nobility of character seemed saintly, they set him apart'.[87]

Hymns. Sermons. Prayers.

All rise.

'The first notes of the anthem,' Weary's first biographer and great friend Sue Ebury chronicles, 'floated through the cathedral like the wind in the trees on a dark night.'

Outside, the six serving military pall-bearers carefully place Weary's coffin on the gun-carriage in preparation for being taken to the Shrine of Remembrance.

The mood of the heavy crowds outside with their heads bowed once more – listening to the funeral live broadcast on the ABC – is exemplified by a hastily scribbled note pinned on a side door of St Paul's: 'I didn't know you personally, but you made me proud to be an Australian. Rest gently.'[88]

While the Australian Army Band, together with soldiers and senior officers of the Australian Army, prepare to lead the cortege in a slow march to the Shrine, journalists are recording reminiscences of many of the POWs and the medical fraternity about Weary's life and times. One of them, Dr Max Lake, recounts a tale to *The Age* that seems emblematic of an emerging theme that while you can take the war hero out of the war, you can't always take the war out of the war hero.

'Weary discovered a man tampering with his car. When challenged, he made his first mistake by taking off. Weary had a blue for running. He made his second mistake by trying to dodge. Weary was a football blue and tackled him. He made his final and most serious mistake by shaping up and having a go. Weary had a blue for boxing and broke his jaw.

'Weary then gathered him up, drove him to hospital, set his jaw and arranged for the discharge and review of the patient at the next convenient outpatient clinic.'[89]

For his part, Tom Uren said of his great friend: 'Weary was a builder looking to the future, not to the past. He will be remembered in the hearts and minds of people and he will be immortalised in the history of Australia, one of the very special people.'[90]

Bill Griffiths, with teary if sightless eyes, tells the press, 'I am grateful to have had the privilege of knowing him.'[91]

Now, no fewer than 20,000 mourners line Swanston Street then up St Kilda Road, as the carriage – behind the band and the solid ranks of marching men and women – makes its way towards the Shrine of Remembrance, where Weary has paid his own respects to deceased veterans so many times, including most Anzac Days.

Among the crowd at the Shrine is a seven-year-old girl, Stephanie Lillis, who is wrapped up against the cold and holding a school exercise book, in which she has newspaper cuttings of her hero, Sir Weary Dunlop.

'If there is another war I want to be just like Weary,' Stephanie tells the *Canberra Times*, albeit noting one difference. 'I want to be just like Weary, except a girl.'[92]

From the Shrine, the cortege – with Weary's coffin now placed in a dark hearse – makes its way to the Springvale crematorium, where his earthly remains are interred, ashes to ashes, dust to dust.

It has been an extraordinary day. The next day, Sir Zelman Cowen will sagely note of proceedings that 'the experience . . . was altogether remarkable and it is surely one which will remain in the collective life of the nation as a celebration of human worth'.[93]

The following Anzac Day, Weary is back at the Thai–Burma Railway. Or at least a fair portion of his ashes is, for he had told his family, 'I would like to be with my comrades.'[94]

So, on the eve of the service, some of his ashes are cast adrift by his sons, Alexander and John, in a metre-long model boat made of plywood that is bedecked with a single candle and 160 orchids – all while a 16-year-old piper[95] from Perth plays 'The Flowers of the Forest'.

The following day, the Anzac Day Dawn Service at Hellfire Pass is attended by 500 people – each bearing a lit candle – and is presided over by Reverend Dr Monty Morris, vicar of Christ Church, Bangkok, with Weary's two sons sitting beside Blue Butterworth in the front row. Alexander is wearing Weary's medals.

This time the piper plays 'Waltzing Matilda' before the remains of Weary's remains are raked into the rocky earth, during a two-minute silence. Breaking the spell, the Reverend Morris invokes the famous words of Kemal Ataturk about Australians interred in the soil of their one-time enemies.

'You, the mothers, who sent their sons from faraway countries, wipe away your tears. Your sons are now lying in our bosom and are in peace. After having lost their lives on this land, they have become our sons as well.'[96]

It is over.

•

Two years later, Blue Butterworth will again be present for a grand occasion to honour 'the boss', as the first of three statues raised for Weary – the other two being one in his hometown of Benalla, unveiled before a crowd of 10,000, a fair effort for a town of just 9000 people; and one at the Australian War Memorial – is unveiled in the park by Melbourne's St Kilda Road. The next day Blue returns, and asks a woman passer-by to photograph him standing beside it.

'I was with him,' he can't resist saying as he poses proudly.

'That's what they all say,'[97] she replies knowingly.

Blue died in December 2011, aged 93, outlasting Ray Parkin by six years.

Bill Griffiths died in July 2012.

Tom Uren filled his final years as an active campaigner for environmental causes, while also coming out staunchly against the wars in Iraq and Afghanistan. He died on 26 January 2015, aged 93, a giant among men. I felt privileged when I met him several times over the years – the first time at an anti-war rally in Sydney – but only wish I had known then what I know now: just what a truly great Australian he was.

•

Strangely, of all the principals and even bit-players in this story, the longest lived is Yi Hak-Nae. Instead of dying at the time that Weary was close to killing him, he actually lived for another . . . eight decades, the last several of which had been spent pursuing the Japanese Government.

In the early 1990s, he and seven other Korean *senpan* brought a suit against the government in the Tokyo District Court seeking compensation. It was the beginning of a legal odyssey which, though it went through many iterations and appeals, finally . . . got nowhere.

Yi Hak-Nae finally died in 2021, aged 96, with his claims still unrealised.

•

And so the story ends.

But if, as George Eliot once famously opined, 'Our dead are never dead to us, until we have forgotten them', Weary Dunlop lives on, at least in legend. Even today, over thirty years after he died, he remains a byword for self-sacrifice, for inspirational leadership, for what it means to be an Australian when we are at our very best.

He embodied our finest values, and lived a life of which all Australians can be proud.

Vale, great Australian, Edward 'Weary' Dunlop.

APPENDIX

At the fall of Singapore there were about 100 Australian medical and dental officers who became prisoners-of-war. There were probably a greater number of MOs from the other Allied forces, such as Captain Dr Jacob Markowitz, a Canadian doctor and fellow POW mentioned in these pages. Forty-four medical officers and five dental officers were sent to Burma and Thailand in support of the POWs on the Line. In my view, as a group they have been insufficiently commemorated and I offer the following list of these officers, provided by Dr John Mitchell of Victoria, together with the identity of the force to which they were attached, with profound respect.

AAMC Officers on the Thai–Burma Railway

A FORCE To Burma, May 1942

HAMILTON, T Lt Col SMO 2/4 CCS NX70505
COATES, AE Lt Col 2/10 AGH VX39198
EADIE, NB Lt Col 2/13 AGH VX14845
HOBBS, AF Maj 2/4 CCS SX10761
FISHER, WE Maj 2/4 CCS NX70506
CHALMERS, JS Maj 2/4 CCS TX2150
KRANTZ, SS Maj 2/4 CCS SX13978
RICHARDS, CRB Capt 2/15 Fd Regt NX70273
ANDERSON, CD Capt 2/4 MGB WX3464
CUMMING, GD Capt 2/10 Fd Amb NX70385
BRERETON, TLG Capt 2/4 CCS NX76108
HIGGIN, JP Capt 2/4 CCS NX34949
WHITE, AJM Capt 2/4 CCS TX6074
SIMPSON, ST Capt (Dentist) 2/4 CCS TX2188
TREVELEVEN, WJK Capt (Dentist) 25 Dental Unit VX39266

D FORCE *To the southern end of the Line, March 1943*

HAZELTON, AR Maj SMO 2/10 Fd Amb NX35134
PARKER, RG Capt 2/10 Fd Amb NX71143
WRIGHT, RG Capt 2/10 AGH NX70664
MILLARD, PT Capt 2/26 Bn NX76511
HINDER, D Capt 2/19 Bn NX76302
DUNCAN, IL Capt RAE NX35135
FINIMORE, LT Capt (Dentist) 32 Dental Unit QX25482

DUNLOP FORCE *To the southern end of the Line, January 1943*

DUNLOP, EE Lt Col 2/2 CCS VX259
MOON, AA Maj 2/2 CCS NX455
CORLETTE, EL Maj 2/2 CCS NX350
CLARKE, JER Maj (Dentist) 2/2 CCS QX6245
GODLEE, T Capt 2/3 MGB WX11057

F FORCE *To Northern Thailand, April 1943*

STEVENS, RH Maj SMO 2/12 Fd Amb NX39043
HUNT, BA Maj 2/13 AGH WX11177
ROGERS, EA Maj 2/13 AGH TX2199
CAHILL, RL Capt (Lloyd) 2/19 Bn NX35149
CAHILL, FJ Capt (Frank) 2/9 Fd Amb VX39702
HENDRY, PIA 2/10 Fd Amb NX35147
TAYLOR, JL Capt 2/30 Bn NX70453
MILLS, RM Capt 2/10 Fd Amb NX35139
BRAND, V Capt 2/29 Bn VX39085
JUTTNER, CP Capt 2/9 Fd Amb SX14044
MANNION, RI Capt (Dentist) 33 Dental Unit QX25481

H FORCE *To the southern end of the Line, 1943*

MARSDEN, EA Maj 2/10 AGH NX39316
FAGAN, KJ Maj 2/10 AGH NX70643
WINCHESTER, Mac K Capt (Dentist) 43 ADU NX76600

K FORCE *Deployed in medical support of labourers, June 1943*

ANDERSON, BH Maj DADMS VX47449
DAVIES, GFS Maj 2/13 AGH NX76351

HOGG, TGH Capt 2/13 AGH TX2185
FREW, JK Capt 2/13 AGH VX39181
DREVERMANN, EB Capt 2/13 AGH VX61260

L FORCE Deployed in medical support of labourers, August 1943

ANDREWS, HL Maj 2/10 AGH VX39316
MURPHY, PF Maj 2/10 Fd Amb NX70489
CRANKSHAW, TP Maj 2/13 AGH VX62081

ENDNOTES

Abbreviations

AWM   Australian War Memorial
NAA   National Archives of Australia
SLV   State Library of Victoria

Epigraph

1   *The Sydney Morning Herald*, 25 April 1991.
2   *The Sunday Times* (Perth), 18 October 1936, p. 9, https://trove.nla.gov.au/newspaper/article/58773112.

Dramatis personae

1   Paper written by Ewan Corlette's son, Andrew, in 2015, sent to the author.
2   *Daily Mail*, 27 February 2010, https://www.dailymail.co.uk/news/article-1254168/Monsters-River-Kwai-One-British-POW-tells-horrifying-story.html.

Chapter One

1   Ebury, *Weary: The Life of Sir Edward Dunlop*, Penguin Books, Australia, 1995, p. 47.
2   Wodehouse, *Very Good, Jeeves*, Herbert Jenkins, 1930, p. 301.
3   Sir Ernest Edward 'Weary' Dunlop interviewed by Dr Hank Nelson, Australian War Memorial, https://www.awm.gov.au/collection/C283448.
4   *Truth*, 12 August 1934, p. 6, https://trove.nla.gov.au/newspaper/article/169325953.
5   Sir Ernest Edward 'Weary' Dunlop interviewed by Dr Hank Nelson, Australian War Memorial, https://www.awm.gov.au/collection/C283448.
6   Dunlop, *Little Sticks, The Story of Two Brothers*, Acacia Press, 1985, p. vii.
7   Dunlop, *Little Sticks, The Story of Two Brothers*, p. vii.
8   *The Herald*, 20 July 1932, p. 4, https://trove.nla.gov.au/newspaper/article/242980325.
9   Woodhouse, 'Sam White', *Australian Dictionary of Biography*, Vol. 18, 2012, https://adb.anu.edu.au/biography/white-sam-14877.
10   Sir Ernest Edward 'Weary' Dunlop interviewed by Dr Hank Nelson, Australian War Memorial, https://www.awm.gov.au/collection/C283448.
11   *Referee*, 27 July 1932, p. 12, https://trove.nla.gov.au/newspaper/article/135326279. Further reading: https://trove.nla.gov.au/newspaper/article/186938169.

12 Dunlop, *Little Sticks, The Story of Two Brothers*, p. xi.

13 Dunlop, *Little Sticks, The Story of Two Brothers*, p. viii.

14 Dunlop, *Little Sticks, The Story of Two Brothers*, p. 21.

15 Ebury, *Weary: The Life of Sir Edward Dunlop*, p. 102.

16 Ebury, *Weary: The Life of Sir Edward Dunlop*, p. 101.

17 Sir Ernest Edward 'Weary' Dunlop interviewed by Dr Hank Nelson, Australian War Memorial, https://www.awm.gov.au/collection/C283448.

18 Sir Ernest Edward 'Weary' Dunlop interviewed by Dr Hank Nelson, Australian War Memorial, https://www.awm.gov.au/collection/C283448.

19 Ebury, *Weary: The Life of Sir Edward Dunlop*, p. 93.

20 Letter, Edward Dunlop to Helen Ferguson, 1 January 1939. Papers of Sir Edward 'Weary' Dunlop, PR00926, item 1/34 Part 1, Australian War Memorial [AWM].

21 Ebury, *Weary: The Life of Sir Edward Dunlop*, p. 111.

22 *Benalla Standard*, 2 August 1938, p. 5, https://trove.nla.gov.au/newspaper/article/269698755.

23 *This is Your Life*, Sir Edward Dunlop, 23 June 1979, https://www.iwm.org.uk/collections/item/object/80012508.

24 *Benalla Standard*, 19 August 1938, p. 6, https://trove.nla.gov.au/newspaper/article/269686947.

25 *Benalla Standard*, 2 May 1939, p. 4, https://trove.nla.gov.au/newspaper/article/269469146.

26 *Benalla Standard*, 2 May 1939, p. 4, https://trove.nla.gov.au/newspaper/article/269469146.

27 Letter, Edward Dunlop to Helen Ferguson, mid-1938, Papers of Sir Edward 'Weary' Dunlop, PR00926, item 1/34 Part 1, AWM.

28 Letter, Edward Dunlop to Helen Ferguson, 1938, Papers of Sir Edward 'Weary' Dunlop, PR00926, item 1/34 Part 1, AWM.

29 Sir Ernest Edward 'Weary' Dunlop interviewed by Dr Hank Nelson, Australian War Memorial, https://www.awm.gov.au/collection/C283448.

30 Sir Ernest Edward 'Weary' Dunlop interviewed by Dr Hank Nelson, Australian War Memorial, https://www.awm.gov.au/collection/C283448 [reported thought].

31 Sir Ernest Edward 'Weary' Dunlop interviewed by Dr Hank Nelson, Australian War Memorial, https://www.awm.gov.au/collection/C283448.

32 *Mirror*, 15 July 1939, p. 17, https://trove.nla.gov.au/newspaper/article/75869223.

33 *Mirror*, 15 July 1939, p. 17, https://trove.nla.gov.au/newspaper/article/75869223.

34 Dunlop, *The War Diaries of Weary Dunlop*, Penguin Books, Australia, 1986, p. xxv.

35 Radio Address by Neville Chamberlain, Prime Minister, 3 September 1939, Yale Law School, https://avalon.law.yale.edu/wwii/gb3.asp.

36 Sir Robert Menzies, 1939 Radio Address, Papers of Sir Robert Menzies, National Library of Australia, https://nla.gov.au/nla.obj-233710278.

37 Milton Butterworth (Blue), Transcript of interview, UNSW Australians at War Film Archive, November 2003.

38 *The Last Post Magazine*, Edition 2, 2011, p. 75, https://thelastpostmagazine.com/wp-content/uploads/2020/05/The-Last-Post-Magazine-Edition-2-Summer-2011.pdf.

39 Milton Butterworth (Blue), Transcript of interview, UNSW Australians at War Film Archive, 21 November 2003, http://australiansatwarfilmarchive.unsw.edu.au/archive/906.

40 Milton Butterworth (Blue), Transcript of interview, UNSW Australians at War Film Archive, 21 November 2003, http://australiansatwarfilmarchive.unsw.edu.au/archive/906.

Chapter Two

1 Letter, Edward Dunlop to Helen Ferguson, 3 September 1939, Papers of Sir Edward 'Weary' Dunlop, PR00926, item 1/34 Part 3, AWM.

2 *Benalla Standard*, 26 September 1939, p. 4, https://trove.nla.gov.au/newspaper/article/269471737.

3 Dunlop, *The War Diaries of Weary Dunlop*, p. xxvi.

4 Dunlop, *The War Diaries of Weary Dunlop*, p. xxvi.

5 Sir Ernest Edward 'Weary' Dunlop interviewed by Dr Hank Nelson, Australian War Memorial, https://www.awm.gov.au/collection/C283448.

6 Sir Ernest Edward 'Weary' Dunlop interviewed by Dr Hank Nelson, Australian War Memorial, https://www.awm.gov.au/collection/C283448.

7 Sir Ernest Edward 'Weary' Dunlop interviewed by Dr Hank Nelson, Australian War Memorial, https://www.awm.gov.au/collection/C283448.

8 Dunlop, *The War Diaries of Weary Dunlop*, p. vi.

9 Sir Ernest Edward 'Weary' Dunlop interviewed by Dr Hank Nelson, Australian War Memorial, https://www.awm.gov.au/collection/C283448.

10 Ebury, *Weary: The Life of Sir Edward Dunlop*, p. 150.

11 Sir Ernest Edward 'Weary' Dunlop interviewed by Dr Hank Nelson, Australian War Memorial, https://www.awm.gov.au/collection/C283448.

12 *Benalla Standard*, 5 March 1940, p. 3, https://trove.nla.gov.au/newspaper/article/269476418.

13 *Benalla Standard*, 5 March 1940, p. 3, https://trove.nla.gov.au/newspaper/article/269476418.

14 Ebury, *Weary: The Life of Sir Edward Dunlop*, p. 164.

15 Sir Ernest Edward 'Weary' Dunlop interviewed by Dr Hank Nelson, Australian War Memorial, https://www.awm.gov.au/collection/C283448.

16 Ebury, *Weary: The Life of Sir Edward Dunlop*, p. 172.

17 Sir Ernest Edward 'Weary' Dunlop interviewed by Dr Hank Nelson, Australian War Memorial, https://www.awm.gov.au/collection/C283448.

18 *The Argus*, 7 June 1940, p. 10 https://trove.nla.gov.au/newspaper/article/12469514.

19 Ebury, *Weary: The Life of Sir Edward Dunlop*, p. 170.

20 Ebury, *Weary: The Life of Sir Edward Dunlop*, p. 171.

21 Peter FitzSimons, *Tobruk*, HarperCollins Publishers, Sydney, 2006, p. 114.

22 Sir Ernest Edward 'Weary' Dunlop interviewed by Dr Hank Nelson, Australian War Memorial.

23 Ebury, *Weary: The Life of Sir Edward Dunlop*, p. 188.

24 Milton Butterworth (Blue), Transcript of interview, UNSW Australians at War Film Archive, 21 November 2003, http://australiansatwarfilmarchive.unsw.edu.au/archive/906.

25 Pitt, *The Crucible of War, Western Desert 1941*, Jonathan Cape Ltd, London, 1980, p. 148.

26 Milton Butterworth (Blue), Transcript of interview, UNSW Australians at War Film Archive, November 2003.

27 Moorehead, *African Trilogy*, Text Publishing Company, 1997, p. 82.

28 Milton Butterworth (Blue), Transcript of interview, UNSW Australians at War Film Archive, November 2003.

29 Ebury, *Weary: The Life of Sir Edward Dunlop*, p. 191.

30 Hill, *Diggers and Greeks: The Australian Campaign in Greece and Crete*, UNSW Press, Australia, 2010, p. 66.

31 Martin and Hardy (eds), *Dark and Hurrying Days, Menzies 1941 Diary*, National Library of Australia, 1993, p. 119.

32 Graham Freudenberg, *Churchill and Australia*, Pan Macmillan, Sydney, 2008, p. 261.

33 Freudenberg, *Churchill and Australia*, p. 256.

34 Freudenberg, *Churchill and Australia*, p. 258.

35 Ebury, *Weary: The Life of Sir Edward Dunlop*, p. 200.

36 Ebury, *Weary: The Life of Sir Edward Dunlop*, pp. 200–201.

37 Ebury, *Weary: The Life of Sir Edward Dunlop*, p. 201.

Chapter Three

1 Freudenberg, *Churchill and Australia*, p. 268.

2 Sir Ernest Edward 'Weary' Dunlop interviewed by Dr Hank Nelson, Australian War Memorial, https://www.awm.gov.au/collection/C283448.

3 Sir Ernest Edward 'Weary' Dunlop interviewed by Dr Hank Nelson, Australian War Memorial, https://www.awm.gov.au/collection/C283448.

4 Sir Ernest Edward 'Weary' Dunlop interviewed by Dr Hank Nelson, Australian War Memorial, https://www.awm.gov.au/collection/C283448.

5 Wright, *Ray Parkin's Odyssey*, Macmillan Publishers, Australia, 2012, pp. 96–97.

6 Wright, *Ray Parkin's Odyssey*, p. 97.

7 *Greece and Crete*, Department of Veterans' Affairs, October 2011, Australia Anzac Portal, https://anzacportal.dva.gov.au/resources/greece-and-crete.

8 Stephens, *Heroes*, Slattery Media Group, Richmond, Vic., 2013, p. 105.

9 Ebury, *Weary: The Life of Sir Edward Dunlop*, p. 220.

10 *Greece and Crete*, Department of Veterans' Affairs, October 2011, Australia Anzac Portal, https://anzacportal.dva.gov.au/resources/greece-and-crete.

11 Long, *Australia in the War of 1939–1945, Series 1 Army, Vol II, Greece, Crete and Syria*, Australian War Memorial, Canberra, 1953, p. 143.

12 *Greece and Crete*, Department of Veterans' Affairs, October 2011, Australia Anzac Portal, https://anzacportal.dva.gov.au/resources/greece-and-crete.

13 Sir Ernest Edward 'Weary' Dunlop interviewed by Dr. Hank Nelson, Australian War Memorial, https://www.awm.gov.au/collection/C283448.

14 Robert Menzies Diary, Museum of Australian Democracy, 27 April 1941.

15 *Westralian Worker*, 18 May 1945, p. 3, https://trove.nla.gov.au/newspaper/article/148366841.

16 Robert Menzies Diary, Museum of Australian Democracy, 28 April 1941.

17 Milton Butterworth (Blue), Transcript of interview, UNSW Australians at War Film Archive, 21 November 2003, http://australiansatwarfilmarchive.unsw.edu.au/archive/906.

18 Milton Butterworth (Blue), Transcript of interview, UNSW Australians at War Film Archive, 21 November 2003, http://australiansatwarfilmarchive.unsw.edu.au/archive/906.

19 Milton Butterworth (Blue), Transcript of interview, UNSW Australians at War Film Archive, 21 November 2003, http://australiansatwarfilmarchive.unsw.edu.au/archive/906.

20 Milton Butterworth (Blue), Transcript of interview, UNSW Australians at War Film Archive, 21 November 2003, http://australiansatwarfilmarchive.unsw.edu.au/archive/906.

21 Milton Butterworth (Blue), Transcript of interview, UNSW Australians at War Film Archive, 21 November 2003, http://australiansatwarfilmarchive.unsw.edu.au/archive/906.

22 Milton Butterworth (Blue), Transcript of interview, UNSW Australians at War Film Archive, 21 November 2003, http://australiansatwarfilmarchive.unsw.edu.au/archive/906.

23 Sir Ernest Edward 'Weary' Dunlop interviewed by Dr Hank Nelson, Australian War Memorial, https://www.awm.gov.au/collection/C283448.

24 Sir Ernest Edward 'Weary' Dunlop interviewed by Dr Hank Nelson, Australian War Memorial, https://www.awm.gov.au/collection/C283448.

25 Geddes, *Remembering Weary*, Viking, Penguin Books, Australia, 1996, p. 70.

26 Ebury, *Weary: The Life of Sir Edward Dunlop*, p. 232.

27 Sir Ernest Edward 'Weary' Dunlop interviewed by Dr Hank Nelson, Australian War Memorial, https://www.awm.gov.au/collection/C283448.

28 Ebury, *Weary: The Life of Sir Edward Dunlop*, p. 236.

29 Milton Butterworth (Blue), Transcript of interview, UNSW Australians at War Film Archive, 21 November 2003, http://australiansatwarfilmarchive.unsw.edu.au/archive/906.

30 Sir Ernest Edward 'Weary' Dunlop interviewed by Dr Hank Nelson, Australian War Memorial, https://www.awm.gov.au/collection/C283448.

31 Milton Butterworth (Blue), Transcript of interview, UNSW Australians at War Film Archive, 21 November 2003, http://australiansatwarfilmarchive.unsw.edu.au/archive/906.

32 Sir Ernest Edward 'Weary' Dunlop interviewed by Dr Hank Nelson, Australian War Memorial [reported speech], https://www.awm.gov.au/collection/C283448.

33 Freudenberg, *Churchill and Australia*, p. 258.

34 Milton Butterworth (Blue), Transcript of interview, UNSW Australians at War Film Archive, 21 November 2003, http://australiansatwarfilmarchive.unsw.edu.au/archive/906.

35 Milton Butterworth (Blue), Transcript of interview, UNSW Australians at War Film Archive, 21 November 2003, http://australiansatwarfilmarchive.unsw.edu.au/archive/906.

36 Milton Butterworth (Blue), Transcript of interview, UNSW Australians at War Film Archive, 21 November 2003, http://australiansatwarfilmarchive.unsw.edu.au/archive/906.

37 Milton Butterworth (Blue), Transcript of interview, UNSW Australians at War Film Archive, 21 November 2003, http://australiansatwarfilmarchive.unsw.edu.au/archive/906.

38 Geddes, *Remembering Weary*, p. 73.

39 Milton Butterworth (Blue), Transcript of interview, UNSW Australians at War Film Archive, 21 November 2003, http://australiansatwarfilmarchive.unsw.edu.au/archive/906.

40 Wright, *Ray Parkin's Odyssey*, p. 110.

41 Geddes, *Remembering Weary*, p. 74.

42 Milton Butterworth (Blue), Transcript of interview, UNSW Australians at War Film Archive, 21 November 2003, http://australiansatwarfilmarchive.unsw.edu.au/archive/906.

43 Milton Butterworth (Blue), Transcript of interview, UNSW Australians at War Film Archive, 21 November 2003, http://australiansatwarfilmarchive.unsw.edu.au/archive/906.

44 Sir Ernest Edward 'Weary' Dunlop interviewed by Dr Hank Nelson, Australian War Memorial, https://www.awm.gov.au/collection/C283448.
45 Milton Butterworth (Blue), Transcript of interview, UNSW Australians at War Film Archive, 21 November 2003, http://australiansatwarfilmarchive.unsw.edu.au/archive/906.
46 Milton Butterworth (Blue), Transcript of interview, UNSW Australians at War Film Archive, 21 November 2003, http://australiansatwarfilmarchive.unsw.edu.au/archive/906.
47 Milton Butterworth (Blue), Transcript of interview, UNSW Australians at War Film Archive, 21 November 2003, http://australiansatwarfilmarchive.unsw.edu.au/archive/906.
48 Freudenberg, *Churchill and Australia*, p. 267.
49 Freudenberg, *Churchill and Australia*, p. 269.
50 *Kalgoorlie Miner*, 31 May 1941, p. 2, https://trove.nla.gov.au/newspaper/article/95123307.

Chapter Four

1 Parker, *Desert Rats, From El Alamein to Basra: The Inside Story of a Military Legend*, Headline Book Publishing, London, 2004, p. 9. Author's note: Although Churchill's book was from 1899, the description from his own experience was still apt for the conditions of most of the North African campaign four decades later.
2 Ebury, *Weary: The Life of Sir Edward Dunlop*, p. 250.
3 Milton Butterworth (Blue), Transcript of interview, UNSW Australians at War Film Archive, 21 November 2003, http://australiansatwarfilmarchive.unsw.edu.au/archive/906.
4 Ebury, *Weary: The Life of Sir Edward Dunlop*, pp. 254–255.
5 Ebury, *Weary: The Life of Sir Edward Dunlop*, p. 255.
6 Ebury, *Weary: The Life of Sir Edward Dunlop*, p. 255.
7 Glassop and Wilmot, *Australian War Classics*, Penguin Books, Ringwood, Vic., first published 2001, this edition 2003, p. 277.
8 Milton Butterworth (Blue), Transcript of interview, UNSW Australians at War Film Archive, 21 November 2003, http://australiansatwarfilmarchive.unsw.edu.au/archive/906.
9 Porch, *Hitler's Mediterranean Gamble: The North African and the Mediterranean Campaigns in World War II*, Weidenfeld & Nicholson, London, 2004, p. 231.
10 McDonald, *War Cameraman – The Story of Damien Parer*, Lothian, Melbourne, 1994, 'The spirit which has made Australia . . .' p. 111.
11 Milton Butterworth (Blue), Transcript of interview, UNSW Australians at War Film Archive, 21 November 2003, http://australiansatwarfilmarchive.unsw.edu.au/archive/906.
12 Milton Butterworth (Blue), Transcript of interview, UNSW Australians at War Film Archive, 21 November 2003, http://australiansatwarfilmarchive.unsw.edu.au/archive/906.
13 Milton Butterworth (Blue), Transcript of interview, UNSW Australians at War Film Archive, 21 November 2003, http://australiansatwarfilmarchive.unsw.edu.au/archive/906.
14 Milton Butterworth (Blue), Transcript of interview, UNSW Australians at War Film Archive, 21 November 2003, http://australiansatwarfilmarchive.unsw.edu.au/archive/906.
15 Glassop and Wilmot, *Australian War Classics*.

16 Freudenberg, *Churchill and Australia*, p. 296.
17 Hetherington, *Blamey: Controversial Soldier*, published jointly by The Australian War Memorial and the Australian Government Publishing Service, Canberra, 1973, p. 183.
18 Ebury, *Weary: The Life of Sir Edward Dunlop*, p. 266.
19 Ebury, *Weary: The Life of Sir Edward Dunlop*, p. 266.
20 Ebury, *Weary: The Life of Sir Edward Dunlop*, p. 266.
21 Milton Butterworth (Blue), Transcript of interview, UNSW Australians at War Film Archive, 21 November 2003, http://australiansatwarfilmarchive.unsw.edu.au/archive/906.
22 Ebury, *Weary: The Life of Sir Edward Dunlop*, p. 272.
23 Ebury, *Weary: The Life of Sir Edward Dunlop*, p. 272.
24 Sir Ernest Edward 'Weary' Dunlop interviewed by Dr Hank Nelson, Australian War Memorial, https://www.awm.gov.au/collection/C283448.
25 Ebury, *Weary: The Life of Sir Edward Dunlop*, p. 280.
26 Ebury, *Weary: The Life of Sir Edward Dunlop*, p. 277.
27 Ebury, *Weary: The Life of Sir Edward Dunlop*, p. 277.
28 Ebury, *Weary: The Life of Sir Edward Dunlop*, p. 278.
29 Letter, Weary Dunlop to Helen Ferguson, 5 November 1941, Papers of Sir Edward 'Weary' Dunlop, PR00926, item 1/34 Part 1, AWM.
30 Letter, Weary Dunlop to Helen Ferguson, 11 November 1941, Papers of Sir Edward 'Weary' Dunlop, PR00926, item 1/34 Part 1, AWM.
31 Ebury, *Weary: The Life of Sir Edward Dunlop*, p. 280.
32 Ebury, *Weary: The Life of Sir Edward Dunlop*, p. 280.
33 Dunlop, *The War Diaries of Weary Dunlop*, p. 3.
34 Sir Ernest Edward 'Weary' Dunlop interviewed by Dr Hank Nelson, Australian War Memorial, https://www.awm.gov.au/collection/C283448.
35 Ebury, *Weary: The Life of Sir Edward Dunlop*, p. 287.
36 Milton Butterworth (Blue), Transcript of interview, UNSW Australians at War Film Archive, 21 November 2003, http://australiansatwarfilmarchive.unsw.edu.au/archive/906.
37 Sir Ernest Edward 'Weary' Dunlop interviewed by Dr Hank Nelson, Australian War Memorial, https://www.awm.gov.au/collection/C283448.

Chapter Five

1 Lewis, *Parer's War. A Study Guide*, ATOM, Australian Teachers of Media, Melbourne, 2014, p. 10; original from AWM PR84/389, three-page typescript entitled 'A Cameraman Looks at a Digger'.
2 Freudenberg, *Churchill and Australia*, p. 326.
3 'Diary of a Labor Man', 1941, published by John Curtin Prime Ministerial Library, 2008, https://john.curtin.edu.au/diary/primeminister/1941.html.
4 MacArthur, 'Reports of General MacArthur', *Japanese Operation in the Southwest Pacific area, Compiled from Japanese Demobilization Bureaux Records*, U.S. Government Printing Office, 1966, p. xiv.
5 Freudenberg, *Churchill and Australia*, p. 354.
6 Freudenberg, *Churchill and Australia*, p. 354.
7 Freudenberg, *Churchill and Australia*, p. 365.
8 Letter, Weary Dunlop to Helen Ferguson, 17 December 1941, Papers of Sir Edward 'Weary' Dunlop, PR00926, item 1/34 Part 8, AWM.

9   *The Age*, 8 September 1945, p. 8, https://trove.nla.gov.au/newspaper/article/205651893.

10 *Northam Advertiser*, 28 October 1949, p. 7, https://trove.nla.gov.au/newspaper/article/211476222.

11 *The Age*, 8 September 1945, p. 8.

12 *The Advertiser*, 3 October 1945, p. 6 https://trove.nla.gov.au/newspaper/article/48670614.

13 Churchill to General Sir Archibald Wavell, Supreme Commander of the South West Pacific, 10 February 1942, https://www.churchillarchive.com/previous-topic-in-focus.

14 Hunter, *The World War Two Diary of Thomas Henry Fagan*, Albury and District Historical Society Papers No. 31, 2018, https://victoriancollections.net.au/media/collectors/53feae1c2162f1087018acb7/items/5c03651e21ea6712f4ca4d5c/item-media/5c03655721ea6712f4ca860b/original.pdf.

15 Hunter, *The World War Two Diary of Thomas Henry Fagan*, Albury and District Historical Society Papers No. 31, 2018.

16 Hackney, 'Dark Evening', a typescript account of the massacre at Parit Sulong, AWM MSS0758.

17 Hackney, 'Dark Evening', a typescript account of the massacre at Parit Sulong, AWM MSS0758.

18 Hackney, 'Dark Evening', a typescript account of the massacre at Parit Sulong, AWM MSS0758.

19 Hackney, 'Dark Evening', a typescript account of the massacre at Parit Sulong, AWM MSS0758.

20 Hackney, 'Dark Evening', a typescript account of the massacre at Parit Sulong, AWM MSS0758.

21 Ben Charles Hackney interviewed by Tim Bowden, July 1983, https://www.awm.gov.au/collection/C1006619.

22 Ben Charles Hackney interviewed by Tim Bowden, July 1983, https://www.awm.gov.au/collection/C1006619.

23 Hackney, 'Dark Evening', a typescript account of the massacre at Parit Sulong, AWM MSS0758.

24 Ben Charles Hackney interviewed by Tim Bowden, July 1983, https://www.awm.gov.au/collection/C1006619.

25 Hackney, 'Dark Evening', a typescript account of the massacre at Parit Sulong, AWM MSS0758.

26 Lee, 'A Case from Australia's War Crime Trials: Lieutenant General Nishimura, 1950', *Deakin Law Review*, Vol. 18, No. 2, 2014, pp. 337–360, http://www.austlii.edu.au/au/journals/DeakinLawRw/2013/14.pdf.

27 Milton Butterworth (Blue), Transcript of interview, UNSW Australians at War Film Archive, 21 November 2003, http://australiansatwarfilmarchive.unsw.edu.au/archive/906.

28 *The Age*, 8 September 1945, p. 8.

29 *The Age*, 8 September 1945, p. 8.

30 'Fall of Singapore', National Museum of Australia, https://www.nma.gov.au/defining-moments/resources/fall-of-singapore#:~:text=In%20London%2C%20Prime%20Minister%20Winston,die%20as%20prisoners%20of%20war.

31 Hunter, *The World War Two Diary of Thomas Henry Fagan*, Albury and District Historical Society Papers No. 31, 2018.

32 Report by Neil MacPherson, 2/2nd Pioneer Battalion, 2nd AIF, Japan POW, Burma Railway, Japan, https://www.wa.gov.au/system/files/2020–01/Macpherson_Neil.pdf.

33 *The Advertiser*, 3 October 1945, p. 6, https://trove.nla.gov.au/newspaper/article/48670614.

34 Sir Ernest Edward 'Weary' Dunlop interviewed by Dr Hank Nelson, Australian War Memorial [reported speech], https://www.awm.gov.au/collection/C283448.

35 Hunter, *The World War Two Diary of Thomas Henry Fagan*, Albury and District Historical Society Papers No. 31, 2018.

36 *Benalla Ensign*, 2 June 1946, p. 6, https://trove.nla.gov.au/newspaper/article/65565403.

37 Corrie, *Survival Against Odds*, Golden Banner Printing Service, Castlemaine, 1983, p. 1.

38 Corrie, *Survival Against Odds*, p. 1.

39 *The Advertiser*, 3 October 1945, p. 6, https://trove.nla.gov.au/newspaper/article/48670614.

40 Corrie, *Survival Against Odds*, p. 1.

41 Corrie, *Survival Against Odds*, pp. 1–2.

42 Hunter, *The World War Two Diary of Thomas Henry Fagan*, Albury and District Historical Society Papers No. 31, 2018 [reported speech].

43 *The Age*, 8 September 1945, p. 8 [reported speech], https://trove.nla.gov.au/newspaper/article/205651893.

44 Corrie, *Survival Against Odds*, p. 2.

45 Corrie, *Survival Against Odds*, p. 2.

46 Corrie, *Survival Against Odds*, p. 2.

47 *The Advertiser*, 3 October 1945, p. 6, https://trove.nla.gov.au/newspaper/article/48670614.

48 *The Age*, 8 September 1945, p. 8.

49 Sir Ernest Edward 'Weary' Dunlop interviewed by Dr Hank Nelson, Australian War Memorial, https://www.awm.gov.au/collection/C283448.

50 Transcript of war diaries of Major John Edward Rea Clarke OBE, 1940–1942, 2007, Australian War Memorial, https://www.awm.gov.au/collection/C2761011.

51 *The Age*, 8 September 1945, p. 8.

52 *The Age*, 8 September 1945, p. 8.

53 *The Age*, 8 September 1945, p. 8.

54 *The Age*, 8 September 1945, p. 8.

Chapter Six

1 Milton Butterworth (Blue), Transcript of interview, UNSW Australians at War Film Archive, 21 November 2003, http://australiansatwarfilmarchive.unsw.edu.au/archive/906.

2 *The Courier Mail*, 4 October 1945, p. 2, https://trove.nla.gov.au/newspaper/article/50286129.

3 Hunter, *The World War Two Diary of Thomas Fagan*, Albury and Districts Historical Society Papers No. 31, 2018.

4 *The Age*, 8 September 1945, p. 8.

5 Report by Neil MacPherson, 2/2nd Pioneer Battalion, 2nd AIF, Japan POW, Burman Railway, Japan https://www.wa.gov.au/system/files/2020-01/Macpherson_Neil.pdf.

6 Freudenberg, *Churchill and Australia*, p. 378.

7 Cablegram, Curtin to Sir Earle Page, Special Representative in the United Kingdom, 19 February 1942, https://www.dfat.gov.au/about-us/publications/historical-documents/Pages/

volume-05/345-mr-john-curtin-prime-minister-to-sir-earle-page-special-representative-in-the-united-kingdom.

8   Sir Ernest Edward 'Weary' Dunlop interviewed by Dr Hank Nelson, Australian War Memorial, https://www.awm.gov.au/collection/C283448.

9   Milton Butterworth (Blue), Transcript of interview, UNSW Australians at War Film Archive, 21 November 2003, http://australiansatwarfilmarchive.unsw.edu.au/archive/906.

10   Dunlop, *The War Diaries of Weary Dunlop*, p. 4.

11   *This is Your Life*, Sir Edward Dunlop, 23 June 1979, https://www.iwm.org.uk/collections/item/object/80012508.

12   Speech by Andrew Corlette, The Australian Ex-Prisoners of War Memorial, Ballarat, Victoria, 2018 [reported speech], https://www.powmemorialballarat.com.au/2018-andrew-corlette/.

13   Speech by Andrew Corlette, The Australian Ex-Prisoners of War Memorial, Ballarat, Victoria, 2018, https://www.powmemorialballarat.com.au/2018-andrew-corlette/.

14   Freudenberg, *Churchill and Australia*, p. 261.

15   Cablegram, Churchill to Curtin, 20 February 1942, https://s3-ap-southeast-2.amazonaws.com/awm-media/collection/RCDIG1070112/document/5519441.PDF.

16   Freudenberg, *Churchill and Australia*, p. 380.

17   Cablegram, Curtin to Sir Earle Page, Special Representative in the United Kingdom, 25 February 1942, https://www.dfat.gov.au/about-us/publications/historical-documents/Pages/volume-05/374-mr-john-curtin-prime-minister-to-sir-earle-page-special-representative-in-the-united-kingdom.

18   David Day, *The Politics of War*, HarperCollins Publishers, Sydney, 2003, p. 21.

19   Cablegram, Churchill to Curtin, 22 February 1942, https://www.dfat.gov.au/about-us/publications/historical-documents/Pages/volume-05/362-mr-clement-attlee-uk-secretary-of-state-for-dominion-affairs-to-mr-john-curtin-prime-minister.

20   Cablegram, Curtin to Mr Clement Attlee, UK Secretary of State for Dominion Affairs, 23 February 1942, https://www.dfat.gov.au/about-us/publications/historical-documents/Pages/volume-05/366-mr-john-curtin-prime-minister-to-mr-clement-attlee-uk-secretary-of-state-for-dominion-affairs.

21   Tom Uren, Transcript of interview, UNSW Australians at War Film Archive, 11 August 2003, http://australiansatwarfilmarchive.unsw.edu.au/archive/728.

22   Diary of a Labor Man, 19 February 1942, published by John Curtin Prime Ministerial Library, 2008, https://john.curtin.edu.au/diary/primeminister/1942.html.

23   Tom Uren, Transcript of interview, UNSW Australians at War Film Archive, 11 August 2003, http://australiansatwarfilmarchive.unsw.edu.au/archive/728.

24   Tom Uren, Transcript of interview, UNSW Australians at War Film Archive, 11 August 2003, http://australiansatwarfilmarchive.unsw.edu.au/archive/728.

25   Tom Uren, Transcript of interview, UNSW Australians at War Film Archive, 11 August 2003, http://australiansatwarfilmarchive.unsw.edu.au/archive/728.

26   Frank McGovern, Transcript of interview, UNSW Australians at War Film Archive, 8 May 2003, https://australiansatwarfilmarchive.unsw.edu.au/archive/19.

27   Carlton, *Cruiser: The Life and Loss of HMAS* Perth *and Her Crew*, William Heinemann, Australia, 2010, p. 445.

28   Parkin, *Out of the Smoke*, William Morrow & Company, New York, 1960, p. 253.

29   Parkin, *Out of the Smoke*, p. 253 [reported speech].

30   *The Quiet Lions*, documentary, directed by Robin Newell, 2008.

31   *The Quiet Lions*, documentary, directed by Robin Newell, 2008.

32 Frank McGovern, Transcript of interview, UNSW Australians at War Film Archive, 8 May 2003, https://australiansatwarfilmarchive.unsw.edu.au/archive/19.

33 Parkin, *Out of the Smoke*, p. 253.

34 Parkin, *Out of the Smoke*, p. 260.

35 Ray Parkin, Transcript of interview, UNSW Australians at War Film Archive, 7 June 2000, https://australiansatwarfilmarchive.unsw.edu.au/archive/2552.

36 Ray Parkin, Transcript of interview, UNSW Australians at War Film Archive, 7 June 2000, https://australiansatwarfilmarchive.unsw.edu.au/archive/2552.

37 Ray Barker, Transcript of interview, UNSW Australians at War Film Archive, 17 May 2003, https://australiansatwarfilmarchive.unsw.edu.au/archive/126.

38 Parkin, *Out of the Smoke*, p. 266 [reported speech].

Chapter Seven

1 Raymond 'Ray' Edward Parkin: Interviews for the Channel 10 program, *Surgeon of the Railway*, 1987, Australian War Memorial, https://www.awm.gov.au/collection/F09396.

2 *The Advertiser*, 3 October 1945, p. 6, https://trove.nla.gov.au/newspaper/article/48670614.

3 *The Advertiser*, 3 October 1945, p. 6, https://trove.nla.gov.au/newspaper/article/48670614.

4 Dunlop, *The War Diaries of Weary Dunlop*, p. 5.

5 Dunlop, *The War Diaries of Weary Dunlop*, p. 5.

6 Dunlop, *The War Diaries of Weary Dunlop*, p. 5 [reported speech].

7 Sir Ernest Edward 'Weary' Dunlop interviewed by Dr Hank Nelson, Australian War Memorial [reported speech], https://www.awm.gov.au/collection/C283448.

8 Milton Butterworth (Blue), Transcript of interview, UNSW Australians at War Film Archive, 21 November 2003, http://australiansatwarfilmarchive.unsw.edu.au/archive/906.

9 Sir Ernest Edward 'Weary' Dunlop interviewed by Dr Hank Nelson, Australian War Memorial [reported speech], https://www.awm.gov.au/collection/C283448.

10 Dunlop, *The War Diaries of Weary Dunlop*, p. 5.

11 *The Quiet Lions*, documentary, directed by Robin Newell, 2008.

12 Milton Butterworth (Blue), Transcript of interview, UNSW Australians at War Film Archive, 21 November 2003, http://australiansatwarfilmarchive.unsw.edu.au/archive/906 [reported thoughts].

13 *The Advertiser*, 3 October 1945, p. 6, https://trove.nla.gov.au/newspaper/article/48670614.

14 Faulkner, *Arthur Blackburn, VC: An Australian Hero, His Men, and Their Two World Wars*, Wakefield Press, Australia, 2008, p. 334.

15 Griffiths with Popham, *Blind to Misfortune*, Leo Cooper, London, 1989, p. 36.

16 Griffiths with Popham, *Blind to Misfortune*, p. 37.

17 Faulkner, *Arthur Blackburn, VC: An Australian Hero, His Men, and Their Two World Wars*, p. 335.

18 Corrie, *Survival Against Odds*, p. 4.

19 *The Courier Mail*, 4 October 1945, p. 2.

20 *The Advertiser*, 3 October 1945, p. 6.

21 *The Advertiser*, 3 October 1945, p. 6.

22 Griffiths with Popham, *Blind to Misfortune*, p. 1.

23 Griffiths with Popham, *Blind to Misfortune*, p. 2.

24 Griffiths with Popham, *Blind to Misfortune*, p. 2.

25 Griffiths with Popham, *Blind to Misfortune*, p. 2.
26 Hunter, *The World War Two Diary of Thomas Fagan*, Albury and Districts Historical Society Papers No. 31, 2018, p. 13.
27 Griffiths with Popham, *Blind to Misfortune*, p. xi.
28 Griffiths with Popham, *Blind to Misfortune*, p. xi.
29 Milton Butterworth (Blue), Transcript of interview, UNSW Australians at War Film Archive, 21 November 2003, http://australiansatwarfilmarchive.unsw.edu.au/archive/906.
30 *This is Your Life*, Sir Edward Dunlop, 23 June 1979, https://www.iwm.org.uk/collections/item/object/80012508.
31 Dunlop, *The War Diaries of Weary Dunlop*, February 1942, p. 6.
32 Dunlop, *The War Diaries of Weary Dunlop*, February 1942, p. 6.
33 *The Courier Mail*, 4 October 1945, p. 2.
34 Griffiths with Popham, *Blind to Misfortune*, p. 6 [reported speech].
35 Griffiths with Popham, *Blind to Misfortune*, p. xi.
36 Griffiths with Popham, *Blind to Misfortune*, p. xi.
37 Griffiths with Popham, *Blind to Misfortune*, p. xi.
38 Griffiths with Popham, *Blind to Misfortune*, p. 6 [reported speech].
39 Geddes, *Remembering Weary*, p. 86.
40 Griffiths with Popham, *Blind to Misfortune*, p. 7.
41 Griffiths with Popham, *Blind to Misfortune*, p. 7.
42 Sir Ernest Edward 'Weary' Dunlop interviewed by Dr Hank Nelson, Australian War Memorial, https://www.awm.gov.au/collection/C283448.
43 Sir Ernest Edward 'Weary' Dunlop interviewed by Dr Hank Nelson, Australian War Memorial, https://www.awm.gov.au/collection/C283448.
44 Griffiths with Popham, *Blind to Misfortune*, p. 10.
45 Sir Ernest Edward 'Weary' Dunlop interviewed by Dr Hank Nelson, Australian War Memorial, https://www.awm.gov.au/collection/C283448.
46 Dunlop, *The War Diaries of Weary Dunlop*, p. 7.
47 Sir Ernest Edward 'Weary' Dunlop interviewed by Dr Hank Nelson, Australian War Memorial, https://www.awm.gov.au/collection/C283448.
48 Sir Ernest Edward 'Weary' Dunlop interviewed by Dr Hank Nelson, Australian War Memorial, https://www.awm.gov.au/collection/C283448.
49 Milton Butterworth (Blue), Transcript of interview, UNSW Australians at War Film Archive, 21 November 2003, http://australiansatwarfilmarchive.unsw.edu.au/archive/906.
50 Parkin, *Wartime Trilogy*, Melbourne University Press, Australia, 1999, p. 437.
51 Dunlop, *The War Diaries of Weary Dunlop*, 20 March 1943, p. 192.
52 Dunlop, *The War Diaries of Weary Dunlop*, p. 10 [reported speech].
53 Dunlop, *The War Diaries of Weary Dunlop*, p. 9.
54 Dunlop, *The War Diaries of Weary Dunlop*, p. 9.
55 Dunlop, *The War Diaries of Weary Dunlop*, p. 9.
56 Dunlop, *The War Diaries of Weary Dunlop*, p. 9.
57 Dunlop, *The War Diaries of Weary Dunlop*, p. 9.
58 Dunlop, *The War Diaries of Weary Dunlop*, p. 9.
59 Dunlop, *The War Diaries of Weary Dunlop*, p. 9.
60 Ebury, *Weary: The Life of Sir Edward Dunlop*, p. 325.
61 Ebury, *Weary: The Life of Sir Edward Dunlop*, p. 325.
62 Dunlop, *The War Diaries of Weary Dunlop*, p. 9.
63 Dunlop, *The War Diaries of Weary Dunlop*, 18 April 1942, p. 10.

64 Sir Ernest Edward 'Weary' Dunlop interviewed by Dr Hank Nelson, Australian War Memorial, https://www.awm.gov.au/collection/C283448.

65 Letter, Edward Dunlop to Helen Ferguson, 21 February 1942, Papers of Sir Edward 'Weary' Dunlop, PR00926, item 1/34 Part 8, AWM.

66 Sir Ernest Edward 'Weary' Dunlop interviewed by Dr Hank Nelson, Australian War Memorial, https://www.awm.gov.au/collection/C283448.

67 Sir Ernest Edward 'Weary' Dunlop interviewed by Dr Hank Nelson, Australian War Memorial, https://www.awm.gov.au/collection/C283448.

68 Dunlop, *The War Diaries of Weary Dunlop*, 18 April 1942, p. 1.

69 *The West Australian*, 22 January 1977.

70 Griffiths with Popham, *Blind to Misfortune*, p. 12.

71 *The Courier Mail*, 4 October 1945, p. 2.

72 Dunlop, *The War Diaries of Weary Dunlop*, 19 April 1942, p. 12.

73 Geddes, *Remembering Weary*, p. 163.

74 Author's note: This is a Malay word used by both guards and POWs.

75 Sir Ernest Edward 'Weary' Dunlop interviewed by Dr Hank Nelson, Australian War Memorial, https://www.awm.gov.au/collection/C283448.

76 Sir Ernest Edward 'Weary' Dunlop interviewed by Dr Hank Nelson, Australian War Memorial, https://www.awm.gov.au/collection/C283448.

77 Geddes, *Remembering Weary*, p. 163.

78 Dunlop, *The War Diaries of Weary Dunlop*, 28 April 1942, p. 17.

79 Dunlop, *The War Diaries of Weary Dunlop*, 28 April 1942, p. 17.

80 Dunlop, *The War Diaries of Weary Dunlop*, 28 April 1942, p. 17.

81 Dunlop, *The War Diaries of Weary Dunlop*, 28 April 1942, p. 17.

82 Dunlop, *The War Diaries of Weary Dunlop*, 29 April 1942, p. 18.

83 Dunlop, *The War Diaries of Weary Dunlop*, 29 April 1942, p. 18.

84 Dunlop, *The War Diaries of Weary Dunlop*, 29 April 1942, p. 18.

Chapter Eight

1 Corrie, *Survival Against Odds*, p. 13.

2 Dunlop, *The War Diaries of Weary Dunlop*, 30 May 1942, p. 33.

3 Dunlop, *The War Diaries of Weary Dunlop*, 30 May 1942, p. 33.

4 Dunlop, *The War Diaries of Weary Dunlop*, 30 May 1942, p. 33.

5 Dunlop, *The War Diaries of Weary Dunlop*, 30 May 1942, p. 33.

6 Transcript of War Diaries of Major John Edward Rea Clarke OBE, 1940–1942, 2007, Australian War Memorial, https://www.awm.gov.au/collection/C2761011.

7 van der Post, *Yet Being Someone Other*, Penguin Books, London, 1984, p. 315.

8 Sir Ernest Edward 'Weary' Dunlop interviewed by Dr Hank Nelson, Australian War Memorial, https://www.awm.gov.au/collection/C283448.

9 Sir Ernest Edward 'Weary' Dunlop interviewed by Dr Hank Nelson, Australian War Memorial, https://www.awm.gov.au/collection/C283448.

10 Dunlop, *The War Diaries of Weary Dunlop*, 6 June 1942, p. 40.

11 Transcript of war diaries of Major John Edward Rea Clarke OBE, 1940–1942, 2007, Australian War Memorial, https://www.awm.gov.au/collection/C2761011.

12 Sir Ernest Edward 'Weary' Dunlop interviewed by Dr Hank Nelson, Australian War Memorial, https://www.awm.gov.au/collection/C283448.

13 Corrie, *Survival Against Odds*, p. 5.

14 Corrie, *Survival Against Odds*, p. 5.

15 Transcript of War Diaries of Major John Edward Rea Clarke OBE, 1940–1942, 2007, Australian War Memorial, https://www.awm.gov.au/collection/C2761011.

16 Transcript of War Diaries of Major John Edward Rea Clarke OBE, 1940–1942, 2007, Australian War Memorial, https://www.awm.gov.au/collection/C2761011.

17 Transcript of War Diaries of Major John Edward Rea Clarke OBE, 1940–1942, 2007, Australian War Memorial, https://www.awm.gov.au/collection/C2761011.

18 Sir Ernest Edward 'Weary' Dunlop interviewed by Dr Hank Nelson, Australian War Memorial, https://www.awm.gov.au/collection/C283448.

19 Dunlop, *The War Diaries of Weary Dunlop*, p. x [reported speech].

20 Dunlop, *The War Diaries of Weary Dunlop*, p. 339.

21 Sir Ernest Edward 'Weary' Dunlop interviewed by Dr Hank Nelson, Australian War Memorial, https://www.awm.gov.au/collection/C283448.

22 Sir Ernest Edward 'Weary' Dunlop interviewed by Dr Hank Nelson, Australian War Memorial, https://www.awm.gov.au/collection/C283448.

23 Sir Ernest Edward 'Weary' Dunlop interviewed by Dr Hank Nelson, Australian War Memorial, https://www.awm.gov.au/collection/C283448.

24 Corrie, *Survival Against Odds*, p. 7 [reported speech].

25 Corrie, *Survival Against Odds*, p. 9.

26 Dunlop, *The War Diaries of Weary Dunlop*, foreword, xi.

27 Dunlop, *The War Diaries of Weary Dunlop*, foreword, xii.

28 Dunlop, *The War Diaries of Weary Dunlop*, foreword, xii.

29 Dunlop, *The War Diaries of Weary Dunlop*, foreword, xii.

30 Dunlop, *The War Diaries of Weary Dunlop*, foreword, xii.

31 Dunlop, *The War Diaries of Weary Dunlop*, foreword, xii.

32 Dunlop, *The War Diaries of Weary Dunlop*, foreword, xii.

33 Dunlop, *The War Diaries of Weary Dunlop*, foreword, xii.

34 Dunlop, *The War Diaries of Weary Dunlop*, foreword, xii.

35 Dunlop, *The War Diaries of Weary Dunlop*, foreword, xii.

36 Dunlop, *The War Diaries of Weary Dunlop*, foreword, xii.

37 Parkin, *Out of the Smoke*, p. ix.

38 Clarke, Comment, *The Monthly*, August 2005, https://www.themonthly.com.au/nation-reviewed-john-clarke-comment--73.

39 Dunlop, *The War Diaries of Weary Dunlop*, 7 August 1942, p. 77.

40 WW2, People's War, Archive of World War Two Memories, BBC Home, https://www.bbc.co.uk/history/ww2peopleswar/stories/58/a4159758.shtml.

41 WW2, People's War, Archive of World War Two Memories, BBC Home, https://www.bbc.co.uk/history/ww2peopleswar/stories/58/a4159758.shtml.

42 Dunlop, *The War Diaries of Weary Dunlop*, 11 August 1942, p. 78.

43 Dunlop, *The War Diaries of Weary Dunlop*, p. 80.

44 Dunlop, *The War Diaries of Weary Dunlop*, p. 80.

45 Dunlop, *The War Diaries of Weary Dunlop*, p. 93 [reported speech].

46 Dunlop, *The War Diaries of Weary Dunlop*, p. 93.

47 Dunlop, *The War Diaries of Weary Dunlop*, 29 August 1942, p. 84.

48 Williams, 'John Clarke's Second World War', *Meanjin*, August 2017 [reported speech], https://meanjin.com.au/latest/john-clarkes-second-world-war/.

49 Williams, 'John Clarke's Second World War', *Meanjin*, August 2017, https://meanjin.com.au/latest/john-clarkes-second-world-war/.

50 Dunlop, *The War Diaries of Weary Dunlop*, 29 August 1942, p. 83.

51 Sir Ernest Edward 'Weary' Dunlop interviewed by Dr Hank Nelson, Australian War Memorial, https://www.awm.gov.au/collection/C283448.

52 Convention of 27 July 1929, Relative to the Treatment of Prisoners of War, Yale Law School, https://avalon.law.yale.edu/20th_century/geneva02.asp.

53 Wright, *Ray Parkin's Odyssey*, p. 282.

54 Jones, *Storyteller: The Many Lives of Laurens van der Post*, John Murray, London, 2001, p. 43 [reported speech].

55 Transcript of war diaries of Major John Edward Rea Clarke OBE, 1940–1942, 2007, Australian War Memorial, https://www.awm.gov.au/collection/C2761011.

56 Dunlop, *The War Diaries of Weary Dunlop*, 9 September 1942, p. 88.

57 Dunlop, *The War Diaries of Weary Dunlop*, 18 September 1942, p. 92.

58 Dunlop, *The War Diaries of Weary Dunlop*, 8 September 1942, p. 87.

59 Sir Ernest Edward 'Weary' Dunlop interviewed by Dr Hank Nelson, Australian War Memorial, https://www.awm.gov.au/collection/C283448.

60 Sir Ernest Edward 'Weary' Dunlop interviewed by Dr Hank Nelson, Australian War Memorial, https://www.awm.gov.au/collection/C283448.

61 Dunlop, *The War Diaries of Weary Dunlop*, 22 September 1942, p. 94.

62 Sir Ernest Edward 'Weary' Dunlop interviewed by Dr Hank Nelson, Australian War Memorial, https://www.awm.gov.au/collection/C283448.

63 Dunlop, *The War Diaries of Weary Dunlop*, 22 September 1942, p. 94.

64 'Audio commentaries', Department of Veterans' Affairs, Anzac Portal, https://anzacportal.dva.gov.au/wars-and-missions/burma-thailand-railway-and-hellfire-pass-1942-1943/resources/audio-commentaries.

65 McCormack and Nelson, *The Burma–Thailand Railway*, Allen & Unwin, Sydney, 1993, p. 87.

66 Sir Ernest Edward 'Weary' Dunlop interviewed by Dr. Hank Nelson, Australian War Memorial, https://www.awm.gov.au/collection/C283448.

67 Dunlop, *The War Diaries of Weary Dunlop*, 1 October 1942, p. 97.

68 Dunlop, *The War Diaries of Weary Dunlop*, 9 October 1942, p. 99.

69 Dunlop, *The War Diaries of Weary Dunlop*, 9 October 1942, p. 99 [reported speech].

70 Dunlop, *The War Diaries of Weary Dunlop*, 2 October 1942, p. 97.

71 Dunlop, *The War Diaries of Weary Dunlop*, 2 October 1942, p. 97.

72 Dunlop, *The War Diaries of Weary Dunlop*, 6 June 1942, p. 40.

73 Dunlop, *The War Diaries of Weary Dunlop*, 5 October 1942, p. 98.

74 Dunlop, *The War Diaries of Weary Dunlop*, 6 October 1942, p. 98.

75 Dunlop, *The War Diaries of Weary Dunlop*, 6 October 1942, p. 98.

76 Dunlop, *The War Diaries of Weary Dunlop*, 6 October 1942, p. 98.

77 Corrie, *Survival Against Odds*, p. 6.

78 Corrie, *Survival Against Odds*, p. 6.

79 Corrie, *Survival Against Odds*, p. 6.

Chapter Nine

1 Ray Parkin, Transcript of interview, UNSW Australians at War Film Archive, 7 June 2000, https://australiansatwarfilmarchive.unsw.edu.au/archive/2552.

2 Dunlop, *The War Diaries of Weary Dunlop*, 7 October 1942, p. 98.

3 Dunlop, *The War Diaries of Weary Dunlop*, 7 October 1942, p. 99.

4 Sir Ernest Edward 'Weary' Dunlop interviewed by Dr Hank Nelson, Australian War Memorial, https://www.awm.gov.au/collection/C283448.

5 Dunlop, *The War Diaries of Weary Dunlop*, 13 October 1942, p. 101.

6 Dunlop, *The War Diaries of Weary Dunlop*, 13 October 1942, p. 102.

7 Dunlop, *The War Diaries of Weary Dunlop*, 5 October 1942, pp. 110–111.

8 Dunlop, *The War Diaries of Weary Dunlop*, 5 October 1942, pp. 110–111.

9 Dunlop, *The War Diaries of Weary Dunlop*, p. 117.

10 Dunlop, *The War Diaries of Weary Dunlop*, p. x.

11 Corrie, *Survival Against Odds*, p. 7.

12 Wright, *Ray Parkin's Odyssey*, pp. 109–110.

13 Wright, *Ray Parkin's Odyssey*, p. 301.

14 Dunlop, *The War Diaries of Weary Dunlop*, 3 November 1942, p. 111.

15 Wright, *Ray Parkin's Odyssey*, p. 297.

16 Transcript of war diaries of Major John Edward Rea Clarke OBE, 1940–1942, 2007, Australian War Memorial, https://www.awm.gov.au/collection/C2761011.

17 Dunlop, *The War Diaries of Weary Dunlop*, 28 December 1942, p. 132.

18 Transcript of war diaries of Major John Edward Rea Clarke OBE, 1940–1942, 2007, Australian War Memorial, https://www.awm.gov.au/collection/C2761011.

19 Dunlop, *The War Diaries of Weary Dunlop*, 9 December 1942, p. 145.

20 Dunlop, *The War Diaries of Weary Dunlop*, 19 December 1942, p. 128.

21 Dunlop, *The War Diaries of Weary Dunlop*, 22 December 1942, p. 128.

22 Telegram, Edward Dunlop to Helen Ferguson, 1942, Papers of Sir Edward 'Weary' Dunlop, PR00926, item 1/34 Part 1, AWM.

23 Transcript of war diaries of Major John Edward Rea Clarke OBE, 1940–1942, 2007, Australian War Memorial, https://www.awm.gov.au/collection/C2761011.

24 Dunlop, *The War Diaries of Weary Dunlop*, 24 December 1942, p. 129.

25 Dunlop, *The War Diaries of Weary Dunlop*, 25 December 1942, p. 130.

26 Dunlop, *The War Diaries of Weary Dunlop*, 25 December 1942, p. 130.

27 Dunlop, *The War Diaries of Weary Dunlop*, 26 December 1942, p. 131.

28 Dunlop, *The War Diaries of Weary Dunlop*, 27 December 1942, p. 131.

29 Dunlop, *The War Diaries of Weary Dunlop*, 27 December 1942, p. 131.

30 Dunlop, *The War Diaries of Weary Dunlop*, 28 December 1942, p. 132.

31 Dunlop, *The War Diaries of Weary Dunlop*, 28 December 1942, p. 132.

32 Dunlop, *The War Diaries of Weary Dunlop*, 30 December 1942, p. 132.

33 Dunlop, *The War Diaries of Weary Dunlop*, 31 December 1942, p. 134.

34 Dunlop, *The War Diaries of Weary Dunlop*, 31 December 1942, p. 134.

35 Dunlop, *The War Diaries of Weary Dunlop*, 2 January 1943, p. 134.

36 Dunlop, *The War Diaries of Weary Dunlop*, 2 January 1943, p. 135.

37 'Dolores' by Louis Alter (song) and Frank Loesser (lyrics), 1941.

38 Dunlop, *The War Diaries of Weary Dunlop*, 4 January 1943, p. 137.

39 Sir Ernest Edward 'Weary' Dunlop interviewed by Dr Hank Nelson, Australian War Memorial, https://www.awm.gov.au/collection/C283448.

40 Sir Ernest Edward 'Weary' Dunlop interviewed by Dr Hank Nelson, Australian War Memorial, https://www.awm.gov.au/collection/C283448.

41 Dunlop, *The War Diaries of Weary Dunlop*, 7 January 1943, p. 141.

42 Dunlop, *The War Diaries of Weary Dunlop*, 7 January 1943, p. 141.

43 Milton Butterworth (Blue), Transcript of interview, UNSW Australians at War Film Archive, 21 November 2003, http://australiansatwarfilmarchive.unsw.edu.au/archive/906.

44 Milton Butterworth (Blue), Transcript of interview, UNSW Australians at War Film Archive, 21 November 2003, http://australiansatwarfilmarchive.unsw.edu.au/archive/906.

45 Milton Butterworth (Blue), Transcript of interview, UNSW Australians at War Film Archive, 21 November 2003, http://australiansatwarfilmarchive.unsw.edu.au/archive/906.

46 Sir Ernest Edward 'Weary' Dunlop interviewed by Dr Hank Nelson, Australian War Memorial, https://www.awm.gov.au/collection/C283448.

47 Geddes, *Remembering Weary*, p. 98.

48 Nelson, *POW. Prisoners of War: Australians Under Nippon*, ABC Enterprises, Australia, 1985, p. 34.
49 Griffin, 'Galleghan, Sir Frederick Gallagher (1897–1971)', *Australian Dictionary of Biography*, National Centre of Biography, Australian National University, Vol. 14, 1996.
50 Sir Ernest Edward 'Weary' Dunlop interviewed by Dr Hank Nelson, Australian War Memorial, https://www.awm.gov.au/collection/C283448.
51 Ebury, *Weary: The Life of Sir Edward Dunlop*, p. 370.
52 Ebury, *Weary: The Life of Sir Edward Dunlop*, p. 370.
53 Ebury, *Weary: The Life of Sir Edward Dunlop*, p. 371.
54 Dunlop, *The War Diaries of Weary Dunlop*, 10 January 1943, p. 145 [reported speech].
55 Dunlop, *The War Diaries of Weary Dunlop*, 10 January 1943, p. 145.
56 Ebury, *Weary: The Life of Sir Edward Dunlop*, p. 371.
57 Ebury, *Weary: The Life of Sir Edward Dunlop*, p. 371 [reported speech].
58 Ebury, *Weary: The Life of Sir Edward Dunlop*, p. 371.
59 Sir Ernest Edward 'Weary' Dunlop interviewed by Dr Hank Nelson, Australian War Memorial, https://www.awm.gov.au/collection/C283448.
60 Dunlop, *The War Diaries of Weary Dunlop*, 10 January 1943, p. 145 [reported speech].
61 Sir Ernest Edward 'Weary' Dunlop interviewed by Dr Hank Nelson, Australian War Memorial, https://www.awm.gov.au/collection/C283448.
62 Dunlop, *The War Diaries of Weary Dunlop*, 10 January 1943, p. 145 [reported speech].
63 Dunlop, *The War Diaries of Weary Dunlop*, 10 January 1943, p. 145.
64 Milton Butterworth (Blue), Transcript of interview, UNSW Australians at War Film Archive, 21 November 2003, http://australiansatwarfilmarchive.unsw.edu.au/archive/906.
65 Dunlop, *The War Diaries of Weary Dunlop*, 4 December 1942, p. 124.
66 Sir Ernest Edward 'Weary' Dunlop interviewed by Dr. Hank Nelson, Australian War Memorial, https://www.awm.gov.au/collection/C283448.
67 Milton Butterworth (Blue), Transcript of interview, UNSW Australians at War Film Archive, 21 November 2003, http://australiansatwarfilmarchive.unsw.edu.au/archive/906.
68 Dunlop, *The War Diaries of Weary Dunlop*, p. xxviii.
69 *The Quiet Lions*, documentary, directed by Robin Newell, 2008.
70 Wright, *Ray Parkin's Odyssey*, p. 317.
71 Wright, *Ray Parkin's Odyssey*, p. 321.
72 Faulkner, *Arthur Blackburn, VC: An Australian Hero, His Men, and Their Two World Wars*, p. 383.
73 Sir Ernest Edward 'Weary' Dunlop interviewed by Dr Hank Nelson, Australian War Memorial, https://www.awm.gov.au/collection/C283448.

Chapter Ten

1 Dunlop, *The War Diaries of Weary Dunlop*, 28 February 1943, p. 178.
2 Dunlop, *The War Diaries of Weary Dunlop*, p. 218.
3 Dunlop, *The War Diaries of Weary Dunlop*, rear panel.
4 Geddes, *Remembering Weary*, p. 163.
5 *Daily Mail*, 27 February 2010.
6 McCormack and Nelson, *The Burma–Thailand Railway*, p. 37.

7 'Audio commentaries', Department of Veterans' Affairs, Anzac Portal, https://anzacportal.dva.gov.au/wars-and-missions/burma-thailand-railway-and-hellfire-pass-1942-1943/resources/audio-commentaries.

8 Milton Butterworth (Blue), Transcript of interview, UNSW Australians at War Film Archive, 21 November 2003, http://australiansatwarfilmarchive.unsw.edu.au/archive/906.

9 Wright, *Ray Parkin's Odyssey*, p. 325.

10 *Daily Mail*, 27 February 2010.

11 Wright, *Ray Parkin's Odyssey*, p. 325.

12 Wright, *Ray Parkin's Odyssey*, p. 326.

13 Wright, *Ray Parkin's Odyssey*, p. 332.

14 Dunlop, *The War Diaries of Weary Dunlop*, 24 January 1943, p. 153.

15 Dunlop, *The War Diaries of Weary Dunlop*, 25 January 1943, p. 153.

16 Raymond 'Ray' Edward Parkin: Interviews for the Channel 10 program, *Surgeon of the Railway*, 1987, Australian War Memorial, https://www.awm.gov.au/collection/F09396.

17 Dunlop, *The War Diaries of Weary Dunlop*, 25 January 1943, p. 153.

18 Ernie Badham, 2/2nd CCS, Prisoner of War Account, p. 4, https://www.burmarailway.com.au/page-4.

19 Dunlop, *The War Diaries of Weary Dunlop*, 25 January 1943, p. 153.

20 Dunlop, *The War Diaries of Weary Dunlop*, 25 January 1943, p. 153.

21 *Daily Mail*, 27 February 2010.

22 Dunlop, *The War Diaries of Weary Dunlop*, 25 January 1943, p. 152.

23 Dunlop, *The War Diaries of Weary Dunlop*, 25 January 1943, p. 155.

24 Wright, *Ray Parkin's Odyssey*, p. 334.

25 Dunlop, *The War Diaries of Weary Dunlop*, 26 January 1943, p. 157.

26 Parkin, *Wartime Trilogy*, pp. 397–398.

27 McCormack and Nelson, *The Burma–Thailand Railway*, p. 38.

28 Dunlop, *The War Diaries of Weary Dunlop*, 26 January 1943, p. 157.

29 Dunlop, *The War Diaries of Weary Dunlop*, 25 January 1943, p. 156.

30 Wright, *Ray Parkin's Odyssey*, p. 327.

31 Dunlop, *The War Diaries of Weary Dunlop*, 25 January 1943, p. 156.

32 Dunlop, *The War Diaries of Weary Dunlop*, 24 February 1943, p. 176.

33 Wright, *Ray Parkin's Odyssey*, p. 328.

34 Parkin, *Wartime Trilogy*, p. 397.

35 Dunlop, *The War Diaries of Weary Dunlop*, 27 January 1943, p. 158.

36 'Dunlop Force – Java Party No. 6 – O and P Battalions', 2/4th Machine Gun Battalion Ex Members Association, February 2018, https://2nd4thmgb.com.au/story/dunlop-force-java-party-no-6-o-p-battalions/.

37 Parkin, *Wartime Trilogy*, p. 402.

38 Milton Butterworth (Blue), Transcript of interview, UNSW Australians at War Film Archive, 21 November 2003, http://australiansatwarfilmarchive.unsw.edu.au/archive/906.

39 Dunlop, *The War Diaries of Weary Dunlop*, 27 January 1943, p. 158.

40 Dunlop, *The War Diaries of Weary Dunlop*, 27 January 1943, p. 158.

41 Dunlop, *The War Diaries of Weary Dunlop*, 27 January 1943, p. 158.

42 Dunlop, *The War Diaries of Weary Dunlop*, 2 February 1943, p. 162.

43 Uren, *Straight Left*, Random House, Australia, 1994, p. 32.

44 Parkin, *Wartime Trilogy*, p. 399.

45 Parkin, *Wartime Trilogy*, p. 417.

46 Dunlop, *The War Diaries of Weary Dunlop*, 25 January 1943, p. 156.

47 Dunlop, *The War Diaries of Weary Dunlop*, 31 January 1943, pp. 161–162.

48 Dunlop, *The War Diaries of Weary Dunlop*, 2 February 1943, p. 162.

49 Dunlop, *The War Diaries of Weary Dunlop*, 2 February 1943, p. 163.

50 Dunlop, *The War Diaries of Weary Dunlop*, 2 February 1943, p. 163.

51 Wright, *The Men of the Line: Stories of the Thai–Burma Railway Survivors*, Melbourne University Publishing, Victoria, 2008, p. 24.

52 Wright, *The Men of the Line: Stories of the Thai–Burma Railway Survivors*, p. 151.

53 Tom Uren, Transcript of interview, UNSW Australians at War Film Archive, 11 August 2003, http://australiansatwarfilmarchive.unsw.edu.au/archive/728.

54 Tom Uren, Transcript of interview, UNSW Australians at War Film Archive, 11 August 2003, http://australiansatwarfilmarchive.unsw.edu.au/archive/728.

55 Parkin, *Wartime Trilogy*, p. 414.

56 Dunlop, *The War Diaries of Weary Dunlop*, 6 February 1943, p. 166.

57 Dunlop, *The War Diaries of Weary Dunlop*, 3 February 1943, p. 164.

58 Dunlop, *The War Diaries of Weary Dunlop*, 3 February 1943, p. 164.

59 Parkin, *Wartime Trilogy*, pp. 428–429.

60 Parkin, *Wartime Trilogy*, pp. 428–429.

61 Dunlop, *The War Diaries of Weary Dunlop*, 3 February 1943, p. 165.

62 Dunlop, *The War Diaries of Weary Dunlop*, 3 February 1943, p. 165.

63 Dunlop, *The War Diaries of Weary Dunlop*, 5 February 1943, p. 165.

64 Dunlop, *The War Diaries of Weary Dunlop*, 7 February 1943, p. 166.

65 Dunlop, *The War Diaries of Weary Dunlop*, 4 April 1943, p. 202.

66 Dunlop, *The War Diaries of Weary Dunlop*, p. 166.

67 *The Canberra Times*, 18 May 1991, p. 19, https://trove.nla.gov.au/newspaper/article/122363608.

68 Clarke, 'Comment', *The Monthly*, August 2005, https://www.themonthly.com.au/nation-reviewed-john-clarke-comment--73.

69 Wright, *Ray Parkin's Odyssey*, p. 359.

70 Dunlop, *The War Diaries of Weary Dunlop*, 6 February 1943, p. 167.

71 Dunlop, *The War Diaries of Weary Dunlop*, 6 February 1943, p. 167.

72 Dunlop, *The War Diaries of Weary Dunlop*, p. 192.

73 Dunlop, *The War Diaries of Weary Dunlop*, p. 192.

74 Speech by Andrew Corlette, The Australian Ex-Prisoners of War Memorial, Ballarat, Victoria, 2018, https://www.powmemorialballarat.com.au/2018-andrew-corlette/.

75 Paper written by Ewan Corlette's son, Andrew, in 2015, sent to the author.

76 Speech by Andrew Corlette, The Australian Ex-Prisoners of War Memorial, Ballarat, Victoria, 2018, https://www.powmemorialballarat.com.au/2018-andrew-corlette/.

77 Speech by Andrew Corlette, The Australian Ex-Prisoners of War Memorial, Ballarat, Victoria, 2018, https://www.powmemorialballarat.com.au/2018-andrew-corlette/.

78 *The Australian Women's Weekly*, 20 October 1945, p. 17, https://trove.nla.gov.au/newspaper/article/51281493.

79 Sir Ernest Edward 'Weary' Dunlop interviewed by Dr. Hank Nelson, Australian War Memorial, https://www.awm.gov.au/collection/C283448.

80 Dunlop, *The War Diaries of Weary Dunlop*, 16 February 1943, p. 171.

81 Dunlop, *The War Diaries of Weary Dunlop*, 16 February 1943, p. 171.

82 Dunlop, *The War Diaries of Weary Dunlop*, 16 February 1943, p. 171.

83 Dunlop, *The War Diaries of Weary Dunlop*, 16 February 1943, p. 171.

84 Dunlop, *The War Diaries of Weary Dunlop*, 16 February 1943, p. 171.

85 Dunlop, *The War Diaries of Weary Dunlop*, 16 February 1943, p. 171.
86 Dunlop, *The War Diaries of Weary Dunlop*, 16 February 1943, p. 171.
87 Dunlop, *The War Diaries of Weary Dunlop*, p. 197.
88 Dunlop, *The War Diaries of Weary Dunlop*, 18 February 1943, p. 173.
89 Dunlop, 'Medical Experiences in Japanese Captivity', *British Medical Journal*, 5 October 1946, p. 486, https://pmc.ncbi.nlm.nih.gov/articles/PMC2057680/.
90 Dunlop, *The War Diaries of Weary Dunlop*, 18 February 1943, p. 173.
91 Milton Butterworth (Blue), Transcript of interview, UNSW Australians at War Film Archive, 21 November 2003 [reported speech], http://australiansatwarfilmarchive. unsw.edu.au/archive/906.
92 Wright, *The Men of the Line: Stories of the Thai–Burma Railway Survivors*, pp. 96–97.
93 Duncan, 'Makeshift Medicine: Combating Disease in Japanese Prison Camps', *The Medical Journal of Australia*, January 1983, p. 31, https://onlinelibrary.wiley.com/ doi/pdf/10.5694/j.1326-5377.1983.tb136020.x.
94 Dunlop, *The War Diaries of Weary Dunlop*, 18 February 1943, p. 173.
95 *The Australian Women's Weekly*, 20 October 1945, p. 17, https://trove.nla.gov.au/ newspaper/article/51281493.
96 Parkin, *Wartime Trilogy*, p. 421.
97 Parkin, *Wartime Trilogy*, p. 421 [reported speech].
98 Tom Uren, Transcript of interview, UNSW Australians at War Film Archive, 11 August 2003, http://australiansatwarfilmarchive.unsw.edu.au/archive/728.
99 Uren, *Straight Left*, p. 33.
100 Uren, *Straight Left*, p. 33.
101 Uren, *Straight Left*, p. 33 [reported speech].
102 Uren, *Straight Left*, p. 33.

Chapter Eleven

1 Convention Relative to the Treatment of Prisoners of War, Geneva, 27 July 1929, https://ihl-databases.icrc.org/assets/treaties/305-IHL-GC-1929-2-EN.pdf.
2 Dunlop, 'Medical Experiences in Japanese Captivity', *British Medical Journal*, 5 October 1946, p. 484, https://pmc.ncbi.nlm.nih.gov/articles/PMC2057680/.
3 Dunlop, *The War Diaries of Weary Dunlop*, 21 February 1943, p. 174.
4 Dunlop, *The War Diaries of Weary Dunlop*, 22 February 1943, p. 175.
5 Wright, *Ray Parkin's Odyssey*, p. 346.
6 Dunlop, *The War Diaries of Weary Dunlop*, 22 February 1943, p. 175.
7 Dunlop, *The War Diaries of Weary Dunlop*, 22 February 1943, p. 175.
8 Dunlop, *The War Diaries of Weary Dunlop*, 22 February 1943, p. 175.
9 Dunlop, *The War Diaries of Weary Dunlop*, 23 February 1943, p. 175.
10 Dunlop, *The War Diaries of Weary Dunlop*, 23 February 1943, p. 175.
11 Dunlop, *The War Diaries of Weary Dunlop*, 23 February 1943, p. 176.
12 Dunlop, *The War Diaries of Weary Dunlop*, 23 February 1943, p. 176.
13 Dunlop, *The War Diaries of Weary Dunlop*, 23 February 1943, p. 176.
14 Dunlop, *The War Diaries of Weary Dunlop*, 23 February 1943, p. 176.
15 Dunlop, *The War Diaries of Weary Dunlop*, 25 February 1943, p. 176.
16 Dunlop, *The War Diaries of Weary Dunlop*, 25 February 1943, p. 176.
17 Dunlop, *The War Diaries of Weary Dunlop*, 25 February 1943, p. 177.
18 Dunlop, *The War Diaries of Weary Dunlop*, 25 February 1943, p. 177.
19 Dunlop, *The War Diaries of Weary Dunlop*, 27 February 1943, p. 177.
20 Dunlop, *The War Diaries of Weary Dunlop*, 27 February 1943, p. 177.

21 Dunlop, *The War Diaries of Weary Dunlop*, 27 February 1943, p. 177.

22 Dunlop, *The War Diaries of Weary Dunlop*, 27 February 1943, p. 177.

23 Dunlop, *The War Diaries of Weary Dunlop*, 27 February 1943, p. 178.

24 *The Australian Women's Weekly*, 20 October 1945, p. 17, https://trove.nla.gov.au/newspaper/article/51281493.

25 Dunlop, *The War Diaries of Weary Dunlop*, 27 February 1943, p. 178.

26 Dunlop, *The War Diaries of Weary Dunlop*, 28 February 1943, p. 178.

27 Dunlop, *The War Diaries of Weary Dunlop*, 28 February 1943, p. 178.

28 Dunlop, *The War Diaries of Weary Dunlop*, 28 February 1943, p. 178.

29 Dunlop, *The War Diaries of Weary Dunlop*, 2 March 1943, p. 180.

30 Dunlop, *The War Diaries of Weary Dunlop*, 2 March 1943, p. 180.

31 Dunlop, *The War Diaries of Weary Dunlop*, 2 March 1943, p. 180.

32 Dunlop, *The War Diaries of Weary Dunlop*, 2 March 1943, p. 180.

33 Dunlop, *The War Diaries of Weary Dunlop*, 2 March 1943, p. 180.

34 Dunlop, *The War Diaries of Weary Dunlop*, 2 March 1943, p. 180.

35 Dunlop, *The War Diaries of Weary Dunlop*, 2 March 1943, p. 180.

36 Dunlop, *The War Diaries of Weary Dunlop*, 2 March 1943, p. 180.

37 Dunlop, *The War Diaries of Weary Dunlop*, 2 March 1943, p. 180.

38 Dunlop, *The War Diaries of Weary Dunlop*, 2 March 1943, p. 180.

39 Dunlop, *The War Diaries of Weary Dunlop*, 2 March 1943, p. 180.

40 Dunlop, *The War Diaries of Weary Dunlop*, 2 March 1943, p. 180.

41 Dunlop, *The War Diaries of Weary Dunlop*, 2 March 1943, p. 180.

42 Dunlop, *The War Diaries of Weary Dunlop*, 2 March 1943, p. 181.

43 Dunlop, *The War Diaries of Weary Dunlop*, 2 March 1943, p. 181.

44 Dunlop, *The War Diaries of Weary Dunlop*, 2 March 1943, p. 181.

45 Dunlop, *The War Diaries of Weary Dunlop*, 1 March 1943, p. 179.

46 Dunlop, *The War Diaries of Weary Dunlop*, 3 March 1943, p. 181.

47 Dunlop, *The War Diaries of Weary Dunlop*, 2 March 1943, p. 181.

48 Dunlop, *The War Diaries of Weary Dunlop*, 2 March 1943, p. 182.

49 Dunlop, *The War Diaries of Weary Dunlop*, 4 March 1943, p. 182.

50 Dunlop, *The War Diaries of Weary Dunlop*, 5 March 1943, p. 183.

51 Dunlop, *The War Diaries of Weary Dunlop*, 5 March 1943, p. 183.

52 Dunlop, *The War Diaries of Weary Dunlop*, 5 March 1943, p. 183.

53 Dunlop, *The War Diaries of Weary Dunlop*, 5 March 1943, p. 183.

54 Dunlop, *The War Diaries of Weary Dunlop*, 5 March 1943, p. 183.

55 Dunlop, *The War Diaries of Weary Dunlop*, 6 March 1943, p. 183.

56 Carter, *G-String Jesters*, Currawong, Sydney, 1966, p. 25.

57 George Formby, 'Bless 'em All', Lyrics.Com, https://www.lyrics.com/lyric/15712045/George+Formby/Bless+%27Em+All#google_vignette. Author's note: 'Fuck 'em All' was effectively the anthem of the British fighting man in World War I, and spread around the forces of the British Empire from there.

58 *The Quiet Lions*, documentary, directed by Robin Newell, 2008.

59 Dunlop, *The War Diaries of Weary Dunlop*, 6 March 1943, p. 183.

60 Dunlop, *The War Diaries of Weary Dunlop*, 7 March 1943, p. 184.

61 Dunlop, *The War Diaries of Weary Dunlop*, 7 March 1943, p. 184.

62 Wright, *Ray Parkin's Odyssey*, p. 411.

63 Wright, *Ray Parkin's Odyssey*, p. 411.

64 Dunlop, *The War Diaries of Weary Dunlop*, 11 March 1943, p. 185.

65 Dunlop, *The War Diaries of Weary Dunlop*, 11 March 1943, p. 185.

66 Dunlop, *The War Diaries of Weary Dunlop*, 11 March 1943, p. 185.

67 Dunlop, *The War Diaries of Weary Dunlop*, 11 March 1943, p. 185.

68 Dunlop, *The War Diaries of Weary Dunlop*, 11 March 1943, p. 185.
69 Dunlop, *The War Diaries of Weary Dunlop*, 11 March 1943, p. 185.
70 Dunlop, *The War Diaries of Weary Dunlop*, 11 March 1943, p. 185.
71 Dunlop, *The War Diaries of Weary Dunlop*, 11 March 1943, p. 185.
72 Dunlop, *The War Diaries of Weary Dunlop*, 11 March 1943, p. 185.
73 Dunlop, *The War Diaries of Weary Dunlop*, 11 March 1943, p. 185.
74 Dunlop, *The War Diaries of Weary Dunlop*, 11 March 1943, p. 185.
75 Dunlop, *The War Diaries of Weary Dunlop*, 11 March 1943, p. 185.
76 Author's note: For the record, I agree with the remarks of Wright, from her own book, *The Men of the Line*: 'After spending some five years or so years looking at, reading about, researching through and talking to the men who were there, I have come to a few conclusions about the Thai–Burma Railway. The pertinent one now is that there is little agreement regarding the various camps. Specifically, their number, location, spelling, their kilometre marks, even the names of the camps cause dissension. And investigation of new camps continues even now.'
77 Dunlop, *The War Diaries of Weary Dunlop*, 11 March 1943, p. 185.
78 Dunlop, *The War Diaries of Weary Dunlop*, 11 March 1943, p. 185.
79 Dunlop, *The War Diaries of Weary Dunlop*, 11 March 1943, p. 185.
80 Dunlop, *The War Diaries of Weary Dunlop*, 11 March 1943, p. 186.
81 Dunlop, *The War Diaries of Weary Dunlop*, 11 March 1943, p. 186.
82 Dunlop, *The War Diaries of Weary Dunlop*, 11 March 1943, p. 186.
83 Dunlop, *The War Diaries of Weary Dunlop*, 13 March 1943, p. 186.
84 Dunlop, *The War Diaries of Weary Dunlop*, 13 March 1943, p. 186.
85 Dunlop, *The War Diaries of Weary Dunlop*, 13 March 1943, p. 186.
86 Dunlop, *The War Diaries of Weary Dunlop*, 13 March 1943, p. 186.
87 Dunlop, *The War Diaries of Weary Dunlop*, 13 March 1943, p. 186.
88 Dunlop, *The War Diaries of Weary Dunlop*, 14 March 1943, p. 187.
89 Dunlop, *The War Diaries of Weary Dunlop*, 14 March 1943, p. 187.
90 Dunlop, *The War Diaries of Weary Dunlop*, 14 March 1943, p. 187.
91 Dunlop, *The War Diaries of Weary Dunlop*, 15 March 1943, p. 187.
92 Dunlop, *The War Diaries of Weary Dunlop*, 16 March 1943, p. 187.
93 Dunlop, *The War Diaries of Weary Dunlop*, 16 March 1943, p. 187.
94 Dunlop, *The War Diaries of Weary Dunlop*, 16 March 1943, p. 187.
95 Dunlop, *The War Diaries of Weary Dunlop*, 16 March 1943, p. 187.
96 Dunlop, *The War Diaries of Weary Dunlop*, 16 March 1943, p. 187.
97 Dunlop, *The War Diaries of Weary Dunlop*, 16 March 1943, p. 187.
98 Dunlop, *The War Diaries of Weary Dunlop*, 16 March 1943, p. 188.
99 Dunlop, *The War Diaries of Weary Dunlop*, 16 March 1943, p. 188.
100 Dunlop, *The War Diaries of Weary Dunlop*, 16 March 1943, p. 188.
101 Parkin, *Wartime Trilogy*, p. 434.
102 Parkin, *Wartime Trilogy*, p. 434.
103 Parkin, *Wartime Trilogy*, p. 434.
104 Parkin, *Wartime Trilogy*, p. 435.
105 Parkin, *Wartime Trilogy*, p. 434.
106 Tom Uren, Transcript of interview, UNSW Australians at War Film Archive, 11 August 2003, http://australiansatwarfilmarchive.unsw.edu.au/archive/728.
107 Bill Haskell, 'Memories of the Burma Siam Railway', http://www.mansell.com/pow_resources/camplists/death_rr/hintok.html.
108 Parkin, *Wartime Trilogy*, p. 437.
109 Parkin, *Wartime Trilogy*, p. 437.
110 Parkin, *Wartime Trilogy*, pp. 436–437.

111 Parkin, *Wartime Trilogy*, p. 435.
112 Photograph of Lieutenant Usuki, Australian War Memorial, https://www.awm.gov.au/collection/C195470.
113 *Daily Mail*, 27 February 2010.
114 *Daily Mail*, 27 February 2010.
115 *Daily Mail*, 27 February 2010.
116 McCormack and Nelson, *The Burma–Thailand Railway*, p. 43.
117 Corrie, *Survival Against Odds*, p. 15.
118 Dunlop, *The War Diaries of Weary Dunlop*, 17 March 1943, p. 189.
119 *The Sydney Morning Herald*, 25 April 1991.
120 Wright, *Ray Parkin's Odyssey*, p. 361.
121 Dunlop, *The War Diaries of Weary Dunlop*, 17 March 1943, p. 189.
122 Dunlop, *The War Diaries of Weary Dunlop*, 17 March 1943, p. 189.
123 Dunlop, *The War Diaries of Weary Dunlop*, 17 March 1943, p. 190.
124 Dunlop, *The War Diaries of Weary Dunlop*, 17 March 1943, p. 190.
125 Dunlop, *The War Diaries of Weary Dunlop*, 17 March 1943, p. 190.
126 Dunlop, *The War Diaries of Weary Dunlop*, 17 March 1943, p. 190.
127 Dunlop, *The War Diaries of Weary Dunlop*, 17 March 1943, p. 190.
128 Dunlop, *The War Diaries of Weary Dunlop*, 17 March 1943, p. 190.
129 Dunlop, *The War Diaries of Weary Dunlop*, 17 March 1943, p. 190.
130 *The Coromandel*, 15 December 1945, p. 3, https://trove.nla.gov.au/newspaper/article/261040610.
131 Dunlop, *The War Diaries of Weary Dunlop*, 18 March 1943, p. 190.
132 Dunlop, *The War Diaries of Weary Dunlop*, 18 March 1943, p. 190.
133 Dunlop, *The War Diaries of Weary Dunlop*, 18 March 1943, p. 190.
134 Dunlop, *The War Diaries of Weary Dunlop*, 18 March 1943, p. 190.
135 Dunlop, *The War Diaries of Weary Dunlop*, 19 March 1943, p. 191.
136 Dunlop, *The War Diaries of Weary Dunlop*, 19 March 1943, p. 191.
137 Dunlop, *The War Diaries of Weary Dunlop*, 19 March 1943, p. 191.
138 Raymond 'Ray' Edward Parkin: Interviews for the Channel 10 program, *Surgeon of the Railway*, 1987, Australian War Memorial, https://www.awm.gov.au/collection/F09396.
139 Dunlop, *The War Diaries of Weary Dunlop*, 20 March 1943, p. 191.
140 Dunlop, *The War Diaries of Weary Dunlop*, 20 March 1943, p. 191.
141 Dunlop, *The War Diaries of Weary Dunlop*, 20 March 1943, p. 192.
142 Dunlop, *The War Diaries of Weary Dunlop*, 20 March 1943, p. 192.
143 Dunlop, *The War Diaries of Weary Dunlop*, 20 March 1943, p. 192.
144 Milton Butterworth (Blue), Transcript of interview, UNSW Australians at War Film Archive, 21 November 2003, http://australiansatwarfilmarchive.unsw.edu.au/archive/906.
145 Dunlop, *The War Diaries of Weary Dunlop*, 20 March 1943, p. 192.
146 Dunlop, *The War Diaries of Weary Dunlop*, 20 March 1943, p. 192.
147 Dunlop, *The War Diaries of Weary Dunlop*, 20 March 1943, p. 192.
148 Dunlop, *The War Diaries of Weary Dunlop*, 20 March 1943, p. 193.
149 Dunlop, *The War Diaries of Weary Dunlop*, 20 March 1943, p. 193.
150 Dunlop, *The War Diaries of Weary Dunlop*, 20 March 1943, p. 193.
151 Dunlop, *The War Diaries of Weary Dunlop*, 20 March 1943, p. 193.
152 Dunlop, *The War Diaries of Weary Dunlop*, 20 March 1943, p. 193.
153 Dunlop, *The War Diaries of Weary Dunlop*, 20 March 1943, p. 193.
154 Dunlop, *The War Diaries of Weary Dunlop*, 20 March 1943, p. 193.
155 Dunlop, *The War Diaries of Weary Dunlop*, 20 March 1943, p. 193.

156 Dunlop, *The War Diaries of Weary Dunlop*, 20 March 1943, p. 193 [reported speech].

157 Dunlop, *The War Diaries of Weary Dunlop*, 20 March 1943, p. 193.

158 Dunlop, *The War Diaries of Weary Dunlop*, 20 March 1943, p. 193.

Chapter Twelve

1 Raymond 'Ray' Edward Parkin: Interviews for the Channel 10 program, *Surgeon of the Railway*, 1987, Australian War Memorial, https://www.awm.gov.au/collection/F09396.

2 Dunlop, *The War Diaries of Weary Dunlop*, 21 March 1943, p. 194.

3 Dunlop, *The War Diaries of Weary Dunlop*, 21 March 1943, p. 194.

4 Dunlop, *The War Diaries of Weary Dunlop*, 21 March 1943, p. 194.

5 Dunlop, *The War Diaries of Weary Dunlop*, 21 March 1943, p. 194.

6 Dunlop, *The War Diaries of Weary Dunlop*, 22 March 1943, p. 195.

7 Dunlop, *The War Diaries of Weary Dunlop*, 22 March 1943, p. 195.

8 Dunlop, *The War Diaries of Weary Dunlop*, 22 March 1943, p. 195.

9 Dunlop, *The War Diaries of Weary Dunlop*, 22 March 1943, p. 195.

10 Dunlop, *The War Diaries of Weary Dunlop*, 22 March 1943, p. 195.

11 Dunlop, *The War Diaries of Weary Dunlop*, 22 March 1943, p. 195.

12 Dunlop, *The War Diaries of Weary Dunlop*, 22 March 1943, p. 195.

13 Dunlop, *The War Diaries of Weary Dunlop*, 22 March 1943, p. 195.

14 *The Canberra Times*, 18 May 1991, p. 19, https://trove.nla.gov.au/newspaper/article/122363608.

15 'Death Railway Shrine', The War Channel, https://www.youtube.com/watch?v=Nr5cPrsoeM0.

16 Wright, *Ray Parkin's Odyssey*, p. 374.

17 Wright, *The Men of the Line: Stories of the Thai–Burma Railway Survivors*, p. 44.

18 Wright, *Ray Parkin's Odyssey*, p. 358.

19 *Daily Mail*, 27 February 2010.

20 Dunlop, *The War Diaries of Weary Dunlop*, 7 April 1943, p. 203.

21 Parkin, *Wartime Trilogy*, p. 447.

22 Parkin, *Wartime Trilogy*, p. 445.

23 'Tom Uren: Back to the Burma Railway', David Brill, The Big Picture, https://www.youtube.com/watch?v=Lp6tHPKnYHc.

24 Tom Uren, Transcript of interview, UNSW Australians at War Film Archive, 11 August 2003, http://australiansatwarfilmarchive.unsw.edu.au/archive/728.

25 Tom Uren, Transcript of interview, UNSW Australians at War Film Archive, 11 August 2003, http://australiansatwarfilmarchive.unsw.edu.au/archive/728.

26 'Tom Uren: Back to the Burma Railway', David Brill, The Big Picture' https://www.youtube.com/watch?v=Lp6tHPKnYHc.

27 Tom Uren, Transcript of interview, UNSW Australians at War Film Archive, 11 August 2003, http://australiansatwarfilmarchive.unsw.edu.au/archive/728.

28 Tom Uren, Transcript of interview, UNSW Australians at War Film Archive, 11 August 2003, http://australiansatwarfilmarchive.unsw.edu.au/archive/728.

29 Tom Uren, Transcript of interview, UNSW Australians at War Film Archive, 11 August 2003, http://australiansatwarfilmarchive.unsw.edu.au/archive/728.

30 Flanagan, 'For Tom Uren: "You were a champion, Tom. You're in the company of legends now"', 4 February 2015, https://speakola.com/eulogy/-tom-uren-martin-flanagan-2015.

31 Tom Uren, Transcript of interview, UNSW Australians at War Film Archive, 11 August 2003, http://australiansatwarfilmarchive.unsw.edu.au/archive/728.

32 Tom Uren, Transcript of interview, UNSW Australians at War Film Archive, 11 August 2003, http://australiansatwarfilmarchive.unsw.edu.au/archive/728.

33 Tom Uren, Transcript of interview, UNSW Australians at War Film Archive, 11 August 2003, http://australiansatwarfilmarchive.unsw.edu.au/archive/728.

34 Tom Uren, Transcript of interview, UNSW Australians at War Film Archive, 11 August 2003, http://australiansatwarfilmarchive.unsw.edu.au/archive/728.

35 *The Herald*, 8 November 1951, p. 5, https://trove.nla.gov.au/newspaper/article/247837683.

36 Ryan, 'The Major Moon Collection', State Library of Victoria, 1 April 2013, https://blogs.slv.vic.gov.au/such-was-life/war-such-was-life/the-major-moon-collection/.

37 Sir Ernest Edward 'Weary' Dunlop interviewed by Dr Hank Nelson, Australian War Memorial, https://www.awm.gov.au/collection/C283448.

38 Dunlop, *The War Diaries of Weary Dunlop*, 23 March 1943, p. 196.

39 Dunlop, *The War Diaries of Weary Dunlop*, 23 March 1943, p. 196.

40 Dunlop, *The War Diaries of Weary Dunlop*, 24 March 1943, p. 196.

41 *The Canberra Times*, 18 May 1991, p. 19, https://trove.nla.gov.au/newspaper/article/122363608.

42 Dunlop, *The War Diaries of Weary Dunlop*, 25 March 1943, p. 197.

43 Dunlop, *The War Diaries of Weary Dunlop*, 25 March 1943, p. 197.

44 Dunlop, *The War Diaries of Weary Dunlop*, 26 March 1943, p. 197.

45 Dunlop, *The War Diaries of Weary Dunlop*, 26 March 1943, p. 197.

46 Dunlop, *The War Diaries of Weary Dunlop*, 26 March 1943, p. 197.

47 Dunlop, *The War Diaries of Weary Dunlop*, 28 March 1943, p. 198.

48 Dunlop, *The War Diaries of Weary Dunlop*, 31 March 1943, p. 200.

49 Dunlop, *The War Diaries of Weary Dunlop*, 31 March 1943, p. 200.

50 Dunlop, *The War Diaries of Weary Dunlop*, 31 March 1943, p. 200.

51 Dunlop, *The War Diaries of Weary Dunlop*, 31 March 1943, p. 201.

52 *The Quiet Lions*, documentary, directed by Robin Newell, 2008.

53 Sir Ernest Edward 'Weary' Dunlop interviewed by Dr Hank Nelson, Australian War Memorial, https://www.awm.gov.au/collection/C283448.

54 Sir Ernest Edward 'Weary' Dunlop interviewed by Dr Hank Nelson, Australian War Memorial, https://www.awm.gov.au/collection/C283448.

55 Dunlop, 'Medical Experiences in Japanese Captivity', *British Medical Journal*, 5 October 1946, p. 485, https://pmc.ncbi.nlm.nih.gov/articles/PMC2057680/.

56 Parkin, *Wartime Trilogy*, p. 442.

57 Ray Parkin, Transcript of interview, UNSW Australians at War Film Archive, 7 June 2000, https://australiansatwarfilmarchive.unsw.edu.au/archive/2552.

58 Wright, *Ray Parkin's Odyssey*, p. 372.

59 Wright, *Ray Parkin's Odyssey*, p. 372.

60 Dunlop, *The War Diaries of Weary Dunlop*, 4 April 1943, p. 202.

61 Dunlop, *The War Diaries of Weary Dunlop*, 4 April 1943, p. 202.

62 Dunlop, *The War Diaries of Weary Dunlop*, 5 April 1943, p. 202.

63 Dunlop, *The War Diaries of Weary Dunlop*, 5 April 1943, p. 202.

64 Dunlop, *The War Diaries of Weary Dunlop*, 5 April 1943, p. 202.

65 Dunlop, *The War Diaries of Weary Dunlop*, 5 April 1943, p. 202.

66 Parkin, *Wartime Trilogy*, p. 522.

67 Dunlop, *The War Diaries of Weary Dunlop*, 17 June 1943, p. 247.

68 Parkin, *Wartime Trilogy*, p. 522.

69 Parkin, *Wartime Trilogy*, p. 522.

70 Parkin, *Wartime Trilogy*, p. 421.

71 *The Australian Women's Weekly*, 20 October 1945, p. 17, https://trove.nla.gov.au/newspaper/article/51281493.

72 Raymond 'Ray' Edward Parkin: Interviews for the Channel 10 program, *Surgeon of the Railway*, 1987, Australian War Memorial [reported speech], https://www.awm.gov.au/collection/F09396.

73 Dunlop, *The War Diaries of Weary Dunlop*, 7 April 1943, p. 203.

74 Dunlop, *The War Diaries of Weary Dunlop*, 7 April 1943, p. 203.

75 Dunlop, *The War Diaries of Weary Dunlop*, 7 April 1943, p. 203.

76 Dunlop, *The War Diaries of Weary Dunlop*, 7 April 1943, p. 203.

77 Dunlop, *The War Diaries of Weary Dunlop*, 7 April 1943, p. 203.

78 Dunlop, *The War Diaries of Weary Dunlop*, 7 April 1943, p. 203.

79 Dunlop, *The War Diaries of Weary Dunlop*, 7 April 1943, p. 203.

80 Dunlop, *The War Diaries of Weary Dunlop*, 7 April 1943, p. 203.

81 Dunlop, *The War Diaries of Weary Dunlop*, 7 April 1943, p. 203.

82 Edward 'Weary' Dunlop, Transcript of interview, Department of Veterans' Affairs, Anzac Portal, https://anzacportal.dva.gov.au/resources/edward-weary-dunlop.

83 Edward 'Weary' Dunlop, Transcript of interview, Department of Veterans' Affairs, Anzac Portal, https://anzacportal.dva.gov.au/resources/edward-weary-dunlop.

84 Geddes, *Remembering Weary*, p. 163.

85 Dunlop, 'Medical Experiences in Japanese Captivity', *British Medical Journal*, 5 October 1946, p. 484, https://pmc.ncbi.nlm.nih.gov/articles/PMC2057680/.

86 Dunlop, 'Medical Experiences in Japanese Captivity', *British Medical Journal*, 5 October 1946, p. 484, https://pmc.ncbi.nlm.nih.gov/articles/PMC2057680/.

87 Nelson, *POW. Prisoners of War: Australians Under Nippon*, p. 52.

88 Wright, *The Men of the Line: Stories of the Thai–Burma Railway Survivors*, p. 15.

89 Wright, *The Men of the Line: Stories of the Thai–Burma Railway Survivors*, p. 17.

90 Nelson, *POW. Prisoners of War: Australians Under Nippon*, p. 52.

91 Thomas Young (Tom), Transcript of interview, UNSW Australians at War Film Archive, 8 October 2003, https://australiansatwarfilmarchive.unsw.edu.au/archive/1021.

92 Dunlop, *The War Diaries of Weary Dunlop*, 8 April 1943, p. 204.

93 Dunlop, *The War Diaries of Weary Dunlop*, 8 April 1943, p. 204.

94 Dunlop, *The War Diaries of Weary Dunlop*, 11 April 1943, p. 206.

95 Dunlop, *The War Diaries of Weary Dunlop*, 11 April 1943, p. 206.

96 Dunlop, *The War Diaries of Weary Dunlop*, 11 April 1943, p. 206.

97 Dunlop, *The War Diaries of Weary Dunlop*, 11 April 1943, p. 206.

98 Dunlop, *The War Diaries of Weary Dunlop*, 11 April 1943, p. 206.

99 Dunlop, *The War Diaries of Weary Dunlop*, 12 April 1943, p. 207.

100 Dunlop, *The War Diaries of Weary Dunlop*, 13 April 1943, p. 207.

101 Dunlop, *The War Diaries of Weary Dunlop*, 13 April 1943, p. 207.

102 Dunlop, *The War Diaries of Weary Dunlop*, 13 April 1943, p. 207.

103 Dunlop, *The War Diaries of Weary Dunlop*, 13 April 1943, p. 207.

104 Dunlop, *The War Diaries of Weary Dunlop*, 13 April 1943, p. 207.

105 Dunlop, *The War Diaries of Weary Dunlop*, 13 April 1943, p. 207.

106 Dunlop, *The War Diaries of Weary Dunlop*, 13 April 1943, p. 207.

107 Dunlop, *The War Diaries of Weary Dunlop*, 14 April 1943, p. 207.

108 Dunlop, *The War Diaries of Weary Dunlop*, 14 April 1943, p. 208.

109 Dunlop, *The War Diaries of Weary Dunlop*, 14 April 1943, p. 208.

110 Finkemeyer, *It Happened to Us*, first published in Melbourne, July 1994, Australian War Memorial Edition 2015, p. 80, https://s3-ap-southeast-2.amazonaws.com/awm-media/collection/MSS2350/document/6187721.PDF.

111 Finkemeyer, *It Happened to Us*, first published in Melbourne, July 1994, Australian War Memorial Edition 2015, p. 80, https://s3-ap-southeast-2.amazonaws.com/awm-media/collection/MSS2350/document/6187721.PDF.

112 Finkemeyer, *It Happened to Us*, first published in Melbourne, July 1994, Australian War Memorial Edition 2015, p. 81 https://s3-ap-southeast-2.amazonaws.com/awm-media/collection/MSS2350/document/6187721.PDF.

113 Dunlop, *The War Diaries of Weary Dunlop*, 14 April 1943, p. 208.

114 Dunlop, *The War Diaries of Weary Dunlop*, 14 April 1943, p. 208.

115 Dunlop, *The War Diaries of Weary Dunlop*, 14 April 1943, p. 208.

116 Dunlop, *The War Diaries of Weary Dunlop*, 14 April 1943, p. 208.

117 *The Australian Women's Weekly*, 20 October 1945, p. 17, https://trove.nla.gov.au/newspaper/article/51281493.

118 Dunlop, *The War Diaries of Weary Dunlop*, 15 April 1943, p. 208.

119 Dunlop, *The War Diaries of Weary Dunlop*, 15 April 1943, p. 208.

120 Wright, *The Men of the Line: Stories of the Thai–Burma Railway Survivors*, p. 13.

121 Sir Ernest Edward 'Weary' Dunlop interviewed by Dr Hank Nelson, Australian War Memorial, https://www.awm.gov.au/collection/C283448.

122 Dunlop, 'Medical Experiences in Japanese Captivity', *British Medical Journal*, 5 October 1946, p. 484, https://pmc.ncbi.nlm.nih.gov/articles/PMC2057680/.

123 Coates, 'Clinical Lessons from Prisoner of War Hospitals in the Far East (Burma and Siam)', *The Medical Journal of Australia*, June 1946, p. 755, https://onlinelibrary.wiley.com/doi/abs/10.5694/j.1326-5377.1946.tb33884.x.

124 Dunlop, *The War Diaries of Weary Dunlop*, 15 April 1943, p. 208.

125 Dunlop, *The War Diaries of Weary Dunlop*, 23 March 1943, p. 196.

126 Dunlop, *The War Diaries of Weary Dunlop*, 15 April 1943, p. 208.

127 Author's note: It is possible that instead of Usuki, it was Okada who committed this atrocity. In Alistair Urquhart's book, *Forgotten Highlander*, which was written 50 years after the event, he does name Usuki as the perpetrator, though in another interview he said it was Okada. Though Weary Dunlop later talked of beheadings on the Line, this was not one he witnessed.

128 Urquhart, *Forgotten Highlander*, Little Brown, London, 2010, p. 173.

129 Urquhart, *Forgotten Highlander*, p. 173.

130 Urquhart, *Forgotten Highlander*, p. 173.

131 Wright, *Ray Parkin's Odyssey*, p. 344.

132 Ray Parkin, Transcript of interview, UNSW Australians at War Film Archive, 7 June 2000, https://australiansatwarfilmarchive.unsw.edu.au/archive/2552.

133 Dunlop, *The War Diaries of Weary Dunlop*, 17 April 1943, p. 210.

134 Dunlop, *The War Diaries of Weary Dunlop*, 17 April 1943, p. 210.

135 Dunlop, *The War Diaries of Weary Dunlop*, 17 April 1943, p. 210.

Chapter Thirteen

1 'Report on Conditions, Life and Work of Prisoners of War in Burma and Siam', by Brigadier C. A. McEachern, 1942–1945, Australian War Memorial, Series No. AWM54, https://s3-ap-southeast-2.amazonaws.com/awm-media/collection/AWM2017.8.197/document/6593514.PDF.

2 Dunlop, *The War Diaries of Weary Dunlop*, 18 April 1943, p. 210.

3 Dunlop, *The War Diaries of Weary Dunlop*, 18 April 1943, p. 210.

4 Dunlop, *The War Diaries of Weary Dunlop*, 18 April 1943, p. 210.

5 Dunlop, *The War Diaries of Weary Dunlop*, 18 April 1943, p. 210.

6 Dunlop, *The War Diaries of Weary Dunlop*, 18 April 1943, p. 210.

7 Dunlop, *The War Diaries of Weary Dunlop*, 18 April 1943, p. 210.

8 Dunlop, *The War Diaries of Weary Dunlop*, 18 April 1943, p. 211.

9 Dunlop, *The War Diaries of Weary Dunlop*, 18 April 1943, p. 211.

10 Dunlop, *The War Diaries of Weary Dunlop*, 18 April 1943, p. 211.

11 Dunlop, *The War Diaries of Weary Dunlop*, 20 April 1943, p. 211.

12 Dunlop, *The War Diaries of Weary Dunlop*, 20 April 1943, p. 211.

13 Dunlop, *The War Diaries of Weary Dunlop*, 20 April 1943, p. 211.

14 Dunlop, *The War Diaries of Weary Dunlop*, 20 April 1943, p. 211.

15 Dunlop, *The War Diaries of Weary Dunlop*, 20 April 1943, p. 211.

16 Dunlop, *The War Diaries of Weary Dunlop*, 20 April 1943, p. 211.

17 Nelson, *POW. Prisoners of War: Australians Under Nippon*, p. 48.

18 Dunlop, *The War Diaries of Weary Dunlop*, 20 April 1943, p. 211.

19 'Now is the Hour' written by Maewa Kaihau and Dorothy Stewart.

20 Dunlop, *The War Diaries of Weary Dunlop*, 11 August 1943, p. 272.

21 Dunlop, *The War Diaries of Weary Dunlop*, 21 April 1943, p. 212.

22 Dunlop, *The War Diaries of Weary Dunlop*, 21 April 1943, p. 212.

23 Dunlop, *The War Diaries of Weary Dunlop*, 21 April 1943, p. 212.

24 Dunlop, *The War Diaries of Weary Dunlop*, 21 April 1943, p. 212.

25 Dunlop, *The War Diaries of Weary Dunlop*, 21 April 1943, p. 212.

26 Dunlop, *The War Diaries of Weary Dunlop*, 21 April 1943, p. 212.

27 Dunlop, *The War Diaries of Weary Dunlop*, 21 April 1943, p. 212.

28 Dunlop, *The War Diaries of Weary Dunlop*, 21 April 1943, p. 212.

29 Dunlop, *The War Diaries of Weary Dunlop*, 21 April 1943, p. 212.

30 Dunlop, *The War Diaries of Weary Dunlop*, 21 April 1943, p. 212.

31 Dunlop, *The War Diaries of Weary Dunlop*, 21 April 1943, p. 213.

32 Dunlop, *The War Diaries of Weary Dunlop*, 21 April 1943, p. 213.

33 Dunlop, *The War Diaries of Weary Dunlop*, 22 April 1943, p. 213.

34 Dunlop, *The War Diaries of Weary Dunlop*, 22 April 1943, p. 213.

35 Dunlop, *The War Diaries of Weary Dunlop*, 22 April 1943, p. 213.

36 Dunlop, *The War Diaries of Weary Dunlop*, 22 April 1943, p. 213.

37 Dunlop, *The War Diaries of Weary Dunlop*, 22 April 1943, p. 213.

38 Dunlop, *The War Diaries of Weary Dunlop*, 24 April 1943, p. 214.

39 Dunlop, *The War Diaries of Weary Dunlop*, 24 April 1943, p. 214.

40 Dunlop, *The War Diaries of Weary Dunlop*, 24 April 1943, p. 214.

41 Dunlop, *The War Diaries of Weary Dunlop*, 24 April 1943, p. 215.

42 Dunlop, *The War Diaries of Weary Dunlop*, 24 April 1943, p. 215.

43 Dunlop, *The War Diaries of Weary Dunlop*, 24 April 1943, p. 215.

44 Dunlop, *The War Diaries of Weary Dunlop*, 25 April 1943, p. 215.

45 Ebury, *Weary: The Life of Sir Edward Dunlop*, p. 408.

46 Dunlop, *The War Diaries of Weary Dunlop*, 2 May 1943, p. 221.

47 Ebury, *Weary: The Life of Sir Edward Dunlop*, p. 408.

48 Ebury, *Weary: The Life of Sir Edward Dunlop*, p. 409.

49 Captain Fred Stahl 'F' Force Thailand Diary, 2/4th Machine Gun Battalion Ex Members Association, 20 June 2023, https://2nd4thmgb.com.au/story/29505/.

50 Author's note: In his diary, Stahl used the word 'fluffing' instead of 'fucking', but in context it is obvious that the word he roared was the latter.

51 Dunlop, *The War Diaries of Weary Dunlop*, 26 April 1943, p. 216.

52 Dunlop, *The War Diaries of Weary Dunlop*, 28 April 1943, p. 217.

53   Dunlop, *The War Diaries of Weary Dunlop*, 28 April 1943, p. 217.

54   Dunlop, *The War Diaries of Weary Dunlop*, 28 April 1943, p. 217.

55   Dunlop, *The War Diaries of Weary Dunlop*, 28 April 1943, p. 217.

56   Dunlop, 'Medical Experiences in Japanese Captivity', *British Medical Journal*, 5 October 1946, p. 486, https://pmc.ncbi.nlm.nih.gov/articles/PMC2057680/.

57   Dunlop, 'Medical Experiences in Japanese Captivity', *British Medical Journal*, 5 October 1946, p. 483, https://pmc.ncbi.nlm.nih.gov/articles/PMC2057680/.

58   Dunlop, *The War Diaries of Weary Dunlop*, 29 April 1943, p. 217.

59   Dunlop, *The War Diaries of Weary Dunlop*, 29 April 1943, p. 218.

60   Dunlop, *The War Diaries of Weary Dunlop*, 29 April 1943, p. 217.

61   Dunlop, *The War Diaries of Weary Dunlop*, 29 April 1943, p. 218.

62   Dunlop, *The War Diaries of Weary Dunlop*, 19 March 1943, p. 191.

63   McCormack, 'Yi Hak-Nae and the Burma–Thailand Railway, *Asia-Pacific Journal: Japan Focus*, Vol. 19, Issue 15, No. 1, August 2021. Author's note: I have made it 'Dunrop', as that's the way Weary reported that the Japanese pronounced his name.

64   McCormack and Nelson, *The Burma–Thailand Railway*, p. 145 [reported speech].

65   Wright, *The Men of the Line: Stories of the Thai–Burma Railway Survivors*, pp. 137–138.

66   Wright, *The Men of the Line: Stories of the Thai–Burma Railway Survivors*, pp. 137–138 [reported speech].

67   Wright, *The Men of the Line: Stories of the Thai–Burma Railway Survivors*, p. 15.

68   Dunlop, *The War Diaries of Weary Dunlop*, 3 May 1943, p. 221.

69   Dunlop, *The War Diaries of Weary Dunlop*, 3 May 1943, p. 221.

70   Dunlop, *The War Diaries of Weary Dunlop*, 4 May 1943, p. 222.

71   Dunlop, *The War Diaries of Weary Dunlop*, 4 May 1943, p. 222.

72   Dunlop, *The War Diaries of Weary Dunlop*, 4 May 1943, p. 222.

73   McCormack and Nelson, *The Burma–Thailand Railway*, p. 144.

74   Dunlop, *The War Diaries of Weary Dunlop*, 5 May 1943, p. 222.

75   Dunlop, *The War Diaries of Weary Dunlop*, 5 May 1943, p. 222.

76   *The Canberra Times*, 15 February 1995, p. 40.

77   *The Canberra Times*, 15 February 1995, p. 40 [reported speech].

78   *The Canberra Times*, 15 February 1995, p. 40.

79   Dunlop, *The War Diaries of Weary Dunlop*, 8 May 1943, p. 224.

80   Dunlop, *The War Diaries of Weary Dunlop*, 8 May 1943, p. 224.

81   Dunlop, *The War Diaries of Weary Dunlop*, 8 May 1943, p. 224.

82   Dunlop, *The War Diaries of Weary Dunlop*, 8 May 1943, p. 224.

83   Dunlop, *The War Diaries of Weary Dunlop*, 8 May 1943, p. 224.

84   Dunlop, *The War Diaries of Weary Dunlop*, 8 May 1943, p. 224.

85   Dunlop, *The War Diaries of Weary Dunlop*, 8 May 1943, p. 224.

86   Dunlop, *The War Diaries of Weary Dunlop*, 8 May 1943, p. 224.

87   Corrie, *Survival Against Odds*, p. 15.

88   *The Australian Women's Weekly*, 20 October 1945, p. 17, https://trove.nla.gov.au/newspaper/article/51281493.

89   *The Australian Women's Weekly*, 20 October 1945, p. 17, https://trove.nla.gov.au/newspaper/article/51281493.

90   *The Australian Women's Weekly*, 20 October 1945, p. 17 [reported speech], https://trove.nla.gov.au/newspaper/article/51281493.

91   Raymond 'Ray' Edward Parkin: Interviews for the Channel 10 program, *Surgeon of the Railway*, 1987, Australian War Memorial, https://www.awm.gov.au/collection/F09396.

92 Raymond 'Ray' Edward Parkin: Interviews for the Channel 10 program, *Surgeon of the Railway*, 1987, Australian War Memorial, https://www.awm.gov.au/collection/F09396.
93 Geddes, *Remembering Weary*, p. 163.
94 Wright, *The Men of the Line: Stories of the Thai–Burma Railway Survivors*, p. 18.
95 Wright, *Ray Parkin's Odyssey*, p. 364. Author's note: I have standardised Parkin's spelling of 'Ba-ge-e-era' to the way I have spelt it in the rest of the manuscript.
96 Tom Uren, Transcript of interview, UNSW Australians at War Film Archive, 11 August 2003, http://australiansatwarfilmarchive.unsw.edu.au/archive/728.
97 Dunlop, *The War Diaries of Weary Dunlop*, 9 May 1943, p. 225.
98 Dunlop, *The War Diaries of Weary Dunlop*, 9 May 1943, p. 225.
99 Dunlop, *The War Diaries of Weary Dunlop*, 9 May 1943, p. 225.
100 Dunlop, *The War Diaries of Weary Dunlop*, 10 May 1943, p. 225.
101 Dunlop, *The War Diaries of Weary Dunlop*, 10 May 1943, p. 225.
102 Dunlop, *The War Diaries of Weary Dunlop*, 10 May 1943, p. 225.
103 Dunlop, *The War Diaries of Weary Dunlop*, 10 May 1943, p. 225.
104 Dunlop, *The War Diaries of Weary Dunlop*, 10 May 1943, p. 226.
105 Dunlop, *The War Diaries of Weary Dunlop*, 10 May 1943, p. 227.
106 Dunlop, *The War Diaries of Weary Dunlop*, 10 May 1943, p. 227.
107 Dunlop, *The War Diaries of Weary Dunlop*, 10 May 1943, p. 227.
108 Dunlop, *The War Diaries of Weary Dunlop*, 10 May 1943, p. 227.
109 Dunlop, *The War Diaries of Weary Dunlop*, 10 May 1943, p. 227.
110 Dunlop, *The War Diaries of Weary Dunlop*, 10 May 1943, p. 227.
111 Dunlop, *The War Diaries of Weary Dunlop*, 10 May 1943, p. 227.
112 Dunlop, *The War Diaries of Weary Dunlop*, 12 May 1943, p. 227.
113 Dunlop, *The War Diaries of Weary Dunlop*, 12 May 1943, p. 227.
114 Dunlop, *The War Diaries of Weary Dunlop*, 12 May 1943, p. 227.
115 Dunlop, *The War Diaries of Weary Dunlop*, 12 May 1943, p. 227.
116 Dunlop, *The War Diaries of Weary Dunlop*, 12 May 1943, p. 227.
117 Dunlop, *The War Diaries of Weary Dunlop*, 13 May 1943, pp. 227–228.
118 Dunlop, *The War Diaries of Weary Dunlop*, 13 May 1943, p. 228.
119 Dunlop, *The War Diaries of Weary Dunlop*, 13 May 1943, p. 228.
120 Dunlop, *The War Diaries of Weary Dunlop*, 13 May 1943, p. 228.
121 Dunlop, *The War Diaries of Weary Dunlop*, 5 May 1943, p. 223.
122 Dunlop, *The War Diaries of Weary Dunlop*, 14 May 1943, p. 228.
123 Dunlop, *The War Diaries of Weary Dunlop*, 14 May 1943, p. 228.
124 Dunlop, *The War Diaries of Weary Dunlop*, 14 May 1943, p. 228.
125 Tom Uren, Transcript of interview, UNSW Australians at War Film Archive, 11 August 2003, http://australiansatwarfilmarchive.unsw.edu.au/archive/728.
126 Wright, *Ray Parkin's Odyssey*, p. 380.
127 Wright, *Ray Parkin's Odyssey*, p. 380.
128 Tom Uren, Transcript of interview, UNSW Australians at War Film Archive, 11 August 2003, http://australiansatwarfilmarchive.unsw.edu.au/archive/728.
129 Dunlop, *The War Diaries of Weary Dunlop*, 18 May 1943, p. 231.
130 Dunlop, *The War Diaries of Weary Dunlop*, 17 June 1943, p. 246.

Chapter Fourteen

1 *The Australian Women's Weekly*, 20 October 1945, p. 17, https://trove.nla.gov.au/newspaper/article/51281493.

2   *Army Magazine*, 1 June 1998, p. 62, https://trove.nla.gov.au/newspaper/article/267398068/29994865.

3   Dunlop, *The War Diaries of Weary Dunlop*, 19 June 1943, p. 247.

4   Dunlop, *The War Diaries of Weary Dunlop*, 19 June 1943, p. 247.

5   Dunlop, *The War Diaries of Weary Dunlop*, 19 June 1943, p. 247.

6   Dunlop, *The War Diaries of Weary Dunlop*, 19 June 1943, p. 247.

7   Dunlop, *The War Diaries of Weary Dunlop*, 19 June 1943, p. 247.

8   Dunlop, *The War Diaries of Weary Dunlop*, 19 June 1943, p. 247.

9   Dunlop, *The War Diaries of Weary Dunlop*, 19 June 1943, p. 247.

10 Wright, *Ray Parkin's Odyssey*, p. 386.

11 *The Quiet Lions*, documentary, directed by Robin Newell, 2008.

12 Wright, *Ray Parkin's Odyssey*, p. 392.

13 Ebury, *Weary: The Life of Sir Edward Dunlop*, p. 369.

14 Ebury, *Weary: The Life of Sir Edward Dunlop*, p. 369.

15 Wright, *The Men of the Line: Stories of the Thai–Burma Railway Survivors*, p. 87.

16 Nelson, *POW. Prisoners of War: Australians Under Nippon*, p. 53.

17 Nelson, *POW. Prisoners of War: Australians Under Nippon*, p. 53.

18 Wright, *Ray Parkin's Odyssey*, p. 377.

19 Dunlop, 'Medical Experiences in Japanese Captivity', *British Medical Journal*, 5 October 1946, p. 483, https://pmc.ncbi.nlm.nih.gov/articles/PMC2057680/.

20 Wright, *The Men of the Line: Stories of the Thai–Burma Railway Survivors*, p. 145.

21 Tom Uren, Transcript of interview, UNSW Australians at War Film Archive, 11 August 2003, http://australiansatwarfilmarchive.unsw.edu.au/archive/728.

22 'Illness and death', Department of Veterans' Affairs, 2024, Anzac Portal, https://anzacportal.dva.gov.au/wars-and-missions/burma-thailand-railway-and-hellfire-pass-1942-1943/events/surviving/illness-and-death.

23 Tom Uren, Transcript of interview, UNSW Australians at War Film Archive, 11 August 2003, http://australiansatwarfilmarchive.unsw.edu.au/archive/728.

24 Milton Butterworth (Blue), Transcript of interview, UNSW Australians at War Film Archive, 21 November 2003, http://australiansatwarfilmarchive.unsw.edu.au/archive/906.

25 Dunlop, *The War Diaries of Weary Dunlop*, p. 253.

26 Sir Ernest Edward 'Weary' Dunlop interviewed by Dr Hank Nelson, Australian War Memorial, https://www.awm.gov.au/collection/C283448.

27 *The Australian Women's Weekly*, 20 October 1945, p. 17, https://trove.nla.gov.au/newspaper/article/51281493.

28 Parkin, *Wartime Trilogy*, p. 441.

29 Ebury, *Weary: The Life of Sir Edward Dunlop*, p. 422.

30 Tom Uren, Transcript of interview, UNSW Australians at War Film Archive, 11 August 2003, http://australiansatwarfilmarchive.unsw.edu.au/archive/728.

31 Thomas Young (Tom), Transcript of interview, UNSW Australians at War Film Archive, 8 October 2003, https://australiansatwarfilmarchive.unsw.edu.au/archive/1021.

32 Tom Uren, Transcript of interview, UNSW Australians at War Film Archive, 11 August 2003, http://australiansatwarfilmarchive.unsw.edu.au/archive/728.

33 Tom Uren, Transcript of interview, UNSW Australians at War Film Archive, 11 August 2003, http://australiansatwarfilmarchive.unsw.edu.au/archive/728.

34 Tom Uren, Transcript of interview, UNSW Australians at War Film Archive, 11 August 2003, http://australiansatwarfilmarchive.unsw.edu.au/archive/728.

35 Thomas Young (Tom), Transcript of interview, UNSW Australians at War Film Archive, 8 October 2003, https://australiansatwarfilmarchive.unsw.edu.au/archive/1021.

36 Dunlop, *The War Diaries of Weary Dunlop*, 21 July 1943, p. 264.

37 Sir Ernest Edward 'Weary' Dunlop interviewed by Dr Hank Nelson, Australian War Memorial, https://www.awm.gov.au/collection/C283448.

38 Wright, *The Men of the Line: Stories of the Thai–Burma Railway Survivors*, p. 58 [reported speech].

39 Wright, *The Men of the Line: Stories of the Thai–Burma Railway Survivors*, p. 58.

40 Wright, *The Men of the Line: Stories of the Thai–Burma Railway Survivors*, p. 58.

41 Wright, *The Men of the Line: Stories of the Thai–Burma Railway Survivors*, p. 58.

42 Wright, *The Men of the Line: Stories of the Thai–Burma Railway Survivors*, p. 90.

43 Wright, *The Men of the Line: Stories of the Thai–Burma Railway Survivors*, p. 91.

44 Parkin, *Wartime Trilogy*, p. 517.

45 Parkin, *Wartime Trilogy*, p. 517.

46 Parkin, *Wartime Trilogy*, p. 517.

47 Dunlop, *The War Diaries of Weary Dunlop*, 13 July 1943, p. 259.

48 Eiji Hirota, War Crimes Military Tribunal, National Archives of Australia, Series No. A471, Item ID, 722378.

49 Eiji Hirota, War Crimes Military Tribunal, National Archives of Australia, Series No. A471, Item ID, 722378.

50 Eiji Hirota, War Crimes Military Tribunal, National Archives of Australia, Series No. A471, Item ID, 722378.

51 Dunlop, *The War Diaries of Weary Dunlop*, 26 June 1943, p. 251.

52 Dunlop, *The War Diaries of Weary Dunlop*, 24 June 1943, p. 250.

53 *The Canberra Times*, 15 February 1995, p. 40.

54 *The Canberra Times*, 15 February 1995, p. 40.

55 *The Canberra Times*, 15 February 1995, p. 40.

56 Dunlop, 'Medical Experiences in Japanese Captivity', *British Medical Journal*, 5 October 1946, p. 484, https://pmc.ncbi.nlm.nih.gov/articles/PMC2057680/.

57 Milton Butterworth (Blue), Transcript of interview, UNSW Australians at War Film Archive, 21 November 2003, http://australiansatwarfilmarchive.unsw.edu.au/archive/906.

58 Milton Butterworth (Blue), Transcript of interview, UNSW Australians at War Film Archive, 21 November 2003 [reported speech], http://australiansatwarfilmarchive.unsw.edu.au/archive/906.

59 *The Sydney Morning Herald*, 3 November 2012 [reported speech], https://www.smh.com.au/national/no-cup-bet-this-year-in-memory-of-a-true-blue-20121102-28p1j.html.

60 Speech by Andrew Corlette, The Australian Ex-Prisoners of War Memorial, Ballarat, Victoria, 2018, https://www.powmemorialballarat.com.au/2018-andrew-corlette/.

61 *The Australian Women's Weekly*, 20 October 1945, p. 17, https://trove.nla.gov.au/newspaper/article/51281493.

62 Milton Butterworth (Blue), Transcript of interview, UNSW Australians at War Film Archive, 21 November 2003, http://australiansatwarfilmarchive.unsw.edu.au/archive/906.

63 Milton Butterworth (Blue), Transcript of interview, UNSW Australians at War Film Archive, 21 November 2003, http://australiansatwarfilmarchive.unsw.edu.au/archive/906.

64 'VX48789 KAPPE, Lt. Col Charles Henry "Gus" – C.O. "F" Force Thailand, Australian POWs', 2/4th Machine Gun Battalion Ex Members Association, 18 June 2023, https://2nd4thmgb.com.au/story/kappe-lt-col-charles-henry-f-force-thailand/.

65 'VX48789 KAPPE, Lt. Col Charles Henry "Gus" – C.O. "F" Force Thailand, Australian POWs', 2/4th Machine Gun Battalion Ex Members Association, 18 June 2023, https://2nd4thmgb.com.au/story/kappe-lt-col-charles-henry-f-force-thailand/.

66 Paper written by Ewan Corlette's son, Andrew, in 2015, sent to the author.

67 Sir Ernest Edward 'Weary' Dunlop interviewed by Dr Hank Nelson, Australian War Memorial, https://www.awm.gov.au/collection/C283448.

68 Tom Uren, Transcript of interview, UNSW Australians at War Film Archive, 11 August 2003, http://australiansatwarfilmarchive.unsw.edu.au/archive/728.

69 *The Canberra Times*, 15 February 1995, p. 40.

70 *Daily Mail*, 27 February 2010.

71 Tom Uren, Transcript of interview, UNSW Australians at War Film Archive, 11 August 2003, http://australiansatwarfilmarchive.unsw.edu.au/archive/728.

72 *Daily Mail*, 27 February 2010.

73 Dunlop, *The War Diaries of Weary Dunlop*, 18 July 1943, p. 261.

74 Geddes, *Remembering Weary*, p. 163.

75 Wright, *Ray Parkin's Odyssey*, p. 380.

76 Wright, *Ray Parkin's Odyssey*, p. 380.

77 'The Australian Prisoners' Accounts', Department of Veterans' Affairs, Anzac Portal, https://anzacportal.dva.gov.au/wars-and-missions/burma-thailand-railway-and-hellfire-pass-1942-1943/resources/australian-prisoners-accounts.

78 Wright, *The Men of the Line: Stories of the Thai–Burma Railway Survivors*, p. 175.

79 Raymond 'Ray' Edward Parkin: Interviews for the Channel 10 program, *Surgeon of the Railway*, 1987, Australian War Memorial, https://www.awm.gov.au/collection/F09396.

80 *The Australian Women's Weekly*, 20 October 1945, p. 17, https://trove.nla.gov.au/newspaper/article/51281493.

81 Parkin, *Wartime Trilogy*, p. 541.

82 Parkin, *Wartime Trilogy*, p. 542.

83 Wright, *Ray Parkin's Odyssey*, p. 402.

84 Parkin, *Wartime Trilogy*, p. 542.

85 Raymond 'Ray' Edward Parkin: Interviews for the Channel 10 program, *Surgeon of the Railway*, 1987, Australian War Memorial, https://www.awm.gov.au/collection/F09396.

86 *The Sydney Morning Herald*, 25 April 1991.

87 Raymond 'Ray' Edward Parkin: Interviews for the Channel 10 program, *Surgeon of the Railway*, 1987, Australian War Memorial, https://www.awm.gov.au/collection/F09396.

88 Raymond 'Ray' Edward Parkin: Interviews for the Channel 10 program, *Surgeon of the Railway*, 1987, Australian War Memorial, https://www.awm.gov.au/collection/F09396.

89 Nelson, *POW. Prisoners of War: Australians Under Nippon*, p. 56.

90 Raymond 'Ray' Edward Parkin: Interviews for the Channel 10 program, *Surgeon of the Railway*, 1987, Australian War Memorial, https://www.awm.gov.au/collection/F09396.

91 Raymond 'Ray' Edward Parkin: Interviews for the Channel 10 program, *Surgeon of the Railway*, 1987, Australian War Memorial, https://www.awm.gov.au/collection/F09396.

92 Dunlop, *The War Diaries of Weary Dunlop*, 19 July 1943, p. 263.

93 Dunlop, *The War Diaries of Weary Dunlop*, 19 July 1943, p. 263.

94 Sir Ernest Edward 'Weary' Dunlop interviewed by Dr Hank Nelson, Australian War Memorial, https://www.awm.gov.au/collection/C283448.

95 Sir Ernest Edward 'Weary' Dunlop interviewed by Dr Hank Nelson, Australian War Memorial, https://www.awm.gov.au/collection/C283448.

96 Sir Ernest Edward 'Weary' Dunlop interviewed by Dr Hank Nelson, Australian War Memorial, https://www.awm.gov.au/collection/C283448.

97 *The Quiet Lions*, documentary, directed by Robin Newell, 2008 [reported speech].

98 Raymond 'Ray' Edward Parkin: Interviews for the Channel 10 program, *Surgeon of the Railway*, 1987, Australian War Memorial, https://www.awm.gov.au/collection/F09396.

99 Nelson, *POW. Prisoners of War: Australians Under Nippon*, p. 49.

100 Sir Ernest Edward 'Weary' Dunlop interviewed by Dr Hank Nelson, Australian War Memorial, https://www.awm.gov.au/collection/C283448.

101 Wright, *The Men of the Line: Stories of the Thai–Burma Railway Survivors*, p. 3.

102 Dunlop, 'Medical Experiences in Japanese Captivity', *British Medical Journal*, 5 October 1946, p. 484, https://pmc.ncbi.nlm.nih.gov/articles/PMC2057680/.

103 McCormack and Nelson, *The Burma–Thailand Railway*, p. 32.

104 *The Canberra Times*, 18 May 1991, p. 19, https://trove.nla.gov.au/newspaper/article/122363608.

105 Milton Butterworth (Blue), Transcript of interview, UNSW Australians at War Film Archive, 21 November 2003, http://australiansatwarfilmarchive.unsw.edu.au/archive/906.

106 *The Australian Women's Weekly*, 20 October 1945, p. 17, https://trove.nla.gov.au/newspaper/article/51281493.

107 *The Australian Women's Weekly*, 20 October 1945, p. 17, https://trove.nla.gov.au/newspaper/article/51281493.

108 Wright, *The Men of the Line: Stories of the Thai–Burma Railway Survivors*, p. 17.

109 Dunlop, *The War Diaries of Weary Dunlop*, 20 September 1943, p. 286.

110 Dunlop, *The War Diaries of Weary Dunlop*, 14 October 1943, p. 295.

111 Dunlop, *The War Diaries of Weary Dunlop*, 3 August 1943, p. 269.

112 Dunlop, *The War Diaries of Weary Dunlop*, 8 August 1943, p. 271.

113 Tom Uren, Transcript of interview, UNSW Australians at War Film Archive, 11 August 2003, http://australiansatwarfilmarchive.unsw.edu.au/archive/728.

114 Tom Uren, Transcript of interview, UNSW Australians at War Film Archive, 11 August 2003, http://australiansatwarfilmarchive.unsw.edu.au/archive/728.

115 Wright, *The Men of the Line: Stories of the Thai–Burma Railway Survivors*, p. 17.

116 Dunlop, *The War Diaries of Weary Dunlop*, 20 August 1943, p. 276.

Chapter Fifteen

1 Parkin, *Wartime Trilogy*, p. 421.

2 Ernie Badham, 2/2nd CCS, Prisoner of War Account, p. 1, https://www.burmarailway.com.au/page-1.

3 Ernie Badham, 2/2nd CCS, Prisoner of War Account, p. 1, https://www.burmarailway.com.au/page-1.

4 Dunlop, *The War Diaries of Weary Dunlop*, 3 October 1943, p. 294.

5 Dunlop, *The War Diaries of Weary Dunlop*, 3 October 1943, p. 294.

6 Dunlop, *The War Diaries of Weary Dunlop*, 11 October 1943, p. 294.

7 Wright, *The Men of the Line: Stories of the Thai–Burma Railway Survivors*, p. 164.

8 Wright, *The Men of the Line: Stories of the Thai–Burma Railway Survivors*, p. 164.

9 Wright, *The Men of the Line: Stories of the Thai–Burma Railway Survivors*, p. 106 [reported speech].

10 Dunlop, *The War Diaries of Weary Dunlop*, 5 November 1943, p. 302.

11 Dunlop, *The War Diaries of Weary Dunlop*, 16 May 1943, p. 230.

12 Dunlop, *The War Diaries of Weary Dunlop*, 25 October 1943, p. 298.

13 Jack Chalker: Interviews for the Channel 10 program, *Surgeon of the Railway*, 1987, Australian War Memorial, https://www.awm.gov.au/collection/C1290394.

14 *The Australian Women's Weekly*, 20 October 1945, p. 17, https://trove.nla.gov.au/newspaper/article/51281493.

15 *The Australian Women's Weekly*, 20 October 1945, p. 17, https://trove.nla.gov.au/newspaper/article/51281493.

16 *The Australian Women's Weekly*, 20 October 1945, p. 17, https://trove.nla.gov.au/newspaper/article/51281493.

17 Dunlop, *The War Diaries of Weary Dunlop*, 5 November 1943, p. 302.

18 Dunlop, *The War Diaries of Weary Dunlop*, 5 November 1943, p. 302.

19 Dunlop, *The War Diaries of Weary Dunlop*, 5 November 1943, p. 303.

20 Author's note: Though the formal word for four is *'shi'*, it also means death and the Japanese of that era avoided saying it when counting. They used *'yon'* instead, another word for four.

21 Dunlop, *The War Diaries of Weary Dunlop*, 5 November 1943, p. 303.

22 Dunlop, *The War Diaries of Weary Dunlop*, 5 November 1943, p. 304.

23 Dunlop, *The War Diaries of Weary Dunlop*, 5 November 1943, p. 304.

24 Dunlop, *The War Diaries of Weary Dunlop*, 5 November 1943, p. 304.

25 Dunlop, *The War Diaries of Weary Dunlop*, 5 November 1943, p. 304.

26 Dunlop, *The War Diaries of Weary Dunlop*, 5 November 1943, p. 304.

27 Dunlop, *The War Diaries of Weary Dunlop*, 5 November 1943, p. 304.

28 *This is Your Life*, Sir Edward Dunlop, 23 June 1979, https://www.iwm.org.uk/collections/item/object/80012508.

29 Wright, *The Men of the Line: Stories of the Thai–Burma Railway Survivors*, p. 137.

30 Nelson, *POW. Prisoners of War: Australians Under Nippon*, p. 34.

31 Nelson, *POW. Prisoners of War: Australians Under Nippon*, p. 68.

32 Christie, *A History of the 2/29 Battalion – 8th Australian Division*, AIF, 1983, first edition, p. 122.

33 Ford-Gaden, 'Memory and Heritage', https://secondtwentiethbattalionaif.wordpress.com/prisoner-of-war-pow/memory-and-heritage/.

34 Dunlop, *The War Diaries of Weary Dunlop*, 25 October 1943, p. 298.

35 Dunlop, *The War Diaries of Weary Dunlop*, 30 December 1943, p. 317.

36 Dunlop, *The War Diaries of Weary Dunlop*, 17 January 1944, p. 322.

37 'The Colonel & the Bombardier, Sir Edward "Weary" Dunlop, artist Jack Bridger Chalker', https://www.cofepow.org.uk/armed-forces-stories-list/the-colonel-the-bombardier.

38 'The Colonel & the Bombardier, Sir Edward "Weary" Dunlop, artist Jack Bridger Chalker', https://www.cofepow.org.uk/armed-forces-stories-list/the-colonel-the-bombardier.

39 'The Colonel & the Bombardier, Sir Edward "Weary" Dunlop, artist Jack Bridger Chalker, https://www.cofepow.org.uk/armed-forces-stories-list/the-colonel-the-bombardier.

40 Raymond 'Ray' Edward Parkin: Interviews for the Channel 10 program, *Surgeon of the Railway*, 1987, Australian War Memorial, https://www.awm.gov.au/collection/F09396.
41 Parkin, *Wartime Trilogy*, p. 637.
42 Parkin, *Wartime Trilogy*, p. 637.
43 Parkin, *Wartime Trilogy*, p. 637.
44 Parkin, *Wartime Trilogy*, p. 637.
45 Parkin, *Wartime Trilogy*, p. 637.
46 Parkin, *Wartime Trilogy*, p. 637.
47 Parkin, *Wartime Trilogy*, p. 637.
48 Wright, *The Men of the Line: Stories of the Thai–Burma Railway Survivors*, p. 47.
49 McCormack and Nelson, *The Burma–Thailand Railway*, p. 38.
50 Wright, *The Men of the Line: Stories of the Thai–Burma Railway Survivors*, p. 110.
51 Thomas Young (Tom), Transcript of interview, UNSW Australians at War Film Archive, 8 October 2003, https://australiansatwarfilmarchive.unsw.edu.au/archive/1021.
52 Thomas Young (Tom), Transcript of interview, UNSW Australians at War Film Archive, 8 October 2003, https://australiansatwarfilmarchive.unsw.edu.au/archive/1021.
53 Thomas Young (Tom), Transcript of interview, UNSW Australians at War Film Archive, 8 October 2003, https://australiansatwarfilmarchive.unsw.edu.au/archive/1021.
54 Parkin, *Wartime Trilogy*, p. 634.
55 Wright, *Ray Parkin's Odyssey*, p. 399.
56 Wright, *Ray Parkin's Odyssey*, p. 399.
57 Raymond 'Ray' Edward Parkin: Interviews for the Channel 10 program, *Surgeon of the Railway*, 1987, Australian War Memorial, https://www.awm.gov.au/collection/F09396.
58 Ray Parkin, Transcript of interview, UNSW Australians at War Film Archive, 7 June 2000 [reported speech], https://australiansatwarfilmarchive.unsw.edu.au/archive/2552.
59 Dunlop, *The War Diaries of Weary Dunlop*, 12 June 1944, p. 359.
60 *The Australian Women's Weekly*, 20 October 1945, p. 17, https://trove.nla.gov.au/newspaper/article/51281493.

Chapter Sixteen

1 Coates, 'Clinical Lessons from Prisoner of War Hospitals in the Far East (Burma and Siam)', *The Medical Journal of Australia*, June 1946, p. 757, https://onlinelibrary.wiley.com/doi/abs/10.5694/j.1326-5377.1946.tb33884.x.
2 Coates, 'Clinical Lessons from Prisoner of War Hospitals in the Far East (Burma and Siam)', *The Medical Journal of Australia*, June 1946, p. 757, https://onlinelibrary.wiley.com/doi/abs/10.5694/j.1326-5377.1946.tb33884.x.
3 Coates and Rosenthal, *The Albert Coates Story*, Hyland House, Melbourne, 1977, p. 185.
4 Dunlop, 'Medical Experiences in Japanese Captivity', *British Medical Journal*, 5 October 1946, p. 486, https://pmc.ncbi.nlm.nih.gov/articles/PMC2057680/.
5 *The Advertiser*, 22 June 1946, p. 5.
6 Jack Chalker: Interviews for the Channel 10 program, *Surgeon of the Railway*, 1987, Australian War Memorial, https://www.awm.gov.au/collection/C1290394.

7   Tom Uren, Transcript of interview, UNSW Australians at War Film Archive, 11 August 2003, http://australiansatwarfilmarchive.unsw.edu.au/archive/728.

8   *The Canberra Times*, 15 February 1995, p. 40.

9   McCormack and Nelson, *The Burma–Thailand Railway*, p. 149 [reported speech].

10 Milton Butterworth (Blue), Transcript of interview, UNSW Australians at War Film Archive, 21 November 2003, http://australiansatwarfilmarchive.unsw.edu.au/archive/906.

11 Swanton, 'Cricket under the Japs', Wisden, 1946, https://www.espncricinfo.com/wisdenalmanack/content/story/152863.html.

12 Swanton, 'Cricket under the Japs', Wisden, 1946, https://www.espncricinfo.com/wisdenalmanack/content/story/152863.html.

13 Swanton, 'Cricket under the Japs', Wisden, 1946, https://www.espncricinfo.com/wisdenalmanack/content/story/152863.html.

14 Swanton, 'Cricket under the Japs', Wisden, 1946, https://www.espncricinfo.com/wisdenalmanack/content/story/152863.html.

15 Swanton, 'Cricket under the Japs', Wisden, 1946, https://www.espncricinfo.com/wisdenalmanack/content/story/152863.html.

16 Swanton, 'Cricket under the Japs', Wisden, 1946, https://www.espncricinfo.com/wisdenalmanack/content/story/152863.html.

17 Swanton, 'Cricket under the Japs', Wisden, 1946, https://www.espncricinfo.com/wisdenalmanack/content/story/152863.html.

18 Milton Butterworth (Blue), Transcript of interview, UNSW Australians at War Film Archive, 21 November 2003, http://australiansatwarfilmarchive.unsw.edu.au/archive/906.

19 Milton Butterworth (Blue), Transcript of interview, UNSW Australians at War Film Archive, 21 November 2003, http://australiansatwarfilmarchive.unsw.edu.au/archive/906.

20 Dunlop, *The War Diaries of Weary Dunlop*, 6 July 1945, p. 430.

21 Dunlop, *The War Diaries of Weary Dunlop*, 6 July 1945, p. 430.

22 Dunlop, *The War Diaries of Weary Dunlop*, 6 July 1945, p. 430.

23 Dunlop, *The War Diaries of Weary Dunlop*, 6 July 1945, p. 430.

24 Dunlop, *The War Diaries of Weary Dunlop*, 6 July 1945, p. 430.

25 Dunlop, *The War Diaries of Weary Dunlop*, 6 July 1945, p. 430.

26 Dunlop, *The War Diaries of Weary Dunlop*, 6 July 1945, pp. 430–431.

27 Dunlop, *The War Diaries of Weary Dunlop*, 6 July 1945, p. 431.

28 Dunlop, *The War Diaries of Weary Dunlop*, 6 July 1945, p. 431.

29 Dunlop, *The War Diaries of Weary Dunlop*, 6 July 1945, p. 431.

30 Dunlop, *The War Diaries of Weary Dunlop*, 6 July 1945, p. 431.

31 Dunlop, *The War Diaries of Weary Dunlop*, 6 July 1945, p. 431.

32 Sides, *Ghost Soldiers: The Epic Account of World War II's Greatest Rescue Mission*, Knopf Doubleday Publishing Group, 2002, pp. 23–24.

33 Wright, *The Men of the Line: Stories of the Thai–Burma Railway Survivors*, p. 152.

34 Paul Tibbets interview, AVWeb, 14 June 2019, https://www.avweb.com/features/paul-tibbets-interview/.

35 Peter Williams, *Japan's Pacific War*, Pen & Sword Books, 2021, p. 158.

36 Williams, *Japan's Pacific War*, p. 158.

37 Ray Parkin, Transcript of interview, UNSW Australians at War Film Archive, 7 June 2000, https://australiansatwarfilmarchive.unsw.edu.au/archive/2552.

38 Ray Parkin, Transcript of interview, UNSW Australians at War Film Archive, 7 June 2000, https://australiansatwarfilmarchive.unsw.edu.au/archive/2552.

39 Tom Uren, Transcript of interview, UNSW Australians at War Film Archive, 11 August 2003, http://australiansatwarfilmarchive.unsw.edu.au/archive/728.

40 Tom Uren, Transcript of interview, UNSW Australians at War Film Archive, 11 August 2003, http://australiansatwarfilmarchive.unsw.edu.au/archive/728.

41 Williams, *Japan's Pacific War*, p. 158.

42 Ebury, *Weary: The Life of Sir Edward Dunlop*, p. 503.

43 Dunlop, *The War Diaries of Weary Dunlop*, 14 August 1945, p. 380.

44 Dunlop, *The War Diaries of Weary Dunlop*, 14 August 1945, p. 380.

45 Dunlop, *The War Diaries of Weary Dunlop*, 15 August 1945, p. 380.

46 Wright, *The Men of the Line: Stories of the Thai–Burma Railway Survivors*, p. 150.

47 Speech by Andrew Corlette, The Australian Ex-Prisoners of War Memorial, Ballarat, Victoria, 2018 [reported speech], https://www.powmemorialballarat.com.au/2018-andrew-corlette/.

48 Dunlop, *The War Diaries of Weary Dunlop*, 16 August 1945, p. 381.

49 Dunlop, *The War Diaries of Weary Dunlop*, 16 August 1945, p. 381.

50 Dunlop, *The War Diaries of Weary Dunlop*, p. 381.

51 Coates and Rosenthal, *The Albert Coates Story*, p. 140.

52 Coates and Rosenthal, *The Albert Coates Story*, p. 140.

53 Coates and Rosenthal, *The Albert Coates Story*, p. 140.

54 Dunlop, *The War Diaries of Weary Dunlop*, 16 August 1945, p. 380.

55 Coates and Rosenthal, *The Albert Coates Story*, p. 141.

56 Dunlop, *The War Diaries of Weary Dunlop*, p. 381.

57 Dunlop, *The War Diaries of Weary Dunlop*, p. 381. Author's note: I suspect Weary was getting this quote mixed up with a similar quote from Oscar Wilde. Or perhaps he was thinking of the Duke of Wellington who said, 'Only a battle lost can be close to as sad as a battle won'.

58 Dunlop, *The War Diaries of Weary Dunlop*, p. 381.

59 Coates and Rosenthal, *The Albert Coates Story*, p. 133.

60 Dunlop, *The War Diaries of Weary Dunlop*, 16 August 1945, p. 381.

61 Coates and Rosenthal, *The Albert Coates Story*, p. 142.

62 Paper written by Ewan Corlette's son, Andrew, in 2015, sent to the author.

63 Geddes, *Remembering Weary*, p. 86.

64 WW2, People's War, Archive of World War Two Memories, BBC Home, https://www.bbc.co.uk/history/ww2peopleswar/stories/39/a4170539.shtml.

65 Sir Ernest Edward 'Weary' Dunlop interviewed by Dr Hank Nelson, Australian War Memorial, https://www.awm.gov.au/collection/C283448.

66 Ebury, *Weary: The Life of Sir Edward Dunlop*, p. 509.

67 Ebury, *Weary: The Life of Sir Edward Dunlop*, p. 509.

68 Ebury, *Weary: The Life of Sir Edward Dunlop*, p. 509.

69 Geddes, *Remembering Weary*, p. 141.

70 Sir Ernest Edward 'Weary' Dunlop interviewed by Dr Hank Nelson, Australian War Memorial, https://www.awm.gov.au/collection/C283448.

71 Dunlop, *The War Diaries of Weary Dunlop*, 5 November 1943, pp. 304–305.

72 Sir Ernest Edward 'Weary' Dunlop interviewed by Dr Hank Nelson, Australian War Memorial, https://www.awm.gov.au/collection/C283448.

73 Sir Ernest Edward 'Weary' Dunlop interviewed by Dr Hank Nelson, Australian War Memorial, https://www.awm.gov.au/collection/C283448.

74 Sir Ernest Edward 'Weary' Dunlop interviewed by Dr Hank Nelson, Australian War Memorial, https://www.awm.gov.au/collection/C283448.

75 Sir Ernest Edward 'Weary' Dunlop interviewed by Dr Hank Nelson, Australian War Memorial, https://www.awm.gov.au/collection/C283448.

76 Wright, *The Men of the Line: Stories of the Thai–Burma Railway Survivors*, p. 5.
77 Author interview, with Wright, Mornington Peninsula, 27 January 2025.
78 Dunlop, *The War Diaries of Weary Dunlop*, p. 9.
79 Dunlop, *The War Diaries of Weary Dunlop*, p. 9.
80 Ebury, *Weary: The Life of Sir Edward Dunlop*, p. 519 [reported speech].
81 Geddes, *Remembering Weary*, p. 346.
82 Geddes, *Remembering Weary*, p. 365.
83 Geddes, *Remembering Weary*, p. 346.
84 Letter, Edward Dunlop to Helen Ferguson, 23 September 1945, Papers of
    Sir Edward 'Weary' Dunlop, PR00926, item 1/30, AWM.
85 Telegram, Edward Dunlop to Helen Ferguson, 13 October 1945, Papers of
    Sir Edward 'Weary' Dunlop, PR00926, item 1/30, Australian War Memorial.
86 *The Australian Women's Weekly*, 20 October 1945, p. 17, https://trove.nla.gov.au/
    newspaper/article/51281493.
87 *The Australian Women's Weekly*, 20 October 1945, p. 17, https://trove.nla.gov.au/
    newspaper/article/51281493.
88 Milton Butterworth (Blue), Transcript of interview, UNSW Australians at War
    Film Archive, 21 November 2003, http://australiansatwarfilmarchive.unsw.edu.au/
    archive/906.
89 Ebury, *Weary: The Life of Sir Edward Dunlop*, p. 529.
90 Ebury, *Weary: The Life of Sir Edward Dunlop*, p. 529.
91 Ebury, *Weary: The Life of Sir Edward Dunlop*, p. 527.
92 Ebury, *Weary: The Life of Sir Edward Dunlop*, p. 530.
93 Ebury, *Weary: The Life of Sir Edward Dunlop*, p. 530.
94 Ebury, *Weary: The Life of Sir Edward Dunlop*, p. 530.
95 Milton Butterworth (Blue), Transcript of interview, UNSW Australians at War
    Film Archive, 21 November 2003, http://australiansatwarfilmarchive.unsw.edu.au/
    archive/906.
96 Milton Butterworth (Blue), Transcript of interview, UNSW Australians at War
    Film Archive, 21 November 2003, http://australiansatwarfilmarchive.unsw.edu.au/
    archive/906.
97 Geddes, *Remembering Weary*, p. 143.
98 Ebury, *Weary: The Life of Sir Edward Dunlop*, p. 532.

Epilogue

1 Raymond 'Ray' Edward Parkin: Interviews for the Channel 10 program, *Surgeon of
   the Railway*, 1987, Australian War Memorial, https://www.awm.gov.au/collection/
   F09396.
2 Ebury, *Weary: The Life of Sir Edward Dunlop*, p. 533.
3 Park, 'The Survivor: Last Korean War Criminal in Japan Wants Recognition',
   Thomson Reuters, 4 August 2020, https://www.reuters.com/article/world/the-
   survivor-last-korean-war-criminal-in-japan-wants-recognition-idUSKCN2500B7/.
4 *The Canberra Times*, 15 February 1995, p. 40.
5 War Crimes Military Tribunal, Hiromura Kakurai, Singapore, 18 and 20 March
   1947, Item ID. 721743, Series No. A471, National Archives of Australia.
6 Green, 'Boon Pong – and Other Forgotten Heroes', Green Writing Room,
   12 January 2024, https://greenwritingroom.com/2014/01/12/boon-pong-and-other-
   forgotten-heroes/.
7 *Benalla Ensign*, 21 June 1946, p. 6, https://trove.nla.gov.au/newspaper/
   article/65565403.

8   *Benalla Ensign*, 21 June 1946, p. 6, https://trove.nla.gov.au/newspaper/article/65565403.

9   Geddes, *Remembering Weary*, p. 155.

10 Tom Uren, Transcript of interview, UNSW Australians at War Film Archive, 11 August 2003, http://australiansatwarfilmarchive.unsw.edu.au/archive/728.

11 Ebury, *Weary: The Life of Sir Edward Dunlop*, p. 554.

12 Geddes, *Remembering Weary*, p. 144.

13 Ray Parkin, Transcript of interview, UNSW Australians at War Film Archive, 7 June 2000, https://australiansatwarfilmarchive.unsw.edu.au/archive/2552.

14 Parkin, *Wartime Trilogy*, p. 361.

15 Parkin, *Wartime Trilogy*, p. 634.

16 Milton Butterworth (Blue), Transcript of interview, UNSW Australians at War Film Archive, 21 November 2003, http://australiansatwarfilmarchive.unsw.edu.au/archive/906.

17 *The Canberra Times*, 10 December 1960, p. 1, https://trove.nla.gov.au/newspaper/article/103111982.

18 *The Canberra Times*, 10 December 1960, p. 1, https://trove.nla.gov.au/newspaper/article/103111982.

19 *The Canberra Times*, 10 December 1960, p. 1, https://trove.nla.gov.au/newspaper/article/103111982.

20 *The Canberra Times*, 10 December 1960, p. 1, https://trove.nla.gov.au/newspaper/article/103111982.

21 *The Canberra Times*, 20 January 1961, p. 5, https://trove.nla.gov.au/newspaper/article/133926531/15105474.

22 *The Canberra Times*, 20 January 1961, p. 5, https://trove.nla.gov.au/newspaper/article/133926531/15105474.

23 Paper written by Ewan Corlette's son, Andrew, in 2015, sent to the author.

24 Paper written by Ewan Corlette's son, Andrew, in 2015, sent to the author.

25 Geddes, *Remembering Weary*, p. 158.

26 Marshall, '"Weary" Dunlop: Surgeon', *Australian and New Zealand Journal of Surgery*, January 1994, https://doi.org/10.1111/j.1445-2197.1994.tb02129.x.

27 Geddes, *Remembering Weary*, p. 217.

28 Marshall, '"Weary" Dunlop: Surgeon', *Australian and New Zealand Journal of Surgery*, January 1994, https://doi.org/10.1111/j.1445-2197.1994.tb02129.x.

29 Geddes, *Remembering Weary*, p. 217.

30 Geddes, *Remembering Weary*, p. 378.

31 Geddes, *Remembering Weary*, p. 382.

32 Raymond 'Ray' Edward Parkin: Interviews for the Channel 10 program, *Surgeon of the Railway*, 1987, Australian War Memorial, https://www.awm.gov.au/collection/F09396.

33 Geddes, *Remembering Weary*, p. 246.

34 McCormack, 'Yi Hak-Nae and the Burma–Thailand Railway', *Asia-Pacific Journal: Japan Focus*, Vol. 19, Issue 15, No. 1, August 2021, https://apjjf.org/2021/15/mccormack.

35 Ebury, *Weary: The Life of Sir Edward Dunlop*, p. 420.

36 Ebury, *Weary: The Life of Sir Edward Dunlop*, p. 420.

37 *The Herald*, 9 November 1946, p. 7, https://trove.nla.gov.au/newspaper/article/245378292.

38 Flanagan, 'For Tom Uren: "You were a champion, Tom. You're in the company of legends now"', 4 February 2015, https://speakola.com/eulogy/-tom-uren-martin-flanagan-2015.

39 Tom Uren (ALP-Reid) – Maiden Speech, 26 February 1959, https://
    australianpolitics.com/1959/02/26/tom-uren-alp-reid-maiden-speech.html/.
40 Tom Uren, Transcript of interview, UNSW Australians at War Film Archive,
    11 August 2003, http://australiansatwarfilmarchive.unsw.edu.au/archive/728.
41 Tom Uren, Transcript of interview, UNSW Australians at War Film Archive,
    11 August 2003, http://australiansatwarfilmarchive.unsw.edu.au/archive/728.
42 Tom Uren, Transcript of interview, UNSW Australians at War Film Archive,
    11 August 2003, http://australiansatwarfilmarchive.unsw.edu.au/archive/728.
43 *The Sydney Morning Herald*, 4 February 2015, https://www.smh.com.au/national/
    nsw/tom-uren--boxer-pow-and-workingclass-hero-20150204-135n3v.html.
44 *The Sydney Morning Herald*, 27 May 2022, https://www.smh.com.au/national/i-
    love-the-boy-the-gift-our-pm-received-from-a-bamboo-prison-20220526-p5aotw.
    html.
45 *The Sydney Morning Herald*, 27 May 2022, https://www.smh.com.au/national/i-
    love-the-boy-the-gift-our-pm-received-from-a-bamboo-prison-20220526-p5aotw.
    html.
46 Geddes, *Remembering Weary*, p. 163.
47 *This is Your Life*, Sir Edward Dunlop, 23 June 1979, https://www.iwm.org.uk/
    collections/item/object/80012508.
48 *This is Your Life*, Sir Edward Dunlop, 23 June 1979, https://www.iwm.org.uk/
    collections/item/object/80012508.
49 *This is Your Life*, Sir Edward Dunlop, 23 June 1979, https://www.iwm.org.uk/
    collections/item/object/80012508.
50 Geddes, *Remembering Weary*, p. 184.
51 Author interview with John Dunlop, 23 February 2025.
52 Author interview with John Dunlop, 23 February 2025.
53 *This is Your Life*, Sir Edward Dunlop, 23 June 1979, https://www.iwm.org.uk/
    collections/item/object/80012508.
54 Ebury, *Weary: The Life of Sir Edward Dunlop*, p. 574.
55 'The Colonel & the Bombardier, Sir Edward "Weary" Dunlop, artist Jack
    Bridger Chalker', https://www.cofepow.org.uk/armed-forces-stories-list/
    the-colonel-the-bombardier.
56 Dunlop, *The War Diaries of Weary Dunlop*, Preface, p. xvii.
57 *Daily Telegraph* (London), 22 September 2001.
58 Jones, *Storyteller: The Many Lives of Laurens van der Post*, p. 363.
59 'Report by Allied Joint Planning Staff, 4 October 1945', cited in Kratoska (ed.),
    The Thailand–Burma Railway, 1942–1946, Documents and Selected Writings,
    Vol. II, London, Routledge, 2006, p. 126.
60 Tom Uren, Transcript of interview, UNSW Australians at War Film Archive,
    11 August 2003, http://australiansatwarfilmarchive.unsw.edu.au/archive/728.
61 *The Sydney Morning Herald*, 27 May 2022, https://www.smh.com.au/national/i-
    love-the-boy-the-gift-our-pm-received-from-a-bamboo-prison-20220526-p5aotw.
    html.
62 Tom Uren, AC Memorial Lecture, 20 June 2021, https://anthonyalbanese.com.au/
    media-centre/tom-uren-ac-memorial-lecture-20-june-2021.
63 *The Sydney Morning Herald*, 27 May 2022, https://www.smh.com.au/national/i-
    love-the-boy-the-gift-our-pm-received-from-a-bamboo-prison-20220526-p5aotw.
    html.
64 Tom Uren, Transcript of interview, UNSW Australians at War Film Archive,
    11 August 2003, http://australiansatwarfilmarchive.unsw.edu.au/archive/728.

65 McCormack, 'Yi Hak-Nae and the Burma–Thailand Railway', *Asia-Pacific Journal: Japan Focus*, Vol. 19, Issue 15, No. 1, August 2021, https://apjjf.org/2021/15/mccormack.

66 Ebury, *Weary: The Life of Sir Edward Dunlop*, p. 636.

67 McCormack and Nelson, *The Burma–Thailand Railway*, p. 5.

68 McCormack, 'Yi Hak-Nae and the Burma–Thailand Railway', *Asia-Pacific Journal: Japan Focus*, Vol. 19, Issue 15, No. 1, August 2021, https://apjjf.org/2021/15/mccormack.

69 Ebury, *Weary: The Life of Sir Edward Dunlop*, p. 637.

70 Ebury, *Weary: The Life of Sir Edward Dunlop*, p. 637.

71 *The Sydney Morning Herald*, 25 April 1991.

72 *The Canberra Times*, 18 May 1991, p. 19.

73 *The Canberra Times*, 18 May 1991, p. 19.

74 *The Sydney Morning Herald*, 25 April 1991.

75 *Royal Australian Naval News*, 6 April 1998, p. 10, https://trove.nla.gov.au/newspaper/article/267312032.

76 *Royal Australian Naval News*, 6 April 1998, p. 10, https://trove.nla.gov.au/newspaper/article/267312032.

77 *The Canberra Times*, 18 May 1991, p. 19, https://trove.nla.gov.au/newspaper/article/122363608.

78 *The Canberra Times*, 18 May 1991, p. 19, https://trove.nla.gov.au/newspaper/article/122363608.

79 *The Canberra Times*, 3 July 1993, p. 16.

80 Ebury, *Weary: The Life of Sir Edward Dunlop*, p. 640.

81 Ebury, *Weary: The Life of Sir Edward Dunlop*, p. 620.

82 Ebury, *Weary: The Life of Sir Edward Dunlop*, p. 641.

83 *The Canberra Times*, 12 July 1993, p. 15.

84 *The Sydney Morning Herald*, 13 July 1993.

85 *The Sydney Morning Herald*, 13 July 1993.

86 *The Sydney Morning Herald*, 13 July 1993.

87 *The Sydney Morning Herald*, 13 July 1993.

88 *The Canberra Times*, 3 July 1993, p. 16, https://trove.nla.gov.au/newspaper/article/127236774.

89 *The Sydney Morning Herald*, 13 July 1993.

90 *The Canberra Times*, 3 July 1993, p. 16, https://trove.nla.gov.au/newspaper/article/127236774.

91 *The Canberra Times*, 3 July 1993, p. 16, https://trove.nla.gov.au/newspaper/article/127236774.

92 *The Canberra Times*, 13 July 1993, p. 1, https://trove.nla.gov.au/newspaper/article/127239134.

93 Ebury, *Weary: The Life of Sir Edward Dunlop*, p. 641.

94 *The Sydney Morning Herald*, 25 April 1994.

95 'Weary Dunlop Hellfire Pass Burial, Anzac Day 1994', https://www.youtube.com/watch?v=tTo1A2qM_tg&t=147s.

96 *The Sydney Morning Herald*, 26 April 1994.

97 *The Sydney Morning Herald*, 21 December 2011, https://www.smh.com.au/national/blue-protected-his-mate-at-all-costs-20111220–1p3sa.html.

BIBLIOGRAPHY

Books

Carlton, Mike, *Cruiser: The Life and Loss of HMAS* Perth *and Her Crew*, William Heinemann, Australia, 2010

Carter, Norman, *G-String Jesters*, Currawong, Sydney, 1966

Christie, Robert, *A History of the 2/29 Battalion – 8th Australian Division, AIF*, first edition 1983

Coates, Albert Ernest and Rosenthal, Newman, *The Albert Coates Story*, Hyland House, Melbourne, 1977

Corrie, E. C. W., *Survival Against Odds*, Golden Banner Printing Service, Castlemaine, 1983

Day, David, *The Politics of War*, HarperCollins Publishers, Sydney, 2004

Dunlop, B. A., *Little Sticks, The Story of Two Brothers*, Acacia Press, 1985

Dunlop, E. E., *The War Diaries of Weary Dunlop*, Thomas Nelson, Melbourne, 1986

Dunlop, E. E., *The War Diaries of Weary Dunlop*, Penguin Books, Australia, 1990

Ebury, Sue, *Weary: The Life of Sir Edward Dunlop*, Penguin Books, Australia, 1995

Faulkner, Andrew, *Arthur Blackburn, VC: An Australian Hero, His Men, and Their Two World Wars*, Wakefield Press, Australia, 2008

FitzSimons, Peter, *Tobruk*, HaperCollins Publishers, Sydney 2006

Freudenberg, Graham, *Churchill and Australia*, Pan Macmillan, Sydney, 2008

Geddes, Margaret, *Remembering Weary*, Viking, Penguin Books, Australia, 1996

Glassop, Lawson and Wilmot, Chester, *Australian War Classics*, Penguin Books, Ringwood, Vic., first published 2001, this edition published 2003

Greece and Crete, Department of Veterans' Affairs, October 2011

Griffiths, Bill with Popham, Hugh, *Blind to Misfortune*, Leo Cooper, London, 1989

Hetherington, John, *Blamey: Controversial Soldier*, published jointly by The Australian War Memorial and the Australian Government Publishing Service, Canberra, 1973

Hill, Maria, *Diggers and Greeks: The Australian Campaign in Greece and Crete*, UNSW Press, Australia, 2010

Jones, J. D. F., *Storyteller: The Many Lives of Laurens van der Post*, John Murray, London, 2001

Kratoska, Paul H. (ed.), *The Thailand–Burma Railway, 1942–1946, Documents and Selected Writings*, Vol. II, London, Routledge, 2006

Lewis, Robert, *Parer's War. A Study Guide*, ATOM, Australian Teachers of Media, Melbourne, 2014

Long, Gavin, *Australia in the War of 1939–1945, Series 1 Army, Vol II, Greece, Crete and Syria*, Australian War Memorial, Canberra, 1953

MacArthur, Douglas, 'Reports of General MacArthur', *Japanese Operation in the Southwest Pacific area, Compiled from Japanese Demobilization Bureaux Records*, U.S. Government Printing Office, 1966

Martin, A. W. and Hardy, Patsy (eds), *Dark and Hurrying Days, Menzies 1941 Diary*, National Library of Australia, 1993

McCormack, Gavan and Nelson, Hank, *The Burma–Thailand Railway*, Allen & Unwin, Sydney, 1993

McDonald, Neil, *War Cameraman – The Story of Damien Parer*, Lothian, Melbourne, 1994

Moorehead, Alan, *African Trilogy*, Text Publishing Company, 1997

Nelson, Hank, *POW. Prisoners of War: Australians Under Nippon*, ABC Enterprises, Australia, 1985

Parker, John, *Desert Rats, From El Alamein to Basra: The Inside Story of a Military Legend*, Headline Book Publishing, London, 2004

Parkin, Ray, *Out of the Smoke*, William Morrow & Company, New York, 1960

Parkin, Ray, *Wartime Trilogy*, Melbourne University Press, Australia, 1999

Pitt, Barrie, *The Crucible of War, Western Desert 1941*, Jonathan Cape Ltd, London, 1980

Porch, Douglas, *Hitler's Mediterranean Gamble: The North African and the Mediterranean Campaigns in World War II*, Weidenfeld & Nicholson, London, 2004

Sides, Hampton, *Ghost Soldiers: The Epic Account of World War II's Greatest Rescue Mission*, Knopf Doubleday Publishing Group, 2002

Stephens, Tony, *Heroes*, Slattery Media Group, Richmond, Vic., 2013

Uren, Tom, *Straight Left*, Random House, Australia, 1994

Urquhart, Alistair, *Forgotten Highlander*, Little Brown, London, 2010

van der Post, Laurens, *Yet Being Someone Other*, Penguin Books, London, 1984

Williams, Peter, *Japan's Pacific War: Personal Accounts of the Emperor's Warriors*, Pen & Sword Books, Yorkshire, 2021

Wodehouse, P. G., *Very Good, Jeeves*, Herbert Jenkins, 1930

Wright, Pattie, *The Men of the Line: Stories of the Thai–Burma Railway Survivors*, Melbourne University Publishing, Victoria, 2008

Wright, Pattie, *Ray Parkin's Odyssey*, Macmillan Publishers, Australia, 2012

Journal and magazine articles

Army Magazine, 1 June 1998, p. 62, https://trove.nla.gov.au/newspaper/article/267398068/29994865

The Australian Women's Weekly, 20 October 1945, p. 17, https://trove.nla.gov.au/newspaper/article/51281493

Clarke, John, 'Comment', *The Monthly*, August 2005, https://www.themonthly.com.au/nation-reviewed-john-clarke-comment--73

Coates, Albert E., 'Clinical Lessons from Prisoner of War Hospitals in the Far East (Burma and Siam)', *The Medical Journal of Australia*, June 1946, p. 755, https://onlinelibrary.wiley.com/doi/abs/10.5694/j.1326-5377.1946.tb33884.x

Duncan, Ian L., 'Makeshift Medicine: Combating Disease in Japanese Prison Camps', *The Medical Journal of Australia*, January 1983, p. 31, https://onlinelibrary.wiley.com/doi/pdf/10.5694/j.1326-5377.1983.tb136020.x

Dunlop, E. E., 'Medical Experiences in Japanese Captivity', *British Medical Journal*, 5 October 1946, p. 486, https://pmc.ncbi.nlm.nih.gov/articles/PMC2057680/

Griffin, David, 'Galleghan, Sir Frederick Gallagher (1897–1971)', *Australian Dictionary of Biography*, National Centre of Biography, Australian National University, Vol. 14, 1996

The Last Post Magazine, Edition 2, 2011, p. 75, https://thelastpostmagazine.com/wp-content/uploads/2020/05/The-Last-Post-Magazine-Edition-2-Summer-2011.pdf

Lee, Lisa, 'A Case from Australia's War Crime Trials: Lieutenant General Nishimura, 1950', *Deakin Law Review*, Vol. 18, No. 2, 2014, pp. 337–360, http://www.austlii.edu.au/au/journals/DeakinLawRw/2013/14.pdf

Marshall, Robert D., '"Weary" Dunlop: Surgeon', *Australian and New Zealand Journal of Surgery*, January 1994, https://doi.org/10.1111/j.1445-2197.1994.tb02129.x

McCormack, Gavan, 'Yi Hak-Nae and the Burma–Thailand Railway', *Asia-Pacific Journal: Japan Focus*, Vol. 19, Issue 15, No. 1, August 2021, https://apjjf.org/2021/15/mccormack

Park, Ju-Min, 'The Survivor: Last Korean War Criminal in Japan Wants Recognition', Thomson Reuters, 4 August 2020, https://www.reuters.com/article/world/the-survivor-last-korean-war-criminal-in-japan-wants-recognition-idUSKCN2500B7/

Royal Australian Naval News, 6 April 1998, p. 10, https://trove.nla.gov.au/newspaper/article/267312032

Williams, Damien, 'John Clarke's Second World War', *Meanjin*, August 2017 [reported speech], https://meanjin.com.au/latest/john-clarkes-second-world-war/

Newspapers

The Advertiser (Adelaide)
The Age
The Argus
Benalla Ensign
Benalla Standard
The Canberra Times
The Coromandel
The Courier Mail
Daily Mail
Daily Telegraph (London)
The Herald (Melbourne)
Kalgoorlie Miner
Mirror
Northam Advertiser
Referee (Sydney)
The Sun
The Sunday Times (Perth)
The Sydney Morning Herald
Truth
The West Australian
Westralian Worker

Archives/State collections

Diaries

Clarke, Major John Edward Rea, Transcript of war diaries of Major John Edward Rea Clarke OBE, 1940–1942, 2007, Australian War Memorial, https://www.awm.gov.au/collection/C2761011

Hunter, Jan (compiled by), *The World War Two Diary of Thomas Henry Fagan*, Albury and District Historical Society Papers No. 31, 2018, https://victoriancollections.net.au/media/collectors/53feae1c2162f1087018acb7/items/5c03651e21ea6712f4ca4d5c/item-media/5c03655721ea6712f4ca860b/original.pdf

Menzies, Robert, Robert Menzies Diary, Museum of Australian Democracy, 27 and 28 April 1941

Letters, telegrams and cablegrams

Cablegram, Churchill to Curtin, 20 February 1942, https://s3-ap-southeast-2.amazonaws.com/awm-media/collection/RCDIG1070112/document/5519441.PDF

Cablegram, Churchill to Curtin, 22 February 1942, https://www.dfat.gov.au/about-us/publications/historical-documents/Pages/volume-05/362-mr-clement-attlee-uk-secretary-of-state-for-dominion-affairs-to-mr-john-curtin-prime-minister

Cablegram, Curtin to Mr Clement Attlee, UK Secretary of State for Dominion Affairs, Cablegram 139 CANBERRA, 23 February 1942, https://www.dfat.gov.au/about-us/publications/historical-documents/Pages/volume-05/366-mr-john-curtin-prime-minister-to-mr-clement-attlee-uk-secretary-of-state-for-dominion-affairs

Cablegram, Curtin to Sir Earle Page, Special Representative in the United Kingdom, 19 February 1942, https://www.dfat.gov.au/about-us/publications/historical-documents/Pages/volume-05/374-mr-john-curtin-prime-minister-to-sir-earle-page-special-representative-in-the-united-kingdom

Letter, Edward Dunlop to Helen Ferguson, mid-1938, Papers of Sir Edward 'Weary' Dunlop, PR00926, item 1/34 Part 1, AWM

Letter, Edward Dunlop to Helen Ferguson, 1938, Papers of Sir Edward 'Weary' Dunlop, PR00926, item 1/34 Part 1, AWM

Letter, Edward Dunlop to Helen Ferguson, 1 January 1939, Papers of Sir Edward 'Weary' Dunlop, PR00926, item 1/34 Part 1, AWM

Letter, Edward Dunlop to Helen Ferguson, 3 September 1939, Papers of Sir Edward 'Weary' Dunlop, PR00926, item 1/34 Part 3, AWM

Letter, Weary Dunlop to Helen Ferguson, 5 November 1941, Papers of Sir Edward 'Weary' Dunlop, PR00926, item 1/34 Part 1, AWM

Letter, Weary Dunlop to Helen Ferguson, 11 November 1941, Papers of Sir Edward 'Weary' Dunlop, PR00926, item 1/34 Part 1, AWM

Letter, Weary Dunlop to Helen Ferguson, 17 December 1941, Papers of Sir Edward 'Weary' Dunlop, PR00926, item 1/34 Part 8, AWM

Letter, Edward Dunlop to Helen Ferguson, 21 February 1942, Papers of Sir Edward 'Weary' Dunlop, PR00926, item 1/34 Part 8, AWM

Letter, Edward Dunlop to Helen Ferguson, 23 September 1945, Papers of Sir Edward 'Weary' Dunlop, PR00926, item 1/30, AWM

Telegram, Edward Dunlop to Helen Ferguson, 1942, Papers of Sir Edward 'Weary' Dunlop, PR00926, item 1/34 Part 1, AWM

Telegram, Edward Dunlop to Helen Ferguson, 13 October 1945, Papers of Sir Edward 'Weary' Dunlop, PR00926, item 1/30, AWM

Other items

Hackney, Ben, 'Dark Evening', a typescript account of the massacre at Parit Sulong, AWM MSS0758

McEachern, Brigadier C. A., 'Report on Conditions, Life and Work of Prisoners of War in Burma and Siam', 1942–1945, Australian War Memorial, Series No. AWM54, https://s3-ap-southeast-2.amazonaws.com/awm-media/collection/AWM2017.8.197/document/6593514.PDF

Menzies, Sir Robert, 1939 Radio Address, Papers of Sir Robert Menzies, National Library of Australia, https://nla.gov.au/nla.obj-233710278

War Crimes Military Tribunal, Eiji Hirota, National Archives of Australia, Series No. A471, Item ID, 722378

War Crimes Military Tribunal, Hiromura Kakurai, Singapore, 18 and 20 March 1947, National Archives of Australia, Series No. A471, Item ID, 721743

Interviews

Barker, Ray, Transcript of interview, UNSW Australians at War Film Archive, 17 May 2003, https://australiansatwarfilmarchive.unsw.edu.au/archive/126

Butterworth, Milton (Blue), Transcript of interview, UNSW Australians at War Archive, 21 November 2003, http://australiansatwarfilmarchive.unsw.edu.au/archive/906

Chalker, Jack, Interviews for the Channel 10 program, *Surgeon of the Railway*, 1987, Australian War Memorial, https://www.awm.gov.au/collection/C1290394

Dunlop, Edward 'Weary', Transcript of interview, Department of Veterans' Affairs, Anzac Portal, https://anzacportal.dva.gov.au/resources/edward-weary-dunlop

Dunlop, Sir Ernest Edward 'Weary', interviewed by Dr Hank Nelson, Australian War Memorial, https://www.awm.gov.au/collection/C283448

Dunlop, John, interview with author, 23 February 2025

Hackney, Ben Charles, interviewed by Tim Bowden, July 1983, https://www.awm.gov.au/collection/C1006619

McGovern, Frank, Transcript of interview, UNSW Australians at War Film Archive, 8 May 2003, https://australiansatwarfilmarchive.unsw.edu.au/archive/19

Parkin, Ray, Transcript of interview, UNSW Australians at War Film Archive, 7 June 2000, https://australiansatwarfilmarchive.unsw.edu.au/archive/2552

Parkin, Raymond 'Ray' Edward, Interviews for the Channel 10 program, *Surgeon of the Railway*, 1987, Australian War Memorial, https://www.awm.gov.au/collection/F09396

Uren, Tom, Transcript of interview, UNSW Australians at War Film Archive, 11 August 2003, http://australiansatwarfilmarchive.unsw.edu.au/archive/728

Wright, Pattie, interview with author, Mornington Peninsula, 27 January 2025

Young, Thomas (Tom), Transcript of interview, UNSW Australians at War Film Archive, 8 October 2003, https://australiansatwarfilmarchive.unsw.edu.au/archive/1021

Online sources

'Audio commentaries', Department of Veterans' Affairs, Anzac Portal, https://anzacportal.dva.gov.au/wars-and-missions/burma-thailand-railway-and-hellfire-pass-1942-1943/resources/audio-commentaries

'The Australian Prisoners' Accounts', Department of Veterans' Affairs, Anzac Portal, https://anzacportal.dva.gov.au/wars-and-missions/burma-thailand-railway-and-hellfire-pass-1942-1943/resources/australian-prisoners-accounts

Badham, Ernie, 2/2nd CCS, Prisoner of War Account, https://www.burmarailway.com.au/page-4

Captain Fred Stahl 'F' Force Thailand Diary, 2/4th Machine Gun Battalion Ex Members Association, 20 June 2023, https://2nd4thmgb.com.au/story/29505/

Churchill to General Sir Archibald Wavell, Supreme Commander of the South West Pacific, 10 February 1942, https://www.churchillarchive.com/previous-topic-in-focus

'The Colonel & the Bombardier, Sir Edward "Weary" Dunlop, artist Jack Bridger Chalker', https://www.cofepow.org.uk/armed-forces-stories-list/the-colonel-the-bombardier

Convention of 27 July 1929, Relative to the Treatment of Prisoners of War, Yale Law School, https://avalon.law.yale.edu/20th_century/geneva02.asp

Convention Relative to the Treatment of Prisoners of War, Geneva, 27 July 1929, https://ihl-databases.icrc.org/assets/treaties/305-IHL-GC-1929–2-EN.pdf

Corlette, Andrew, Speech, The Australian Ex-Prisoners of War Memorial, Ballarat, Victoria, 2018, https://www.powmemorialballarat.com.au/2018-andrew-corlette/

'Death Railway Shrine', The War Channel, https://www.youtube.com/watch?v=Nr5cPrsoeM0

'Diary of a Labor Man', 1941, published by John Curtin Prime Ministerial Library, 2008, https://john.curtin.edu.au/diary/primeminister/1941.html

'Dunlop Force – Java Party No. 6 – O and P Battalions', 2/4th Machine Gun Battalion Ex Members Association, February 2018, https://2nd4thmgb.com.au/story/dunlop-force-java-party-no-6-o-p-battalions/

'Fall of Singapore', National Museum of Australia, https://www.nma.gov.au/defining-moments/resources/fall-of-singapore#:~:text=In%20London%2C%20Prime%20Minister%20Winston,die%20as%20prisoners%20of%20war

Flanagan, Martin, 'For Tom Uren: "You were a champion, Tom. You're in the company of legends now"', 4 February 2015, https://speakola.com/eulogy/-tom-uren-martin-flanagan-2015

Ford-Gaden, Caroline, 'Memory and Heritage', https://secondtwentiethbattalionaif.wordpress.com/prisoner-of-war-pow/memory-and-heritage/

Green, Hilary Custance, 'Boon Pong – and Other Forgotten Heroes', Green Writing Room, 12 January 2024, https://greenwritingroom.com/2014/01/12/boon-pong-and-other-forgotten-heroes/

Haskell, Bill, 'Memories of the Burma Siam Railway', http://www.mansell.com/pow_resources/camplists/death_rr/hintok.html

'Illness and death', Department of Veterans' Affairs, 2024, Anzac Portal, https://anzacportal.dva.gov.au/wars-and-missions/burma-thailand-railway-and-hellfire-pass-1942-1943/events/surviving/illness-and-death

MacPherson, Neil, 2/2nd Pioneer Battalion, 2nd AIF, Japan POW, Burma Railway, Japan https://www.wa.gov.au/system/files/2020-01/Macpherson_Neil.pdf

Radio Address by Neville Chamberlain, Prime Minister, 3 September 1939, Yale Law School, https://avalon.law.yale.edu/wwii/gb3.asp

Ryan, Sarah, 'The Major Moon Collection', State Library of Victoria, 1 April 2013, https://blogs.slv.vic.gov.au/such-was-life/war-such-was-life/the-major-moon-collection/

Swanton, E. W., 'Cricket under the Japs', Wisden, 1946, https://www.espncricinfo.com/wisdenalmanack/content/story/152863.html

Tibbets, Paul, interview, AVWeb, 14 June 2019, https://www.avweb.com/features/paul-tibbets-interview/

'Tom Uren: Back to the Burma Railway', David Brill, The Big Picture, https://www.youtube.com/watch?v=Lp6tHPKnYHc

Uren, Tom, (ALP-Reid) – Maiden Speech, 26 February 1959, https://australianpolitics.com/1959/02/26/tom-uren-alp-reid-maiden-speech.html/

'VX48789 KAPPE, Lt. Col Charles Henry "Gus" – C.O. "F" Force Thailand, Australian POWs', 2/4th Machine Gun Battalion Ex Members Association, 18 June 2023, https://2nd4thmgb.com.au/story/kappe-lt-col-charles-henry-f-force-thailand/

Woodhouse, Fay, 'White, Sam (1913–1988)', *Australian Dictionary of Biography*, National Centre of Biography, Australian National University, https://adb.anu.edu.au/biography/white-sam-14877/text26067, published first in hardcopy 2012

WW2, People's War, Archive of World War Two Memories, BBC Home, https://www.bbc.co.uk/history/ww2peopleswar/stories/58/a4159758.shtml

TV shows and movies

This is Your Life, Sir Edward Dunlop, 23 June 1979, https://www.iwm.org.uk/collections/item/object/80012508

The Quiet Lions, documentary, directed by Robin Newell, 2008

Songs

'Dolores' by Louis Alter (song) and Frank Loesser (lyrics), 1941

George Formby, 'Bless 'em All', Lyrics.Com, https://www.lyrics.com/lyric/15712045/George+Formby/Bless+%27Em+All#google_vignette

'Now is the Hour', lyrics written by Maewa Kaihau and Dorothy Stewart

INDEX